The Handbook of Country and Political Risk Analysis

Third Edition

Edited by
Llewellyn D. Howell, Ph.D.

Published by
The PRS Group, Inc.
6320 Fly Road, Suite 102, P.O. Box 248
East Syracuse, NY 13057-0248 USA
Tel: +1 (315) 431-0511 • Fax: +1 (315) 431-0200
www.prsgroup.com ~ www.countrydata.com

© The PRS Group, Inc., 2001
The Handbook of Country and Political Risk Analysis (Third Edition)
ISBN: 1-931077-01-0

Printed in U.S.A.
Manufactured by Dupli Envelope & Graphics Corporation

Table of Contents
The Handbook of Country and Political Risk Analysis
3rd Edition

Preface

This third edition of *The Handbook of Country and Political Risk Analysis* represents the continuation of The PRS Group's effort to bridge the gap between the academic world and the real world of politics, government, and economics. The *Handbook* is designed to enhance understanding of how to identify and assess country and political risks for international businesses for their decision-making in such areas as strategic planning, marketing, finance, corporate security, government affairs, and risk management.

The Handbook of Country and Political Risk Analysis is a convenient compilation of analysis descriptions and samples provided by the world's leading commercial publishers of country and political risk analysis. Our thanks go to each of the contributors represented in these pages.

In this edition, readers will find most chapters fully updated, providing readers with the most up-to-date discussions of the various methods employed in conducting country and political risk analysis. In addition, this edition includes a new chapter from the IHS Energy Group, providing an excellent working example of the application of country and political analysis by a major international corporation, giving the reader insight into the use of this kind of analysis in strategic planning.

The 3rd edition includes two unique appendices. Appendix A is new in this edition and provides a full range of internet resources to enhance the reader's own research into the field of country and political risk analysis. Appendix B provides a case example from the records of the Overseas Private Investment Corporation (OPIC), a US agency that provides political risk insurance. We hope that these additions will enhance readers' use of the publication, and that the *Handbook* will continue to be informative for current students and future users of risk publications.

We appreciate hearing from faculty, students, and researchers. We have demonstrated that we welcome comments or new ideas for *The Handbook of Country and Political Risk Analysis* by using readers' comments to plan the expansion of this new edition.

Both PRS and the editor would like to give special thanks to Suzy Howell, managing editor of the *Thunderbird International Business Review*, for her editorial assistance and organizational skill in putting the publication together.

Ben McTernan
Managing Editor
The PRS Group, Inc.

Section I
Introduction

Chapter I

Introduction
Country and Political Risk Analysis:
Applications for Management

Llewellyn D. Howell, Ph.D.
Thunderbird — The American Graduate School of International Management

Politics, Society, and Risk to Investment Success

In the age of globalization, the integrated and integral relationship between the global economy and domestic politics, society, and culture is far from being well understood. From both host country and foreign investor participants, there is often an expectation that somehow business and politics can be separate entities with no penetration of the delicate partition that has historically (or at least conceptually) divided them. This is not to argue that there has been no recognition of the fact that there is a relationship between politics and business, and especially business success. Rather, its nature is not understood and its consequences are resisted.

Misunderstanding the nature of the relationship results in inappropriate and misleading analysis for investors. Resisting its consequences has meant that host countries view attempts at risk management by foreign investors as intrusion and interference in sovereign matters. Some efforts at risk management have been viewed as cultural intrusion, especially in Asia where the concept of "Asian values" has been promoted in defense of forms of what are called nepotism and corruption in the West. Analysis of the sources of country and political risk becomes an extremely delicate matter in that the analyst might miss a cultural characteristic that is the source of a threat (especially in areas of religious advocacy, for instance) and host countries have come to see foreign investors as agents of imperialism and sources of unwanted change. While both investor and host country recognize that politics and business are intertwined, they both shy away from the intimacy that the relationship seems to require.

However, developing a recognition of the relationship between business and politics is unavoidable. A formal recognition has been on the table for more than 30 years in the form of political risk insurance. In the last decade, investors have begun to move rapidly into regions of new opportunity, while trying to keep a close eye on the political situations in these states, wary of processes that seem alien and events that seem unpredictable. But more than just a "close eye" is necessary to sort out causal relationships in situations that may come to a head three, four, or five years in the future, just as an investment begins to mature. How does a foreign investor, in particular, sort out the characteristics of an unfamiliar environment and project how they might come together at some point in the future? What elements of the very complex and unfamiliar political situation require attention and assessment before the new investor risks personnel and critical amounts of capital? An analytical structure is needed to sort the multitude of factors that contribute to the puzzles and riddles that often seem the best characterizations of politics and society in the new world of business opportunity. Such structures, provided for observers in the field, are referred to as "country risk analysis" or "political risk analysis."

Political risk assessment is a practice that has been around for probably thousands of years. *Assessment* refers to a measure, in this case a probability measure, which acts as a warning of the *level* of threat. In political risk *analysis*, the origins or causes of the threat – whatever its level – are the object of attention. There is, therefore, a small but important difference between the terms *assessment* and *analysis*, although they are often used interchangeably.

The term **political risk** by itself refers to the possibility that *political decisions* or *political or social events* in a country will affect the business climate in such a way that investors will lose money or not make as much money as they expected when the investment was made. **Country risk** is of a larger scale, incorporating *economic* and *financial* characteristics of a system, along with the political and social, in the same effort to forecast situations in which foreign investors will find problems in specific national environments. Some approaches to political risk analysis describe this as being an effort to project or forecast "harm" to the investor by political and social forces in the host country or resulting from political decisions. Again we find that the terms assessment and analysis are used interchangeably for both country and political risk, although they actually have different (although related) objectives.

For international management, the immediate managerial need is for assessment. But the more important goal is analysis since it is through determination of causes of future behavior that the right assessment can be made and the right management tools can be brought to bear. In the discussion below, I will emphasize the term "analysis" and the goal of useful theory in trying to shape our knowledge of the political risk field for productive use by managers.

In many approaches to risk assessment, political risk is subsumed in country risk[1]. However, there is a need to report political risk separately. First, there is an availability of political risk insurance. As will be discussed below, this insurance covers losses that are due to political acts only, not to economic or financial conditions or circumstances. Therefore, a country risk rating that includes these other aspects of general risk will not be useful guidance as to the need for political risk insurance or to the level of premium that an investor should be willing to pay. Second, the tools for managing political risk are very different from those that would be employed in managing economic or financial risk. A country risk rating, which incorporates a variety of characteristics of the investment situation, is not good guidance for a manager trying to deal with specific political or social elements in the investment environment. It is therefore important to deal with country risk and political risk separately even though many theories and methods combine them.

In focusing on *political* risk analysis, it is useful to construct a definition of what counts as "political" by beginning with political risk coverage for insurance. Insurance from the Overseas Private Investment Corporation (OPIC) of the U.S. federal government and the Multilateral Investment Guarantee Agency (MIGA) of the World Bank is characteristic as well as prominent in considerations of insurance availability.[2] Both OPIC and MIGA cover four major types of losses to investors that are typical of the harm that can come from the political and social environments in which they operate. These major types of losses are as follows:

(1) *Inconvertibility*, action taken by a government to prevent conversion of local currency to some form of foreign exchange such as dollars

(2) *Expropriation* or *Nationalization*, an action taken by a government to seize property or assets of the foreign investor without full compensation to the foreign investor

(3) *War Damage*, losses resulting from an international conflict

(4) *Civil Strife Damage*, losses generated by internal conflict

In addition, MIGA and private insurers such as AIG provide a fifth form of political risk insurance covering (5) *Contract Repudiation*. Also known as "contract frustration" or "breach of contract," this loss results from government termination of contracts without compensation for existing investment in the project or service. The AIG list of political categories of contract repudiation is instructive. They include unilateral termination of a contract by a government, payment defaults, license cancellations, embargoes, war or civil war (occurrence, not damage), default on an arbitration award, and government acts, laws, decrees, or regulations that result in breach or alteration of an agreement.

Three more broad categories complete the range of losses that stem from political sources. Probably the most common source of losses to foreign businesses is from (6) *Negative Government Actions*. Governments often formally decide to reduce or restrict earnings or participation of foreign investors in ways that are less direct than expropriation or inconvertibility. Ordinarily, losses that result are not covered by insurance, although almost anything can be insured through private insurers. Political Risk Services (PRS) includes the following among their list of possible sources of loss that fit in this category.[3] *Equity Restrictions* would be a government decision or a decision by a segment of the government, such as a ministry. *Personnel/Procurement Interference* occurs in many political systems. *Taxation Discrimination* directed at particular companies or particular nationalities is the result of a decision of someone in government and may reflect social issues or prejudices. *Repatriation Restrictions, Exchange Controls, Tariff Imposition, Non-Tariff Barrier Imposition*, and *Fiscal/Monetary Expansion*, all of which may affect businesses negatively, are the result of government decisions. *Labor Cost Expansion, Payment Delays* and *Bureaucratic Sluggishness* may be functions of government policy or simply government inefficiency, but all are affected by government decisions at some level in the system.

A related type, (7) *Process Deterioration* includes those losses to businesses that result from indirect government action, government attributes (rather than decisions), and societal processes or characteristics. Examples of these, respectively, are lack of enforcement of copyright agreements (where the government may be simply incapable of enforcement), government interference in operations (such as with racial quotas in hiring of managers), and bribery and systemic corruption (where American investors need to be sensitive to the application of the Foreign Corrupt Practices Act).

A final type of loss – not typically insured – is (8) *Event Intervention*. This loss results from some event that is political in its nature or source, while not being a result of a known government decision or indecision. Examples of event interventions that affect businesses negatively would be kidnapping of managers or executives, strikes or production stoppages that occur with political rather than economic or financial objectives, and sabotage or damage to a plant or service that originates with a political or religious group in the host country.

Political risk analysis is directed at locating the sources of risk and determining assessment, projecting the probability of these eight types of losses, and thus acting as advisement to investors regarding both choices about management tools and insurance.

The Assessment of Political Risk

The primary objective in both political risk assessment and analysis is to forecast these losses. A secondary objective stemming from the first is to suggest means of managing the risk or avoiding the loss. Analysis typically involves identification of variables, determination of their relationship to each other, establishing their contribution to a particular situation (data), and then projecting the future for purposes of a specific application. The loss projection or assessment serves in a way that is very similar to a weather forecast in meteorology. Just as the forecast (e.g., rain in the afternoon) is a probability of a weather condition that one uses to decide whether or not to take an umbrella, a political risk forecast is a probabilistic characterization of a social or political condition (e.g., that an oil pipeline would be attacked by a guerrilla group). If the probability is at or changes to a specified level, some management action, equivalent to carrying an umbrella, would be taken. Some oil companies, for example, have hired armed personnel to protect their oil lines. In both cases—rain or guerrilla action—there is also a possibility that the forecast is wrong. Even so, we weigh the cost of not managing the problem along with the cost of managing it when we make a decision. Political risk has received considerably more attention in recent years because of the increased cost and increased losses when investment environments are not addressed with some management tool or loss protection.

Modeling the Risk Situation: A useful projection of risk involves some form of causal analysis in which connections are drawn between historical or existing attributes or behaviors and future actions or decisions, with a projection out into the future. For example, if a highly nationalist or socialist party takes over a government, corollaries in history would suggest that there would be increased government interference in business operations or even nationalization of foreign enterprises. Or if ethnic tension in the country is high and rising, corollaries would lead us to project civil strife and, thus, civil strife damage to facilities or production. Or if the government of a neighboring country is rattling sabers, we might project international conflict and war damage. For each of the loss categories listed above (1-8), there are predictors in the social, political, or international system that can tell us something about the likelihood that a particular type of loss will occur.

Figure 1 *(on the next page)* portrays the simplest version of this sequence. In this civil strife damage example, the origins of the risk lie in the existence of one variable—ethnic fractionalization. Of course, we live in a complex society and variables combine and interact to bring about the conditions we are trying to forecast. It might therefore be a combination of ethnic fractionalization, societal conditions, and authoritarian government that brings about civil strife. The challenge to the political risk analyst and to the forecasting methodology is to determine both which variable(s) *and* which combination are likely to result in the threat of loss to the investor. The calculation of the combination must include some weights for the variables involved.

The systematic methods for forecasting political (and country) risk typically result in an index that is composed of a variety of weighted variables that is an additive sum for the country as a whole and for any type of foreign investment. In a country risk method presented in *The Economist*[4] political variables were given a total weight of 50 points, social variables 17 points, and economic variables 33 points, for a total of 100 in the index. Within the political variables, "Bad Neighbors" were weighted at three points but ongoing "War and Armed Insurrection" was weighted at 20. One is roughly seven times more important a contribution to risk than the other.[5] The model used to derive the index has underlying theory that determines these relative contributions to risk. Models that vary from each other in the choice of included variables and in varied weightings presumably are derived from differing theories on the sources of loss to foreign investors. Before applying a particular method of risk analysis, it is important to ask what its underlying theory is.

Figure 1: Forecasting Risk

Linkages

Societal Attributes
(Ethnic Fractionalization)

Political Choices and Actions
(Ethnic Conflict)

Effective Outcomes
(Civil Strife Damage)

Loss to Investor
(Damage to Facilities)

The attributes to be examined are analyzed in two different ways. One is to portray *trends*, the other is to assess current but *compared characteristics*. In the case of trends, the matter is relatively simple, although perhaps somewhat deceptive. If there is a record of expropriation in the country (the dependent variable), the new investor obviously needs to be concerned. If the current government of a host country has previously expropriated foreign firms on a repeated basis, potential investors obviously need to pay attention to the possibility that they, too, could be nationalized. Similarly, a history of civil strife and especially the occurrence of ongoing wars indicate a high likelihood that direct damage could occur to the investment or that contracts could be repudiated under war circumstances. Trends in countries with similar attributes to the one being examined could be employed in an extrapolation or reasoning by analogy to project risk.

The second approach is to examine current societal attributes and the circumstances (the independent variables) under which losses have occurred before, either in that same country or others like it. If high levels of ethnic tension are often followed by open ethnic conflict, for example, that civil strife could result in damage to businesses or in forced abandonment of the investment, as happened in the 1990s in Algeria. Most of the formal forecasting methods, such as that presented by *The Economist*, rely on this approach, the representation of independent variables that might have a causal relationship with losses. [6]

In designing a model, the relationships between abstract concepts, such as authoritarianism, and acts of damage to the investor need to be grounded in social science knowledge and research. A variety of approaches have been put forth by corporate analysts and by political risk organizations in their efforts to describe the circumstances of incipient loss. Larger corporations such as oil companies or banks may have "in-house" advisory groups to examine the context in which the investment will occur. They may have their own models that encompass selected sets of variables and relationships among them that they have determined are appropriate forecasting tools for the types of decisions they will make with regard to investment. Chase Manhattan Bank, for example, has included the bases of *political stability*, *social cohesiveness*, *corruption*, and *external factors* such as war and vulnerability to fanaticism in a model employed in the 1980s. Other firms, and especially smaller firms, may rely wholly or in part on political risk advisory services such as Political Risk Services or International Country Risk Guide (both products of

The PRS Group, Inc.), or the Business Environment Risk Intelligence (BERI) Index. The choice of the system of analysis, with sometimes quite different sets of independent variables, can affect the investment decision dramatically.

Forecasting: The method of forecasting itself can determine the picture of some future harm that is presented to the investor.[7] The method should be considered by the user of risk indices. Forecasting for political and country risk has taken four basic forms in the models that have been in recent use.[8] For a variety of reasons, all are linear projections with multiple indicators from which the forecasts are made. **Type I** is a correlation from current attributes of countries to potential (and hypothetical) types of harm. A list of attributes that are deemed significant correlates of future trouble are scored by experts and specialists to create a numerical index that should project to an equivalent level of danger (and loss) to the firm. The attributes are seen in the present, losses are expected to follow in time.

An example of a Type I forecast is that provided in the *Economist* article. The article presented a list of factors that it described as economic, political, and social and provided a scheme for weighing their individual impact and relative roles (measures of "risk" contribution). They offered an additive method for combining the risk scores and ranking them in such a way as to advise the reader of useful directions to take in investment. The index of up to 100 points provided a ranking of countries by level of risk.

Type II forecasts are those that ask experts to project the attributes out into the future. If this approach were applied in the *Economist* case, the question to the expert would be "what will the level of ethnic tension be five years from now in country X?" rather than what is the level of ethnic tension now. That having been done, there would be no time lag between the attribute and the problem for the business.

The Business Environment Risk Intelligence (BERI) Political Risk Index (PRI) is an example of a Type II forecast. Like the Economist's ratings, the BERI Index is based on scores assigned to ten "political" variables by experts. Also like the Economist, the BERI PRI is clearly identified as being "socio-political." The ten variables are divided into three categories: "Internal causes of political risk," "External causes of political risk", and "Symptoms of political risk".

BERI's consultant analysts complete three different assessments. Assessments on a zero to seven scale are provided for each of the ten variables to describe present conditions, conditions one year from now, and conditions five years from now. In each of the projections, it is the task of the country expert to extrapolate from the present to the future. If this were done in writing (which it is not), support for the current level ratings would be a description of the related conditions that would support, for example, a rating of five out of seven on the variable "political fractionalization." To support a rating of six (instead of five) for the one-year projection, the analyst would be required to develop a scenario that logically would show how current conditions would improve over the course of a year. Then another scenario would be needed to demonstrate how the one-year projection would turn into the five-year projection.

Type III forecasting is a straightforward projection of the losses or the actions that account for the losses themselves out into the future. For example, it is easy to understand how a war going on today could be damaging infrastructure necessary for successful business activity. But will there be a war going on five years from now? Or a more difficult question, will there be bureaucratic inefficiency five years or ten years from now? This process skips the intervening stage of trying to project first whether there will be ethnic tension at some point in the future and then whether that ethnic tension will result in civil strife that could damage physical plant in that same future. It is the dependent variable that is judgmentally forecast. An example of the Type III forecast also comes from BERI in its Operations Risk Index (ORI). In Operations Risk, the analyst assesses the likely occurrence, in the future, of *nationalization, bureaucratic delays, currency convertibility, enforceability of contracts, availability of communications and transportation infrastructures,* and *availability of capable local management and partners.*

Type IV provides a distinct approach. In this method, future governments are projected by the analyst (stage 1), and then the behaviors of those governments toward businesses are similarly projected (stage 2). An example of Type IV forecasting is the Political Risk Services (PRS) approach and their use of the PRINCE model.

In this approach, the PRS experts forecast the three most likely governments (or "regimes") to be in power 18 months or five years from the present, and then predict how they will behave toward businesses at that time. Behaviors are projected as was the case in Type III, rather than system attributes as in Types I and II. PRS – with one exception – examines direct but future government actions or economic functions. PRS adds the dimension of the combined effect of likely governments at the future points. If three potential governments have likelihoods of 60%, 30%, and 10%, for example, each of their possible behaviors are combined in the forecast at the level of their likelihood of being in a position to carry out that behavior.

The issue here is how projection or forecasting is done. There are obviously a variety of approaches. What needs to be considered by the user is whether any actual forecast has been provided or are the data simply descriptions of current conditions, with the forecasting left to the user.

The Analysis of Political Risk

Analytical Focus: Every process of analysis and assessments that are derived from them are dependent on underlying theory about the causes of politically sourced losses. The theory determines what kind of predictive variables are examined, how they are measured, and how they are combined to generate an overall risk rating. Although theories are seldom explicated by the various ratings systems, they exist nevertheless and can usually be derived from an examination of the system or model utilized. In assessing a risk level, the analytical process must take into consideration factors on both the side of the host country and on the side of the foreign investor.

On the side of the host country, there are three theoretical divisions that need to be considered. The first is that theories are divided into those that attribute causality to (A) underlying **characteristics** and conditions in the country, versus those that take (B) a more "rational actor" or **government decision-making** approach. BERI, ICRG, and EIU, for example, rely on underlying conditions[9] such as the level of Ethnic fractionalization or the extent of democracy present in the host country government.

PRS, on the other hand, focuses explicitly on national government decisions such as those relating to levels of non-tariff barriers, repatriation restrictions, or operations interference. The Euromoney assessment is based on the perceived likelihood that governments will repay debt, a rather singular reliance on government decision-making.

There is no reason that the two should not be combined. Political risk in a country could be the combination of both a government's inclination to interfere in operations *and* the presence of ethnic division and strife. A more important theoretical question is whether particular national circumstances—such as a dominant religious culture (e.g. "Islamic Fundamentalism" from the *Economist* model) that emphasizes a hierarchical system of rule coincides with a decision type (e.g. "Restrictions on Operations" from the PRS model). It could be argued that characteristics are a causal factor in particular decisions.

Similarly, in political risk analysis we have to be concerned about relationships among the variables in the assessment model. Several models, for example (ICRG, *The Economist*), include both extent of democracy and involvement of the military in politics as separate variables in calculating the assessment. It can be easily argued that these two variables are so interrelated that they are really one. Including them both in an assessment would therefore be tantamount to counting the same variable twice, therefore distorting the assessment. These questions must be addressed in the theory phase of building risk assessment systems but usually are not.

The second theoretical division is that between what has been described as (C) **macro** and (D) **micro** approaches. This division has been characterized in several ways but usually with reference to macro analysis as being concerned with government decisions that would relate to all foreign investors in a country, while micro analysis is addressing "government policies and actions that influence selected sectors of the economy or specific foreign businesses in the country."[10] The latter would include assessments related to particular firms. While the macro/micro differentiation is usually discussed in the context of government decisions, it can be applied as well to country characteristics, where, for example, ethnic divisions in a country might affect manufacturing facilities but wouldn't have any direct effect on financial investors in host country stock markets.

A third division that must be considered is the unit level for either characteristics or government decisions. We might divide this into categories (E) **national** and (F) **local**, although this is really a spectrum that could be divided much more finely. As we know well in the case of the United States, there may be cases where the national government does not interfere in foreign investment but a state or local government does. In Vietnam, there are government divisions that run from national to provincial to city or even village, with a variety of policies. The differentiation applies to risk characteristics as well, where, for example, corruption may be denounced and inhibited at the national level while it is rampant at some local levels (but not necessarily others).

Risk is differentiated on the side of the investor as well, with some firms being more vulnerable to risk problems than others. It is useful to think in terms of firm *exposure*[11] to political risk, with the exposure varying according to attributes other than simply those of the host country. PRS begins the process of narrowing in its applications by defining the effective variables differently for each of three major **Types of International Business** (that I will refer to as Category G of foreign investor attributes). For PRS these are 1) Financial Transfers (the banking and financial industry), 2) Direct Investment (manufacturing, mining, agriculture in the host country), and 3) Exports (sales and perhaps distribution).[12] Their method assumes, for example, that *political turmoil* will affect the Direct Investment and Export industries but not Finance and Banking. Changes in tariffs will affect Exports but not the others. This makes sense. Not all investors in every industry will be affected by actions or conditions in the same way.

Several other variations in investor characteristics need to be considered as well. Category H – **Industry Character**: If a banking institution has personnel and physical facilities within the host country, they of course could be subject to the negative effects of political turmoil or ethnic conflict. Political rioting might result in damaged facilities, a banking shutdown, or loss of employees. A foreign lending institution, on the other hand, might not be subject to any physical damage. As another example, if an industry is the source of considerable foreign exchange earnings for the host country or is the vehicle for important technology transfer, it might be subject to less government interference than one that is not such a source. Such factors would need to be taken into consideration for a specific industry's risk to be determined.

Category J – **Physical Environment**: Especially in emerging economies where agricultural and extractive industries are primary areas of investment, much FDI is located in remote or rural areas. As such they will be more vulnerable to guerrillas and civil warfare that takes place out of the reach of government authorities. Conversely, urban investment could be more subject to mass demonstrations and direct political interference than a firm operating in a remote area.

Category K – **Investor Attributes**: Race, religion, and culture are often matters of compatibility in investment situations. Jews and Chinese, among others, are often subject to challenges as investors that other ethnic groups would not be likely to face. In Southeast Asia, Chinese businesses are more likely to be attacked in circumstances of socio-economic deprivation than are businesses of others, and Chinese are more likely to be kidnapped under an assumption that they have wealth that they will easily part with in a ransom circumstance. Because of the prominent role of the U.S. in international affairs, American companies are more likely to be the target of nationalists than those of Belgium or Singapore. Risk depends, at least in part, on who the investor is.

One condition applies to the overall risk situation, impacting host country and investor as well. Category L – **Time Frame**: It is not a static world. As global circumstances change, so do the actions that result in losses to foreign investors. OPIC's recent reports[13] indicate a notable shift in the nature of claims paid over the years that it has been in existence. In the 1960s, there were significant numbers of expropriations, which would mean that the nature of the government would have been a critical predictor variable. In the 1970s and 1980s, inconvertibility became the dominant type of loss, indicating the importance of government operations and perhaps economic variables impacting on host governments. Since 1991 and the end of the Cold War, the preponderance of claims paid have been for damage due to civil strife. In most cases, the strife was the result of ethnic divisions. Thus, while government attributes would have been important and weighted heavily in the 1970s, variables like *Ethnic Tension* (*The Economist*) or *Ethnic Fragmentation* (BERI) should have been weighted more heavily leading into the 1990s. That is, as times change, the models must also be adapted to fit the circumstance.

While only the PRS model explicitly includes the means of adaptation, if the principle is understood, users can reconstruct the models to fit their own circumstances. Recent history would indicate that this is probably necessary. Users should at least be aware of the need for political risk assessments that are narrower than a country analysis.

The Nature of "Risk"

In examining the models underlying various risk analyses, it is critical that the concept of "risk" be clearly understood. The term risk implies a probabilistic assessment. That is, political risk analysis does *not* result in a prediction. It has as its product a *forecast*. The difference is that there are elements to the analytical process that prevent the projection of specific events. The projection is that given a history, *usually* or "*there is a high probability that*" history will repeat itself. Or given a set of circumstances, an outcome has a high probability of following.

A number of elements of the analytical method and model prevent precise prediction. One is the model itself. Modelers select a sample of variables as representative of the situations that they believe will precede investor harm. Social systems are notably complex and some representative approximations of a complete range of societal attributes are utilized in any model. The projection of outcomes from the situation becomes probabilistic because a) a complex set of circumstances is necessarily simplified and abbreviated in any model, and b) the selection of representative variables and their relationships may not be the optimal one.

Even with the best of models, variables that are not included will still have *some* effect on the situation and will eliminate the possibility of perfect prediction. There is always the possibility, and perhaps high probability, that some unforeseen event outside the scope of the analysis will affect the government processes that result in losses. For example, a heavy rainstorm up river could result in flooding that, in turn, causes great damage to crops that is followed by food riots that bring the downfall of a democratic government and the installation of an authoritarian one that imposes strict controls on foreign business that deal in food products. While the probability of such events is low, they do occur and would not likely be included in even a good country risk model.

A second element that prevents prediction is partial information. Even if an optimal model is employed, the information that is incorporated as the basis of the assessment and forecast is inevitably incomplete and sometimes inaccurate. Whether there are direct observations of such phenomena as "press freedom," or media reports or authoritative testimony, there is no perfect description of such circumstances that can be introduced into the analysis. Variations in the data introduce some margin of error in the projection. This is unavoidable in social science analysis. It is important to note, however, that increased availability of information, especially through the Internet, has helped reduce this data problem. Verbal information on risk variables is not only more widely available, it is much more timely.[14]

A third problem is that human intervention also prevents prediction. Just as the person who is predicted to die in an automobile accident can stay away from automobiles for the rest of her life and thereby avoid the prediction circumstance, political risk analysis is provided with the specific intention that investors will somehow prevent the forecast from coming true. Unfortunately, many investors still don't pay attention to political risk (and very few foreign investors in emerging markets take advantage of political risk insurance). And many proceed to take the risks because the opportunity seems far greater than the risk. Many forecasted losses therefore do occur but the ones that are avoided result in a differentiation between forecast and outcome. Thus the forecast inevitably appears as a probability that is less than one hundred percent.

Many host country governments and some analysts have argued that political risk forecasts are inaccurate because "ethnic tension" did not turn into "civil strife" and subsequently did not become damage or harm to an investor. Equivalent arguments have been made on the other end of the spectrum as well, where it is argued that good risk ratings were followed by some catastrophic political event that had not been accounted for in a risk assessment. This by no means is an indication that the risk was not there. If the forecast is for rain and it doesn't rain, this is not an indication that the forecast was wrong. It might have been characterized as a 75% chance of rain. This means that there is a 25% forecast of something other than rain. It is important to emphasize again that risk assessments are not predictions but are probabilistic forecasts. But in contrast to a weather forecast, it is possible to change the odds once the political risk forecast is known. Model variation, sampling issues, data quality, and human intervention all can cause variation in the level of risk. And, of course, political risk management is explicitly intended to alter the odds.

Managing Political Risk

Host Country Management: Political and Country Risk Analysis was invented at the behest of investors and their home governments. The objective was to avoid loss. But just as firms may undertake strategies to reduce risks, so may host governments beat the odds or prove them wrong by altering behavior or changing characteristics. That is, governments may alter the risk attributed to them. This has become a very important by-product of the country and political risk assessments that are being done today. Host country governments are very concerned about how they appear in risk ratings.

There is a great competition in the global economy to draw in foreign investment. Interestingly, countries like Malaysia compete with the United States for Japanese (for example) foreign direct investment. The relative standing of opportunity is, of course, important but so is the investor's perception of the likelihood of civil strife or operations interference. Good ratings are always an objective of a government seeking an edge in the FDI competition.

There are two clear alternative types of reactions of host governments to country and political risk ratings. The first (often) is to criticize the assessments and their derivation. Complaints are often leveled at the method or the capability of the analysts themselves. Methods are argued to be "Western" in origin and therefore not appreciative of local values or circumstances. Analysts are argued to be biased or remote from the "real" circumstances. While such errors in assessment are always possible, it is often the case that this is an effort to "kill the messenger" rather than face the alternative response to the bad news. Risk analysis firms often face challenge and even retribution from host country governments when risk ratings are lower than officials think they should be.

The second response possibility is to address the risk ratings as if they were regression equations. That is, if they can see that corruption levels contribute so much to a negative rating, they can say "if we reduce our corruption rating by X points,[15] our risk rating will improve by Y points." They can then set out to improve that perception by actually reducing corruption and thereby improve the actual level of overall risk. That this is an option doesn't mean that it is readily chosen. There is still a strong inclination of governments to be defensive about risk ratings, but there is also increasing awareness that actual problems inhibit foreign investment and that these problems can be realistically addressed.

Investor Management: The original and still primary goal of political risk assessment and analysis is to enable risk management by the investors. After receiving a risk assessment, investors presumably take some action as a result. A number of alternatives are represented in the toolkit of political risk management.

The most obvious approach for an investors is to choose to go to an entirely different country. Some investors are now leaving Vietnam, after an initial rush, to avoid social and political problems they have encountered. Others see the risk levels there and encounter the disinvestment phenomenon and simply choose not to go to a particular country.

A common and sometimes inadvertent approach is *adaptation*. The firm may proceed with the investment and ignore the risks or simply count them as risks as they do with economic risk. A part of adaptation might be to elevate prices to cover possible losses. By *changing location*, investors may try to modify the arrangements or circumstances of their investment. For example, if one part of a country has civil strife and another does not, they may choose to operate in the less dangerous part of the country and leave the other until the situation changes.

Another approach to managing political risk is to *negotiate an improved agreement* with the host country government. If there is a high level of government interference in personnel decisions, for example, prior to the investment the investor can seek (and often obtain) a variation in convertibility limits or in tax levels in exchange for accommodating the government on the personnel issues. This can only be done, however, if the investor knows the social environment of the personnel issue and its implications for business operations. The risk assessment can be turned directly into an asset.

In some circumstances, the risk can be managed by *direct action*, including physical protection. In the case of kidnapping possibilities, for example, some firms have hired bodyguards or taken other protective measures to prevent situations from arising where a kidnapping could take place. Some firms have hired protective services that amount to private armies or even have created their own armed forces. Such measures entail some cost, of course, but would presumably be commensurate with minimizing the cost or harm to the investor.

Investors can *develop alliances* within the host country and even within the government that can elevate their position and help avoid the risk circumstance. This may be risky in itself if the faction or government they have aligned themselves with falls into disfavor. But it does constitute one method of active management of risk. *Strategic debt management* involves explicit disbursement of capital investment across high and low risk sites.[16]

Perhaps the most common method of dealing with risk is to obtain *political risk insurance[17]*. Political risk insurance, as indicated above, is available in the public and private sectors and is widely held by international investors and businesses. That OPIC insurance was originally provided under the auspices of the U.S. Agency for International Development (AID) is an indication of the argument that risk should not lead to limitations on investment. Risk analysis offers advice to the investor on how to manage risk in a world full of political and social danger but also full of extraordinary opportunity. OPIC's reasonable premium rates for all countries covered are an indication that international investment is being encouraged, despite the difficulties to be faced, not discouraged.

But political risk insurance, in its base form, is not really risk management. It is instead a method of salvaging the situation when risk management has failed. In addition to whatever deductible there might be with any insurance policy, considerable expenses are added in the claim and recovery process. Plus, the asset has presumably been lost and the investment process must begin anew. No insurance claim recovers anything near the investment amount and effort. It is clearly more advantageous, financially and practically, to not lose the investment in the first place.

Political risk insurance, however, *can be* a management tool. In this case, the existence of a political risk insurance policy can be used as a shield against some forms of political risk, particularly those that emanate from host governments. Assuming rational decision-makers, if an insurance policy from MIGA (i.e. the World Bank) is in place for a foreign investor, the host government might be less likely to interfere with the investment for fear of retribution from the parent body. For many insurers, an action against an investment would mean negative exposure for the host government and a discouragement of other needed foreign investment. While the existence of an insurance policy might mean nothing to a rebel group or to conflicting ethnic or tribal groups, in many cases the simple existence of a political risk insurance policy will act as a deterrent to much of the damage that might be done to a foreign investment project.[18]

Political risk analysis and political risk management are intricately and intimately intertwined. The prudent investor doesn't always avoid risk but instead takes advantage of available knowledge to deal with societies in the same manner that he would deal with economic or financial uncertainties. To do that, the assessment of risk must be a reasonable guide to actual probabilities of specific problems that will require a response with specific management tools. Theory, at the beginning of the process, must fit with management applications at the end of the process.

In this third revised edition of *The Handbook of Country and Political Risk Analysis*, a variety of successful political and country risk forecasting methods are presented in updated formats. These should be useful both to the experienced foreign investor and to the new investor seeking to determine how unfamiliar political systems and societies should be approached. They will be particularly useful if the user is aware of the critical elements of country and political risk analysis and especially of the utility of adapting methods and analyses to the focused needs of the firm.

ENDNOTES

[1] See the description of the country risk method provided by Standard & Poors, for example, where political risk composes a part of the calculation of country risk ratings but it is the country risk rating that is reported on an AAA to D scale. Political risk is not reported separately.

[2] For a discussion and further references on political risk insurance, see John O'Connell, "Political Risk Insurance," in John O'Connell, ed., *The Blackwell Encyclopedic Dictionary of International Management*, Cambridge, MA: Blackwell Publishers, 1997, pp. 230-233.

[3] William D. Coplin, Michael K. O'Leary, and Tom Sealy, *A Business Guide to Political Risk for International Decisions*, Syracuse, NY: Political Risk Services, 1991, p. 28.

[4] See "Countries in Trouble," *The Economist*, December 20, 1986, pp. 25-28. A variety of other constructed indices appear in this volume.

[5] For the political risk portion of the index, *The Economist* chose six political variables and four social variables. They are, with weights: *bad neighbors* (3 negative points), *authoritarianism* (7 points), *staleness* (5 points), *illegitimacy* (9 points), *generals in power* (6 points), *war/armed insurrection* (20 points), *urbanization pace* (3 points), *Islamic fundamentalism* (4 points), *corruption* (6 points), and *ethnic tension* (4 points).

[6] For a full discussion of this approach, see Llewellyn D. Howell, "Political Risk and Political Loss for Foreign Investment," *The International Executive*, Vol. 34, No. 6 (November/December 1992), pp. 485–498. A discussion of how a model can be reconstructed to improve its forecasting ability is presented in Llewellyn D. Howell and Donald Xie, "Asia at Risk: The Impact of Methodology in Forecasting," *Management Decision*, Vol. 34, Issue 9, November 1996, pp. 6-16.

[7] In practice, most risk forecasting techniques are what are referred to as "judgmental approaches" as distinct from quantitative approaches. This distinction is discussed in Spyros Makridakis and Steven Wheelwright, *Forecasting Methods for Management*, Fifth Edition, New York: John Wiley & Sons, 1989, pp. 240-256.

[8] Llewellyn D. Howell, "Forecasting Political Risk," in John O'Connell, ed., *The Blackwell Encyclopedic Dictionary of International Management*, Cambridge, MA: Blackwell Publishers, 1997, pp. 119-122.

[9] EIU, for example, employs variables such as social unrest, politically motivated violence, and institutional effectiveness in determining its risk assessment.

[10] See Richard M. Hodgetts and Fred Luthans, *International Management*, New York: McGraw-Hill, Inc., 1991, pp. 118-119.

[11] From Gerald T. West, "Managing Project Political Risk: The Role of Investment Insurance," *Journal of Project Finance*, Vol. 2, No. 4 (Winter 1996), p. 7.

[12] See Coplin, O'Leary, and Sealy, *A Business Guide to Political Risk for International Decisions*, p. 26.

[13] OPIC, "Insurance Claims Experience to Date: OPIC and Its Predecessor Agency," Washington, DC: OPIC, September 30, 2000.

[14] Marydee Ojala, "Using Databases to Determine Political Risk," *Database*, Vol. 19, No. 2 (April-May 1996), pp. 80-84.

[15] Corruption perception ratings from Transparency International have become increasingly influential in describing investment climates for potential investors. See their website www.ti.com.

[16] A more extended list of management tools is proposed in Louis T. Wells, Jr., "God and Fair Competition: Does the Foreign Investor Face Still Other Risks in Emerging Markets?" in Theodore H. Moran, ed., *Managing International Political Risk*, Malden, Mass.: Blackwell Publishers, 1998, pp. 15-43.

[17] A review of insurance options for political risk management is presented in James F. Quirk, "Protecting Multinational Investments With Political Risk Coverage," in *Viewpoint Quarterly*, Marsh & McLennan Companies, Fall 1996, 7 pp.

[18] For a further discussion of this role for political risk insurance, see Gerald T. West, "Managing Political Risk Insurance: The Role of Investment Insurance," *Journal of Project Finance*, Winter 1996, pp. 5-11 and Gerald T. West and Keith Martin, "Political Risk Investment Insurance: The Renaissance Revisited," in Theodore H. Moran, ed., *International Political Risk Management: Exploring New Frontiers*, Washington, DC: The World Bank, 2001, pp. 207-230.

Section II
Comprehensive
Country Risk

International Country Risk Guide (ICRG)
The PRS Group, Inc.

Business Environment Risk Intelligence (BERI) S.A.

Economist Intelligence Unit (EIU)

Euromoney

Moody's Investor Services

S.J. Rundt & Associates

Standard & Poor's Ratings Group

Chapter 2

International Country Risk Guide (ICRG)
The PRS Group, Inc.

The ICRG Rating System

The *International Country Risk Guide* (ICRG) model for forecasting financial, economic, and political risk was created in 1980 by the editors of *International Reports*, the widely respected weekly newsletter on international finance and economics. To meet the needs of clients for an in-depth and exhaustively researched analysis of the potential risks to international business operations, the editors created a statistical model to calculate risks and backed it up with analyses that explain the numbers and examine what the numbers do not show. The result is a comprehensive system that enables various types of risk to be measured and compared between countries. In 1992, ICRG, its editor and analysts moved from *International Reports* to The PRS Group, becoming an integral part of the company's services to the international business community. In 2001, PRS launched ICRG online at www.ICRGOnline.com.

The *International Country Risk Guide* (ICRG) rating comprises 22 variables in three subcategories of risk: political, financial, and economic. A separate index is created for each of the subcategories. The Political Risk index is based on 100 points, Financial Risk on 50 points, and Economic Risk on 50 points. The total points from the three indices are divided by two to produce the weights for inclusion in the composite country risk score. The composite scores, ranging from zero to 100, are then broken into categories from Very Low Risk (80 to 100 points) to Very High Risk (zero to 49.5 points).

The Political Risk Rating includes 12 weighted variables covering both political and social attributes. ICRG advises users on means of adapting both the data and the weights in order to focus the rating on the needs of the particular investing firm.

ICRG incorporates a "Type II" forecast (see Chapter 1, Introduction) in which its experts provide a current assessment, a one-year assessment, and a five-year assessment. The projections of future conditions are framed in "best" case and "worst" case scenarios. This provides managers with a probabilistic future in which to make judgements about risk management or insurance needs.

Country reports include descriptive assessments and economic data. ICRG provides ratings for 140 countries on a monthly basis.

One advantage of the ICRG model is that it allows users to make their own risk assessments based on the ICRG model or to modify the model to meet their specific requirements. If particular risk factors have greater bearing on business or investments, composite risk ratings can be recalculated by giving greater weight to those factors. Used by institutional investors, banks, multinational corporations, importers, exporters, foreign exchange traders, shipping concerns, and a multitude of others, the ICRG model can determine how financial, economic, and political risk might affect their business and investments now and in the future.

The system is based on a set of 22 components grouped into three major categories of risk: political, financial, and economic, with political risk comprising 12 components, financial risk five components, and economic risk five components. Each component is assigned a maximum numerical value (risk points), with the highest number of points indicating the lowest potential risk for that component and the lowest number (0) indicating the highest potential risk. The maximum points able to be awarded to any particular risk component is preset within the system and depends on the importance (weighting) of that component to the overall risk of a country.

The ICRG staff collects political information and financial and economic data, converting these into risk points for each individual risk component on the basis of a consistent pattern of evaluation. The political risk assessments are made on the basis of subjective analysis of the available information, while the financial and economic risk assessments are made solely on the basis of objective data. In addition to the 22 individual ratings, the ICRG model also produces a rating for each of the three risk factor groups plus an overall score for each country.

After a risk assessment (rating) has been awarded to each of the 22 risk components, the components within each category of risk are added together to provide a risk rating for each risk category (Political, Financial, or Economic). The risk ratings for these categories are then combined on the basis of a formula to provide the country's overall, or composite, risk rating. As with the risk component ratings, the higher the rating computed for the political, financial, economic, or composite rating, the lower the risk, and vice versa.

Consequently, the ICRG system presents a comprehensive risk structure for the country with ratings for its overall, or composite, risk, for its political, financial, and economic risk and for the risk components that make up these broad risk categories. This approach enables the user to track the effect of a single risk component, or group of components, on the overall risk of a country.

In addition, ICRG also produces the information and data on which the ratings for the individual risk components are determined, together with its interpretation of that informat'... or data. This enables the user of the system to balance his/her own interpretation of the information and   'nst that of the ICRG staff.

Changes to the System

As the international business scene has evolved since 1980, so has ICRG. Over the   ICRG model has been changed and refined to reflect the needs of clients and the subtle changes in risks to international business since the 1980s. The most recent changes occurred in 1997, when the total number of risk components was reduced from 24 to 22, and the components of the economic and financial risk categories were altered to produce a more objective measurement of risk in these areas.

Changes to the Political Risk Components. The total number of political risk components was reduced from 13 to 12 by merging two old categories ("Political Violence" and "Civil War Threat") into the single category "Internal Conflict." Other changes include the replacement of "Economic Planning" in the old system by "Investment Profile," the replacement of "Party Development" from the old system by "Democratic Accountability," and a slight adjustment in the weighting of two components ("External Conflict" has been increased by two points and "Bureaucracy Quality" has been decreased by two points).

Changes to the Financial Risk Components. Although the total number of risk components remained the same, some changes were introduced to make the assessment of risk more objective. However, the old categories have not disappeared completely. "Foreign Debt Stress" can still be seen, we hope more accurately, in two new components: "Foreign Debt as a Percentage of Exports of Goods and Services" and "Foreign Debt Service as a Percentage of Exports of Goods and Services." "Net Liquidity as Months of Import Cover" has replaced the old category of "Delayed Payments." In a similar way, "Exchange Rate Stability" has replaced the more subjective assessment of risk of "Exchange Control Losses." Two of the old financial risk categories, "Contract Viability" and "Expropriation," are now taken into account as part of the "Investment Profile" component of political risk.

Changes to the Economic Risk Components. Although most of the old components have been replaced, they have not disappeared entirely. "Foreign Debt Service as a Percentage of Goods and Services," "Current Account as a Percentage of Goods and Services," and "Net Liquidity as Months of Import Cover" are now financial risk components, and are calculated in the same way using the same scale. The old category "Collection Experience" can be deduced from "Net Liquidity as Months of Import Cover," while "Foreign Exchange (Parallel Market Indicators)" can be deduced from the financial risk component "Exchange Rate Stability."

The Risk Components

The 22 risk components and the maximum possible number of points assigned to them are:

POLITICAL RISK COMPONENTS

Sequence	Component	Points (max.)
A	Government Stability	12
B	Socioeconomic Conditions	12
C	Investment Profile	12
D	Internal Conflict	12
E	External Conflict	12
F	Corruption	6
G	Military in Politics	6
H	Religious Tensions	6
I	Law and Order	6
J	Ethnic Tensions	6
K	Democratic Accountability	6
L	Bureaucracy Quality	4
Maximum total points		**100**

FINANCIAL RISK COMPONENTS

Sequence	Component	Points (max.)
A	Foreign Debt as a Percentage of GDP	10
B	Foreign Debt Service as a Percentage of XGS*	10
C	Current Account as a Percentage of XGS*	15
D	Net Liquidity as Months of Import Cover	5
E	Exchange Rate Stability	10
Maximum total points		**50**

* XGS = *Exports of Goods and Services*

ECONOMIC RISK COMPONENTS

Sequence	Component	Points (max.)
A	GDP per Head of Population	5
B	Real Annual GDP Growth	10
C	Annual Inflation Rate	10
D	Budget Balance as a Percentage of GDP	10
E	Current Account Balance as a Percentage of GDP	15
Maximum total points		**50**

As already noted, the political, financial, and economic risk rating is determined by adding together the ratings assigned to each individual risk component within the risk category to produce an aggregate risk rating in which the higher the rating the lower the risk and vice versa.

The method of calculating the **Composite Political, Financial and Economic Risk Rating** remains unchanged. The political risk rating contributes 50% of the composite rating, while the financial and economic risk ratings each contribute 25%.

The following formula is used to calculate the aggregate political, financial and economic risk:

$$CPFER\ (country\ X) = 0.5\ (PR + FR + ER)$$

CPFER = Composite political, financial and economic risk ratings

PR = Total political risk indicators
FR = Total financial risk indicators
ER = Total economic risk indicators

Degree of Risk

The risk points awarded to each risk component or calculated for each Risk Category or the Composite Risk show the degree of risk. In each case, the higher the number, the lower the risk. This enables the degree of risk to be seen within a single risk component, a Risk Category or the Composite Risk (the relative position of the actual risk points (ARP) within the total risk points (TRP), or in comparison with one or more other countries.

The ARP can also be expressed within a range of risk from, Very High to Very Low, and compared on that basis by Risk Component, Risk Category, or Composite Risk.

This is done by calculating the proportion of the TRP presented by the ARP [(ARP/TRP)X100] and reading its range from the following table. As Composite Risk is always a proportion of 100 no calculation is necessary.

Very High Risk	00.0 to 49.9 percent
High Risk	50.0 to 59.9 percent
Moderate Risk	60.0 to 69.9 percent
Low risk	70.0 to 79.9 percent
Very Low Risk	80.0 to 100 percent

For example:
An Investment Profile of 10. ARP = 10; the TRP = 12. (10/12)x100 = 83.3 = Very Low Risk.
A Financial Risk Rating of 32. ARP = 32; the TRP = 50 (32/50)x100 = 64.0% = Moderate Risk.
A Composite Risk Rating of 53. This is 53% of the total and puts it in the High Risk band.

Assessing Current Risk

The risk assessment process begins with assessing the current risk of the country in question. This is carried out for each risk component within each risk category. The actual ratings assigned to each risk component are determined from available information and data according to a set of guidelines for each risk component, as follows:

The Political Risk Rating

The aim of the political risk rating is to provide a means of assessing the political stability of the countries covered by ICRG on a comparable basis. This is done by assigning risk points to a pre-set group of factors, termed political risk components. The minimum number of points that can be assigned to each component is zero, while the maximum number of points depends on the fixed weight that component is given in the overall political risk assessment. In every case the lower the risk point total, the higher the risk, and the higher the risk point total the lower the risk.

To ensure consistency, both between countries and over time, points are assigned by ICRG editors on the basis of a series of pre-set questions for each risk component. For most components, the set of questions used depends in turn on the type of governance applicable to the country in question. For this purpose we have defined the following types of governance.

Accountable (Alternating) Democracy. The essential features of an accountable democracy are:
- A government/executive that has not served more than two successive terms;
- Free and fair elections for the legislature and executive as determined by constitution or statute;
- The active presence of more than one political party and a viable opposition;
- Evidence of checks and balances among the three elements of government: executive, legislative and judicial;
- Evidence of an independent judiciary;
- Evidence of the protection of personal liberties through constitutional or other legal guarantees.

Dominated Democracy. The essential features of a dominated democracy are:
- A government/executive that has served more than two successive terms;
- Free and fair elections for the legislature and executive as determined by constitution or statute;
- The active presence of more than one political party;
- Evidence of checks and balances between the executive, legislature, and judiciary;
- Evidence of an independent judiciary;
- Evidence of the protection of personal liberties.

De facto One-Party State. The essential features of a de facto one-party state are:
- A government/executive that has served more than two successive terms, or where the political/electoral system is designed or distorted to ensure the domination of governance by a particular government/executive;
- Holding of regular elections as determined by constitution or statute;
- Evidence of restrictions on the activity of non-government political parties (such as disproportionate media access between the governing and non-governing parties, harassment of the leaders and/or supporters of non-government political parties, the creation impediments and obstacles affecting only the non-government political parties, electoral fraud, etc).

De jure One-Party State. The identifying features of a one-party state are:
- A constitutional requirement that there be only one governing party;
- Lack of any legally recognized political opposition.

Autarchy. The identifying feature of an autarchy is:
- Leadership of the state by a group or single person, without being subject to any franchise, either through military might or inherited right.

In an autarchy, the leadership might indulge in some quasi-democratic processes. In its most developed form this allows competing political parties and regular elections, through popular franchise, to an assembly with restricted legislative powers (approaching the category of a de jure or de facto one party state).

However, the defining feature is whether the leadership, i.e., the head of government, is subject to election where political opponents are allowed to stand.

These classifications are fundamental to the ICRG rating process because our assessments of political risk in all categories are based on the premise that the more democratic the society is, the more accountable it is; and the more accountable it is, the less susceptible it is to sudden or explosive political shocks.

Assessing Political Risk

As pointed out earlier, points are awarded to each risk component on a scale from zero up to a pre-set maximum, either 12, 6, or 4. In general terms if the points awarded are less than 50% of the total, that component can be considered as very high risk. If the points are in the 50-60% range as high risk, in the 60%-70% range as moderate risk, in the 70-80% range as low risk and in the 80-100% range as very low risk. However, this is only a general guideline as a better rating in other components can compensate for a poor risk rating in one component.

Overall, a political risk rating of 0.0% to 49.9% indicates a Very High Risk; 50.0% to 59.9% High Risk; 60.0% to 69.9% Moderate Risk; 70.0% to 79.9% Low Risk; and 80.0% or more Very Low Risk. Once again, however, a better financial and/or economic risk rating can compensate for a poor political risk rating.

Government Stability – 12 Points

This is a measure both of the government's ability to carry out its declared program(s), and its ability to stay in office. This will depend on the type of governance, the cohesion of the government and governing party or parties, the closeness of the next election, the government's command of the legislature, popular approval of government policies, and so on.

Socioeconomic Conditions – 12 Points

This is an attempt to measure general public satisfaction, or dissatisfaction, with the government's economic policies. In general terms, the greater the popular dissatisfaction with a government's policies, the greater the chances that the government will be forced to change tack, possibly to the detriment of business, or will fall.

Socioeconomic conditions cover a broad spectrum of factors ranging from infant mortality and medical provision to housing and interest rates. Within this range different factors will have different weight in different societies. We attempt to identify those factors that are important for the society in question, i.e. those with the greatest political impact, and assess the country on that basis.

It is therefore quite possible for a highly developed industrialized democracy to have a lower point score, i.e., higher risk, in this category than a poor, developing country. For example a three percentage point rise in unemployment could have a significant political impact in a country that has enjoyed an unemployment rate of just 2%, but would be barely noticed in a society where unemployment is in excess of 30%. Similarly a sharp rise in interest rates, which hit the housing market in a developed society, would have a negligible impact in a society where most people secure their everyday needs by barter.

Investment Profile – 12 Points

This is a measure of the government's attitude to inward investment. The investment profile is determined by our assessment of four sub-components:
- risk of expropriation or contract viability (scored from zero [very high risk] to four [very low]);
- taxation (scored from zero to three, corresponding to very high, high, medium, and low risk);
- repatriation (scored from zero to three);
- and labor costs (scored from zero to two, corresponding to high, medium and low).

Internal Conflict – 12 points

This is an assessment of political violence in the country and its actual or potential impact on governance. The highest rating is given to those countries where there is no armed opposition to the government and the government does not indulge in arbitrary violence, direct or indirect, against its own people. The lowest rating is given to a country embroiled in an on-going civil war.

The intermediate ratings are awarded on the basis of whether the threat posed is to government and business or only business (e.g. kidnapping for ransom); whether acts of violence are carried out for a political objective (i.e. terrorist operations); whether such groups are composed of a few individuals with little support, or are well-organized movements operating with the tacit support of the people they purport to represent; whether acts of violence are sporadic or sustained; and whether they are restricted to a particular locality or region, or are carried out nationwide.

External Conflict – 12 Points

The external conflict measure is an assessment of the risk to both the incumbent government and inward investment. It ranges from trade restrictions and embargoes, whether imposed by a single country, a group of countries, or the whole international community, through geopolitical disputes, armed threats, exchanges of fire on borders, border incursions, foreign-supported insurgency, and full-scale warfare.

External conflicts can adversely affect foreign business in many ways, ranging from restrictions on operations, to trade and investment sanctions, to distortions in the allocation of economic resources, to violent change in the structure of society.

Corruption – 6 Points

This is a measure of corruption within the political system. Such corruption is a threat to foreign investment for several reasons: it distorts the economic and financial environment, it reduces the efficiency of government and business by enabling people to assume positions of power through patronage rather than ability, and, last but not least, introduces an inherent instability into the political process.

The most common form of corruption met directly by business is financial corruption in the form of demands for special payments and bribes connected with import and export licenses, exchange controls, tax assessments, police protection, or loans. Such corruption can make it difficult to conduct business effectively, and in some cases may force the withdrawal or withholding of an investment.

Although our measure takes such corruption into account, it is more concerned with actual or potential corruption in the form of excessive patronage, nepotism, job reservations, "favor-for-favors," secret party funding, and suspiciously close ties between politics and business. In our view these insidious sorts of corruption are potentially of much greater risk to foreign business in that they can lead to popular discontent, unrealistic and inefficient controls on the state economy, and encourage the development of the black market.

The greatest risk in such corruption is that at some time it will become so overweening, or some major scandal will be suddenly revealed, as to provoke a popular backlash, resulting in a fall or overthrow of the government, a major reorganizing or restructuring of the country's political institutions, or, at worst, a breakdown in law and order, rendering the country ungovernable.

As events in recent years have shown, such corruption can affect both rich and poor countries as well as countries with democratic and non-democratic institutions. For example, corruption, of one kind or another, played a key role in the change of government in Japan, the reorganization of the political system in Italy, and the collapse of governmental authority and law and order in Zaire.

One of the difficulties in assessing the degree to which political corruption represents a potential risk is that much of it is hidden from general view until it suddenly erupts in a major scandal. However, one possible early indicator of potential corruption is the length of time a government has been in power continuously. The one feature that all three countries quoted above – Japan, Italy, and Zaire – have in common is that they have had the same party or parties in government for decades.

In assessing the corruption risk, therefore, we look first at how long a government has been in power continuously. In the case of a one-party state or non-elected government, corruption, in the form of patronage and nepotism, is an essential prerequisite and it is therefore corrupt, to a greater or lesser degree, from its inception. In the case of a democratic government, it has been our experience, almost without exception, that things begin to go wrong after an elected government has been in office for more than two consecutive terms, that is, eight to ten years.

On that basis, the highest risk ratings tend to signify an accountable democracy whose government has been in office for less than five years. An intermediate rating often indicates a country whose government has been in office for more than 10 years and where a large number of officials are appointed rather than elected. The lowest ratings are usually given to one-party states and autarchies.

Military in Politics – 6 Points
The military is not elected by anyone. Therefore, its involvement in politics, even at a peripheral level, is a diminution of democratic accountability. However, it also has other significant implications.

The military might, for example, become involved in government because of an actual or created internal or external threat. Such a situation would imply the distortion of government policy in order to meet this threat, for example by increasing the defense budget at the expense of other budget allocations.

In some countries, the threat of military take-over can force an elected government to change policy or cause its replacement by another government more amenable to the military's wishes. A military takeover or threat of a takeover may also represent a high risk if it is an indication that the government is unable to function effectively and that the country therefore has an uneasy environment for foreign businesses.

A full-scale military regime poses the greatest risk. In the short term a military regime may provide a new stability and thus reduce business risks. However, in the longer term the risk will almost certainly rise, partly because the system of governance will be become corrupt and partly because the continuation of such a government is likely to create an armed opposition.

In some cases, military participation in government may be a symptom rather than a cause of underlying difficulties. Overall, lower risk ratings indicate a greater degree of military participation in politics and a higher level of political risk.

Religious Tensions – 6 Points
Religious tensions may stem from the domination of society and/or governance by a single religious group that seeks to replace civil law by religious law and to exclude other religions from the political and/or social process; the desire of a single religious group to dominate governance; the suppression of religious freedom; the desire of a religious group to express its own identity, separate from the country as a whole.

The risk involved in these situations range from inexperienced people imposing inappropriate policies through civil dissent to civil war.

Law and Order – 6 Points
Law and Order are assessed separately, with each sub-component comprising zero to three points. The Law sub-component is an assessment of the strength and impartiality of the legal system, while the Order sub-component is an assessment of popular observance of the law. Thus, a country can enjoy a high rating (3.0) in terms of its judicial system, but a low rating (1.0) if the law is ignored for a political aim, e.g. widespread strikes involving illegal practices.

Ethnic Tensions – 6 Points
This component measures the degree of tension within a country attributable to racial, nationality, or language divisions. Lower ratings are given to countries where racial and nationality tensions are high because opposing groups are intolerant and unwilling to compromise. Higher ratings are given to countries where tensions are minimal, even though such differences may still exist.

Democratic Accountability – 6 Points
This is a measure of how responsive government is to its people, on the basis that the less responsive it is, the more likely it is that the government will fall, peacefully in a democratic society, but possibly violently in a non-democratic one.

However, assessing democratic accountability is more complex than simply determining whether the country has free and fair elections. Even democratically elected governments, particularly those that are apparently popular, can delude themselves into thinking they know what is good for their people even when the people have made it abundantly clear that they do not approve particular policies. Close to an election, such an attitude can have disastrous consequences (e.g., Prime Minister Thatcher's poll tax).

Therefore, it is possible for an accountable democracy to have a lower score, i.e. a higher risk, for this component than a less democratic form of government.

Bureaucracy Quality – 4 Points
The institutional strength and quality of the bureaucracy is another shock absorber that tends to minimize revisions of policy when governments change. Therefore, high points are given to countries where the bureaucracy has the strength and expertise to govern without drastic changes in policy or interruptions in government services. In these low-risk countries, the bureaucracy tends to be somewhat autonomous from political pressure and to have an established mechanism for recruitment and training. Countries that lack the cushioning effect of a strong bureaucracy receive low points because a change in government tends to be traumatic in terms of policy formulation and day-to-day administrative functions.

The Financial Risk Rating

The overall aim of the Financial Risk Rating is to provide a means of assessing a country's ability to pay its way. In essence this requires a system of measuring a country's ability to finance its official, commercial, and trade debt obligations.

This is done by assigning risk points to a pre-set group of factors, termed financial risk components. The minimum number of points for each component is zero, while the maximum number of points depends on the fixed weight that component is given in the overall financial risk assessment. In every case the lower the risk point total, the higher the risk, and the higher the risk point total the lower the risk.

To ensure comparability between countries the components are based on accepted ratios between measured data within the national economic/financial structure. It is the ratios that are compared, not the data themselves. The risk points assigned to each component (ratio) are taken from a fixed scale.

Assessing Financial Risk

As noted above, points are awarded to each risk component on a scale from zero to a pre-set maximum. In general, if the points awarded are less than 50% of the total, that component can be considered as very high risk. If the points are in the 50-60% range as high risk, in the 60%-70% range as moderate risk, in the 70-80% range as low risk and in the 80-100% range as very low risk. However, this is only a general guideline as a better rating in other components can compensate for a poor risk rating in one component.

Overall, a financial risk rating of 0.0% to 24.5% indicated a Very High Risk; 25.0% to 29.9% High Risk; 30.0% to 34.9% Moderate Risk; 35.0% to 39.9% Low Risk; and 40.0% or more Very Low Risk. Once again, however, a poor financial risk rating can be compensated for by a better political and/or economic risk rating.

Foreign Debt as a Percentage of GDP — 10 points
The estimated gross foreign debt in a given year, converted into US dollars at the average exchange rate for that year, is expressed as a percentage of the gross domestic product converted into US dollars at the average exchange rate for that year. The risk points are then assigned according to the following scale:

Ratio (%)	Points	Ratio (%)	Points
0.0–5.0	10.0	60.1–70.0	4.5
5.1–10.0	9.5	70.1–80.0	4.0
10.1–15.0	9.0	80.1–90.0	3.5
15.1–20.0	8.5	90.1–100.0	3.0
20.1–25.0	8.0	100.1–110.0	2.5
25.1–30.0	7.5	110.1–120.0	2.0
31.1–35.0	7.0	120.1–130.0	1.5
35.1–40.0	6.5	130.1–150.0	1.0
40.1–45.0	6.0	150.1–200.0	0.5
45.1–50.0	5.5	200.1 and over	0.0
50.1 – 60.0	5.0		

Foreign Debt Service as a Percentage of Exports of Goods and Services — 10 points
The estimated foreign debt service, for a given year, converted into US dollars at the average exchange rate for that year, is expressed as a percentage of the sum of the estimated total exports of goods and services for that year, converted into US dollars at the average exchange rate for that year. The risk points are then assigned according to the following scale:

Ratio (%)	Points	Ratio (%)	Points
0.0–4.9	10.0	45.0–48.9	4.5
5.0–8.9	9.5	49.0–52.9	4.0
9.0–12.9	9.0	53.0–56.9	3.5
13.0–16.9	8.5	57.0–60.9	3.0
17.0–20.9	8.0	61.0–65.9	2.5
21.0–24.9	7.5	66.0–70.9	2.0
25.0–28.9	7.0	71.0–75.9	1.5
29.0–32.9	6.5	76.0–80.9	1.0
33.0–36.9	6.0	81.0–84.9	0.5
37.0–40.9	5.5	85.0 and over	0.0
41.0–44.9	5.0		

Current Account as a Percentage of Exports of Goods and Services — 15 points

The balance of the current account of the balance of payments for a given year, converted into US dollars at the average exchange rate for that year, is expressed as a percentage of the sum of the estimated total exports of goods and services for that year, converted into US dollars at the average exchange rate for that year. The risk points are then assigned according to the following scale:

Ratio (%)	Points	Ratio (%)	Points
+25 and over	15.0	-50.1 to -55.0	7.0
20.1 to 25.0	14.5	-55.1 to -60.0	6.5
15.1 to 20.0	14.0	-60.1 to -65.0	6.0
10.1 to 15.0	13.5	-65.1 to -70.0	5.5
5.1 to 10.0	13.0	-70.1 to -75.0	5.0
0.0 to 5.0	12.5	-75.1 to -80.0	4.5
-0.1 to -5.0	12.0	-80.1 to -85.0	4.0
-5.1 to -10.0	11.5	-85.1 to -90.0	3.5
-10.1 to -15.0	11.0	-90.1 to -95.0	3.0
-15.1 to -20.0	10.5	-95.1 to -100.0	2.5
-20.1 to -25.0	10.0	-100.1 to -105.0	2.0
-25.1 to -30.0	9.5	-105.1 to -110.0	1.5
-30.1 to -35.0	9.0	-110.1 to -115.0	1.0
-35.1 to -40.0	8.5	-115.1 to -120.0	0.5
-40.1 to -45.0	8.0	Below -120.1	0.0
-45.1 to -50.0	7.5		

Net International Liquidity as Months of Import Cover — 5 points

The total estimated official reserves for a given year, converted into US dollars at the average exchange rate for that year, including official holdings of gold converted into US dollars at the free market price for the period, but excluding the use of IMF credits and the foreign liabilities of the monetary authorities, is divided by the average monthly merchandise import cost, converted into US dollars at the average exchange rate for the period. This provides a comparative liquidity risk ratio that indicates how many months of imports can be financed with reserves. The risk points are then assigned according to the following scale:

Months	Points	Months	Points
Over 15	5.0	3.1–4.0	2.0
12.1–15.0	4.5	2.1–3.0	1.5
9.1–12.0	4.0	1.1–2.0	1.0
6.1–9.0	3.5	0.6–1.0	0.5
5.1–6.0	3.0	0.0–0.5	0.0
4.1–5.0	2.5		

Exchange Rate Stability — 10 points

The appreciation or depreciation of a currency against the US dollar (against the German mark in the case of the US) over a calendar year or the most recent 12-month period is calculated as a percentage change. The risk points are then assigned according to the following scale:

Appreciation Change, plus	Points	Depreciation Change, minus	Points
0.0–9.9	10.0	0.1–4.9	10.0
10.0–14.9	9.5	5.0–7.4	9.5
15.0–19.9	9.0	7.5–9.9	9.0
20.0–22.4	8.5	10.0–12.4	8.5
22.5–24.9	8.0	12.5–14.9	8.0
25.0–27.4	7.5	15.0–17.4	7.5
27.5–29.9	7.0	17.5–19.9	7.0
30.0–34.9	6.5	20.0–22.4	6.5
35.0–39.9	6.0	22.5–24.9	6.0
40.0–49.9	5.5	25.0–29.9	5.5
50 or more	5.0	30.0–34.9	5.0
		35.0–39.9	4.5
		40.0–44.9	4.0
		45.0–49.9	3.5
		50.0–54.9	3.0
		55.0–59.9	2.5
		60.0–69.9	2.0
		70.0–79.9	1.5
		80.0–89.9	1.0
		90.0–99.9	0.5
		100 or more	0.0

The Economic Risk Rating

The overall aim of the Economic Risk Rating is to provide a means of assessing a country's current economic strengths and weaknesses. In general terms where its strengths outweigh its weaknesses it will present a low economic risk and where its weaknesses outweigh its strengths it will present a high economic risk.

These strengths and weaknesses are assessed by assigning risk points to a pre-set group of factors, termed economic risk components. The minimum number of points that can be assigned to each component is zero, while the maximum number of points depends on the fixed weight that component is given in the overall economic risk assessment. In every case the lower the risk point total, the higher the risk, and the higher the risk point total the lower the risk.

To ensure comparability between countries the components are based on accepted ratios between measured data within the national economic/financial structure. It is the ratios that are compared, not the data themselves. The points assigned to each component (ratio) are taken from a fixed scale.

Assessing Economic Risk

As noted above, points are awarded to each risk component on a scale from zero up to a pre-set maximum. In general terms if the points awarded are less than 50% of the total, that component can be considered as very high risk. If the points are in the 50-60% range as high risk, in the 60%-70% range as moderate risk, in the 70-80% range as low risk, and in the 80-100% range as very low risk. However, this is only a general guideline as a better rating in other components can compensate for a poor risk rating in one component.

Overall, an economic risk rating of 0.0% to 24.5% indicates a Very High Risk; 25.0% to 29.9% High Risk; 30.0% to 34.9% Moderate Risk; 35.0% to 39.9% Low Risk; and 40.0% or more Very Low Risk. Once again, however, a poor economic risk rating can be compensated for by a better political and/or financial risk rating.

GDP Per Head — 5 points

The estimated GDP per head for a given year, converted into US dollars at the average exchange rate for that year, is expressed as a percentage of the average of the estimated total GDP of all the countries covered by ICRG. The risk points are then assigned according to the following scale:

% of average	Points	% of average	Points
250 +	5.0	40–49.9	2.0
200–249.9	4.5	30–39.9	1.5
150–199.9	4.0	20–29.9	1.0
100–149.9	3.5	10–19.9	0.5
75–99.9	3.0	Up to 9.9	0.0
50–74.9	2.5		

Real GDP Growth — 10 points

The annual change in the estimated GDP, at constant 1990 prices, of a given country is expressed as a percentage increase or decrease. The risk points are then assigned according to the following scale:

Change (%)	Points	Change (%)	Points
6.0 +	10.0	-0.5 to- 0.9	4.5
5.0 to 5.9	9.5	-1.0 to -1.4	4.0
4.0 to 4.9	9.0	-1.5 to -1.9	3.5
3.0 to 3.9	8.5	-2.0 to -2.4	3.0
2.5 to 2.9	8.0	-2.5 to -2.9	2.5
2.0 to 2.4	7.5	-3.0 to -3.4	2.0
1.5 to 1.9	7.0	-3.5 to -3.9	1.5
1.0 to 1.4	6.5	-4.0 to -4.9	1.0
0.5 to 0.9	6.0	-5.0 to -5.9	0.5
0.0 to 0.4	5.5	-6 or more	0.0
-0.1 to -0.4	5.0		

Annual Inflation Rate — 10 points

The estimated annual inflation rate (the unweighted average of the Consumer Price Index(is calculated as a percentage change. The risk points are then assigned according to the following scale:

Change (%)	Points	Change (%)	Points
0–1.9	10.0	22.0–24.9	4.5
2.0–2.9	9.5	25.0–30.9	4.0
3.0–3.9	9.0	31.0–40.9	3.5
4.0–5.9	8.5	41.0–50.9	3.0
6.0–7.9	8.0	51.0–65.9	2.5
8.0–9.9	7.5	66.0–80.9	2.0
10.0–11.9	7.0	81.0–95.9	1.5
12.0–13.9	6.5	96.0–110.9	1.0
14.0–15.9	6.0	111.0–129.9	0.5
16.0–18.9	5.5	130.0 +	0.0
19.0–21.9	5.0		

Budget Balance as a Percentage of GDP — 10 points

The estimated general government budget balance (excluding grants) for a given year in the national currency is expressed as a percentage of the estimated GDP for that year in the national currency. The risk points are then assigned according to the following scale:

Ratio (%)	Points	Ratio (%)	Points
4.0 +	10.0	-6.0 to -6.9	4.5
3.0 to 3.99	9.5	7.0 to -7.9	4.0
2.0 to 2.99	9.0	-8.0 to -8.9	3.5
1.0 to 1.99	8.5	-9.0 to -9.9	3.0
0.0 to 0.99	8.0	-10.0 to -11.9	2.5
-0.1 to -0.9	7.5	-12.0 to -14.9	2.0
-1.0 to -1.9	7.0	-15.0 to -19.9	1.5
-2.0 to -2.9	6.5	-20.0 to -24.9	1.0
-3.0 to -3.9	6.0	-25.0 to -29.9	0.5
-4.0 to -4.9	5.5	-30.0+	0.0
-5.0 to -5.9	5.0		

Current Account as a Percentage of GDP — 15 points

The estimated balance on the current account of the balance of payments for a given year, converted into US dollars at the average exchange rate for that year, is expressed as a percentage of the estimated GDP of the country concerned, converted into US dollars at the average rate of exchange for the period covered. The risk points are then assigned according to the following scale:

Ratio (%)	Points	Ratio (%)	Points
10.0+	15.0	-16.0 to -16.9	7.0
8.0-9.9	14.5	-17.0 to -17.9	6.5
6.0-7.9	14.0	-18.0 to -18.9	6.0
4.0-5.9	13.5	-19.0 to -19.9	5.5
2.0-3.9	13.0	-20.0 to -20.9	5.0
1.0-1.9	12.5	-21.0 to -21.9	4.5
0.0-0.9	12.0	-22.0 to -22.9	4.0
-0.1 to -0.9	11.5	-23.0 to -23.9	3.5
-1.0 to -1.9	11.0	-24.0 to -24.9	3.0
-2.0 to -3.9	10.5	-25.0 to -26.9	2.5
4.0 to 5.9	10.0	-27.0 to -29.9	2.0
-6.0 to -7.9	9.5	-30.0 to -32.4	1.5
-8.0 to -9.9	9.0	-32.5 to -34.9	1.0
-10.0 to -11.9	8.5	-35.0 to -39.9	0.5
-12.0 to -13.9	8.0	-40.0+	0.0
-14.0 to -15.9	7.5		

Making Risk Forecasts

At the same time as the current risk assessments are produced, one- and five-year risk forecasts are produced using the same methodology.

Three forecasts are produced for each time period – a Worst Case Forecast (WC Forecast), a Most Probable Forecast (MP Forecast) and a Best Case Forecast (BC Forecast).

The WC Forecast is produced by extrapolating the worst-case trend for each risk component in each risk category to produce a WC Forecast for Political, Economic, and Financial Risk.

The MP Forecast is produced by extrapolating the most probable trend for each risk component in each risk category to produce a MP Forecast for Political, Economic, and Financial Risk.

The BC Forecast is produced by extrapolating the best-case trend for each risk component in each risk category to produce a BC Forecast for Political, Economic, and Financial Risk.

A Composite Risk Rating is also produced for each of the three forecasts in both time periods.

Worst Case and Best Case Forecasts

The WC and BC Forecasts do not represent the possible extremes of risk, but a "reasonably possible" outcome of the negative and positive trends within each risk component. Such trends could be an accelerating build-up of debt, political fragmentation, worsening ethnic or religious tensions, adequate arrangements for government takeover in the case of the death or assassination of a leader, and so on. In approaching the forecasting exercise we make a judgment as to the "reasonableness" of the trend or event identified and the ability of the government to counteract such trends. This is the basis on which the WC and BC forecasts are determined.

Thus, it is possible for a country to produce a worse performance than our WC forecast or a better performance than our BC forecast, but we do not see such an outcome as likely.

Most Probable Forecast

The MP Forecasts is not a mean or median measure between the WCF and BCF, but a trend established by assuming that a government is aware of the negative trends we have established to produce the WCF and takes action to avoid them or mitigate their affects.

Analyzing the Forecasts

The forecasts lend themselves to a variety of analyses. We find the following the most useful – Risk Stability, Downside Risk, and Upside Risk.

Risk Stability

A country can appear to present a solid basis for investment on the basis of an acceptable level of risk in terms of its current Composite Risk Rating and its MP Forecast Composite Risk Rating. However, these numbers give no indication of how stable that assessed situation is. – i.e. to what degree that risk assessment might vary.

We have made an attempt to measure this stability or instability by introducing the concept of Risk Stability.

In our forecasting system the Risk Stability of an individual country is the difference between the WCF and the BCF and represents the volatility or stability of risk for that country. The greater the difference, the greater is the volatility or the less the stability.

Downside Risk

This is a measure of the degree to which a Risk Category could reasonably be expected to deteriorate if the negative trends noted in the risk components are not compensated for, and is expressed as the difference between the MP forecast and the WC Forecast. The greater the difference, the greater the downside risk.

Upside Risk

This is a measure of the positive potential of the country that could be realized if the positive trends identified in the risk components are fully exploited in conjunction with a generally favorable environment. It is expressed as the difference between the MP Forecast and the BC Forecast. The greater the difference, the greater the upside risk.

Tailoring the System

The ICRG system as it stands is produced for the general user, that is, it looks at the overall risk of country in terms of the general risk it represents.

Some users may require a more specific risk assessment that is geared to their own particular interests. For example, a company engaged in international tourism will be interested in country risk as it applies to its desirability as a vacation destination. In this case the general risk assessment may not be of much help – it is possible for a country to present a High Risk in its Composite Risk Rating, but not present a significant risk to holidaymakers because its composite risk is pulled down by such factors as low financial or economic risk, a poor investment climate, and other non-threatening factors. On the other hand, a different country might enjoy a Moderate Risk in its Composite Risk Rating because it has a stable government and acceptable economic/financial management, but still present a risk to tourists because of high crime, religious conflict, and so on.

In such cases, a better understanding of the specific risk presented can be the ascertained by looking at the assessments for individual risk components, such as internal conflict, external conflict, law and order, religious tensions, etc.

Another approach to making ICRG more specific to a particular user needs is for the user to change the weighting (Total Risk Points) of the components he/she is interested in, while reducing the weight of components of lesser interest. For example, keeping with the international travel company, one could increase the weighting of the Religious and Ethnic tensions components from 6 to, say 12, while reducing the weighting of, say, the Investment Profile, Bureaucracy Quality, and Democratic Accountability components to compensate.

Cross-Checking

ICRG provides not only the risk ratings for the countries it covers, but also the political information and financial and economic data on which those ratings are based. It is therefore possible for the user to check through the information and data so as to assess the ratings given against his or her own assessments or against some other risk rating system.

Conclusion

This, then, is the working system by which ICRG assesses the possibilities of a successful venture into a foreign market. Learning to apply either the ICRG or Political Risk Services system can play a vital role in your investment and business decisions. Know the risks and you will be miles ahead of the competition as you seek business opportunities around the globe.

Example of ICRG Ratings and Forecasts

On the following pages, there appears a sample region (North Africa, Middle East, & Central Asia) from the ICRG issue of March 2001, as well as the risk rating tables (including all 140 countries monitored by ICRG) from the same issue.

North Africa, Middle East and Central Asia

	RISK RATINGS - CURRENT ASSESSMENTS AND ONE-YEAR FORECASTS						
	CURRENT RATINGS			COMPOSITE RATINGS			
COUNTRY	Political Risk 03/01	Financial Risk 03/01	Economic Risk 03/01	Year Ago 04/00	Current Month 03/01	One Year Forecast	Five Year Forecast
Algeria	41.0	38.5	41.0	56.3	60.3	53.5	67.0
Armenia	55.0	31.5	31.5	57.0	59.0	60.0	68.0
Azerbaijan	59.0	36.5	31.5	58.8	63.5	57.5	66.0
Bahrain	66.0	43.5	37.5	71.8	73.5	74.0	71.5
Egypt	66.0	37.5	35.5	70.3	69.5	69.0	68.5
Iran	60.0	41.5	41.0	65.8	71.3	68.5	71.5
Iraq	36.0	30.5	29.5	46.8	48.0	44.0	52.5
Israel	57.0	39.0	38.5	70.3	67.3	65.0	70.0
Jordan	69.0	36.5	36.0	70.8	70.8	74.0	74.0
Kazakstan	68.0	39.0	37.0	64.8	72.0	67.0	67.0
Kuwait	68.0	48.5	44.5	80.5	80.5	72.5	72.0
Lebanon	63.0	30.5	23.5	58.5	58.5	55.5	57.5
Libya	59.0	44.0	39.0	68.8	71.0	63.5	68.0
Morocco	68.0	37.0	36.5	73.0	70.8	72.0	70.5
Oman	76.0	41.0	43.0	78.3	80.0	72.0	71.0
Qatar	75.0	29.0	36.0	69.0	70.0	62.5	65.0
Saudi Arabia	66.0	45.5	42.0	73.0	76.8	70.5	74.5
Sudan	36.0	30.0	33.0	46.3	49.5	47.0	54.5
Syria	65.0	38.0	40.0	71.5	71.5	70.0	69.0
Tunisia	75.0	35.0	36.5	73.5	73.3	71.0	69.0
Turkey	53.0	26.0	31.0	55.0	55.0	64.5	69.5
United Arab Em'ts	72.0	45.5	45.5	79.3	81.5	75.5	75.0
Yemen Republic	61.0	31.0	35.5	62.0	63.8	63.5	69.0

For historical risk ratings and key economic data on these and other countries in ICRG, please go to
www.CountryData.com.

IRAN

POLITICS

Government Stability

In a further deterioration of the already fraught relations between the pro-reform parliamentarians and the anti-reform clerical establishment, March 3 saw Deputy Interior Minister Mostafa Tajzadeh sentenced to a year in jail for his alleged complicity in rigging the February 2000 legislative elections.

In addition to the jail term, he was banned from holding public office for 39 months and banned from overseeing elections for six years. The sentence is to be appealed and Tajzadeh was released pending the outcome of those proceedings.

Compared with other sentences recently handed down to pro-reformists *(see below)*, Tajzadeh got off lightly. However, its significance is twofold. He is one of President Mohammad Khatami's most outspoken and fervent allies and, before this ruling, he would have been responsible for the supervision of presidential elections due to take place in June this year.

At the time of Tajzadeh's sentencing, it was unclear whether or not Khatami, who is at the forefront of the campaign for social and democratic reforms in Iran, will stand for reelection at those polls. Despite vocal encouragement from his supporters, he held off announcing his candidacy, apparently concerned that to do so would intensify the crackdown already taking place against the reform movement.

According to that movement, Tajzadeh's conviction and sentence was part of that crackdown and was aimed at discouraging Khatami from standing. It is a position that is difficult to dispute. Aside from removing his ally from fulfilling his role as election overseer, the sentence appears to be further evidence of the clerics' attempts to undermine his broad popular support base.

Although it will fall to Khatami to replace Tajzadeh, the anti-reformists, led by Iran's supreme spiritual leader, Ayatollah Ali Khamenei, hope that by having attacked one of his closest allies with seeming impunity, they have made him appear weak in the eyes of his grassroots support.

Underlying the clerics' attempts to do so is their desperate desire to avoid the presidential elections turning into a re-run of the 2000 legislative polls.

2000 Elections

Those polls resulted in Khatami's pro-reform supporters gaining control of parliament *(Majlis)* from the theocratic elite for the first time since Iran's 1979 revolution.

The clerics were outraged and immediately charged that the outcome of the poll could only be explained in terms of fraud on the part of the reformists, hence Tajzadeh's conviction.

However, the clerics provided no public evidence to support their claims.

In part, the failure to do so is simply symptomatic of Iran's judicial system, in which alleged miscreants are often tried in the absence of obvious evidence, and whose sentences are not revealed until the outcome of appeal procedures is known.

That said, given the significance of the February 2000 polls, it might reasonably have been assumed that the clerical establishment would have used any evidence of wrongdoing to its maximum public advantage.

Whether any real evidence against Tajzadeh exists or not is a matter of speculation. What is not is that, having lost control of parliament, the theocrats set about ensuring that the reformists' victory was rendered hollow by attacking any and all institutions and individuals allied to their cause.

Berlin Conference

The clerics' campaign began in earnest in April last year after a conference held in the German capital, Berlin. Sponsored by a foundation associated with the German Green Party, the conference was held to assess progress, or the lack of it, towards reform Iran. However, it was deemed by Iranian clerics to have been un-Islamic and a threat to the country.

Aside from its overall content, the conference was marked by some of those attending assuming various degree of undress in a deliberate and perhaps unnecessary attempt to offend Iran's religious leaders.

As a result, the judiciary, which remains firmly under the control of Khamenei and the clerics, issued arrest warrants against numerous delegates to the conference.

January Verdicts

In all, 17 people were tried as a result of the Berlin conference. The least fortunate of those was dissident cleric, Hasan Yousefi-Eshkevari. Because of his position, he was tried by Iran's special court for the clergy. In late 2000, he was sentenced to death. His appeal has yet to be heard.

The remaining 16 defendants were tried by Tehran's revolutionary court in mid-January this year. Six were acquitted, while the other ten received sentences ranging from four to ten years.

One of those sentenced to ten years was Saeed Sadr, a translator for the German Embassy in Tehran who, aside from helping organize the conference, was accused of using diplomatic privileges to smuggle propaganda into Iran.

The other person to receive a ten-year sentence was Akbar Ganji, a journalist who had alleged high-level clerical involvement in a string of politically motivated murders in Iran. In addition to his jail sentence, Ganji was further ordered to serve a five-year period of internal exile, the first such ruling against an academic since the revolution.

Reactions

The sentences drew guarded criticism from both the European Union (EU) and Germany, which summoned Iran's ambassador to the Foreign Ministry to hear the government's *"profound concerns"*. However, both were loathe to take formal action against Iran, lest they exacerbate the tensions already at play in the country.

Legislators' Petition

Those tensions were underlined when, on January 23, a petition signed by some 150 reformist legislators was read out in the parliament. The document, which took the form of an open letter to the head of the judiciary, Ayatollah Mahmud Hashemi-Shahrudi, accused the judicial system of acting illegally and spreading mistrust among the population.

In addition to its parliamentary reading, the petition was published in the handful of pro-reform newspapers that had not previously been subjected to judiciary-inspired shutdowns. At the time of the sentences, the total number of publications to have been closed by the authorities stood at 32.

The publication of the petition coincided with the start of Deputy Interior Minister Tajzadeh's trial and was seen as an act of support for him and Khatami.

Intelligence Agents Sentenced

Meanwhile, on January 27, three former intelligence agents were sentenced to death for their parts in the murder of four pro-reform activists in 1998. The three were part of a larger group of 15 agents tried, three of whom were acquitted, while the remainder received various jail terms.

On the face of it, the sentences might have been expected to ease tensions between the pro- and anti-reformists. However, pro-reformists quickly condemned the trials as a deliberate attempt by the clerical establishment to support its claims of "rogue agents" being responsible for the murders.

In doing so, they reiterated the jailed journalist, Akbar Ganji's claims that no fewer than eight clerics, including judges and two former intelligence ministers, were responsible for ordering the killings and that the total number of politically motivated murders was a deal higher than four.

The reformists' claims appeared to have been given weight during the intelligence agents' trial when one of them accused former intelligence minister, Ghorban-Ali Dorri-Najafabadi, of ordering the killings. However, the trial judge ruled that he had already been cleared of involvement in a previous inquiry.

Protests

It was against that backdrop that early February saw a series of pro-reform demonstrations take place in Tehran and beyond as groups of mainly young people called for greater freedom of expression and, in some cases, an end to the Islamic regime. The police, allegedly using tear gas and baton charges, brought the protests under control.

Khatami Versus Khamenei

In the wake of the protests, Khatami warned the clerical establishment that its determination to *"crush and destroy"* those who disagreed with what he described as its *"parochial and dark"* viewpoint, ran the risk of a social explosion.

The warning brought an uncharacteristically swift response from Khamenei, who counter-accused that the reformists were deliberately trying to undermine Iran's judiciary and questioned their motivation for so doing.

Clerical Protest

However, the degree of unity behind Khamenei's position was thrown into some doubt shortly after his comments when several hundred clerical protestors took to the streets of Iran's holiest city, Qom. The demonstrators were angry with the establishment of a breakaway movement within conservative religious ranks.

According to them, the new group, which espouses a religious democracy as opposed to a totalitarian theocracy, was being encouraged by articles published in the pro-conservative *Entekhab* newspaper that promoted *"new religious thinking"* as against old-fashioned *"reactionary Islam"*.

For his part, *Entekhab* editor, Mohammad Mehdi Faqihi, claimed that the new grouping would put forward a candidate for the June presidential elections. Although regarded as having close ties to the clerical establishment, *Entekhab* has increasingly followed the line put forward by its managing editor, Taha Hashemi, that Iran's Islamic state could, through a process of gradual reforms, become a modern state in which the people hold a degree of sovereignty.

There are no immediate indications of the degree of support such a radical idea enjoys among Iranian clerics. However, as was demonstrated by the protestors, there are at least some who would like to see *Entekhab* join the sea of liberal publications that have been closed down.

Outlook

All this, coupled with still more arrests of reformists and the sentencing of Tajzadeh, provides a distinct impression of impending doom. As the June elections approach, that impression is likely to deepen, especially if, as seems likely, Khatami bites the bullet and announces his candidacy.

The one potential bright spot lies in the possible establishment of a more conciliatory wing of the clerical establishment as suggested by the *Entekhab* protests. However, the degree to which such a movement, even if it truly exists, will be able to persuade the more extreme conservatives of the need for compromise is open to serious question.

Unfortunately, the movement might easily become tarred with the same brush as the reformists, with its supporters suffering similar fates.

Internal Conflict

Meanwhile, as if the political battle between theocracy and democracy was not enough to contend with, January saw a resurgence in activity by the Iraq-based rebel Mujahideen e Khalq Organization (MKO).

On January 7, five mortar shells exploded in northern Tehran near a military base belonging to the elite Islamic Republic Guards Corps, while on January 20, a similar attack took place on the Central Islamic Revolutionary Court in Tehran.

Claiming responsibility for the attacks, the MKO said that they were in response to the *"executions and brutal sentences"* passed on young people by Iran's *"criminal"* judiciary. The organization subsequently tried to link itself with the reform protests that took place in February and voiced its support for them

For its part, the government claimed at the end of January, to have foiled more than 25 operations by the MKO, seizing a number of rebels and weapons in the process.

External Conflict
USA

Foreign Minister Kamal Kharrazi is hoping that the new US administration will look kindly on Iran in terms of loosening the trade and diplomatic sanctions against it. To that end, mid-January saw Kharrazi call on President George W Bush's incoming administration to make drastic changes in US policy.

Tehran hopes that the new Republican administration will be persuaded so to do by the large US oil companies who are gagging to do business with Tehran.

The US Act of Congress under which American companies are banned from investing in Iranian oil and gas industries is due to expire in August this year.

Jordan

In the latest sign of improved relations between the two countries, late January saw the Speaker of the Iranian parliament, Mehdi Karrubi, begin a three-day visit to Jordan. In doing so, he became the highest-ranking official to visit the country since Iran's 1979 revolution.

Relations between the two countries cooled rapidly in the wake of that revolution because of the close links between the ousted Shah of Iran and Jordan's King Hussein. Tensions were further heightened by Jordan's subsequent support of Iraq in its eight year-long war with Iran.

However, since Khatami's assumption of the presidency in 1997 and the 1999 succession of Hussein's son, King Abdullah, relations have improved considerably. Queen Rania of Jordan visited Iran in July and King Abdullah is due to visit by the end of February. Like Karrubi, but grander, he will be the first Jordanian monarch to make the trip since the revolution.

Karrubi was accompanied on his trip by a large business delegation and numerous trade agreements were signed.

Syria

Meanwhile, late January also saw Syrian President Bashar al-Assad make his first visit to Iran since coming to power in mid-2000. The visit was somewhat less significant than Jordanian moves in that Bashar's late father had maintained relations with Iran even when Tehran was seen as hostile by the Gulf Arab states.
For his part, Bashar described relations with Tehran as *"excellent"*, adding that both countries have a similar outlook on the Palestinian issue and insist on the right of return for Palestinian refugees.

Similarly, the two countries regard US sanctions against Baghdad as regionally dangerous and are considering jointly improving relations with Iraq.

ISRAEL

POLITICS

Democratic Accountability

As expected, Ariel Sharon of the Likud party won a landslide victory in the premiership election on February 6, taking 62.6% of the vote against 37.2% for outgoing prime minister and Labor Party leader Ehud Barak. This was better result for Sharon than had been indicated by opinion polls, which gave him a 20 percentage point lead over Barak.

Nevertheless, the turnout was low in Israeli terms at less than 59% of the electorate. It would seem that a large number of disillusioned Labor voters had given up on Barak, but could not bring themselves to vote for Sharon.

The stay-aways included about 60% of the one million Arabs entitled to vote. The Arab vote traditionally goes to Labor or to the Arab parties. However, in this election, about one quarter of the 20% of Arabs who did cast their ballots voted for Sharon.

An important factor in reducing Arab participation was a boycott to register a protest against the shooting of members of the Arab community by the Israeli security forces in the early days of the Intifada.

Election Campaign

The election campaign was really a no contest. Against the background of the collapse of the peace negotiations, the on-gong Palestinian Intifada, and, particularly, the deaths of Israelis at the hands of Palestinians, Ehud Barak, who had won the May 1999 election on a peace platform, was a busted flush.

No Israeli genuinely believes that Sharon can succeed where Barak failed, as far as the peace process is concerned. However, on the basis of Sharon's reputation and his rhetoric they have allowed themselves to be deluded into believing that he can stop the killing. The fact that even if this doubtful goal is achieved it will mean that Israel will be doomed to remain the nation state equivalent of a medieval siege city for the foreseeable future is simply not addressed.

Government Stability
Unity Deal

After his election victory, Sharon pledged to restore the security of Israel's citizens and to achieve "*real peace*" and stability in the region. He also called for a government of national unity to bring this about. Critical to the formation of a unity government would be the inclusion of the Labor party.

Late on February 15, it appeared that Sharon had achieved his goal. Ehud Barak announced he was willing to join the government. Conditionally, Barak was penciled in as defense minister and Shimon Peres as foreign minister. However, the deal, which would remove dependence on the smaller ultra-nationalist or religious parties, was dependent on Likud and Labor working out an agreed set of policies.

In the event that proved too great a hurdle. On February 21, Barak announced that he would not join Sharon's government and intended to retire from politics. In a bitter letter to Sharon, Barak wrote that the prime minister-elect had ``*seriously harmed the trust*'' between them with his recent actions, presumed to be a reference to Sharon's public suggestions that Barak would not be a partner in decision-making.

Composition of the Parliament

Parties	Seats	Orientation
The Right	*60*	
Likud	19	Ariel Sharon's party. Its aim is to retain the Jordan Valley, the unity of Jerusalem and hold onto most settlements in the peace process.
Shas	17	Ultra-orthodox party of Sephardic Jews of North African and Middle Eastern origin. Shas supported Ariel Sharon in the election campaign.
Ysrael Beitenu/ National Union	7	Grouping of ultra-Russian nationalists and others, some of whom advocate the expulsion of Israeli Arab citizens and the bombing of Aswan Dam and Tehran.
National Religious Party	5	The settler's party: takes a similar line to Likud.
United Judaism Torah	5	Ultra-orthodox party of Ashkenazi Jews of non Middle-East origin.
Ysrael B'Aliyah	4	Russian immigrant party. Nationalist and more hard-line than Likud.
Gesher	2	Its main focus is on social issues but hawkish on peace.
Herut	1	Ultra-nationalist party.
The Center	*12*	
Center Party	6	Evenly split on supporting Likud or Labor.
Shinui	6	Leans to the right on the question of Palestine and to the left on religious issues.
The Left	*48*	
Labor Party	24	Deeply divided. Small Barak camp outnumbered by those wanting to keep Jerusalem and refugee issue off the agenda.
Meretz	10	Coming round to ending the occupation of the West Bank and Gaza.
United Arab List	5	Its aim is to end occupation.
Hadash	3	Same aims as the United Arab List.
One Nation	2	Could support either camp. Its agenda is dominated by social and labor affairs.
Democratic Choice	2	Russian immigrant supporters of Barak camp.
Balad	1	Israeli-Arab party.
Ta-Al	1	Israeli-Arab party.

Unity Government Agreed

Shimon Peres, who favors the unity government, was appointed temporary chairman of the party on February 26 and the party subsequently voted to participate. However, Labor is deeply divided on the issue with about one third of the delegates to the party convention voting against.

The decision is a lifesaver for Sharon. Likud has only 19 seats in the 120-seat parliament. Even with his natural allies counted in he would still be able to command only 60 seats, forcing him to lean on, and make concessions to, one or both of the center parties to get his program through. It would have been a shaky and uncertain government.

Also, Sharon has given Labor only eight of the 30 cabinet posts, meaning that while Labor will be in government it will have limited opportunities to shape policy.

That could be a major stumbling block. Labor still wants to pursue the peace process from where it was left off by Barak. Sharon, on the other hand, has declared the process to be dead and wants to start negotiations again with a clean slate, and only after the Intifada has been brought to an end.

Internal Conflict

That end is nowhere in sight. In the five months of violence up to the end of February 409 people have been killed, including 337 Palestinians, 57 Israeli Jews, and 15 others.

KAZAKSTAN

ECONOMY

The economy performed substantially better than expected last year on the back of the improving Russian economy and, particularly, the massive increase in the international oil price.

Growth and Inflation

Real GDP growth hit an estimated 8% in the year – a huge jump from the 1.7% growth recorded in 1999 and hugely better than the 3% growth projected under the program agreed with the International Monetary Fund (IMF) in December 1999. This was supported by a US$453 million Extended Fund Facility.

In addition the inflation rate was pulled down an estimated 9% at the end of 2000 compared with 17.8% at end-1999.

Budget Balance

Despite the enormous pressure for a commensurate rise in public spending on the back of the huge jump in budget revenues, the government held back. As a result, the budget balance was a positive 23 billion tenge (Kt) in the first nine months of last year. Overall, the general government budget is estimated to have ended the year in near balance – about –0.1% of GDP – against a deficit of 5.3% of GDP in 1999.

Current Account

With last year's rise in oil prices and restrained growth in imports, the trade balance surged to 14.3% of GDP compared with 4.4% of GDP in 1999. The current account balance more than tripled, rising from 1.1% of GDP in 1999 to an estimated 4.8% of GDP last year.

Reflecting these developments, the seven-year Eurobond of US$350 million issued by Kazakhstan in April 2000 was priced to yield 11.25%, about 500 basis points above a comparable benchmark yield.

Liquidity and Debt

Higher oil prices meant that Kazakhstan was awash with dollars last year. The government's share of this booty pushed up the country's gross international reserves to a record US$2.2 billion in September from US$2 billion at end-1999. In May last year the National Bank of Kazakhstan (NBK) repaid all its outstanding obligations to the IMF, amounting to some US$385 million. This, coupled with other debt repayments, reduced the public external debt stock at the end of June 2000 to US$3.9 billion, or 23% of GDP.

Monetary Policy

Against the background of economic recovery and a strong balance of payments, monetary aggregates have expanded significantly. With signs of a recovery in demand for tenge, the NBK loosened monetary policy in 2000. Given the strong growth in deposits and the confidence of market participants in a stable exchange rate, interest rates have declined. Rates on 3-month treasury bills have declined by about one-half in the year ending October 2000 to reach around 8%.

Structural Reforms

When the economy was in deep trouble the government began to accelerate its reform process as a prerequisite for IMF support. However, this acceleration was moderate and took place from a virtual standstill. With the economy now buoyant again, the reform process, such as it is, has slowed again.

On the plus side, the government has eliminated trade restrictions introduced at the outset of the Russian crisis and has converted most specific tariffs into *ad-valorem* tariffs. On the other hand, there have been delays in the reform of the tariff regime and some ad-hoc trade restrictions have been introduced to address perceived problems in domestic markets.

Even more importantly, perhaps, the privatization of large-scale companies has slowed to a stop, as have the adoption of promised fiscal sector measures and reforms in the land and social sectors.

There is unlikely to be much rapid progress in these areas until such time as Kazakhstan is again in dire need of Western money.

Despite technical support form the IMF and other agencies, Kazakhstan's official economic and financial data remain almost as dodgy as ever. In particular, the IMF has complained about the paucity of information on budget projections and formulation and the management of public resources. Despite the recent provision of some on the oil sector, the Fund has called for transparency of the oil sector's operations and its linkages with public finance.

Kazakhstan: Selected Economic Indicators						
	1995	1996	1997	1998	1999	2000 Proj.
Real economy	*(Changes in percent)*					
Real GDP	-8.2	0.5	1.7	-1.9	1.7	8.0
CPI (end-of-period)	60.3	28.7	11.2	1.9	17.8	9.0
Public finance	*(In percent of GDP)*					
Government revenue and grants	16.9	13.2	13.3	18.3	18.6	24.1
Government expenditures	20.1	18.6	20.1	26.0	23.9	24.2
General government balance[1]	-2.7	-5.3	-7.0	-7.7	-5.3	-0.1
General government debt (end-of-period)	14.5	14.5	16.4	22.4	33.5	30.9
Money and Credit	*(Changes in percent)*					
Base money	91.8	26.4	42.0	-23.8	55.0	3.7
Broad money	106.1	13.8	29.2	-14.1	83.4	39.7
Banking sector credit to the economy	-36.7	-11.5	23.1	30.0	51.8	45.7
Yield on three-month treasury bill, percent per annum (end-period)	58.8	32.3	16.1	25.8	16.3	8.3[2]
Balance of Payments	*(In percent of GDP)*					
Trade balance	0.7	-1.6	-1.2	-3.4	4.4	14.3
Current account balance[3]	1.3	-3.6	-3.6	-5.6	1.1	3.9
External public debt	...	18.7	20.3	17.9	25.3	24.1
Gross international reserves (in millions of US$)	1,653	1,961	2,252	1,967	2,003	2,215[4]
(in month of imports of goods and nonfactor services)	3.3	3.1	3.3	3.5	3.3	2.7
Exchange Rate						
End-of-period level (Tenge/US$)	64.0	73.8	75.9	84.0	138.3	144.1[5]
Real exchange rate vis-à-vis US$[6]	32.4	7.9	6.4	-9.5	-29.8	-0.7[7]
Real exchange rate vis-à-vis Russian Ruble[6]	-19.0	8.0	4.9	68.5	-30.9	-3.4[7]

Source: IMF, December 2000.
1-This definition of the general government balance treats revenue from privatization as a financing item. 2-End-October. 3-Reported figures for the 1999 current account have been adjusted for estimates of the underinvoicing of exports. 4-End-September. 5-End-November. 6-End-of-period from end of previous year. 7-End-July.

SAUDI ARABIA

POLITICS

Internal Conflict

In early February, three Westerners appeared on state-run Saudi television and confessed to involvement in the series of bombings that have claimed one life and injured five other people since last November. All of the victims have been British.

Car Bombings

The first device exploded on November 17, killing a British engineer, Christopher Rodway, and injuring his wife as they drove through the capital, Riyadh. Another bomb exploded on November 22 in Riyadh, injuring two British men and an Irish woman. The third car bomb exploded on December 15 in Khobar, Eastern province, seriously injuring another British citizen, David Brown.

In the most recent attack on January 14, an Irish citizen escaped with his life when he noticed the device under his car. The bomb was safely defused.

As the bombings followed shortly after the Palestinian uprising in Gaza and the West Bank, the attacks had been attributed to anti-Israeli, anti-Western groups in Saudi Arabia, with the finger of suspicion falling on the group that carried out two bomb attacks on US military installations in the mid-1990s, in which over 20 US servicemen were killed.

Also, in August last year a lone gunman, later said to be deranged, opened fire outside a complex housing British and US workers at an airbase.

This interpretation was backed up by a leading Saudi dissident based in London, Dr Saad Al-Faqih. According to Dr Faqih the car bombs were planted by small local groups with a grudge against the West. They are going for soft targets such as British expatriates because they do not have the resources to mount a major attack like the one on a US warship in Aden harbor in October last year.

Westerners Arrested

However, the arrest and apparent public confessions of the three Westerners – a Briton, Alexander Mitchell, who was born in Scotland, a Canadian, William Sampson, who was also born in Scotland, and a Belgian, Raf Schifter - throw a completely different light on the situation.

In his televised confession, Mitchell, who was head of the anesthesia department at Internal Security Hospital in Riyadh, said: "*I confirm and confess that I received orders to carry out the bombing here in Riyadh which took place on November 17.*" Mitchell claimed he planted the explosive device on a car belonging to Rodway. Then, he said he and Sampson followed the victim and his wife to a main thoroughfare where Sampson detonated the explosive by remote control.

Sampson, who was an economist at the Saudi Industrial Development Fund, described himself as a marketing consultant during his televised confession. He claimed he was ordered by Mitchell to make preparations for the second bombing with the help of a Belgian he identified as Raf Schifter.

Schifter, who worked as an emergency coordinator at another military hospital, the King Fahd Hospital for the National Guard, claimed that he was at Mitchell's home and heard a conversation between Mitchell and Sampson about the first explosion.

He claimed that Mitchell later told him he would need his help in the second bombing. He said he received an explosive device from Sampson, which he was ordered to plant on a car parked near his car outside a residential complex. He said he followed the car and saw it explode. When it did so *"I immediately stopped my car behind it and helped the wounded people."* He concluded his confession by saying: *"What I have said is the truth."*

Drink Link

The Saudi Interior Ministry has said that nine others are also under arrest in connection with the car bombings: four are apparently Britons, one is Lebanese, and one is believed to be a US citizen.

As for motive, the authorities have rejected any possible link to an internal dissident group or to the Palestinian Intifada. Instead, they claim the bombings are linked to illegal trading in alcohol among expatriate workers in the Kingdom. They also claim that the explosives used in the bombings are of foreign origin and were smuggled into the Kingdom and then assembled *"by experts"*.

Questions

Although the arrests and confessions seem to tie up the affair, they also present a number of questions. First, who is the mysterious figure who gave Mitchell his orders? His confession appears to be full and frank, but omits this vital piece of information. Of course it is possible that the police refused to let Mitchell disclose his name for security reasons, but it does beg the question as to whether such a person actually exists.

Second, why should Sampson simply obey Mitchell's orders to plant a bomb? It is not the sort of thing one normally asks a friend to do. Third, Schifter's explanation for his involvement is even less credible – he overhears a conversation about killing someone, and then volunteers to help out?

Fourth, who planted the bombs on December 15 and January 14? The three televised confessions refer only to the two bombings in November. Also, Mitchell was arrested and detained in December on alcohol-related charges.

Judicial Process

In the West these confessions would be tested in court. In Saudi Arabia a confession is an absolute admission of guilt and cannot be retracted, leaving the court, presided over by judges without the benefit of a jury, only to deliberate the degree of culpability rather than the question of guilt or innocence. On the rare occasions that defense council are allowed to present a defendant's case, this is only to enter a plea of mitigation.

The reason for this is that confession is a cornerstone of Islamic law (Shari'a), particularly when there are no eyewitnesses. Consequently, the police will not take a case to court unless there is a confession and suspects are be held, often incommunicado, until such confessions are secured. In this case, the British, Canadian and Belgian embassies did not know of their nationals' involvement in the bombing inquiry or of their confessions until they heard them on television.

As one person has been killed, there can be no mitigation in this case unless the relatives of the victim are prepared to accept payment (blood money) in place of vengeance. This has reportedly been rejected by the father of Christopher Rodway. So, unless something dramatic happens, Mitchell at least will be beheaded, while the best that Sampson and Schifter can hope for is life imprisonment.

Foreign Reaction

So far the British, Canadian and Belgian embassies have made a low-key response to the confessions saying only that they are seeking access to their nationals and clarification of their legal position. However, the real fuss will start when they are found guilty and sentenced. There could also be a rumpus when the other Western detainees make their confessions, particularly if they too confess to a capital crime.

TUNISIA

POLITICS

Government Stability

On 23 January, President Zine El Abidine Ben Ali reshuffled the cabinet and removed the hard-line interior minister, Abdallah Kallel, and defense minister, Mohamed Jegham. No explanation was given for the move, but it is interesting that although some other ministers were moved around, these were the most important ministers to be dismissed from the cabinet.

The interior minister plays a key role in the governance of Tunisia – it was from that position that Ben Ali ousted President Bourguiba in a bloodless coup in November 1987. Obviously, if an incumbent interior minister were plotting a coup, it would be critical to have the military on side as well.

Of course, the sudden removals could well have nothing to do with coup plots. Tunisia is anxious to deepen its relations with the European Union (EU), but faces constant criticism in the European parliament and by European human rights' groups for such abuses as the harassment, arrest, torture and 'disappearance' of opposition activists. So, it could be that the dismissals are merely an attempt to change the mood. If that is so, mood is all that will be changed – harassment of the opposition continues as before.

Ben Ali appointed a' technocrat', Abdallah Kaabi as his new interior minister and one the minister delegate to the prime minister, Dali Jazi, as his new defense minister. In his former job Jazi had special responsibility for human rights.

In all, six new ministers joined the cabinet. However, apart from the dismissals of Kallel and Jegham, the only interesting feature of the reshuffle was the appointment of a raft of junior ministers (ministers of state), whose number was increased from 11 to 24. They are meant to bring new skills to the cabinet and assist ministers in deepening economic reforms and other future challenges.

The previous government shuffle came in November 1999, a month after the presidential and legislative elections.

New Cabinet

Cabinet as of January 23, 2001		
Ministry	**Minister**	**Previously**
Prime Minister	Mohamed Ben Hassouna Ghannouchi	No Change
Minister of State, Special Advisor to the President	Abdelaziz Ben Dhia	No change
Minister of State, Head of the Presidential Office	Ahmed Eyadh Ouederni	Education
Foreign Affairs	Habib Ben Yahia	No Change
National Defense	Dali Jazi	Minister delegate to the prime minister human rights, communications and relations with the parliament
Interior	Abdallah Kaabi	Secretary-general to the government
Women's and Family Affairs	Neziha Zarrouk	No Change
Justice	Bechir Takali	No Change
Religious Affairs	Jelloul Jribi	No Change
Youth, Childhood and Sport	Abderrahim Zouari	New
Agriculture	Sadok Rabeh	No Change
Education	Moncer Rouissi	Vocational training and employment minister
Social Affairs	Hedi M'henni	Public health minister
State Properties and Property Affairs	Ridha Grira	No Change
Minister of Higher Education	Sadok Chaabane	No Change
Minister of Communications Technologies	Ahmed Friaa	No Change
International Cooperation and Foreign Investment	Fethi Merdassi	No Change
Tourism, Entertainment and Handicraft	Mondher Zenaidi	Trade minister
Finance	Taoufik Baccar	No change
Industry	Moncef Ben Abdallah	No Change
Culture	Abdelbaki Hermassi	No change
Transport	Hassine Chouk	No Change
Equipment and Housing	Slaheddine Belaid	No change
Vocational Training and Employment	Faiza Kefi	Environment and land development minister
Economic Development	Abdellatif Saddam	No Change
Minister Delegate to the Prime Minister for Human Rights, communications and Relations with the House of Deputies	Afif Hindaoui	New
Public Health	Abdelkrim Zbidi	New
Trade	Taher Sioud	New
Environment and Land Development	Mohamed Nabli	New
Secretary-General of the Government	Mohamed Rachid Kechiche	New

New Party Leadership

Although Tunisia has the trappings of a democratic state it is in reality a one-party state, with the one party being the Democratic Constitutional Rally (Rassemblement Constitutionelle et Démocratique - RCD). Elections are held, but these are arranged to ensure an overwhelming majority in the parliament for the RCD. This is so over the top, that special provision is made in the constitution to ensure that the 'acceptable' opposition receives 34 of the 182 parliamentary seats to preserve the fiction of democratic accountability.

From this it follows that control of the party is an absolute prerequisite for the head of state. In that context it is interesting that three days after dismissing he interior and defense ministers, President Ben Ali appointed a new political bureau to the RCD.

RCD Political Bureau: January 26, 2001	
First deputy	Hamed Karoui
Second deputy	Mohamed Ghannouchi
Secretary-general	Ali Chaouch
Treasurer	Abdallah Kallel
Members	Fouad M'Bazaa, Abdelaziz Ben Dhia, Abderrahim Zouari, Chedli Neffati, Habib Ben Yahia, Mrs Naziha Zarrouk, Dali Jazi.

Democratic Accountability

On January 29, President Ben Ali gave a speech to mark the new administrative year in which he said he was committed to furthering the democratic course in his country "*until it goes along with all aspects of development and reform*". He added that on the '13th Anniversary of Change' (the anniversary of Ben Ali's takeover on November 7, 1987) His government had increased the state funding for political parties and their press and introduced reforms to strengthen the freedom of expression. He also pointed to reforms in the penal system that have "*promoted human rights*" in the country. He was positive about relations with the EU and various African organizations.

However, he spent most of his speech on Israel and that Palestinians and Syria should have their land returned. This, and Tunisia's assertion that the UN embargo on Iraq should end, will not be welcome to Western ears, but is unlikely to damage the country's reputation as one of the safest Middle Eastern havens for investment.

Crackdown on Activists

Reports surfaced in early February of a crackdown on human rights activists, trade unions and left wing political groups, in which various leaders were placed under a form of unofficial house arrest. On February 6, the office of the chairman of the Tunisian Human Rights League [LTDH], Mokhtar Trifi, was cordoned off.

On February 12, a court ordered that the leadership of the LTDH be dissolved and fresh elections held. Four LTDH members had complained to the court that the organization broke its own regulations when it elected a new leadership last October. Two of the four are known to be members of the ruling party and the LTDH leaders and membership have accused them of infiltrating the group to hamper its work and stifle criticism of human rights abuses.

The LTDH is one of the last remaining centers of opposition to Ben Ali's administration. The group has been under judicial supervision, which effectively meant it was shut down, since October last year when it elected a new, more independent leadership, critical of Tunisia's poor human rights record and Ben Ali's regime.

Foreign Relations
Syria

Relations with Syria took a positive step forward on January 23, with the signing of agreement and programs in the spheres of energy, environment, sport, health, social affairs, posts, information, air transport, tourism, investment, media, and justice.

ECONOMY
Growth and Inflation

In its report on the economy in February, the International Monetary Fund (IMF) noted that Tunisia's real GDP growth strengthened to an average rate of 5.7% between 1996 and 2000. GDP growth has been robust in all sectors, particularly services and manufacturing, while domestic demand growth has been buoyed by rising real incomes and strong investment, particularly in the services and export-oriented manufacturing sectors.

Real GDP growth slipped slightly last year to an estimated 5%, from 6.2% in 1999, largely due to drought-depressed agricultural output. However, the prospects are that growth will bounce back up to 6% this year on the back of an expected rebound in agricultural production.

A prudent monetary policy and an active incomes policy kept annual inflation stable at just under 3% in 2000, despite higher food and energy prices.

Socioeconomic Conditions

Tunisia's social indicators remain outstanding by regional standards, notably in terms of education, health provision, gender gaps and housing.

On the other hand, despite significant job creation, high labor force growth has left the unemployment rate roughly unchanged over the past five years at around 15%.

Structural Reforms

The government has made some progress in implementing reforms in the banking sector, enterprise restructuring, and in developing the private sector. The privatization program was boosted by the sale of three major cement factories in 1998 and 2000, and a new privatization drive involving 41 public enterprises has been announced for 2001.

In the past, weak lending practices and banking supervision resulted in the accumulation of a large stock of non-performing loans. Banking sector reforms and public enterprise restructuring have succeeded in reversing this trend, but bad loans still stood at 20% of GDP at the end of 1999, although over half of this amount is covered by loan loss provisions.

Tunisia began reducing tariffs against European Union (EU) manufactured goods in 1996. However, overall trade protection remains high and the IMF points out that significant restructuring is still needed to meet the challenges of free trade with the EU.

Also, the state still retains extensive control over the economy through a large public enterprise sector and controls on prices and market access.

Budget Balance

The budget deficit target set for 2000 (3.7% of GDP) appears to have been comfortably met, as supplementary spending on petroleum price supports were more than offset by higher tax revenues. With the inclusion of the social security surplus, the consolidated deficit is estimated at 2.9% of GDP last year.

Thanks in part to large privatization proceeds (1.3% of GDP), government debt is estimated to have declined to 54% of GDP in 2000.

Monetary Policy

During 1999 and 2000, the monetary authorities had to accommodate large portfolio shifts out of liquid treasury paper into time deposits, stemming from the phasing out of liquid treasury bills and their replacement with auctioned bills and bonds. Although this led to a marked increase in the growth of broad money, there was little impact on real activity or interest rates as overall liquidity increased only moderately, and in line with the authorities' target. Growth in credit to the economy (private and public enterprises) was kept slightly below nominal GDP growth.

Current Account

Reflecting a rising investment rate, a deterioration in agricultural trade, a slowdown in the growth of tourism receipts and the rise in oil prices, the Fund projected that the external current account deficit would rise to 3.2% of GDP last year. In fact, recent data from the Central Bank of Tunisia puts the 2000 external current account deficit at about 3.8% of GDP. Nevertheless, the IMF sees a narrowing of the current account deficit this year as the agricultural sector picks up.

Debt

Strong non-debt creating capital inflows linked to the privatization of a large state cement enterprise limited the external borrowing requirement in 2000. Consequently, medium and long-term external debt is estimated to have declined from 52% of GDP in 1999 to 49% of GDP last year.

Riding on an improved credit rating (Standard & Poor's long-term foreign currency rating was upgraded to BBB in early 2000 and Moody's outlook went from "stable" to "positive"), the authorities tapped international financial markets at a much lower spread (130 basis points on a 10-year yen issue) than in 1999 (280 basis points on a 10-year euro issue).

Currency Stability

In the face of a weakening euro, the central bank departed from its fixed real exchange rate rule during 2000 and allowed the dinar to depreciate slightly in real effective terms.

Tunisia: Selected Economic Indicators						
	1995	1996	1997	1998	1999	2000
Real sector	*(In percent)*					
Real GDP	2.4	7.0	5.4	5.0	6.2	5.0
GDP deflator	5.5	4.5	4.0	3.5	3.5	3.2
Consumer price index (CPI, period average)	6.3	3.8	3.7	3.1	2.7	3.0
External sector	*(In millions of U.S. dollars, unless otherwise indicated)*					
Exports of goods, f.o.b.	5,469	5,519	5,559	5,733	5,864	5,992
Imports of goods, f.o.b.	7,458	7,280	7,514	7,887	8,003	8,278
Current account, excluding capital grants (in percent of GDP)	-4.3	-2.4	-3.1	-3.4	-2.1	-3.2
Foreign direct investment, net	308	262	388	685	357	651
Capital and financial account balance	928	838	710	621	878	568
Total reserves minus gold	1,616	1,916	1,985	1,866	2,289	2,222
External MLT debt (in billions of US$)	9.8	9.9	9.6	10.0	10.3	9.8
Debt service ratio (in percent of exports of goods and nonfactor services)	20.9	21.4	19.4	19.2	18.6	22.4
Real effective exchange rate (in percent)	2.2	0.7	-0.1	-0.1	1.0	-0.7
Financial variables	*(In percent of GDP, unless otherwise indicated)*					
Fiscal balance[2]	-4.5	-5.1	-4.2	-2.8	-2.6	-2.9
Revenues[3]	29.9	30.3	28.4	29.1	28.9	29.1
Expenditures and net lending	34.5	35.5	32.6	32.0	31.5	32.0
Gross saving	20.2	22.4	23.2	23.5	24.5	24.5
Gross domestic investment	24.7	25.1	26.5	26.9	26.6	27.7
Change in liquidity (M4) (in percent)	10.6	12.4	8.7	9.3	9.4	5.1
Interest rate (money market rate, in percent)	8.8	7.8	6.9	6.9	5.9	5.9

Source. IMF, February 2001.
1-Projection. 2-Overall deficit excluding grants and privatization. 3-Excluding grants.

TURKEY

ECONOMY

In its latest review of Turkey's economic program in December, the International Monetary Fund (IMF) approved the immediate disbursement of about US$577 million from the US$3.8 billon standby-credit initially approved in December 1999. This brings the total disbursed under the credit to about US$865 million, leaving an undisbursed balance of about US$2.9 billion.

The Fund also approved additional resources under the stand-by credit available under the Supplemental Reserve Facility (SRF) totaling some US$7.5 billion, or 600% of Turkey's quota in the IMF, to alleviate balance of payments difficulties stemming from the recent financial crisis. Of this amount, about US$2.2 billion, or 180% of quota, was made available immediately.

Financial Crisis

This extra support was necessitated by a financial crisis that emerged in late November when some medium-sized banks ran into liquidity problems. The roots of these problems lay, in part, with the economic program agreed with the IMF in December 1999. The change in the monetary framework and the strong fiscal and structural reform within the program resulted in the rapid fall in domestic interest rates in early 2000. While the introduction of the preannounced exchange rate path provided an anchor to interest rates, the effect on inflation expectations was not as strong.

This combination of a sharp decline in interest rates and inertia in inflation expectations spurred domestic demand to well-above program expectations. The surge in domestic demand, coupled with external shocks, such as the increase in international energy prices and interest rates, and the appreciation of the US dollar vis-à-vis the euro also led to a deterioration of the external current account.

The significant deterioration in the external current account and a weakening of confidence hit parts of the banking system as rises in interest rates translated into a fall in profit margins due to a mismatch in the asset/liability composition.

In this context, and following a major relaxation of liquidity, a disturbance in the interbank market also resulted in a substantial loss of foreign reserves.

To secure the extra support, the government agreed to strengthen measures to restore the program's credibility. These include rapid measures to strengthen the banking sector and fiscal tightening geared to reduce the use of external savings.

Growth and Inflation

The economy recovered strongly from the 1999 recession in 2000 with real GNP growth turning in at an estimated 5.9% from –6.1%. Growth is projected to moderate this year to about 4-4.5%.

The latest estimates put consumer price inflation last year at about 38% last year, its lowest level since the mid-1980s, but still 13 percentage points above the program target. CPI inflation is forecast to fall to about 12% by end-2001.

Budget Balance

Fiscal accounts improved dramatically last year with the primary public sector balance shifting to a projected surplus of 3% of GNP from a deficit of 1.9% of GNP in 1999. The operational deficit is expected to have fallen even more as a result of the drop in domestic interest rates.

The central government budget target for 2001 is to be achieved through revenue and expenditure measures. In the banking sector, the government is following a multi-pronged strategy that includes providing a government guarantee on depositors and creditors, implementing a law to remove tax obstacles to mergers of banks, accelerating the resolution of intervened banks, and the strengthening of bank supervision.

Monetary Policy

In the first half of 2001, monetary policy is to focus on recovering part of the foreign exchange that was lost during the crisis, in the context of the preannounced crawling peg with no band. As envisaged in the original program, monetary and exchange rate policies will become gradually more flexible starting on July 1, this year, with the opening of an exchange rate band around the preannounced mid-point.

Current Account

The external account deficit is estimated to have widened to about 5% of GNP last year from just under 1% of GNP in 1999. It is projected to fall this year to 3.5% of GNP.

Turkey: Selected Economic Indicators						
	1996	**1997**	**1998**	**1999**	**2000**	**2001**
Real economy	*(Change in %)*					
Real GNP	7.2	8.2	3.9	-6.1	5.9	4.0
Domestic demand	10.0	7.5	0.6	-4.0	12.0	2.2
CPI (end-of-period)	79.8	99.1	69.7	65.4	25.0	12.0
Unemployment rate (in %)[1]	6.0	6.4	5.9	7.7	5.6	...
Gross national saving[2,3]	18.9	20.8	22.5	20.5	18.2	20.9
Gross domestic investment[2,3]	23.4	24.6	24.0	21.5	24.1	25.0
Public finance	*(In percent of GNP)*					
Central government						
Primary balance	1.2	-0.2	3.6	1.5	4.9	5.7
Overall balance	-8.4	-7.6	-7.7	-11.6	-11.3	-4.8
Central government debt	48.0	46.6	48.5	63.2	62.1	58.6
Consolidated public sector						
Primary balance	-1.2	-2.1	0.9	-1.9	3.6	5.0
Operational balance	-7.1	-3.0	-4.6	-14.1	-5.6	-3.3
Consolidated net debt	46.5	42.9	43.7	61.2	62.3	57.5
Money and credit	*(End-year, percentage change)*					
Broad liquidity[4]	113.1	117.6	76.0	82.6	42.0	23.0
Credit to private sector	125.8	120.5.	81.7	58.3	61.8	23.0
Interest rates	*(Year average)*					
Treasury bill rate[5]	132.4	105.2	115.7	106.2	38.4	...
Overnight money market rate[6]	115.8	101.4	111.9	107.0	49.7	...
Balance of payments						
Trade balance[2]	-5.7	-8.0	-7.0	-5.6	-11.6	-10.0
Current account balance (including shuttle trade)[2]	-1.3	-1.4	0.9	-0.8	-5.3	-3.5
Reserves (US$ billions, end-of-period)[7]	17,695	19,575	20,112	24,274	22,787	
Reserve cover (in months of imports of GNFS)	3.9	3.8	4.0	5.3	4.0	

Source: IMF, December 2000.
1-As of the third quarter of 2000.2-In percent of GNP.3-Difference between balance of payments and the national income accounts comes from the treatment of shuttle trade and related services receipts.4-Includes foreign currency deposits and repos.5-Simple average across maturities ranging from three months to one year, net of tax, in the primary auction.6-Average during January 1 to November 17, 2000.7-For 2000, estimates for end-December.

* * *

An Extract of ICRG's
STATISTICAL
SECTION
March 2001 Issue

TABLE 1

COUNTRY RISK, RANKED BY COMPOSITE RISK RATING
(March 2001 versus April 2000)

Rank In 03/01	Country	Composite Risk Rating 03/01	Composite Risk Rating 04/00	03/01 versus 04/00	Rank In 04/00
	Very Low Risk				
1 Norway		91.5	88.5	3.0	5
2 Singapore		90.3	89.0	1.3	2
3 Luxembourg		89.5	89.8	-0.3	1
4 Netherlands		89.0	87.8	1.2	6
5 Finland		88.5	88.8	-0.3	3
6 Denmark		88.3	86.8	1.5	7
6 Switzerland		88.3	88.8	-0.5	3
8 Ireland		86.8	85.8	1.0	8
9 Brunei		86.3	85.3	1.0	10
10 Sweden		84.5	84.0	0.5	12
11 Austria		84.0	82.3	1.7	18
11 Germany		84.0	84.0	0.0	12
13 Canada		83.8	85.5	-1.8	9
14 Japan		83.5	82.8	0.7	17
15 United Kingdom		83.3	85.3	-2.1	10
16 Belgium		82.0	80.8	1.2	21
17 United States		81.8	80.0	1.8	24
18 Taiwan		81.5	83.0	-1.5	16
18 United Arab Emirates		81.5	79.3	2.2	29
20 France		80.5	81.5	-1.0	19
20 Hong Kong		80.5	79.3	1.2	29
20 Kuwait		80.5	80.5	0.0	22
23 Australia		80.0	83.8	-3.8	14
23 Oman		80.0	78.3	1.7	32
	Low Risk				
25 Italy		79.8	79.8	0.0	28
25 Spain		79.8	78.0	1.8	34
27 Korea, Republic		79.5	80.0	-0.5	24
27 Portugal		79.5	81.0	-1.5	20
29 Malta		79.3	80.0	-0.8	24
30 Botswana		79.0	83.5	-4.5	15
31 Cyprus		78.3	79.3	-1.1	29
31 New Zealand		78.3	80.0	-1.8	24
33 Iceland		78.0	80.3	-2.3	23
34 Slovenia		77.0	77.3	-0.3	35
35 Saudi Arabia		76.8	73.0	3.8	50
36 Costa Rica		76.5	76.8	-0.3	36
36 Greece		76.5	76.3	0.2	37
38 Estonia		76.3	74.5	1.8	42
38 Namibia		76.3	78.3	-2.1	32

Rank In 03/01	Country	Composite Risk Rating 03/01	Composite Risk Rating 04/00	03/01 versus 04/00	Rank In 04/00
40	Malaysia	75.0	75.5	-0.5	40
41	Hungary	74.5	74.5	0.0	42
41	Panama	74.5	74.0	0.5	47
41	Poland	74.5	76.3	-1.8	37
44	Bahamas	74.3	73.8	0.5	48
44	Chile	74.3	74.5	-0.3	42
46	Slovak Republic	74.0	72.5	1.5	53
46	Trinidad & Tobago	74.0	74.8	-0.8	41
46	Uruguay	74.0	73.0	1.0	50
49	China, Peoples' Rep.	73.8	72.3	1.5	54
49	Czech Republic	73.8	76.3	-2.6	37
51	Bahrain	73.5	71.8	1.7	56
51	El Salvador	73.5	74.5	-1.0	42
51	Thailand	73.5	74.3	-0.8	46
51	Tunisia	73.3	73.5	-0.3	49
55	Croatia	72.5	70.0	2.5	67
55	Dominican Republic	72.5	71.8	0.7	56
55	Mexico	72.5	70.0	2.5	67
58	Kazakstan	72.0	64.8	7.2	80
59	Lithuania	71.8	71.3	0.5	59
60	Latvia	71.5	72.3	-0.8	54
60	Syria	71.5	71.5	0.0	58
62	Iran	71.3	65.8	5.5	79
62	Vietnam	71.3	67.3	4.0	77
64	Libya	71.0	68.8	2.2	71
65	Jamaica	70.8	68.8	2.0	71
65	Jordan	70.8	70.8	0.0	61
65	Morocco	70.8	73.0	-2.3	50
68	Qatar	70.0	69.0	1.0	70
	Medium Risk				
69	Egypt	69.5	70.3	-0.8	63
69	Guatemala	69.5	70.3	-0.8	63
71	Argentina	69.3	71.3	-2.1	59
72	Bolivia	69.0	68.3	0.7	74
72	South Africa	69.0	70.0	-1.0	67
74	Peru	68.8	67.8	1.0	76
75	Venezuela	68.5	64.5	4.0	83
76	Bulgaria	68.0	70.8	-2.8	61
77	Gabon	67.8	68.3	-0.5	74
78	Israel	67.3	70.3	3.1	63
79	Mongolia	67.0	64.5	2.5	83
79	Suriname	67.0	59.3	7.7	106
81	Russian Federation.	66.5	55.3	11.2	122
82	Paraguay	66.3	63.8	2.5	87
83	Philippines	66.0	70.3	-4.3	63
84	Gambia	65.8	68.8	-3.1	71
84	Uganda	65.8	63.5	2.3	88
86	Papua New Guinea	65.3	63.3	2.0	89
87	Senegal	64.8	64.8	0.0	80

Rank In 03/01	Country	Composite Risk Rating 03/01	Composite Risk Rating 04/00	03/01 versus 04/00	Rank In 04/00
88	Guyana	64.3	64.0	0.3	86
88	Romania	64.3	61.3	3.0	97
88	Ukraine	64.3	58.3	6.0	112
91	Honduras	64.0	63.0	1.0	90
91	India	64.0	64.3	-0.3	85
93	Madagascar	63.8	62.0	1.8	94
93	Yemen, Republic	63.8	62.0	1.8	94
95	Azerbaijan	63.5	58.8	4.7	108
95	Brazil	63.5	64.8	-1.3	80
95	Cameroon	63.5	60.3	3.2	101
95	Mali	63.5	66.0	-2.5	78
99	Burkina Faso	63.0	63.0	0.0	90
99	Cuba	63.0	61.3	1.7	97
101	Albania	62.3	62.5	-0.3	93
102	Nigeria	61.8	54.8	7.0	124
103	Bangladesh	61.5	61.8	-0.3	96
103	Togo	61.5	60.3	1.2	101
105	Kenya	60.5	56.8	3.7	117
106	Algeria	60.3	56.3	4.0	119
107	Niger	60.0	63.0	-3.0	90
	High Risk				
108	Ethiopia	59.5	57.0	2.5	114
108	Moldova	59.5	54.5	5.0	125
108	Zambia	59.5	60.0	-0.5	103
111	Tanzania	59.3	59.5	-0.3	105
112	Armenia	59.0	57.0	2.0	114
112	Belarus	59.0	58.8	0.2	108
112	Congo, Republic	59.0	48.8	10.2	130
115	Colombia	58.8	57.0	1.8	114
115	Ecuador	58.8	50.0	8.8	129
115	Malawi	58.8	61.0	-2.3	99
115	Mozambique	58.8	56.0	2.8	121
119	Lebanon	58.5	58.5	0.0	111
119	Sri Lanka	58.5	60.5	-2.0	100
121	Guinea	58.3	59.8	-1.6	104
122	Myanmar	57.8	58.8	-1.1	108
123	Haiti	56.8	56.3	0.5	119
124	Ghana	56.3	57.8	-1.6	113
125	Cote d'Ivoire	55.8	56.5	-0.8	118
125	Nicaragua	55.8	51.8	4.0	127
127	Turkey	55.0	55.0	0.0	123
128	Pakistan	54.0	54.3	-0.3	126
129	Indonesia	53.8	59.0	-5.3	107
	Very High Risk				
130	Sudan	49.5	46.3	3.2	134
131	Guinea-Bissau	49.3	46.3	3.0	134
131	Somalia	49.3	39.8	9.5	139
133	Liberia	49.0	48.5	0.5	131
134	Angola	48.8	45.5	3.3	136

Rank In 03/01	Country	Composite Risk Rating 03/01	Composite Risk Rating 04/00	03/01 versus 04/00	Rank In 04/00
135	Congo, Dem. Republic	48.3	44.8	3.5	137
135	Korea, D.P.R.	48.3	47.5	0.8	132
137	Iraq	48.0	46.8	1.2	133
138	Yugoslavia	47.8	43.3	4.5	138
139	Sierra Leone	41.0	37.8	3.2	140
140	Zimbabwe	40.5	51.8	-11.3	127

TABLE 2A

COMPOSITE RISK RATINGS OVER THE PERIOD APRIL 2000 THROUGH MARCH 2001

Country	04/00	05/00	06/00	07/00	08/00	09/00	10/00	11/00	12/00	01/01	02/01	03/01
Albania	62.5	62.5	62.5	63.0	63.0	62.5	62.5	62.5	62.3	62.3	62.8	62.3
Algeria	56.3	55.5	56.3	56.8	56.0	55.0	55.5	55.3	59.0	62.3	61.8	60.3
Angola	45.5	45.5	45.5	46.0	45.8	49.0	49.0	49.5	49.3	51.3	48.8	48.8
Argentina	71.3	70.3	69.3	68.8	68.5	69.0	68.8	70.3	68.8	69.5	69.5	69.3
Armenia	57.0	56.5	56.0	56.0	56.0	56.0	56.0	56.0	56.8	58.3	57.8	59.0
Australia	83.8	83.0	81.8	82.5	81.5	81.8	80.8	81.8	80.5	81.0	80.8	80.0
Austria	82.3	81.0	81.8	82.8	82.8	82.0	82.8	82.8	81.5	82.5	83.8	84.0
Azerbaijan	58.8	58.5	58.3	58.8	58.8	58.8	58.3	59.3	59.5	62.5	63.0	63.5
Bahamas	73.8	73.8	73.5	73.5	73.5	73.5	73.5	73.5	73.5	74.3	74.3	74.3
Bahrain	71.8	71.8	71.8	71.8	71.8	71.8	71.8	71.8	71.8	73.0	73.0	73.5
Bangladesh	61.8	61.8	62.3	62.3	62.5	62.0	62.0	62.0	62.5	61.8	62.3	61.5
Belarus	58.8	57.8	57.8	57.8	58.8	58.3	57.8	60.0	59.8	59.5	59.5	59.0
Belgium	80.8	80.0	78.5	79.3	79.5	78.8	79.5	78.3	79.3	80.3	81.0	82.0
Bolivia	68.3	68.3	67.5	67.5	67.5	68.0	68.5	68.5	69.5	69.8	69.0	69.0
Botswana	83.5	83.0	82.5	82.8	80.8	80.8	80.5	80.0	79.3	79.0	79.0	79.0
Brazil	64.8	64.0	64.8	64.8	64.3	64.3	64.3	64.3	64.5	64.3	64.0	63.5
Brunei	85.3	85.3	85.8	85.8	85.8	85.8	85.8	85.8	85.8	86.3	86.3	86.3
Bulgaria	70.8	69.5	70.0	69.3	70.3	69.5	68.8	68.0	67.3	68.3	69.0	68.0
Burkina Faso	63.0	62.3	62.3	63.0	63.0	61.3	61.0	60.3	61.8	62.8	63.0	63.0
Cameroon	60.3	59.5	59.5	60.3	60.3	59.5	59.8	58.5	59.0	62.8	63.5	63.5
Canada	85.5	85.5	84.5	84.5	84.5	84.5	84.5	84.5	84.8	84.5	84.3	83.8
Chile	74.5	73.5	73.8	75.3	75.0	74.5	74.3	74.5	74.8	75.3	74.8	74.3
China, Peoples' Rep.	72.3	72.3	73.3	73.3	73.3	73.5	73.5	73.8	73.8	73.5	73.5	73.8
Colombia	57.0	58.0	57.5	57.3	59.3	59.8	59.8	60.0	60.3	60.0	59.0	58.8
Congo, Dem. Rep.	44.8	44.8	44.8	44.8	45.0	45.0	45.0	44.5	45.0	47.8	46.3	48.3
Congo, Republic	48.8	48.8	48.8	50.3	49.8	49.5	49.8	49.0	55.3	59.0	59.5	59.0
Costa Rica	76.8	75.3	75.0	75.0	75.5	75.8	75.5	75.8	75.8	75.5	75.5	76.5
Cote d'Ivoire	56.5	55.8	55.5	56.3	57.0	55.8	54.0	54.3	54.0	55.5	56.5	55.8
Croatia	70.0	70.0	69.8	70.8	70.3	69.8	69.5	69.0	70.3	72.0	72.5	72.5
Cuba	61.3	61.3	61.3	61.3	62.3	62.3	62.3	62.3	62.3	63.0	63.0	63.0
Cyprus	79.3	78.8	79.3	80.0	79.8	78.5	78.5	77.5	77.5	78.0	78.3	78.3
Czech Republic	76.3	75.3	75.0	76.0	74.8	74.3	74.0	72.8	73.3	72.8	73.0	73.8
Denmark	86.8	85.8	85.5	86.3	87.0	86.3	85.5	85.3	86.3	88.5	89.0	88.3
Dominican Rep.	71.8	71.8	74.3	74.3	74.3	73.3	74.3	73.8	73.8	73.0	73.0	72.5
Ecuador	50.0	50.3	49.5	49.5	49.5	47.0	49.8	51.3	52.8	56.8	57.3	58.8
Egypt	70.3	70.5	70.3	70.3	69.8	69.8	69.8	69.0	69.3	69.8	69.5	69.5
El Salvador	74.5	74.5	74.5	74.5	75.0	75.0	75.0	75.0	75.0	74.5	74.5	73.5
Estonia	74.5	73.8	73.8	74.8	74.5	73.8	74.0	73.3	73.8	75.5	76.5	76.3
Ethiopia	57.0	57.5	58.5	59.5	60.8	61.3	60.8	61.3	61.3	60.0	59.5	59.5
Finland	88.8	88.0	88.3	88.5	88.8	88.0	87.8	87.0	87.0	87.8	89.0	88.5
France	81.5	80.8	80.8	81.5	81.5	80.3	79.5	78.8	78.5	80.0	81.3	80.5
Gabon	68.3	67.5	67.5	68.3	66.5	65.8	65.5	63.5	64.5	67.8	67.8	67.8
Gambia	68.8	68.8	68.5	68.0	67.5	67.3	66.8	66.0	66.3	65.5	65.5	65.8
Germany	84.0	83.3	84.3	85.0	85.0	83.5	83.3	83.3	84.3	83.8	84.5	84.0
Ghana	57.8	57.5	55.5	55.3	54.3	54.3	54.8	54.8	53.8	55.5	55.8	56.3
Greece	76.3	76.0	75.0	76.0	76.3	75.5	75.3	74.3	73.3	75.5	76.5	76.5
Guatemala	70.3	70.3	70.3	70.3	70.0	69.5	69.8	69.8	69.8	69.5	69.5	69.5
Guinea	59.8	60.0	60.5	60.0	59.8	60.0	58.8	57.0	57.0	56.8	58.0	58.3
Guinea-Bissau	46.3	45.5	44.5	45.8	45.8	45.5	44.8	44.0	45.0	48.5	49.0	49.3

Country	04/00	05/00	06/00	07/00	08/00	09/00	10/00	11/00	12/00	01/01	02/01	03/01
Guyana	64.0	61.8	64.3	64.3	59.3	59.3	64.0	64.3	63.5	65.3	64.3	64.3
Haiti	56.3	56.0	59.3	58.3	56.3	56.0	55.5	55.3	55.5	57.8	58.0	56.8
Honduras	63.0	62.5	62.0	62.0	62.0	62.0	62.0	62.0	63.0	64.0	64.0	64.0
Hong Kong	79.3	79.3	79.8	79.3	79.5	79.5	79.5	79.5	79.3	78.8	78.8	80.5
Hungary	74.5	75.0	73.8	74.8	74.8	73.3	73.0	72.5	72.0	74.0	75.8	74.5
Iceland	80.3	80.3	80.3	80.3	80.0	79.8	80.8	79.3	77.5	78.3	78.0	78.0
India	64.3	63.8	63.8	63.5	63.5	63.3	63.3	62.5	61.8	63.0	63.8	64.0
Indonesia	59.0	59.3	56.8	56.0	54.3	56.0	56.5	54.8	54.8	54.5	54.8	53.8
Iran	65.8	64.8	65.3	65.3	65.8	65.3	65.3	65.3	68.5	71.8	71.8	71.3
Iraq	46.8	46.8	46.8	46.8	45.5	45.5	46.5	46.5	47.0	47.5	47.5	48.0
Ireland	85.8	85.5	85.3	86.0	85.5	83.5	83.3	83.0	84.3	86.3	87.0	86.8
Israel	70.3	69.3	69.5	70.0	70.3	70.3	67.8	67.8	68.0	66.8	66.3	67.3
Italy	79.8	78.5	79.0	78.8	79.5	79.0	78.3	78.5	78.8	80.3	81.0	79.8
Jamaica	68.8	68.5	68.5	68.5	68.5	69.0	68.8	68.0	67.8	70.5	70.8	70.8
Japan	82.8	83.3	82.8	83.3	83.8	83.5	83.5	83.5	83.8	84.0	83.3	83.5
Jordan	70.8	70.8	70.3	71.3	71.3	71.3	71.3	70.8	70.8	70.8	70.8	70.8
Kazakhstan	64.8	65.3	66.3	66.0	66.0	65.5	66.0	66.0	66.0	72.0	72.0	72.0
Kenya	56.8	57.8	59.3	58.0	58.5	61.3	61.8	61.5	60.3	60.3	59.3	60.5
Korea, D.P.R.	47.5	47.5	48.0	48.0	48.5	48.5	48.5	48.5	48.5	48.3	48.3	48.3
Korea, Republic	80.0	79.5	80.0	78.0	78.5	78.5	78.5	78.5	78.0	78.5	79.0	79.5
Kuwait	80.5	80.5	80.5	80.5	80.3	80.3	80.3	80.3	80.3	80.5	79.0	80.5
Latvia	72.3	71.3	71.8	71.8	71.3	71.3	71.3	70.8	71.0	71.3	71.3	71.5
Lebanon	58.5	58.5	61.5	61.5	61.3	60.8	60.3	60.3	61.0	58.5	58.5	58.5
Liberia	48.5	49.5	49.0	48.5	48.5	48.5	48.5	50.0	50.0	49.0	49.0	49.0
Libya	68.8	68.5	69.3	68.5	68.5	68.5	68.0	66.5	66.8	70.0	70.3	71.0
Lithuania	71.3	71.3	71.3	71.3	71.3	71.3	71.3	71.8	71.8	71.3	71.8	71.8
Luxembourg	89.8	88.8	89.3	90.0	89.8	89.0	89.0	88.0	88.5	89.5	90.0	89.5
Madagascar	62.0	61.8	63.8	64.3	64.3	63.0	63.0	62.5	63.0	63.8	63.8	63.8
Malawi	61.0	61.3	61.5	59.8	59.5	59.3	57.5	57.3	56.8	58.8	58.8	58.8
Malaysia	75.5	75.8	76.0	76.0	76.0	76.0	76.0	76.5	75.8	75.3	75.3	75.0
Mali	66.0	65.8	65.8	66.5	66.5	65.3	65.0	61.3	61.8	62.5	63.0	63.5
Malta	80.0	79.8	79.5	78.8	78.8	78.3	78.8	78.3	78.5	79.0	79.3	79.3
Mexico	70.0	69.8	69.5	70.3	72.5	72.5	72.5	72.5	73.0	74.0	74.0	72.5
Moldova	54.5	55.8	54.8	54.8	51.5	48.3	48.3	48.5	49.5	57.3	56.8	59.5
Mongolia	64.5	65.8	63.8	62.3	67.5	67.5	67.0	67.0	67.0	67.0	67.0	67.0
Morocco	73.0	72.0	71.5	72.0	71.5	71.0	70.8	70.5	67.8	70.0	70.3	70.8
Mozambique	56.0	54.5	54.5	54.5	54.5	54.5	55.0	55.3	55.3	58.8	58.8	58.8
Myanmar	58.8	59.3	59.5	59.0	59.0	58.5	58.0	58.3	58.3	58.5	58.8	57.8
Namibia	78.3	78.0	76.0	76.5	76.8	76.5	76.5	76.0	75.8	75.8	75.8	76.3
Netherlands	87.8	87.0	87.8	88.5	88.8	88.5	88.3	87.5	88.0	88.5	89.3	89.0
New Zealand	80.0	80.3	79.5	80.3	79.5	78.8	78.0	77.3	77.5	77.8	78.3	78.3
Nicaragua	51.8	51.3	51.3	51.3	51.5	51.3	51.5	51.3	52.3	55.0	55.3	55.8
Niger	63.0	62.3	62.3	63.3	63.0	62.3	62.0	61.3	61.8	59.5	60.0	60.0
Nigeria	54.8	55.5	57.8	57.8	57.3	59.3	59.0	57.8	59.3	60.3	60.3	61.8
Norway	88.5	88.3	88.0	88.8	89.0	89.5	89.8	89.3	90.5	91.3	91.5	91.5
Oman	78.3	78.3	78.3	78.3	78.3	78.3	78.3	78.3	78.3	80.0	80.0	80.0
Pakistan	54.3	54.0	54.3	54.3	54.0	53.8	53.3	53.0	53.8	54.0	54.3	54.0
Panama	74.0	74.0	73.0	72.8	72.3	72.3	72.3	72.8	72.8	73.5	73.5	74.5
Papua N. G.	63.3	65.3	65.3	65.3	65.3	65.0	64.8	66.8	66.5	66.3	66.3	65.3
Paraguay	63.8	64.3	65.8	65.8	65.8	65.8	65.8	65.8	65.8	64.0	64.3	66.3
Peru	67.8	67.8	67.5	69.3	68.8	68.5	67.5	68.0	69.5	68.5	68.5	68.8
Philippines	70.3	68.5	68.3	68.0	67.5	67.8	67.3	65.0	65.0	64.3	66.5	66.0
Poland	76.3	75.3	72.3	72.5	73.0	72.8	73.0	73.3	73.8	75.0	75.0	74.5
Portugal	81.0	80.5	80.5	81.3	81.0	80.0	78.8	78.0	78.8	79.3	80.0	79.5
Qatar	69.0	69.0	69.0	69.0	69.0	69.0	69.0	69.0	69.0	70.0	70.0	70.0

Country	04/00	05/00	06/00	07/00	08/00	09/00	10/00	11/00	12/00	01/01	02/01	03/01
Romania	61.3	61.5	61.3	59.8	60.0	60.5	59.5	59.5	58.5	62.8	64.3	64.3
Russian Fed.	55.3	59.5	59.8	61.8	63.0	62.8	62.0	65.0	66.3	66.0	66.0	66.5
Saudi Arabia	73.0	73.0	73.0	73.5	73.5	73.5	73.5	73.5	76.0	76.8	76.8	76.8
Senegal	64.8	63.5	63.5	63.8	63.8	63.0	62.8	62.0	62.5	64.3	64.8	64.8
Sierra Leone	37.8	37.8	35.0	34.8	38.0	36.8	37.3	37.3	37.8	35.8	41.3	41.0
Singapore	89.0	89.0	90.8	90.8	90.8	90.8	90.8	90.5	90.5	90.5	90.5	90.3
Slovak Rep.	72.5	72.8	72.3	72.8	71.8	71.0	70.3	69.5	71.5	73.0	73.5	74.0
Slovenia	77.3	76.3	76.5	77.8	77.0	75.3	75.0	75.5	75.8	76.3	76.8	77.0
Somalia	39.8	40.3	41.3	41.3	41.3	41.3	42.3	44.3	44.8	51.8	49.3	49.3
South Africa	70.0	69.8	68.3	68.8	69.0	69.0	68.5	68.0	68.0	68.5	68.5	69.0
Spain	78.0	77.0	77.5	79.0	79.5	78.8	78.3	78.5	79.0	79.8	80.5	79.8
Sri Lanka	60.5	60.5	59.8	59.3	59.8	58.8	58.5	59.0	59.0	58.0	58.5	58.5
Sudan	46.3	48.8	49.3	48.8	48.8	48.8	48.8	48.8	49.5	49.5	49.5	49.5
Suriname	59.3	59.3	60.8	61.3	65.0	65.0	66.3	64.5	64.5	65.8	67.5	67.0
Sweden	84.0	83.8	83.8	84.5	84.8	84.3	84.0	83.8	84.0	84.8	85.0	84.5
Switzerland	88.8	88.5	88.0	90.3	90.3	89.0	89.8	88.8	89.5	88.3	88.5	88.3
Syria	71.5	69.0	68.0	69.3	70.3	69.0	69.5	67.0	69.3	69.5	70.5	71.5
Taiwan	83.0	83.0	83.5	83.5	83.8	83.8	83.5	82.5	82.5	82.0	81.8	81.5
Tanzania	59.5	59.0	59.3	59.3	60.0	60.0	60.3	59.8	59.5	59.8	59.8	59.3
Thailand	74.3	74.3	74.0	74.0	73.5	75.8	75.8	75.3	75.3	73.0	72.8	73.5
Togo	60.3	59.5	59.5	60.3	60.3	58.5	58.8	58.0	58.5	61.0	61.5	61.5
Trinidad & Tob.	74.8	74.3	74.3	74.3	74.3	74.3	74.3	73.8	72.8	74.0	73.5	74.0
Tunisia	73.5	73.0	72.8	73.5	73.3	72.8	72.5	71.8	72.5	74.0	74.5	73.3
Turkey	55.0	55.3	56.5	58.0	58.3	58.0	58.3	57.8	55.5	59.5	60.0	55.0
Uganda	63.5	62.8	63.0	63.5	64.5	64.0	64.0	64.3	64.3	65.8	65.8	65.8
Ukraine	58.3	59.0	59.5	59.5	59.5	60.5	60.5	60.8	61.8	64.0	64.8	64.3
United Arab Em'tes	79.3	79.3	79.5	79.5	79.0	79.0	79.0	79.3	80.0	81.5	81.5	81.5
United Kingdom	85.3	85.0	84.3	84.5	84.0	83.5	82.8	83.5	83.5	83.3	82.8	83.3
United States	80.0	80.8	84.5	84.8	84.3	84.0	83.8	83.5	82.0	82.0	82.3	81.8
Uruguay	73.0	73.3	73.0	73.3	73.3	73.3	73.3	73.3	73.3	74.0	74.0	74.0
Venezuela	64.5	64.5	66.5	65.5	65.8	66.8	68.8	69.5	70.0	69.0	69.3	68.5
Vietnam	67.3	67.3	66.8	66.8	68.3	71.0	71.0	70.0	70.0	71.8	71.8	71.3
Yemen, Republic	62.0	62.5	62.5	63.3	58.5	63.0	63.0	63.5	63.5	64.3	64.3	63.8
Yugoslavia	43.3	43.3	42.8	42.8	42.8	42.8	39.3	44.3	45.5	51.8	42.3	47.8
Zambia	60.0	59.5	59.8	59.8	59.0	57.5	57.8	57.0	57.3	58.5	58.8	59.5
Zimbabwe	51.8	53.5	49.3	49.3	47.0	44.5	44.8	43.0	40.3	40.8	41.3	40.5

TABLE 2B

CURRENT RISK RATINGS AND COMPOSITE RISK FORECASTS

COUNTRY	CURRENT RATINGS			COMPOSITE RATINGS			
	Political Risk 03/01	Financial Risk 03/01	Economic Risk 03/01	Year Ago 04/00	Current 03/01	One Year Forecast	Five Year Forecast
Albania	59.0	33.0	32.5	62.5	62.3	64.0	68.5
Algeria	41.0	38.5	41.0	56.3	60.3	53.5	67.0
Angola	47.0	24.0	26.5	45.5	48.8	47.0	58.5
Argentina	72.0	28.5	38.0	71.3	69.3	69.5	76.5
Armenia	55.0	31.5	31.5	57.0	59.0	60.0	68.0
Australia	87.5	33.0	39.5	83.8	80.0	81.0	83.0
Austria	85.5	42.0	40.5	82.3	84.0	85.0	87.0
Azerbaijan	59.0	36.5	31.5	58.8	63.5	57.5	66.0
Bahamas	82.0	31.0	35.5	73.8	74.3	74.5	75.0
Bahrain	66.0	43.5	37.5	71.8	73.5	74.0	71.5
Bangladesh	53.5	36.0	33.5	61.8	61.5	62.5	64.5
Belarus	56.0	33.0	29.0	58.8	59.0	55.0	58.5
Belgium	82.0	38.5	43.5	80.8	82.0	80.0	81.0
Bolivia	70.0	35.0	33.0	68.3	69.0	68.0	71.5
Botswana	77.0	42.5	38.5	83.5	79.0	82.5	83.5
Brazil	62.0	29.5	35.5	64.8	63.5	61.5	71.5
Brunei	77.0	49.0	46.5	85.3	86.3	79.5	81.0
Bulgaria	65.5	35.5	35.0	70.8	68.0	74.5	77.0
Burkina Faso	64.0	32.0	30.0	63.0	63.0	65.0	66.5
Cameroon	57.0	31.5	38.5	60.3	63.5	63.0	63.0
Canada	88.0	39.0	40.5	85.5	83.8	82.0	84.0
Chile	74.0	37.0	37.5	74.5	74.3	73.5	76.5
China, Peoples' Rep.	63.0	45.5	39.0	72.3	73.8	72.5	76.5
Colombia	46.0	37.0	34.5	57.0	58.8	58.0	62.0
Congo, Dem. Republic	32.0	35.0	29.5	44.8	48.3	42.5	55.5
Congo, Republic	51.0	29.5	37.5	48.8	59.0	51.0	54.5
Costa Rica	81.0	38.0	34.0	76.8	76.5	75.5	77.5
Cote d'Ivoire	52.0	27.0	32.5	56.5	55.8	63.3	64.0
Croatia	71.0	37.5	36.5	70.0	72.5	71.0	70.5
Cuba	60.0	31.5	34.5	61.3	63.0	60.5	63.5
Cyprus	74.0	43.0	39.5	79.3	78.3	75.0	76.0
Czech Republic	74.0	39.0	34.5	76.3	73.8	75.0	77.0
Denmark	92.0	41.0	43.5	86.8	88.3	87.0	87.0
Dominican Republic	72.0	37.0	36.0	71.8	72.5	73.5	71.5
Ecuador	55.0	33.0	29.5	50.0	58.8	57.0	63.0
Egypt	66.0	37.5	35.5	70.3	69.5	69.0	68.5
El Salvador	70.0	41.5	35.5	74.5	73.5	77.0	75.5
Estonia	77.0	37.0	38.5	74.5	76.3	73.5	74.0
Ethiopia	59.0	27.5	32.5	57.0	59.5	59.5	63.5
Finland	93.0	37.5	46.5	88.8	88.5	86.5	86.0
France	79.0	39.0	43.0	81.5	80.5	80.5	85.0
Gabon	62.0	35.5	38.0	68.3	67.8	70.5	70.5
Gambia	68.0	30.5	33.0	68.8	65.8	71.0	72.5
Germany	88.0	39.0	41.0	84.0	84.0	84.0	87.0
Ghana	65.0	21.0	26.5	57.8	56.3	62.0	64.5
Greece	80.0	33.0	40.0	76.3	76.5	78.5	80.5
Guatemala	64.0	40.0	35.0	70.3	69.5	68.0	71.5

| COUNTRY | CURRENT RATINGS | | | COMPOSITE RATINGS | | | |
	Political Risk 03/01	Financial Risk 03/01	Economic Risk 03/01	Year Ago 04/00	Current 03/01	One Year Forecast	Five Year Forecast
Guinea	50.0	32.5	34.0	59.8	58.3	59.8	62.0
Guinea-Bissau	54.0	20.0	24.5	46.3	49.3	52.5	60.5
Guyana	68.0	30.5	30.0	64.0	64.3	64.0	67.0
Haiti	49.0	33.0	31.5	56.3	56.8	60.5	62.5
Honduras	62.0	35.5	30.5	63.0	64.0	60.0	67.5
Hong Kong	70.0	44.0	47.0	79.3	80.5	75.5	75.5
Hungary	75.0	37.5	36.5	74.5	74.5	76.0	77.0
Iceland	89.0	31.5	35.5	80.3	78.0	82.5	81.0
India	54.0	40.0	34.0	64.3	64.0	64.0	68.0
Indonesia	42.5	30.0	35.0	59.0	53.8	52.5	64.5
Iran	60.0	41.5	41.0	65.8	71.3	68.5	71.5
Iraq	36.0	30.5	29.5	46.8	48.0	44.0	52.5
Ireland	87.0	41.0	45.5	85.8	86.8	87.0	86.0
Israel	57.0	39.0	38.5	70.3	67.3	65.0	70.0
Italy	80.0	39.0	40.5	79.8	79.8	78.5	80.0
Jamaica	74.0	35.0	32.5	68.8	70.8	70.0	75.0
Japan	80.0	48.0	39.0	82.8	83.5	84.5	85.5
Jordan	69.0	36.5	36.0	70.8	70.8	74.0	74.0
Kazakhstan	68.0	39.0	37.0	64.8	72.0	67.0	67.0
Kenya	54.0	35.5	31.5	56.8	60.5	63.5	64.5
Korea, D.P.R.	59.0	20.5	17.0	47.5	48.3	40.5	48.5
Korea, Republic	75.5	39.0	44.5	80.0	79.5	76.0	80.0
Kuwait	68.0	48.5	44.5	80.5	80.5	72.5	72.0
Latvia	68.0	39.5	35.5	72.3	71.5	71.5	72.0
Lebanon	63.0	30.5	23.5	58.5	58.5	55.5	57.5
Liberia	44.0	19.5	34.5	48.5	49.0	44.0	48.0
Libya	59.0	44.0	39.0	68.8	71.0	63.5	68.0
Lithuania	66.0	40.5	37.0	71.3	71.8	74.5	74.0
Luxembourg	92.0	41.0	46.0	89.8	89.5	90.3	88.5
Madagascar	64.0	33.0	30.5	62.0	63.8	67.5	68.5
Malawi	65.0	21.5	31.0	61.0	58.8	60.0	61.5
Malaysia	66.0	42.0	42.0	75.5	75.0	69.0	64.0
Mali	65.0	31.5	30.5	66.0	63.5	65.3	68.0
Malta	86.0	37.0	35.5	80.0	79.3	80.5	77.5
Mexico	72.0	36.5	36.5	70.0	72.5	65.5	69.5
Moldova	59.0	28.5	31.5	54.5	59.5	52.0	59.5
Mongolia	70.0	34.0	30.0	64.5	67.0	65.0	66.0
Morocco	68.0	37.0	36.5	73.0	70.8	72.0	70.5
Mozambique	63.0	29.0	25.5	56.0	58.8	59.8	62.0
Myanmar	44.0	35.5	36.0	58.8	57.8	56.0	54.5
Namibia	75.0	40.5	37.0	78.3	76.3	77.0	76.0
Netherlands	97.0	37.0	44.0	87.8	89.0	87.5	86.5
New Zealand	88.0	28.5	40.0	80.0	78.3	79.0	79.5
Nicaragua	63.0	22.5	26.0	51.8	55.8	49.0	54.0
Niger	61.0	29.0	30.0	63.0	60.0	63.5	64.0
Nigeria	48.0	39.0	36.5	54.8	61.8	55.0	63.5
Norway	90.0	46.5	46.5	88.5	91.5	88.0	89.5
Oman	76.0	41.0	43.0	78.3	80.0	72.0	71.0
Pakistan	44.5	30.0	33.5	54.3	54.0	58.0	60.5
Panama	76.0	34.5	38.5	74.0	74.5	73.5	75.0
Papua New Guinea	56.0	38.5	36.0	63.3	65.3	64.5	68.0
Paraguay	61.0	39.5	32.0	63.8	66.3	59.5	66.0

COUNTRY	CURRENT RATINGS			COMPOSITE RATINGS			
	Political Risk 03/01	Financial Risk 03/01	Economic Risk 03/01	Year Ago 04/00	Current 03/01	One Year Forecast	Five Year Forecast
Peru	64.0	37.5	36.0	67.8	68.8	67.5	69.5
Philippines	60.0	35.0	37.0	70.3	66.0	69.0	70.0
Poland	76.0	38.0	35.0	76.3	74.5	78.5	77.0
Portugal	89.0	33.5	36.5	81.0	79.5	80.5	81.5
Qatar	75.0	29.0	36.0	69.0	70.0	62.5	65.0
Romania	68.0	30.5	30.0	61.3	64.3	58.0	64.0
Russian Federation.	55.0	40.0	38.0	55.3	66.5	52.0	60.0
Saudi Arabia	66.0	45.5	42.0	73.0	76.8	70.5	74.5
Senegal	59.0	34.0	36.5	64.8	64.8	63.8	63.5
Sierra Leone	40.0	16.5	25.5	37.8	41.0	35.0	54.0
Singapore	86.0	45.5	49.0	89.0	90.3	82.5	78.0
Slovak Republic	79.0	36.5	32.5	72.5	74.0	74.5	77.0
Slovenia	80.0	39.0	35.0	77.3	77.0	79.0	80.5
Somalia	34.0	36.0	28.5	39.8	49.3	37.5	46.5
South Africa	65.0	36.0	37.0	70.0	69.0	65.5	66.0
Spain	82.0	37.5	40.0	78.0	79.8	81.0	85.0
Sri Lanka	52.0	33.0	32.0	60.5	58.5	62.5	67.5
Sudan	36.0	30.0	33.0	46.3	49.5	47.0	54.5
Suriname	66.0	37.0	31.0	59.3	67.0	69.5	69.5
Sweden	88.0	35.0	46.0	84.0	84.5	84.0	83.5
Switzerland	90.0	41.5	45.0	88.8	88.3	89.0	88.5
Syria	65.0	38.0	40.0	71.5	71.5	70.0	69.0
Taiwan	76.0	44.5	42.5	83.0	81.5	83.0	80.5
Tanzania	62.0	22.0	34.5	59.5	59.3	57.0	61.0
Thailand	70.0	38.0	39.0	74.3	73.5	70.0	70.5
Togo	55.0	34.0	34.0	60.3	61.5	61.0	63.0
Trinidad & Tobago	71.0	40.0	37.0	74.8	74.0	73.5	73.0
Tunisia	75.0	35.0	36.5	73.5	73.3	71.0	69.0
Turkey	53.0	26.0	31.0	55.0	55.0	64.5	69.5
Uganda	61.0	37.0	33.5	63.5	65.8	62.0	63.0
Ukraine	55.0	39.0	34.5	58.3	64.3	56.0	62.0
United Arab Emirates	72.0	45.5	45.5	79.3	81.5	75.5	75.0
United Kingdom	90.0	35.5	41.0	85.3	83.3	80.0	83.0
United States	87.0	36.5	40.0	80.0	81.8	82.5	80.5
Uruguay	74.0	36.0	38.0	73.0	74.0	70.5	72.0
Venezuela	56.0	43.5	37.5	64.5	68.5	61.0	72.0
Vietnam	67.0	36.5	39.0	67.3	71.3	61.0	63.0
Yemen, Republic	61.0	31.0	35.5	62.0	63.8	63.5	69.0
Yugoslavia	52.0	16.0	27.5	43.3	47.8	51.5	60.5
Zambia	67.0	24.5	27.5	60.0	59.5	56.5	63.5
Zimbabwe	43.0	23.0	15.0	51.8	40.5	45.0	55.0

TABLE 2C

COMPOSITE RISK FORECASTS

Country	Current Rating	One Year Ahead				Five Years Ahead			
		Worst Case	Most Probable	Best Case	Risk Stability	Worst Case	Most Probable	Best Case	Risk Stability
Albania	62.3	44.0	64.0	66.5	22.5	53.0	68.5	70.5	17.5
Algeria	60.3	49.5	53.5	59.0	9.5	51.5	67.0	70.0	18.5
Angola	48.8	34.0	47.0	49.0	15.0	36.5	58.5	64.0	27.5
Argentina	69.3	66.5	69.5	72.5	6.0	65.0	76.5	79.5	14.5
Armenia	59.0	57.5	60.0	63.0	5.5	55.5	68.0	71.5	16.0
Australia	80.0	77.5	81.0	83.0	5.5	73.0	83.0	85.5	12.5
Austria	84.0	79.5	85.0	88.0	8.5	77.5	87.0	91.5	14.0
Azerbaijan	63.5	52.0	57.5	60.0	8.0	55.0	66.0	73.0	18.0
Bahamas	74.3	73.0	74.5	76.0	3.0	71.0	75.0	77.5	6.5
Bahrain	73.5	68.0	74.0	75.0	7.0	65.0	71.5	75.0	10.0
Bangladesh	61.5	58.0	62.5	65.5	7.5	51.0	64.5	69.5	18.5
Belarus	59.0	52.0	55.0	58.0	6.0	50.5	58.5	62.0	11.5
Belgium	82.0	76.5	80.0	82.0	5.5	71.5	81.0	85.0	13.5
Bolivia	69.0	62.5	68.0	70.0	7.5	63.0	71.5	74.5	11.5
Botswana	79.0	77.5	82.5	84.5	7.0	76.0	83.5	85.5	9.5
Brazil	63.5	51.0	61.5	63.0	12.0	59.0	71.5	76.5	17.5
Brunei	86.3	76.5	79.5	81.5	5.0	74.5	81.0	83.0	8.5
Bulgaria	68.0	68.0	74.5	78.0	10.0	66.0	77.0	80.5	14.5
Burkina Faso	63.0	59.0	65.0	66.5	7.5	56.5	66.5	69.0	12.5
Cameroon	63.5	55.5	63.0	65.0	9.5	57.0	63.0	66.0	9.0
Canada	83.8	77.5	82.0	84.0	6.5	72.0	84.0	87.5	15.5
Chile	74.3	67.5	73.5	76.0	8.5	68.5	76.5	79.5	11.0
China, Peoples' Rep.	73.8	68.0	72.5	74.5	6.5	67.0	76.5	81.0	14.0
Colombia	58.8	48.5	58.0	62.0	13.5	50.5	62.0	69.0	18.5
Congo, Dem. Republic	48.3	34.0	42.5	49.0	15.0	42.0	55.5	61.0	19.0
Congo, Republic	59.0	41.0	51.0	54.5	13.5	40.0	54.5	59.5	19.5
Costa Rica	76.5	73.0	75.5	77.5	4.5	69.0	77.5	80.0	11.0
Cote d'Ivoire	55.8	58.0	63.3	67.3	9.3	57.0	64.0	69.0	12.0
Croatia	72.5	66.5	71.0	73.5	7.0	64.0	70.5	75.0	11.0
Cuba	63.0	52.5	60.5	63.0	10.5	49.5	63.5	69.5	20.0
Cyprus	78.3	63.5	75.0	76.5	13.0	59.5	76.0	79.5	20.0
Czech Republic	73.8	73.0	75.0	77.0	4.0	72.5	77.0	80.5	8.0
Denmark	88.3	81.5	87.0	88.5	7.0	77.5	87.0	90.5	13.0
Dominican Republic	72.5	66.0	73.5	75.5	9.5	59.0	71.5	75.5	16.5
Ecuador	58.8	51.0	57.0	61.0	10.0	52.0	63.0	67.0	15.0
Egypt	69.5	60.5	69.0	72.5	12.0	55.0	68.5	70.5	15.5
El Salvador	73.5	74.0	77.0	78.0	4.0	67.5	75.5	79.0	11.5
Estonia	76.3	69.5	73.5	76.0	6.5	66.5	74.0	79.5	13.0
Ethiopia	59.5	54.0	59.5	60.5	6.5	57.5	63.5	67.0	9.5
Finland	88.5	80.5	86.5	88.0	7.5	75.5	86.0	90.0	14.5
France	80.5	79.0	80.5	83.0	4.0	75.0	85.0	89.0	14.0
Gabon	67.8	61.5	70.5	72.0	10.5	58.0	70.5	73.5	15.5
Gambia	65.8	65.0	71.0	72.5	7.5	61.0	72.5	76.0	15.0
Germany	84.0	77.5	84.0	86.5	9.0	75.5	87.0	91.5	16.0
Ghana	56.3	60.0	62.0	64.0	4.0	59.0	64.5	66.0	7.0
Greece	76.5	72.0	78.5	81.5	9.5	72.5	80.5	84.0	11.5
Guatemala	69.5	66.0	68.0	70.0	4.0	64.0	71.5	75.0	11.0
Guinea	58.3	55.5	59.8	61.5	6.0	52.0	62.0	64.0	12.0

Country	Current Rating	One Year Ahead				Five Years Ahead			
		Worst Case	Most Probable	Best Case	Risk Stability	Worst Case	Most Probable	Best Case	Risk Stability
Guinea-Bissau	49.3	46.5	52.5	53.5	7.0	50.5	60.5	63.5	13.0
Guyana	64.3	60.0	64.0	66.0	6.0	59.0	67.0	69.5	10.5
Haiti	56.8	50.5	60.5	62.0	11.5	46.5	62.5	66.5	20.0
Honduras	64.0	57.5	60.0	62.5	5.0	60.0	67.5	72.0	12.0
Hong Kong	80.5	71.0	75.5	77.5	6.5	65.5	75.5	81.5	16.0
Hungary	74.5	73.0	76.0	78.5	5.5	68.0	77.0	81.0	13.0
Iceland	78.0	80.5	82.5	84.5	4.0	74.0	81.0	85.0	11.0
India	64.0	58.0	64.0	66.5	8.5	60.0	68.0	70.5	10.5
Indonesia	53.8	45.0	52.5	55.0	10.0	46.5	64.5	68.5	22.0
Iran	71.3	63.5	68.5	70.0	6.5	60.5	71.5	76.0	15.5
Iraq	48.0	32.5	44.0	46.5	14.0	32.5	52.5	65.0	32.5
Ireland	86.8	82.5	87.0	89.5	7.0	74.5	86.0	90.0	15.5
Israel	67.3	62.0	65.0	70.0	8.0	58.0	70.0	75.5	17.5
Italy	79.8	75.0	78.5	80.0	5.0	71.0	80.0	83.5	12.5
Jamaica	70.8	68.5	70.0	72.0	3.5	64.0	75.0	78.5	14.5
Japan	83.5	79.5	84.5	88.0	8.5	78.5	85.5	91.0	12.5
Jordan	70.8	72.0	74.0	76.0	4.0	66.5	74.0	77.5	11.0
Kazakhstan	72.0	64.0	67.0	68.5	4.5	58.0	67.0	70.0	12.0
Kenya	60.5	57.5	63.5	65.0	7.5	54.0	64.5	68.5	14.5
Korea, D.P.R.	48.3	25.0	40.5	41.5	16.5	26.5	48.5	59.0	32.5
Korea, Republic	79.5	71.0	76.0	77.5	6.5	61.5	80.0	83.0	21.5
Kuwait	80.5	69.5	72.5	74.0	4.5	65.5	72.0	77.5	12.0
Latvia	71.5	68.5	71.5	73.0	4.5	64.0	72.0	76.5	12.5
Lebanon	58.5	48.5	55.5	57.0	8.5	45.0	57.5	63.5	18.5
Liberia	49.0	35.0	44.0	44.5	9.5	35.0	48.0	53.0	18.0
Libya	71.0	53.0	63.5	67.0	14.0	49.5	68.0	75.0	25.5
Lithuania	71.8	70.0	74.5	76.0	6.0	65.5	74.0	79.5	14.0
Luxembourg	89.5	89.0	90.3	91.5	2.5	83.0	88.5	91.5	8.5
Madagascar	63.8	63.5	67.5	69.5	6.0	60.0	68.5	71.0	11.0
Malawi	58.8	58.0	60.0	62.0	4.0	51.5	61.5	67.0	15.5
Malaysia	75.0	65.5	69.0	72.0	6.5	57.5	64.0	71.5	14.0
Mali	63.5	58.5	65.3	68.5	10.0	54.0	68.0	71.0	17.0
Malta	79.3	79.0	80.5	81.5	2.5	73.5	77.5	81.0	7.5
Mexico	72.5	60.0	65.5	67.5	7.5	58.0	69.5	75.5	17.5
Moldova	59.5	48.5	52.0	53.5	5.0	50.0	59.5	67.0	17.0
Mongolia	67.0	60.5	65.0	67.0	6.5	54.0	66.0	69.5	15.5
Morocco	70.8	65.5	72.0	73.5	8.0	61.5	70.5	73.5	12.0
Mozambique	58.8	51.5	59.8	61.5	10.0	45.0	62.0	65.0	20.0
Myanmar	57.8	51.0	56.0	57.5	6.5	42.5	54.5	63.0	20.5
Namibia	76.3	72.0	77.0	77.5	5.5	69.0	76.0	78.0	9.0
Netherlands	89.0	86.5	87.5	88.0	1.5	80.5	86.5	88.5	8.0
New Zealand	78.3	76.0	79.0	81.5	5.5	73.0	79.5	84.5	11.5
Nicaragua	55.8	44.5	49.0	52.0	7.5	43.5	54.0	60.0	16.5
Niger	60.0	57.5	63.5	64.5	7.0	53.0	64.0	67.5	14.5
Nigeria	61.8	44.0	55.0	58.5	14.5	44.5	63.5	69.0	23.5
Norway	91.5	85.5	88.0	91.0	5.5	79.0	89.5	94.0	15.0
Oman	80.0	70.5	72.0	74.0	3.5	65.5	71.0	74.5	9.0
Pakistan	54.0	49.5	58.0	60.0	10.5	46.5	60.5	64.0	17.5
Panama	74.5	65.5	73.5	76.0	10.5	60.0	75.0	80.5	20.5
Papua New Guinea	65.3	59.0	64.5	67.0	8.0	51.5	68.0	73.0	21.5
Paraguay	66.3	46.5	59.5	63.5	17.0	42.5	66.0	69.0	26.5
Peru	68.8	57.0	67.5	69.5	12.5	55.0	69.5	72.5	17.5
Philippines	66.0	60.5	69.0	71.0	10.5	61.5	70.0	74.5	13.0

| Country | Current Rating | One Year Ahead | | | | Five Years Ahead | | | |
		Worst Case	Most Probable	Best Case	Risk Stability	Worst Case	Most Probable	Best Case	Risk Stability
Poland	74.5	70.5	78.5	80.0	9.5	70.0	77.0	80.5	10.5
Portugal	79.5	77.0	80.5	83.5	6.5	72.5	81.5	85.5	13.0
Qatar	70.0	60.0	62.5	64.5	4.5	57.5	65.0	68.5	11.0
Romania	64.3	54.5	58.0	60.5	6.0	50.0	64.0	69.0	19.0
Russian Federation.	66.5	44.0	52.0	56.0	12.0	40.0	60.0	70.0	30.0
Saudi Arabia	76.8	61.0	70.5	72.5	11.5	60.0	74.5	78.0	18.0
Senegal	64.8	60.0	63.8	64.0	4.0	52.5	63.5	66.0	13.5
Sierra Leone	41.0	28.0	35.0	45.5	17.5	30.0	54.0	59.5	29.5
Singapore	90.3	81.0	82.5	85.0	4.0	64.5	78.0	85.5	21.0
Slovak Republic	74.0	69.5	74.5	78.0	8.5	69.5	77.0	81.5	12.0
Slovenia	77.0	73.0	79.0	82.5	9.5	70.5	80.5	84.0	13.5
Somalia	49.3	33.0	37.5	43.5	10.5	32.0	46.5	55.5	23.5
South Africa	69.0	61.5	65.5	67.0	5.5	56.5	66.0	71.5	15.0
Spain	79.8	75.0	81.0	84.5	9.5	74.5	85.0	90.0	15.5
Sri Lanka	58.5	55.0	62.5	65.0	10.0	52.5	67.5	72.0	19.5
Sudan	49.5	39.8	47.0	49.0	9.3	43.0	54.5	62.0	19.0
Suriname	67.0	58.5	69.5	71.5	13.0	57.5	69.5	74.0	16.5
Sweden	84.5	81.0	84.0	86.0	5.0	73.5	83.5	88.0	14.5
Switzerland	88.3	86.0	89.0	92.0	6.0	79.0	88.5	94.0	15.0
Syria	71.5	62.0	70.0	71.0	9.0	57.5	69.0	71.0	13.5
Taiwan	81.5	76.5	83.0	87.0	10.5	65.5	80.5	84.0	18.5
Tanzania	59.3	54.0	57.0	59.0	5.0	55.0	61.0	64.0	9.0
Thailand	73.5	66.0	70.0	73.5	7.5	58.0	70.5	75.5	17.5
Togo	61.5	54.0	61.0	62.0	8.0	54.0	63.0	68.0	14.0
Trinidad & Tobago	74.0	72.0	73.5	75.0	3.0	67.5	73.0	74.5	7.0
Tunisia	73.3	63.5	71.0	74.0	10.5	59.0	69.0	74.5	15.5
Turkey	55.0	57.5	64.5	66.5	9.0	60.5	69.5	73.0	12.5
Uganda	65.8	58.0	62.0	64.0	6.0	54.0	63.0	67.5	13.5
Ukraine	64.3	50.0	56.0	58.0	8.0	48.5	62.0	68.5	20.0
United Arab Emirates	81.5	73.0	75.5	78.0	5.0	68.5	75.0	79.0	10.5
United Kingdom	83.3	78.5	80.0	84.0	5.5	71.5	83.0	86.5	15.0
United States	81.8	75.0	82.5	85.5	10.5	73.0	80.5	84.0	11.0
Uruguay	74.0	66.0	70.5	73.5	7.5	64.0	72.0	76.0	12.0
Venezuela	68.5	54.5	61.0	65.5	11.0	51.5	72.0	76.0	24.5
Vietnam	71.3	57.5	61.0	63.0	5.5	52.5	63.0	68.0	15.5
Yemen, Republic	63.8	62.0	63.5	66.0	4.0	57.5	69.0	71.5	14.0
Yugoslavia	47.8	32.5	51.5	54.0	21.5	40.0	60.5	65.0	25.0
Zambia	59.5	55.0	56.5	58.0	3.0	52.0	63.5	64.0	12.0
Zimbabwe	40.5	41.0	45.0	53.5	12.5	42.0	55.0	66.0	24.0

TABLE 3A

POLITICAL RISK RATINGS OVER THE PERIOD APRIL 2000 THROUGH MARCH 2001

COUNTRY	04/00	05/00	06/00	07/00	08/00	09/00	10/00	11/00	12/00	01/01	02/01	03/01
Albania	59.0	59.0	60.0	60.0	60.0	60.0	60.0	61.0	60.0	60.0	60.0	59.0
Algeria	45.0	44.0	45.0	45.0	43.0	43.0	44.0	44.0	44.0	44.0	43.0	41.0
Angola	45.0	45.0	45.0	46.0	45.0	46.0	46.0	47.0	47.0	47.0	47.0	47.0
Argentina	74.0	72.0	72.0	71.0	71.0	72.0	71.0	74.0	72.0	72.0	72.0	72.0
Armenia	56.0	55.0	54.0	54.0	54.0	54.0	54.0	54.0	54.0	54.0	53.0	55.0
Australia	89.0	89.0	89.0	89.0	89.0	89.0	89.0	89.0	89.0	88.0	88.0	87.5
Austria	82.0	81.0	82.0	82.0	82.0	82.0	84.0	84.0	83.0	83.0	84.0	85.5
Azerbaijan	57.0	57.0	56.0	57.0	57.0	57.0	57.0	57.0	57.0	57.0	58.0	59.0
Bahamas	82.0	82.0	82.0	82.0	82.0	82.0	82.0	82.0	82.0	82.0	82.0	82.0
Bahrain	64.0	64.0	64.0	64.0	64.0	64.0	64.0	64.0	64.0	65.0	65.0	66.0
Bangladesh	54.0	54.0	55.0	55.0	55.0	55.0	55.0	55.0	56.0	54.0	55.0	53.5
Belarus	58.0	56.0	56.0	56.0	58.0	57.0	56.0	57.0	57.0	57.0	57.0	56.0
Belgium	79.0	79.0	77.0	77.0	77.0	77.0	79.0	78.0	79.0	79.0	79.0	82.0
Bolivia	68.0	68.0	67.0	67.0	67.0	68.0	69.0	69.0	71.0	71.0	70.0	70.0
Botswana	77.0	77.0	77.0	77.0	77.0	77.0	77.0	77.0	77.0	77.0	77.0	77.0
Brazil	65.0	64.0	64.0	64.0	63.0	63.0	63.0	63.0	63.0	63.0	63.0	62.0
Brunei	76.0	76.0	77.0	77.0	77.0	77.0	77.0	77.0	77.0	77.0	77.0	77.0
Bulgaria	73.0	70.0	71.0	70.0	70.0	70.0	69.0	69.0	67.0	66.0	66.0	65.5
Burkina Faso	63.0	63.0	63.0	63.0	63.0	63.0	63.0	63.0	65.0	65.0	64.0	64.0
Cameroon	56.0	56.0	56.0	56.0	56.0	56.0	56.0	56.0	56.0	57.0	57.0	57.0
Canada	88.0	88.0	88.0	88.0	88.0	88.0	88.0	88.0	88.0	88.0	88.0	88.0
Chile	71.0	70.0	70.0	73.0	73.0	74.0	74.0	74.0	74.0	74.0	74.0	74.0
China, P. Rep.	61.0	61.0	63.0	63.0	63.0	63.0	63.0	63.0	63.0	63.0	63.0	63.0
Colombia	47.0	48.0	47.0	47.0	51.0	51.0	51.0	51.0	49.0	49.0	47.0	46.0
Congo, D. Rep	31.0	31.0	31.0	31.0	31.0	31.0	31.0	30.0	31.0	31.0	28.0	32.0
Congo, Rep.	46.0	47.0	47.0	49.0	49.0	49.0	50.0	50.0	52.0	52.0	52.0	51.0
Costa Rica	81.0	78.0	78.0	78.0	79.0	79.0	79.0	79.0	79.0	79.0	79.0	81.0
Cote d'Ivoire	51.0	51.0	51.0	51.0	51.0	50.0	47.0	49.0	53.0	51.0	52.0	52.0
Croatia	68.0	69.0	69.0	69.0	68.0	68.0	68.0	69.0	70.0	71.0	71.0	71.0
Cuba	58.0	58.0	58.0	58.0	60.0	60.0	60.0	60.0	60.0	60.0	60.0	60.0
Cyprus	75.0	75.0	77.0	77.0	77.0	76.0	76.0	76.0	75.0	74.0	74.0	74.0
Czech Rep.	78.0	78.0	78.0	78.0	75.0	75.0	75.0	74.0	74.0	73.0	73.0	74.0
Denmark	93.0	93.0	92.0	92.0	93.0	93.0	92.0	93.0	94.0	94.0	94.0	92.0
Dominican R.	68.0	68.0	73.0	73.0	73.0	73.0	73.0	72.0	72.0	72.0	72.0	72.0
Ecuador	56.0	57.0	55.0	55.0	55.0	53.0	56.0	57.0	57.0	57.0	57.0	55.0
Egypt	65.0	65.0	65.0	65.0	65.0	65.0	65.0	65.0	64.0	66.0	66.0	66.0
El Salvador	70.0	70.0	70.0	70.0	71.0	71.0	71.0	71.0	71.0	72.0	72.0	70.0
Estonia	75.0	75.0	75.0	75.0	75.0	75.0	76.0	76.0	76.0	76.0	77.0	77.0
Ethiopia	58.0	59.0	61.0	63.0	64.0	64.0	64.0	64.0	64.0	60.0	59.0	59.0
Finland	94.0	94.0	94.0	93.0	93.0	93.0	93.0	93.0	92.0	92.0	93.0	93.0
France	81.0	81.0	81.0	81.0	81.0	80.0	79.0	79.0	78.0	78.0	79.0	79.0
Gabon	62.0	62.0	62.0	62.0	62.0	62.0	62.0	62.0	63.0	63.0	62.0	62.0
Gambia	69.0	69.0	69.0	68.0	67.0	67.0	67.0	67.0	68.0	68.0	68.0	68.0
Germany	87.0	87.0	89.0	89.0	89.0	88.0	88.0	88.0	89.0	88.0	88.0	88.0
Ghana	61.0	61.0	61.0	61.0	61.0	61.0	61.0	61.0	61.0	65.0	65.0	65.0
Greece	79.0	80.0	80.0	80.0	80.0	80.0	80.0	79.0	79.0	79.0	80.0	80.0
Guatemala	65.0	65.0	65.0	65.0	65.0	64.0	64.0	64.0	64.0	64.0	64.0	64.0
Guinea	55.0	55.0	56.0	55.0	54.0	54.0	53.0	50.0	50.0	50.0	50.0	50.0

COUNTRY	04/00	05/00	06/00	07/00	08/00	09/00	10/00	11/00	12/00	01/01	02/01	03/01
Guinea-Bissau	51.0	51.0	49.0	50.0	50.0	51.0	50.0	50.0	51.0	54.0	54.0	54.0
Guyana	70.0	70.0	70.0	70.0	70.0	70.0	70.0	70.0	70.0	70.0	68.0	68.0
Haiti	46.0	46.0	53.0	51.0	48.0	48.0	49.0	49.0	49.0	50.0	50.0	49.0
Honduras	62.0	61.0	60.0	60.0	60.0	60.0	60.0	60.0	62.0	62.0	62.0	62.0
Hong Kong	71.0	71.0	71.0	70.0	70.0	70.0	70.0	70.0	70.0	70.0	70.0	70.0
Hungary	79.0	79.0	79.0	79.0	79.0	77.0	77.0	77.0	76.0	76.0	77.0	75.0
Iceland	88.0	88.0	88.0	88.0	88.0	88.0	90.0	89.0	89.0	89.0	89.0	89.0
India	55.0	54.0	54.0	54.0	54.0	54.0	54.0	53.0	53.0	53.0	54.0	54.0
Indonesia	47.0	47.0	46.0	45.0	43.0	43.0	43.0	44.0	43.0	44.0	44.0	42.5
Iran	63.0	61.0	62.0	62.0	62.0	61.0	61.0	61.0	61.0	61.0	61.0	60.0
Iraq	32.0	32.0	32.0	32.0	32.0	32.0	34.0	34.0	35.0	35.0	35.0	36.0
Ireland	86.0	87.0	87.0	87.0	86.0	84.0	84.0	85.0	86.0	87.0	87.0	87.0
Israel	62.0	60.0	61.0	62.0	62.0	62.0	57.0	57.0	56.0	56.0	55.0	57.0
Italy	77.0	76.0	78.0	77.0	77.0	77.0	76.0	80.0	80.0	80.0	80.0	80.0
Jamaica	74.0	74.0	74.0	74.0	74.0	74.0	74.0	73.0	73.0	73.0	73.0	74.0
Japan	80.0	81.0	80.0	81.0	81.0	81.0	81.0	81.0	81.0	82.0	81.0	80.0
Jordan	69.0	69.0	68.0	70.0	70.0	70.0	70.0	69.0	69.0	69.0	69.0	69.0
Kazakhstan	71.0	71.0	71.0	71.0	71.0	70.0	70.0	70.0	70.0	68.0	68.0	68.0
Kenya	48.0	48.0	51.0	50.0	51.0	54.0	55.0	55.0	54.0	54.0	54.0	54.0
Korea, D.P.R.	57.0	57.0	58.0	58.0	59.0	59.0	59.0	59.0	59.0	59.0	59.0	59.0
Korea, Rep.	75.0	74.0	75.0	75.0	76.0	76.0	76.0	76.0	76.0	76.0	76.0	75.5
Kuwait	68.0	68.0	68.0	68.0	68.0	68.0	68.0	68.0	68.0	68.0	65.0	68.0
Latvia	69.0	67.0	68.0	68.0	68.0	68.0	68.0	68.0	68.0	68.0	68.0	68.0
Lebanon	58.0	58.0	64.0	64.0	65.0	64.0	63.0	63.0	63.0	63.0	63.0	63.0
Liberia	42.0	44.0	43.0	42.0	42.0	42.0	42.0	45.0	45.0	44.0	44.0	44.0
Libya	61.0	61.0	61.0	61.0	61.0	61.0	62.0	59.0	59.0	59.0	59.0	59.0
Lithuania	66.0	66.0	66.0	66.0	66.0	66.0	66.0	67.0	67.0	66.0	66.0	66.0
Luxembourg	91.0	91.0	92.0	92.0	92.0	92.0	92.0	92.0	92.0	92.0	92.0	92.0
Madagascar	63.0	63.0	63.0	63.0	63.0	63.0	63.0	63.0	63.0	64.0	64.0	64.0
Malawi	66.0	67.0	68.0	67.0	67.0	67.0	66.0	66.0	65.0	65.0	65.0	65.0
Malaysia	67.0	67.0	67.0	67.0	67.0	67.0	67.0	68.0	67.0	66.0	66.0	66.0
Mali	64.0	65.0	65.0	65.0	65.0	64.0	64.0	64.0	64.0	64.0	64.0	65.0
Malta	87.0	87.0	87.0	85.0	85.0	85.0	86.0	86.0	86.0	86.0	86.0	86.0
Mexico	69.0	67.0	66.0	68.0	72.0	72.0	72.0	72.0	72.0	72.0	72.0	72.0
Moldova	65.0	64.0	62.0	62.0	62.0	55.0	55.0	55.0	56.0	55.0	55.0	59.0
Mongolia	70.0	70.0	69.0	65.0	71.0	71.0	70.0	70.0	70.0	70.0	70.0	70.0
Morocco	70.0	69.0	68.0	68.0	68.0	68.0	68.0	68.0	68.0	68.0	68.0	68.0
Mozambique	59.0	59.0	59.0	59.0	59.0	59.0	60.0	60.0	60.0	62.0	62.0	63.0
Myanmar	47.0	47.0	47.0	46.0	46.0	45.0	45.0	45.0	45.0	45.0	45.0	44.0
Namibia	76.0	76.0	74.0	74.0	74.0	74.0	75.0	75.0	75.0	75.0	75.0	75.0
Netherlands	94.0	94.0	96.0	96.0	96.0	97.0	97.0	97.0	97.0	97.0	97.0	97.0
New Zealand	89.0	89.0	89.0	89.0	88.0	88.0	88.0	88.0	88.0	88.0	88.0	88.0
Nicaragua	61.0	60.0	60.0	60.0	60.0	60.0	60.0	60.0	62.0	62.0	62.0	63.0
Niger	61.0	61.0	61.0	61.0	61.0	61.0	61.0	61.0	61.0	61.0	61.0	61.0
Nigeria	44.0	45.0	45.0	45.0	46.0	47.0	48.0	46.0	46.0	46.0	46.0	48.0
Norway	85.0	86.0	86.0	86.0	87.0	87.0	88.0	88.0	89.0	90.0	90.0	90.0
Oman	76.0	76.0	76.0	76.0	76.0	76.0	76.0	76.0	76.0	76.0	76.0	76.0
Pakistan	44.0	44.0	44.0	44.0	45.0	45.0	45.0	44.0	44.0	44.0	45.0	44.5
Panama	76.0	76.0	76.0	76.0	75.0	75.0	75.0	76.0	76.0	76.0	76.0	76.0
Papua N. G.	62.0	62.0	62.0	62.0	62.0	62.0	61.0	61.0	60.0	60.0	60.0	56.0
Paraguay	56.0	57.0	58.0	58.0	58.0	58.0	58.0	58.0	58.0	57.0	57.0	61.0
Peru	60.0	60.0	60.0	63.0	63.0	62.0	60.0	61.0	64.0	64.0	64.0	64.0
Philippines	66.0	62.0	62.0	62.0	62.0	62.0	61.0	59.0	57.0	57.0	61.0	60.0
Poland	77.0	77.0	74.0	74.0	74.0	73.0	74.0	75.0	75.0	76.0	76.0	76.0
Portugal	90.0	90.0	90.0	90.0	90.0	90.0	88.0	88.0	89.0	89.0	89.0	89.0

COUNTRY	04/00	05/00	06/00	07/00	08/00	09/00	10/00	11/00	12/00	01/01	02/01	03/01
Qatar	75.0	75.0	75.0	75.0	75.0	75.0	75.0	75.0	75.0	75.0	75.0	75.0
Romania	66.0	66.0	66.0	63.0	63.0	64.0	63.0	63.0	60.0	65.0	68.0	68.0
Russian Fed.	47.0	54.0	54.0	58.0	58.0	57.0	55.0	55.0	55.0	54.0	54.0	55.0
Saudi Arabia	66.0	66.0	66.0	67.0	67.0	67.0	67.0	67.0	66.0	66.0	66.0	66.0
Senegal	60.0	59.0	59.0	58.0	58.0	58.0	58.0	58.0	58.0	59.0	59.0	59.0
Sierra Leone	42.0	42.0	36.0	37.0	39.0	39.0	39.0	38.0	40.0	40.0	41.0	40.0
Singapore	86.0	86.0	86.0	86.0	86.0	86.0	86.0	86.0	86.0	86.0	86.0	86.0
Slovak Rep.	76.0	77.0	77.0	77.0	75.0	75.0	75.0	75.0	78.0	78.0	78.0	79.0
Slovenia	79.0	79.0	80.0	81.0	80.0	78.0	78.0	80.0	80.0	80.0	80.0	80.0
Somalia	29.0	30.0	32.0	32.0	32.0	32.0	35.0	38.0	39.0	39.0	34.0	34.0
South Africa	65.0	65.0	64.0	64.0	65.0	65.0	65.0	65.0	65.0	65.0	65.0	65.0
Spain	78.0	78.0	78.0	79.0	80.0	80.0	80.0	82.0	82.0	82.0	82.0	82.0
Sri Lanka	54.0	52.0	51.0	50.0	52.0	50.0	50.0	51.0	51.0	51.0	52.0	52.0
Sudan	34.0	34.0	35.0	34.0	34.0	34.0	34.0	34.0	35.0	36.0	36.0	36.0
Suriname	60.0	60.0	63.0	64.0	64.0	64.0	64.0	64.0	64.0	66.0	66.0	66.0
Sweden	86.0	86.0	86.0	86.0	87.0	87.0	87.0	88.0	88.0	88.0	88.0	88.0
Switzerland	88.0	88.0	88.0	89.0	89.0	89.0	89.0	89.0	89.0	90.0	90.0	90.0
Syria	67.0	67.0	65.0	65.0	67.0	67.0	67.0	66.0	65.0	65.0	65.0	65.0
Taiwan	77.0	77.0	78.0	78.0	78.0	78.0	78.0	76.0	76.0	76.0	76.0	76.0
Tanzania	65.0	64.0	64.0	64.0	64.0	64.0	64.0	63.0	63.0	63.0	63.0	62.0
Thailand	72.0	72.0	72.0	72.0	72.0	72.0	72.0	72.0	72.0	71.0	71.0	70.0
Togo	53.0	53.0	53.0	53.0	53.0	51.0	52.0	52.0	52.0	55.0	55.0	55.0
Trinidad & T.	73.0	72.0	72.0	72.0	72.0	72.0	72.0	71.0	69.0	71.0	70.0	71.0
Tunisia	75.0	75.0	75.0	75.0	75.0	75.0	75.0	75.0	75.0	75.0	75.0	75.0
Turkey	57.0	58.0	60.0	63.0	63.0	61.0	61.0	60.0	60.0	58.0	58.0	53.0
Uganda	55.0	55.0	56.0	56.0	59.0	59.0	60.0	61.0	61.0	61.0	61.0	61.0
Ukraine	56.0	58.0	59.0	59.0	59.0	59.0	59.0	59.0	59.0	58.0	56.0	55.0
United Arab E.	72.0	72.0	72.0	72.0	72.0	72.0	72.0	72.0	72.0	72.0	72.0	72.0
United K'dom	91.0	91.0	90.0	90.0	89.0	89.0	88.0	90.0	90.0	90.0	90.0	90.0
United States	90.0	91.0	91.0	91.0	90.0	90.0	90.0	90.0	87.0	87.0	87.0	87.0
Uruguay	74.0	74.0	74.0	74.0	74.0	74.0	74.0	74.0	74.0	74.0	74.0	74.0
Venezuela	57.0	56.0	57.0	55.0	55.0	57.0	57.0	58.0	58.0	58.0	58.0	56.0
Vietnam	68.0	68.0	67.0	67.0	70.0	70.0	70.0	68.0	68.0	68.0	68.0	67.0
Yemen, Rep.	61.0	61.0	61.0	62.0	62.0	62.0	62.0	62.0	62.0	62.0	62.0	61.0
Yugoslavia	38.0	38.0	37.0	37.0	37.0	37.0	30.0	40.0	42.0	50.0	41.0	52.0
Zambia	68.0	68.0	68.0	68.0	68.0	66.0	66.0	66.0	67.0	67.0	67.0	67.0
Zimbabwe	45.0	48.0	47.0	47.0	46.0	46.0	47.0	44.0	43.0	45.0	46.0	43.0

TABLE 3B

POLITICAL RISK POINTS BY COMPONENT - MARCH 2001

This table lists the total points for each of the following political risk components out of the maximum points indicated. The symbol ↑ indicates a rise in the points awarded to that specific risk component from the previous month (an improving risk), while the symbol ↓ indicates a decrease (deteriorating risk). The final columns in the table show the overall political risk rating (the sum of the points awarded to each component) and the change from the preceding month.

A	Government Stability	12	E	External Conflict	12	J	Ethnic Tensions		6
B	Socioeconomic Conditions	12	F	Corruption	6	K	Democratic Accountability		6
			G	Military in Politics	6				
C	Investment Profile	12	H	Religious Tensions	6	L	Bureaucracy Quality		4
D	Internal Conflict	12	I	Law and Order	6				

COUNTRY	A	B	C	D	E	F	G	H	I	J	K	L	Political Risk Rating	
Albania	10.0	2.0	6.0	9.0	↓8.0	2.0	4.0	5.0	2.0	5.0	5.0	1.0	59.0	-1.0
Algeria	↓7.0	3.0	7.0	4.0	9.0	2.0	0.0	0.0	2.0	2.0	3.0	2.0	41.0	-2.0
Angola	11.0	2.0	2.0	8.0	7.0	2.0	1.0	4.0	3.0	3.0	3.0	1.0	47.0	0.0
Argentina	10.0	5.0	5.0	10.0	10.0	3.0	4.0	6.0	5.0	6.0	5.0	3.0	72.0	0.0
Armenia	↑8.0	3.0	4.0	8.0	↑8.0	2.0	4.0	5.0	3.0	5.0	4.0	1.0	55.0	2.0
Australia	↓9.5	10.0	10.0	11.0	10.0	5.0	6.0	6.0	6.0	4.0	6.0	4.0	87.5	-0.5
Austria	10.0	10.0	10.0	10.0	↑10.0	↑4.5	6.0	6.0	6.0	4.0	5.0	4.0	85.5	1.5
Azerbaijan	11.0	2.0	9.0	8.0	↑8.0	2.0	4.0	4.0	4.0	4.0	2.0	1.0	59.0	1.0
Bahamas	11.0	6.0	10.0	11.0	12.0	4.0	6.0	6.0	4.0	5.0	4.0	3.0	82.0	0.0
Bahrain	11.0	6.0	9.0	8.0	10.0	3.0	3.0	3.0	5.0	4.0	↑2.0	2.0	66.0	1.0
Bangladesh	↓7.5	2.0	6.0	7.0	10.0	2.0	3.0	3.0	2.0	5.0	4.0	2.0	53.5	-1.5
Belarus	↓9.0	2.0	4.0	7.0	10.0	3.0	5.0	5.0	4.0	5.0	1.0	1.0	56.0	-1.0
Belgium	↑11.0	↑8.0	9.0	11.0	11.0	4.0	6.0	5.0	5.0	3.0	5.0	4.0	82.0	3.0
Bolivia	9.0	6.0	10.0	10.0	11.0	3.0	3.0	6.0	3.0	3.0	4.0	2.0	70.0	0.0
Botswana	11.0	4.0	11.0	12.0	11.0	3.0	6.0	5.0	4.0	5.0	3.0	2.0	77.0	0.0
Brazil	↓9.0	4.0	6.0	9.0	10.0	3.0	4.0	6.0	2.0	3.0	4.0	2.0	62.0	-1.0
Brunei	11.0	10.0	8.0	12.0	11.0	3.0	5.0	3.0	6.0	5.0	0.0	3.0	77.0	0.0
Bulgaria	↓6.5	2.0	10.0	10.0	9.0	2.0	5.0	5.0	4.0	5.0	5.0	2.0	65.5	-0.5
Burkina Faso	11.0	5.0	8.0	8.0	9.0	2.0	3.0	5.0	4.0	4.0	4.0	1.0	64.0	0.0
Cameroon	11.0	4.0	8.0	8.0	9.0	2.0	4.0	4.0	2.0	2.0	2.0	1.0	57.0	0.0
Canada	11.0	9.0	10.0	10.0	11.0	6.0	6.0	6.0	6.0	3.0	6.0	4.0	88.0	0.0
Chile	11.0	5.0	9.0	9.0	9.0	4.0	4.0	6.0	5.0	5.0	4.0	3.0	74.0	0.0
China, P. Rep.	12.0	4.0	10.0	10.0	10.0	1.0	2.0	3.0	4.0	4.0	1.0	2.0	63.0	0.0
Colombia	↓9.0	2.0	3.0	4.0	8.0	2.0	2.0	5.0	1.0	5.0	3.0	2.0	46.0	-1.0
Congo, D. Rep.	↑9.0	1.0	1.0	↑7.0	7.0	1.0	0.0	4.0	1.0	0.0	1.0	0.0	32.0	4.0
Congo, Rep.	10.0	2.0	6.0	↓9.0	9.0	4.0	0.0	3.0	2.0	4.0	1.0	1.0	51.0	-1.0
Costa Rica	10.0	6.0	10.0	↑11.0	11.0	5.0	6.0	5.0	4.0	6.0	5.0	2.0	81.0	2.0
Cote d'Ivoire	↑11.0	7.0	2.0	↓7.0	9.0	3.0	1.0	6.0	3.0	2.0	1.0	0.0	52.0	0.0
Croatia	10.0	2.0	7.0	10.0	10.0	4.0	5.0	5.0	5.0	5.0	5.0	3.0	71.0	0.0
Cuba	11.0	4.0	6.0	9.0	9.0	2.0	3.0	4.0	4.0	6.0	0.0	2.0	60.0	0.0
Cyprus	10.0	9.0	8.0	9.0	8.0	4.0	5.0	4.0	5.0	2.0	6.0	4.0	74.0	0.0
Czech Rep.	↑7.0	7.0	8.0	11.0	9.0	4.0	6.0	6.0	5.0	3.0	5.0	3.0	74.0	1.0
Denmark	10.0	10.0	10.0	↓10.0	12.0	6.0	6.0	6.0	6.0	6.0	6.0	4.0	92.0	-2.0
Dominican R.	11.0	5.0	11.0	9.0	10.0	4.0	3.0	5.0	4.0	4.0	5.0	1.0	72.0	0.0

A	*Government Stability*	*12*	E	*External Conflict*	*12*	J	*Ethnic Tensions*	*6*
B	*Socioeconomic*	*12*	F	*Corruption*	*6*	K	*Democratic*	*6*
	Conditions		G	*Military in Politics*	*6*		*Accountability*	
C	*Investment Profile*	*12*	H	*Religious Tensions*	*6*	L	*Bureaucracy Quality*	*4*
D	*Internal Conflict*	*12*	I	*Law and Order*	*6*			

COUNTRY	A	B	C	D	E	F	G	H	I	J	K	L	Political Risk Rating	
Ecuador	↓8.0	3.0	5.0	8.0	9.0	3.0	2.0	5.0	3.0	3.0	4.0	2.0	55.0	-2.0
Egypt	11.0	6.0	10.0	9.0	9.0	2.0	3.0	2.0	4.0	6.0	2.0	2.0	66.0	0.0
El Salvador	10.0	↓2.0	9.0	9.0	12.0	4.0	3.0	6.0	3.0	6.0	4.0	2.0	70.0	-2.0
Estonia	10.0	6.0	9.0	11.0	10.0	6.0	5.0	5.0	4.0	3.0	5.0	3.0	77.0	0.0
Ethiopia	12.0	4.0	6.0	9.0	7.0	2.0	1.0	5.0	5.0	3.0	4.0	1.0	59.0	0.0
Finland	10.0	10.0	9.0	12.0	12.0	6.0	6.0	6.0	6.0	6.0	6.0	4.0	93.0	0.0
France	10.0	9.0	9.0	9.0	10.0	3.0	5.0	6.0	5.0	4.0	5.0	4.0	79.0	0.0
Gabon	10.0	5.0	9.0	9.0	10.0	1.0	2.0	5.0	3.0	3.0	3.0	2.0	62.0	0.0
Gambia	10.0	5.0	9.0	8.0	11.0	3.0	2.0	5.0	5.0	5.0	3.0	2.0	68.0	0.0
Germany	11.0	10.0	10.0	11.0	11.0	4.0	6.0	6.0	5.0	5.0	5.0	4.0	88.0	0.0
Ghana	11.0	4.0	9.0	9.0	11.0	3.0	3.0	6.0	2.0	2.0	3.0	2.0	65.0	0.0
Greece	11.0	6.0	11.0	9.0	9.0	5.0	5.0	6.0	3.0	6.0	6.0	3.0	80.0	0.0
Guatemala	11.0	3.0	8.0	9.0	10.0	4.0	2.0	6.0	2.0	3.0	4.0	2.0	64.0	0.0
Guinea	10.0	4.0	8.0	6.0	5.0	3.0	2.0	3.0	3.0	2.0	2.0	2.0	50.0	0.0
Guinea-Bissau	10.0	3.0	5.0	10.0	10.0	2.0	2.0	5.0	1.0	3.0	2.0	1.0	54.0	0.0
Guyana	8.0	6.0	8.0	7.0	9.0	3.0	6.0	6.0	4.0	3.0	5.0	3.0	68.0	0.0
Haiti	11.0	1.0	4.0	6.0	9.0	↓1.0	3.0	6.0	2.0	4.0	2.0	0.0	49.0	-1.0
Honduras	10.0	2.0	8.0	10.0	10.0	2.0	3.0	4.0	2.0	5.0	4.0	2.0	62.0	0.0
Hong Kong	11.0	5.0	8.0	9.0	10.0	3.0	3.0	6.0	5.0	5.0	2.0	3.0	70.0	0.0
Hungary	↓7.0	6.0	9.0	11.0	10.0	↓3.0	6.0	5.0	4.0	↑4.0	6.0	4.0	75.0	-2.0
Iceland	11.0	7.0	8.0	12.0	11.0	6.0	6.0	6.0	6.0	6.0	6.0	4.0	89.0	0.0
India	9.0	4.0	5.0	6.0	7.0	3.0	3.0	2.0	4.0	2.0	6.0	3.0	54.0	0.0
Indonesia	↓7.5	2.0	5.0	4.0	9.0	1.0	2.0	1.0	2.0	2.0	4.0	3.0	42.5	-1.5
Iran	↓8.0	5.0	5.0	7.0	9.0	4.0	5.0	2.0	5.0	5.0	3.0	2.0	60.0	-1.0
Iraq	11.0	1.0	4.0	4.0	↑6.0	1.0	0.0	5.0	2.0	2.0	0.0	0.0	36.0	1.0
Ireland	11.0	11.0	7.0	12.0	11.0	2.0	6.0	5.0	6.0	6.0	6.0	4.0	87.0	0.0
Israel	↑8.0	6.0	7.0	5.0	6.0	3.0	4.0	2.0	5.0	1.0	6.0	4.0	57.0	2.0
Italy	10.0	8.0	9.0	10.0	11.0	3.0	6.0	5.0	6.0	5.0	4.0	3.0	80.0	0.0
Jamaica	10.0	5.0	9.0	↑9.0	12.0	2.0	6.0	6.0	2.0	5.0	5.0	3.0	74.0	1.0
Japan	↓8.0	8.0	8.0	12.0	10.0	3.0	6.0	5.0	5.0	6.0	5.0	4.0	80.0	-1.0
Jordan	11.0	5.0	10.0	7.0	10.0	3.0	5.0	3.0	4.0	5.0	4.0	2.0	69.0	0.0
Kazakhstan	11.0	3.0	9.0	10.0	11.0	2.0	5.0	5.0	4.0	5.0	1.0	2.0	68.0	0.0
Kenya	10.0	↓2.0	7.0	8.0	↑10.0	2.0	3.0	3.0	2.0	2.0	3.0	2.0	54.0	0.0
Korea, D.P.R.	11.0	1.0	7.0	10.0	10.0	2.0	1.0	6.0	5.0	6.0	0.0	0.0	59.0	0.0
Korea, Rep.	↓8.5	6.0	8.0	9.0	11.0	3.0	5.0	6.0	4.0	6.0	6.0	3.0	75.5	-0.5
Kuwait	↑10.0	8.0	5.0	11.0	10.0	2.0	5.0	2.0	5.0	5.0	3.0	2.0	68.0	3.0
Latvia	10.0	4.0	7.0	10.0	9.0	3.0	5.0	5.0	5.0	3.0	5.0	2.0	68.0	0.0
Lebanon	10.0	5.0	7.0	9.0	9.0	1.0	3.0	3.0	4.0	3.0	5.0	2.0	63.0	0.0
Liberia	10.0	1.0	3.0	8.0	5.0	5.0	1.0	3.0	2.0	3.0	3.0	0.0	44.0	0.0
Libya	10.0	4.0	9.0	7.0	10.0	4.0	3.0	4.0	4.0	2.0	1.0	1.0	59.0	0.0
Lithuania	9.0	4.0	7.0	9.0	10.0	3.0	5.0	5.0	4.0	3.0	5.0	2.0	66.0	0.0
Luxembourg	11.0	10.0	10.0	12.0	12.0	5.0	6.0	6.0	6.0	5.0	5.0	4.0	92.0	0.0
Madagascar	10.0	3.0	7.0	9.0	12.0	4.0	3.0	5.0	3.0	2.0	5.0	1.0	64.0	0.0
Malawi	9.0	3.0	10.0	7.0	12.0	3.0	4.0	3.0	4.0	4.0	4.0	2.0	65.0	0.0
Malaysia	10.0	5.0	8.0	9.0	10.0	3.0	5.0	4.0	3.0	4.0	2.0	3.0	66.0	0.0
Mali	↑10.0	5.0	8.0	10.0	11.0	2.0	4.0	4.0	3.0	4.0	4.0	0.0	65.0	1.0
Malta	11.0	9.0	9.0	12.0	11.0	4.0	6.0	4.0	5.0	6.0	6.0	3.0	86.0	0.0

A	Government Stability	12	E	External Conflict	12	J	Ethnic Tensions	6
B	Socioeconomic Conditions	12	F	Corruption	6	K	Democratic Accountability	6
C	Investment Profile	12	G	Military in Politics	6			
			H	Religious Tensions	6	L	Bureaucracy Quality	4
D	Internal Conflict	12	I	Law and Order	6			

COUNTRY	A	B	C	D	E	F	G	H	I	J	K	L	Political Risk Rating	
Mexico	11.0	5.0	9.0	9.0	10.0	4.0	3.0	5.0	2.0	5.0	6.0	3.0	72.0	0.0
Moldova	↑10.0	2.0	3.0	9.0	9.0	2.0	4.0	6.0	5.0	4.0	3.0	2.0	59.0	4.0
Mongolia	11.0	1.0	7.0	11.0	12.0	3.0	5.0	5.0	4.0	5.0	4.0	2.0	70.0	0.0
Morocco	10.0	4.0	9.0	9.0	9.0	3.0	4.0	4.0	6.0	5.0	3.0	2.0	68.0	0.0
Mozambique	11.0	2.0	8.0	↑10.0	12.0	2.0	2.0	6.0	3.0	4.0	3.0	0.0	63.0	1.0
Myanmar	↓9.0	3.0	4.0	6.0	8.0	1.0	0.0	6.0	3.0	3.0	0.0	1.0	44.0	-1.0
Namibia	11.0	5.0	9.0	10.0	8.0	3.0	6.0	6.0	6.0	5.0	4.0	2.0	75.0	0.0
Netherlands	11.0	10.0	12.0	12.0	12.0	6.0	6.0	6.0	6.0	6.0	6.0	4.0	97.0	0.0
New Zealand	10.0	8.0	9.0	12.0	12.0	5.0	6.0	6.0	6.0	4.0	6.0	4.0	88.0	0.0
Nicaragua	↑10.0	1.0	6.0	10.0	10.0	4.0	2.0	4.0	4.0	5.0	6.0	1.0	63.0	1.0
Niger	10.0	3.0	8.0	10.0	11.0	1.0	4.0	3.0	2.0	3.0	5.0	1.0	61.0	0.0
Nigeria	↑10.0	2.0	5.0	7.0	10.0	1.0	3.0	1.0	3.0	↑2.0	3.0	1.0	48.0	2.0
Norway	10.0	10.0	10.0	12.0	11.0	5.0	6.0	5.0	6.0	5.0	6.0	4.0	90.0	0.0
Oman	11.0	9.0	8.0	12.0	11.0	3.0	5.0	4.0	5.0	5.0	1.0	2.0	76.0	0.0
Pakistan	↓9.5	5.0	3.0	7.0	7.0	2.0	0.0	1.0	3.0	5.0	0.0	2.0	44.5	-0.5
Panama	10.0	7.0	10.0	10.0	10.0	2.0	5.0	5.0	3.0	5.0	6.0	3.0	76.0	0.0
Papua N. G.	↓8.0	3.0	↓7.0	9.0	11.0	↓1.0	3.0	5.0	2.0	2.0	3.0	2.0	56.0	-4.0
Paraguay	↑10.0	5.0	5.0	↑9.0	11.0	2.0	2.0	6.0	3.0	5.0	2.0	1.0	61.0	4.0
Peru	10.0	6.0	7.0	7.0	10.0	4.0	4.0	6.0	3.0	3.0	2.0	2.0	64.0	0.0
Philippines	↓8.0	5.0	8.0	6.0	9.0	2.0	4.0	3.0	2.0	5.0	5.0	3.0	60.0	-1.0
Poland	9.0	5.0	9.0	9.0	11.0	3.0	6.0	5.0	4.0	6.0	6.0	3.0	76.0	0.0
Portugal	11.0	7.0	10.0	12.0	12.0	5.0	6.0	6.0	5.0	6.0	6.0	3.0	89.0	0.0
Qatar	11.0	6.0	10.0	12.0	10.0	2.0	4.0	4.0	6.0	6.0	2.0	2.0	75.0	0.0
Romania	11.0	3.0	7.0	9.0	11.0	3.0	5.0	4.0	4.0	4.0	6.0	1.0	68.0	0.0
Russian Fed.	11.0	2.0	6.0	↑9.0	9.0	1.0	4.0	4.0	3.0	2.0	3.0	1.0	55.0	1.0
Saudi Arabia	10.0	6.0	9.0	9.0	10.0	2.0	5.0	3.0	5.0	5.0	0.0	2.0	66.0	0.0
Senegal	10.0	5.0	7.0	9.0	9.0	3.0	2.0	3.0	3.0	3.0	4.0	1.0	59.0	0.0
Sierra Leone	9.0	2.0	2.0	↓7.0	8.0	3.0	0.0	4.0	3.0	2.0	0.0	0.0	40.0	-1.0
Singapore	11.0	10.0	11.0	12.0	9.0	4.0	6.0	5.0	6.0	6.0	2.0	4.0	86.0	0.0
Slovak Rep.	10.0	7.0	8.0	11.0	11.0	4.0	6.0	5.0	4.0	↑4.0	6.0	3.0	79.0	1.0
Slovenia	10.0	5.0	10.0	11.0	11.0	4.0	5.0	6.0	5.0	5.0	5.0	3.0	80.0	0.0
Somalia	5.0	1.0	5.0	6.0	7.0	1.0	1.0	3.0	2.0	2.0	1.0	0.0	34.0	0.0
South Africa	10.0	5.0	7.0	8.0	10.0	3.0	5.0	6.0	2.0	3.0	4.0	2.0	65.0	0.0
Spain	11.0	9.0	11.0	7.0	11.0	4.0	5.0	6.0	4.0	4.0	6.0	4.0	82.0	0.0
Sri Lanka	10.0	4.0	6.0	0.0	12.0	4.0	2.0	4.0	3.0	1.0	4.0	2.0	52.0	0.0
Sudan	10.0	2.0	3.0	4.0	10.0	1.0	0.0	0.0	2.0	0.0	3.0	1.0	36.0	0.0
Suriname	10.0	6.0	5.0	8.0	11.0	3.0	3.0	6.0	3.0	4.0	5.0	2.0	66.0	0.0
Sweden	10.0	8.0	9.0	10.0	12.0	6.0	6.0	6.0	6.0	5.0	6.0	4.0	88.0	0.0
Switzerland	10.0	10.0	9.0	12.0	11.0	5.0	6.0	6.0	6.0	5.0	6.0	4.0	90.0	0.0
Syria	11.0	6.0	6.0	11.0	9.0	2.0	2.0	5.0	5.0	6.0	1.0	1.0	65.0	0.0
Taiwan	9.0	8.0	10.0	11.0	9.0	2.0	4.0	6.0	4.0	5.0	5.0	3.0	76.0	0.0
Tanzania	10.0	3.0	8.0	7.0	↓9.0	2.0	4.0	5.0	5.0	4.0	4.0	1.0	62.0	-1.0
Thailand	9.0	5.0	9.0	10.0	↓10.0	2.0	4.0	5.0	5.0	5.0	4.0	2.0	70.0	-1.0
Togo	10.0	5.0	6.0	9.0	10.0	2.0	1.0	5.0	3.0	2.0	2.0	0.0	55.0	0.0
Trinidad & T.	↑10.0	6.0	9.0	9.0	11.0	3.0	5.0	5.0	4.0	2.0	4.0	3.0	71.0	1.0
Tunisia	11.0	6.0	10.0	11.0	11.0	3.0	4.0	5.0	5.0	5.0	2.0	2.0	75.0	0.0
Turkey	↓7.0	2.0	↓6.0	8.0	8.0	3.0	3.0	4.0	4.0	2.0	4.0	2.0	53.0	-5.0

A	Government Stability	12	E	External Conflict	12	J	Ethnic Tensions	6
B	Socioeconomic	12	F	Corruption	6	K	Democratic	6
	Conditions		G	Military in Politics	6		Accountability	
C	Investment Profile	12	H	Religious Tensions	6	L	Bureaucracy Quality	4
D	Internal Conflict	12	I	Law and Order	6			

COUNTRY	A	B	C	D	E	F	G	H	I	J	K	L	Political Risk Rating	
Uganda	11.0	5.0	8.0	7.0	10.0	2.0	2.0	4.0	4.0	4.0	2.0	2.0	61.0	0.0
Ukraine	↓7.0	3.0	3.0	7.0	11.0	2.0	5.0	6.0	4.0	4.0	2.0	1.0	55.0	-1.0
United Arab E.	10.0	8.0	7.0	12.0	11.0	2.0	5.0	4.0	4.0	4.0	2.0	3.0	72.0	0.0
United K'dom	11.0	11.0	11.0	10.0	9.0	5.0	6.0	6.0	6.0	5.0	6.0	4.0	90.0	0.0
United States	11.0	11.0	9.0	11.0	9.0	4.0	6.0	6.0	6.0	5.0	5.0	4.0	87.0	0.0
Uruguay	10.0	4.0	10.0	9.0	12.0	3.0	5.0	5.0	3.0	6.0	5.0	2.0	74.0	0.0
Venezuela	↓9.0	3.0	4.0	8.0	8.0	3.0	2.0	5.0	4.0	5.0	4.0	1.0	56.0	-2.0
Vietnam	11.0	4.0	7.0	12.0	11.0	2.0	2.0	6.0	↓4.0	5.0	1.0	2.0	67.0	-1.0
Yemen, Rep.	11.0	3.0	8.0	7.0	10.0	3.0	4.0	4.0	2.0	5.0	↓3.0	1.0	61.0	-1.0
Yugoslavia	11.0	2.0	5.0	5.0	↓9.0	1.0	3.0	4.0	↑3.0	3.0	4.0	2.0	52.0	0.0
Zambia	10.0	3.0	10.0	10.0	8.0	2.0	5.0	5.0	4.0	5.0	4.0	1.0	67.0	0.0
Zimbabwe	↑10.0	2.0	2.0	↓6.0	↓7.0	↓0.0	↓3.0	4.0	2.0	3.0	2.0	2.0	43.0	-3.0

TABLE 3C

POLITICAL RISK FORECASTS

Country	Current Rating	One Year Ahead				Five Years Ahead			
		Worst Case	Most Probable	Best Case	Risk Stability	Worst Case	Most Probable	Best Case	Risk Stability
Albania	59.0	45.0	60.0	63.0	18.0	48.0	67.0	69.0	21.0
Algeria	41.0	39.0	42.0	50.0	11.0	38.0	60.0	63.0	25.0
Angola	47.0	30.0	48.0	50.0	20.0	30.0	65.0	68.0	38.0
Argentina	72.0	69.0	70.0	73.0	4.0	67.0	76.0	78.0	11.0
Armenia	55.0	55.0	58.0	62.0	7.0	55.0	68.0	70.0	15.0
Australia	87.5	85.0	89.0	90.0	5.0	79.0	88.0	90.0	11.0
Austria	85.5	79.0	88.0	92.0	13.0	81.0	90.0	92.0	11.0
Azerbaijan	59.0	50.0	57.0	59.0	9.0	55.0	67.0	72.0	17.0
Bahamas	82.0	80.0	80.0	82.0	2.0	80.0	80.0	82.0	2.0
Bahrain	66.0	60.0	68.0	68.0	8.0	58.0	67.0	72.0	14.0
Bangladesh	53.5	49.0	56.0	60.0	11.0	49.0	58.0	63.0	14.0
Belarus	56.0	54.0	58.0	62.0	8.0	56.0	60.0	64.0	8.0
Belgium	82.0	75.0	80.0	82.0	7.0	70.0	82.0	84.0	14.0
Bolivia	70.0	63.0	70.0	72.0	9.0	68.0	73.0	75.0	7.0
Botswana	77.0	75.0	78.0	79.0	4.0	76.0	78.0	79.0	3.0
Brazil	62.0	57.0	68.0	70.0	13.0	60.0	70.0	73.0	13.0
Brunei	77.0	70.0	73.0	75.0	5.0	70.0	78.0	78.0	8.0
Bulgaria	65.5	65.0	76.0	78.0	13.0	65.0	79.0	82.0	17.0
Burkina Faso	64.0	55.0	64.0	66.0	11.0	55.0	65.0	68.0	13.0
Cameroon	57.0	50.0	58.0	58.0	8.0	50.0	56.0	58.0	8.0
Canada	88.0	82.0	88.0	90.0	8.0	75.0	90.0	92.0	17.0
Chile	74.0	65.0	73.0	76.0	11.0	70.0	78.0	79.0	9.0
China, Peoples' Rep.	63.0	58.0	63.0	65.0	7.0	60.0	70.0	74.0	14.0
Colombia	46.0	40.0	55.0	60.0	20.0	48.0	58.0	62.0	14.0
Congo, Dem. Republic	32.0	25.0	35.0	45.0	20.0	35.0	48.0	52.0	17.0
Congo, Republic	51.0	35.0	45.0	50.0	15.0	35.0	47.0	52.0	17.0
Costa Rica	81.0	78.0	81.0	82.0	4.0	78.0	82.0	84.0	6.0
Cote d'Ivoire	52.0	50.0	58.0	65.0	15.0	50.0	58.0	65.0	15.0
Croatia	71.0	62.0	69.0	72.0	10.0	65.0	70.0	75.0	10.0
Cuba	60.0	48.0	60.0	62.0	14.0	48.0	58.0	65.0	17.0
Cyprus	74.0	50.0	71.0	72.0	22.0	50.0	75.0	78.0	28.0
Czech Republic	74.0	78.0	80.0	82.0	˙4.0	78.0	82.0	84.0	6.0
Denmark	92.0	85.0	94.0	95.0	10.0	85.0	94.0	96.0	11.0
Dominican Republic	72.0	60.0	73.0	75.0	15.0	60.0	70.0	75.0	15.0
Ecuador	55.0	53.0	60.0	65.0	12.0	58.0	65.0	68.0	10.0
Egypt	66.0	50.0	65.0	70.0	20.0	50.0	68.0	68.0	18.0
El Salvador	70.0	70.0	74.0	74.0	4.0	68.0	73.0	75.0	7.0
Estonia	77.0	70.0	75.0	78.0	8.0	70.0	76.0	80.0	10.0
Ethiopia	59.0	60.0	65.0	66.0	6.0	65.0	67.0	70.0	5.0
Finland	93.0	85.0	95.0	96.0	11.0	83.0	94.0	96.0	13.0
France	79.0	79.0	80.0	83.0	4.0	79.0	90.0	93.0	14.0
Gabon	62.0	50.0	63.0	65.0	15.0	50.0	65.0	67.0	17.0
Gambia	68.0	65.0	73.0	75.0	10.0	65.0	74.0	77.0	12.0
Germany	88.0	80.0	91.0	94.0	14.0	82.0	92.0	95.0	13.0
Ghana	65.0	63.0	65.0	67.0	4.0	63.0	67.0	68.0	5.0
Greece	80.0	73.0	84.0	88.0	15.0	78.0	86.0	90.0	12.0
Guatemala	64.0	65.0	67.0	69.0	4.0	68.0	72.0	76.0	8.0
Guinea	50.0	50.0	55.0	57.0	7.0	50.0	58.0	59.0	9.0

Country	Current Rating	One Year Ahead				Five Years Ahead			
		Worst Case	Most Probable	Best Case	Risk Stability	Worst Case	Most Probable	Best Case	Risk Stability
Guinea-Bissau	54.0	48.0	55.0	56.0	8.0	50.0	58.0	60.0	10.0
Guyana	68.0	65.0	68.0	70.0	5.0	65.0	70.0	72.0	7.0
Haiti	49.0	40.0	56.0	57.0	17.0	40.0	56.0	60.0	20.0
Honduras	62.0	60.0	63.0	66.0	6.0	58.0	66.0	68.0	10.0
Hong Kong	70.0	69.0	73.0	74.0	5.0	65.0	75.0	80.0	15.0
Hungary	75.0	80.0	83.0	86.0	6.0	78.0	84.0	86.0	8.0
Iceland	89.0	86.0	88.0	90.0	4.0	83.0	88.0	90.0	7.0
India	54.0	50.0	60.0	63.0	13.0	58.0	65.0	67.0	9.0
Indonesia	42.5	40.0	48.0	50.0	10.0	40.0	60.0	64.0	24.0
Iran	60.0	58.0	67.0	67.0	9.0	55.0	67.0	70.0	15.0
Iraq	36.0	25.0	38.0	40.0	15.0	25.0	45.0	60.0	35.0
Ireland	87.0	80.0	87.0	90.0	10.0	77.0	88.0	92.0	15.0
Israel	57.0	56.0	60.0	68.0	12.0	54.0	70.0	75.0	21.0
Italy	80.0	73.0	77.0	78.0	5.0	70.0	78.0	80.0	10.0
Jamaica	74.0	73.0	74.0	76.0	3.0	70.0	78.0	79.0	9.0
Japan	80.0	76.0	83.0	88.0	12.0	76.0	85.0	94.0	18.0
Jordan	69.0	70.0	72.0	74.0	4.0	68.0	74.0	78.0	10.0
Kazakhstan	68.0	66.0	69.0	70.0	4.0	60.0	68.0	70.0	10.0
Kenya	54.0	50.0	56.0	58.0	8.0	50.0	58.0	63.0	13.0
Korea, D.P.R.	59.0	25.0	55.0	55.0	30.0	25.0	55.0	60.0	35.0
Korea, Republic	75.5	70.0	78.0	80.0	10.0	65.0	80.0	82.0	17.0
Kuwait	68.0	68.0	70.0	71.0	3.0	66.0	70.0	72.0	6.0
Latvia	68.0	65.0	68.0	69.0	4.0	65.0	70.0	76.0	11.0
Lebanon	63.0	50.0	59.0	60.0	10.0	45.0	60.0	62.0	17.0
Liberia	44.0	30.0	45.0	45.0	15.0	30.0	48.0	55.0	25.0
Libya	59.0	40.0	58.0	63.0	23.0	35.0	58.0	65.0	30.0
Lithuania	66.0	63.0	68.0	69.0	6.0	63.0	70.0	74.0	11.0
Luxembourg	92.0	91.0	92.0	93.0	2.0	88.0	90.0	93.0	5.0
Madagascar	64.0	61.0	66.0	67.0	6.0	60.0	67.0	68.0	8.0
Malawi	65.0	68.0	70.0	73.0	5.0	58.0	68.0	75.0	17.0
Malaysia	66.0	60.0	65.0	69.0	9.0	58.0	60.0	70.0	12.0
Mali	65.0	55.0	63.0	66.0	11.0	50.0	65.0	67.0	17.0
Malta	86.0	86.0	87.0	88.0	2.0	80.0	84.0	87.0	7.0
Mexico	72.0	62.0	69.0	70.0	8.0	60.0	70.0	75.0	15.0
Moldova	59.0	58.0	64.0	67.0	9.0	60.0	65.0	70.0	10.0
Mongolia	70.0	60.0	67.0	69.0	9.0	55.0	68.0	70.0	15.0
Morocco	68.0	60.0	71.0	72.0	12.0	60.0	70.0	72.0	12.0
Mozambique	63.0	50.0	63.0	65.0	15.0	50.0	65.0	67.0	17.0
Myanmar	44.0	40.0	47.0	48.0	8.0	30.0	47.0	55.0	25.0
Namibia	75.0	70.0	77.0	77.0	7.0	68.0	75.0	78.0	10.0
Netherlands	97.0	93.0	94.0	94.0	1.0	88.0	93.0	94.0	6.0
New Zealand	88.0	85.0	89.0	92.0	7.0	85.0	90.0	95.0	10.0
Nicaragua	63.0	56.0	60.0	63.0	7.0	48.0	58.0	64.0	16.0
Niger	61.0	53.0	63.0	65.0	12.0	50.0	60.0	63.0	13.0
Nigeria	48.0	40.0	55.0	60.0	20.0	45.0	65.0	67.0	22.0
Norway	90.0	83.0	88.0	92.0	9.0	80.0	90.0	95.0	15.0
Oman	76.0	76.0	77.0	78.0	2.0	68.0	72.0	74.0	6.0
Pakistan	44.5	40.0	55.0	57.0	17.0	40.0	58.0	62.0	22.0
Panama	76.0	65.0	77.0	80.0	15.0	60.0	78.0	82.0	22.0
Papua New Guinea	56.0	55.0	62.0	65.0	10.0	48.0	65.0	68.0	20.0
Paraguay	61.0	38.0	55.0	60.0	22.0	30.0	60.0	63.0	33.0
Peru	64.0	50.0	66.0	68.0	18.0	50.0	68.0	69.0	19.0
Philippines	60.0	55.0	70.0	72.0	17.0	65.0	70.0	74.0	9.0

Country	Current Rating	One Year Ahead				Five Years Ahead			
		Worst Case	Most Probable	Best Case	Risk Stability	Worst Case	Most Probable	Best Case	Risk Stability
Poland	76.0	70.0	84.0	85.0	15.0	76.0	82.0	86.0	10.0
Portugal	89.0	83.0	88.0	92.0	9.0	83.0	90.0	94.0	11.0
Qatar	75.0	73.0	75.0	77.0	4.0	70.0	75.0	78.0	8.0
Romania	68.0	67.0	72.0	74.0	7.0	60.0	70.0	74.0	14.0
Russian Federation.	55.0	46.0	58.0	63.0	17.0	40.0	60.0	70.0	30.0
Saudi Arabia	66.0	55.0	70.0	72.0	17.0	55.0	70.0	73.0	18.0
Senegal	59.0	53.0	58.0	58.0	5.0	50.0	58.0	58.0	8.0
Sierra Leone	40.0	28.0	36.0	50.0	22.0	25.0	57.0	59.0	34.0
Singapore	86.0	84.0	85.0	88.0	4.0	65.0	78.0	88.0	23.0
Slovak Republic	79.0	73.0	80.0	85.0	12.0	76.0	80.0	85.0	9.0
Slovenia	80.0	78.0	84.0	87.0	9.0	76.0	88.0	92.0	16.0
Somalia	34.0	28.0	35.0	45.0	17.0	28.0	50.0	56.0	28.0
South Africa	65.0	60.0	66.0	66.0	6.0	55.0	65.0	70.0	15.0
Spain	82.0	70.0	80.0	85.0	15.0	74.0	88.0	94.0	20.0
Sri Lanka	52.0	48.0	58.0	62.0	14.0	50.0	65.0	68.0	18.0
Sudan	36.0	30.0	42.0	45.0	15.0	37.0	52.0	60.0	23.0
Suriname	66.0	50.0	66.0	68.0	18.0	50.0	66.0	68.0	18.0
Sweden	88.0	84.0	88.0	90.0	6.0	80.0	88.0	92.0	12.0
Switzerland	90.0	84.0	88.0	92.0	8.0	80.0	88.0	92.0	12.0
Syria	65.0	55.0	69.0	69.0	14.0	48.0	68.0	70.0	22.0
Taiwan	76.0	70.0	82.0	87.0	17.0	60.0	78.0	80.0	20.0
Tanzania	62.0	63.0	65.0	67.0	4.0	60.0	65.0	68.0	8.0
Thailand	70.0	64.0	70.0	75.0	11.0	60.0	70.0	75.0	15.0
Togo	55.0	48.0	54.0	55.0	7.0	48.0	57.0	63.0	15.0
Trinidad & Tobago	71.0	72.0	73.0	73.0	1.0	70.0	72.0	73.0	3.0
Tunisia	75.0	60.0	73.0	76.0	16.0	58.0	68.0	76.0	18.0
Turkey	53.0	57.0	68.0	70.0	13.0	63.0	68.0	70.0	7.0
Uganda	61.0	50.0	56.0	58.0	8.0	50.0	58.0	63.0	13.0
Ukraine	55.0	57.0	66.0	67.0	10.0	57.0	67.0	72.0	15.0
United Arab Emirates	72.0	70.0	72.0	74.0	4.0	65.0	70.0	72.0	7.0
United Kingdom	90.0	85.0	86.0	92.0	7.0	78.0	90.0	93.0	15.0
United States	87.0	78.0	90.0	93.0	15.0	80.0	85.0	88.0	8.0
Uruguay	74.0	68.0	75.0	78.0	10.0	68.0	74.0	77.0	9.0
Venezuela	56.0	50.0	60.0	67.0	17.0	50.0	70.0	74.0	24.0
Vietnam	67.0	63.0	68.0	70.0	7.0	55.0	68.0	72.0	17.0
Yemen, Republic	61.0	60.0	62.0	64.0	4.0	55.0	68.0	69.0	14.0
Yugoslavia	52.0	30.0	58.0	58.0	28.0	40.0	60.0	65.0	25.0
Zambia	67.0	68.0	69.0	70.0	2.0	65.0	70.0	73.0	8.0
Zimbabwe	43.0	40.0	45.0	60.0	20.0	48.0	60.0	70.0	22.0

TABLE 4A

FINANCIAL RISK RATINGS OVER THE PERIOD APRIL 2000 THROUGH MARCH 2001

COUNTRY	04/00	05/00	06/00	07/00	08/00	09/00	10/00	11/00	12/00	01/01	02/01	03/01
Albania	33.0	33.0	32.0	33.0	33.0	32.0	32.0	31.0	31.5	32.0	33.0	33.0
Algeria	32.5	32.0	32.5	33.5	35.0	33.0	33.0	32.5	37.0	38.5	38.5	38.5
Angola	23.5	23.5	23.5	23.5	23.5	26.0	26.0	26.0	25.5	29.0	24.0	24.0
Argentina	29.5	29.5	27.5	27.5	27.5	27.5	29.0	29.0	28.5	28.5	28.5	28.5
Armenia	32.0	32.0	32.0	32.0	32.0	32.0	32.0	32.0	29.5	31.0	31.0	31.5
Australia	35.0	33.5	33.0	34.5	34.0	34.5	32.5	34.5	31.5	34.0	33.5	33.0
Austria	42.5	41.0	41.0	42.5	42.5	41.0	40.5	40.5	39.5	41.0	42.5	42.0
Azerbaijan	31.5	31.0	31.5	31.5	31.5	31.5	30.5	32.5	33.0	36.5	36.5	36.5
Bahamas	31.0	31.0	31.0	31.0	31.0	31.0	31.0	31.0	31.0	31.0	31.0	31.0
Bahrain	42.5	42.5	42.5	42.5	42.5	42.5	42.5	42.5	42.5	43.5	43.5	43.5
Bangladesh	36.0	36.0	36.0	36.0	36.5	35.5	35.5	35.5	35.5	36.0	36.0	36.0
Belarus	33.5	33.5	33.5	33.5	33.5	33.5	33.5	33.5	33.5	33.0	33.0	33.0
Belgium	38.0	36.5	36.5	38.0	38.0	36.5	36.0	34.5	35.5	37.5	39.0	38.5
Bolivia	34.5	34.5	34.5	34.5	34.5	34.5	34.5	34.5	34.5	35.0	34.5	35.0
Botswana	46.5	45.5	44.5	45.0	44.0	44.0	43.5	42.5	42.5	42.0	42.0	42.5
Brazil	31.5	31.0	31.5	31.5	31.5	31.5	31.5	31.5	32.0	30.5	30.0	29.5
Brunei	48.5	48.5	48.5	48.5	48.5	48.5	48.5	48.5	48.5	49.0	49.0	49.0
Bulgaria	31.5	31.5	31.5	31.5	35.5	34.0	33.5	32.0	33.0	34.5	36.0	35.5
Burkina Faso	31.5	30.0	30.0	31.5	31.5	30.0	29.5	28.0	29.0	30.5	32.0	32.0
Cameroon	30.0	28.5	28.5	30.0	30.0	28.5	29.0	26.5	27.5	30.0	31.5	31.5
Canada	39.0	39.0	39.0	39.0	39.0	39.0	39.0	39.0	39.0	39.5	39.0	39.0
Chile	38.5	38.0	38.5	38.5	38.0	37.0	36.5	37.0	37.0	38.0	37.0	37.0
China, Peoples' Rep.	44.0	44.0	44.0	44.0	44.0	45.0	45.0	45.5	45.5	45.5	45.5	45.5
Colombia	33.0	34.0	34.0	33.5	34.0	35.0	35.0	35.5	38.0	37.0	37.0	37.0
Congo, Dem. Republic	30.5	30.5	30.5	30.5	30.5	30.5	30.5	30.5	30.5	35.0	35.0	35.0
Congo, Republic	19.5	18.5	18.5	19.5	19.0	18.5	18.0	16.5	21.0	28.5	29.5	29.5
Costa Rica	37.5	37.5	37.5	37.5	37.5	38.0	37.5	38.0	38.0	38.0	38.0	38.0
Cote d'Ivoire	26.0	24.5	24.5	26.0	26.5	25.0	24.5	23.0	23.0	26.5	27.5	27.0
Croatia	36.0	35.0	34.5	36.5	36.5	35.5	35.0	33.0	34.5	36.5	37.5	37.5
Cuba	31.5	31.5	31.5	31.5	31.5	31.5	31.5	31.5	31.5	31.5	31.5	31.5
Cyprus	43.0	42.0	42.0	43.5	43.0	41.5	41.5	39.5	40.5	42.5	43.0	43.0
Czech Republic	39.5	38.0	37.5	38.5	38.5	37.5	37.0	36.0	37.0	38.0	38.5	39.0
Denmark	38.0	36.5	36.5	38.0	38.0	36.5	36.0	34.5	35.5	39.5	40.5	41.0
Dominican Republic	38.0	38.0	38.0	38.0	38.0	36.0	38.0	38.0	38.0	38.0	38.0	37.0
Ecuador	21.0	21.0	21.0	21.0	21.0	18.5	18.5	20.5	23.5	27.0	28.0	33.0
Egypt	39.0	39.0	39.0	39.0	39.0	39.0	39.0	37.5	38.0	38.0	37.5	37.5
El Salvador	42.5	42.5	42.5	42.5	42.5	42.5	42.5	42.5	42.5	41.5	41.5	41.5
Estonia	36.5	35.0	35.0	37.0	36.5	35.0	34.5	33.0	34.0	36.5	37.5	37.0
Ethiopia	25.0	25.0	25.0	25.0	26.5	27.3	26.5	27.5	27.5	27.5	27.5	27.5
Finland	37.0	35.5	35.5	37.0	37.0	35.5	35.0	33.5	34.5	36.5	38.0	37.5
France	38.5	37.0	37.0	38.5	38.5	37.0	36.5	35.0	35.5	38.0	39.5	39.0
Gabon	35.0	33.5	33.5	35.0	34.0	32.5	32.0	30.5	31.5	34.5	35.5	35.5
Gambia	34.0	34.0	34.0	34.0	34.0	34.5	33.5	32.0	31.5	30.0	30.0	30.5
Germany	39.0	37.5	37.5	39.0	39.0	37.5	37.0	35.5	36.5	38.0	39.5	39.0
Ghana	23.5	23.0	21.5	21.0	20.5	20.5	21.5	21.5	20.5	20.5	21.0	21.0
Greece	34.0	32.5	31.5	33.5	33.5	32.0	31.5	30.5	28.5	32.0	33.0	33.0
Guatemala	39.5	40.0	40.5	40.5	40.0	40.0	40.5	40.5	40.5	40.0	40.0	40.0
Guinea	30.5	31.0	31.0	31.0	31.5	32.0	30.5	30.0	30.0	29.5	32.0	32.5

COUNTRY	04/00	05/00	06/00	07/00	08/00	09/00	10/00	11/00	12/00	01/01	02/01	03/01
Guinea-Bissau	18.0	16.5	16.5	18.0	18.0	16.5	16.0	14.5	15.5	18.5	19.5	20.0
Guyana	28.5	24.0	29.0	29.0	19.0	19.0	28.5	29.0	30.0	30.5	30.5	30.5
Haiti	34.5	34.5	34.0	34.0	33.0	32.5	30.5	30.0	30.5	32.5	34.5	33.0
Honduras	35.5	35.5	35.5	35.5	35.5	35.5	35.5	35.5	35.5	35.5	35.5	35.5
Hong Kong	44.0	44.0	44.0	44.0	44.0	44.0	44.0	44.0	44.0	44.0	44.0	44.0
Hungary	36.0	34.0	33.5	35.5	35.0	34.0	33.5	32.5	32.5	35.0	37.5	37.5
Iceland	35.0	35.0	35.0	35.0	34.5	34.0	34.0	32.0	30.5	31.0	31.5	31.5
India	39.0	39.0	39.0	39.5	39.5	39.0	39.0	38.5	39.0	39.5	40.0	40.0
Indonesia	35.5	36.0	32.0	31.5	31.0	34.5	34.5	30.0	30.5	30.0	30.5	30.0
Iran	34.5	34.5	34.5	34.5	34.5	34.5	34.5	34.5	40.5	41.5	41.5	41.5
Iraq	33.0	33.0	33.0	33.0	30.5	30.5	30.5	30.5	30.5	30.5	30.5	30.5
Ireland	40.5	39.0	39.0	40.5	40.5	39.0	38.5	37.0	38.0	40.0	41.5	41.0
Israel	38.5	38.5	39.0	39.0	39.0	39.0	39.0	39.0	39.0	39.0	39.0	39.0
Italy	40.0	38.5	38.5	39.0	40.0	38.5	38.0	35.5	36.5	38.5	40.0	39.0
Jamaica	35.5	35.0	35.0	35.0	35.0	36.0	35.5	35.0	35.0	35.5	36.0	35.0
Japan	47.0	47.0	47.0	47.0	47.5	48.0	48.0	48.0	47.5	47.0	46.5	48.0
Jordan	37.0	37.0	37.0	37.0	37.0	37.0	37.0	37.0	37.0	36.5	36.5	36.5
Kazakhstan	32.0	33.0	35.5	35.0	35.0	35.0	36.0	36.0	36.0	39.0	39.0	39.0
Kenya	33.0	34.5	35.0	34.5	35.0	36.0	36.0	35.5	36.0	35.5	33.5	35.5
Korea, D.P.R.	20.5	20.5	20.5	20.5	20.5	20.5	20.5	20.5	20.5	20.5	20.5	20.5
Korea, Republic	40.5	40.5	40.5	39.5	39.5	39.5	39.5	39.5	39.0	40.0	38.5	39.0
Kuwait	48.0	48.0	48.0	48.0	48.0	48.0	48.0	48.0	48.0	48.5	48.5	48.5
Latvia	39.0	39.0	39.0	39.0	39.0	39.0	39.0	38.0	38.5	39.0	39.0	39.5
Lebanon	30.5	30.5	30.5	30.5	30.5	30.5	30.5	30.5	30.5	30.5	30.5	30.5
Liberia	20.0	20.0	20.0	20.0	20.0	20.0	20.0	20.0	20.0	19.5	19.5	19.5
Libya	41.5	41.0	42.5	41.0	41.0	41.0	39.0	39.0	39.5	42.0	42.5	44.0
Lithuania	40.0	40.0	40.0	40.0	40.0	40.0	40.0	40.0	40.0	40.0	40.5	40.5
Luxembourg	41.5	40.0	40.0	41.5	41.5	40.0	40.0	38.0	39.0	41.0	42.0	41.0
Madagascar	28.0	27.5	32.0	33.0	33.0	33.0	33.0	32.0	33.0	33.0	33.0	33.0
Malawi	29.5	29.0	28.0	25.5	25.0	24.5	22.0	21.5	21.5	21.5	21.5	21.5
Malaysia	42.0	42.0	42.0	42.0	42.0	42.0	42.0	42.0	42.0	42.0	42.0	42.0
Mali	31.5	30.0	30.0	31.5	31.5	30.0	29.5	27.5	28.5	30.5	31.5	31.5
Malta	37.5	37.0	37.0	37.5	37.5	36.5	36.5	35.5	36.0	36.5	37.0	37.0
Mexico	36.0	36.0	36.0	35.5	36.0	36.0	36.0	36.0	36.0	36.0	36.0	36.5
Moldova	25.0	28.5	28.5	28.5	27.5	28.0	28.0	28.5	29.5	28.0	27.0	28.5
Mongolia	33.0	34.0	34.0	35.0	34.0	34.0	34.0	34.0	34.0	34.0	34.0	34.0
Morocco	38.0	37.0	37.0	38.0	38.0	37.0	36.5	36.0	35.0	36.0	36.5	37.0
Mozambique	28.5	25.5	25.5	25.5	25.5	25.5	25.5	26.0	26.0	29.5	29.5	29.0
Myanmar	35.5	35.5	35.5	35.5	35.5	35.5	34.5	35.0	35.0	36.0	36.5	35.5
Namibia	43.5	43.0	41.0	42.0	42.5	42.0	41.0	40.0	39.5	39.5	39.5	40.5
Netherlands	37.0	35.5	35.5	37.0	37.0	35.5	35.0	33.5	34.5	36.0	37.5	37.0
New Zealand	28.5	29.0	27.5	29.0	29.0	27.5	26.0	25.5	26.0	27.5	28.5	28.5
Nicaragua	22.0	22.0	22.0	22.0	22.5	22.0	22.5	22.0	22.0	22.0	22.5	22.5
Niger	30.0	28.5	28.5	30.5	30.0	28.5	28.0	26.5	27.5	28.0	29.0	29.0
Nigeria	34.0	34.5	34.5	34.5	34.0	36.0	34.5	34.0	36.5	38.0	38.0	39.0
Norway	45.5	44.5	44.0	45.5	45.0	44.5	44.0	43.0	44.5	45.5	46.5	46.5
Oman	40.0	40.0	40.0	40.0	40.0	40.0	40.0	40.0	40.0	41.0	41.0	41.0
Pakistan	31.5	31.0	31.5	31.5	31.5	31.0	30.0	30.5	31.0	31.0	30.5	30.0
Panama	34.0	34.0	34.0	33.5	33.5	33.5	33.5	33.5	33.5	34.0	34.0	34.5
Papua New Guinea	32.5	36.5	36.5	36.5	36.5	36.0	36.5	37.0	37.5	36.5	36.5	38.5
Paraguay	38.0	38.5	41.0	41.0	41.0	41.0	41.0	41.0	41.0	39.0	39.5	39.5
Peru	37.5	37.5	37.0	37.5	37.0	37.5	37.5	37.5	38.0	37.5	37.5	37.5
Philippines	36.5	36.5	36.0	35.5	35.0	35.5	35.5	33.0	34.5	34.0	34.5	35.0
Poland	40.0	38.0	35.5	36.0	36.5	37.0	36.5	36.0	37.5	38.0	38.0	38.0
Portugal	34.0	32.5	32.5	34.0	34.0	32.5	32.0	30.5	30.5	32.0	33.5	33.5

COUNTRY	04/00	05/00	06/00	07/00	08/00	09/00	10/00	11/00	12/00	01/01	02/01	03/01
Qatar	28.5	28.5	28.5	28.5	28.5	28.5	28.5	28.5	28.5	29.0	29.0	29.0
Romania	32.0	32.5	32.0	32.0	31.5	31.5	30.5	30.5	30.0	30.5	30.5	30.5
Russian Federation.	32.0	32.5	32.0	32.0	32.5	33.0	33.5	36.5	38.0	40.0	40.0	40.0
Saudi Arabia	42.0	42.0	42.0	42.0	42.0	42.0	42.0	42.0	44.5	45.5	45.5	45.5
Senegal	33.0	31.5	31.5	33.0	33.0	31.5	31.0	29.5	30.5	33.0	34.0	34.0
Sierra Leone	13.5	13.5	14.0	12.5	17.0	14.5	15.5	16.5	15.5	9.5	19.5	16.5
Singapore	45.5	45.5	45.5	45.5	45.5	45.5	45.5	45.0	45.0	45.5	45.5	45.5
Slovak Republic	38.0	38.0	37.0	38.0	38.0	36.5	35.0	33.5	34.5	35.5	36.5	36.5
Slovenia	38.5	37.5	37.5	39.0	38.5	37.0	36.5	35.5	36.0	37.5	38.5	39.0
Somalia	22.0	22.0	22.0	22.0	22.0	22.0	21.0	22.0	22.0	36.0	36.0	36.0
South Africa	38.0	37.5	35.5	36.5	37.0	37.0	36.0	35.0	35.0	35.0	35.0	36.0
Spain	38.0	36.5	36.5	38.0	38.0	36.5	36.0	34.5	35.5	36.5	38.0	37.5
Sri Lanka	36.0	36.5	36.0	36.0	35.0	35.0	34.5	34.5	34.5	33.0	33.0	33.0
Sudan	25.0	30.0	30.0	30.0	30.0	30.0	30.0	30.0	30.5	30.0	30.0	30.0
Suriname	28.0	28.0	28.0	28.0	35.5	35.5	38.0	34.5	34.5	34.5	38.0	37.0
Sweden	37.0	36.5	36.0	37.0	36.5	35.5	34.5	33.0	33.5	35.0	35.5	35.0
Switzerland	44.5	44.0	44.0	45.5	45.5	43.0	44.5	42.5	44.0	41.0	41.5	41.5
Syria	36.0	31.0	31.0	33.5	33.5	31.0	32.0	28.0	33.5	34.0	36.0	38.0
Taiwan	45.0	45.0	45.0	45.0	45.0	45.0	45.0	45.0	45.0	45.0	44.5	44.5
Tanzania	21.5	21.5	22.0	22.0	23.5	23.5	23.0	23.0	23.0	22.0	22.0	22.0
Thailand	38.5	38.5	38.0	38.0	37.5	39.5	39.5	38.5	38.0	36.0	35.5	38.0
Togo	33.5	32.0	32.0	33.5	33.5	32.0	31.5	30.0	31.0	33.0	34.0	34.0
Trinidad & Tobago	39.5	39.5	39.5	39.5	39.5	39.5	39.5	39.5	39.5	40.0	40.0	40.0
Tunisia	34.5	33.5	33.5	35.0	34.5	33.5	33.0	31.5	33.0	35.0	36.0	35.0
Turkey	27.5	27.0	27.5	27.5	27.5	29.0	29.5	29.5	24.0	30.5	31.5	26.0
Uganda	37.0	36.0	35.5	36.5	35.5	34.5	33.5	33.0	33.0	37.0	37.0	37.0
Ukraine	32.0	31.5	31.5	31.5	31.5	33.5	33.5	34.0	36.0	38.5	39.0	39.0
United Arab Emirates	42.0	42.0	42.0	42.0	42.0	42.0	42.0	42.5	44.0	45.5	45.5	45.5
United Kingdom	37.0	37.0	36.5	37.0	37.0	36.0	35.5	35.0	35.0	36.0	35.0	35.5
United States	28.0	28.5	36.0	36.5	36.5	36.0	35.5	35.0	35.0	36.0	36.5	36.5
Uruguay	36.0	36.0	36.0	36.0	36.0	36.0	36.0	36.0	36.0	36.0	36.0	36.0
Venezuela	38.0	38.5	41.5	41.5	42.0	42.0	42.0	42.5	43.5	43.0	43.5	43.5
Vietnam	32.0	32.0	32.0	32.0	32.0	34.0	34.0	34.0	34.0	36.5	36.5	36.5
Yemen, Republic	29.0	30.0	30.0	30.5	21.0	30.0	30.0	31.0	31.0	31.0	31.0	31.0
Yugoslavia	24.0	24.0	24.0	24.0	24.0	24.0	24.0	24.0	24.5	26.0	16.0	16.0
Zambia	25.0	24.0	24.5	24.5	23.0	22.0	22.5	21.0	20.5	21.5	22.0	24.5
Zimbabwe	33.0	33.5	30.5	30.5	30.5	25.5	25.0	24.5	24.0	23.0	23.0	23.0

TABLE 4B

FINANCIAL RISK POINTS BY COMPONENT - MARCH 2001

This table lists the total points for each of the following financial risk indicators out of the maximum points indicated in parentheses. The final columns in the table show the overall financial risk rating (the sum of the points awarded to each component) and the change from the preceding month. Changes in the points awarded to the individual risk components are shown in Tables 12 through 16.

COUNTRY	Total Foreign Debt as percent of GDP (10 points)	Debt Service as percent of Exports of Goods and Services (10 points)	Current Account as percent of Exports of Goods and Services (15 points)	Inter-national Liquidity as months of import cover (5 points)	Exchange Rate Stability as percentage change (10 points)	Financial Risk Rating	
Albania	7.5	4.5	9.5	1.5	10.0	33.0	0.0
Algeria	5.0	6.0	15.0	3.5	9.0	38.5	0.0
Angola	1.0	9.0	13.5	0.5	0.0	24.0	0.0
Argentina	5.0	1.0	9.5	3.0	10.0	28.5	0.0
Armenia	6.0	7.0	7.0	1.5	10.0	31.5	0.5
Australia	5.0	9.0	11.0	1.5	6.5	33.0	-0.5
Austria	9.5	10.0	11.5	2.0	9.0	42.0	-0.5
Azerbaijan	8.5	9.5	7.5	1.0	10.0	36.5	0.0
Bahamas	0.0	9.5	9.5	2.0	10.0	31.0	0.0
Bahrain	10.0	9.0	12.0	2.5	10.0	43.5	0.0
Bangladesh	5.5	8.0	12.0	1.0	9.5	36.0	0.0
Belarus	9.0	8.0	11.0	0.0	5.0	33.0	0.0
Belgium	8.5	7.5	12.5	1.0	9.0	38.5	-0.5
Bolivia	6.0	7.5	9.0	3.0	9.5	35.0	0.5
Botswana	7.5	10.0	12.5	5.0	7.5	42.5	0.5
Brazil	6.5	3.5	8.5	3.0	8.0	29.5	-0.5
Brunei	10.0	10.0	14.0	5.0	10.0	49.0	0.0
Bulgaria	4.0	8.5	11.5	2.5	9.0	35.5	-0.5
Burkina Faso	4.5	9.0	7.0	2.0	9.5	32.0	0.0
Cameroon	4.0	7.5	10.5	0.0	9.5	31.5	0.0
Canada	10.0	6.5	12.0	1.0	9.5	39.0	0.0
Chile	5.5	7.0	12.0	4.0	8.5	37.0	0.0
China, Peoples' Rep.	9.0	9.5	13.0	4.0	10.0	45.5	0.0
Colombia	6.0	8.0	12.0	3.5	7.5	37.0	0.0
Congo, Dem. Rep.	0.0	9.5	15.0	0.5	10.0	35.0	0.0
Congo, Republic	0.5	8.5	11.0	0.0	9.5	29.5	0.0
Costa Rica	6.5	8.5	11.5	2.0	9.5	38.0	0.0
Cote d'Ivoire	1.0	5.5	11.0	0.0	9.5	27.0	-0.5
Croatia	6.5	9.0	10.5	2.0	9.5	37.5	0.0
Cuba	5.5	5.5	10.0	0.5	10.0	31.5	0.0
Cyprus	10.0	8.5	12.5	3.0	9.0	43.0	0.0
Czech Republic	5.5	9.0	12.0	2.5	10.0	39.0	0.5
Denmark	8.5	8.5	12.5	2.5	9.0	41.0	0.5
Dominican Republic	7.5	8.0	12.0	0.5	9.0	37.0	-1.0
Ecuador	2.0	6.0	12.5	2.5	10.0	33.0	5.0
Egypt	7.5	9.0	11.5	1.5	8.0	37.5	0.0
El Salvador	8.5	9.0	11.0	3.0	10.0	41.5	0.0
Estonia	9.0	6.0	11.5	1.5	9.0	37.0	-0.5
Ethiopia	1.0	4.0	11.5	1.0	10.0	27.5	0.0
Finland	5.0	8.5	13.0	2.0	9.0	37.5	-0.5

COUNTRY	Total Foreign Debt as percent of GDP (10 points)	Debt Service as percent of Exports of Goods and Services (10 points)	Current Account as percent of Exports of Goods and Services (15 points)	Inter- national Liquidity as months of import cover (5 points)	Exchange Rate Stability as percentage change (10 points)	Financial Risk Rating	
France	8.0	8.0	12.5	1.5	9.0	39.0	-0.5
Gabon	4.5	9.0	12.5	0.0	9.5	35.5	0.0
Gambia	2.5	9.0	11.0	2.5	5.5	30.5	0.5
Germany	9.0	7.5	12.0	1.5	9.0	39.0	-0.5
Ghana	3.0	7.0	10.0	0.5	0.5	21.0	0.0
Greece	6.5	4.0	10.5	3.5	8.5	33.0	0.0
Guatemala	8.5	8.5	11.0	2.0	10.0	40.0	0.0
Guinea	5.0	8.0	11.0	1.0	7.5	32.5	0.5
Guinea-Bissau	0.0	8.0	2.5	0.0	9.5	20.0	0.5
Guyana	0.0	9.0	11.5	0.0	10.0	30.5	0.0
Haiti	7.0	9.5	11.0	0.0	5.5	33.0	-1.5
Honduras	4.0	8.0	11.0	2.5	10.0	35.5	0.0
Hong Kong	8.5	10.0	12.5	3.0	10.0	44.0	0.0
Hungary	5.5	8.0	11.5	2.5	10.0	37.5	0.0
Iceland	4.0	8.0	10.0	2.5	7.0	31.5	0.0
India	8.0	7.5	11.5	3.5	9.5	40.0	0.0
Indonesia	3.0	6.5	13.0	2.5	5.0	30.0	-0.5
Iran	9.5	6.0	15.0	1.0	10.0	41.5	0.0
Iraq	3.5	2.5	12.5	2.0	10.0	30.5	0.0
Ireland	8.5	10.0	12.5	1.0	9.0	41.0	-0.5
Israel	5.0	8.5	12.0	3.5	10.0	39.0	0.0
Italy	9.5	7.0	12.0	1.5	9.0	39.0	-1.0
Jamaica	5.5	8.0	12.0	1.5	8.0	35.0	-1.0
Japan	10.0	10.0	14.0	4.0	10.0	48.0	1.5
Jordan	3.0	8.0	12.5	3.0	10.0	36.5	0.0
Kazakhstan	5.5	8.5	13.0	2.0	10.0	39.0	0.0
Kenya	5.0	8.0	11.5	1.5	9.5	35.5	2.0
Korea, D.P.R.	3.0	3.0	4.5	0.0	10.0	20.5	0.0
Korea, Republic	7.0	9.0	12.5	2.0	8.5	39.0	0.5
Kuwait	10.0	10.0	15.0	3.5	10.0	48.5	0.0
Latvia	7.5	9.5	10.5	2.0	10.0	39.5	0.5
Lebanon	6.0	9.5	0.0	5.0	10.0	30.5	0.0
Liberia	0.0	2.0	7.5	0.0	10.0	19.5	0.0
Libya	9.5	9.5	13.5	3.5	8.0	44.0	1.5
Lithuania	9.0	9.5	10.5	1.5	10.0	40.5	0.0
Luxembourg	10.0	10.0	12.5	0.5	8.0	41.0	-1.0
Madagascar	3.0	8.0	11.5	0.5	10.0	33.0	0.0
Malawi	0.5	8.0	10.0	1.5	1.5	21.5	0.0
Malaysia	6.0	9.5	13.5	3.0	10.0	42.0	0.0
Mali	2.0	8.5	9.5	2.0	9.5	31.5	0.0
Malta	3.5	9.0	12.0	3.0	9.5	37.0	0.0
Mexico	7.5	6.5	11.0	1.5	10.0	36.5	0.5
Moldova	4.0	5.5	9.0	0.0	10.0	28.5	1.5
Mongolia	4.0	8.5	10.5	1.0	10.0	34.0	0.0
Morocco	4.5	7.5	11.5	3.5	10.0	37.0	0.5
Mozambique	3.0	9.5	8.5	3.0	5.0	29.0	-0.5
Myanmar	9.5	8.5	8.5	0.0	9.0	35.5	-1.0
Namibia	9.5	10.0	13.0	1.5	6.5	40.5	1.0
Netherlands	7.0	7.0	13.0	1.0	9.0	37.0	-0.5

COUNTRY	Total Foreign Debt as percent of GDP (10 points)	Debt Service as percent of Exports of Goods and Services (10 points)	Current Account as percent of Exports of Goods and Services (15 points)	International Liquidity as months of import cover (5 points)	Exchange Rate Stability as percentage change (10 points)	Financial Risk Rating	
New Zealand	2.5	5.5	10.5	2.0	8.0	28.5	0.0
Nicaragua	0.0	5.0	7.5	0.0	10.0	22.5	0.0
Niger	4.5	6.0	9.0	0.0	9.5	29.0	0.0
Nigeria	4.5	9.5	15.0	1.5	8.5	39.0	1.0
Norway	10.0	9.5	15.0	3.0	9.0	46.5	0.0
Oman	7.5	9.0	12.5	2.0	10.0	41.0	0.0
Pakistan	4.5	7.0	11.0	0.0	7.5	30.0	-0.5
Panama	5.0	7.0	11.5	1.0	10.0	34.5	0.5
Papua New Guinea	6.5	8.5	12.0	1.5	10.0	38.5	2.0
Paraguay	7.5	9.5	11.5	1.5	9.5	39.5	0.0
Peru	5.5	7.0	11.0	4.0	10.0	37.5	0.0
Philippines	4.5	8.5	13.5	1.5	7.0	35.0	0.5
Poland	6.5	8.5	10.0	3.0	10.0	38.0	0.0
Portugal	4.5	8.0	9.5	2.0	9.5	33.5	0.0
Qatar	3.0	7.5	8.5	0.0	10.0	29.0	0.0
Romania	7.5	7.0	10.5	1.5	4.0	30.5	0.0
Russian Federation.	4.5	9.0	15.0	1.5	10.0	40.0	0.0
Saudi Arabia	9.0	9.5	13.5	3.5	10.0	45.5	0.0
Senegal	4.5	8.0	11.5	0.5	9.5	34.0	0.0
Sierra Leone	0.5	3.5	2.5	0.0	10.0	16.5	-3.0
Singapore	9.0	10.0	13.0	3.5	10.0	45.5	0.0
Slovak Republic	6.5	9.0	11.5	1.0	8.5	36.5	0.0
Slovenia	9.5	9.0	10.5	2.0	8.0	39.0	0.5
Somalia	5.0	9.0	12.0	0.0	10.0	36.0	0.0
South Africa	7.5	9.0	12.0	1.0	6.5	36.0	1.0
Spain	8.5	7.5	11.0	1.5	9.0	37.5	-0.5
Sri Lanka	4.5	8.5	11.5	1.0	7.5	33.0	0.0
Sudan	0.5	10.0	9.5	0.0	10.0	30.0	0.0
Suriname	9.5	9.0	12.0	0.0	6.5	37.0	-1.0
Sweden	6.5	6.5	12.5	1.5	8.0	35.0	-0.5
Switzerland	10.0	5.5	13.5	2.5	10.0	41.5	0.0
Syria	7.0	8.0	12.5	0.5	10.0	38.0	2.0
Taiwan	9.0	10.0	12.5	3.5	9.5	44.5	0.0
Tanzania	0.0	6.5	5.0	0.5	10.0	22.0	0.0
Thailand	5.5	8.5	13.0	2.5	8.5	38.0	2.5
Togo	3.5	9.0	11.0	1.0	9.5	34.0	0.0
Trinidad & Tobago	8.5	8.5	11.5	1.5	10.0	40.0	0.0
Tunisia	5.5	7.5	11.5	1.5	9.0	35.0	-1.0
Turkey	6.0	6.0	11.0	2.0	1.0	26.0	-5.5
Uganda	5.0	9.0	14.0	1.5	7.5	37.0	0.0
Ukraine	7.0	8.5	12.5	1.0	10.0	39.0	0.0
United Arab Emirates	8.0	10.0	15.0	2.5	10.0	45.5	0.0
United Kingdom	9.5	5.5	12.0	0.0	8.5	35.5	0.5
United States	9.5	7.0	9.5	0.5	10.0	36.5	0.0
Uruguay	6.0	6.0	11.5	3.5	9.0	36.0	0.0
Venezuela	7.5	8.0	15.0	3.5	9.5	43.5	0.0
Vietnam	4.0	8.5	13.0	1.0	10.0	36.5	0.0
Yemen, Republic	0.5	7.0	12.5	1.0	10.0	31.0	0.0
Yugoslavia	5.0	4.5	6.5	0.0	0.0	16.0	0.0

COUNTRY	Total Foreign Debt as percent of GDP (10 points)	Debt Service as percent of Exports of Goods and Services (10 points)	Current Account as percent of Exports of Goods and Services (15 points)	International Liquidity as months of import cover (5 points)	Exchange Rate Stability as percentage change (10 points)	Financial Risk Rating	
Zambia	0.5	7.5	11.0	0.0	5.5	24.5	2.5
Zimbabwe	3.5	5.0	10.5	0.0	4.0	23.0	0.0

TABLE 4C

FINANCIAL RISK FORECASTS

Country	Current Rating	One Year Ahead				Five Years Ahead			
		Worst Case	Most Probable	Best Case	Risk Stability	Worst Case	Most Probable	Best Case	Risk Stability
Albania	33.0	23.0	35.0	36.0	13.0	30.0	35.0	36.0	6.0
Algeria	38.5	30.0	32.0	34.0	4.0	30.0	38.0	40.0	10.0
Angola	24.0	20.0	26.0	27.0	7.0	25.0	30.0	32.0	7.0
Argentina	28.5	30.0	34.0	35.0	5.0	30.0	37.0	39.0	9.0
Armenia	31.5	30.0	31.0	32.0	2.0	28.0	34.0	36.0	8.0
Australia	33.0	33.0	35.0	36.0	3.0	32.0	39.0	41.0	9.0
Austria	42.0	42.0	43.0	44.0	2.0	39.0	44.0	48.0	9.0
Azerbaijan	36.5	29.0	31.0	33.0	4.0	30.0	35.0	38.0	8.0
Bahamas	31.0	30.0	31.0	32.0	2.0	30.0	32.0	34.0	4.0
Bahrain	43.5	39.0	42.0	43.0	4.0	36.0	38.0	40.0	4.0
Bangladesh	36.0	35.0	36.0	37.0	2.0	28.0	36.0	39.0	11.0
Belarus	33.0	27.0	28.0	29.0	2.0	25.0	30.0	31.0	6.0
Belgium	38.5	38.0	39.0	40.0	2.0	38.0	40.0	42.0	4.0
Bolivia	35.0	32.0	34.0	35.0	3.0	30.0	35.0	37.0	7.0
Botswana	42.5	40.0	44.0	45.0	5.0	38.0	45.0	47.0	9.0
Brazil	29.5	20.0	28.0	28.0	8.0	28.0	35.0	40.0	12.0
Brunei	49.0	44.0	45.0	46.0	2.0	44.0	46.0	48.0	4.0
Bulgaria	35.5	36.0	37.0	38.0	2.0	34.0	37.0	39.0	5.0
Burkina Faso	32.0	30.0	32.0	33.0	3.0	30.0	34.0	35.0	5.0
Cameroon	31.5	28.0	33.0	35.0	7.0	30.0	35.0	37.0	7.0
Canada	39.0	36.0	37.0	38.0	2.0	33.0	38.0	41.0	8.0
Chile	37.0	34.0	36.0	38.0	4.0	34.0	37.0	40.0	6.0
China, Peoples' Rep.	45.5	40.0	43.0	44.0	4.0	38.0	44.0	46.0	8.0
Colombia	37.0	30.0	33.0	35.0	5.0	28.0	34.0	38.0	10.0
Congo, Dem. Republic	35.0	23.0	28.0	30.0	7.0	25.0	33.0	37.0	12.0
Congo, Republic	29.5	20.0	25.0	26.0	6.0	20.0	27.0	30.0	10.0
Costa Rica	38.0	36.0	37.0	38.0	2.0	30.0	38.0	39.0	9.0
Cote d'Ivoire	27.0	29.0	30.5	30.5	1.5	29.0	33.0	34.0	5.0
Croatia	37.5	35.0	36.0	37.0	2.0	30.0	36.0	38.0	8.0
Cuba	31.5	28.0	30.0	32.0	4.0	26.0	33.0	36.0	10.0
Cyprus	43.0	42.0	43.0	44.0	2.0	39.0	42.0	44.0	5.0
Czech Republic	39.0	38.0	39.0	40.0	2.0	37.0	38.0	40.0	3.0
Denmark	41.0	37.0	38.0	39.0	2.0	35.0	40.0	42.0	7.0
Dominican Republic	37.0	35.0	36.0	37.0	2.0	30.0	36.0	38.0	8.0
Ecuador	33.0	24.0	27.0	28.0	4.0	23.0	31.0	33.0	10.0
Egypt	37.5	37.0	37.0	38.0	1.0	30.0	34.0	37.0	7.0
El Salvador	41.5	41.0	42.0	43.0	2.0	37.0	40.0	42.0	5.0
Estonia	37.0	35.0	36.0	37.0	2.0	33.0	36.0	39.0	6.0
Ethiopia	27.5	20.0	23.0	23.0	3.0	22.0	25.0	27.0	5.0
Finland	37.5	37.0	38.0	39.0	2.0	33.0	38.0	40.0	7.0
France	39.0	38.0	39.0	40.0	2.0	36.0	40.0	42.0	6.0
Gabon	35.5	33.0	36.0	37.0	4.0	30.0	36.0	37.0	7.0
Gambia	30.5	33.0	34.0	34.0	1.0	30.0	36.0	38.0	8.0
Germany	39.0	37.0	38.0	39.0	2.0	35.0	44.0	46.0	11.0
Ghana	21.0	30.0	31.0	32.0	2.0	28.0	32.0	33.0	5.0
Greece	33.0	34.0	35.0	36.0	2.0	32.0	37.0	39.0	7.0
Guatemala	40.0	35.0	36.0	37.0	2.0	30.0	36.0	37.0	7.0
Guinea	32.5	30.0	31.5	32.0	2.0	26.0	32.0	33.0	7.0

Country	Current Rating	One Year Ahead				Five Years Ahead			
		Worst Case	Most Probable	Best Case	Risk Stability	Worst Case	Most Probable	Best Case	Risk Stability
Guinea-Bissau	20.0	20.0	24.0	24.0	4.0	26.0	30.0	32.0	6.0
Guyana	30.5	25.0	28.0	29.0	4.0	25.0	30.0	31.0	6.0
Haiti	33.0	33.0	34.0	35.0	2.0	28.0	34.0	36.0	8.0
Honduras	35.5	30.0	31.0	32.0	2.0	30.0	34.0	38.0	8.0
Hong Kong	44.0	39.0	42.0	44.0	5.0	36.0	40.0	44.0	8.0
Hungary	37.5	35.0	36.0	37.0	2.0	30.0	35.0	38.0	8.0
Iceland	31.5	35.0	36.0	37.0	2.0	30.0	34.0	37.0	7.0
India	40.0	37.0	38.0	39.0	2.0	34.0	38.0	39.0	5.0
Indonesia	30.0	30.0	34.0	35.0	5.0	25.0	36.0	38.0	13.0
Iran	41.5	40.0	40.0	42.0	2.0	38.0	42.0	43.0	5.0
Iraq	30.5	20.0	26.0	27.0	7.0	20.0	30.0	37.0	17.0
Ireland	41.0	41.0	42.0	43.0	2.0	37.0	40.0	43.0	6.0
Israel	39.0	34.0	35.0	36.0	2.0	32.0	35.0	38.0	6.0
Italy	39.0	38.0	40.0	41.0	3.0	37.0	42.0	43.0	6.0
Jamaica	35.0	35.0	36.0	37.0	2.0	30.0	38.0	40.0	10.0
Japan	48.0	45.0	47.0	48.0	3.0	43.0	47.0	48.0	5.0
Jordan	36.5	39.0	40.0	41.0	2.0	35.0	39.0	40.0	5.0
Kazakhstan	39.0	35.0	36.0	37.0	2.0	30.0	34.0	36.0	6.0
Kenya	35.5	33.0	36.0	37.0	4.0	30.0	36.0	37.0	7.0
Korea, D.P.R.	20.5	18.0	18.0	18.0	0.0	18.0	22.0	28.0	10.0
Korea, Republic	39.0	35.0	36.0	37.0	2.0	30.0	40.0	42.0	12.0
Kuwait	48.5	43.0	45.0	46.0	3.0	37.0	40.0	43.0	6.0
Latvia	39.5	36.0	38.0	39.0	3.0	30.0	37.0	39.0	9.0
Lebanon	30.5	27.0	29.0	30.0	3.0	25.0	30.0	35.0	10.0
Liberia	19.5	18.0	20.0	21.0	3.0	20.0	23.0	25.0	5.0
Libya	44.0	38.0	39.0	40.0	2.0	36.0	42.0	46.0	10.0
Lithuania	40.5	38.0	39.0	40.0	2.0	33.0	38.0	41.0	8.0
Luxembourg	41.0	43.0	43.5	44.0	1.0	40.0	43.0	44.0	4.0
Madagascar	33.0	32.0	33.0	35.0	3.0	30.0	34.0	36.0	6.0
Malawi	21.5	20.0	21.0	22.0	2.0	20.0	25.0	27.0	7.0
Malaysia	42.0	38.0	39.0	40.0	2.0	30.0	35.0	38.0	8.0
Mali	31.5	32.0	33.5	34.0	2.0	28.0	35.0	37.0	9.0
Malta	37.0	37.0	38.0	38.0	1.0	34.0	36.0	38.0	4.0
Mexico	36.5	28.0	30.0	32.0	4.0	28.0	33.0	36.0	8.0
Moldova	28.5	22.0	22.0	22.0	0.0	20.0	26.0	30.0	10.0
Mongolia	34.0	34.0	35.0	36.0	2.0	30.0	36.0	37.0	7.0
Morocco	37.0	35.0	36.0	37.0	· 2.0	33.0	35.0	37.0	4.0
Mozambique	29.0	30.0	30.5	31.0	1.0	20.0	32.0	35.0	15.0
Myanmar	35.5	37.0	38.0	39.0	2.0	30.0	35.0	38.0	8.0
Namibia	40.5	38.0	40.0	40.0	2.0	34.0	40.0	40.0	6.0
Netherlands	37.0	38.0	38.0	39.0	1.0	36.0	38.0	39.0	3.0
New Zealand	28.5	30.0	31.0	32.0	2.0	28.0	32.0	35.0	7.0
Nicaragua	22.5	15.0	17.0	19.0	4.0	17.0	20.0	24.0	7.0
Niger	29.0	30.0	31.0	31.0	1.0	28.0	34.0	35.0	7.0
Nigeria	39.0	23.0	28.0	29.0	6.0	23.0	30.0	34.0	11.0
Norway	46.5	45.0	45.0	46.0	1.0	40.0	45.0	47.0	7.0
Oman	41.0	35.0	36.0	38.0	3.0	33.0	35.0	38.0	5.0
Pakistan	30.0	28.0	29.0	30.0	2.0	25.0	28.0	30.0	5.0
Panama	34.5	31.0	32.0	33.0	2.0	30.0	34.0	39.0	9.0
Papua New Guinea	38.5	30.0	33.0	34.0	4.0	27.0	35.0	38.0	11.0
Paraguay	39.5	35.0	37.0	38.0	3.0	30.0	37.0	38.0	8.0
Peru	37.5	34.0	36.0	37.0	3.0	30.0	36.0	38.0	8.0
Philippines	35.0	35.0	36.0	37.0	2.0	30.0	35.0	37.0	7.0

Country	Current Rating	One Year Ahead				Five Years Ahead			
		Worst Case	Most Probable	Best Case	Risk Stability	Worst Case	Most Probable	Best Case	Risk Stability
Poland	38.0	37.0	38.0	39.0	2.0	34.0	37.0	38.0	4.0
Portugal	33.5	34.0	35.0	36.0	2.0	30.0	35.0	38.0	8.0
Qatar	29.0	25.0	26.0	27.0	2.0	23.0	28.0	30.0	7.0
Romania	30.5	22.0	23.0	24.0	2.0	20.0	28.0	32.0	12.0
Russian Federation.	40.0	23.0	26.0	28.0	5.0	20.0	30.0	35.0	15.0
Saudi Arabia	45.5	38.0	40.0	41.0	3.0	36.0	44.0	45.0	9.0
Senegal	34.0	32.0	33.5	34.0	2.0	25.0	34.0	36.0	11.0
Sierra Leone	16.5	8.0	10.0	15.0	7.0	15.0	25.0	30.0	15.0
Singapore	45.5	43.0	44.0	45.0	2.0	38.0	45.0	47.0	9.0
Slovak Republic	36.5	36.0	37.0	38.0	2.0	33.0	38.0	40.0	7.0
Slovenia	39.0	38.0	41.0	42.0	4.0	35.0	38.0	39.0	4.0
Somalia	36.0	18.0	19.0	20.0	2.0	18.0	20.0	27.0	9.0
South Africa	36.0	33.0	34.0	35.0	2.0	30.0	34.0	35.0	5.0
Spain	37.5	40.0	41.0	42.0	2.0	38.0	42.0	44.0	6.0
Sri Lanka	33.0	30.0	33.0	34.0	4.0	27.0	35.0	38.0	11.0
Sudan	30.0	22.5	23.0	23.0	0.5	24.0	27.0	29.0	5.0
Suriname	37.0	37.0	41.0	42.0	5.0	35.0	38.0	43.0	8.0
Sweden	35.0	34.0	35.0	36.0	2.0	30.0	35.0	37.0	7.0
Switzerland	41.5	46.0	47.0	48.0	2.0	40.0	45.0	48.0	8.0
Syria	38.0	32.0	33.0	34.0	2.0	33.0	35.0	36.0	3.0
Taiwan	44.5	43.0	43.0	45.0	2.0	36.0	43.0	45.0	9.0
Tanzania	22.0	15.0	17.0	17.0	2.0	20.0	22.0	23.0	3.0
Thailand	38.0	35.0	36.0	37.0	2.0	28.0	35.0	37.0	9.0
Togo	34.0	30.0	33.0	34.0	4.0	30.0	34.0	36.0	6.0
Trinidad & Tobago	40.0	37.0	38.0	39.0	2.0	35.0	38.0	38.0	3.0
Tunisia	35.0	33.0	34.0	36.0	3.0	30.0	35.0	36.0	6.0
Turkey	26.0	30.0	31.0	32.0	2.0	30.0	36.0	37.0	7.0
Uganda	37.0	31.0	32.0	33.0	2.0	28.0	33.0	35.0	7.0
Ukraine	39.0	23.0	24.0	26.0	3.0	20.0	27.0	30.0	10.0
United Arab Emirates	45.5	38.0	40.0	42.0	4.0	36.0	40.0	44.0	8.0
United Kingdom	35.5	36.0	37.0	38.0	2.0	35.0	38.0	40.0	5.0
United States	36.5	34.0	35.0	36.0	2.0	30.0	36.0	38.0	8.0
Uruguay	36.0	32.0	33.0	34.0	2.0	30.0	35.0	37.0	7.0
Venezuela	43.5	33.0	35.0	36.0	3.0	30.0	38.0	39.0	9.0
Vietnam	36.5	27.0	28.0	29.0	2.0	25.0	28.0	30.0	5.0
Yemen, Republic	31.0	31.0	32.0	33.0	2.0	30.0	34.0	36.0	6.0
Yugoslavia	16.0	15.0	17.0	18.0	3.0	20.0	27.0	30.0	10.0
Zambia	24.5	16.0	17.0	18.0	2.0	16.0	20.0	25.0	9.0
Zimbabwe	23.0	20.0	21.0	22.0	2.0	18.0	23.0	30.0	12.0

TABLE 5A

ECONOMIC RISK RATINGS OVER THE PERIOD APRIL 2000 THROUGH MARCH 2001

COUNTRY	04/00	05/00	06/00	07/00	08/00	09/00	10/00	11/00	12/00	01/01	02/01	03/01
Albania	33.0	33.0	33.0	33.0	33.0	33.0	33.0	33.0	33.0	32.5	32.5	32.5
Algeria	35.0	35.0	35.0	35.0	34.0	34.0	34.0	34.0	37.0	42.0	42.0	41.0
Angola	22.5	22.5	22.5	22.5	23.0	26.0	26.0	26.0	26.0	26.5	26.5	26.5
Argentina	39.0	39.0	39.0	39.0	38.5	38.5	37.5	37.5	37.0	38.5	38.5	38.0
Armenia	26.0	26.0	26.0	26.0	26.0	26.0	26.0	26.0	30.0	31.5	31.5	31.5
Australia	43.5	43.5	41.5	41.5	40.0	40.0	40.0	40.0	40.5	40.0	40.0	39.5
Austria	40.0	40.0	40.5	41.0	41.0	41.0	41.0	41.0	40.5	41.0	41.0	40.5
Azerbaijan	29.0	29.0	29.0	29.0	29.0	29.0	29.0	29.0	29.0	31.5	31.5	31.5
Bahamas	34.5	34.5	34.0	34.0	34.0	34.0	34.0	34.0	34.0	35.5	35.5	35.5
Bahrain	37.0	37.0	37.0	37.0	37.0	37.0	37.0	37.0	37.0	37.5	37.5	37.5
Bangladesh	33.5	33.5	33.5	33.5	33.5	33.5	33.5	33.5	33.5	33.5	33.5	33.5
Belarus	26.0	26.0	26.0	26.0	26.0	26.0	26.0	29.5	29.0	29.0	29.0	29.0
Belgium	44.5	44.5	43.5	43.5	44.0	44.0	44.0	44.0	44.0	44.0	44.0	43.5
Bolivia	34.0	34.0	33.5	33.5	33.5	33.5	33.5	33.5	33.5	33.5	33.5	33.0
Botswana	43.5	43.5	43.5	43.5	40.5	40.5	40.5	40.5	39.0	39.0	39.0	38.5
Brazil	33.0	33.0	34.0	34.0	34.0	34.0	34.0	34.0	34.0	35.0	35.0	35.5
Brunei	46.0	46.0	46.0	46.0	46.0	46.0	46.0	46.0	46.0	46.5	46.5	46.5
Bulgaria	37.0	37.5	37.5	37.0	35.0	35.0	35.0	35.0	34.5	36.0	36.0	35.0
Burkina Faso	31.5	31.5	31.5	31.5	31.5	29.5	29.5	29.5	29.5	30.0	30.0	30.0
Cameroon	34.5	34.5	34.5	34.5	34.5	34.5	34.5	34.5	34.5	38.5	38.5	38.5
Canada	44.0	44.0	42.0	42.0	42.0	42.0	42.0	42.0	42.5	41.5	41.5	40.5
Chile	39.5	39.0	39.0	39.0	39.0	38.0	38.0	38.0	38.5	38.5	38.5	37.5
China, P. Rep.	39.5	39.5	39.5	39.5	39.5	39.0	39.0	39.0	39.0	38.5	38.5	39.0
Colombia	34.0	34.0	34.0	34.0	33.5	33.5	33.5	33.5	33.5	34.0	34.0	34.5
Congo, D. Rep	28.0	28.0	28.0	28.0	28.5	28.5	28.5	28.5	28.5	29.5	29.5	29.5
Congo, Rep.	32.0	32.0	32.0	32.0	31.5	31.5	31.5	31.5	37.5	37.5	37.5	37.5
Costa Rica	35.0	35.0	34.5	34.5	34.5	34.5	34.5	34.5	34.5	34.0	34.0	34.0
Cote d'Ivoire	36.0	36.0	35.5	35.5	36.5	36.5	36.5	36.5	32.0	33.5	33.5	32.5
Croatia	36.0	36.0	36.0	36.0	36.0	36.0	36.0	36.0	36.0	36.5	36.5	36.5
Cuba	33.0	33.0	33.0	33.0	33.0	33.0	33.0	33.0	33.0	34.5	34.5	34.5
Cyprus	40.5	40.5	39.5	39.5	39.5	39.5	39.5	39.5	39.5	39.5	39.5	39.5
Czech Rep.	35.0	34.5	34.5	35.5	36.0	36.0	36.0	35.5	35.5	34.5	34.5	34.5
Denmark	42.5	42.0	42.5	42.5	43.0	43.0	43.0	43.0	43.0	43.5	43.5	43.5
Dominican R.	37.5	37.5	37.5	37.5	37.5	37.5	37.5	37.5	37.5	36.0	36.0	36.0
Ecuador	23.0	22.5	23.0	23.0	23.0	22.5	25.0	25.0	25.0	29.5	29.5	29.5
Egypt	36.5	37.0	36.5	36.5	35.5	35.5	35.5	35.5	36.5	35.5	35.5	35.5
El Salvador	36.5	36.5	36.5	36.5	36.5	36.5	36.5	36.5	36.5	35.5	35.5	35.5
Estonia	37.5	37.5	37.5	37.5	37.5	37.5	37.5	37.5	37.5	38.5	38.5	38.5
Ethiopia	31.0	31.0	31.0	31.0	31.0	31.0	31.0	31.0	31.0	32.5	32.5	32.5
Finland	46.5	46.5	47.0	47.0	47.5	47.5	47.5	47.5	47.5	47.0	47.0	46.5
France	43.5	43.5	43.5	43.5	43.5	43.5	43.5	43.5	43.5	44.0	44.0	43.0
Gabon	39.5	39.5	39.5	39.5	37.0	37.0	37.0	34.5	34.5	38.0	38.0	38.0
Gambia	34.5	34.5	34.0	34.0	34.0	33.0	33.0	33.0	33.0	33.0	33.0	33.0
Germany	42.0	42.0	42.0	42.0	42.0	41.5	41.5	43.0	43.0	41.5	41.5	41.0
Ghana	31.0	31.0	28.5	28.5	27.0	27.0	27.0	27.0	26.0	25.5	25.5	26.5
Greece	39.5	39.5	38.5	38.5	39.0	39.0	39.0	39.0	39.0	40.0	40.0	40.0
Guatemala	36.0	35.5	35.0	35.0	35.0	35.0	35.0	35.0	35.0	35.0	35.0	35.0
Guinea	34.0	34.0	34.0	34.0	34.0	34.0	34.0	34.0	34.0	34.0	34.0	34.0

COUNTRY	04/00	05/00	06/00	07/00	08/00	09/00	10/00	11/00	12/00	01/01	02/01	03/01
Guinea-Bissau	23.5	23.5	23.5	23.5	23.5	23.5	23.5	23.5	23.5	24.5	24.5	24.5
Guyana	29.5	29.5	29.5	29.5	29.5	29.5	29.5	29.5	27.0	30.0	30.0	30.0
Haiti	32.0	31.5	31.5	31.5	31.5	31.5	31.5	31.5	31.5	33.0	31.5	31.5
Honduras	28.5	28.5	28.5	28.5	28.5	28.5	28.5	28.5	28.5	30.5	30.5	30.5
Hong Kong	43.5	43.5	44.5	44.5	45.0	45.0	45.0	45.0	44.5	43.5	43.5	47.0
Hungary	34.0	37.0	35.0	35.0	35.5	35.5	35.5	35.5	35.5	37.0	37.0	36.5
Iceland	37.5	37.5	37.5	37.5	37.5	37.5	37.5	37.5	35.5	36.5	35.5	35.5
India	34.5	34.5	34.5	33.5	33.5	33.5	33.5	33.5	31.5	33.5	33.5	34.0
Indonesia	35.5	35.5	35.5	35.5	34.5	34.5	35.5	35.5	36.0	35.0	35.0	35.0
Iran	34.0	34.0	34.0	34.0	35.0	35.0	35.0	35.0	35.5	41.0	41.0	41.0
Iraq	28.5	28.5	28.5	28.5	28.5	28.5	28.5	28.5	28.5	29.5	29.5	29.5
Ireland	45.0	45.0	44.5	44.5	44.5	44.0	44.0	44.0	44.5	45.5	45.5	45.5
Israel	40.0	40.0	39.0	39.0	39.5	39.5	39.5	39.5	41.0	38.5	38.5	38.5
Italy	42.5	42.5	41.5	41.5	42.0	42.5	42.5	41.5	41.0	42.0	42.0	40.5
Jamaica	28.0	28.0	28.0	28.0	28.0	28.0	28.0	28.0	27.5	32.5	32.5	32.5
Japan	38.5	38.5	38.5	38.5	39.0	38.0	38.0	38.0	39.0	39.0	39.0	39.0
Jordan	35.5	35.5	35.5	35.5	35.5	35.5	35.5	35.5	35.5	36.0	36.0	36.0
Kazakhstan	26.5	26.5	26.0	26.0	26.0	26.0	26.0	26.0	26.0	37.0	37.0	37.0
Kenya	32.5	33.0	32.5	31.5	31.0	32.5	32.5	32.5	30.5	31.0	31.0	31.5
Korea, D.P.R.	17.5	17.5	17.5	17.5	17.5	17.5	17.5	17.5	17.5	17.0	17.0	17.0
Korea, Rep.	44.5	44.5	44.5	41.5	41.5	41.5	41.5	41.5	41.0	41.0	43.5	44.5
Kuwait	45.0	45.0	45.0	45.0	44.5	44.5	44.5	44.5	44.5	44.5	44.5	44.5
Latvia	36.5	36.5	36.5	36.5	35.5	35.5	35.5	35.5	35.5	35.5	35.5	35.5
Lebanon	28.5	28.5	28.5	28.5	27.0	27.0	27.0	27.0	28.5	23.5	23.5	23.5
Liberia	35.0	35.0	35.0	35.0	35.0	35.0	35.0	35.0	35.0	34.5	34.5	34.5
Libya	35.0	35.0	35.0	35.0	35.0	35.0	35.0	35.0	35.0	39.0	39.0	39.0
Lithuania	36.5	36.5	36.5	36.5	36.5	36.5	36.5	36.5	36.5	36.5	37.0	37.0
Luxembourg	47.0	46.5	46.5	46.5	46.0	46.0	46.0	46.0	46.0	46.0	46.0	46.0
Madagascar	33.0	33.0	32.5	32.5	32.5	30.0	30.0	30.0	30.0	30.5	30.5	30.5
Malawi	26.5	26.5	27.0	27.0	27.0	27.0	27.0	27.0	27.0	31.0	31.0	31.0
Malaysia	42.0	42.5	43.0	43.0	43.0	43.0	43.0	43.0	42.5	42.5	42.5	42.0
Mali	36.5	36.5	36.5	36.5	36.5	36.5	36.5	31.0	31.0	30.5	30.5	30.5
Malta	35.5	35.5	35.0	35.0	35.0	35.0	35.0	35.0	35.0	35.5	35.5	35.5
Mexico	35.0	36.5	37.0	37.0	37.0	37.0	37.0	37.0	38.0	40.0	40.0	36.5
Moldova	19.0	19.0	19.0	19.0	13.5	13.5	13.5	13.5	13.5	31.5	31.5	31.5
Mongolia	26.0	27.5	24.5	24.5	30.0	30.0	30.0	30.0	30.0	30.0	30.0	30.0
Morocco	38.0	38.0	38.0	38.0	37.0	37.0	37.0	37.0	32.5	36.0	36.0	36.5
Mozambique	24.5	24.5	24.5	24.5	24.5	24.5	24.5	24.5	24.5	26.0	26.0	25.5
Myanmar	35.0	36.0	36.5	36.5	36.5	36.5	36.5	36.5	36.5	36.0	36.0	36.0
Namibia	37.0	37.0	37.0	37.0	37.0	37.0	37.0	37.0	37.0	37.0	37.0	37.0
Netherlands	44.5	44.5	44.0	44.0	44.5	44.5	44.5	44.5	44.5	44.0	44.0	44.0
New Zealand	42.5	42.5	42.5	42.5	42.0	42.0	42.0	41.0	41.0	40.0	40.0	40.0
Nicaragua	20.5	20.5	20.5	20.5	20.5	20.5	20.5	20.5	20.5	26.0	26.0	26.0
Niger	35.0	35.0	35.0	35.0	35.0	35.0	35.0	35.0	35.0	30.0	30.0	30.0
Nigeria	31.5	31.5	36.0	36.0	34.5	35.5	35.5	35.5	36.0	36.5	36.5	36.5
Norway	46.5	46.0	46.0	46.0	46.0	47.5	47.5	47.5	47.5	47.0	46.5	46.5
Oman	40.5	40.5	40.5	40.5	40.5	40.5	40.5	40.5	40.5	43.0	43.0	43.0
Pakistan	33.0	33.0	33.0	33.0	31.5	31.5	31.5	31.5	32.5	33.0	33.0	33.5
Panama	38.0	38.0	36.0	36.0	36.0	36.0	36.0	36.0	36.0	37.0	37.0	38.5
Papua N.G.	32.0	32.0	32.0	32.0	32.0	32.0	32.0	35.5	35.5	36.0	36.0	36.0
Paraguay	33.5	33.0	32.5	32.5	32.5	32.5	32.5	32.5	32.5	32.0	32.0	32.0
Peru	38.0	38.0	38.0	38.0	37.5	37.5	37.5	37.5	37.0	35.5	35.5	36.0
Philippines	38.0	38.5	38.5	38.5	38.0	38.0	38.0	38.0	38.5	37.5	37.5	37.0
Poland	35.5	35.5	35.0	35.0	35.5	35.5	35.5	35.5	35.0	36.0	36.0	35.0
Portugal	38.0	38.5	38.5	38.5	38.0	37.5	37.5	37.5	38.0	37.5	37.5	36.5

COUNTRY	04/00	05/00	06/00	07/00	08/00	09/00	10/00	11/00	12/00	01/01	02/01	03/01
Qatar	34.5	34.5	34.5	34.5	34.5	34.5	34.5	34.5	34.5	36.0	36.0	36.0
Romania	24.5	24.5	24.5	24.5	25.5	25.5	25.5	25.5	27.0	30.0	30.0	30.0
Russian Fed.	31.5	32.5	33.5	33.5	35.5	35.5	35.5	38.5	39.5	38.0	38.0	38.0
Saudi Arabia	38.0	38.0	38.0	38.0	38.0	38.0	38.0	38.0	41.5	42.0	42.0	42.0
Senegal	36.5	36.5	36.5	36.5	36.5	36.5	36.5	36.5	36.5	36.5	36.5	36.5
Sierra Leone	20.0	20.0	20.0	20.0	20.0	20.0	20.0	20.0	20.0	22.0	22.0	25.5
Singapore	46.5	46.5	50.0	50.0	50.0	50.0	50.0	50.0	50.0	49.5	49.5	49.0
Slovak Rep.	31.0	30.5	30.5	30.5	30.5	30.5	30.5	30.5	30.5	32.5	32.5	32.5
Slovenia	37.0	36.0	35.5	35.5	35.5	35.5	35.5	35.5	35.5	35.0	35.0	35.0
Somalia	28.5	28.5	28.5	28.5	28.5	28.5	28.5	28.5	28.5	28.5	28.5	28.5
South Africa	37.0	37.0	37.0	37.0	36.0	36.0	36.0	36.0	36.0	37.0	37.0	37.0
Spain	40.0	39.5	40.5	41.0	41.0	41.0	40.5	40.5	40.5	41.0	41.0	40.0
Sri Lanka	31.0	32.5	32.5	32.5	32.5	32.5	32.5	32.5	32.5	32.0	32.0	32.0
Sudan	33.5	33.5	33.5	33.5	33.5	33.5	33.5	33.5	33.5	33.0	33.0	33.0
Suriname	30.5	30.5	30.5	30.5	30.5	30.5	30.5	30.5	30.5	31.0	31.0	31.0
Sweden	45.0	45.0	45.5	46.0	46.0	46.0	46.5	46.5	46.5	46.5	46.5	46.0
Switzerland	45.0	45.0	44.0	46.0	46.0	46.0	46.0	46.0	46.0	45.5	45.5	45.0
Syria	40.0	40.0	40.0	40.0	40.0	40.0	40.0	40.0	40.0	40.0	40.0	40.0
Taiwan	44.0	44.0	44.0	44.0	44.5	44.5	44.0	44.0	44.0	43.0	43.0	42.5
Tanzania	32.5	32.5	32.5	32.5	32.5	32.5	33.5	33.5	33.0	34.5	34.5	34.5
Thailand	38.0	38.0	38.0	38.0	37.5	40.0	40.0	40.0	40.5	39.0	39.0	39.0
Togo	34.0	34.0	34.0	34.0	34.0	34.0	34.0	34.0	34.0	34.0	34.0	34.0
Trinidad & T.	37.0	37.0	37.0	37.0	37.0	37.0	37.0	37.0	37.0	37.0	37.0	37.0
Tunisia	37.5	37.5	37.0	37.0	37.0	37.0	37.0	37.0	37.0	38.0	38.0	36.5
Turkey	25.5	25.5	25.5	25.5	26.0	26.0	26.0	26.0	27.0	30.5	30.5	31.0
Uganda	35.0	34.5	34.5	34.5	34.5	34.5	34.5	34.5	34.5	33.5	33.5	33.5
Ukraine	28.5	28.5	28.5	28.5	28.5	28.5	28.5	28.5	28.5	31.5	34.5	34.5
United Arab E.	44.5	44.5	45.0	45.0	44.0	44.0	44.0	44.0	44.0	45.5	45.5	45.5
United K'dom	42.5	42.0	42.0	42.0	42.0	42.0	42.0	42.0	42.0	40.5	40.5	41.0
United States	42.0	42.0	42.0	42.0	42.0	42.0	42.0	42.0	42.0	41.0	41.0	40.0
Uruguay	36.0	36.5	36.0	36.5	36.5	36.5	36.5	36.5	36.5	38.0	38.0	38.0
Venezuela	34.0	34.5	34.5	34.5	34.5	34.5	38.5	38.5	38.5	37.0	37.0	37.5
Vietnam	34.5	34.5	34.5	34.5	34.5	38.0	38.0	38.0	38.0	39.0	39.0	39.0
Yemen, Rep.	34.0	34.0	34.0	34.0	34.0	34.0	34.0	34.0	34.0	35.5	35.5	35.5
Yugoslavia	24.5	24.5	24.5	24.5	24.5	24.5	24.5	24.5	24.5	27.5	27.5	27.5
Zambia	27.0	27.0	27.0	27.0	27.0	27.0	27.0	27.0	27.0	28.5	28.5	27.5
Zimbabwe	25.5	25.5	21.0	21.0	17.5	17.5	17.5	17.5	13.5	13.5	13.5	15.0

TABLE 5B

ECONOMIC RISK POINTS BY COMPONENT - MARCH 2001

This table lists the risk points awarded to each of the Economic Risk components. The maximum points available for each component are given in parentheses in the column heading. The final columns in the table show the overall economic risk rating (the sum of the points awarded to each component) and the change from the preceding month. Changes in the points awarded to the individual risk components are shown in Tables 7 through 11.

COUNTRY	GDP per head of Population (5)	Real Annual GDP Growth (10)	Annual Inflation Rate (10)	Budget Balance as percent of GDP (10)	Current Account as percent of GDP (15)	Economic Risk Rating	
Albania	0.5	10.0	9.5	3.0	9.5	32.5	0.0
Algeria	1.0	9.5	8.0	8.5	14.0	41.0	-1.0
Angola	0.0	9.5	0.0	8.5	8.5	26.5	0.0
Argentina	3.5	7.5	10.0	6.5	10.5	38.0	-0.5
Armenia	0.0	10.0	8.0	8.5	5.0	31.5	0.0
Australia	5.0	8.0	8.5	8.0	10.0	39.5	-0.5
Austria	5.0	7.5	10.0	7.5	10.5	40.5	-0.5
Azerbaijan	0.0	10.0	8.5	6.0	7.0	31.5	0.0
Bahamas	4.0	7.5	9.5	6.5	8.0	35.5	0.0
Bahrain	3.5	9.0	9.5	6.0	9.5	37.5	0.0
Bangladesh	0.0	9.5	7.5	5.5	11.0	33.5	0.0
Belarus	0.5	8.5	2.5	7.0	10.5	29.0	0.0
Belgium	5.0	7.5	10.0	8.0	13.0	43.5	-0.5
Bolivia	0.5	8.5	8.5	6.0	9.5	33.0	-0.5
Botswana	2.0	9.5	7.5	6.5	13.0	38.5	-0.5
Brazil	2.0	9.0	8.5	5.5	10.5	35.5	0.5
Brunei	5.0	9.0	9.0	10.0	13.5	46.5	0.0
Bulgaria	1.0	9.0	7.5	7.0	10.5	35.0	-1.0
Burkina Faso	0.0	9.5	9.5	3.5	7.5	30.0	0.0
Cameroon	0.0	9.5	9.5	8.5	11.0	38.5	0.0
Canada	5.0	7.5	9.0	8.0	11.0	40.5	-1.0
Chile	2.5	9.0	8.5	7.0	10.5	37.5	-1.0
China, Peoples' Rep.	0.5	10.0	10.0	6.0	12.5	39.0	0.5
Colombia	1.5	8.5	8.0	6.0	10.5	34.5	0.5
Congo, Dem. Republic	0.0	9.0	0.0	5.5	15.0	29.5	0.0
Congo, Republic	0.5	9.0	9.0	9.5	9.5	37.5	0.0
Costa Rica	2.0	9.0	7.0	6.0	10.0	34.0	0.0
Cote d'Ivoire	0.5	6.0	9.0	7.0	10.0	32.5	-1.0
Croatia	2.5	9.0	8.5	7.0	9.5	36.5	0.0
Cuba	1.5	9.5	7.0	6.0	10.5	34.5	0.0
Cyprus	4.0	9.0	8.5	5.5	12.5	39.5	0.0
Czech Republic	2.5	8.5	8.5	4.5	10.5	34.5	0.0
Denmark	5.0	7.5	9.5	9.0	12.5	43.5	0.0
Dominican Republic	1.0	10.0	6.0	8.5	10.5	36.0	0.0
Ecuador	0.5	7.5	3.0	6.5	12.0	29.5	0.0
Egypt	0.5	9.0	8.5	7.0	10.5	35.5	0.0
El Salvador	1.0	8.0	10.0	6.5	10.0	35.5	0.0
Estonia	2.5	9.5	9.0	8.0	9.5	38.5	0.0

COUNTRY	GDP per head of Population (5)	Real Annual GDP Growth (10)	Annual Inflation Rate (10)	Budget Balance as percent of GDP (10)	Current Account as percent of GDP (15)	Economic Risk Rating	
Ethiopia	0.0	9.5	8.0	4.5	10.5	32.5	0.0
Finland	5.0	8.5	9.5	10.0	13.5	46.5	-0.5
France	5.0	7.5	10.0	7.5	13.0	43.0	-1.0
Gabon	2.0	3.0	9.5	10.0	13.5	38.0	0.0
Gambia	0.0	9.0	9.0	6.5	8.5	33.0	0.0
Germany	5.0	7.5	10.0	7.0	11.5	41.0	-0.5
Ghana	0.0	8.5	4.5	4.5	9.0	26.5	1.0
Greece	4.0	9.0	9.0	7.5	10.5	40.0	0.0
Guatemala	1.0	9.0	7.5	7.0	10.5	35.0	0.0
Guinea	0.5	9.0	8.5	6.0	10.0	34.0	0.0
Guinea-Bissau	0.0	10.0	9.5	1.0	4.0	24.5	0.0
Guyana	0.5	8.5	8.0	5.5	7.5	30.0	0.0
Haiti	0.0	8.5	7.5	6.0	9.5	31.5	0.0
Honduras	0.5	7.5	7.5	5.5	9.5	30.5	0.0
Hong Kong	5.0	9.0	10.0	10.0	13.0	47.0	3.5
Hungary	3.5	9.5	7.5	6.0	10.0	36.5	-0.5
Iceland	4.5	7.0	8.5	6.5	9.0	35.5	0.0
India	0.0	9.5	8.5	5.0	11.0	34.0	0.5
Indonesia	0.0	9.0	8.0	6.0	12.0	35.0	0.0
Iran	2.5	9.5	5.5	9.0	14.5	41.0	0.0
Iraq	1.5	9.0	3.5	3.5	12.0	29.5	0.0
Ireland	5.0	10.0	8.5	10.0	12.0	45.5	0.0
Israel	4.5	8.5	9.0	6.0	10.5	38.5	0.0
Italy	5.0	7.5	9.5	7.0	11.5	40.5	-1.5
Jamaica	1.5	7.5	8.0	5.0	10.5	32.5	0.0
Japan	5.0	7.5	10.0	3.5	13.0	39.0	0.0
Jordan	0.5	9.0	8.5	5.5	12.5	36.0	0.0
Kazakhstan	0.5	9.5	5.5	8.0	13.5	37.0	0.0
Kenya	0.0	6.5	8.5	7.0	9.5	31.5	0.5
Korea, D.P.R.	0.0	2.0	4.0	2.5	8.5	17.0	0.0
Korea, Republic	3.5	9.5	9.5	8.5	13.5	44.5	1.0
Kuwait	4.0	7.5	9.0	9.0	15.0	44.5	0.0
Latvia	1.5	8.5	9.0	7.0	9.5	35.5	0.0
Lebanon	2.5	10.0	7.0	1.5	2.5	23.5	0.0
Liberia	0.0	10.0	8.5	7.0	9.0	34.5	0.0
Libya	3.0	9.0	5.0	9.0	13.0	39.0	0.0
Lithuania	2.0	9.0	10.0	6.5	9.5	37.0	0.0
Luxembourg	5.0	8.5	9.5	8.5	14.5	46.0	0.0
Madagascar	0.0	9.0	7.5	5.0	9.0	30.5	0.0
Malawi	0.0	8.5	5.0	8.0	9.5	31.0	0.0
Malaysia	2.5	9.5	9.0	6.0	15.0	42.0	-0.5
Mali	0.0	9.0	9.5	3.0	9.0	30.5	0.0
Malta	3.5	8.5	9.0	4.5	10.0	35.5	0.0
Mexico	2.5	8.5	7.5	7.5	10.5	36.5	-3.5
Moldova	0.0	9.5	6.5	6.0	9.5	31.5	0.0
Mongolia	0.0	8.5	7.0	5.5	9.0	30.0	0.0
Morocco	0.5	10.0	9.0	6.5	10.5	36.5	0.5
Mozambique	0.0	10.0	8.0	1.5	6.0	25.5	-0.5
Myanmar	2.5	7.5	7.0	7.5	11.5	36.0	0.0

COUNTRY	GDP per head of Population (5)	Real Annual GDP Growth (10)	Annual Inflation Rate (10)	Budget Balance as percent of GDP (10)	Current Account as percent of GDP (15)	Economic Risk Rating	
Namibia	1.0	9.0	7.5	6.0	13.5	37.0	0.0
Netherlands	5.0	8.5	9.0	8.0	13.5	44.0	0.0
New Zealand	4.5	7.5	9.5	8.5	10.0	40.0	0.0
Nicaragua	0.0	9.0	8.0	7.0	2.0	26.0	0.0
Niger	0.0	8.5	9.0	4.0	8.5	30.0	0.0
Nigeria	0.0	8.5	9.0	6.5	12.5	36.5	0.0
Norway	5.0	7.5	9.0	10.0	15.0	46.5	0.0
Oman	3.0	9.0	10.0	8.5	12.5	43.0	0.0
Pakistan	0.0	9.0	8.5	5.0	11.0	33.5	0.5
Panama	2.0	9.0	10.0	8.0	9.5	38.5	1.5
Papua New Guinea	0.5	8.0	8.5	7.5	11.5	36.0	0.0
Paraguay	1.0	7.5	7.5	6.0	10.0	32.0	0.0
Peru	1.5	8.0	9.0	7.0	10.5	36.0	0.5
Philippines	0.5	8.0	8.0	6.0	14.5	37.0	-0.5
Poland	2.5	8.5	8.0	6.5	9.5	35.0	-1.0
Portugal	4.0	8.0	9.0	7.0	8.5	36.5	-1.0
Qatar	4.5	8.5	9.0	8.0	6.0	36.0	0.0
Romania	1.0	8.0	3.5	7.0	10.5	30.0	0.0
Russian Federation.	0.5	8.5	6.0	8.0	15.0	38.0	0.0
Saudi Arabia	3.0	7.5	9.5	8.0	14.0	42.0	0.0
Senegal	0.0	9.5	10.0	7.0	10.0	36.5	0.0
Sierra Leone	0.0	9.5	4.0	2.5	9.5	25.5	3.5
Singapore	5.0	9.5	9.5	10.0	15.0	49.0	-0.5
Slovak Republic	2.5	8.5	6.5	5.5	9.5	32.5	0.0
Slovenia	3.5	8.5	7.5	7.0	8.5	35.0	0.0
Somalia	0.0	5.5	4.0	8.0	11.0	28.5	0.0
South Africa	2.0	8.5	8.5	7.5	10.5	37.0	0.0
Spain	4.5	8.5	9.0	7.5	10.5	40.0	-1.0
Sri Lanka	0.5	9.0	9.0	3.5	10.0	32.0	0.0
Sudan	0.0	10.0	6.0	7.0	10.0	33.0	0.0
Suriname	3.5	7.5	4.0	5.5	10.5	31.0	0.0
Sweden	5.0	8.0	10.0	10.0	13.0	46.0	-0.5
Switzerland	5.0	7.5	10.0	7.5	15.0	45.0	-0.5
Syria	2.5	8.5	10.0	7.0	12.0	40.0	0.0
Taiwan	4.0	9.0	10.0	7.5	12.0	42.5	-0.5
Tanzania	0.0	9.5	8.5	8.0	8.5	34.5	0.0
Thailand	1.0	8.5	9.5	6.5	13.5	39.0	0.0
Togo	0.0	9.0	8.5	6.5	10.0	34.0	0.0
Trinidad & Tobago	2.5	8.5	8.5	7.5	10.0	37.0	0.0
Tunisia	1.5	9.0	9.0	6.5	10.5	36.5	-1.5
Turkey	2.0	9.0	4.0	5.5	10.5	31.0	0.5
Uganda	0.0	10.0	8.0	6.5	9.0	33.5	0.0
Ukraine	0.5	9.0	5.0	7.0	13.0	34.5	0.0
United Arab Emirates	5.0	9.0	8.5	8.0	15.0	45.5	0.0
United Kingdom	5.0	7.5	9.5	8.0	11.0	41.0	0.5
United States	5.0	7.5	9.0	8.0	10.5	40.0	-1.0
Uruguay	3.0	9.0	8.5	7.0	10.5	38.0	0.0
Venezuela	2.5	8.5	6.5	6.0	14.0	37.5	0.5
Vietnam	0.0	9.5	10.0	6.5	13.0	39.0	0.0

COUNTRY	GDP per head of Population (5)	Real Annual GDP Growth (10)	Annual Inflation Rate (10)	Budget Balance as percent of GDP (10)	Current Account as percent of GDP (15)	Economic Risk Rating	
Yemen, Republic	0.0	9.5	7.0	6.5	12.5	35.5	0.0
Yugoslavia	0.5	10.0	3.5	4.5	9.0	27.5	0.0
Zambia	0.0	8.5	4.0	6.0	9.0	27.5	-1.0
Zimbabwe	0.0	0.0	2.5	0.5	12.0	15.0	1.5

TABLE 5C

ECONOMIC RISK FORECASTS

Country	Current Rating	One Year Ahead				Five Years Ahead			
		Worst Case	Most Probable	Best Case	Risk Stability	Worst Case	Most Probable	Best Case	Risk Stability
Albania	32.5	20.0	33.0	34.0	14.0	28.0	35.0	36.0	8.0
Algeria	41.0	30.0	33.0	34.0	4.0	35.0	36.0	37.0	2.0
Angola	26.5	18.0	20.0	21.0	3.0	18.0	22.0	28.0	10.0
Argentina	38.0	34.0	35.0	37.0	3.0	33.0	40.0	42.0	9.0
Armenia	31.5	30.0	31.0	32.0	2.0	28.0	34.0	37.0	9.0
Australia	39.5	37.0	38.0	39.0	2.0	35.0	39.0	40.0	5.0
Austria	40.5	38.0	39.0	40.0	2.0	35.0	40.0	43.0	8.0
Azerbaijan	31.5	25.0	27.0	28.0	3.0	25.0	30.0	36.0	11.0
Bahamas	35.5	36.0	38.0	38.0	2.0	32.0	38.0	39.0	7.0
Bahrain	37.5	37.0	38.0	39.0	2.0	36.0	38.0	38.0	2.0
Bangladesh	33.5	32.0	33.0	34.0	2.0	25.0	35.0	37.0	12.0
Belarus	29.0	23.0	24.0	25.0	2.0	20.0	27.0	29.0	9.0
Belgium	43.5	40.0	41.0	42.0	2.0	35.0	40.0	44.0	9.0
Bolivia	33.0	30.0	32.0	33.0	3.0	28.0	35.0	37.0	9.0
Botswana	38.5	40.0	43.0	45.0	5.0	38.0	44.0	45.0	7.0
Brazil	35.5	25.0	27.0	28.0	3.0	30.0	38.0	40.0	10.0
Brunei	46.5	39.0	41.0	42.0	3.0	35.0	38.0	40.0	5.0
Bulgaria	35.0	35.0	36.0	37.0	2.0	33.0	38.0	40.0	7.0
Burkina Faso	30.0	33.0	34.0	34.0	1.0	28.0	34.0	35.0	7.0
Cameroon	38.5	33.0	35.0	37.0	4.0	34.0	35.0	37.0	3.0
Canada	40.5	37.0	39.0	40.0	3.0	36.0	40.0	42.0	6.0
Chile	37.5	36.0	38.0	38.0	2.0	33.0	38.0	40.0	7.0
China, Peoples' Rep.	39.0	38.0	39.0	40.0	2.0	36.0	39.0	42.0	6.0
Colombia	34.5	27.0	28.0	29.0	2.0	25.0	32.0	38.0	13.0
Congo, Dem. Republic	29.5	20.0	22.0	23.0	3.0	24.0	30.0	33.0	9.0
Congo, Republic	37.5	27.0	32.0	33.0	6.0	25.0	35.0	37.0	12.0
Costa Rica	34.0	32.0	33.0	35.0	3.0	30.0	35.0	37.0	7.0
Cote d'Ivoire	32.5	37.0	38.0	39.0	2.0	35.0	37.0	39.0	4.0
Croatia	36.5	36.0	37.0	38.0	2.0	33.0	35.0	37.0	4.0
Cuba	34.5	29.0	31.0	32.0	3.0	25.0	36.0	38.0	13.0
Cyprus	39.5	35.0	36.0	37.0	2.0	30.0	35.0	37.0	7.0
Czech Republic	34.5	30.0	31.0	32.0	2.0	30.0	34.0	37.0	7.0
Denmark	43.5	41.0	42.0	43.0	2.0	35.0	40.0	43.0	8.0
Dominican Republic	36.0	37.0	38.0	39.0	2.0	28.0	37.0	38.0	10.0
Ecuador	29.5	25.0	27.0	29.0	4.0	23.0	30.0	33.0	10.0
Egypt	35.5	34.0	36.0	37.0	3.0	30.0	35.0	36.0	6.0
El Salvador	35.5	37.0	38.0	39.0	2.0	30.0	38.0	41.0	11.0
Estonia	38.5	34.0	36.0	37.0	3.0	30.0	36.0	40.0	10.0
Ethiopia	32.5	28.0	31.0	32.0	4.0	28.0	35.0	37.0	9.0
Finland	46.5	39.0	40.0	41.0	2.0	35.0	40.0	44.0	9.0
France	43.0	41.0	42.0	43.0	2.0	35.0	40.0	43.0	8.0
Gabon	38.0	40.0	42.0	42.0	2.0	36.0	40.0	43.0	7.0
Gambia	33.0	32.0	35.0	36.0	4.0	27.0	35.0	37.0	10.0
Germany	41.0	38.0	39.0	40.0	2.0	34.0	38.0	42.0	8.0
Ghana	26.5	27.0	28.0	29.0	2.0	27.0	30.0	31.0	4.0
Greece	40.0	37.0	38.0	39.0	2.0	35.0	38.0	39.0	4.0
Guatemala	35.0	32.0	33.0	34.0	2.0	30.0	35.0	37.0	7.0
Guinea	34.0	31.0	33.0	34.0	3.0	28.0	34.0	36.0	8.0

Country	Current Rating	One Year Ahead				Five Years Ahead			
		Worst Case	Most Probable	Best Case	Risk Stability	Worst Case	Most Probable	Best Case	Risk Stability
Guinea-Bissau	24.5	25.0	26.0	27.0	2.0	25.0	33.0	35.0	10.0
Guyana	30.0	30.0	32.0	33.0	3.0	28.0	34.0	36.0	8.0
Haiti	31.5	28.0	31.0	32.0	4.0	25.0	35.0	37.0	12.0
Honduras	30.5	25.0	26.0	27.0	2.0	32.0	35.0	38.0	6.0
Hong Kong	47.0	34.0	36.0	37.0	3.0	30.0	36.0	39.0	9.0
Hungary	36.5	31.0	33.0	34.0	3.0	28.0	35.0	38.0	10.0
Iceland	35.5	40.0	41.0	42.0	2.0	35.0	40.0	43.0	8.0
India	34.0	29.0	30.0	31.0	2.0	28.0	33.0	35.0	7.0
Indonesia	35.0	20.0	23.0	25.0	5.0	28.0	33.0	35.0	7.0
Iran	41.0	29.0	30.0	31.0	2.0	28.0	34.0	39.0	11.0
Iraq	29.5	20.0	24.0	26.0	6.0	20.0	30.0	33.0	13.0
Ireland	45.5	44.0	45.0	46.0	2.0	35.0	44.0	45.0	10.0
Israel	38.5	34.0	35.0	36.0	2.0	30.0	35.0	38.0	8.0
Italy	40.5	39.0	40.0	41.0	2.0	35.0	40.0	44.0	9.0
Jamaica	32.5	29.0	30.0	31.0	2.0	28.0	34.0	38.0	10.0
Japan	39.0	38.0	39.0	40.0	2.0	38.0	39.0	40.0	2.0
Jordan	36.0	35.0	36.0	37.0	2.0	30.0	35.0	37.0	7.0
Kazakhstan	37.0	27.0	29.0	30.0	3.0	26.0	32.0	34.0	8.0
Kenya	31.5	32.0	35.0	35.0	3.0	28.0	35.0	37.0	9.0
Korea, D.P.R.	17.0	7.0	8.0	10.0	3.0	10.0	20.0	30.0	20.0
Korea, Republic	44.5	37.0	38.0	38.0	1.0	28.0	40.0	42.0	14.0
Kuwait	44.5	28.0	30.0	31.0	3.0	28.0	34.0	40.0	12.0
Latvia	35.5	36.0	37.0	38.0	2.0	33.0	37.0	38.0	5.0
Lebanon	23.5	20.0	23.0	24.0	4.0	20.0	25.0	30.0	10.0
Liberia	34.5	22.0	23.0	23.0	1.0	20.0	25.0	26.0	6.0
Libya	39.0	28.0	30.0	31.0	3.0	28.0	36.0	39.0	11.0
Lithuania	37.0	39.0	42.0	43.0	4.0	35.0	40.0	44.0	9.0
Luxembourg	46.0	44.0	45.0	46.0	2.0	38.0	44.0	46.0	8.0
Madagascar	30.5	34.0	36.0	37.0	3.0	30.0	36.0	38.0	8.0
Malawi	31.0	28.0	29.0	29.0	1.0	25.0	30.0	32.0	7.0
Malaysia	42.0	33.0	34.0	35.0	2.0	27.0	33.0	35.0	8.0
Mali	30.5	30.0	34.0	37.0	7.0	30.0	36.0	38.0	8.0
Malta	35.5	35.0	36.0	37.0	2.0	33.0	35.0	37.0	4.0
Mexico	36.5	30.0	32.0	33.0	3.0	28.0	36.0	40.0	12.0
Moldova	31.5	17.0	18.0	18.0	1.0	20.0	28.0	34.0	14.0
Mongolia	30.0	27.0	28.0	29.0	2.0	23.0	28.0	32.0	9.0
Morocco	36.5	36.0	37.0	38.0	2.0	30.0	36.0	38.0	8.0
Mozambique	25.5	23.0	26.0	27.0	4.0	20.0	27.0	28.0	8.0
Myanmar	36.0	25.0	27.0	28.0	3.0	25.0	27.0	33.0	8.0
Namibia	37.0	36.0	37.0	38.0	2.0	36.0	37.0	38.0	2.0
Netherlands	44.0	42.0	43.0	43.0	1.0	37.0	42.0	44.0	7.0
New Zealand	40.0	37.0	38.0	39.0	2.0	33.0	37.0	39.0	6.0
Nicaragua	26.0	18.0	21.0	22.0	4.0	22.0	30.0	32.0	10.0
Niger	30.0	32.0	33.0	33.0	1.0	28.0	34.0	37.0	9.0
Nigeria	36.5	25.0	27.0	28.0	3.0	23.0	32.0	37.0	14.0
Norway	46.5	43.0	43.0	44.0	1.0	38.0	44.0	46.0	8.0
Oman	43.0	30.0	31.0	32.0	2.0	30.0	35.0	37.0	7.0
Pakistan	33.5	31.0	32.0	33.0	2.0	28.0	35.0	36.0	8.0
Panama	38.5	35.0	38.0	39.0	4.0	30.0	38.0	40.0	10.0
Papua New Guinea	36.0	33.0	34.0	35.0	2.0	28.0	36.0	40.0	12.0
Paraguay	32.0	20.0	27.0	29.0	9.0	25.0	35.0	37.0	12.0
Peru	36.0	30.0	33.0	34.0	4.0	30.0	35.0	38.0	8.0
Philippines	37.0	31.0	32.0	33.0	2.0	28.0	35.0	38.0	10.0

Country	Current Rating	One Year Ahead				Five Years Ahead			
		Worst Case	Most Probable	Best Case	Risk Stability	Worst Case	Most Probable	Best Case	Risk Stability
Poland	35.0	34.0	35.0	36.0	2.0	30.0	35.0	37.0	7.0
Portugal	36.5	37.0	38.0	39.0	2.0	32.0	38.0	39.0	7.0
Qatar	36.0	22.0	24.0	25.0	3.0	22.0	27.0	29.0	7.0
Romania	30.0	20.0	21.0	23.0	3.0	20.0	30.0	32.0	12.0
Russian Federation.	38.0	19.0	20.0	21.0	2.0	20.0	30.0	35.0	15.0
Saudi Arabia	42.0	29.0	31.0	32.0	3.0	29.0	35.0	38.0	9.0
Senegal	36.5	35.0	36.0	36.0	1.0	30.0	35.0	38.0	8.0
Sierra Leone	25.5	20.0	24.0	26.0	6.0	20.0	26.0	30.0	10.0
Singapore	49.0	35.0	36.0	37.0	2.0	26.0	33.0	36.0	10.0
Slovak Republic	32.5	30.0	32.0	33.0	3.0	30.0	36.0	38.0	8.0
Slovenia	35.0	30.0	33.0	36.0	6.0	30.0	35.0	37.0	7.0
Somalia	28.5	20.0	21.0	22.0	2.0	18.0	23.0	28.0	10.0
South Africa	37.0	30.0	31.0	33.0	3.0	28.0	33.0	38.0	10.0
Spain	40.0	40.0	41.0	42.0	2.0	37.0	40.0	42.0	5.0
Sri Lanka	32.0	32.0	34.0	34.0	2.0	28.0	35.0	38.0	10.0
Sudan	33.0	27.0	29.0	30.0	3.0	25.0	30.0	35.0	10.0
Suriname	31.0	30.0	32.0	33.0	3.0	30.0	35.0	37.0	7.0
Sweden	46.0	44.0	45.0	46.0	2.0	37.0	44.0	47.0	10.0
Switzerland	45.0	42.0	43.0	44.0	2.0	38.0	44.0	48.0	10.0
Syria	40.0	37.0	38.0	39.0	2.0	34.0	35.0	36.0	2.0
Taiwan	42.5	40.0	41.0	42.0	2.0	35.0	40.0	43.0	8.0
Tanzania	34.5	30.0	32.0	34.0	4.0	30.0	35.0	37.0	7.0
Thailand	39.0	33.0	34.0	35.0	2.0	28.0	36.0	39.0	11.0
Togo	34.0	30.0	35.0	35.0	5.0	30.0	35.0	37.0	7.0
Trinidad & Tobago	37.0	35.0	36.0	38.0	3.0	30.0	36.0	38.0	8.0
Tunisia	36.5	34.0	35.0	36.0	2.0	30.0	35.0	37.0	7.0
Turkey	31.0	28.0	30.0	31.0	3.0	28.0	35.0	39.0	11.0
Uganda	33.5	35.0	36.0	37.0	2.0	30.0	35.0	37.0	7.0
Ukraine	34.5	20.0	22.0	23.0	3.0	20.0	30.0	35.0	15.0
United Arab Emirates	45.5	38.0	39.0	40.0	2.0	36.0	40.0	42.0	6.0
United Kingdom	41.0	36.0	37.0	38.0	2.0	30.0	38.0	40.0	10.0
United States	40.0	38.0	40.0	42.0	4.0	36.0	40.0	42.0	6.0
Uruguay	38.0	32.0	33.0	35.0	3.0	30.0	35.0	38.0	8.0
Venezuela	37.5	26.0	27.0	28.0	2.0	23.0	36.0	39.0	16.0
Vietnam	39.0	25.0	26.0	27.0	2.0	25.0	30.0	34.0	9.0
Yemen, Republic	35.5	33.0	33.0	35.0	2.0	30.0	36.0	38.0	8.0
Yugoslavia	27.5	20.0	28.0	32.0	12.0	20.0	34.0	35.0	15.0
Zambia	27.5	26.0	27.0	28.0	2.0	23.0	37.0	30.0	7.0
Zimbabwe	15.0	22.0	24.0	25.0	3.0	18.0	27.0	32.0	14.0

Chapter 3

Business Environment Risk Intelligence S.A.
http://www.beri.com
Tomorrow's Intelligence Today

BERI provides a complete picture of country risk based on a set of quantitative indices developed and refined over 25 years. A comprehensive Profit Opportunity Recommendation (POR) is a macro risk measure and is an average of three ratings, each on a 100-point scale. The Political Risk Index (PRI) includes ratings on 10 political and social variables. The Operations Risk Index (ORI) includes weighted ratings on 15 political, economic, financial, and structural variables. The third index, the R Factor (Remittance & Repatriation), is also a weighted index, covering the country's legal framework, foreign exchange, hard currency reserves, and foreign debt. The POR thus represents all aspects of country risk. Risk is calculated for the present, as well as one-year and five-year time frames.

At the micro level, BERI provides a Mineral Exploration & Resource Assessment (MERA) measure, constructed specifically for clients in the petroleum industry and can provide other industry-specific assessments and briefings on request.

BERI's Business Risk Service provides quantitative rankings on Government Proficiency, Labor Force Evaluation, and Market Opportunity. The early development of the indices, basic premises, and underlying theory are described in F. T. Haner with John S Ewing, *Country Risk Assessment: Theory and Worldwide Practice*, New York: Praeger, 1985.

PRODUCTS

Multiclient services

- **BRS (Business Risk Service)** is published three times per year. It provides two-page country briefings, risk ratings, and forecasts about the future operating environment in each of 50 countries.

- **FORELEND (Country Risk Forecasts for International Lenders)**, also published three times per year, provides two-page briefings, lender risk ratings, and forecasts about the future in each of 50 countries. The perspective is that of a bank or company with credit exposure.

- **The Automobile Industry in Emerging Growth Markets.** Annual statistical updates and forecasts for 70 non-OECD countries published in September each year.

- **Optional supplements** for BRS and FORELEND include the Labor Force Evaluation Measure (LFEM), Government Proficiency Measure (GPM), ratings for 60 additional countries, and the Market Opportunity Rating (MOR).

Proprietary Services

- *Historical Ratings Research Package.* The *Composite Score*, *Operations Risk Index* (ORI), *Political Risk Index* (PRI), and *Remittance & Repatriation Factor* (R Factor) ratings for each year during 1980 to the most recent complete year for 58 countries are supplied on a CD-ROM disk. The ratings for individual criteria and subindices are included for ORI, PRI, and R Factor.

- *Quick Response.* The service provides answers to a client's question(s) by e-mail and/or fax within hours. Simple Retrieval, Retrieval and Analysis, and Retrieval, Analysis, and Forecasts are levels of complexity and cost.

- *Mineral Exploration & Resource Assessment (MERA).* The CROIL ratings, named for the dominance of petroleum industry clients, are available for any country. The service can include risk ratings only, or it can be supplemented with explanations of the forecasts. Historical and present assessments are supplemented by five-, ten-, and fifteen-year projections.

- *Industry-specific country briefings* tailored to the clients preferred length and in-depth Country Forecast Reports. These services provide outside perspective for important decisions. In some cases the reports are repeated each year as an integral component of the client's strategic planning process. Proprietary country rating systems can be designed to meet the specific requirements.

RATINGS SYSTEMS

Business Risk Service (BRS)

BRS monitors 50 countries three times per year. General uses include: (1) a subscriber can follow important developments in a country and have BERI S.A.'s qualitative analyses and forecasts; (2) a quantitative assessment of risk is provided that is comprehensive and that has survived over three decades of usage; and (3) a table of historical statistics and political information shows trends that assist in providing an independent view of a country's future.

USE OF QUALITATIVE CONTENT

The key applications include:

- The quality of decision making about existing operations in a country is improved by frequent updating of knowledge and perspective. The incisive content presented on two pages per country makes the task relatively easy.

- Perspective from the analyses and forecasts prepared by professional staff is independent of mainstream viewpoints and those of large corporate clients. Their insights are refined by the many times per year reports that are prepared for BRS and other services.

- Language and style in the paragraphs consider that English may be a second or third language for many subscribers. Short sentences that minimize use of specialized jargon facilitate comprehension of BRS country reports.

USE OF QUANTITATIVE CONTENT

The *Composite Score* for each country involves 57 criteria, three separate indices that move independently of each other, and hundreds of calculations to apply time-tested weightings. The results offer subscribers:

- Ratings that are comparable over two decades. Historical data by index and *Composite Score* are available in each issue for the 1990s, and ratings for the 1980s and part of the 1970s can be provided upon request. (See also the Historical Ratings Research Package.)

- Quantitative risk assessments to provide a means of (1) comparing risk exposure and return on investment for existing operations, (2) structuring the composition of global or regional asset deployment that is compatible with executive management's preferences on risk exposure, (3) deciding on proposed projects, comparing net cash flow, resources required, and risk exposure, and (4) judging the merits of divestitures.

- A ratings basis for short-term decisions on extending trade credits, specifying the type of letters of credit, requesting insurance, hedging for foreign exchange rate risk, and level of security required for facilities and personnel.

- A signal from discontinuity in the trend of ratings between Present and +One-Year and/or +Five-Year forecasts that provides an alert about an anticipated major event.

GENERAL USE OF CONTENT

- The statistics, whether in the paragraphs or the table, are from such reliable sources as the International Monetary Fund, World Bank, etc. Information provided by magazines, newsletters, or newspapers is checked for accuracy at two levels of the BERI staff.

- If the BRS is provided on disk or CD-ROM for use on a company-wide information system, the service becomes a common asset for several departments.

- Three supplements to BRS are optional and expand the benefits of subscribing. The *Labor Force Evaluation Measure* (LFEM) assesses the quality of employed workers in a country. The ratings for 50 countries in addition to the 50 in the services are published at mid-year. The *Market Opportunity Rating* (MOR) provides an appraisal of quality, scope, and trends in country markets.

PRINCIPLES OF THE RATING SYSTEM

- The three primary causes of risk for international companies are assessed. The *Political Risk Index* (PRI) measures sociopolitical changes. The *Operations Risk Index* (ORI) measures the degree to which complex operating conditions affect production and profits earned in the local currency by a foreign firm. The third, measured by the *R Factor*, is the risk affected by degree of access to foreign exchange and remittances of profits and repatriation of capital in a convertible currency.

  Forecasts of the three measures of risk are integrated into an overall assessment, the ***Profit Opportunity Recommendation (POR)***. The time needed to bring a venture from a feasibility study to actual operation can be years, and a "+Five Year" forecast of the three measures of risk is used for assigning a POR rating. A "+One-Year" forecast is also provided.

- The quality and continuity of information are fundamental. Comparability over many years is essential. BERI S.A.'s system includes qualitative judgments by two panels of experts, and the quality of these judgments is the foundation for PRI and ORI. Also, the approach selected includes the Delphi method, which reduces bias and conflict of interest in the results. Economic and financial statistics for the *R Factor* are taken from reliable, regularly published sources.

- Results of the three measures of risk serve as parameters for qualitative evaluations in addition to assigning the POR rating. Explanations giving the background on events and the reasoning behind forecasts are required to supplement quantitative ratings. Two-page summaries are given in each subscription issue for the 50 countries regularly monitored by the service.

Users of the BERI S.A. service should consider the following two factors in applying the information:

1. Ratings and recommendations apply to general conditions. It is necessary to distinguish between risk exposure of a capital-intensive facility involving a huge investment at one end of the spectrum and an assembly operation using leased equipment at the other end. Extractive ventures

depleting nonrenewable resources have been targets for nationalization, and this adds to the risk of a capital-intensive investment. The criteria scores, from which ratings are derived, are provided in statistical appendices, and adjustments can be made that fine-tune the system to the profile of the business involved.

2. In some cases, a specific industry within a country justifies a better rating than the country's rating. Less frequently, a company may have a special relationship with a country. Consider, however, that the three measures are sensitive indicators of risk exposure and that relationships change as governments and economic conditions change. Nevertheless, specific operations can be evaluated by country risk analysts and other company personnel, and adjustments to the POR can be made.

Primary Rating - The Profit Opportunity Recommendation (POR)

The POR is based on a composite score derived by adding the (1) *Operations Risk Index* (ORI), (2) *Political Risk Index* (PRI), and (3) *Remittance and Repatriation Factor* (R Factor), and dividing by three. ORI, PRI, and R Factor are explained on the following pages.

Investment Quality – Conditions merit commitment of equity and incurrence of debt to be serviced from operations in the country. Expectations for currency convertibility and dividend remittances are good.

1A	The POR composite score is 75 - 100.	↓Increasing need
1B	The POR composite score is 65 - 74.	↓for high early
1C	The POR composite score is 55 - 64.	↓remittable profits

Nondividend Cash Flow – Conditions generally merit minimum commitment of financial resources. Profits, however, can be earned from fees for transfer of technology, training of nationals, management, and sales of other professional services. Multiyear relationships are involved in the contracts, and when highly successful, a few ventures will generate extraordinary profits and justify a major commitment of financial resources.

2A	The composite score is 55 or more, but investment is not recommended due to such special conditions as excessive regulation and taxation.
2B	The composite score is 45-54.
2C	The composite score is 45-54, but the receiver of technology and services has the potential to use the assistance as a means of penetrating markets traditionally held by the supplier.

Trade Only – Conditions merit only a transaction by transaction relationship.

3A	The composite score is 40-44. Payment delays are probable.	↓Increasing level ↓of problems
3B	The composite score is 35-39. Extreme caution about obtaining payment is required.	↓with payments

No Business Transactions – Conditions merit no business relationship of any kind except those involving cash payments or valid third party guarantees.

4A	The composite score is less than 35.

Operations Risk Index (ORI, 33.3% of POR)

The objective of ORI is to gauge the business operations climate. There are two variables being measured: (1) the degree to which nationals are given preferential treatment and (2) the general quality of the business climate, including bureaucratic and policy continuity.

Definition of the Index. A permanent panel of ±105 experts around the world rate present conditions for the 15 criteria that measure the country's business environment from 0 (unacceptable conditions) to 4 (superior conditions). The criteria are weighted to emphasize critical success factors, and this expands the 15 to a weighted total of 25. A rating of 4 for each criterion gives a perfect environment of 100.

- The quality of the panel members is the foundation of the concept. Executives in companies, banks, governments, and institutions volunteer their ratings. All have extensive international experience. Geographic distribution is worldwide.

- A version of the Delphi method is used. Data are from a permanent panel. The first reply prepared by a panel member requires research and care in matching the rating with the definitions of the criteria. A panelist is supplied with his previous reply and the overall panel average per criterion as input for decisions on current ratings.

Criteria and Weightings. The following have been used for over 25 years. ORI ratings are comparable since 1974.

Criteria	Weighting	Criteria	Weighting
Policy Continuity	3.0	Labor Cost/Productivity	2.0
Attitude: Foreign Investors and Profits	1.5	Professional Services	
Degree of Privatization	1.5	and Contractors	0.5
Monetary Inflation	1.5	Communications and Transporta-	1.0
Balance of Payments	1.5	Local Management and Partners	1.0
Bureaucratic Delays	1.0	Short-Term Credit	2.0
Economic Growth	2.5	Long-Term Loans	
Currency Convertibility	2.5	and Venture Capital	2.0
Enforceability of Contracts	1.5		

Forecast of ORI. Each panel member rates a country for a +1 year and +5 years period by giving a whole number for the overall rating, such as 70, 62, etc. The high and the low ORI forecasts are discarded, and a panel-wide average is used for a country.

Guidelines on Risk. The categories below have been developed to assist in interpreting the ratings.

- 65-100   Stable environment typical of an advanced industrialized economy. Problems for foreign businesses are offset by the country's efficiency, market opportunities, financial system, and advanced infrastructure.

- 50-64   Moderate-risk countries with complications in day-to-day operations. Usually the political structure is sufficiently stable to permit consistent operations without serious disruption. Dynamic economic expansion often has the potential for attractive profits.

- 35-49   High risk for foreign-owned businesses. Only special situations should be considered, e.g., scarce raw materials or unusual profit potential. Selection of management is critical to success in this risk range.

- 0-34   Unacceptable business conditions for foreign-owned businesses.

Political Risk Index (PRI, 33.3% of POR)

The PRI concept focuses wholly on sociopolitical conditions in a country by:

1. Creating a multicomponent system with flexibility to weigh key factors.
2. Utilizing a permanent panel of experts with diplomatic careers and training in a political science.
3. Providing data that can move independently of other BERI S.A. risk measures.

Four time periods are involved:

Present Conditions   +1 Year Conditions   +5 Years Conditions   +10Years Conditions
■   ■   ■   ■

First Step in the System. The expert rates the present conditions for each of the eight causes shown below from 7 (no problems) to zero (prohibitive problems). Then, the two symptoms are rated on the same scale in the present. The perspective is from the viewpoint of an international company rather than private enterprise owned by nationals. This subtotal involves a maximum of 70 for the perfect country.

Six Internal Causes of Political Risk:

♦ Fractionalization of the political spectrum and the power of these factions.

♦ Mentality, including xenophobia, nationalism, corruption, nepotism, willingness to compromise, etc.

♦ Fractionalization by language, ethnic and/or religious groups

♦ Social conditions, including population density and wealth distribution.

♦ Restrictive (coercive) measures required to retain power.

♦ Organization and strength of forces for a radical government.

Two External Causes of Political Risk:

♦ Dependence on and/or importance to a major hostile power.

♦ Negative influences of regional political forces.

Two Symptoms of Political Risk:

♦ Societal conflict involving demonstrations, strikes, and street violence.

♦ Instability as perceived by nonconstitutional changes, assassinations, and guerrilla wars.

Second Step in the System. One or more of the causes may have an overwhelming impact on the overall political stability. The second subtotal of the system allocates a total of 30 points to causes (not symptoms) to reward especially advantageous situations. The expert can apply the points to one, two, etc., causes or opt to allocate no additional points. The lowest risk country could receive a rating of 100 as a result of steps one and two.

Forecast of PRI. Each panel member rates a country for a +1 year, +5 years, and +10 years periods by giving a whole number for the overall rating, such as 70, 62, etc. The high and the low PRI forecasts are discarded, and a panel-wide average is used for a country.

Interpretation of the Ratings. Four categories of political risk have become apparent from usage. Judgment is necessary because country ratings near the threshold of another category, e.g., 53 and 56, are likely to be very similar in degree of risk.

- 65-100   **Low Risk.** Political changes will not lead to conditions seriously adverse to business. No major sociopolitical disturbances are expected.
- 50-64   **Moderate Risk.** Political changes seriously adverse to business have occurred in the past, but governments in power during the forecast period have a low probability of introducing such changes. Some demonstrations and strikes have a high probability of occurring.
- 35-49   **High Risk.** Political developments seriously adverse to business exist or could occur during the forecast period. Major sociopolitical disturbances, including sustained rioting, have a high probability of occurring periodically.
- 0-34   **Prohibitive Risk.** Political conditions severely restrict business operations. Loss of assets from rioting and insurgencies is possible. Disturbances are part of daily life.

Remittance & Repatriation Factor (R Factor, PRI, 33.3% of POR)

The purpose of the **R Factor** is to estimate a country's capacity and willingness for private foreign companies to (1) convert profits and capital in the local currency to foreign exchange and transfer the funds and (2) have access to convertible currency to import components, equipment, and raw materials. The computer program manipulates over 14,000 cells of data and makes hundreds of calculations for each *R Factor* rating and the four subindices described below.

Legal Framework Subindex (20% of R Factor). Each of the six criteria are rated from 5 (best case) to zero (worst case) and weighted by either four or three. The weighted total of 20 times 5 equals the perfect legal framework.

Laws as Written	Weighting	Actual Practices	Weighting
Dividend, Profit, and Salary Remittances	4	Practices on Dividends, Royalties, and Other Periodic Compensation	4
Royalties, Fees, and Remuneration for Nondividend Cash Flow Services	3	Practices on Repatriation of Capital	3
Repatriation of Capital	3	Hedging Opportunities Against a Devaluing Currency	3
	10		10

Foreign Exchange Generation Subindex (30% of R Factor). IMF data published in *International Financial Statistics* (IFS) are used. Certain statistics were converted to "standard normal variates." This technique makes meaningful comparisons possible despite an immense range in the data across countries.

- Current account performance is half the subindex, or 50 points. Breakeven is 25 points. A rolling average is used to dampen the impact of unusual years.
- Three measures are used to award the 50 points for capital flows. First, overall capital account points up to a maximum of 30 are awarded by establishing breakeven as 15. Second, portfolio capital flows attracted by the potential for capital gain and high interest rate differentials earn a maximum of 10 points. Third, *safe haven* currencies also attract capital, and a maximum of 10 points is awarded.

Accumulated International Reserves Subindex (30% of R Factor). *First*, months of coverage for imports of merchandise and services are used as a means of relating convertible currency reserves to the scope of needs. The country with the most coverage each year receives 50 points; the country with the fewest months of coverage earns zero. *Second*, the international reserve total is added to the London valuation for gold holdings to give a complete total on reserves. A ratio is then calculated using total public and private foreign debt as the numerator.

Foreign Debt Assessment Subindex (20% of R Factor). The developing country data for public foreign debt published by the World Bank are the basic sources. Industrialized countries require several sources.

- A ratio using gross domestic product converted to US$ as the denominator is used to put the debt into perspective with the economy. Creditor nations receive all 50 points; the largest result receives zero.

- Capacity to service debt is measured by a ratio of annual public foreign loan obligations (numerator) and foreign exchange earned (denominator). Fifty points go to creditor nations.

Riskiness and the +5 Years Forecast. Risk categories are the same groupings as for ORI and PRI. Data used for the forecast are the result of regression analyses, trends in the ratings, and senior staff judgment. Wholly quantitative forecasts proved unreliable.

Country Risk Forecasts for International Lenders (FORELEND)

FORELEND has a wholly different rating system than BRS. This service for lenders provides qualitative analyses and quantitative ratings for decision making about:

1. Terms and structure of new loans.
2. Participation in syndications.
3. Rescheduling terms and negotiating objectives.
4. Extending credit on purchases of goods and services.
5. Financial factors such as committing to guarantees and the timing of progress payments in construction contracts.

The emphasis is on a +5 years forecast for each of the 50 countries and those countries supplementing this multiclient service at mid-year. The present situation and many years of historical data are provided for independent trend analysis.

FORELEND monitors 50 countries three times per year. General uses of the service include: ① following important developments in a country and having BERI S.A.'s qualitative analyses and forecasts, ② having quantitative measures of risk that are comprehensive and have survived over two decades of testing, and ③ referring to historical statistics and political information that assist the subscriber in developing an independent view of a country's future.

USE OF QUALITATIVE CONTENT

❖ Improvement in the quality of decision making about extending credit in a country from frequent updating of knowledge and perspective. The incisive content presented on two pages per country makes the task relatively easy.

❖ Perspective from the analyses and forecasts prepared by professional staff that is independent of mainstream viewpoints and those of large corporate clients. Their insights are refined by the many times per year reports are prepared for FORELEND and other services.

❖ Language and style in the paragraphs consider that English may be a second or third language for many subscribers. Short sentences that minimize use of specialized jargon facilitate comprehension of a quick review of FORELEND country reports.

USE OF QUANTITATIVE CONTENT

The *Composite Score* for each country involves 66 criteria, three separate indices that move independently of each other, and hundreds of calculations to apply time-tested weightings. The results offer subscribers:

• Ratings that are comparable over two decades. Historical data by index and *Composite Score* are available in each issue for the 1990s, and ratings for the 1980s can be provided upon request.

❖ Quantitative risk assessments to provide a means of ① comparing risk exposure and revenues from credit extended to existing borrowers, ② structuring a loan portfolio that is compatible with executive management's preferences on risk exposure, ③ deciding on proposed loans, comparing interest and fees, resources required, and risk exposure, and ④ preparing for de facto defaults, rescheduling negotiations, and other post-credit developments.

❖ A ratings basis for short-term decisions on extending trade credits, specifying the type of letters of credit, requesting insurance, hedging for exchange rate risk, and acting on nonperforming loans.

❖ A signal from discontinuity in the trend of ratings between Present and +One-Year and/or +Five-Year forecasts that provides an alert about an anticipated major event.

GENERAL USE OF CONTENT

Other benefits result from the subscription.

❖ The statistics, whether in the paragraphs or the table, are from such reliable sources as the International Monetary Fund, World Bank, etc. Information provided by magazines, newsletters, and newspapers is checked for accuracy at two levels of the BERI staff.

❖ If the FORELEND is provided on disk for use on a companywide information system, the service becomes a common asset for several departments.

❖ Three supplements to FORELEND are optional and expand the benefits of subscribing. The *Government Proficiency Measure* (GPM) assesses performance by bureaucrats and politicians in a country. The ratings for 60 countries in addition to the 50 in the services are published at mid-year. The *Market Opportunity Rating* (MOR) provides an appraisal of quality, scope, and trends in country markets.

The Composite Score and Lender's Risk Rating - FORELEND's Primary Ratings

FORELEND uses a sensitive measure of a country's capacity and willingness to meet its contractual obligations in convertible currency. This measure is called LR, an acronym for *Lender's Risk Rating*. LR has the 1 (prime borrower) to 8 (de facto default) range that is shown below. The eight ratings are based on a composite score for a country, and components and methods for compiling this score are explained in the next section of the User Guide.

Each LR has a "Recommended Lender Action." LR1 to LR4 countries receive *lend* recommendations, but risk increases as LR increases, and terms should reflect higher levels of risk. Countries with LR5 or more should receive neither new loans nor credit on purchases. In the case of an LR5 country, the jeopardy to principal is generally too great regardless of the premium obtained on interest rates, profit margins, etc., but a valid foreign-party guarantee may justify credit and loans in individual cases.

Composite Score	LR	Recommended Lender Action
65 - 100	1	Lend. Prime Borrower.
60 - 64	2	Lend at a slightly higher rate than offered to prime borrowers but with similar other terms.
55 - 59	3	Lend at a high rate. Generally tighten terms when compared to LR2 borrowers.
50 - 54	4	Lend at the highest rate without a valid guarantee. Only lend to private parties with such a guarantee.
45 - 49	5	Offer funds only with an institutional guarantee. Provide rollovers only to improve terms.
40 - 44	6	Prepare rescheduling strategy. Implement expediting tactics on interest payments to keep them on schedule. Principal payments are sometimes delayed.
35 - 39	7	Prepare "worst case" actions. Control time and expenses in recovering funds. Interest payments are sometimes delayed. Principal payments require rescheduling.
0 – 34	8	De facto default. Selectively implement "worst case" actions. Control time and expenses in recovering funds.

The composite score, which is the basis of a country's LR, establishes a quantitative framework for the two-page qualitative analysis of each country. The supplementary mid-year ratings have no qualitative analysis. The composite score involves three components that measure the causes of lender risk in a country.

1. A wholly quantitative rating integrates statistics on performance in generating foreign exchange, maintaining reserve levels, accumulating foreign debt, balancing budgets, and other related factors. Reliable, regularly published data by the International Monetary Fund, World Bank, and similar sources are used. This measure is called **LRquant**.

2. A wholly qualitative rating has been created to evaluate technocratic competence, loan structure, related regulatory framework, resolve to honor international obligations, and such sensitive issues as corruption. The regular monitoring of over 100 countries by BERI S.A. analysts provides criteria ratings. A structured format is used, and the Delphi method acts as a quality control mechanism. This measure is called **LRqual**.

3. A rating that moves independently of LRquant and LRqual has been created from BERI S.A.'s panel-based political and operations risk indices to assess the political and socioeconomic situation in each country. Criteria have been selected to tailor the assessment to the international lender's perspective. Social indicators, such as per capita daily calorie consumption, are 20% of this subindex. This measure is called **LRenvir**.

LRquant is 50% of LR. LRqual and LRenvir comprise the other half, each contributing 25%. This composition gives equal emphasis to criteria for which statistics are available and to those that require subjective judgment. An example of a composite score is given below using Korea's ratings for mid-2000.

LRquant	59	x	50%	=	29.50
LRqual	58	x	25%	=	14.50
LRenvir	52	x	25%	=	13.00
Composite Score					57
LR					3

Note that all ratings are rounded to the nearest whole number. Countries on the threshold of another LR rating will be monitored continuously, especially when the change is from LR5 to LR6, as in the case of Korea. All three measures, LRquant, LRqual, and LRenvir, use the same risk scale. This is shown schematically below:

	Prohibitive		High		Moderate		Low	
0		40		55		70		100

LRquant (50% of LR). The purpose of LRquant is to estimate a country's capacity to meet its contractual obligations in convertible currency. This includes both public and private obligations. The computer program manipulates more than 15,000 cells of data and makes hundreds of calculations for each LRquant rating and the four subindices described below.

① *Foreign Exchange Generation Subindex (30% of LRquant)*. IMF data published in "International Financial Statistics" (IFS) are used. Certain statistics were converted to standard normal varieties. This technique makes meaningful comparisons possible despite an immense range in the data sources across countries.

❖ Current account performance is the critical component of the subindex, receiving 80 points. Break-even receives 40 points. A two-year rolling average is used to dampen the impact of unusual years.

❖ Capital flows receive up to a maximum of 20 points by establishing break-even as 10.

② *Foreign Debt Assessment Subindex* (30% of LRquant). The World Bank's *World Debt Tables* are the starting point for developing data on public foreign debt of developing countries. Industrialized countries also require several sources, primarily central bank reports.

❖ A ratio using gross domestic product converted to US$ as the denominator is used to put the debt into perspective with the economy. Creditor nations receive all 50 points; the largest result receives zero.

❖ Capacity to service debt is measured by a ratio of annual public foreign loan obligations (numerator) and foreign exchange earned (denominator); 50 points go to creditor nations.

③ *Accumulated International Reserves Subindex* (30% of LRquant).

❖ First, months of coverage for imports of merchandise and services are used as a means of relating convertible currency reserves to scope of needs. The most coverage each year receives 50 points; the least fraction of a month earns zero.

❖ Second, the international reserve total is added to the London valuation for gold holdings to give a complete total on reserves. A ratio is then calculated using total public foreign debt as the numerator.

(4). *Budget Performance Subindex* (10% of LRquant). *Government Finance Statistics Yearbook* data published by IMF are used. The annual data are updated in the IFS in most instances.

❖ Deficit/surplus of the national budget as a decimal of gross domestic product. Surplus or break-even receives 30 points; 0.09 (9%) or more receives zero.

❖ Percent growth of revenues minus percent growth of expenditures. Three-year rolling averages. Zero (percentages are equal) receives 20 points. Positive results receive up to 40 points in increments of 0.5%; negative results decrease incrementally to zero.

❖ Expenditures as a decimal of gross domestic product. 0.10 or less receives all 30 points; one point is lost for each 0.01 over 0.10. Therefore, 0.40 or more receives zero.

Data used for the +1 year and +5 years forecasts are the result of research staff judgment. Forecasts using wholly quantitative techniques proved unreliable.

LRqual (25% of LR). The objective of the index is to measure factors that have a direct influence on meeting international obligations, but that cannot be assessed through regularly published statistics. The criteria used in LRqual are identified below.

Criteria	Weighting	Criteria	Weighting
Level of resolve toward honoring international obligations	3.0	Corruption in financial transactions: Direct fraud	2.0
Foreign ban structure and terms		Indirect diversion of funds	1.5
Range, concessionary to short term	2.0	Concessionary loans and grants: Level of access	1.5
Current market terms	1.0	Influence of strategic importance	1.5
Net technocratic competence:		Legal framework:	
Overall assessment	2.5	Convertibility for principal,	
Political interference	1.5	interest, fees	2.0
		Taxation constraints	1.5

The 11 criteria have a weighted total of 20. Each criterion for each country is rated from 5 (best case) to zero (worst case). Therefore, a perfect country would receive 100 (20 x 5). The research and analysis undertaken to develop historical data beginning in 1978 required many man-years of effort. The accumulated expertise and information are being applied to current LRqual ratings and the forecasts. A version of the Delphi technique is being used to obtain convergence within staff ratings.

The forecasts do not involve criterion-by-criterion ratings. Instead, the staff estimates LRqual in +one- year and +five years using a single number, such as 57. A mean of the contributions is used after the senior staff estimates are given double weighting.

LRenvir (25% of LR). This measure has three components: ① BERI S.A.'s *Political Risk Index*, 40%; ② selected criteria with adjusted weightings from the *Operations Risk Index*, 40%; and ③ a *Social Conditions Subindex* with eight commonly used criteria for gauging the quality of living conditions, 20%. The purpose of LRenvir is to evaluate the political and socioeconomic environment. The net impact of different value systems, religious practices, traditions, etc., from the viewpoint of the international lender is also estimated. The production of goods and services needed to pay foreign creditors depends upon this environment. The content and methodology involved in each of the three components are explained below.

Political Risk Index. The index focuses wholly on sociopolitical conditions in a country. It uses a multicomponent system with flexibility to weigh key factors. Three time periods are involved: present conditions and conditions in one and five years. The PRI is explained in the BRS rating system.

Adjusted Operations Risk Index. Instead of the fifteen criteria used in BRS, the panel ratings for the following eight criteria are used with different weightings.

Criteria	Weighting	Criteria	Weighting
Monetary inflation	4.0	Professional services and contractors	1.0
Bureaucratic delays	3.5	Communications and transportation	3.0
Economic growth	5.0	Short-term credit	2.5
Enforceability of contracts	3.5	Long-term loans and venture capital	2.5

Social Conditions Subindex. The eight criteria shown below are measured quantitatively. The mean for the countries receives a rating of five in each criterion. An increment is established for data above and below the mean, thereby providing a basis for increasing the rating to a maximum of 10 and decreasing it to zero. The eight criteria have a weighted total of 10, and a perfect country would have a rating of 100 (10 x 10).

Criteria	Weighting	Criteria	Weighting
Per capita income in US$	2	Population growth	2
Government spending for social development per capita	1	Per capita daily calorie consumption	1
Life expectancy	1	Unemployment rate	1
Infant mortality	1	Adult literacy rate	1

Example of the Business Risk Service for a Selected Country

CHINA (P.R.C.)
1 August 2000

PROFIT OPPORTUNITY RECOMMENDATION
1C. INVEST. COMMIT TO PROJECTS WITH HIGH EARLY RETURNS.

Most Probable Political Scenario: Factions led by President Jiang Zemin, Premier Zhu Rongji, and others seek to dominate decision making within the existing organizational structure in Beijing. Recovery of Taiwan within the one-China policy is an objective that has broad consensus. However, use of military force has such immense impact on other priorities like joining the World Trade Organization and confirming China's stature as a world economic power that no invasion takes place during 2000-2004. Only a few of the internal political tactics become public, and the process involves minimal violence. Jiang Zemin, having gained dominance, receives recognition as *modern leader*. Premier Zhu Rongji's position as the senior technocrat who manages the Chinese financial and socioeconomic system is gradually eroded by problems in reforming state industry and managing the debt overhang.

CHINA'S RATINGS

	Combined Score	Political Risk Index	Operations Risk Index	Remittance and Repatriation Factor
1994	56	55	51	61
1995	56	54	51	62
1996	56	55	51	63
1997	58	56	52	66
1998	58	56	51	67
1999	57	56	49	65
Present	56	56	49	64
+1 Year	57	56	49	65
+5 Years	57	56	50	66

CHINA'S OUTLOOK

❖ Political risk will be unchanged during the five-year forecast period. The live ammunition maneuvers, rhetoric, and massing of military facilities and hardware across from Taiwan continues in mid-2000. In addition, leaders of China have been traveling to communicate the one-China-two-systems policy to leaders around the world. China will risk war only when the components of the invasion strategy are ready in five years. An attack has high probability if the issue is not resolved by then. In domestic affairs, President Jiang Zemin has introduced a program to establish the work of the Communist Party (CCP) in the non-state economy. Recognizing that the share of GDP by state-run industries has dropped to 39%, the power of the CCP will be undermined by the recruitment of members in private enterprise. The President has decided to resign as CCP chairman in 2002.

❖ Operating conditions are difficult, especially for non-Mandarin/Cantonese speakers. Corruption is endemic, and efforts to control bribery, extortion, favor trading, etc., usually are aimed at officials being disciplined for other issues. Real GDP grew 8.1% in the first quarter, compared with the

❖ 1999 period. The export drive will result in expansion of 7.8% this year. Industrial production rose 11.2% during January-June from a year earlier, and the average in 2000 will be 10.75% (9.8% in 1999). Retail prices were 0.1% higher in May than a year earlier, ending a long period of deflation. This year oil prices have been raised three times, and drivers pay Rmb3.05 (US$0.37) per liter for gasoline. Banks had Rmb11,263.87 billion in assets at end-March, and 23.8% were considered to be bad loans. Their capital adequacy ratio was only 5.1% at that time.

❖ R Factor ratings reflect a strong foreign exchange reserve position (US$156.820 billion at end-March) and consistently strong current account surpluses since 1993. The merchandise trade surplus increased to US$16.285 billion during January-May, compared with US$10.732 billion in the 1999 period. While imports rose 34.1% to US$76.503 billion with the increase in energy costs, exports jumped 36.9% to US$92.788 billion in a determined effort to cover soaring oil prices. Sales abroad have been assisted by strong demand in Europe and North America. The invisibles deficit during the five months was US$8.995 billion because of increased freight and insurance costs partially offset by net tourism receipts. As a result, the current account surplus was US$7.290 billion (US$15.681 billion in all of 1999).

CHINA'S ECONOMIC AND FINANCIAL INFORMATION

(US$ Millions unless otherwise indicated)					
	1997	1998	1999E	2000F	2001F
Population (millions, 0.85%/year)	1237.6	1248.1	1258.7	1269.4	1280.2
Gross Fixed Capital Formation, % of GDP	33.6	35.3	35.6	35.0	34.5
Production–Industrial (% change)	13.2	9.6	8.5	9.2	8.8
Economic Growth (% change)	8.9	7.8	7.1	7.6	7.5
Consumer Price Index (% change)	2.8	-0.8	-1.3	1.2	0.5
Budget Deficit (% of GDP)	0.7	1.1	1.8	2.1	2.2
Foreign Debt	152044	156554	161088	167500	172500
Debt Service*	36050	37160	37865	38750	39500
Foreign Exchange Earned	215902	217828	231553	241750	230000
Current Account Balance	-29718	29325	15681	5500	12500
Foreign Exchange Reserves (year-end)	139890	144959	154675	160000	165000
Average Exchange Rate: US$1=Chinese	8.2898	8.2790	8.2783	8.2800	9.5000
yuan (Rmb) 21 July 2000:	8.2804				

* Interest paid plus one-seventh of the previous year's outstanding debt.

Profile of the Economy: China is an agricultural nation, producing rice, tobacco, pork, corn, barley, and soybeans. It has important coal deposits and is a petroleum producer. In addition to the country's heavy industry, a large manufacturing base, especially for textiles, has been established. In 1998 exports of goods and services were 21.5% of GDP.

CHINA'S POLITICAL INFORMATION

Governmental System: One-party Socialist republic led by the Chinese Communist Party (CCP). The CCP wields supreme political authority and institutional power through the Politburo according to the state's guiding Marxist-Leninist principles. A new constitution was adopted on 4 December 1982, and amendments were made in 1993. Deng Xiaoping earned the position of *senior leader*, but he held no titles from 1990 until the time of his death on 19 February 1997. The president and vice president are elected by the National People's Congress, and the president appoints the government. The functions of the legislative and judicial branches of government have grown in recent years but remain largely symbolic.

Changes in Government: At the March 1993 government election, Jiang Zemin became president. At the Chinese Communist Party's 15th Congress in September 1997 a new Politburo composed of 22 members, including 7 new members, was appointed. At the National People's Congress on 18 March 1998, Zhu Rongji became the new premier, taking over from Li Peng. Hu Jintao, a young technocrat, was appointed vice president. The cabinet includes four vice premiers (Li Langing, Qian Qichen, Wu Bangguo and Wen Jiabao), Tang Jiaxuan, minister of foreign affairs; Sheng Huaren, minister of State Economic and Trade Commission; Xiang Huaicheng, as minister of finance; and Dai Xianglong as governor of People's Bank of China.

Example of the FORELEND Service for a Selected Country

INDONESIA
1 August 2000

PRESENT LENDER'S RISK RATING – 7 (prohibitive risk)
De facto default exists. Avoid commercial bank lending.

Most Probable Political Scenario: President Abdurrahman Wahid and his selected technocrats have great difficulty in addressing the country's economic problems. Authorities squabble with each other, and the government requires excessive time to develop a political agenda and to implement a coherent reform program. Ethnic, ideological, and religious unrest reach unbearable levels. However, senior military leaders believe that a coup d'état and forcibly restoring order would involve an intolerable loss of life. A presidential impeachment process is begun in late 2000 or early 2001, but this causes chaos. The highly fragmented political structure is an obstacle to decisive action, and new leaders with various power bases emerge. The army periodically is asked to maintain order, but the democratic structure is maintained during 2000-2002.

INDONESIA'S RATINGS

	LR	Composite	LRquant	LRqual	LRenvir
1994	6	41	40	40	43
1995	6	41	40	39	44
1996	6	41	40	39	45
1997	7	39	38	37	43
1998	7	35	37	31	36
1999	7	35	39	30	33
Present	7	37	41	32	33
+1 Year	7	37	41	31	33
+5 Years	7	38	42	34	38

INDONESIA'S OUTLOOK

❖ LRquant ratings are recovering. Growth in foreign exchange reserves (US$28.263 billion at end-March) is being sustained by large current account surpluses. Merchandise imports increased 22.5% during January-May from the 1999 period, reaching US$14.784 billion. The gain resulted from pent-up demand since the start of the crisis. Export receipts jumped 25.7% to US$23.987 billion, yielding a trade surplus of US$9.203 billion for the five months. It is probable that the total for the year will exceed 1999's US$20.705 billion (revised). The invisibles deficit was US$8.024 billion, high because of increased insurance and interest payments. The current account surplus was US$1.017 billion. This year the current account performance will decline from last year's record high. A recession in key markets late in 2001 will reduce but not eliminate the surplus.

❖ LRqual ratings are in the prohibitively high-risk category. The chaos in government is exemplified by the dispute between the President and Sjahril Sabirin, the central bank's governor, Coordinating Economic Minister Kwik Gie's remark that he saw no reason for foreign investors to come to Indonesia, and accusations that the army is tolerating the Laskar Jihad's attack against Christians in Maluku. The rebuilding of the financial system has been placed in doubt by the collapse of the shrimp farm valued by the Indonesian Bank Restructuring Agency at US$2.5 billion. The asset was pledged to pay the debt left by the failure of the Nursalim family's bank, and it is probably worth less than US$400 million. It is believed that the IBRA is holding a large percentage of overvalued assets.

❖ LRenvir ratings are in the prohibitively high-risk category. Law and order is diminishing, and President Abdurrahman Wahid is clearly an incompetent leader. It is doubtful that he will serve a full five-year term, and he may not survive 2000. Impeachment rather than a military coup d'état is becoming probable because of insecurity, rioting, declining economic confidence, and the loss of life it would take to restore order. Vice President Megawati Sukarnoputri would complete the term under the constitution, but she lacks support from the Muslim politicians. In addition, Wahid is the former leader of Nahdlatul Ulama, a Muslim organization with over 30 million members, and the process of deposing the President is likely to add to the chaos.

❖ Operating conditions for private business are dreadful. Real GDP grew 3.2% in the fiscal year ending 31 March, and 4.25% expansion is expected in 2000, mostly because of petroleum industry revenue. Nonetheless, consumer demand is recovering, and steady interest rates (prime of 13.5% in late June but an average lending rate of 19.3%) are assisting durable goods sales. Consumer prices rose only 1.2% in the year through May. (Note: the 20.5% shown in the table for 1999 compares average indices for 1998 and 1999, but prices stabilized in late 1998.)

INDONESIA'S ECONOMIC AND FINANCIAL INFORMATION

(US$ Millions unless otherwise indicated)	1997	1998	1999E	2000F	2001F
Population (millions, 1.55%/year)	201.43	204.42	207.90	211.43	215.02
Gross Fixed Capital Formation, % of GDP	31.3	14.0	14.5	15.0	16.5
Production–Crude Oil (% change)	-1.1	-1.2	-3.0	0.8	1.0
Economic Growth (% change)*	4.7	-13.6	1.8	3.5	-0.5
Consumer Price Index (% change)	6.5	57.6	20.5	2.0	4.5
Central Govt. Budget Deficit (% of GDP)*	0.5	2.4	3.8	4.2	4.5
Foreign Private and Public Debt	140244	140611	143741	147500	152500
Debt Service	23393	36845	22841	22250	23950
Foreign Exchange Earned	66127	58098	62211	65750	60000
Current Account Balance	-4890	4096	7017	3750	1750
Foreign Exchange Reserves (year-end)	16088	22401	26245	27500	24500
Average Exchange Rate: US$1= *rupiahs* (Rp)	2909.4	10013.6	7855.2	8475.0	8850.0
			21 July 2000:	8895.0	

* Fiscal year begins 1 April through 31 March. However, the present fiscal period will be April-December 2000. Calendar years thereafter.

   Profile of the Economy: Until the depression and current slow recovery, Indonesia was reducing its economic dependence on declining petroleum resources. Oil and liquefied natural gas accounted for 7.4% of GDP and 14.6% of exports in 1998, compared with 9.6% of GDP and 39.5% of exports in 1990. Manufacturing grew from 8.4% to 22.7% of GDP in the same period. Principal nonoil exports in 1998 were timber and plywood, textiles, rubber, shrimp, and coffee. In 2000 these trends have been disrupted by the sharply higher hydrocarbon receipts and the decrease in business confidence.

INDONESIA'S POLITICAL INFORMATION

Governmental System: Republic evolving from de facto military control. Constitution of 1969 provided for a presidential system with a unicameral parliament. Three political bills were signed into law at the end of 1998 to introduce far-reaching changes. Elections for the Dewan Perwakilan Rakyat (DPR, House of Representatives) now require candidates to win at local district levels, greatly enhancing local participation in politics. The Majelis Permusyawaratan Rakyat (MPR, People's Consultative Assembly), which elects the president, has been cut in size from 1000 members to 700. The president serves a five-year term and may be reelected.

Changes in Government: Following mass protests, outbreaks of violence, and the shootings of student demonstrators in Jakarta by government forces, President Suharto was pressured by top leaders to resign on 21 May 1999. Habibie succeeded him as interim president. In the parliamentary elections on 7 June, Megawati Sukarnoputri's Indonesian Democratic Party for Struggle won 153 of 500 seats with 34% of the vote. Golkar, the former ruling party, obtained 22% and 120 seats. The United Development Party got 58, the National Awakening Party received 51, and PAN won 34. The remaining 46 seats were spread over several parties; 38 unelected seats are reserved for the military. Muslim leader Abdurrahman Wahid won the presidential election on 20 October 1999 with 373 votes. Megawati Sukarnoputri obtained 313 votes and became vice president.

Chapter 4

Economist Intelligence Unit (*EIU*)
Guide to Ratings

Objective

The purpose of the Country Risk Service (CRS) is to provide complete internationally comparable and regularly updated country risk analysis for 100 developing and highly indebted countries, and to generate credit ratings of the relative risks from a macroeconomic and financial standpoint. The CRS model tries to identify explicitly and, as far as possible, to quantify the risks that concern institutions lending money, financing trade or conducting other types of business which generate crossborder risk.

Frequency

CRS reports are written for 100 countries on a quarterly basis. Country risk ratings accompany all reports, each of which contains the fully updated CRS database. Of the four reports every year, two are Main reports and two are Updaters. A subset of 38 countries have one Main report and three Updaters during the year owing to data limitations and/or more restricted financial opportunities.

The *Risk Ratings Review* is also produced every quarter, listing and comparing the performance of all 100 countries covered by our service. The *Risk Ratings Review* highlights the countries whose ratings have changed in the previous quarter and identifies which ones are likely to improve or deteriorate in the next 3-6 months.

The *Country Risk Service Handbook* is published monthly. It provides an alert service, updating subscribers on country developments that may impact either positively or negatively on the risk ratings. It also includes an annual publication schedule for all 100 country risk service reports and gives a detailed guide to the ratings and a listing of standard definitions and sources.

Format

CRS reports are written to a standard format for all countries to facilitate comparative assessments.

> EIU's Country Risk Service (CRS) assesses composite macro indicator of Country Risk through four types of risk to investors: Political Risk (22% of the composite), Economic Policy Risk (28%), Economic Structure Risk (27%), and Liquidity Risk (23%). It also provides a micro indicator of investment risk for financial instruments.
>
> The political risk component is of the attribute type and includes two subcategories: a) political stability, represented in five indicators—war, social unrest, orderly political transfer, politically motivated violence, and international disputes; and b) political effectiveness, with six indicators—change in government orientation, institutional effectiveness, bureaucracy, transparency/ fairness, corruption, and crime. This is a macro indicator for any type of investment.
>
> Economic policy risk is determined with 27 variables in five categories: monetary policy, fiscal policy, exchange rate policy, trade policy, and regulatory environment. Economic structure risk incorporates global environment, growth, current account, debt, and financial structure groupings with 28 variables. Liquidity risk is covered employs 10 variables. In each of the four categories, numerical scores are converted to letter grades ranging from A to E.
>
> EIU also provides "specific investment risk" in the form of Currency Risk, Sovereign Debt Risk, and Banking Sector Risk. Each is also rated on a 100-point scale and converted to a letter grade. The CRS ratings are supplemented by extensive data and written assessments in each major category. CRS reports cover 100 countries on a quarterly basis, with updates on a monthly basis in the CRS Handbook.

Front page

The front page of each report contains a textual résumé, a breakdown of the country's credit risk ratings and a statistical forecast summary.

Structural review

The structural review in each Main report is a one-page synopsis of the country's economic and political structure, providing a summary of its key economic policies and foreign debt position.

Text and two-year forecasts

The analytical section of each CRS report assesses the country's political risk outlook, its economic prospects, its domestic and external financing requirements and its creditworthiness. The analysis in all Main reports is supplemented by text tables covering a two-year forecast horizon.

Statistical appendices

The CRS statistical appendices aim to provide for each country a complete, compatible and up-to-date selection of the economic data used for country risk analysis and debt management. To this end, most of the data in the tables at the back of each report are presented in a single currency (the US dollar) using standard definitions. Estimates for unpublished historical data are made whenever possible and are based upon partial information or on initial estimates made by national institutions.

Emerging markets coverage

To cover issues arising from the surge in portfolio investment flows in recent years, two additional sections are provided in the Main reports of 26 key emerging markets. One section, called "Domestic financial markets," is incorporated in the main body of the text, while the other, called "Pointers for portfolio investors," can be found at the end of each report. Updaters mirror the basic structure of the Main reports.

Methodology

Our revised risk ratings methodology (introduced in January 1997) examines risk from two distinct perspectives: 1) broad categories of risk grouped in analytical categories of political, economic policy, economic structure and liquidity factors; and 2) risk exposure associated with investing in particular types of financial instruments, namely specific investment risk. This includes risk associated with taking on foreign exchange exposure against the dollar, foreign currency loans to sovereigns and foreign currency loans to banks. The model operates by asking the EIU's country expert to answer a series of quantitative and qualitative questions on recent and expected political and economic trends in the relevant country.

Letter scores range from "A" (the lowest risk) to "E" (the highest risk). Overall scores are awarded in one-point increments, and can range from 0 ("A" category) to a maximum of 100 points ("E" category) for the highest-risk countries.

Broad categories of risk

In terms of broad analytical categories of risk, a country's current and previous ratings, for example, may break down as shown below. The four types of general political and macroeconomic risk (*political risk, economic policy risk, economic structure risk* and *liquidity risk*) are assessed independently of their association with a particular investment vehicle. They are each given a letter grade. These factors are then used to compile an overall score and rating for the country. This overall country risk assessment can be used for making a general assessment of the risk of a crisis in the country's financial markets, where foreign investors may have exposure. It is also useful for investors wishing to get a snapshot of the generalised risk of investing in the country or for those investing in the country in an investment vehicle which is not expressly covered in the EIU's specific investment risk categories.

	Overall rating	Overall score	Political risk	Economic policy risk	Economic structure risk	Liquidity risk
Current	C	42	C	B	C	C
Previous	B	40	B	B	C	C

Political risk

The political risk factors are the least quantifiable of all the factors in the risk ratings model. Indeed, all 11 political risk questions are entirely subjective. However, there is considerable written guidance given to analysts to ensure consistency. *Political risk* is divided into two subcategories: political stability and political effectiveness. Political stability asks the question whether the political scene is free of internal or external threats to security. An environment in which the analyst perceives a low risk of such events occurring scores favourably on the model. Political effectiveness addresses issues pertaining to good governance and the outcome of good governance. Political risk is given a weighting of 22% of the overall score.

Political Stability

1. war
2. social unrest
3. orderly political transfer
4. politically motivated violence
5. international disputes

Political Effectiveness

6. change in government/pro-business orientation
7. institutional effectiveness
8. bureaucracy
9. transparency/fairness
10. corruption
11. crime

Economic policy risk

The economic policy risk factors assessed in the model relate to the quality and consistency of economic policy management and performance. Five sub-categories are considered: monetary policy; fiscal policy; exchange rate policy; trade policy; and regulatory policy. A country with a low and stable inflation rate, a consistently low public deficit/GDP ratio and public-sector debt/GDP ratio, an appropriately valued exchange rate, an open trade policy and liberal and transparent regulatory policies is rewarded with a low score. There are 27 questions in this category, of which 15 are subjective. Economic policy risk is given a weighting of 28% of the overall score, making it the most heavily weighted general category of risk in the overall score and overall rating.

Economic structure risk

Monetary policy

1. inflation rate
2. inflation rate, direction
3. policies favourable to savers
4. ability to boost interest rates
5. monetary stability
6. use of indirect instruments
   of monetary policy
7. real lending rates
8. boom/bust scenario
9. financial liberalisation

Fiscal policy

10. public-sector budget
    balance/GDP
11. cumulative years of a
    public-sector budget balance
12. government's ability to
    generate tax revenue
13. public debt/GDP
14. public debt/GDP, direction

Exchange rate policy

15. real appreciation
16. real appreciation, evaluation
17. exchange rate regime
18. change in prospects
19. expectations of a regime change
20. interest differentials
21. black market/dual exchange rate

Trade policy

22. trade liberalisation
23. exports/GDP

Regulatory environment

24. official data (quality/timeliness)
25. policy towards foreign capital
26. popular attitudes towards foreign capital
27. restrictions on transfers

Economic structure risk examines economic variables central to solvency. Countries are rewarded with favourable scores when growth and investment are high, but are accompanied by a low reliance on external savings, especially debt capital. This risk category also includes an assessment of the global economic environment. There are 29 questions included in the *economic structure risk* category, of which 11 are subjective. The subcategories are: the global environment; growth; the current account; debt; and financial structure. *Economic structure risk* is given a weighting of 27% of the overall score, making it the second most heavily weighted general category of risk in computing the overall score and overall rating.

Global environment
1. global short-term interest rates
2. global real GDP growth
3. international financial support
4. "contagion" effect

Growth
5. national savings/GDP
6. fixed investment/GDP
7. pension system
8. investment efficiency
9. real GDP growth, average
10. real GDP growth, latest
11. real GDP growth, volatility

Debt
19. default history
20. total external debt/exports
21. debt-service ratio
22. interest due/exports

Financial structure
23. asset price decline
24. performance of bank stocks
25. incidence of bank failures
26. banking sector ratings
27. reliance on external debt
28. government involvement
    in the banking sector

Current account
12. cumulative years of a current-account deficit
13. current-account, direction
14. current account, magnitude
15. current-account deficit,
    investment/consumption driven
16. reliance on single raw material export
17. reliance on single export category
18. export receipts, annual rate of growth

Liquidity risk

Liquidity risk examines the risk of potential imbalances between resources and obligations which could result in disruption of the financial markets. *Liquidity risk* also measures the stability of a country's funding base. It rewards countries with high levels of reserves, financing surpluses, financing requirements funded by heavy reliance on foreign direct investment rather than portfolio investment or short-term flows and stable local-currency debt structures. It also rewards countries which have steady and cheap access to the capital markets. *Liquidity risk* is weighted 23% of the overall score and overall rating. There are no subcategories of risk in this category and only two subjective questions.

Liquidity

1. external short-term debt/exports
2. % decline in official reserves, actual
3. % decline in official reserves, forecast
4. net direct investment/financing
   requirement
5. import cover
6. "means"/"spending" ratio
7. net portfolio inflows/financing requirement
8. $M2/reserves
9. access to the capital markets
10. domestic debt maturity structure

Specific investment risk

In terms of specific investment risk, a country's current and previous ratings, for example, may break down as follows.

	Overall rating	Overall score	Political risk	Economic policy risk	Economic structure risk	Liquidity risk
Currency risk						
Current	D	72	E	D	D	E
Previous	D	75	E	D	E	E
Sovereign debt risk						
Current	C	57	C	C	B	C
Previous	C	56	C	C	B	C
Banking sector risk						
Current	C	59	C	B	C	C
Previous	C	59	C	B	C	C

Currency risk

A score and ratings are derived to assess the risk of a devaluation against the dollar of 20% or more in real terms over the forecast period. Political, economic policy, economic structure and liquidity risk factors are taken into account in assessing the risk associated with this specific investment. Each is given a letter grade to evaluate its contribution to the overall score and rating as it pertains to foreign currency exchange rate risk.

Sovereign debt risk

A score and ratings are derived to assess the risk of a build-up in arrears of principal and/or interest on foreign currency debt which are the direct obligation of the sovereign or guaranteed by the sovereign. Political, economic policy, economic structure and liquidity risk factors are taken into account in assessing the risk associated with this specific investment. Each is given a letter grade to evaluate its contribution to the overall score and rating as it pertains to sovereign debt risk.

Banking sector risk

A score and ratings are derived to assess the risk of a build-up in arrears of principal and/or interest on foreign currency debt which are the obligation of the country's private banking institutions. In the case of banking sector risk, the model assesses whether there are likely to be payment problems within the banking sector, but not whether one particular bank is likely to experience payment problems. Political, economic policy, economic structure and liquidity risk factors are taken into account in assessing the risk associated with exposure to this sector. Each is given a letter grade to evaluate its contribution to the overall score and rating as it pertains to banking sector risk.

Ratings bands

The meaning of the ratings bands of "A" to "E" as they pertain to a country's overall risk rating are described below. The ratings bands of "A" to "E" as they pertain to *political risk*, *economic policy risk*, *economic structure risk* and *liquidity risk* are a convenient summary for translating the score obtained in the model into a letter category. For example, an "A" rating signifies the country is very strong in a particular category, and conversely an "E" underscores a severe weakness.

Band A (0-20 points)

Contains countries which have no foreign exchange constraints on their debt-service ability and no problems financing their trade activities. Their economic policies are deemed to be effective and correct regarding the conditions they face (whether in a boom or a recession) and they have a working government (not always a multiparty democracy in the European mould) capable of effective policy implementation. These countries have no significant constraints on any international financial transactions.

Band B (21-40 points)

Contains countries which also have no significant foreign exchange constraint, but whose economic policies or political structure may be a cause for concern. B-rated countries have access to commercial capital markets. There are no major risks with respect to international financial transactions, but *political risk* and *economic policy risk* often need to be watched carefully.

Band C (41-60 points)

Contains countries which have a record of periodic foreign exchange crises and political problems. Many of these countries will have negotiated external debt-rescheduling agreements and could be in the process of successfully carrying out an economic reform programme. These economies will usually be in a state of flux with persistent, but controllable, internal and external imbalances. However, some will have access to commercial capital markets. With caution, this set of countries will often offer exciting opportunities for foreign investors.

Band D (61-80 points)

Contains countries which are currently suffering from serious economic and political problems. Arrears, debt rescheduling and restricted access to official lending are common characteristics. Many have a narrow commodity-dependent export base, resulting in potentially large and frequent fluctuations in export earnings and lengthening remittance delays. Many of these economies will be heavily regulated in the initial phases of restructuring or will have failed to implement such reforms. Any investment or other international financial transactions should be very carefully considered and would best be postponed.

Band E (81-100 points)

Contains countries which are likely to have a high and rising level of arrears. They will be characterised by severe fiscal imbalances and hyperinflation. Foreign exchange will be scarce, and their relations with multilateral lenders severely strained. Often they are in or on the verge of civil war or undergoing violent political change. Political risk is usually extremely high.

Example of regional analysis from *Risk Ratings Review*

Latin America & the Caribbean

Third quarter 1997

Winners	Losers
Bolivia, Ecuador Mexico	El Salvador

The average score for the countries in Latin America & the Caribbean improved by one point to 52 in the third quarter. This kept the region in the "C" category overall and in third position among the six regions covered by the Country Risk Service.

Latin America & the Caribbean is a medium-risk region with respect to the four broad risk categories, *political risk, economic policy risk, economic structure risk and liquidity risk*. The average regional grade for each category was unchanged at "C". The countries in the region tend to cluster around the mean in each of the four broad risk categories, although two significant changes were made in the third quarter. Venezuela was upgraded to "A" for *liquidity risk* owing to rising foreign reserves and its strong current-account position. This raised to four the total of "A" ratings in the broad categories of risk that Latin America & the Caribbean earn—the other three are awarded to Chile. The improvement at the top end of the scale was offset by a deterioration at the bottom end. Paraguay's rating on *political risk* worsened to an "E". It becomes the second country in the region to merit the lowest risk rating for one of the broad categories of risk. Cuba is the other, with an E rating for *liquidity risk.*

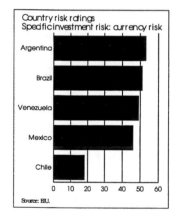

Country risk ratings
Specific investment risk: currency risk

Source: EIU.

The regional averages for specific investment risk categories followed divergent trends in the third quarter; as *banking risk* and *sovereign risk* each improved by one point while *currency risk* worsened by one point. The small changes in the average scores masked some sharp changes within the three specific investment risk categories for individual countries. For example, there was a four-point deterioration in El Salvador's score for *banking risk* because of liquidity crises affecting several financial institutions. El Salvador's score for *sovereign debt risk* also worsened, by seven points, because of a worsening of the fiscal position and worries about the fixed exchange rate. Bolivia's *sovereign debt risk* score improved by five points, owing to an easing of political concerns following the orderly transfer of power to the new president, Hugo Banzer Suárez.

Losers in the *currency risk* specific investment risk category were El Salvador (nine points) Colombia (seven points) and Jamaica (seven points). Mexico's score for *currency risk* improved by a remarkable ten points. We expect the long-term economic policy environment to become more stable as a more open political system creates checks and balances and makes for more accountable government. Venezuela was another winner in this category (five points) because of its strong external position.

Mexico is upgraded to a "C" rating

Mexico was upgraded to a C-rating on a four-point improvement in its overall risk score to 57. This reflects the peaceful manner in which the elections were held on July 6, and the acceptance by the ruling Partido Revolucionario Institucional (PRI) of the loss of its congressional majority for the first time. The elections mark an important step in Mexico's transition to a modern multiparty democracy. A more open political system should encourage people to express their discontent about income and social inequality through the ballot box rather than violence. This reduces the risk of rebel activity becoming more widespread.

The PRI's loss of its majority in the lower house of Congress will complicate economic policy-making in the second half of the term of President Ernesto Zedillo. Previously Congress had rubber-stamped government proposals. Now legislation will have to be approved through negotiation with the opposition. But wider debate should encourage a more consensual approach to policy formation, and help Mexico find solutions to structural flaws, such as a low domestic savings rate and an inability to attract sufficient long-term capital inflows. As government in Mexico becomes more accountable, there will be less risk of the economic crises which have accompanied the last three transfers of power between presidents.

Bolivia's score improves as it cements good relations with the USA

Bolivia's score improved by five points to 52, keeping its overall risk rating at "C". The danger of an immediate cooling of relations with the USA and with creditors following the election of Hugo Banzer Suárez has passed. It had been feared that Mr Banzer's inclusion of the Movimiento de la Izquierda Revolucionaria (MIR) in his government coalition would present problems, since the MIR leader has been denied a US visa following accusations that he had accepted drugs money during the 1993 election campaign. Mr Banzer's new government has moved quickly to cement good relations with the USA, and has already agreed on ambitious coca eradication targets. Having opposed many aspects of the economic reforms introduced under the outgoing government, the parties of the new ruling coalition have also given reassurances that the reform process will be continued. This means that a section of conservative opinion and even some of the left-wing opponents of reform have been brought into the reform camp.

Political risk still remains a concern in Bolivia

The receding danger of difficulties with creditors has brought an improvement in risk scores in all specific risk categories, although the ratings are unchanged. However, these positive developments have not altered the political and economic policy environment sufficiently to improve *political risk* and *economic policy risk* ratings, which still stand at "D" and "C" respectively. Political conflict has receded for now, but underlying tensions are likely to resurface. Further resistance to coca eradication from coca growers and obstruction to institutional reform from vested interest groups remains possible. Corruption remains widespread and social divisions are deep. *Economic structure risk* retains a "D" rating. With a high level of indebtedness, large current-account deficit and dependence on a small number of primary exports, vulnerability to external shocks is high. However, international reserves remain high enough to keep Bolivia's *liquidity risk* at a "B" rating.

Ecuador is upgraded to a "C"

Ecuador was upgraded from the "D" band to the "C" band because of a four-point improvement in its overall risk score to 57. The improvement chiefly reflected a better score for *liquidity risk*, which is now "B" rated. International reserves have risen steadily, reaching $2.3bn by the close of the second quarter. Providing the sale of EMETEL (the state telephone company) goes through before December, reserves could reach $2.8bn by the end of the year. This would put Ecuador in a comfortable external position, with over seven months' import cover. The EIU believes that the upgrade is also justified by the likelihood that an IMF agreement will soon be reached and by a less pessimistic fiscal deficit forecast. An IMF agreement would be conditional upon settlement of debt arrears with bilateral Paris Club creditors. This would improve Ecuador's creditworthiness and enable it to tap the international capital markets on better terms.

However, developments on the political front have been less encouraging. The threat of renewed political instability connected with next year's presidential and congressional elections and with the establishment of a constitutional assembly keeps *political risk* high at "D".

El Salvador's overall score worsened by five points to 57. It remains in the "C" category but is now uncomfortably close to the threshold for a "D". The mid-term elections in March were an unexpected setback for the Calderón Sol administration and its hopes for the re-election of an ARENA president in 1999. Internal strife within the ruling party is increasing, and is costing the president some of his closest advisers. Since June the administration has had to negotiate its policy initiatives with an opposition-dominated Legislative Assembly. *Political risk* continues to be high, with a *"D"* rating. *Economic policy risk* remains "C" rated, but there has been some deterioration in its score. The state modernisation and privatisation programme, at the centre of the administration's policy, has been damaged by the resignation of the presidential commissioner, Mr Mena Lagos, and there are fears that pressure from interest groups will succeed in undermining parts of the programme. Monetary policy remains tight, and the finance ministry is committed to reducing the public-sector deficit. But we do not expect fiscal targets to be met in 1997-98.

Political risk is rising in El Salvador

The most marked deterioration was for *liquidity risk,* which was downgraded to a "D". Import cover is forecast to remain below the 3.5 months required for a reasonable payments position. El Salvador will tap international capital markets with a Eurobond issue this year, but the sale of the state telecoms company, ANTEL, which should attract substantial FDI inflows, has been postponed, probably until early 1998.

There is a risk of a maxi-devaluation in Jamaica

Jamaica's score on currency risk worsened for the second consecutive quarter, this time from 65 to 72 points, although the overall country risk rating remained a "D". This deterioration was mainly due to our decision to reclassify the exchange rate as quasi-pegged, rather than as a managed float. It also reflects recent rapid growth in the money supply, which has added to the risks represented by the overvaluation of the Jamaican dollar and the dependence of the exchange rate parity upon inflows of short-term capital attracted by comparatively high domestic interest rates. The precarious nature of these capital flows has been demonstrated by pressure on the exchange rate and a small net outflow on the capital account. Reserves have fallen as the Bank of Jamaica has intervened to prop up the exchange rate.

The EIU expects a maxi-devaluation of the Jamaica dollar following the general election, likely to take place in the first quarter of 1998. There is a risk that the government will not succeed in defending the exchange rate until then, and developments in the exchange market should be followed closely.

Watchlist

Possible winners	Possible losers
None	Brazil, Argentina

For several months after the onset of the financial turmoil in East Asia in the middle of this year, the view prevailed that differences in economic fundamentals would protect Latin American currencies from speculative attacks. The private sector in Latin America is not as heavily indebted as its counterpart in East Asia. The banking systems are stronger and better regulated. Over-investment, which has created surplus capacity in sectors such as electronics in East Asia, is not a problem in Latin America. But while the markets were focusing on Latin America's differences from East Asia, there was a tendency to overlook the fact that, despite improving fundamentals, Latin American economies continue to suffer from weaknesses. The most important weakness in the current environment is the widespread use of the exchange rate as a nominal anchor for controlling prices.

In late October the markets stopped overlooking these vulnerabilities and the financial turmoil in East Asia spread to Latin America. There was a sell-off in all of the region's stock markets and the prices of Latin American debt fell. Brazil was the country most affected. The São Paulo stock market index lost one-third of its value within a week. As investors converted the proceeds from equity sales into dollars, the Central Bank had to draw down its reserves to keep the Real within its band. Rumours that some Brazilian banks were experiencing liquidity difficulties caused by the fall in asset prices added to a sense of panic.

The Real is vulnerable to a devaluation

The Real is vulnerable to a devaluation owing to the government's failure to consolidate the 1994 stabilisation plan with fiscal reform, leaving policymakers dependent upon a strong exchange rate and high interest rates to keep price pressures under control. Although the fiscal deficit has declined this year, it remains large at around 4.5% of GDP (nominal measure). Dependence upon external savings to finance the fiscal deficit is reflected in a current-account deficit of $33bn (around 4.3% of GDP) in 1997. An increasing proportion of the financing for the external deficit is being provided by long-term capital attracted by Brazil's large privatisation programme. But Brazil still needs more than $10bn in short-term financing to cover the rest of the current-account deficit, plus an extra $12bn to meet external debt repayments falling due in 1998. The government will also have to roll over part of its $220bn of internal debt, which has an average maturity of around nine months. The turmoil in the international financial markets has temporarily interrupted Brazil's access to external funding. Even when access is restored, the tightening of international liquidity will increase the country risk premium which Brazil will have to pay on new debt issues over the coming months.

The Central Bank has shown its commitment to the stabilisation plan

The Central Bank has shown its commitment to the stabilisation plan with a firm defence of the Real. In late October it increased its key money market rate to over 43%, around 38% in real terms, and spent an estimated $10bn of its $60bn in foreign-exchange reserves to keep the Real within its band. These measures have been supported by a fiscal package of tax increases and spending cuts representing a fiscal saving of around $18bn (2.3% of GDP) in 1998. Faster progress is now expected on reforms to the civil service and social security, needed for long-term fiscal balance. These reforms, which require three-fifths congressional majorities, have been obstructed by Congress since President Cardoso took office in 1995. The current turmoil may shake Congress and the government out of their complacency.

Brazil's overall rating is expected to deteriorate in the fourth quarter

Provided the government secures approval for the necessary constitutional reforms and for all of the measures in its fiscal package, Brazil may be able to attract the foreign capital needed to maintain its exchange-rate policy. The sharp slowdown in economic growth caused by higher interest rates and the austerity measures will be unpopular, particularly as 1998 is an election year. But the measures will reduce the current-account deficit and financing requirement. In the long term, the fiscal adjustments would lay the foundations for higher investment rates, productivity gains and sustainable growth. The Country Risk Service will revise its forecasts in the fourth quarter on the basis of these assumptions. Brazil's risk rating will worsen, because of higher interest rates, slower growth and the recent fall in reserves. Among specific investment risks, *currency risk* in particular will worsen. These negative factors will be offset by improvements in the fiscal and current accounts and by the strength of Brazil's large private-sector banks. Brazil's country credit rating will worsen but it will remain within the C-band.

Example of *Country Risk Service* report

COUNTRY RISK SERVICE   MAIN REPORT

4th quarter 1997

Mexico

Risk ratings	Overall rating •	Overall score	Political risk	Economic policy risk	Economic structure risk	Liquidity risk
Current	C	55	C	C	C	C
Previous	C	57	D	C	C	D

Political risk

Political uncertainty will intensify as the opposition-controlled Chamber of Deputies tests the extent of its new powers. A clash over the budget could paralyze the government in 1998, although a more conciliatory approach by all sides suggests that a compromise will be reached.

Economic outlook

After approaching 6% this year, GDP growth will slow to more sustainable rates in 1998-99. Progress on price stabilisation will be slow as easier monetary policy and a widening trade deficit weaken the peso.

Financial market trends

Easier monetary policy will exert downward pressure on money-market yields. Falling interest rates will help to bolster company earnings, underpinning stock prices but this year's returns are unlikely to be matched.

Debt outlook

Export growth and a lower repayment schedule will ease the debt-service ratio in 1998-99. But the debt stock will grow as the government borrows to finance the fiscal deficit and the private sector taps the markets for funds.

Economic forecast summary

	1997	1998	1999
Real GDP (% change)	5.9	4.9	4.3
Consumer prices (% change; av)	21.0	14.0	10.7
Exchange rate Ps:$ (av)	7.873	8.472	9.123
Current account ($ m)			
Goods: exports fob	109,048	120,197	132,470
Goods: imports fob	−110,064	−126,454	−143,532
Trade balance	−1,016	−6,258	−11,061
Current-account balance	−8,480	−14,503	−18,993
% of GDP	−2.0	−3.2	−3.9
External financing ($ m)			
Financing balance	−37,286	−30,475	−36,380
Total debt	177,493	188,946	198,920
Total debt service	41,134	29,468	30,721
Debt-service ratio, paid (%)	31.6	20.6	20.2
Financial markets			
Stock-market index (end-period)	5,500	7,500	–

Structural review

Foreign debt

Mexico precipitated the Latin American debt crisis of the 1980s by suspending service payments in August 1982. It was the first country to secure a Brady Plan debt-restructuring deal in February 1991. External debt rose rapidly during the economic liberalisation of the 1990s. Following a depletion of reserves and the devaluation of the peso in December 1994, Mexico would have defaulted on its debt-service obligations in 1995 without a $50bn emergency loan package led by the USA and the IMF. Because of these loans, Mexico's external debt rose by $25.7bn in 1995 to $165.7bn, equivalent to 57.8% of GDP. Of this, $94bn was long-term public or publicly guaranteed debt.

Key policies

Policy priorities following the devaluation of the peso were to control inflation, stabilise the exchange rate, strengthen the banking system and restore confidence among domestic and foreign investors. Now that progress towards these goals has been achieved, the government hopes to raise the level of long-term sustainable growth through further deregulation and liberalisation of the economy. In 1994 Mexico became a member of the North American Free Trade Agreement (NAFTA) with the USA and Canada. Trade and investment liberalisation is being deepened by agreements with other Latin American countries. The introduction of private pensions in 1997 is designed to encourage domestic savings and lessen the country's dependence upon speculative foreign investment.

Economic structure

In 1996 services accounted for 60% of Mexico's output, followed by industry (33%) and agriculture (7%). Since the early 1980s oil has been overtaken as the country's main export by manufactures, which accounted for 44% of merchandise exports in 1996. The maquila (in-bond assembly for re-export) sector has also grown strongly. The USA is Mexico's dominant trading partner, buying 84% of Mexico's exports in 1996 and supplying 75% of its imports.

Financial markets structure

With a capitalisation of over $107bn at the end of 1996, the stock market is one of the largest emerging equity markets. Trading tends to be concentrated in a few companies, in particular the telecommunications company, Telmex. Investors can also access Mexican stocks via many American Depository Receipts (ADRs) traded in New York. The money market is dominated by government paper; the benchmark is the 28-day local-currency Treasury bill (Cetes). In mid-1997 $17.6bn of long-term dollar-denominated Brady par bonds and $6.2bn of Brady discount bonds were outstanding. The stock of Eurobonds is expanding steadily and reached $32.5bn in mid-1997.

Political structure

Mexican politics is undergoing a transition from a system in which the Partido Revolucionario Institucional (PRI) has dominated the three branches of government to a competitive multiparty democracy. In the July 1997 mid-term congressional elections the PRI lost its majority in the Chamber of Deputies for the first time. The opposition parties have formed an alliance and control key congressional committees. Congress will no longer rubber-stamp legislation but will provide checks and balances to the powerful executive.

Political risk outlook

Congress

Mexico has entered a new political era following the mid-term congressional elections of July 6. The four opposition parties, which have 262 of the 500 seats in the lower house, the Chamber of Deputies, have formed a working alliance and wrested control of key positions and committees from the ruling Partido Revolucionario Institucional (PRI). For the first time, Congress will provide checks and balances to the powerful executive. In the past, when the PRI dominated all branches of government, differences between the executive and legislature were discussed and solved in private negotiations. Now most of those discussions will be in the open, and the government will have to get used to the idea that Congress will no longer rubber-stamp its proposals.

Congress's new role will make for more transparent and accountable government and encourage a more representative democracy. But in the short term it may be a source of delay and instability. One of the first measures taken by deputies was to increase the period of analysis of legislative initiatives from five to 30 days. When the new Chamber of Deputies convened at the start of September for the president's annual state of the nation speech (informe), PRI deputies threatened to form a parallel legislature in protest at the opposition's increased influence. The president, Ernesto Zedillo, helped to avert a constitutional crisis by persuading the PRI deputies to take their seats alongside the opposition and by using his speech as a platform to stress the need for cooperation between the parties and for a consensual approach to economic policies. The appeal for moderation elicited the desired response from Porfirio Muñoz Ledo of the broad left Partido de la Revolución Democrática (PRD) who, as president of the new chamber, was the first opposition deputy to respond to a president's informe.

The budget

The next big test will be the budget, which has to be approved in December. The Chamber of Deputies has complete legislative authority over the budget, with no intervention from the upper house, the Senate, in which PRI retains a majority. The two main opposition parties, the right-wing Partido Acción Nacional (PAN) and the PRD, have both argued for measures which would undermine the government's fiscal targets, which are already on the loose side. These measures include a 33% cut in value-added tax (VAT) to 10% and a pay rise for civil servants, although both main opposition parties have been more conciliatory on their VAT demand of late, not least because a cut would reduce an important source of revenue for state and municipal governments, many of which are now are in their hands. The government is insisting that its fiscal targets must be met and dismisses the PRD's claims that a fiscal deficit of 3% of GDP would be acceptable. As there are no contingency measures to roll over the previous year's budget in the event of the new one not being approved, stalemate could lead to government grinding to a halt in early 1998. The budget proposal is to be presented to Congress two weeks before the November 15 deadline to allow more time for analysis. The most likely outcome will be for the government to get its way on the fiscal targets in return for concessions on individual spending items, including the president's discretionary funds.

PRI   The opposition is not the only threat to the government. The PRI's disappointing election results in July have deepened the resentment among hardline PRI elements of the political and economic reforms enacted under the past three technocratic governments. Some nationalist PRI members have defected to the PRD and in the Senate the PRI's simple majority is in jeopardy following the formation of a PRI splinter group, which has said that it will no longer automatically toe the party line. The presidential aura ensures that Mr Zedillo, whose public standing has been raised by electoral reform and economic recovery, is still able to exert considerable influence on his party. But the risk of a backlash by PRI hardliners will remain if the opposition uses its control of legislative committees to press for investigations into corruption and abuses of power by PRI members.

Chiapas   There has been no progress on talks between the government and peasant rebels in the poor southern state of Chiapas. The Ejército Zapatista de Liberación Nacional (EZLN) has founded a civilian front but will not transform itself into a political party or contest elections. The government claims to be willing to resume talks but is clearly in no hurry to do so. The EZLN is demanding that a series of conditions be met before restarting negotiations. These are unacceptable to the government. The stalemate is likely to persist, but with little risk of the stand-off getting out of control.Economic outlook

World assumptions   Fears that tightness in the labour market will fuel inflationary pressures in the USA will cause the Federal Reserve Board to raise short-term interest rates by 50 basis points by early 1998. On average the interest rate on $ three-month commercial paper will be around 30 basis points higher in 1998 than this year. A moderate monetary tightening will be enough to ease concern about rising US wages and allow the Federal Reserve to ease policy again in 1999 when the average rate on $ three-month commercial paper will fall to 5.4%. Despite higher US interest rates in 1998, Mexican assets will remain relatively attractive to foreign investors. The impact of higher US interest rates on Mexico's debt-service bill will be mitigated by the government's successful debt refinancing programme. The monetary tightening in the USA will slow economic growth in Mexico's largest export market from 3.8% this year to a more sustainable 2.5% in 1998 and 2.2% in 1999. The Mexican government's fiscal revenue will be affected by a slight fall in world oil prices in 1998-99.

Assumptions

	1997	1998	1999
International assumptions			
OECD GDP growth (%)	3.1	2.9	2.6
World trade growth (%)	8.2	7.7	7.2
World oil price ($/b)	19.3	18.7	18.3
Non-oil commodities (%)	−3.8	0.2	−1.7
DM:$ (end-period)	1.80	1.79	1.72
¥:$ (end-period)	120.0	111.0	109.0
$ 3-month commercial paper rate (%)	5.6	5.9	5.4
Domestic policy indicators			
Budget balance (% of GDP)	−0.5	−1.4	−1.1
Domestic interest rate (%)	22.0	17.0	15.0

Money supply M2 (% change)	25.0	32.0	25.0
Exchange rate Ps:$ (av)	7.873	8.472	9.122

Domestic assumptions

By the end of this year the government will negotiate an agreement on the 1998 budget with the opposition-controlled Chamber of Deputies which will enable it to stick to the fiscal targets in its three-year development plan, termed the Programa Nacional de Financiamiento del Desarrollo (Pronafide), launched in June. A tighter fiscal stance would be appropriate at this stage in the business cycle, given Mexico's need to raise domestic savings and to reduce its dependence upon foreign capital. But the government faces the additional costs of social security reform and debtor relief schemes and will be under pressure from the opposition and its own party to raise spending on social programmes. Although the fiscal deficits are likely to be modest by international standards, they will have a negative impact on the private sector, exerting upward pressure on interest rates and the peso. This will complicate matters for the Banco de México (the central bank), which is finding it difficult to prevent the peso from appreciating in the face of strong capital inflows. We expect the central bank to ease its monetary stance and make changes to its exchange rate policies to discourage inflows of speculative capital. These changes, together with a widening current-account deficit, should guide the peso lower in 1998-99, lessening the risk of a large and potentially damaging correction. A successful shift to private pension schemes (the initial take-up rate is around 80% of workers) should foster domestic savings. These will gradually raise the level of sustainable growth, although Mexico will remain dependent upon external capital in 1998-99. The government will sign a three-year extended agreement with the IMF, which will enable it to roll over the large repayments falling due in 1998-99 and to enjoy the Fund's seal of approval during the sensitive period in the run-up to the presidential elections in 2000.

Fiscal policy

In the first half of the year the public-sector accounts posted an overall surplus of Ps18.3bn ($2.4bn) while the primary balance (which excludes interest payments) was Ps68.8bn. Total expenditure reached Ps315.4bn, 8.5% higher in real terms than a year earlier, while non-interest spending increased by 12.2%. These rates outstripped the rise in total revenue which reached Ps335.2bn, 4.5% higher in real terms. In the second half of the year the fiscal accounts will move into deficit because of the cost of the shift to private pensions. But the positive impact of strong demand on tax collection and the fact that spending was front-loaded into the first half of the year before the July elections suggest that the government will not overrun its target of a deficit of 0.5% of GDP in 1997.

According to Pronafide, the fiscal deficit will widen to 1.3% of GDP in 1998 and then narrow to 0.9% of GDP in 1999. The expected deterioration is primarily due to the cost of social security reform, which is projected to rise from 0.7% of GDP in 1997 to 1.4% of GDP in 1998 and 1999. The PAN and the PRD have moderated their calls for a cut in VAT from 15% to 10%, which would have jeopardised the fiscal targets. Mr Zedillo's attempts to foster a consensual approach on economic policy and his warnings against a dash for growth through deficit spending appear to be working. The EIU expects the government to come close to meeting its fiscal targets in 1998-99.

Monetary policy

The monetary base on October 14 was Ps81.2bn, Ps4.3bn above the central bank's projections at the start of the year. A higher than expected rate of monetary growth has been matched by rising demand for cash. The latter reflects stronger than expected GDP growth, exchange rate stability and changes in the banking system, including an expansion in automatic teller machines. The central bank has maintained tight control of net domestic credit (the monetary base minus net foreign assets), which has contracted in the year to date. Sterilisation of foreign capital inflows has curbed growth in the broad monetary aggregates. Much of the expansion in bank deposits has been due to interest capitalisation rather than inflows of new deposits.

In September the central bank announced a shift from a restrictive to a neutral monetary stance. Commercial banks are still expected to maintain zero average balances in their current accounts with the central bank. But now the central bank leaves the commercial banks "long" (ie with a positive daily balance in their current accounts) to signal when it wants interest rates to come down and the peso to weaken. The central bank had been operating an asymmetrical policy, restricting itself to a neutral stance (a zero daily balance) or a tight one (leaving the commercial banks overdrawn or "short" when the peso came under pressure). The shift will not result in large injections of liquidity into the economy because any long positions will amount to no more than a fraction of the monetary base. The central bank has assured the markets that it will leave the commercial banks "long" only if conditions in the money markets are preventing the exchange rate and interest rates from behaving as expected (ie if an appreciation of the peso is not accompanied by falling domestic interest rates).

In 1998 we expect the central bank to reduce its open-market operations and leave more foreign capital inflows unsterilised. The release of external resources to the financial system will allow banks to resume lending, thereby sustaining the economic recovery. Easier monetary policy may be accompanied by changes in foreign exchange policy aimed at increasing the exchange rate risk to foreign investors. This will be necessary to reduce Mexico's attractions as a destination for speculative flows. But the central bank will not want to frighten off high-quality investment. Strict control of domestic credit creation will be maintained and the central bank will tighten its monetary stance if the currency comes under pressure as a result of its own policies, fiscal laxity or changes in the international environment.

Growth and inflation
(% real change)

	1997	1998	1999
GDP	5.9	4.9	4.3
Gross fixed investment	22.0	9.0	8.0
Exports of goods & services	10.5	7.9	7.1
Imports of goods & services	22.9	12.1	9.8
Industrial growth	8.0	5.1	4.0
Consumer prices (av)	21.0	14.0	10.7

Growth prospects

The economy surpassed expectations in the second quarter, growing by 8.8% year on year. Investment surged by 24.7%. Export volume growth held up well at 15.3%. Growth in private consumption quickened to 6.9% from 2% in the first quarter, confirming the broadening of the recovery to the domestic economy. The strengthening of demand was evident in import growth of 27%, with capital and consumer goods imports both buoyant. On the supply side, growth was broadly based. Even agriculture, which has lagged in recent years, grew by 10%. The second-quarter surge took growth for the first half to 7%. Strengthening retail sales figures and sustained growth in industrial output indicate that the economy remained strong in the third quarter. In August the unemployment rate fell to 3.5%, the second lowest in the last 32 months, while the number of workers registered at the Instituto Mexicano de Seguridad Social (IMSS, Mexican Institute of Social Security) was 10% higher than a year earlier. We have revised our growth forecast for the full year upward to 5.9%, the highest rate for more than 20 years.

We have also revised upward our forecast for GDP growth in 1998, to 4.9%. The change in monetary policy will stimulate a gradual recovery of bank lending. Private consumption will strengthen as workers take advantage of a tightening labour market to press for pay claims above the rate of inflation to recoup some of the purchasing power lost in 1995-97. Recent investments, particularly in the maquila (in-bond assembly for re-export) sector, will keep exports growing firmly. But the failure of small and medium-sized companies to supply more inputs to the export sector will keep Mexico's propensity to import high. A rising import bill will lead to a widening trade and current-account deficits which, with slowing demand in the USA, will constrain growth to below 4.5% in 1999.

Prices

The peso's stability kept the annual inflation rate on a downward trend in the third quarter. But the monthly rate has stopped falling, remaining stuck at 0.9% in July and August and rising to 1.3% in September. The recovery of domestic demand appears to be tempting some producers and retailers to raise prices to compensate for squeezed margins during the recession. In September additional inflationary pressures were caused by rises in government-controlled milk and tortilla prices and by seasonal increases associated with the new academic year. The year-end inflation rate will largely depend upon whether public tariff and wage increases agreed in November are implemented this year, as in 1995 and 1996, or held over until 1998. The central bank appears to want the rises deferred until next year in order to get close to its year-end target of 15% in 1997. On the assumption that it gets its way, we forecast a year-end rate of 16.1%.

In 1998 we expect inflation to subside only gradually, ending the year at 13.1%. This forecast reflects the expected loosening of monetary and fiscal policies, a weaker peso and strengthening domestic demand. Because of the tightening labour market, most pay settlements are likely to be above the official year-end inflation target of 12.5%. In 1999 we forecast further gradual progress on price stabilisation, taking the year-end rate into single digits.

Currency outlook

The peso's strength continues to surprise the markets. In mid-October the peso was trading at Ps7.737:$1, representing a nominal appreciation of 1.7% in the year to date. The inflation differential with the USA over the same period was around 10%. The real appreciation this year maintains the trend in 1996 when the peso appreciated by almost 17% against the dollar. On the basis of consumer price differentials, the competitive cushion provided by the maxi-devaluation of late 1994 has almost disappeared. Productivity gains and cuts in real wages since 1995 mean that the peso is more competitive against the dollar when the price adjustment is made on the basis of unit labour costs. This is borne out by continued high rates of export growth, but only to the US market. Mexican producers are finding it difficult to maintain their market share in other markets, where the loss of competitiveness has been magnified by the dollar's appreciation against the yen and the D-mark in 1996-97.

With the trade account moving into deficit in July, the Central Bank loosening of monetary policy and a possible rise in the US Federal Fund rates in November, a long-expected adjustment of around 5% in the exchange rate is expected by year end. We are forecasting a year-end exchange rate of Ps8.013:$1.

In 1998-99 looser fiscal and monetary policies and a worsening current account will contribute to a weaker peso. Our forecasts for 1998-99 assume that the nominal exchange rate moves in line with consumer price inflation differentials with the USA. Mexican policy-makers would like to see this result achieved through a gradual depreciation in the nominal exchange rate. But the pattern since late 1995 of periods of stability interrupted by sudden corrections is likely to persist. Investors with unhedged peso exposure will run risks, depending on the timing of the corrections.

Domestic financial markets

The money market

Although money-markets yields have been more volatile than the exchange rate, they have remained on a downward trend in the year to date. Demand for Certificados del Tesoro (Cetes, the benchmark 28-Treasury-bill rate) has remained strong, with primary auctions for paper of all maturities usually several times oversubscribed. The average annualised yield of the Cetes in the primary market fell from 23.55% in January to 18.93% in August. It fell further in September, reaching 16.65% by the end of the month. Despite continued inflows of foreign capital, a strong peso and a declining annual rate of inflation, the downward trend in money-market yields has stalled in recent weeks. In mid-October yields were back up to 17.78%. Downward rigidity in interest rates was one of the reasons cited by the central bank for its relaxation of monetary policy. But as the change will not result in large injections of liquidity into the money markets, the markets may not react as expected. The money markets are likely to be volatile in the fourth quarter because of a pre-Christmas surge in liquidity, concern about the budget, fears of a rise in US short-term interest rates and the expected correction in the exchange rate. In 1998 we expect the central bank to announce a further easing of monetary policy, which will allow yields to resume a downward trend. Volatility should diminish as inflation and nominal and real yields decline.

Financial market forecasts

	1997	1998	1999
Exchange rate Ps:$ (end-period)	8.013	8.825	9.362
Interest rates on 28-day Cetes (end-period; %)	17.0	13.5	11.0
Stock-market index (end-period)	5,500	7,500	–

The bond market

Inflation-indexed Ajustabonos and Bondes, which pay interest linked to the rates on Cetes, are the benchmark instruments in the domestic debt market. In mid-October three-year Ajustabonos offered a real yield of 5.6% per year in the primary market. The one- and two-year Bondes both offered a premium of 0.8 of a percentage point over 28-day Cetes, down from 1.17 of a percentage point six months earlier. At the October 21 auction the central bank is to offer Ps700m of three-year Bondes, the first time that Bondes with a term of more than two years are to be sold. The real yield on Ajustabonos is likely to fall in 1998 as inflation slows and volatility declines. There is little scope for a further narrowing of the premium on Bondes.

The equity market

The Mexican stock market rose to a high of 5,360 on October 7. It has since fallen back as a decline in US stock prices was transmitted to the Mexican market. Even so, the Mexican IPC index is still showing a dollar return of more than 60% in the year to date. The rally is being driven by currency stability, the sustained recovery of the economy and expectations of strong corporate results in the third quarter, due to be announced in the second half of October. Trading volumes have been moderate. Unless leading companies turn in exceptional results, the market may be subject to profit-taking in the fourth quarter, traditionally a volatile time. For these reasons, we are keeping to our conservative year-end forecast for the IPC index at 5,500.

In 1998 the Mexican stock-market rally will resume as companies benefit from sustained economic recovery, further progress on price stabilisation and lower interest rates. Increased consumer purchasing power will allow for some recovery of margins. But this year's surge in stock prices from low valuations is unlikely to be matched, and inflows of foreign investment will be deterred by a weaker peso and a widening current-account deficit. Our forecasts for the IPC index and the exchange rate imply a dollar return of 23.8% for 1998.

External finance and credit risk

Current account
($ m)

	1997	1998	1999
Goods: exports fob	109,048	120,197	132,470
Goods: imports fob	−110,064	−126,454	−143,532
Trade balance	−1,016	−6,258	−11,061
Services: credit	12,031	12,974	13,870
Services: debit	−11,105	−12,089	−13,298
Services balance	926	885	573
Income: credit	4,984	5,483	6,031
Income: debit	−18,270	−19,802	−20,037
Income balance	−13,285	−14,319	−14,006
Current transfers: credit	4,926	5,222	5,535

Current transfers: debit	−31	−32	−33
Current transfers balance	4,895	5,190	5,502
Current-account balance	-8,480	-14,503	-18,993

Current-account outlook

In the first half of this year the current account posted a deficit of $1.7bn, compared with a surplus of $450m in the year-earlier period. The deterioration is largely due to an erosion of the trade surplus. Export growth is holding up well, with earnings of $70.9bn in the first eight months of this year, or 15.5% higher year on year. But imports grew more strongly, reaching $68.8bn, or 21.8% higher than in the first eight months of 1996. Imports of consumer and capital goods are particularly buoyant, reflecting strong domestic demand and the real appreciation of the peso. The trade account swung into deficit in July after 30 consecutive months of surplus. Although export growth will strengthen in the fourth quarter because of a surge in car production capacity, the trade deficit will continue to widen to around $1bn for the full year, compared with a surplus of $6.5bn in 1996. The current-account deficit will widen sharply in the second half to reach $8.5bn (2.2% of GDP).

The 1997 current-account deficit would have been higher without the central bank's sterilisation of foreign exchange reserves. This has prevented part of the external savings which Mexico has attracted from boosting demand. In 1998-99 we expect the central bank to reduce its sterilisation of foreign exchange reserves in order to stimulate bank lending and to ease upward pressure on the peso. Investment in export projects will keep export earnings rising at a healthy rate but they will not keep pace with the import bill. The high propensity to import in part reflects a lack of domestic suppliers for companies in the export sector. Until this structural problem is addressed, periods of strong economic growth will be accompanied by widening trade and current-account deficits.

Financing requirement

In 1997 we estimate Mexico's financing requirement at a hefty $37.3bn. This is partly due to voluntary prepayments, which will ease the amortisation schedule in 1998-99. Inflows of long-term debt, foreign direct investment and portfolio investment will enable Mexico to meet its financing requirement this year while accumulating foreign exchange reserves. In 1998 lower principal prepayments will offset a widening current-account deficit, reducing the financing requirement by almost $7bn to $30.4bn, which will be almost wholly covered by long-term debt and investment inflows. In 1999 a further widening of the current-account deficit will leave Mexico dependent upon speculative capital to cover around $5bn of a $36.4bn financing requirement.

Financing
($ m)

	1997	1998	1999
Current-account balance	−8,480	−14,503	−18,993
Principal repayments due	−28,806	−15,972	−17,387
Financing requirement	−37,286	−30,475	−36,380
Medium- & long-term debt inflows	25,716	20,321	20,368
Commercial bank loans	8,716	8,170	7,040
Official guaranteed loans	4,500	3,151	2,828
International bond issues	12,500	9,000	10,500

Net direct investment flows	11,000	10,000	10,500
Net portfolio investment flows	10,350	6,300	5,900
IMF credit	0	1,349	1,372
Increase in interest arrears (if any)	0	0	0
Other capital flows (net)	220	–3,294	–1,261

Foreign currency bonds

According to the Salomon Brothers' Brady Bond Index, Mexican Brady bonds yielded a dollar return of 28.5% in the year to mid-October. This compares favourably with Brazil (22.3%) but unfavourably with Argentina (34.4%). Mexican Brady bond prices have been boosted by the orderly and peaceful manner in which the July elections were conducted and by the strength of the economy in the second quarter. Like other emerging market debt, Mexican Brady bond prices benefited from buyback operations by Argentina, Venezuela and Panama in September, before falling back on expectations of a rise in US short-term interest rates in the fourth quarter. Uncertainty over the budget is likely to continue to dull sentiment about Mexican Brady bonds in the short term. Upside potential lies in another buyback operation, which is possible given the Mexican government's innovative approach to refinancing. But after this year's rise, the scope for further capital gains has diminished.

External debt
($ m)

	1997	1998	1999
Total foreign debt stock	177,493	188,946	198,920
of which:			
short-term debt	50,121	54,442	58,547
Total foreign debt service	41,134	29,468	30,721
Principal repayments	28,806	15,972	17,387
of which:			
official creditors	5,319	4,366	5,975
private creditors	19,880	9,997	9,406
Interest payments	12,328	13,495	13,334
of which:			
official creditors	2,514	2,596	2,360
private creditors	6,166	6,965	7,145
Total debt (% of GDP)	42.9	41.1	40.4
Debt-service ratio, paid (%)	31.6	20.6	20.2

Debt outlook

According to the finance ministry, gross external public debt fell by $1.4bn in the first half of this year to $96.9bn, mainly because of currency adjustments. Of the total, only $5.5bn was short-term debt. We expect the external public debt stock to rise in the second half of this year and in 1998-99 as the government borrows to fund its fiscal deficit. An active debt management programme has reduced repayments due from the federal government to under $1bn per year in 1998-99. But the central bank faces a heavy repayment schedule in these years on debt to the IMF from the 1995 emergency loan package. The authorities will probably try to roll over some of this debt with a new IMF loan and to refinance the rest from bond issues. Most of the financing will be raised in the international capital markets although the development of the private pension fund system will provide a growing pool of domestic funding. Private debt will also rise in the forecast period as blue-chip Mexican companies turn to the external markets for funds. But firm export growth and lower repayments will reduce the debt-service ratio to around 20%. We do not expect Mexican borrowers to experience difficulties in meeting their obligations.

Specific investment risk ratings

	Overall rating	Overall score	Political risk	Economic policy risk	Economic structure risk	Liquidity risk
Currency risk						
Current	C	49	C	C	D	C
Previous	C	46	C	B	C	D
Sovereign debt risk						
Current	C	55	C	C	C	C
Previous	C	56	D	C	C	D
Banking sector risk						
Current	C	55	C	C	C	C
Previous	C	56	D	B	C	D

Specific investment risk

The system of a floating exchange rate, supported by monetary tightening when the peso comes under pressure, has worked well in stabilising the economy. But there is now a risk that capital inflows could strengthen the peso to a level where there would be a risk of a sharp correction. The risk is all the greater because the government will be running a fiscal deficit in 1998-99. The central bank is unlikely to move from a float in 1998-99 but it may make some changes to increase exchange rate risk for speculative inflows. Looser monetary policy may be combined with changes in the monthly auctions of peso call options to the commercial banks. The commitment may be dropped to sell $200m worth of dollars at the previous day's exchange rate if the peso devalues by more than 2% in a day. Such measures, together with a deterioration in the trade account, should help to guide the peso lower in 1998-99. But for the time being *currency risk* remains a "C".

Mexico's score for *sovereign debt* is dragged down by a troubled debt-service history and a tendency to suffer economic crises at the end of each six-year presidential term. Risk of sovereign default was averted in 1995 only by a $50bn emergency loan package led by the USA and the IMF. This year uncertainties have been created by the new balance of forces in Congress but even the PRD, which has advocated rescheduling in the past, appears to be adopting a more friendly stance towards foreign investors and creditors. The government's commitment to meeting its external obligations is not in doubt and its skilful debt management programme has eased the country's debt-service burden in 1998-99. Public short-term debt is low at less than $6bn. Mexico continues to merit a "C" for *sovereign debt*.

The government prevented a systemic banking collapse following the peso's devaluation by a costly series of measures to assist debtors and the banks. The risk of moral hazard was averted by providing support to institutions rather than shareholders. Many banks have been recapitalised, some with foreign capital. Despite the cleaning-up of banks' balance-sheets, the quality of loan portfolios remains poor. But asset quality will improve as interest rates decline and the economy grows, while a recovery of credit activity will lead to an improvement in operating results. The banking crisis in 1995 exposed failings in regulation and lending practices following the privatisation of the banks during the presidency of Carlos Salinas (1988-94). Regulation has been tightened and prudential standards improved, with the phased introduction of US accounting standards. These changes will improve *banking sector risk* in the medium and long term but at present it remains towards the lower end of the "C" band.

Risk ratings summary

	Overall rating	Overall score	Political risk	Economic policy risk	Economic structure risk	Liquidity risk
Current	C	55	C	C	C	C
Previous	C	57	D	C	C	D

Risk ratings summary

Mexico remains a C-rated country, with a two-point improvement in its score to 55. *Political risk* has been upgraded from a "D" to a "C". Electoral reforms promoted by Mr Zedillo helped to make the mid-term elections of July 6 peaceful and fair. The ruling PRI has accepted the loss of its majority in the Chamber of Deputies and of three more state governorships. Despite some early posturing by the opposition parties, there of signs that they are becoming less confrontational and are rising to their new responsibilities. The untested relationship between the legislature and the government will create some political noise. The budget could be contentious and the risk of a backlash by hardliners in the PRI remains if the opposition parties use their new-found influence to press for investigations into corruption and abuses. But the July elections were undoubtedly an important step in Mexico's transition to a modern multiparty democracy. A more representative political system should encourage people to express their discontent and opposition through the ballot box rather than violence. This will reduce the risk of insurgency in poor southern states spreading.

Economic policy risk remains a "C". The PRI's loss of its majority in the lower house of Congress will complicate economic policy-making in the second half of Mr Zedillo's term. Previously, Congress had rubber-stamped government proposals. Now legislation will have to be approved through negotiation with the opposition. Logjams on important legislation are possible. The 1998 budget might not be approved, which could lead to government grinding to a halt in 1998. Yet neither of the main opposition parties will find it to be in its own interests to push for irresponsible policies. The economy's improving fundamentals will help Mr Zedillo to build consensus on the need for fiscal and monetary discipline. The extensive liberalisation and deregulation of the economy since the mid-1980s is unlikely to be reversed.

Economic structure risk remains a "C". The increased accountability under which the PRI will now operate should reduce the risk of the economic crises which have tended to afflict Mexico at the end of each six-year presidential term. The government is trying to build consensus for a medium-term programme aimed at addressing structural flaws such as low savings and investment rates.

Liquidity risk has been upgraded from "D" to "C" to reflect the continued accumulation of international reserves. According to the IMF, gross reserves reached $25.4bn in August, $6.4bn higher than at the beginning of the year. Import cover remains low at 3 months, but rises to 4.7 months when maquila imports are stripped out. The rise in reserves has reduced the ratio of M2 to reserves from five to four.

Pointers for portfolio investors

Three-month outlook

- The financial markets will react negatively to any difficulties experienced by the government in securing the opposition's agreement for its 1998 budget.

- Money-market yields are likely to be volatile in the fourth quarter, influenced by factors such as the pre-Christmas surge in liquidity and uncertainty about next year's monetary programme.

- The futures market is expecting the peso, which has appreciated in nominal and real terms against the dollar so far this year, to suffer a correction of around 5% by year-end.

- Stock prices have risen to record highs as strong economic growth has fuelled expectations of good company third-quarter earnings. This could leave the market vulnerable to profit-taking in the fourth quarter, if the results are disappointing.

- An expected rise in the US Federal Funds rate in November would hit Mexican asset prices. But if political worries prove unfounded, Mexican stock prices could benefit from a rally around the turn of the year as foreign funds rebalance their portfolios.

Outlook to end-1998

- The markets will be looking for the government and the opposition parties in Congress to develop a working relationship. Disagreements between the two sides would deflate the feeling of optimism about political risk in Mexico, hitting all Mexican asset prices.

- The central bank's announcement of its 1998 monetary programme will be keenly awaited as it could contain some important changes from the targeting of the monetary base and net domestic credit in 1995-97. The central bank will want to shift to a less restrictive stance, possibly leaving some foreign reserve accumulation unsterilised.

- A less restrictive monetary stance will allow bank lending to recover, which would help to sustain the economic recovery. But if the trade balance worsens too rapidly, it will put the peso under pressure and exert upward pressure on interest rates.

- Prospects for corporate earnings growth will remain good. Stocks with exposure to the recovery in consumer demand may outperform. Following three lean years, banks' earnings should benefit from the pick-up in lending.

- The federal government will issue fewer foreign currency bonds than in recent years as its debt management programme has reduced funding requirements to less than $1bn and part of the fiscal deficit will be financed in the domestic market.

Mexico: Quarterly indicators

	1995 4 Qtr	1996 1 Qtr	2 Qtr	3 Qtr	4 Qtr	1997 1 Qtr	2 Qtr
Exchange rate (Ps:$)							
Average	7.338	7.528	7.483	7.561	7.827	7.862	7.919
End-period	7.643	7.548	7.611	7.537	7.851	7.891	7.958
Domestic indicators (% change)							
Consumer prices (av)	48.7	48.0	34.1	30.5	28.1	25.5	21.3
Money supply M2	33.3	29.0	29.9	29.5	26.2	33.5	28.7
Industrial production	−6.9	1.4	11.1	13.5	13.3	6.3	11.2
Interest rate (av)	43.7	38.4	30.6	27.2	26.7	22.1	19.5
Energy indicators							
Petroleum production ('000 b/d)	2,700	2,836	2,869	2,855	2,873	2,878	–
External trade ($ m)							
Goods: exports fob	20,313	21,781	23,688	24,247	26,275	26,323	23,378
Goods: imports fob	19,404	19,935	21,601	22,835	25,288	23,529	26,800
Trade balance	909	1,846	2,087	1,412	987	2,794	−3,422
Current account ($ m)							
Current-account balance	−128	46	404	−845	−1,527	−271	−1,396
International reserves ($ m)							
Total reserves minus gold	16,847	16,878	16,472	17,140	19,433	21,056	23,775
Foreign exchange	15,250	15,701	15,717	17,140	19,176	20,743	23,472
Commercial banks' foreign assets	6,271	7,456	6,349	6,010	6,152	5,565	4,984
Commercial banks' foreign liabilities	20,129	19,675	18,597	17,800	17,937	16,239	15,258
Commercial banks' net foreign assets	−13,858	−12,219	−12,248	−11,790	−11,785	−10,674	−10,274
Financial indicators ($ m)							
Assets with BIS-reporting banks	33,514	33,879	35,075	36,695	36,960	37,376	–
Liabilities with BIS-reporting banks	73,311	71,926	70,188	72,771	73,213	73,773	–
IMF credit (net)	1,376	−253	−263	−1,241	−291	−2,492	–
External bank loans	140	0	0	75	520	140	2,280 [a]
External bond issues	1,416	3,330	4,833	9,433	1,781	4,033	4,105 [a]
Secondary market debt prices (cents per $ of face value)							
Par: bid	60.14	66.66	64.53	66.39	71.63	74.91	72.46
Par: offer	60.56	66.91	64.83	66.51	71.75	75.03	72.60
Discount: bid	67.88	74.17	77.18	80.77	84.30	90.25	88.85
Discount: offer	68.29	74.42	77.57	80.90	84.42	90.43	89.02
Financial market indicators							
Stock-market index (end-period)	2,779	3,072	3,211	3,236	3,361	3,748	4,771
Change in $ value of stock-market index (%)	−2.4	12.0	3.6	1.8	−0.3	11.0	26.2
Dividend yield (%)	1.1	0.9	1.2	1.4	1.5	1.4	1.5
Price/earnings ratio (%)	28.4	18.6	10.5	17.1	16.8	16.1	20.7
Market capitalisation ($ m)	90,694	102,735	110,700	113,670	106,540	114,952	131,779
No of listed companies	185	185	191	193	193	192	189
Volume traded ($ m)	8,483	12,811	13,617	8,628	7,985	10,086	10,845

[a] April May

Symbols

0, 0.0 *nil or negligible*

– *not applicable or not available*

Mexico: Economic structure

	1993 [a]	1994 [a]	1995 [a]	1996 [a]	1997 [b]	1998 [b]	1999 [b]
GDP at market prices							
Nominal GDP ($ m)	403,197	421,724	286,837	334,792	413,828	459,731	492,886
Nominal GDP (Ps bn)	1,256,200	1,423,360	1,841,320	2,544,220	3,258,215	3,894,910	4,496,467
Real GDP (Ps '000 at 1980 prices)	5,655,267	5,853,201	5,488,446	5,766,202	6,104,706	6,402,847	6,679,863
Expenditure on GDP (% real change)							
GDP	0.7	3.5	−6.2	5.1	5.9	4.9	4.3
Private consumption	0.2	3.7	−9.5	2.3	4.5	5.0	4.0
Government consumption	2.0	2.5	−1.3	3.7	4.0	3.0	3.0
Gross fixed investment	−1.2	8.1	−29.0	17.7	22.0	9.0	8.0
Exports of goods & services	3.7	7.3	33.0	18.7	10.5	7.9	7.1
Imports of goods & services	−1.3	12.9	−12.8	27.8	22.9	12.1	9.8
Origin of GDP (% real change)							
Agriculture	1.4	2.0	−3.8	1.2	4.0	2.0	2.5
Industry	0.2	3.0	−10.0	10.4	8.0	5.1	4.0
of which: manufacturing	−0.8	1.5	−6.4	10.9	8.0	6.0	4.0
Services	0.9	3.4	−4.4	3.1	4.9	5.1	4.7
Ratios, GDP at market prices (%)							
Gross fixed investment/GDP	18.6	19.3	16.1	17.2	17.7	18.3	18.5
Exports of goods & services/GDP	15.2	16.9	31.3	31.9	29.3	29.0	29.7
Imports of goods & services/GDP	13.2	15.7	22.0	23.7	23.9	24.9	26.4
Gross national savings/investment	72.4	68.2	98.9	97.3	90.5	85.8	82.9
Ratios, GDP at factor cost (%)							
Agriculture/GDP	7.3	7.2	7.4	7.1	7.0	6.8	6.7
Industry/GDP	32.8	33.0	31.7	33.3	33.9	34.0	33.9
Services/GDP	59.8	59.8	60.9	59.6	59.0	59.2	59.4
Energy indicators							
Petroleum production ('000 b/d)	2,673	2,685	2,670	2,860	3,146	3,366	3,501
Petroleum reserves (m barrels)	64,516	63,220	62,058	64,000	66,000	68,000	68,000
Policy indicators (% of GDP)							
Budget balance	0.7	−0.3	−0.2	0.0	−0.5	−1.4	−1.1
Money supply (% change)							
M1	17.7	1.1	3.5	36.9	38.0	27.0	18.0
M2	14.5	21.7	48.9	22.3	25.0	32.0	25.0
Prices and exchange rates							
Interest rate (%; av)	18.6	15.5	45.1	30.7	22.0	17.0	15.0
Consumer prices (% change; av)	9.7	6.9	35.0	35.2	21.0	14.0	10.7
Consumer prices (% change; end-period)	8.0	7.1	52.0	27.7	16.1	13.1	9.1
Exchange rate Ps:$ (av)	3.116	3.375	6.419	7.599	7.873	8.472	9.123
Exchange rate Ps:$ (end-period)	3.106	5.325	7.643	7.851	8.013	8.825	9.362
Real exchange rate (1990=100)	126.99	122.19	84.36	93.63	106.76	110.10	110.07
Population and income							
Population (m)	90.00	91.85	93.67	95.10	96.91	98.75	100.62
Population growth (%)	2.1	2.0	2.0	1.9	1.9	1.9	1.9
Labour force (m)	34.33	35.38	36.46	37.45	38.47	39.50	40.55
GDP per head ($)	4,480	4,592	3,062	3,520	4,270	4,656	4,898
GDP per head ($)—PPP	5,287	5,632	5,440	5,635	5,995	6,337	6,669

[a] Actual. [b] EIU forecasts.

Mexico: Foreign payments

	1993[a]	1994[a]	1995[a]	1996[a]	1997[b]	1998[b]	1999[b]
Current account ($ m)							
Current-account balance	−23,400	−29,418	−651	−1,922	−8,480	−14,503	−18,993
Goods: exports fob	51,885	60,879	79,543	96,000	109,048	120,197	132,470
Goods: imports fob	−65,366	−79,346	−72,454	−89,469	−110,064	−126,454	−143,532
Trade balance	−13,481	−18,467	7,089	6,531	−1,016	−6,258	−11,061
Services: credit	9,517	10,323	10,281	10,779	12,031	12,974	13,870
Services: debit	−12,046	−12,925	−9,407	−10,231	−11,105	−12,089	−13,298
Services balance	−2,529	−2,602	874	548	926	885	573
Income: credit	2,694	3,348	3,705	4,154	4,984	5,483	6,031
Income: debit	−13,724	−15,709	−16,284	−17,686	−18,270	−19,802	−20,037
Income balance	−11,030	−12,361	−12,579	−13,532	−13,285	−14,319	−14,006
Current transfers: credit	3,656	4,042	3,993	4,561	4,926	5,222	5,535
Current transfers: debit	−16	−30	−31	−30	−31	−32	−33
Current transfers balance	3,640	4,012	3,965	4,531	4,895	5,190	5,502
Financing ($ m)							
Financing requirement	−39,517	−42,124	−13,081	−27,085[c]	−37,286	−30,475	−36,380
of which: principal repayments due	−16,117	−12,706	−12,430	−25,162[c]	−28,806	−15,972	−17,387
Medium- & long-term debt inflows	17,436	16,130	13,927	28,541[c]	25,716	20,321	20,368
Inward direct investment	4,389	10,972	6,963	7,619	11,000	10,000	10,500
Outward direct investment	–	–	–	–	–	–	–
Net direct investment flows	4,389	10,972	6,963	7,619	11,000	10,000	10,500
Inward portfolio investment							
(net of fc bonds)	22,171	6,460	−14,461	3,902	11,000	7,000	6,500
Outward portfolio investment	−564	−615	−663	−600[c]	−650	−700	−600
Net portfolio investment flows	21,607	5,845	−15,124	3,302	10,350	6,300	5,900
IMF credit	0	0	13,288	0	0	1,349	1,372
Increase in interest arrears (if any)	0	0	0	0	0	0	0
Increase in principal arrears (if any)	0	0	0	0	0	0	0
Other capital flows (net)	2,253	−9,655	4,596	−9,792[c]	220	−3,294	−1,261
Change in international reserves							
(− indicates increase)	−6,168	18,832	−10,569	−2,586	−10,000	−4,200	−500
International reserves ($ m)							
Total	25,110	6,278	16,847	19,433	29,433	33,633	34,133
Foreign exchange reserves	24,886	6,101	15,250	19,176	29,044	33,188	33,682
Commercial banks' foreign assets	5,945	5,752	6,271	6,152	7,000	8,000	–
Commercial banks' foreign liabilities	22,871	24,054	20,129	17,937	20,000	22,500	–
Commercial banks' net foreign assets	−16,926	−18,302	−13,858	−11,785	−13,000	−14,500	–
Months of import cover	3.9	0.8	2.5	2.3	4.5	2.9	2.6
Ratios (%)							
Current-account balance/GDP	−5.8	−7.0	−0.2	−0.6	−2.0	−3.2	−3.9
Trade balance/GDP	−3.3	−4.4	2.5	2.0	−0.2	−1.4	−2.2
Exports of goods & services/imports of							
goods & services	115.2	107.2	142.5	134.8	122.4	116.4	112.4
Exports of goods/exports of goods							
& services	84.5	85.5	88.6	89.9	90.1	90.3	90.5
Imports of goods/imports of goods							
& services	84.4	86.0	88.5	89.7	90.8	91.3	91.5
Services balance/GDP	−0.6	−0.6	0.3	0.2	0.2	0.2	0.1
Income balance/GDP	−2.7	−2.9	−4.4	−4.0	−3.2	−3.1	−2.8
Current transfers balance/GDP	0.9	1.0	1.4	1.4	1.2	1.1	1.1
Memorandum items ($ m)							
Net export credits	2,324	1,953	−2,208	287	5,755	4,580	4,771
Capital flight	11,804	−7,239	−8,506	−12,600	3,860	−1,316	535
Workers' remittances	3,332	3,694	2,600	3,150	4,000	4,200	4,500

[a] Actual. [b] EIU forecasts. [c] EIU estimate.

Mexico: External debt stock

	1993 [a]	1994 [a]	1995 [a]	1996 [b]	1997 [c]	1998 [c]	1999 [c]
Foreign debt stock ($ m)							
Total	131,572	139,955	165,743	174,734	177,493	188,946	198,920
Public medium- & long-term	74,989	79,284	94,027	98,183	96,841	102,919	108,189
Private medium- & long-term	15,538	17,489	18,587	19,862	21,722	22,950	24,039
IMF	4,787	3,860	15,828	13,278 [a]	8,810	8,634	8,146
Short-term	36,257	39,323	37,300	43,411	50,121	54,442	58,547
of which: interest arrears	0	0	0	0	0	0	0
official creditors	0	0	0	0	0	0	0
private creditors	0	0	0	0	0	0	0
Ratios (%)							
Total debt/exports of goods & services	195.1	178.9	172.4	153.2	136.5	132.3	130.5
Total debt/GDP	32.6	33.2	57.8	52.2	42.9	41.1	40.4
International reserves/total debt	19.1	4.5	10.2	11.1	16.6	17.8	17.2
Debt per head ($)	1,462	1,524	1,769	1,837	1,832	1,913	1,977
Net debt ($ m)							
Total	106,462	133,677	148,896	155,301	148,060	155,313	164,787
Ratios (%)							
Net debt/exports of goods & services	157.9	170.8	154.9	136.1	113.8	108.7	108.1
Net debt/GDP	26.4	31.7	51.9	46.4	35.8	33.8	33.4
Medium- and long-term debt ($ m)							
Total	90,528	96,772	112,614	118,045	118,563	125,869	132,228
Official creditors	26,094	27,466	38,432	35,269	34,450	34,584	32,809
Bilateral	10,017	10,391	19,790	16,936	15,521	15,120	13,272
Multilateral	16,077	17,075	18,642	18,332	18,929	19,464	19,537
Private creditors	64,434	69,307	74,183	82,777	84,113	91,285	99,419
Memorandum items ($ m)							
Export credits	24,968	26,921	24,713	25,000	30,755	35,335	40,107
Principal arrears	0	0	0	0	0	0	0
Official creditors	0	0	0	0	0	0	0
Private creditors	0	0	0	0	0	0	0
Debt owed to BIS banks ($ m)							
Total	53,896	61,731	52,043	61,335 [a]	–	–	–
0-1 year	26,120	33,025	26,019	28,080 [a]	–	–	–
1-2 years	2,345	2,086	3,403	3,999 [a]	–	–	–
over 2 years	25,431	26,620	22,621	26,235 [a]	–	–	–
Memorandum items ($ m)							
BIS banks' undisbursed credit commitments	5,202	5,806	4,143	5,914 [a]	4,500	5,000	–
Crossborder liabilities of BIS-reporting banks	25,482	26,095	30,278	37,355 [a]	48,000	54,000	–

[a] Actual. [b] EIU estimates. [c] EIU forecasts.

Mexico: External debt service

	1993[a]	1994[a]	1995[b]	1996[b]	1997[c]	1998[c]	1999[c]
Foreign debt service ($ m)							
Total paid	24,218	21,943	23,556	37,097	41,134	29,468	30,721
Medium- & long-term debt	20,795	18,057	19,256	31,528	33,879	23,924	24,886
Official creditors	4,709	4,713	5,747	10,531	7,833	6,962	8,335
Private creditors	16,087	13,344	13,509	20,996	26,046	16,962	16,551
IMF debits & charges	1,601	1,437	1,689	3,385[a]	4,629	2,440	2,763
Short-term debt (interest only)	1,822	2,448	2,611	2,184	2,625	3,104	3,072
Total due	24,218	21,943	23,556	37,097	41,134	29,468	30,721
Ratios (%)							
Debt-service ratio, paid	35.9	28.0	24.5	32.5	31.6	20.6	20.2
Debt-service ratio, due	35.9	28.0	24.5	32.5	31.6	20.6	20.2
Debt service/GDP	6.0	5.2	8.2	11.1	9.9	6.4	6.2
Principal repayments ($ m)							
Total paid	16,117	12,706	12,430	25,162	28,806	15,972	17,387
Medium- & long-term debt	14,942	11,501	11,285	23,110	25,199	14,363	15,381
Official creditors	2,790	2,719	3,081	7,663	5,319	4,366	5,975
Private creditors	12,152	8,782	8,204	15,447	19,880	9,997	9,406
IMF debits	1,175	1,204	1,144	2,052[a]	3,607	1,609	2,006
Total due	16,117	12,706	12,430	25,162	28,806	15,972	17,387
Interest payments ($ m)							
Total paid	8,101	9,237	11,126	11,934	12,328	13,495	13,334
Medium- & long-term debt	5,854	6,556	7,971	8,418	8,680	9,561	9,505
Official creditors	1,919	1,994	2,666	2,868	2,514	2,596	2,360
Private creditors	3,935	4,562	5,305	5,549	6,166	6,965	7,145
IMF charges	426	233	545	1,332[a]	1,022	830	757
Interest on short-term debt	1,822	2,448	2,611	2,184	2,625	3,104	3,072
Total due	8,101	9,237	11,126	11,934	12,328	13,495	13,334
Ratios (%)							
Interest paid/debt service paid	33.5	42.1	47.2	32.2	30.0	45.8	43.4
Interest paid/exports of goods & services	12.0	11.8	11.6	10.5	9.5	9.4	8.8
Interest due/exports of goods & services	12.0	11.8	11.6	10.5	9.5	9.4	8.8
Interest paid/GDP	2.0	2.2	3.9	3.6	3.0	2.9	2.7
Memorandum items							
Effective interest rate (%)	7.2	7.2	8.2	7.5	7.4	8.1	7.6
Effective maturity (years)	5.5	7.9	8.6	4.9	4.7	8.3	8.2

[a] Actual. [b] EIU estimates. [c] EIU forecasts.

Mexico: External trade

	1993[a]	1994[a]	1995[a]	1996[a]	1997[b]	1998[b]	1999[b]
Goods: exports fob ($ m)							
Total	30,191	34,589	47,276	59,079	65,571	71,080	77,939
of which:							
manufactured goods	19,832	24,133	35,455	43,384	44,580	48,406	52,870
crude petroleum	7,418	7,393	8,423	11,654	12,008	–	–
agricultural products	2,504	2,678	4,016	3,592	3,509	–	–
mining products	278	357	400	449	480	–	–
Services							
Tourism receipts	4,019	4,254	4,051	4,647	5,019	5,421	5,854
Goods: imports cif ($ m)							
Total	47,399	61,083	46,249	58,964	74,142	85,873	98,477
of which:							
intermediate goods	30,025	36,049	32,242	41,385	–	–	–
capital goods	11,056	13,322	8,697	10,922	–	–	–
consumer goods	7,842	9,511	5,335	6,657	–	–	–
Volume and prices (%)							
Export volume of goods	20.6	13.4	17.8	22.3	19.1	9.1	6.8
Import volume of goods	6.7	16.8	–19.0	16.7	27.2	13.1	9.9
Export prices	–6.8	3.4	10.9	–1.3	–4.7	1.0	3.2
Import prices	–1.4	4.0	12.7	5.8	–3.3	1.6	3.3
Terms of trade (1985=100)	84.7	84.3	83.0	77.4	76.3	75.8	75.7

[a] Actual. [b] EIU forecasts.

Mexico: Trends in foreign trade

	1993[a]	1994[a]	1995[a]	1996[a]	1997[b]	1998[b]	1999[b]
Main destinations of exports (% share)							
USA	78.6	85.1	83.6	83.9	–	–	–
Canada	5.7	2.4	2.5	2.3	–	–	–
Spain	1.9	1.4	1.0	1.0	–	–	–
Japan	2.1	1.6	1.2	1.4	–	–	–
Main origins of imports (% share)							
USA	69.1	72.0	74.5	75.5	–	–	–
Japan	6.6	4.8	5.0	4.6	–	–	–
Germany	4.3	3.9	3.7	3.5	–	–	–
France	1.4	1.9	1.4	1.1	–	–	–
Principal exports (% share)							
Manufactured goods	38.2	39.6	44.6	40.3	40.9	40.3	39.9
Crude petroleum	14.3	12.1	10.6	12.1	11.0	–	–
Agricultural products	4.8	4.4	5.0	3.7	3.2	–	–
Mining products	0.5	0.6	0.5	0.5	0.4	–	–
Principal imports (% share)							
Intermediate goods	45.9	45.4	44.5	46.3	–	–	–
Capital goods	16.9	16.8	12.0	12.2	–	–	–
Consumer goods	12.0	12.0	7.4	7.4	–	–	–

[a] Actual. [b] EIU forecasts.

Chapter 5

Euromoney
Methodology: Country Risk Ratings

To obtain the overall country risk score, *Euromoney* assigns a weighting to the nine categories listed below. The best underlying value per category achieves the full weighting (25, 10 or 5); the worst scores zero and all other values are calculated relative to these two. The formula used is the following: A - (A / (B-C)) x (D–C), where A = category weighting; B = lowest value* in range; C = highest value* in range, D = individual value.

*NB for Debt indicators and Debt in default, B and C are reversed in the formula, as the lowest score receives the full weighting and the highest gets zero.

• **Political risk** (25% weighting): the risk of non-payment or non-servicing of payment for goods or services, loans, trade-related finance and dividends, and the non-repatriation of capital. Risk analysts give each country a score between 10 and zero - the higher, the better. This does not reflect the creditworthiness of individual counterparties.

Euromoney provides a full country risk rating based on nine individual variables. These include Political Risk (25%), Economic Performance (25%), Debt Indicators (10%), Debt in Default or Rescheduled (10%), Credit Ratings (10%), Access to Bank Finance (5%), Access to Short-term Finance (5%), Access to Capital Markets (5%), and Discount on Forfaiting (5%).

The Political Risk assessment is a single indicator created on a 0-10 scale (before weighting) derived from country experts, brokers, and banking officers. It is specifically derived as risk of non-payment or non-serving of payment for goods or services, loans, trade-related finance and dividends, and the non-repatriation of capital. The PR assessment would be regarded as an industry-specific assessment.

In a separate *Euromoney* Economic Projection, responses from 30 economists at leading institutions are rated comparatively on a basis of zero to 100, with the best in a given year at 100 and the worst at zero.

• **Economic performance** (25%): based (1) on GNP* figures per capita and (2) on results of *Euromoney* poll of economic projections, where each country's score is obtained from average projections for 1999 and 2000. The sum of these two factors, equally weighted, makes up this column – the higher the result, the better.

*GNP figures were unavailable for the following countries, so GDP data were used instead: Afghanistan, Antigua & Barbuda, Bahamas, Bahrain, Barbados, Bosnia-Herzegovina, Cuba, Cyprus, Djibouti, Iraq, North Korea, Kuwait, Liberia, Libya, Macau, Myanmar, New Caledonia, Oman, Qatar, Singapore, Somalia.

• **Debt indicators** (10%): calculated using these ratios from the World Bank's *Global Development Finance 2000*: total debt stocks to GNP (A), debt service to exports (B); current account balance to GNP (C). Scores are calculated as follows: A + (B x 2) – (C x 10). The lower this score, the better. Figures are for 1998.
Because of lack of consistent economic data for OECD and rich oil-producing countries, these score the full weighting, except where they report debt figures to the IMF. Developing countries which do not report complete debt data get zero.

• **Debt in default or rescheduled** (10%): scores are based on the ratio of rescheduled debt to debt stocks, taken from the World Bank's *Global Development Finance 2000*. The lower the ratio, the better. OECD and developing countries which do not report under the debtor reporting system (DRS) score 10 and zero respectively.

- **Credit ratings** (10%): nominal values are assigned to sovereign ratings from Moody's, S&P and Fitch IBCA. The higher the average value, the better. Where there is no rating, countries score zero.

- **Access to bank finance** (5%): calculated from disbursements of private, long-term, unguaranteed loans as a percentage of GNP. The higher the result, the better. OECD and developing countries not reporting under the DRS score five and zero respectively. Source: the World Bank's *Global Development Finance 2000.*

- **Access to short-term finance** (5%): takes into account OECD consensus groups (source: ECGD) and short-term cover available from the US Exim Bank and NCM UK. The higher the score, the better.
- **Access to capital markets** (5%): heads of debt syndicate and loan syndications rated each country's accessibility to international markets at the time of the survey. The higher the average rating out of 10, the better.

- **Discount on forfaiting** (5%): reflects the average maximum tenor for forfaiting and the average spread over riskless countries such as the US. The higher the score, the better. Countries where forfaiting is not available score zero. Data were supplied by Deutsche Bank, Standard Bank and WestLB.

Economic Projections Methodology

Euromoney received replies from 30 economists at leading financial and economic institutions. They gave each country's economic performance for 2001 and 2002 a score out of 100. The world's fastest-growing, best-performing economy in an ideal year would score 100; the worst economy in a disastrous year would score zero.

Respondents were asked to consider economic growth, monetary stability, current-account, budget deficit or surplus, unemployment and structural imbalances. Economists also gave their GNP growth forecasts for 2000 and 2001. Countries which received no votes were excluded from this table.

Our thanks go to the 44 political analysts and economists who took part in our surveys. Those who did not wish to remain anonymous were:

Dr. Michael O'Leary, The PRS Group; Bernard Butticker, UBS AG; Chi-Y Tan, Bank of Taiwan; Conrad Schuller, Erste Bank; Dennis Readman, Barclays; Douglas Porter, Nesbitt Burns Canada; Eva Christina Horwitz, Handelsbanken Markets; Ewoud Schuitemaker, ABN AMRO; Nicollas Francois, Credit Lyonnais; George Samu, Royal Bank of Canada; Gregor Eder, Dresdner Bank; Guy Seyler, Banque et Caisse D'Epargne De L'etat; Johan Lumprecht, First National Bank SA; John Krijgsman, CIBC; Karla Schestauber ,Creditanstalt; Kurt von dem Hagen, Royal Bank of Canada; Luigi Ruggerone, Banca Commerciale Italiana; Marijke Zewuster, ABN AMRO Bank, Paul Papadopoulos, Arab Banking Corp; Penelope Forde, Central Bank of Trinidad and Tobago; Reijo Heiskanen, Merita Nordbanken; Richard McGuire and Team, Dun & Bradstreet; Shamus Mok, Bank of East Asia ; Sruti Patel, Afrinvest; Stephen King, HSBC; Veronika Lammer, Erste Bank; Elwin De Groot, Fortis Bank; Arjuna Mahendran, SG Securities

Sep-00	Mar-00		Total Score	Political Risk	Economic Performance	Debt Indicators	Debt in Default or Rescheduled	Credit Ratings	Access to Bank Finance	Access to Short-Term Finance	Access to Capital Markets	Discount on Forfaiting
		Weighting:	100	25	25	10	10	10	5	5	5	5
1	1	Luxembourg	99.02	24.38	25.00	10.00	10.00	10.00	5.00	5.00	5.00	4.64
2	2	Switzerland	96.89	25.00	21.89	10.00	10.00	10.00	5.00	5.00	5.00	4.99
3	4	United States	94.25	24.94	19.30	10.00	10.00	10.00	5.00	5.00	5.00	5.00
4	3	Norway	94.24	23.90	20.42	10.00	10.00	10.00	5.00	5.00	5.00	4.92
5	6	Netherlands	92.90	24.66	18.27	10.00	10.00	10.00	5.00	5.00	5.00	4.98
6	5	Denmark	92.77	23.09	19.95	10.00	10.00	9.79	5.00	5.00	5.00	4.94
7	11	Germany	92.77	24.52	18.27	10.00	10.00	10.00	5.00	5.00	5.00	4.98
8	8	France	92.33	24.34	18.01	10.00	10.00	10.00	5.00	5.00	5.00	4.98
9	7	Austria	92.29	23.69	18.63	10.00	10.00	10.00	5.00	5.00	5.00	4.97
10	12	United Kingdom	91.54	24.63	16.92	10.00	10.00	10.00	5.00	5.00	5.00	4.99
11	9	Finland	91.38	23.52	18.23	10.00	10.00	9.69	5.00	5.00	5.00	4.94
12	10	Sweden	91.12	23.65	18.65	9.50	10.00	9.38	5.00	5.00	5.00	4.94
13	14	Japan	90.70	23.51	18.41	10.00	10.00	9.58	5.00	5.00	5.00	4.19
14	15	Singapore	90.04	22.39	19.07	10.00	10.00	9.58	5.00	5.00	5.00	3.99
15	16	Ireland	89.71	23.42	16.53	10.00	10.00	9.79	5.00	5.00	5.00	4.96
16	13	Belgium	89.63	23.07	17.84	10.00	10.00	8.75	5.00	5.00	5.00	4.97
17	17	Canada	89.10	23.75	16.24	10.00	10.00	9.17	5.00	5.00	5.00	4.94
18	18	Australia	88.01	22.69	16.60	10.00	10.00	9.17	5.00	5.00	5.00	4.56
19	20	Spain	87.29	23.03	14.93	10.00	10.00	9.38	5.00	5.00	5.00	4.96
20	19	Italy	87.11	22.61	16.14	10.00	10.00	8.44	5.00	5.00	5.00	4.93
21	21	Iceland	86.72	19.91	18.71	10.00	10.00	8.54	5.00	5.00	5.00	4.56
22	22	New Zealand	85.27	21.42	14.54	10.00	10.00	9.38	5.00	5.00	5.00	4.94
23	23	Portugal	83.25	22.21	13.72	10.00	10.00	8.75	5.00	4.11	5.00	4.46
24	24	Taiwan	80.65	20.46	14.95	9.87	10.00	8.75	5.00	5.00	3.00	3.63
25	25	Greece	78.66	20.13	13.35	10.00	10.00	6.25	5.00	5.00	5.00	3.93
26	27	Hong Kong	77.42	18.22	15.95	10.00	10.00	7.08	5.00	4.29	4.00	2.88
27	26	Cyprus	76.62	18.18	13.49	9.76	10.00	7.50	5.00	4.29	5.00	3.40
28	29	United Arab Emirates	75.59	18.07	14.59	9.98	10.00	6.88	5.00	5.00	2.30	3.77
29	30	Bermuda	73.67	18.67	13.71	10.00	10.00	8.96	5.00	5.00	2.33	0.00
30	28	Kuwait	73.28	16.35	15.45	9.64	10.00	6.67	5.00	4.11	2.33	3.74
31	33	Malta	72.89	18.40	14.20	9.95	10.00	7.08	0.00	4.29	5.00	3.97
32	31	Israel	72.68	16.56	13.70	9.74	10.00	6.88	5.00	4.11	3.42	3.28

Sep-00	Mar-00		Total Score	Political Risk	Economic Performance	Debt Indicators	Debt in Default or Rescheduled	Credit Ratings	Access to Bank Finance	Access to Short-Term Finance	Access to Capital Markets	Discount on Forfaiting
		Weighting:	100	25	25	10	10	10	5	5	5	5
33	32	Slovenia	68.93	17.43	12.31	5.66	10.00	7.29	5.00	3.39	3.75	4.11
34	38	Saudi Arabia	68.27	16.74	10.85	9.79	10.00	4.38	5.00	4.29	3.45	3.77
35	34	Qatar	68.14	16.10	12.20	8.50	10.00	5.31	5.00	4.29	3.00	3.74
36	35	Brunei	66.84	16.40	18.44	10.00	10.00	0.00	5.00	5.00	2.00	0.00
37	40	Korea South	66.28	17.50	12.43	9.05	10.00	5.83	1.19	4.11	3.00	3.17
38	36	Oman	66.17	15.57	10.27	9.49	10.00	5.00	5.00	4.11	3.00	3.74
39	41	Chile	65.83	18.24	10.39	8.67	10.00	6.88	1.73	3.39	2.50	4.03
40	42	Hungary	65.24	17.06	10.78	8.35	10.00	6.04	2.51	2.50	4.00	3.99
41	39	Bahrain	65.20	15.22	10.56	10.00	10.00	3.75	5.00	4.29	2.61	3.77
42	43	Poland	63.59	16.56	9.92	9.26	10.00	6.25	0.47	2.86	4.00	4.26
43	44	Czech Republic	63.14	17.11	9.96	8.94	10.00	6.46	0.55	2.86	4.00	3.26
44	45	Malaysia	61.11	15.86	10.08	8.88	10.00	5.42	2.25	3.04	3.00	2.60
45	48	China	59.75	15.64	9.46	9.58	10.00	5.83	0.19	2.32	4.00	2.73
46	49	Mexico	59.68	15.68	9.28	8.81	10.00	4.58	0.83	3.48	3.17	3.85
47	54	Thailand	59.55	14.89	8.55	8.44	10.00	4.79	3.64	3.04	3.00	3.21
48	37	Bahamas	59.46	16.50	6.03	10.00	10.00	5.31	5.00	4.29	2.33	0.00
49	47	Mauritius	59.08	14.16	11.44	8.90	10.00	5.00	1.03	3.21	2.83	2.51
50	51	South Africa	57.71	13.85	9.51	9.41	10.00	4.79	0.23	3.39	3.33	3.18
51	46	Tunisia	57.48	13.87	10.00	8.80	10.00	5.21	0.09	3.39	2.42	3.70
52	75	Barbados	57.32	15.62	10.71	9.43	10.00	6.56	0.00	3.66	1.33	0.00
53	50	Uruguay	56.79	14.19	9.41	8.83	10.00	4.79	0.14	4.11	2.22	3.10
54	52	Egypt	56.36	14.48	9.21	9.19	9.90	4.79	0.02	2.74	2.42	3.63
55	55	Estonia	55.69	13.85	9.31	9.61	10.00	5.63	0.16	2.10	2.00	3.04
56	53	Morocco	55.11	12.76	9.27	8.55	10.00	4.38	0.12	2.86	3.56	3.63
57	57	Argentina	54.97	12.81	9.58	7.68	10.00	3.13	1.10	4.38	2.97	3.33
58	60	Trinidad & Tobago	54.18	14.10	10.95	9.10	10.00	5.00	0.17	3.04	1.83	0.00
59	58	India	53.75	13.79	7.90	9.11	10.00	3.96	0.08	3.21	2.00	3.70
60	67	Costa Rica	53.42	13.07	10.88	9.20	10.00	3.54	0.18	2.86	1.67	2.03
61	59	Latvia	53.11	12.84	8.56	9.62	10.00	5.42	0.11	1.92	2.00	2.64
62	66	Slovak Republic	52.95	12.86	8.57	8.76	10.00	4.38	1.46	1.92	2.38	2.63
63	56	Philippines	52.81	13.23	7.61	8.75	10.00	4.38	0.48	3.21	2.00	3.16
64	65	Turkey	52.74	14.07	8.54	8.74	10.00	2.08	0.22	3.48	2.69	2.92
65	64	Panama	52.20	12.02	9.34	8.54	10.00	4.38	0.59	3.04	1.78	2.52

Sep-00	Mar-00		Total Score	Political Risk	Economic Performance	Debt Indicators	Debt in Default or Rescheduled	Credit Ratings	Access to Bank Finance	Access to Short-Term Finance	Access to Capital Markets	Discount on Forfaiting
		Weighting:	100	25	25	10	10	10	5	5	5	5
66	62	Botswana	51.83	15.14	9.93	9.82	10.00	0.00	0.00	3.39	1.25	2.31
67	69	Brazil	51.31	12.49	8.66	7.51	9.96	2.29	1.72	3.39	2.10	3.18
68	63	E Salvador	51.12	10.98	9.63	9.29	10.00	4.58	0.09	3.21	1.33	2.00
69	61	Lithuania	50.79	12.54	8.28	9.49	10.00	3.96	0.06	1.92	2.00	2.54
70	70	Croatia	49.67	11.69	8.49	9.14	7.67	4.58	0.08	2.08	3.00	2.94
71	68	Colombia	48.88	11.26	7.13	8.64	10.00	3.96	0.56	3.21	2.22	1.90
72	71	Fiji	47.38	10.12	9.18	9.68	10.00	3.75	0.32	2.32	2.00	0.00
73	76	Guatemala	47.31	9.77	8.84	9.33	10.00	3.13	0.06	3.21	1.11	1.86
74	73	Lebanon	46.85	10.33	7.29	8.62	10.00	2.50	0.48	2.14	2.50	2.99
75	74	Jordan	46.32	11.22	7.96	7.56	8.49	3.44	0.06	2.41	2.13	3.05
76	78	Venezuela	43.85	10.71	6.85	8.72	10.00	1.67	0.33	2.74	2.25	0.58
77	77	Dominican Republic	43.84	10.25	8.81	9.45	9.19	1.25	0.00	3.04	0.00	1.86
78	90	Jamaica	42.70	7.73	8.76	8.74	10.00	2.19	0.15	3.13	2.00	0.00
79	85	Bolivia	42.52	8.54	7.10	8.08	10.00	2.81	0.02	2.14	1.67	2.15
80	84	Bulgaria	42.51	10.46	6.69	8.23	10.00	1.88	0.82	1.56	1.00	1.87
81	88	Kazakhstan	42.46	9.28	6.65	9.21	10.00	2.29	0.72	1.56	2.00	0.74
82	86	Paraguay	41.31	9.74	7.01	9.45	10.00	1.88	0.05	2.68	0.50	0.00
83	80	Iran	40.64	8.99	7.09	9.25	10.00	1.25	0.04	1.55	1.00	1.46
84	82	Belize	40.61	10.81	5.30	8.82	10.00	3.13	0.00	2.50	0.05	0.00
85	79	Sri Lanka	39.81	9.37	5.82	9.08	10.00	0.00	0.03	2.50	1.00	2.01
86	91	Seychelles	39.71	9.14	6.32	9.14	10.00	0.00	0.00	4.11	1.00	0.00
87	94	Macau	39.59	14.15	12.75	0.00	0.00	5.63	0.00	3.57	1.00	2.50
88	125	Maldives	39.22	9.64	8.23	9.03	10.00	0.00	0.00	2.32	0.00	0.00
89	92	Peru	39.12	10.63	7.50	9.15	1.25	3.33	0.02	2.32	2.45	2.47
90	93	Syria	38.95	9.67	6.62	7.96	10.00	0.00	0.00	1.61	0.88	2.21
91	116	Honduras	38.77	8.00	7.12	8.13	10.00	1.25	0.83	1.61	0.05	1.77
92	136	Dominica	38.60	7.39	9.98	9.08	10.00	0.00	0.00	2.14	0.00	0.00
93	115	Indonesia	38.48	7.98	5.96	6.65	8.65	0.63	5.00	2.62	1.00	0.00
94	87	Vietnam	38.36	9.82	6.01	8.64	9.96	1.88	0.00	2.05	0.00	0.00
95	133	Russia	37.88	8.02	6.65	8.62	8.26	0.42	2.37	1.61	0.75	1.18
96	99	Algeria	37.71	8.27	6.77	7.94	8.90	0.00	0.00	2.32	1.00	2.51
97	72	Ghana	37.64	8.57	6.61	7.92	10.00	0.00	0.11	2.32	0.33	1.77
98	89	Kenya	37.64	7.41	7.37	8.61	10.00	0.00	0.00	2.41	0.05	1.77

Sep-00	Mar-00		Total Score	Political Risk	Economic Performance	Debt Indicators	Debt in default or Rescheduled	Credit Ratings	Access to Bank Finance	Access to Short-Term Finance	Access to Capital Markets	Discount on Forfaiting
		Weighting:	100	25	25	10	10	10	5	5	5	5
99	102	Gambia	37.63	7.85	7.67	9.43	10.00	0.00	0.00	2.68	0.00	0.00
100	120	Macedonia (FYR)	37.37	6.30	7.67	8.18	10.00	0.00	0.86	2.17	1.00	1.18
101	83	Papua New Guinea	37.17	8.49	5.33	8.74	10.00	2.29	0.00	2.32	0.00	0.00
102	103	Azerbaijan	36.94	8.42	6.72	9.22	10.00	0.00	0.03	1.55	1.00	0.00
103	107	Romania	36.62	8.17	5.32	8.89	10.00	0.83	0.18	1.56	1.00	0.67
104	100	Lesotho	36.42	8.47	6.74	8.54	10.00	0.00	0.00	2.68	0.00	0.00
105	98	St Lucia	35.91	9.98	4.57	8.69	10.00	0.00	0.00	2.32	0.33	0.00
106	118	Kyrgyz Republic	35.76	8.05	8.13	8.59	10.00	0.00	0.10	0.89	0.00	0.00
107	110	Equatorial Guinea	35.69	4.19	9.88	8.93	10.00	0.00	0.00	2.68	0.00	0.00
108	95	Bangladesh	34.96	7.73	5.48	9.24	10.00	0.00	0.00	2.50	0.00	0.00
109	96	Senegal	34.28	6.28	7.03	8.22	10.00	0.00	0.16	2.14	0.45	0.00
110	164	Uzbekistan	34.15	6.76	6.35	9.43	10.00	0.00	0.06	1.55	0.00	0.00
111	137	Yemen	33.99	7.57	5.86	8.38	9.95	0.00	0.00	1.80	0.42	0.00
112	101	Uganda	33.73	6.77	6.68	8.95	7.72	0.00	0.00	2.14	0.00	1.48
113	112	Zimbabwe	33.43	4.22	5.04	7.88	10.00	0.00	3.28	2.50	0.50	0.00
114	105	Cape Verde	33.06	6.33	4.95	8.89	10.00	0.00	0.00	2.86	0.04	0.00
115	134	Ukraine	33.06	6.05	5.68	9.26	9.61	0.00	0.48	1.55	0.44	0.00
116	97	Gabon	33.03	6.86	8.42	8.42	8.26	0.00	0.00	1.07	0.00	0.00
117	81	Swaziland	32.92	9.09	8.96	0.00	10.00	0.00	0.00	2.86	0.00	2.01
118	131	Cambodia	32.90	3.81	9.40	8.80	10.00	0.00	0.00	0.89	0.00	0.00
119	106	Nepal	32.72	6.24	5.38	8.96	10.00	0.00	0.00	2.14	0.00	0.00
120	123	Côte d'Ivoire	32.47	5.84	6.56	7.29	8.70	0.00	1.73	1.96	0.39	0.00
121	114	St Vincent & the Grenadines	32.14	7.53	4.27	7.70	10.00	0.00	0.00	2.14	0.50	0.00
122	108	Nigeria	32.09	4.88	6.20	8.48	10.00	0.00	0.02	1.52	1.00	0.00
123	129	Pakistan	31.99	6.36	4.87	8.61	10.00	0.94	0.32	0.89	0.00	0.00
124	119	Burkina Faso	31.95	6.27	4.65	8.85	10.00	0.00	0.00	2.14	0.04	0.00
125	132	Turkmenistan	31.81	5.98	5.96	7.32	10.00	0.94	0.07	1.55	0.00	0.00
126	109	Malawi	31.66	4.99	5.55	7.73	10.00	0.00	0.00	3.39	0.00	0.00
127	147	Samoa	31.28	7.75	0.87	8.52	10.00	0.00	0.00	2.14	2.00	0.00
128	130	Ethiopia	30.95	4.79	7.62	7.41	9.80	0.00	0.00	1.34	0.00	0.00
129	140	Belarus	30.74	5.77	3.24	9.82	10.00	0.00	0.01	0.89	1.00	0.00
130	139	Mongolia	30.64	6.10	3.68	8.71	10.00	1.25	0.00	0.89	0.00	0.00

Sep-00	Mar-00		Total Score	Political Risk	Economic Performance	Debt Indicators	Debt in default or rescheduled	Credit Ratings	Access to Bank Finance	Access to Short-Term Finance	Access to Capital Markets	Discount on Forfaiting
		Weighting:	100	25	25	10	10	10	5	5	5	5
131	144	Armenia	30.47	6.22	3.44	8.91	10.00	0.00	0.00	0.89	1.00	0.00
132	121	Grenada	30.41	8.09	1.46	8.71	10.00	0.00	0.00	2.14	0.00	0.00
133	155	Georgia	30.40	4.19	6.05	9.26	10.00	0.00	0.00	0.89	0.00	0.00
134	135	Solomon Islands	30.39	6.86	0.79	9.25	10.00	0.00	0.00	2.50	1.00	0.00
135	146	Albania	30.38	5.40	4.56	9.49	10.00	0.00	0.03	0.89	0.00	0.00
136	127	Vanuatu	30.02	6.19	0.92	9.58	10.00	0.00	0.00	2.32	1.00	0.00
137	126	Cameroon	29.74	5.64	5.52	7.73	7.72	0.00	0.13	2.95	0.04	0.00
138	117	Madagascar	29.48	3.90	5.66	7.87	9.37	0.00	0.00	2.68	0.00	0.00
139	153	Ecuador	29.28	3.90	5.34	7.94	10.00	0.00	0.32	0.89	0.89	0.00
140	142	Moldova	29.24	4.90	2.42	8.37	10.00	0.94	0.04	1.56	1.00	0.00
141	113	Tanzania	28.89	4.96	6.12	6.63	8.79	0.00	0.03	0.89	0.00	1.48
142	145	Mozambique	28.63	4.60	5.48	6.31	8.84	0.00	0.15	0.89	0.00	2.36
143	111	Togo	28.63	5.46	3.61	7.69	9.19	0.00	0.00	2.68	0.00	0.00
144	157	Bhutan	28.53	6.19	0.71	9.22	10.00	0.00	0.00	2.41	0.00	0.00
145	141	Benin	28.51	4.00	3.69	8.64	10.00	0.00	0.00	2.14	0.04	0.00
146	152	Guyana	28.27	6.69	3.79	6.10	10.00	0.00	0.00	1.52	0.17	0.00
147	104	Mali	28.15	4.66	3.52	8.02	9.99	0.00	0.00	1.96	0.00	0.00
148	150	Chad	27.79	3.04	3.51	8.73	9.82	0.00	0.00	2.68	0.00	0.00
149	149	Mauritania	27.19	3.52	5.33	5.66	10.00	0.00	0.00	2.68	0.00	0.00
150	138	Zambia	27.04	3.86	6.35	6.57	9.32	0.00	0.06	0.89	0.00	0.00
151	122	Guinea	26.77	5.02	3.19	8.04	9.62	0.00	0.00	0.89	0.00	0.00
152	171	Myanmar	26.35	5.03	3.24	7.19	10.00	0.00	0.00	0.89	0.00	0.00
153	158	Nicaragua	26.34	4.71	5.76	4.29	8.72	1.25	0.00	0.89	0.72	0.00
154	154	Sudan	25.45	2.41	3.33	8.82	10.00	0.00	0.00	0.89	0.00	0.00
155	124	Niger	25.43	2.67	3.17	8.26	9.89	0.00	0.55	0.89	0.00	0.00
156	-	Micronesia (Fed. States)	25.24	13.06	0.93	0.00	10.00	0.00	0.00	1.25	0.00	0.00
157	156	Central African Republic	25.13	2.86	4.27	8.11	9.00	0.00	0.00	0.89	0.00	0.00
158	168	Djibouti	24.63	3.30	0.91	9.17	10.00	0.00	0.00	1.25	0.00	0.00
159	148	Haiti	24.32	2.71	0.69	9.40	10.00	0.00	0.00	1.52	0.00	0.00
160	128	Tonga	24.01	8.64	1.06	0.00	10.00	0.00	0.00	2.32	2.00	0.00
161	163	Laos	23.99	6.06	0.00	7.04	10.00	0.00	0.00	0.89	0.00	0.00
162	143	Namibia	23.65	10.29	7.58	0.00	0.00	0.00	0.00	2.32	1.17	2.29

Sep-00	Mar-00		Total Score	Political Risk	Economic Performance	Debt Indicators	Debt in default or rescheduled	Credit Ratings	Access to Bank Finance	Access to Short-Term Finance	Access to Capital Markets	Discount on Forfaiting
		Weighting:	100	25	25	10	10	10	5	5	5	5
163	176	Suriname	23.11	7.36	3.22	0.00	10.00	1.25	0.00	0.89	0.39	0.00
164	162	Sierra Leone	23.06	2.62	2.96	6.62	9.97	0.00	0.00	0.89	0.00	0.00
165	161	Dem. Rep. of the Congo (Zaire)	22.87	2.35	2.61	7.01	10.00	0.00	0.00	0.89	0.00	0.00
166	-	Eritrea	22.18	1.33	0.64	9.31	10.00	0.00	0.00	0.89	0.00	0.00
167	159	Congo	22.03	3.66	3.44	5.75	9.19	0.00	0.00	0.00	0.00	0.00
168	151	Rwanda	21.13	1.52	0.77	9.55	8.40	0.00	0.00	0.89	0.00	0.00
169	167	Angola	20.97	3.30	3.29	4.44	8.42	0.00	0.00	1.52	0.00	0.00
170	-	Burundi	20.81	2.29	0.62	7.01	10.00	0.00	0.00	0.89	0.00	0.00
171	166	Guinea-Bissau	20.04	4.19	2.56	2.47	9.93	0.00	0.00	0.89	0.00	0.00
172	165	New Caledonia	19.96	12.86	3.67	0.00	0.00	0.00	0.00	1.43	2.00	0.00
173	-	Marshall Islands	19.44	12.19	1.00	0.00	0.00	0.00	0.00	1.25	5.00	0.00
174	174	Antigua & Barbuda	19.43	4.61	2.87	0.00	10.00	0.00	0.00	1.79	0.17	0.00
175	169	Libya	19.30	9.20	8.19	0.00	0.00	0.00	0.00	1.90	0.00	0.00
176	172	Tajikistan	17.76	3.09	4.42	8.99	0.00	0.00	0.37	0.89	0.00	0.00
177	160	Sao Tome & Principe	16.67	2.41	0.65	0.00	10.00	0.00	0.00	2.86	0.75	0.00
178	-	Bosnia-Herzegovina	15.82	3.38	3.25	8.16	0.00	0.00	0.00	0.54	0.50	0.00
179	173	Liberia	15.30	3.91	0.85	0.00	10.00	0.00	0.00	0.54	0.00	0.00
180	175	Yugoslavia (Fed. Republic)	14.81	1.99	1.73	0.00	10.00	0.00	0.00	0.71	0.38	0.00
181	170	Somalia	14.76	2.29	0.74	0.00	10.00	0.00	0.00	0.89	0.83	0.00
182	177	Cuba	10.67	3.80	5.81	0.00	0.00	0.00	0.00	0.89	0.17	0.00
183	178	Iraq	9.04	2.36	5.80	0.00	0.00	0.00	0.00	0.54	0.33	0.00
184	179	Korea North	4.72	2.98	0.85	0.00	0.00	0.00	0.00	0.89	0.00	0.00
185	180	Afghanistan	2.81	0.00	1.56	0.00	0.00	0.00	0.00	1.25	0.00	0.00

Chapter 6

Moody's Investors Services
Sovereign Credit Risk Analysis

SOVEREIGN NATIONS

Analytically, the objective of sovereign risk assessment is to answer a single question — one that is as simple to pose as it is ultimately difficult to answer — "Will borrowers from a particular country have access to the foreign currency they need to be able to service their future obligations on foreign-currency debt securities?" In other words, what is the likelihood of an international default?

Moody's Investors Services provides a Sovereign Credit Risk Analysis that assesses the ability of countries (sovereigns) to service their future obligations on foreign currency debt securities. While some of the variables analyzed might be useful in forecasting other forms of risk, the credit risk rating derived by Moody's is explicitly focused on this one form of risk and should not be applied for an alternate exposure. Moody's is a country risk assessment and industry specific. It relies on an attribute model in constructing its assessment.

In establishing credit risk for both short-term and long-term projections, Moody's analysts assess both political and economic variables. In the *political* category they include:
1. The degree and nature of political intrusiveness on the cultivation of wealth.
2. Depth and experience of government bureaucrats.
3. Political intrusiveness on economic management.
4. Political links with foreign partners.
5. Past behavior under stress.
6. Regime legitimacy.

For *economic* fundamentals they examine:
1. The nation's resources.
2. Resource exploitation.
3. Quality of national economic management.
4. Structural dependencies on export/import sectors.
5. Export mix.
6. International capital flows.
7. Austerity programs.

The Moody's assessment examines the liabilities of the country as a whole, not just the government. Country evaluations include economic statistical data to lend depth to their ratings and specify both absolute and relative debt.

The country, or "sovereign", rating is a measure of the ability and willingness of the country's central bank to make available foreign currency to service debt, including that of the central government itself. It follows that this rating is not directly an evaluation of the creditworthiness of the government, but rather it relates to the total foreign debt of the country, including both public and private-sector borrowers. For example, a particular government could be viewed as having an Aaa level of capacity to repay debt denominated in its own currency; yet, the country rating on foreign-currency debt could be lower because of the nation's large external debt or other political or economic factors.

In assessing a sovereign state's ability to repay, the analyst's attention focuses on two often interrelated ways in which a country may fail to meet international debt obligations. First, a nation may default because of chronically deficient foreign exchange earnings, most often due to ongoing vulnerabilities in the country's pattern of wealth generation. The situation could result, for example, from exceedingly inept economic management of the nation's wealth over a period of time; or it could be the result of prolonged economic vicissitudes, such as a dearth of valuable natural resources, protectionism in the nation's chief foreign markets, or, for a commodity-producing nation, a secular decline in world commodity prices.

Second, a country's borrowers may default because of a short-term condition of illiquidity — for example, if it suffers a sudden cash flow interruption from foreign exchange earnings. In both cases, the process of evaluating the nation's ability to repay can be described as a search for structural problems, anomalies, or rigidities that may point to long-term vulnerabilities in a country's pattern of wealth generation. This involves an analysis of a host of interrelated political, economic, social, and cultural facets of the nation — all of which are related to the nation's susceptibility to a long-term wealth decline and the efficacy of programmes designed to correct such a decline once it occurs.

A sovereign's unwillingness to repay often arises out of changes such as a revolution or radical shift in leadership, which may make the option not to service debt attractive politically — or less costly than continuing to service the obligation. An overt repudiation of the whole debt or a segment of it that is deemed "odious" or "imperialistic" may occur, as happened with Russia in 1917 and China in 1949. Or, for a variety of reasons, a newly-elected leader may unilaterally announce that future debt servicing will be restricted to a certain portion of export earnings, as the president of Peru chose to do in 1985. The likelihood of such events hinges largely on political factors, but these in turn relate to cultural, social, and other elements that cannot be evaluated in isolation.

Assessment of the country's debt burden is often more amenable to a quantitative totalling of expected obligations, but here, too, political-economic factors may come into play. The question of how each type of debt should be treated in the analysis may introduce surprising complexities, as outlined in "Defining external debt" (below). The final stage of the analysis, outlined in "Forecasting outcomes" (below), involves a "what-if" forecasting of the degree to which the nation would be likely to avoid default under a variety of plausible stress scenarios, including a potential liquidity crisis.

SOVEREIGN RATINGS AND SOVEREIGN CEILINGS

The country rating acts in virtually all cases as a "sovereign ceiling" or cap on ratings of foreign-currency denominated securities of any entity that falls under the political control of a particular sovereign. In other words, in a country with an Aa2 sovereign ceiling, foreign-currency issues of a top-quality corporate issuer would be rated Aa2, even if the issuer's domestic-currency bonds are rated Aaa.

Moody's particular concern with foreign currency debt parallels what economists call "transfer risk" — that is, the probability that a borrower facing the obligation to make a payment in foreign currency might not be able to convert its own domestic-currency cash flow into the required foreign exchange in a timely fashion. Such transfer risk may occur, for example, because of a liquidity crisis in the international currency markets.

The ceiling role of sovereign ratings derives partly from the fact that all payments of foreign currency must pass through the control mechanisms of the country's central bank. In addition, the central government has the authority in an emergency to require that all foreign-currency earnings of enterprises or public-sector entities be brought back under centralised allocation if the situation should require drastic action. Central banks also have legal authority to impose direct controls on funds flowing in or out of the nation.

In addition to foreign exchange controls, governments have other powers that may serve directly to limit the ability of borrowers within their borders to meet debt payments. For example, the legal powers of the government can force all companies to surrender a share of profits, or they may freeze access to bank deposits, or impose restrictions on external transactions, among many other possible actions.

In a broader context, the sovereign's ultimate control over private sector borrowers can also be seen as one part of the sovereign's overall role as provider of the economic, social, political, diplomatic, regulatory and other conditions conducive to the national welfare — which, for modern states includes an international perception of creditworthiness.

Short of an explicit government guarantee, the creditworthiness of individual borrowers within a nation thus depends on a variety of factors which only the sovereign can provide. These include such conditions as fair and stable regulations for the issuer's industry, an equitable legal structure for the settlement of disputes, a political structure that suits the attitudes and demands of the nation's population while avoiding political upheaval, provision of a national infrastructure, allocation of resources, or fiscal and monetary policy that is conducive to the issuer's economic performance. Such "services" (or indirect "sovereign supports") are ultimately critical for the ability of any issuer domiciled in the nation to generate sufficient cash to pay its debts or to maintain sufficient asset values, liquidity, and other debtholder protections.

As a consequence, the rating process for a foreign-currency issue of any issuer can be divided into two stages. First, the issuer is evaluated for inherent credit quality (ie, credit quality in its own currency). Second, if the resulting rating is higher than the sovereign's foreign-currency ceiling, the ceiling rating applies on the issuer's foreign currency debt; if it is lower, then the issuer's domestic currency rating would also apply to senior foreign-currency obligations. The same analytical procedure applies to all long or short-term foreign-currency debt, including, for example, bonds, commercial paper, and structured finance issues such as asset-backed securities.

The sovereign ceiling for bank deposit ratings is generally handled in the same fashion.

WHAT SOVEREIGN CREDIT RATING IS NOT

From Moody's perspective, the assessment of sovereign risk is intended to be no more than an evaluation of that country's foreign currency credit risk. Since it is a long-term assessment, the factors deemed important are not necessarily the political personalities of the day, quarterly balance of payments results, interest rate or exchange rate fluctuations, this year's scheduled amortisation, or even next year's annual budget. Although useful as indicators of potential changes in underlying trends, all of these factors are regarded as potentially transitory phenomena.

Moody's sovereign risk assessments involve an examination of the political system in each nation, but they should not be regarded as evaluations of the virtues of that nation's specific political ideology or leadership, except as such factors relate to the question of creditworthiness. For example, a country with a highly-centralised or "totalitarian" government could warrant a high credit assessment — provided, that is, that the government is stable, that there is reason to believe it will maintain its legitimacy, and that other positive factors are in place, such as strong export markets and an efficient economic structure for resource exploitation. By contrast, a country with a strong commitment to democracy and a free market economy could — from the narrow perspective of credit assessment — be regarded as a higher credit risk. This might be the case, for example, in a nation that lacked a strong political consensus as to how the nation's economy should be managed, or that did not have a continuing bureaucratic infrastructure keeping economic policies related to foreign export earnings amid the winds of political change.

Similarly, a sovereign credit risk opinion should be clearly differentiated from other categories of country risk opinion. The latter may be intended, for example, to forecast the risk that a foreign-owned mine or plant may be nationalised or the risk that a nation undergoing an international liquidity crisis may choose to cut off foreign currency transfers of foreign bank branches (even though it may continue to honour its own foreign debt servicing). In both cases, a host of political-economic factors would be analysed, but the conclusions could differ radically from those related to the nation's credit risk. Conceivably, for instance, a government could nationalise a company with strong export earnings in order to improve its foreign exchange position; however, a nation such as the Cayman Islands, with extensive international banking facilities, may be unable or unwilling to stop foreign exchange transfers on international banks, regardless of its own foreign currency position.

FUNDAMENTAL FOREIGN CURRENCY REPAYMENT RISKS

The analyst's first problem in assessing a nation's creditworthiness is that he or she faces an information overload. There are literally mountains of relevant political, economic, and sociological information, even with regard to countries such as the Soviet Union or The People's Republic of China, which until recently have been closed to most international research. A wealth of information is available from other in-country sources such as business or labour leaders, academics, private associations, and journalists, as well as from international organisations, such as the Organisation for Economic Cooperation and Development, or country experts at major universities. With no lack of raw data, the problem is to find a way to digest and fit that information into a series of likely socio-political outcomes that could eventually end in default on foreign debt. As anyone familiar with the social sciences knows, there is no agreed-upon conceptual framework for thinking about society, history, and political economy.

In sovereign analysis, as in the study of human affairs generally, rival perspectives never disappear into a consensus. Further, in contrast with the natural sciences, empirical observation of "facts" is not a means of settling disputed issues because the "facts" of history and human behaviour do not speak for themselves without interpretation — and rival interpretations derive from strongly differing presuppositions, values, and interests.

In light of this diversity of theories, the country risk analyst is best advised to take an eclectic approach, borrowing from a variety of traditions of thought and avoiding dogmatic limitation to a single one. In the following, we outline several schematic approaches used by Moody's, ranging from a broad mapping of the credit-related factors in the nation's social structure to a more specific analysis of financial statistics and forecasts.

STRUCTURES OF SOCIAL INTERACTION

The process begins with a wide-ranging analysis of the basic patterns of social interaction that characterise society within the nation. This analysis may involve use of a variety of traditional concepts — class, status hierarchy, interest group, etc. It is also important to understand the lines of conflict which run through the society. Some examples of these are the distribution of income and wealth; religious, ethnic, or linguistic differences; conflicts over lifestyle and ethical norms; or ideological splits reflected in struggles for control of institutions, including the state itself. Fundamentally, we try to understand all attempts to create or mobilise power, in whatever form it occurs.

Several other aspects of social-political structure should be mentioned. Human social groups often take an explicitly organisational form, and effective organisation can magnify many times the force thereby exerted in comparison with looser, more informal groupings. The strength of organisations such as labour unions, business federations, trade and professional associations, and single-issue political movements can be an important factor in economic outcomes.

Beyond the narrow dimension of government institutions, the analyst should examine the nation's overall political structure to determine how state power is achieved and retained, as well as the mechanisms for the transfer of power. A useful concept here is "legitimacy", or the underlying source of authority that sustains a particular type of regime. The analyst should try to understand the systematic belief patterns and habitual behaviours that create consent and willing subordination to that exercise of authority. Legitimacy can derive, for example, from traditional religion-based belief systems (such as the "divine right of kings") or from a modern "goal-directed rationality", by which the regime is widely accepted as the best available leader in the process of creating sustained economic expansion. In examining a particular country, we try to understand the sources of legitimacy that are operating and their degrees of stability.

There are also more narrowly-economic structures to be brought into play, such as the composition of production, the levels and types of technology incorporated into the productive apparatus, the regional location pattern of production, and the natural resources a country possesses, along with the cost requirements of exploiting them. Especially important is the institutional pattern of decision-making power with respect to economic policy. Examples of this are the degree of independence on critical monetary policies that the central bank has over the treasury of finance ministry, or the existence of special structures for consultation between government and labour market mobility, or social welfare policies.

Finally, there is another area of structural analysis — perhaps the most difficult to specify — that we can call the "psycho-cultural". This involves an examination of the deep-seated attitudes and norms that regulate everyday behaviour. Changes in this sphere can sometimes come suddenly and have strong effects on consumption patterns, work performance and productivity, and political party allegiance. In particular, evaluation of the likely response to programmes of economic retrenchment — often instituted in reaction to a build up in foreign debt — can depend in part on the degree to which habitual patterns of consumption and saving can be altered without provoking a sharp political counterreaction. Equally, changes in human fertility and other demographic variables can have important consequences for long-term shifts in the structure of production and imports.

SOCIAL ACTION

Structural analysis has the weakness that it can tend to be static — that is, a description of the balance of forces at a single moment in time. This weakness can only be overcome by maintaining constant awareness that social patterns are constantly evolving as they interact and that what we need most is an understanding of the dynamics of social change — how power is gained and lost, how consensus and conflict are created or destroyed, and how norms and values may change, sometimes gradually, sometimes suddenly. We also try to avoid the natural analytical tendency to present institutions as being more regular and predictable in their functioning than they really are.

The knowledge gained through the structural investigation outlined above is not an end in itself. Its purpose is to feed into an understanding of the actions taken by people — whether individually or in organisations — in response to changes in the social-economic structure of their nation. In recent times, research on social action has often emphasised the role of the state apparatus. In many ways, this is appropriate. During the 20th Century, the state has moved to the centre of social determination. Socio-economic life turns increasingly on the policy decisions of the state, particularly its economic organs, and on the responses and reactions of the other social actors. This focus on the state is true both in the developing countries, where the state acts as regulator and often as the engine of growth, and it is also true in the advanced industrial countries, where state redistribution of resources, subsidies, credit controls and general macroeconomic policy have dominating effects on the results achievable by private economic initiatives.

In analysing social actions (and reactions), the analyst strives to forecast the relative strength of the groups that would play a part in the state's policy arena, the positions they would be likely to take, and the probable outcome. Simultaneously, we assess non-governmental reactions to those policies. These could range from mere grumbling, laxity in implementation, or undermining (through, for instance, capital flight, tax evasion, "underground" or illegal activities), to organised protest, electoral upheaval, or — at the extreme — armed efforts to topple the regime in power. We also look for counterreactions on the part of the state because protest will bring about either a hardening or a modification of state policy.

All of the structural dimensions discussed earlier have to be synthesised into a picture of policy-reaction outcomes as they emerge in such arenas as the labour market (wage growth and employment changes), the government budget balance, the degree of fiscal stimulus or drag imparted to the economy, price movements, credit market variables such as interest rates and money supply, and the nation's international trade and payments balance.

At the risk of oversimplification, the understanding of the broad social trends gathered in the above analysis can shed light on several specific political and economic factors that may point to a nation's risk of default on its foreign currency debt.

POLITICAL DYNAMICS

As American money centre banks learned to their chagrin in the 1980s, financial ratios and econometric models alone can be very misleading indicators. Countries as diverse as Poland, Argentina, South Africa, and the Philippines have defaulted on or have rescheduled their foreign debts to commercial banks for other than strictly economic or financial reasons. Very often, an admixture of political, social, and cultural considerations — such as the inability to impose economic austerity, radical or political uprisings, or lack of public confidence in the central authorities — were at the root of a country's liquidity crisis.

The following questions may help the sovereign analyst to focus on these and other credit-related political fundamentals.

The Degree and Nature of Political Intrusiveness on the Cultivation of Wealth

A country's political system may enhance or detract from the nation's ability to create wealth and thus to maintain the strong export earnings needed to meet future foreign debt servicing. Are the laws and judicial system conducive to commerce, capital investment, and the release and protection of creative economic energies? Do fiscal or administrative rules hamper the efficient flow of goods, services, and capital? Are entrepreneurs in export industries rewarded or penalised by tax laws or cultural biases?

Depth and Experience of Government Bureaucrats

Obviously, inexperienced administrators and corrupt public officials can delay the most efficacious economic plans or reforms and undercut the noblest policy intentions, thus siphoning off resources from the legitimate pursuit of wealth creation. Are the middle levels of the government bureaucracy staffed with competent civil servants who can translate policy into action with a minimum of delay and drain on public resources? Among the political and managerial elite of a nation, are there well-trained and experienced technocrats who are adept at managing internal and external debt?

Political Intrusiveness on Economic Management

Extensive or unwarranted involvement of political considerations in the management process can lead to a failure to meet debt-servicing obligations. How politicised are key agencies of the government? Can the central bank, for example, act independently of the political process, or is it a tool of partisan decision-makers? How entrenched and immobile are budgetary expenditures for political constituencies and favoured groups? Where it exists, how severe a drain on resources is pre-election vote-buying or pump priming?

Political Links With Foreign Partners

Membership of regional organisations such as the European Community or the Association of South East Asian Nations or bodies that imply a certain economic status (such as the OECD or the Commonwealth countries) may provide a cushion of support in times of stress and a commonality of interest in general policy matters. Are there political factors that create ties of alliance with the major industrial powers and that would offer a safety net in the form of continued access to funds when other sources are closed off?

Past Behaviour Under Stress

Are the nation's institutions responsive to challenges, resilient to shocks, and flexible under pressure? How have authorities managed existing debt obligations in both favourable and unfavourable economic circumstances? Have they been able, under adverse conditions, to draw up and implement a coherent programme of economic restraint, perhaps including higher taxes and lower spending? Have strongly entrenched groups with political clout been able to reverse or water down austerity plans, undermining their sustainability?

Regime Legitimacy

Is the political system under fundamental stress from severely disaffected groups? Are the laws of the land being questioned? Would a change in government bring to power a set of leaders with a different political philosophy or a new strategy of economic development that could undermine investor confidence and upset policy continuity? Would a change of regime bring to power exponents of debt repudiation?

ECONOMIC FUNDAMENTALS

Ultimately, a sovereign's ability to repay its debts, including foreign-currency debt securities, depends on the country's wealth. In the domestic economy, through the proper mix of human ingenuity, natural resources, land, and capital, the nation must generate enough growth and employment to match population increases as well as to supply operating revenues to the government through taxes. Not to do so will necessitate unending deficits financing, primarily through the issuance of domestic bond debt, but also through external borrowing if attractive terms are available. In the external sector, the country must be able — through the sale of goods and services on world markets — to earn enough foreign exchange to buy necessary imports and have enough remaining to repay outstanding debt and maintain an adequate level of reserves. If a positive balance does not obtain in the external accounts, then further borrowing will be required, thus increasing the nation's international debt burden.

Some countries in the early stages of economic development may find themselves chronically in deficit on their current account balance and therefore have a growing mountain of external debt. The United States, for example, imported capital from Europe in the 19th Century to finance its expanding infrastructure. A wide variety of countries are now in a similar situation. There is nothing inherently wrong with this, provided the country's export capacity grows at a pace that meets both debt-servicing requirements and other demands for foreign exchange. However, should debt-servicing requirements overwhelm the country's other foreign exchange needs, then the question arises as to how far the nation is willing or able to go to reshape its internal and external accounts to accommodate lenders.

The Nation's Resources

Debt payments must in the final analysis derive from a nation's accumulated wealth, which may be measured in terms of its natural resources, labour supply and capital. What kinds of natural resources can the nation draw upon economically within its borders? How exploitable are newly-discovered reserves of these resources? What are the legal, economic, and political constraints to their exploitation? What bottlenecks in labour supply, labour skills, and labour motivation can be anticipated in the production of export goods and services? Are there any disincentives to labour mobility, such as taxation or occupational barriers? Finally, to what extent can capital for investment be generated locally? What is the historical savings rate, and what are the incentives to capital formation?

Resource Exploitation

All the ingredients for wealth generation can be present, but if their utilisation is not sustained or efficient, the domestic economy will fall short of its potential and will thereby exhibit a heightened vulnerability to interruption of debt repayments. What is the level of entrepreneurship in the society, and is it encouraged? Do bureaucracy and regulation, both private and public, stifle efficiency? Do controls, subsidies, and tariffs distort the efficient flow of resources? Is there a black market, a parallel market, or an underground economy of significant size, which indicates the misallocation of resources? Is technology developed indigenously or imported? What are the political barriers to gains in industrial and agricultural efficiency? Does organized labour have the power to "veto" improvements in employment and wage-setting practices? Are there other factors that could inhibit the competitiveness of specific product segments in the nation's major overseas markets?

Quality of National Economic Management

In virtually all cases, this is one of the most critical variables in sovereign risk assessment, because it can affect the level of external debt that a nation undertakes as well as foreign perceptions of confidence in the national authorities. Obviously, the quality of national management depends greatly on the political and social factors mentioned above. From an economic perspective, analysts may also need to assess whether the officials in charge of economic management are prepared to recognize and respond to both economic and financial problems in a timely manner. How well have they dealt with economic cycles and crises in the past? Do they communicate policies and intentions clearly to relevant domestic and foreign constituencies? Is fiscal policy — including taxes, spending, and national budget deficit levels — under control? Are national monetary policies (money supply and deficit financing) rational and consistent? Are they sending the correct and appropriate signals with regard to the crucial prices in the economy: interest rates, foreign exchange rates, wages, utility rates, and prices at the farm gate, mine mouth, and well head?

Structural Dependencies on Export/Import Sectors

Dependencies on certain export products or markets — or, conversely, on certain imports — can prevent the domestic economy from re-configuring to meet internal or external challenges. These dependencies can also inhibit the economy's ability to develop a greater capacity to compete in world markets. Is the economy locked into a set of exports, such as mineral commodities, which are subject to worldwide swings in price, thereby causing a highly-variable and unpredictable cash flow from external earnings? Are markets for exported materials subject to protectionism? Is the economy dependent on a relatively fixed state of imported goods or services that are difficult to alter without upsetting the flow of inputs necessary for re-export products? Is there a lack of self-sufficiency in hydrocarbons such that the next rapid upward ratcheting of international oil prices could cause major disruption in the economy?

Export Mix

What are the current sources of the nation's foreign exchange earnings? How cyclical and reliable are they? Is there heavy dependence on any one or two major sources? What is the country's competitive position in world markets for its mix of exports? Is it gaining or losing world market share? Is the nation a high or a low-cost producer? Do import volumes shrink when the prices of imported items increase in local currency terms, or are certain imports so essential and irreplaceable to the local economy that their volume changes little with price increases?

International Capital Flows

Capital flows in and out of the nation need to be analysed to understand the nature of a country's accumulation of obligations, in debt or equity terms, to the outside world. Is imported capital used to finance foreign exchange-generating projects or non-productive conspicuous consumption? Do a country's rules facilitate or hinder capital inflows? What are the levels of autonomous lending and private transfers? In the other direction, is capital flowing out of the country to increase the foreign asset base, or is it fleeing controls and political instability? The size of the "net errors and omissions" line in the balance of payments accounts is usually an indicator of just such unrecorded capital flows.

Austerity Programmes

A nation's ability to implement and sustain an effective austerity programme is an important indicator of how well a nation can respond to difficulties in its external accounts. Will such a programme be introduced in time to prevent serious deterioration in the accounts and in the confidence of foreign markets? How long can the programme be maintained in the face of growing political pressures by entrenched interest groups, such as farms, urban consumers, industrial labour, or civil servants? Will the tough economic adjustments — often involving higher taxes and higher prices for food, transportation, capital, and other necessities — cause a political backlash which jeopardises the government's standing?

DEFINING EXTERNAL DEBT

In all sovereign risk analysis, it is of prime importance to specify the nature and extent of the external debt burden weighing on the country's financial position. This is so because it is plausible to presume that the higher the relative burden of debt that a country is faced with, the greater will be the probability of a situation arising in which servicing of the debt is interrupted. Moody's begins by looking at the grand total of all the liabilities of a nation to the rest of the world but then proceeds to distinguish among types of liability by risk level, in order to generate a series of debt totals from the broadest to the narrowest.

First of all, we distinguish between two alternative senses of the word "external" — one which depends on currency differences and the other on the residence status of the lender. If the latter criterion is used, then we add together all liabilities to non-residents of the country, regardless of whether these are payable in domestic or foreign currency. On the other hand, if the criterion is the presence of an obligation to pay foreign currency (regardless of where the creditor resides), all foreign-currency obligations are added together, whether they are to foreign or local lenders (perhaps to the local branch of a foreign bank). Obviously, the difference can be very great. The United States, for example, has a rather small foreign-currency debt (mostly owed by corporations and agencies in the Euromarket). But, including obligations to non-residents in US dollars, it is one of the largest debtors in the world.

Because the balance of payments accounts of countries are kept on a residence basis, it is common for most debt ratios to be defined in that way. We believe, however, that a foreign-currency definition is to be preferred, because governments can, if necessary, meet their local currency obligations through taxation or money creation. Additionally, it should be remembered that servicing a domestic-currency obligation places no direct pressure on the value of the country's currency in the foreign exchange markets.

Moody's also attaches a lower risk weight to two other types of liabilities: direct investment and foreign ownership of shares in companies. Both create a profit stream that is payable in domestic currency only; unlike the fixed charges associated with debt instruments, both pay a profit only if the activities being financed are successful.

The highest risk element of external debt thus comprises the liabilities of a country payable in foreign currencies. Although Moody's pays careful attention to the range of possible debt measures for each country, this one is regarded as the most significant since it indicates the direct foreign currency call on the central bank. That call can theoretically be met from four sources:

- the country's own foreign currency reserves;

- its power to appropriate foreign currency assets of individuals or enterprises;

- its access to additional credit in the currencies demanded; and

- its current foreign-currency earnings from exports of goods and services.

Note that liabilities of the country as a whole are being counted, not just those of the government. This is because private-sector liabilities in foreign currency can — and most likely will — become an obligation of the central bank in a debt crisis, as we have seen recently in several Latin American countries. Whether the private sector borrows overseas or not ultimately depends on policy decisions of the government that affect interest rates and the country's exchange rate so that the mix of public-sector versus private-sector borrowing is a variable that is subject to policy discretion. What counts is the total size of the nation's current account deficit and the degree to which it is financed by adding to the outstanding stock of national foreign-currency debt.

As discussed below under the title "Liberalised capital flows and sovereign risk in the OECD nations," the liberalisation of cross-border borrowing and lending, especially between the developed nations, and the consequent privatisation of debt flows does not remove the sovereign risks. In fact, it makes the nation's total debt burden more difficult to measure; and it may reduce the sovereign's ability to manage its credit status.

NET DEBT

In a separate calculation, Moody's also credits some of the county's foreign assets against its liabilities to derive a limited net debt figure. One common procedure in the sovereign analysis field is to subtract total liabilities to non-residents from total claim on them to give what is known as the net investment position. This, however, mixes debt and equity elements while it ignores currency distinctions and is not very informative, for the reasons explained above. Also, private overseas assets cannot easily be accessed by the government, short of total political expropriation.

A more common procedure is to subtract official foreign exchange reserves (with or without gold holdings) from gross debt. This is typically done because reserves generally consist of liquid assets, but, for a variety of reasons, this procedure distorts the use of debt ratios for country comparisons. In some cases, for example, the reserves may include claims on countries with debt-servicing difficulties. Reserves, moreover, are held primarily to iron out very short-term speculative attacks on the currency and are not available for normal debt servicing. Also, a country may have access to short-term funding from other central banks or even directly from the credit markets, which can be suitable alternative to actual reserves. Taking these and other factors into account, Moody's pays closest attention to a gross debt number that is netted for the short-term liquid interbank claims of the banking system only.

COMPARATIVE DEBT BURDEN

The next technical step is to normalise the absolute debt numbers such that they can be compared across countries. There are two widely-used means for doing this:

- dividing external debt by Gross Domestic Product (GDP); and

- dividing external debt by total exports of goods and services, including earnings on the country's foreign assets and net unilateral transfers (when positive).

Which method gives an accurate ranking of countries? The answer, unfortunately, is both and neither.

Consider two countries ("X" and "Y"). X is large (GDP = 1,000) but is relatively closed, in the sense that exports of goods and services comprise only 20% of GDP (200). Y is smaller (GDP = 200), but much more open to trade with the rest of the world — exports comprise 50% of GDP (100). Now assume X has an external debt of 300 while Y's is 100. What do our debt ratios look like?

	X	Y
Debt/GDP	30%	50%
Debt/exports	150%	100%

Measured in relation to GDP, Y is the more indebted country, while, relative to exports, X takes the prize. Which ratio is correct?

The debt/GDP ratio is clearly favourable to relatively closed economies such as the United States, Brazil, Australia, Spain, and Italy; while the debt/export ratio would be biased in favour of more open economies such as Norway, Ireland, Belgium, Portugal and South Korea. Many economists would argue that openness is a strength both in the general process of economic development and, more specifically, in the ability to adjust to demand or price shocks coming from the external environment. The pre-existing export orientation of the open economies may make it easier for them to shift productive resources into the sectors producing internationally-traded goods. This is, indeed, a good argument in favour of the superior value of the debt/export ratio.

On the other hand, countries that are already very open may have little potential for further expansion of exports. It may be difficult for them to get expansion of foreign sales at the margin, but large closed economies tend to have tremendous capacity for shifting resources into sectors that will generate foreign-currency receipts.

What is really at issue in the interpretation of debt ratios is the long-term adjustment capacity of the economy, which cannot be summarised by any single ratio or even by a set of ratios. Calculating both ratios is a useful starting point in order to delineate the magnitude of the debt burden, as long as the above-mentioned technical difficulties are taken into account. However, it does not take us very far into the detailed judgements that need to be made about what a socio-economic system is capable of and willing to undertake in order to control the growth of external debt. As we have emphasised elsewhere, the debt-rating process cannot be ratio-driven because the ratios are based on past experience, and they provide only a glimmering of guidance in forecasting the future.

INTERPRETING ECONOMIC STATISTICS

The same analytical pitfalls appear as the analyst attempts to interpret the variety of secondary measures of creditworthiness that are available. A country's current account, for example, is often regarded as the "bottom line" of its transactions with the rest of the world. If it is in deficit for any given year, the nation's current account necessarily has to be covered by an outflow of reserves or an inflow of capital from abroad. The inflow could be in the form of direct investment or borrowing. For a corporation, the former would be labelled "equity", and the latter "fixed income." The borrowing, of course, represents more of a burden for the receiver of the funds.

By the same token, a long-term forecast of the country's current account outlook (combined with estimates of future inward investment) would seem to be a powerful tool for evaluating the country's future availability of foreign exchange — and thus its credit strength. The problem is that current account balances are notoriously difficult to forecast. Reasonable estimates of the direction of the future developments can only be made through a careful analysis of the fundamental factors that will drive changes in the current account over time, such as export competitiveness, worldwide capacity utilisation in the country's main exports, labour policies, and terms of trade. Moreover, these changes may come about in surprisingly short order, rendering past statistics meaningless. In many countries, for example, policy initiatives have proven successful, resulting in a quick turnaround of a disadvantaged trade position. An austerity programme, possibly implemented by a devaluation of the nation's currency, can be helpful in both limiting the demand for imports by cutting consumption and by boosting exports after wages have been lowered in export industries.

Even an indicator that is very popular with country-risk analysts — import coverage — cannot be used without a judgemental evaluation. The ratio measures the number of months that a country could cover its imports out of current reserves. However, some highly-creditworthy countries show up at the bottom of the list.

On each of the three dozen countries rated, *Moody's Sovereign Credit Reports* present the financial statistics most commonly used by country risk analysts internationally. (See Figure 6.2 for a sample front-page from *Moody's Sovereign Credit Reports,* along with definitions of key ratios and forecasts presented.) In all such reports, statistical trends for the country being analysed are compared with medians for a relevant group of peer countries — the composition of which will change according to the relevance for the country concerned. For example, in the case of Denmark, an OECD comparator group is used; in the case of Hungary, 14 advanced developing countries compose the comparator group.

Needless to say, these statistics must be interpreted carefully in the context of the major short and long-term dynamics that will drive the nation's foreign-currency default risk over the long-term, as summarised in the opinion on page one and in the more detailed write-up inside on key political, economic, and other credit-related factors.

FORECASTING OUTCOMES

In the final stage of analysis, the analyst's task is to judge the effects that broad trends in social action will have on known economic relationships over the near and long term.

For example, a nation's current-account balance is known to depend on:

- relative demand pressure at home and in foreign markets;
- relative cost movements among the country and its trading rivals and customers; and
- changes in exchange rates.

Financing of the nation's deficit — if it exists — can come from:

- foreign willingness to add to domestic-currency holdings;

- inflows of funds to direct investment in plant equipment; or

- adding to foreign-currency debt.

Each of these elements can be traced back to the structural and behavioural determinants already described and interpreted. Since each causal factor is predictable not with certainty but only over a range of degrees of confidence, a set of scenarios results, each of which contains a certain subjective probability weight. Ultimately, what is sought is a forecast of the probabilities of a variety of plausible "worst-case" or crisis scenarios. The higher the statistical weight ascribed to potential crises, the lower the risk rating should be on the scale compared to other countries.

This necessitates one more analytical task — that of creating a narrative version of plausible crisis scenario. How exactly could Country X, with its given socio-economic structures, debt structure, policy parameters and action-reaction mechanisms, get into financial trouble so serious that it would lead to a risk, however small, of default on an external obligation?

SHORT-TERM DEBT AND SUPPORT MECHANISMS

In addition to all that we have discussed so far, the analyst assesses the extent and nature of the nation's short-term debt as well as its access to financial supports capable of preventing temporary shocks from escalating into a full-blown monetary crisis.

Short-term debt (debts that matures in less than one year), can be the obligations of the government or private companies through commercial paper or deposit markets. However, it is more commonly the result of financing external needs throughout the banking system. In many countries, banks have taken on short-term foreign-currency liabilities far in excess of their foreign assets, and then they have passed the proceeds to public and private domestic borrowers, sometimes creating a maturity mismatch in the process.

The debt-servicing capacity of a country with large short-term debt is much more vulnerable to destabilising capital flows than countries with less short-term debt. If an expectation of the depreciation of a country's currency arises for any reason (political turmoil, suspicions about the probity of economic policy, publicity about deteriorating external accounts, etc), massive speculative short-term capital outflows can emerge. Banks can cut their exposure more readily than in the case of long-term assets. Sudden swings in capital flows contribute to, or further, loss of confidence, making it difficult for any debtor to refinance their short-term obligations.

Thus, the sovereign is left with one of two unpalatable options: devaluation, perhaps large-scale, or a drawdown from foreign-exchange reserves. If, on top of the short-term pressure, a poor maturity-profile exists on long-term debt, such that a bunching of principal repayments coincides in time with the exchange-market crisis, an even more difficult situation would arise. In such cases, reorganisation or rescheduling of debt may be required. Therefore, the existence of financial support mechanisms to provide guaranteed funding to ride through short-term disturbances is always a relevant consideration for sovereign analysts. This support can come from swap lines with other governments, financing from international organisations such as the IMF and BIS, and from regional groupings like the European Monetary System.

Consequently, in evaluating country creditworthiness, account should be taken not only of the long-term structural trends but also of the presence or absence of short-term debt and access to financial support and buffering mechanisms capable of arresting a crisis situation in its early stages.

See Table 6.1 for a listing of Moody's sovereign credit ratings as of January 1991. Figures 6.1a and 6.1b summarise how the analytical approach described above resulted in credit opinions on two very different nations, Hungary and the Kingdom of Denmark. Figure 6.2 defines the key statistical data presented on the front page of these and other sovereign credit reports published by Moody's.

SUBNATIONAL GOVERNMENTS

Moody's ratings of bonds issued by subnational governmental entities outside the United States has expanded in recent years. Subnational refers to any issuer that is a political subdivision of a nation, including provinces, regions, states, and local authorities and municipalities, or an enterprise owned by a subnational entity whose debt-servicing capacity is directly dependent on or strongly supported by its links to that governmental unit. Influenced by

deregulation, financial engineering, and internationalisation of capital markets, those borrowers are shifting the blend of funding sources, issuing bonds directly to meet a larger portion of their financing needs.

There are three key aspects in rating the credit quality of debt issued by subnational government borrowers:

- the actual and potential revenue sources available to the borrower;

- the ability of the borrower to make use of those revenue sources at its own initiative and in an effective manner;

- and the political climate affecting public finance decisions.

In analysing the real potential financial resources of a subnational, a profile of the issuer's economic base is constructed. Various measures of the structure of the local economy (for example, the degree of diversification in the economic structure), employment and unemployment, and demographic trends provide a view on the resources available to the subnational government and give an indication of the demands for social services and infrastructure that the issuer could face in the future. The existing tax rates also measure the extent to which additional revenues could be extracted from the same tax base.

CONTROL OF FINANCIAL CONDITIONS

An issue of overriding concern in the credit quality of subnational government debt outside the United States is the relationship between the subnational government and the central government. The ability of a subnational government to control financial conditions is a key element in our rating analysis. In many countries, constraints on the subnational issuer's revenue-raising capacity may be imposed by the central government. However, those constraints may also be compensated by clearly defined and well-established mechanisms through which the central government can offer support for meeting debt-servicing obligations of subnational governmental borrowers, either explicitly or implicitly, conditionally or unconditionally.

Consideration is also given to the degree of flexibility that subnational authorities may have in controlling expenditures and revenues. Some proportion of any budget's expenditures is likely to be fixed, including the servicing of debt and other contractual obligations and contributions to employee pensions. How large a portion is important in determining how flexible the government can be in controlling expenditures.

THREE SUBNATIONAL EXAMPLES

Following is a brief illustration of how the structure governing relations between the central government and subnational governmental entities has influenced Moody's ratings in three different cases: the Commonwealth of Australia; the Federal Republic of Germany; and the Scandinavian countries of Denmark, Norway, and Sweden.

In Australia, the Commonwealth government is dominant over the states in virtually all legal, financial, political, and economic spheres. Economic and social conditions in the states are closely aligned as a result of (1) massive Commonwealth financial assistance to the states, (2) federal control over macroeconomic policy settings, as well as foreign borrowing, and (3) a national political philosophy of fiscal equalisation among the states.

As a result, there are only relatively narrow distinctions between ratings on the domestic currency debt issues of the different Australian states. However, divergent fiscal behaviour among the states, along with a lessening of central support, would open up wider distinctions.

Similarly, that the relationship between states and the central government in the Federal republic of Germany (FRG) creates potentially wide differences in credit risks. Provisions contained in the FRG's constitution establish the states' autonomy and independence from the central government and can outweigh the provision calling for homogeneous living conditions throughout the FRG. Also, revenue-sharing arrangements between the states and centre do not guarantee preservation of fiscal balances in each state and, by their nature, could be difficult to revise in a timely fashion. Moreover, the central government has somewhat limited control over state expenditures, and a provision exists in the FRG's constitution that limits borrowing to finance the state's investment only, not recurrent expenditures. This provision does not offer investors protection that debt-financed investments will generate adequate returns to provide revenues for debt service.

The central governments in Scandinavian countries impose debt limitations on subsovereign governmental borrowers that are similar to that imposed by the central government on the states in the FRG. However, the Scandinavian cities and counties have greater flexibility in raising revenues than in the case of the German states. As of year-end 1990, that added flexibility was one of the major reasons why Moody's assigned ratings at the sovereign-ceiling level to debt issued by the city and county of Copenhagen in Denmark, by Stockholm and Gothenburg in Sweden, and by Oslo in Norway. (See the sample report on the City of Copenhagen, Figure 6.3.)

**Table 6.1. Moody's Sovereign Foreign-Currency Debt Ratings
25 January 1991**

	Long term	Short term
Australia	Aa2[1]	P-1
Austria	Aaa	P-1
Belgium	Aa1	P-1[2]
Brazil	B2	—
Canada	Aaa	P-1[2]
China (People's Republic of)	Baa1	—
Cyprus	—	P-1
Denmark	Aa1[1]	P-1
Finland	Aa1	P-1[2]
France	Aaa	P-1
Germany	Aaa[2]	P-1[2]
Greece	Baa1	—
Hong Kong	A3[1,2]	P-1[2]
Hungary	Ba1	—
Iceland	A2	P-1
India	Baa1	P-2[2]
Ireland	Aa3	P-1
Italy	Aaa	P-1
Japan	Aaa	P-1[2]
Korea	A1	—
Luxembourg	Aaa[2]	P-1[2]
Malaysia	A3	—
Mexico	Ba2	—
Netherlands	Aaa[2]	P-1[2]
New Zealand	Aa3	P-1
Norway	Aa1[1]	P-1
Portugal	A1	—
Singapore	Aa3[2]	P-1[2]
Spain	Aa2	P-1
Sweden	Aa1	P-1
Switzerland	Aaa[2]	P-1[2]
Thailand	A2	P-1
United Kingdom	Aaa	P-1[2]
United States	Aaa	P-1[2]
Venezuela	Ba3	—

Figure 6.1a. Sample Credit Opinion on the Republic of Hungary
January 1991

Ratings			Contacts	
Category	Moody's Rating		Analyst	Phone
Long-Term Bonds & Notes	Ba1		Guillermo Estebanez	(212) 553-1653
			Tulio P. Vera	
			David H. Levey	

☐ Foreign Currency Debt/GDP (%)   **☐ Foreign Currency Debt/Exports (%)**

Debt and Trade Data for Hungary Pertain to Convertible Currencies.

Domestic Statistics (%)

Hungary (Statistics in bold type)
Median for Advanced Developing Countries (ADC) (Statistics in light type)

	1986		1987		1988		1989		E1990		F1991
Real GDP Growth Rate	**1.5**	5.1	**4.0**	5.2	**4.6**	6.8	**-0.9**	4.1	**-2.0**	—	**-1.5**
Inflation (GDP Deflator)	**3.7**	2.9	**8.3**	8.7	**9.8**	12.2	**22.2**	11.0	**25.0**	—	**33.0**
Indust. Prod. (1985=100)	**101.9**	110.3	**105.6**	119.6	**105.2**	130.0	**101.6**	130.0	—	—	—
Investment/GDP	**26.9**	19.4	**26.7**	19.7	**25.4**	20.4	**25.9**	20.5	**27.0**	—	**27.8**

International Statistics (%)

☐ Hungary
Median for Advanced Developing Countries (ADC)

	1986		1987		1988		1989		E1990		F1991
Foreign Curr. Debt (US$ Bil.)	**16.9**	—	**19.6**	—	**19.6**	—	**20.6**	—	**20.5**	—	**21.4**
Foreign Curr. Debt/GDP	**71.2**	44.4	**75.0**	47.8	**70.2**	47.5	**71.3**	45.1	**63.2**	—	**59.7**
Debt Service Ratio	**74.8**	25.8	**50.1**	25.0	**42.5**	27.2	**38.3**	26.8	**41.1**	—	**42.1**
Foreign Curr. Debt/Exports	**-312.7**	267.7	**294.6**	259.4	**270.4**	255.6	**242.5**	235.0	**217.3**	—	**215.5**
Current Account Balance/GDP	**-2.0**	0.2	**0.1**	0.1	**1.7**	-1.5	**1.9**	-2.0	**5.4**	—	**3.0**
Trade Balance/GDP	**-5.7**	3.0	**-3.3**	3.4	**-2.8**	1.0	**-5.1**	1.3	**0.2**	—	**-2.0**

☐ Data are for Convertible Currencies.   ☐ (Interest + Currently Maturing Long-Term Debt)/Exports.

Opinion

Moody's assigns a Ba1 country rating to Hungary. All rated debt has been issued by the Republic of Hungary through the Magyar Nemzeti Bank (National Bank of Hungary). The rating, at the top of the speculative grade, reflects the view that Hungary will face significant difficulties servicing its foreign debt. Hungary's bonds — which represent only 10% of total debt — are likely to be serviced punctually.

Hungary had experimented with economic reform before the end of the communist regime. The country had gone farther than the rest of Eastern Europe in dismantling subsidies, in allowing a degree of market-determined pricing, and in moving towards positive real interest rates.

A key factor behind the speculative-grade rating is Hungary's high external debt burden, a legacy of the communist regime that will seriously constrain the new government's effort towards a market economy. This move would entail substantial recourse to external credit under most scenarios. Unfortunately, Hungary has to cope also with the effects of the breakdown of the COMECON trading system and — at least temporarily — with high oil prices. The willingness of private lenders to roll over their exposure to Hungary has eroded. Notwithstanding the likelihood of higher levels of lending by official sources, Hungary's debt position will therefore be quite fragile in the near future. Another major policy challenge will be to dismantle the state sector — or at least to keep it under financial control — in order to make room for private initiative. Soft controls of the large state sector in a contest of political liberalization can lead to entrenched inflationary pressures. However, the emergence of a market economy will require stable macroeconomic conditions, if the private sector is to commit permanent resources and open up new sectors of activity.

Figure 6.1b. Sample Credit Opinion on the Kingdom of Denmark
January 1991

Ratings			Contacts	

Category	Moody's Rating		Analyst	Phone
Foreign Currency Bonds & Notes	Aa1		Uwe Bott	(212) 553-1653
Domestic Currency Bonds & Notes	Aaa		Guillermo Estebanez	
Short Term	P-1		David H. Levey	

Guaranteed Entities

Foreign Currency Bonds & Notes	Aa1
Domestic Currency Bonds & Notes	Aaa

Foreign Currency Debt/GDP (%) | **□ Foreign Currency Debt/Exports (%)**

① Exports of goods and services and, when positive, net transfers.

Domestic Statistics (%)

Denmark (Statistics in bold type)
OECD Median (Statistics in light type)

	1986		1987		1988		1989		E1990		F1991
General Government Bal/GDP	**3.4**	-3.2	**2.5**	-2.2	**0.3**	-2.1	**-0.4**	-1.7	**-0.5**	-1.1	**0.0**
Real GDP Growth Rate	**3.6**	2.5	**-0.6**	3.3	**-0.2**	3.8	**1.1**	3.4	**1.1**	2.9	**1.6**
Inflation (GDP Deflator)	**4.6**	4.5	**5.0**	4.9	**4.2**	4.2	**4.4**	4.6	**3.5**	4.3	**4.3**
Unemployment Rate	**7.8**	7.6	**7.8**	7.3	**8.6**	6.6	**9.3**	6.2	**9.6**	6.5	**9.7**
Investment/GDP	**20.8**	19.9	**19.1**	19.9	**18.4**	20.2	**18.1**	20.6	**18.0**	20.8	**18.5**
Short-Term Interest Rate[2]	**9.1**	6.0	**9.9**	5.8	**8.2**	6.7	**9.5**	8.1	**10.8**	7.5	**11.0**

② Right column, Auction Average of 3-month US Treasury bills.

International Statistics (%)

Denmark
OECD Median

	1986		1987		1988		1989		E1990		F1991
Foreign Curr. Debt (US$ Bil.)	**49.7**	–	**62.6**	–	**61.9**	–	**67.0**	–	**74.2**	–	**69.6**
Foreign Curr. Debt/GDP	**60.4**	36.4	**61.5**	35.8	**57.5**	32.5	**64.0**	33.2	**57.9**	31.0	**50.6**
Debt Service Ratio ③	**57.2**	20.6	**47.4**	19.3	**45.6**	18.8	**40.7**	16.6	**40.2**	16.8	**36.9**
Foreign Curr. Debt/Exports	**167.6**	109.0	**172.9**	107.1	**153.0**	95.1	**156.6**	95.0	**160.3**	93.5	**138.9**
Current Account Balance/GDP	**-5.5**	0.0	**-2.9**	-0.8	**-1.6**	-1.3	**-1.3**	-1.3	**0.0**	-1.3	**0.2**
Trade Balance/GDP	**-1.3**	-0.3	**0.8**	-0.2	**1.7**	-0.3	**2.3**	-0.2	**3.1**	0.0	**3.6**

³ (Interest + Currently Maturing Long-Term Debt)/Exports.

Opinion

Moody's rates the foreign currency obligations of the Kingdom of Denmark Aa1. Since 1989, Danish creditworthiness has gotten stronger. The current account deficit of the country continued to decline to 1.3% of GDP in 1989. For 1990 the gap may have turned into a small surplus. Weak imports and a relatively healthy export performance, especially in the services sector, are the two main factors behind Denmark's improved credits. The relative wage-cost differential between Denmark and its main trading partners improved 2% this year, but the Danish krone appreciated, pushing net competitiveness down by 4%. The government is obviously willing to continue its tight fiscal policies and called for new elections because of a budget dispute. A major objective of all political parties is a reduction of the country's dependence on foreign debt. However, this process should be expected to be a gradual one.

As of January 1, 1990, the government lowered company tax rates from 50% to 40%. The budget proposal for 1991 provides for a reduction of marginal income tax rates from 68% to 62%. Meanwhile, the revenue shortfall is to be compensated by a broadening of the tax base. A continued drag on the budget as well as on the country's social fabric is the chronically high unemployment rate — a percentage likely to increase in 1991. Unemployment benefits are very generous in Denmark so high unemployment severely weakens efforts to balance the budget.

Debt ratios should be somewhat lower because of improvements in the current account deficit. Denmark's membership in the European Community and in the European Monetary System (EMS), its proximity to a reunited, import-hungry Germany, and strong links to other Scandinavian countries are all significant factors that reduce the risk of balance-of-payments difficulties.

Figure 6.2. Moody's Sovereign Credit Research Guide

Ratings	Contacts
Category Moody's Rating Long- and short-term ratings on the sovereign's securities are shown here.	Analyst Phone Members of the research team at Moody's are available to respond to subscriber inquiries on sovereign or sovereign-related issues.

Relative Size of Foreign Currency Debt Graphs

The year-end stock of total debt payable in foreign currencies by all entities of the country. The currency-of-denomination criterion is preferred over a residency criterion as it more accurately reflects the truly external burden on the sovereign itself and its need to mobilize external resources. Graphed here is this debt both as a percentage of annual gross domestic product and as a percentage of current-account receipts, for both the sovereign and the median country of the comparison group.

Comparative Domestic Statistics

General Gov't. Bal./GDP: Aggregate financial budget balance for general government (central, state, and local) on a national accounts basis, as a percentage of GDP.
Real GDP Growth Rate: The percentage change from the previous year in the economy's total domestic production of goods and services at constant prices. Data are based on the UN System of National Accounts (SNA) methodology.
GDP Deflator: Percentage change over the previous year in the economy's implicit aggregate price index. As the Ratio of nominal GDP to real GDP, the deflator is the broadest measure of inflation.
Unemployment Rate: Percent of the labor force that is unemployed. Definitions vary across countries, and thus rates may not be strictly comparable.
Investment Rate: Private and public expenditure on gross fixed capital formation as a proportion of GDP drawn from the country's national accounts.
Short-Term Interest Rate: The annual average market yield for three-month US Treasury Bills is shown along with the most comparable short-term rate for the sovereign.

Comparative International Statistics

Foreign Curr. Debt/GDP: (See description above).
Debt Service Ratio: Ratio of foreign-currency debt service payments to the value of current receipts from abroad. The numerator is defined as the sum of all interest plus principal paid on long-term foreign-currency debt in a particular year: the denominator is the value of all receipts from exports of goods and services, foreign investment income, and, when positive, net private transfers. The ratio provides a relative indication of the amount of foreign exchange receipts absorbed by servicing of the external debt.
Foreign Curr. Debt/Exports: (See above description).
Current Account Balance/GDP: The balance on the current account of the balance of payments as a percentage of nominal GDP. The current account balance is the measure of all export receipts on goods, services, and unilateral transactions, minus the corresponding import payments. The deficit on the current account is an indicator of the country's net external financing requirements for a particular year.
Trade Balance/GDP: The balance of merchandise exports minus merchandise imports as a percentage of nominal GDP.

Opinion

This summary explains the basis for the sovereign rating and assesses the key elements supporting Moody's rating judgment. It highlights the fundamental political and economic factors affecting the sovereign's creditworthiness and outlook.

Figure 6.3. Sample Credit Opinion on the City of Copenhagen
January 1991

Ratings

Category	Moody's Rating
Long-Term Bonds & Notes	Aa1

Contacts

Analyst	Phone
Uwe Bott	(212) 553-1653
Tulio P. Vera	
David H. Levey	

1 **Operating Balance (%)**

1 Operating balance as % of operating revenues.

Debt/Revenues (%)

Operating Statistics

	1 1986	1987	1988	1989	B1990
Population (Mil.)	473.0	469.7	468.7	467.9	466.7
Operating Bal./Oper. Rev. (%)	1.8	-0.6	1.7	1.3	0.6
2 Budget Balance/Revenues (%)	-3.9	-4.7	-4.2	-4.6	-2.6
Operating Ratio (%)	98.2	100.6	98.3	98.7	99.4
Interest Coverage (X)	1.60	0.80	1.59	1.52	1.76

1 For the twelve months ended December 31. 2 All figures are net of borrowings.

Debt Statistics

	1 1986	1987	1988	1989	B1990
Total Funded Debt (DKr Bil.)	6.56	7.32	7.90	7.95	8.50
Debt Per Capita (DKr Thou.)	13.9	15.6	16.9	17.0	18.2
Debt/Revenues (%)	22.7	23.0	23.8	22.2	23.6
Debt/Own-Tax Cap. (%)	62.1	65.8	65.2	58.9	62.5
Debt Serv./Oper. Rev. (%)	5.5	4.6	4.5	5.3	2.9

1 As of December 31.

Opinion

Moody's Aa1 rating on the long-term debt of the city of Copenhagen is based on the city's strong financial position, the stable economic prospects for the country and the region, and the solid institutional framework in which Danish localities operate.

As a municipality, the city has the constitutional independence to manage its own affairs under the supervision of the Ministry of the Interior. The city borrows to finance capital expenditures, the only outlay that municipalitites can finance through debt in Denmark. The debt burden represents about 23% of the city's total revenues. The bulk of investment is in the city-owned utilities which will generate future income through charges.

Both the population of Copenhagen and its share of gross income represent about 9% of the country's total. The main source of revenue are taxes — income, capital gains, property, and other types of taxation — which contributed to 40% of outlays budgeted for 1989. Social and health services represent the largest expenditure item (about 52% of total current outlays in 89), with the central government covering about half of this item through grants.

Economic growth is expected to be slow in Denmark over the medium term, and this will slow down growth in the city's tax base. However, the capacity of local governments to incur debt is limited and, in addition, the central government will continue to impose tight fiscal guidelines on local authorities. Consequently, the city's financial position is expected to remain strong.

Copenhagen is the capital of Denmark and has population of approximately 468,000. It is the nation's financial and industrial center and an important commercial and shipping hub in Scandinavia.

Chapter 7

S.J. Rundt & Associates

S.J. Rundt & Associates, a consulting group that soon will be 50 years old, provides a systematic evaluation of country risk conducted by specialized analysts around the world. The company's mission statement reads: "S.J. Rundt & Associates, Inc. was established in New York in 1952 to provide a seamlessly integrated range of services delivering independent, unbiased, practical and business-oriented country risk information. In the pursuit of this objective we will at all times put our clients and subscribers first and regard their interests as our own. We will present the truth as we see it, without pulling punches or attempting to be 'politically correct.' We will safeguard our integrity and independence at all cost and endeavor to give our customers the best, most carefully researched information and advice possible."

S.J. Rundt & Associates provides a systematic evaluation of country risk based on three equally weighted composite indicators: Socio-Political Risk, Domestic Economic Risk, and External Accounts Risk. Averaging these three creates an overall country risk score.

Within each measure of risk, a set of variables is rated by S.J Rundt's country specialists on a 1-10 scale, with one representing the best circumstance and 10 the worst. S. J. Rundt's assessments are derived through an attribute model rather than from political decision forecasts. The Socio-Political Risk category assesses 12 variables, including stability of the government, social stability, and government intervention in the economy. In addition to the score assigned, each variable is given a weight signifying its contribution to overall Socio-Political Risk.

Domestic Economic Risk includes 16 variables, weighted as in Socio-Political Risk and graded on a 1-10 scale. External Accounts Risk also includes 16 variables and is similarly scored.

S.J. Rundt's country reports present the individual as well as the combined scores for all 44 variables, plus written descriptions of current circumstances, important economic indicators, and key trends.

S.J. Rundt & Associates have spent half a century building up and strengthening a global network of associates with many areas of knowledge and expertise. This network allows them to gather and evaluate information "on the ground" and then put it in a global context. The company's approach to country risk assessment is based on the belief that in a world in which markets are becoming increasingly integrated, yet where the only constant is change, business and finance must take a global approach to succeed.

With this premise in mind, country risk analysis is useful only if it is

- Neutral -- showing opportunities as well as dangers
- Objective -- free of bias or preconceived notions
- Relevant -- purpose-, company-, even product-specific.

"Neutral" means that the company never relies on in-country sources of information alone, but compares such assessments routinely with the views of outside observers. "Objective" means that the country assignments of supervising analysts are changed from time to time to prevent biases from developing. "Relevant" means that the many variables tracked in the analyses are given different weights depending on the purpose of the risk assessment, whether it is for long-term, direct investment, medium-term bank loans or bond offerings, or short-term export credit. The risks faced by, say, a mining operation in Bolivia are, after all, quite different from those incurred by a distributor in Brazil, or those confronted by an export credit manager contemplating open-account sales to South Africa.

S.J. Rundt & Associates provides a systematic evaluation of country risk based on three weighted composite indicators. These are Socio-Political Risk, Domestic Economic Risk, and External Accounts Risk. The three are averaged to create an overall country risk score.

Within each measure of risk, a set of variables is rated by S.J Rundt's country specialists on a 1-10 scale, with one representing the best circumstance and 10 the worst. The Socio-Political Risk category assesses 12 variables (with 24 sub-categories), including stability of the government, social stability, and government intervention in the economy. In addition to the score assigned, each variable is given a weight signifying its contribution to overall Socio-Political Risk.

The weight, a largely judgmental element, is determined by (a) the purpose of the assessment, (b) whether it is short-, medium-, or long-term risk that is being gauged, and (c) the country under review. Even within a given country, the importance of individual variables and, thus, the weights can change from time to time, depending on social, political, general economic and external-accounts developments.

Domestic Economic Risk includes 16 variables (with 32 subcategories), weighted as in Socio-Political Risk and graded on a 1-10 scale. External Accounts Risk also includes 16 variables (with 32 sub-categories) and is similarly scored. S.J. Rundt's country reports present the individual as well as the combined scores for all 44 dominant variables, plus written descriptions of current circumstances, important economic indicators, and key trends.

The evaluations and forecasts contained in Rundt publications are by necessity general, requiring subscribers to draw their own conclusions as to what the predicted developments and trends mean for their companies' specific operations. In ad-hoc assessments and consulting assignments, these conclusions are being drawn for the client. S.J. Rundt & Associates use three types of publications for conveying their risk reviews to subscribers and clients, all of which are available in print, on disk, by e-mail or on-line:

(1) The Financial Executive's Country Risk Alert
A unique combination of forecasts and survey results geared specifically to short-term trade credit, published three times a year, with intermittent country updates, for 82 countries. The review contains a single numerical risk rating for each country as well as a bias (positive, stable or negative). The heaviest weights in the assessment are attributed to factors influencing short-term hard-currency cash-flow prospects.

(2) World Risk Analysis Package
For companies with ongoing business interests in the countries under review. These are comprehensive risk reports with an at-a-glance overview, a thorough textual analysis of political and economic developments, charts to summarize key macro-economic trends, two pages of statistical information, and a risk rating model that can be customized for specific needs.

(3) Rundt's World Business Intelligence
Published weekly, RWBI covers around 180 countries, some 60 of major international importance regularly, another 80 of lesser significance roughly once every month, and a further 40 when major trends warrant it.

Samples of each of these publications can be found below.

COUNTRY RISK ALERT
ECUADOR

11/02/00

Credit Risk Rating: 8
Bias: Stable

FORECAST FOR THE NEXT 12 MONTHS

INTERNAL FINANCIAL:

The economy has begun to grow again. Real GDP in the second quarter of this year was up 2.4% from January-March, which was more than four times the 0.5% advance registered in the first quarter. Six of the nine sectors showed gains (agriculture, manufacturing, electricity, construction, trade, transportation and domestic services), while only three decreased (oil, financial and government services). The expansion apparently continued in the third quarter, as industrial production in August was 5.5% higher than in July. The Central Bank's anticipation of 1.9% growth for all of 2000 is probably on the conservative side. Inflation has started to come under control (the government is probably correct with its assumption that it will not surpass 80% this year, against the IMF's prediction of 100.6%), unemployment is declining, and capital flight has partially reversed as some companies and individuals are bringing funds back home. Short-term interest rates are down to about one-tenth of what they were just before the dollarization process began.

EXTERNAL FINANCIAL:

Thanks to the high price of oil, the foreign trade balance is now in good shape. It improved to a surplus of USD 1,566 million last year from a deficit of USD 995 million in 1998. In January-August 2000, the surplus increased to USD 1,313 million from one of USD 1,016 million in the first eight months of 1999, as exports jumped by 13.5% (with oil revenues having more than doubled to USD 1,616 million from USD 805 million) while imports rose only 4.8%. The favorable trend will persist so long as international market quotations for hydrocarbons stay near present levels. Official international monetary reserves were last reported by the CB at USD 1,185 million, up from USD 872 million at the start of 2000. A bond swap completed in late August a debt restructuring deal agreed upon with the London Club of commercial creditors and will take around USD 1.5 billion off Ecuador's debt servicing burden over the next five years. It paved the way for a similar accord with the Paris Club of government creditors, consolidating USD 880 million of outstanding foreign obligations until the end of April 2001. The Paris Club has agreed in principle to review the case for a further restructuring of IOUs due to be repaid after April 30,2001. All of this is encouraging, but it does not mean that the nation is totally out of the woods yet. Much remains to be done to consolidate the economic stabilization, kindle growth sufficient to break decisively with a generation of stagnation, and guarantee a constant source of dollars (since Ecuador can no longer print money for the liquidity it needs).

POLITICAL:

Congress ended a month of chaos in late-August with the election of a new legislative chief, the Right-wing Deputy Hugo Quevedo, who won the contest with help from Center-Left Congressmen and pledged to work with President Noboa. But the legislature remains deeply divided and it remains to be seen to what extent the body will now support government initiatives. Socio-political stability also continues to be threatened by the interventionist military, by restive indigenous groups, and by the risk of a spill-over of violence from neighboring Colombia. On the other hand, Pres. Noboa has proven to be a more decisive and adept political leader than most pundits were initially willing to give him credit for, and his approval ratings in public opinion polls have been rising.

CURRENCY:

The sucre is now pegged to the U.S. dollar at ECS 25,000 per USD 1. The CB retains limited powers to act as a lender of last resort to troubled banks.

REGULATORY:

The completion of dollarization by the September 9 deadline came off without a major hitch. All wages and prices must now be set in U.S. currency and only a few (dollar-backed) sucres can still change hands for very small transactions.

(Ecuador continued)

CREDIT INSURANCE:	Eximbank in the U.S. does not cover transactions with public sector entities, but has – selective – facilities for private sector short- and medium-term transactions. Discretionary limits under Short Term Insurance Policies are withdrawn, but while Exim is closed for certain routine trade finance transactions, it will consider certain structured financing arrangements. Cover in Europe is even more difficult to get. But this may now change in the not too distant future, considering that Ecuador has obtained a restructuring of Paris Club and private bond debt.
TRADING TERMS:	There are companies dealing with Ecuador on open account, but only with affiliates and even traditionally reliable distributors are still having problems making payment on time. Many Ecuadorean importers remain unable to open letters of credit and we expect this situation to improve only slowly. In dealing with those who can, one finds that, under certain conditions, some U.S. banks have windows open to confirm such L/Cs, but these facilities are rare and expensive. With traditionally good customers, U.S. exporters are in many instances doing business on terms, but usually one shipment at a time. Credit lines have been slashed. Local currency liquidity remains extremely tight and customer requests for moratoria or debt rescheduling deals are plentiful. Many exporters now say they want to receive payment on previous shipments and clear the funds before releasing new orders. Exporters to Ecuador will be well advised to remain cautious for a while longer.

PERFORMANCE IN THE LAST FOUR MONTHS

General Condition: Very Poor
Exporters Using L/C: 66.6%, with 98.4% of all business (including PIA)
Trends In Credit Terms: More liberal: 0.0%; Less liberal: 32.4 %; No change, 67.6%
Average DSO Over 90 Days

Collection Experience Past Four Months			Risk Perception Past Four Months		
Payment Made	**Commercial Buyers**	**Government Buyers**	**Risk Seen As**	**Commercial Transactions**	**Government Transactions**
Prompt	5.5%	0.0%	Minimal	0.0%	0.0%
In 10-30 days	4.1%	12.2%	Low	0.0%	0.0%
In 31-60 days	46.6%	40.7%	Moderate	15.1%	0.0%
In 61-90 days	20.5%	33.8%	High	47.5%	55.5%
Over 90 days	23.3%	13.3%	Extremely High	37.4%	44.5%

INTERNAL COMPANY TRADE & COLLECTION EXPERIENCE
(indicate your in-house experience below)

A) Shipping Terms	B) Payment Delays
B) Payment/Credit Terms	D) Overall Impressions

COLOMBIA

11/02/00

Credit Risk Rating: 7
Bias: Stable

FORECAST FOR THE NEXT 12 MONTHS

INTERNAL FINANCIAL:

BoP results (q.v., below), are the only encouraging feature of an economy that shows increasing difficulty in trying to pull out of last year's sharp recession. Real GDP, to be sure, gained by 3.53% in the second quarter (y/y), and the advance for the first semester of 2000 was clocked at 2.86%, fueled by headway in manufacturing and agriculture. But the increment is measured against dismal year-ago results and there are aspects in the second-quarter rise that bode ill for the future: Financial services declined by 8.89%, for instance, and the key mining sector, which includes the oil industry, reported a 6.4% drop in output. GDP contracted by 4.48% in all of last year, Colombia's worst recession on record. The government has targeted 3.0% growth for 2000, but it is becoming increasingly less likely that this goal will be hit. Consumer prices rose 0.43% in September, to where they were 7.73% higher than at the outset of this year. In the 12 months through September, their escalation came to 9.20%, meaning that inflation is fast approaching the 10% limit the government has set for calendar 2000. There is, thus, no room for the Central Bank to ease monetary policy and lower interest rates, especially not as the peso has been showing vulnerability in the exchange markets. Also, the Finance Ministry, heralding a period of "sweat and tears," has just introduced to Congress a budget for 2001 that seeks to raise the equivalent of USD 1.6 billion (1.8% of GDP) in extra revenues with higher and expanded taxes.

EXTERNAL FINANCIAL:

Thanks to high world market prices for oil, Colombia's principal legal source of foreign exchange earnings, overall exports in January-August were 19% ahead of the like 1999 period, at USD 8.61 billion (measured fob). The value of shipments abroad of crude jumped by 45.5% in the period, to USD 3.1 billion. Thus, even though revenues from coffee exports dropped by more than 20% in the eight-month span, to USD 699.1 million (partly due to a smaller harvest and in part because of lower prices), and although inflows of direct foreign investment plunged 54% in January-June to just USD 362 million from USD 800 million in the first half of 1999, official international monetary reserves climbed to USD 8,838.4 million as of October 11 from USD 8,107 million at the start of this year.

POLITICAL:

The international press has made much of the fact that the October 29 municipal and provincial elections, in which voters cast their ballots for governors, mayors, provincial delegates and town councilors in all 1,093 municipalities, were, for the most part, peaceful. What the media appear to have overlooked is that the rebel groups on both sides of the political spectrum, which back in 1997 wanted to prevent elections from being held (and failed in this endeavor), are now much more interested in manipulating the outcome. Close to 40 candidates for mayor, council representation and other offices were killed in the runup to the balloting. More than 50 were kidnapped and many others withdrew their candidacy under death threats or were told in no uncertain terms what their fate would be if, once elected, they failed to serve the interests of whichever group of insurgents holds local sway.

CURRENCY:

The peso has been falling from one low to another as investors worry about lack of progress in the peace process, the government's weakness, and vulnerabilities in the economy and the banking system. For the foreseeable future, the currency's travails are likely to persist.

REGULATORY:

The much-touted "Plan Colombia," to which the U.S. is contributing USD 1.3 billion, already shows signs of falling apart. Viewed primarily as a (politically motivated) U.S. scheme to fight drug production, it is not attracting the financial assistance from other industrial nations that the government hoped for. Nor has the administration itself made much progress in detailing the various social aspects of the scheme.

(Colombia continued)

CREDIT INSURANCE: Insurance from public and private sector sources should remain readily available in Europe. The U.S. Eximbank is open for public as well as private sector buyers for all maturities, without special restrictions. Some European public agencies have special conditions. The private sector offers cover mainly for short-term transactions, but also for long-term deals if these involve priority goods. Secure terms are preferred, and buyer credit-worthiness is being carefully reviewed. Many insurers demand Central Bank L/Cs or guarantees.

TRADING TERMS: Open account remains among the most used term, and we see nothing in recent developments that should dissuade exporters from staying with liberal terms so long as the customer is well known, reliable and creditworthy. Customer risks have been growing sharply, however, both those arising from economic conditions that weaken the position of non-financial companies and those affecting the banking system. Some exporters have all along insisted on draft terms (letras de cambio, pagares), conceivably even with avals, to obtain a negotiable instrument that is easier to discount or present to a local court for collection than an open account position. Lately, there has also been a marked increase in the use of L/Cs. Exporters should review their exposure carefully at this stage, since in the short-term, at least, conditions will not improve markedly and since the bank problems loom large. This is also how our (unchanged) risk rating should be interpreted. It has a stable bias because of the absence of a serious near-term threat to Colombia's international liquidity position, but with a grade of 7 that indicates high customer and bank risks.

PERFORMANCE IN THE LAST FOUR MONTHS

General Condition: Fair to poor
Exporters Using L/C: 23.7%, with 45.6% of all business
Trends In Credit Terms: More liberal: 0.0%; Less liberal: 11.7%; No change, 88.3%
Average DSO 56 Days

	Collection Experience Past Four Months			Risk Perception Past Four Months	
Payment Made	**Commercial Buyers**	**Government Buyers**	**Risk Seen As**	**Commercial Transactions**	**Government Transactions**
Prompt	13.7%	9.4%	Minimal	3.3%	7.7%
In 10-30 days	24.6%	27.5%	Low	16.6%	16.3%
In 31-60 days	48.3%	46.3%	Moderate	60.4%	59.2%
In 61-90 days	11.0%	16.8%	High	12.0%	12.9%
Over 90 days	2.4%	0.0%	Extremely High	7.7%	3.9%

INTERNAL COMPANY TRADE & COLLECTION EXPERIENCE
(indicate your in-house experience below)

C) Shipping Terms	B) Payment Delays
D) Payment/Credit Terms	D) Overall Impressions

WORLD RISK ANALYSIS PACKAGE
MEXICO

INDEX

WORLD RISK ANALYSIS PACKAGE

MEXICO

Date of latest revision: August 7, 2000

GENERIC RISKS	Latest Score	5/07/00 Score	1/06/00 Score	7/25/99 Score	5/17/99 Score	1/18/98 Score
Socio-Political	3.52	3.72	3.54	4.08	3.82	3.70
Domestic-Economic	3.42	3.36	3.54	4.25	4.43	5.11
External Accounts	4.03	4.04	4.16	3.84	4.09	4.63
Index Average	3.66	3.71	3.75	4.06	4.11	4.48

Note: Lowest Risk = 1, Highest Risk = 10

SPECIFIC RISKS	High 10	9	8	7	6	5	4	3	2	Low 1
Currency Risk					0	X				
Bank Loan Problems							0	X		
Supplier Credit Risk									0X	
Expropriation										0X

Note: X = Current Outlook; 0 = 4 Months Ago

KEY TRENDS IN THE NEXT 12 MONTHS

The outcome of the July 2 elections was in many respects the best that could be hoped for. While President-Elect Vicente Fox of the previously opposition National Action Party faces an uphill fight with his ambitious program, he is trying hard to enlist all of the country's political groups in what he hopes will be a government of "harmony and inclusion." He is fortunate in that the economic fundamentals are now excellent. Real GDP growth will be 6.0%-6.5% this year, slowing in the second semester without any serious cave-in. Inflation will come close to the official target of 9.3% after 12.3% in 1999. Despite a continued widening of the foreign trade deficit, the external accounts are and will remain in good shape. Inflows of foreign direct investment are likely to surge. The country not only can now service its external debt with ease but is making substantial prepayments to ease its load. The large cushion of "rainy day" credits built up last year has been expanded and extended so that it can be drawn on until end-2001, in the event of an emergency. Against this backdrop, the peso will most likely remain stronger than the authorities would like it, but the CB will prevent an excessive appreciation.

SOCIO-POLITICAL OUTLOOK

The outcome of the July 2 elections – a surprisingly large victory for PAN candidate Vicente Fox in the presidential contest and a demotion in congress of the long-dominant PRI – was the best one could have hoped for. Of all the possible results of the presidential and congressional balloting, a narrow victory by the Institutional Revolutionary Party or PRI – which has run the country autocratically since 1929, winning 14 elections in a row (most of them fixed) and providing a succession of 12 presidents – would probably have been the worst, since it would undoubtedly have triggered charges of fraud by the vanquished. A small-margined triumph by the National Action Party or PAN, linked to the little-known Green Party in Mr. Fox's Alliance for Change, would not have been much better, since it would have deprived the opposition of a clear mandate and would have made governing difficult for it.

A solid victory by the PRI and its candidate Francisco Labastida Ochoa would have been acceptable to the international business & financial communities, but it took a convincing win by Vicente Fox Quesada and his Alliance for Change to prove conclusively that reformers led by the outgoing President Ernesto Zedillo meant what they said when they insisted that they were out to turn their country into a real democracy. This will have a salutary effect not only on Mexico's relations with the United States and Canada, with which it is becoming ever more closely linked through the NAFTA accord, but also on the rest of Latin America, where Mexico, with its over 100 million people, is the largest and most populous of the Spanish-speaking nations.

A Victory With Qualifications

The elections were the cleanest in modern Mexican history. They were conducted and supervised by an electoral institute, the IFE, which for the first time was truly independent of the government. They gave Mr. Fox 42.82% of the vote, compared to 35.66% for Mr. Labastida. The Left-wing Cuauhtemoc Cardenas ran a poor third, with 16.55% of the ballots. But this is not to say that Mr. Fox, when he takes office on December 1, will have a free hand to do as he pleases. While the Alliance for Change bumped the PRI from first place in congress, gaining a two-point edge with 38.42% in the Senate and 38.49% in the House, it will not have an absolute majority. The new government will have to make deals in order to pass major legislation. Moreover, the PRI still rules in half of the nation's 32 states, even though the PAN won control of two significant ones in Central Mexico, Morelos and Guanajuato.

What to Expect From the Next Government

The PAN is a deeply conservative, Catholic and business-oriented party with Rightist roots, but its platform has been tempered in recent years, helping it to make growing inroads against the PRI. Mr. Fox, who turned 58 on election day and is a divorced father of four adopted children, proved to be a strong-willed, hard-driving and blunt-speaking candidate. During the campaign, he steered deliberately clear of any detailed definition of his plans, so much so that detractors called him "a question mark in boots," but he lost little time after the elections clarifying some of the issues on which he previously had appeared excessively vague.

Inter alia, Mr. Fox wants to rebuild the country's Federal law enforcement system, moving toward an American-style model of justice as a way to fight corruption. More specifically, he has promised to remove police functions from the highly politicized Interior Ministry and the Attorney General's office and establish a new, more professional Ministry of Security and Justice. He not only wants to maintain Mexico's close NAFTA relations with the United States but hopes to expand them in the direction of a much more ambitious common market in which migration problems and Customs disputes can be more easily resolved and – eventually – coordinated monetary policies can be established. Mr. Fox hopes for a sharp increase in the number of U.S. visas granted to Mexican nationals, which, coupled with disincentives against illegal emigration, is to help stanch the flow of undocumented Mexicans to the United States. He also expects to talk the U.S. into spending large amounts of money on infrastructure projects in Mexico. These, he says, are essential to expand the Mexican market.

Tax Reform

He has promised to present a budget and announce a Cabinet three months before taking office in December, which would be an unprecedented feat. The fiscal household plan is to include a reform aimed at broadening the tax base (currently, tax revenues are equivalent to only about 11% of GDP, against 21% in the U.S.) and increasing social spending. The budget must be presented to Congress in November, to be passed by December 15. Past governments routinely had difficulties meeting these deadlines and the legislature had to arrange for extraordinary emergency sessions to finish the job in an 11th-hour tug of war. How much better Mr. Fox will do remains to be seen.

The National Action Party will have only 208 seats in the 500-member Chamber of Deputies. So, the government will have to attract 43 additional votes to reach the required 251-vote majority. The PRI will have 209 seats and the PRD 53. In the 128-seat Senate, Mr. Fox's party will have 46 mandates, the PRI 60, the PRD 15, and small parties the rest. The "Greens" (PVEM), in alliance with Fox's PAN, will not be much help, especially as they don't even have the support of the country's main ecological groups. The PRD, mauled in the elections, has been hesitant to say anything positive about the President-Elect. The PRI is still reeling from the shock of its election loss and a couple of weeks of chaotic infighting during which the party's top leader, Dulce Maria Sauri, resigned her post, the presidential candidate Francisco Labastida Ochoa went into seclusion, several hardliners severely criticized President Ernesto Zedillo (breaking an age-old taboo) and at least three rival factions sought to gain control of the party.

Ms. Sauri was ultimately persuaded to remain in office for a few months while the PRI decides how to choose a replacement for her. But the party is only now beginning to pull itself together. It has to select legislative leaders for the new Congress that begins its session on September 1. It faces local elections in three states before the end of the year. And it has obviously not made up its mind yet about what posture it will adopt toward the PAN and Mr. Fox. The PRD, meanwhile, has released to the media a computer list of some 2,300 loans that were part of USD 1.5 billion in possibly illegal loans absorbed by the taxpayers as a result of the USD 100-billion bank bailout of 1994/95, an "indiscretion" that does not make life any easier for the incoming administration.

Government of Inclusion

Fox, however, is nothing like his predecessors with their presumption of king-like powers and their often regal arrogance. He comes from a business background and says that he intends to run his government like a business. A large part of his Cabinet is being picked by a team of executive recruiters rather than being established on the basis of the traditional crony system. In his evident pursuit of a meritocracy, Mr. Fox may well seek to attract people from the PRI as well as the PRD. He has also made (for Mexico highly unusual) overtures to the heads of these two parties, going so far as to apologize for some of his campaign remarks about them in an effort to create a climate of cooperation rather than confrontation – to form a government "of harmony, inclusion, agreement and consensus."

Tasks to Behold

To what extent he will succeed is, of course, still open to question. His plans are ambitious, to put it mildly. He expects to promote extensive reforms in the hitherto jealously guarded energy sector, although he does not seem eager to privatize Pemex. He hopes to open up both the electric power and petrochemical industries to private investment, plans that are fervently opposed by the unions. The President-Elect says he will seek to strengthen the authority of the Central Bank by giving it full control over the management of the peso's exchange rate (the widely respected incumbent CB Governor Guillermo Ortiz has already indicated that he will serve out his term, which extends through 2003). In fulfillment of his pledge to create "an economy with a human face" the President-Elect will aim to hike outlays from the public till that benefit poor Mexicans, but says that this will be done without disrupting public finances.

In fact, with 85%-90% of budgetary expenditures already pre-assigned and therefore non-discretionary, there is some risk that an administration under Fox will not take fiscal discipline quite as seriously as the outgoing Zedillo team has done. We find it somewhat disturbing that Mr. Luis Ernesto Derbez, who spent many years at the World Bank and now is one of the key men in Mr. Fox's transition team, proposes to improve the lot of Mexico's poor by raising taxes and channeling the extra money thus raised back through the bureaucracy, which supposedly will use it to increase social outlays and spending on infrastructure. But the financial markets are on the alert. They will quickly punish any deviation from the path of caution and put a swift end to any serious overspending.

A Better Guarantor of Continued Reform

None of the President-Elect's goals will be as easy to achieve in practice as they appear on paper. Moreover, Mr. Fox will be seriously challenged by long-standing problems against which Pres. Zedillo was unable to make much headway, including a yawning rich-poor gap that prevails throughout the nation, an especially pronounced one that exists between the wealthy North of the country and the backward South, a simmering rebel conflict in the southern state of Chiapas, powerful drug gangs, and rampant crime that has frayed the nation's social fabric.

At the end of the day, though, economic policy under President Fox will not be vastly different from what it would have been under the defeated Francisco Labastida. And Mr. Fox is a better guarantor of continued political reform. While his task as Mexico's first non-PRI Chief

Executive in 71 years will not be an easy one, the country will manage the transition well, helped by strong economic fundamentals.

DOMESTIC MARKET FORECAST

The economy has been forging ahead at a pretty much undiminished pace since it hit a real GDP growth rate of 7.9% in the first quarter of this year. Retail sales in May were 12.5% ahead of the like 1999 month, while wholesale turnover showed an increment of 12.0%. A new statistical gauge, the so-called Global Indicator of Economic Activity (INEGI), which is a fairly close proxy of gross domestic product (excluding only the fishing and forestry sectors), advanced by 8.5% in May (year-on-year). Most local economists expect real GDP figures for the second quarter to reflect growth of at least 6.2%, and we believe that this anticipation could be substantially underestimating the actual result.

Revival of Bank Lending?

Industrial production in the first five months of this year was up by 8.0% (y/y). Open unemployment declined to 2.11% of the labor force in June from 2.14% in May. Perhaps most importantly, after six years during which the battered banks had virtually no taste for expanding their lending to the corporate sector, the appear to have begun – gingerly – to increase their loan portfolios in April-June, a period during which Bancomer, for instance, showed an increase of 3.2% in its outstanding business loans, Banamex one of 7.0%, Banorte one of 7.0%, Santander Mexicano one of 15.6%, and Probursa one of 1.9%.

During the bank-lending drought, which began right after the 1994/95 crisis, department stores, appliance outlets and other retail establishments tried to fill the yawning gap in consumer credit availability, offering installment plans for major purchases. But they did not come close to making up for the banks, which – having been nearly buried by an avalanche of loan defaults in 1995 and 1996 – remained extremely tightfisted. Even now, lending from commercial banks to the private sector is still 9.8% lower than it was at mid-1999. The bank bailout program is far from complete and last month the head of the Institute For Protection of Bank Savings (IPAB, the body charged with sorting out the aftermath of the bailout), Vicente Corta, called it quits because of political pressure against his drive for greater transparency involving those who benefitted from the rescue. A full credit recovery, most analysts believe, is still a couple of years away. But at least a beginning seems to have been made.

Inflation Will Be Kept Under Control

Indeed, some economy watchers believe that Mexico is still at a real risk of overheating. Consumer prices rose 0.59% in June, to where they were 9.41% ahead of January 1.

Any continuation of this trend would make it impossible for the Central Bank to fulfill its vow of keeping inflation for 2000 as a whole at or below 9.3%, compared to 12.3% in 1999. Not willing to let itself be derailed, however, the CB tightened monetary policy on July 31 for the fourth time this year by raising to MXN 280 million from MXN 230 million the so-called "short," i.e., the amount by which it keeps local money markets short of liquidity every day. It also rolled out a new weapon in its anti-inflation arsenal last week by selling a first batch of

Monetary Regulatory Bonds (BREMS) to absorb money market liquidity and ratchet up interest rates as needed. Since monetary policy may not be sufficient by itself to dampen surging consumer demand, the Finance Ministry has let it be known that it stands ready to tighten the fiscal reins as well.

Withal, we feel fairly confident that inflation will be kept under control and will be near the official target by the end of this year. The economy will cool during the second semester, dampened by somewhat lower oil prices as well as slower growth in the United States, leaving average growth for 2000 at around 6%, with a further deceleration expected for 2001. But there will be no cave-in, in part because inflows of foreign investment into Mexico will stay strong.

EXTERNAL ACCOUNTS PROJECTIONS

Externally, Mexico faces a deterioration of its foreign trade balance this year which will get worse as oil prices decline and as the pace of the U.S. economy slackens. Including a preliminary deficit of USD 654 million in June, the country's merchandise trade balance was in the red by USD 2,801 million in January-June, for an increase in the shortfall by 27.3% compared to the first half of 1999. But these are not numbers the government needs to be overly concerned about. A big portion of the imports consists of capital goods that in time will help to strengthen the nation's export capacity. The country's earnings from petroleum exports will recede only gradually. The U.S. economy appears headed for a soft landing rather than a crash.

FDI Boom Ahead?

Foreign direct investment in Mexico, which offsets much of the red-ink spill in trade, increased 10.4% in the first four months of this year and will become even more buoyant now that the political uncertainties are out of the way. Many established multinationals, from Goodyear, Solectron and I.G. Electronics to Peugeot and Volkswagen, have plans to expand their commitment substantially. The influx could gain even more momentum if President-Elect Fox proved able to make good on his promise to accelerate privatization or, as he prefers to call it, "demonopolization." Back in 1997, Mexico took in a record USD 12.83 billion in foreign direct investment (FDI). The influx slowed to USD 11.311 billion in 1998 and then increased slightly to USD 11.568 billion in 1999. Mr. Fox wants to nearly double it to USD 20 billion per annum, and rightly so, since his goal of sustainable GDP growth of 7.0% yearly will not be achievable in the absence of a marked increase in the inflow of venture funds from abroad.

Such aspirations will look quite realistic if the President-Elect can deepen Mexico's ties with NAFTA, as he intends to do, and implements the free trade agreement with the European Union that the government signed in April this year. The latter pact, inked on the sidelines of an EU summit in Lisbon, is the most comprehensive accord of its kind ever negotiated by Brussels. It includes the gamut of trade in manufactured and agricultural goods and services as well as rules of origin, public procurement and dispute settlement mechanisms. Mexico's tariffs for industrial products from the EU would be eliminated by 2007, whereas Europe is expected to drop its duties by 2003.

Mexico also signed (in July) an agreement with the United States to cooperate more closely on anti-trust issues. Under the accord, each country agreed to notify the other of anti-trust enforcement actions that may affect it, to minimize any conflicts and consider the other country's interests during all phases of the enforcement action. The U.S. agreed to carefully consider requests from Mexico to take action against illegal contracts in the United States. Mexican authorities are to give equal consideration to requests for action from Washington. Both countries agreed to share information on enforcement policies and activities and pledged to consider coordinating enforcement activities. Each country, moreover, agreed to maintain the confidentiality of sensitive information provided by the other.

Strong FX Position

Mexico's official international monetary assets stood at a handsome USD 30,843 million on July 21. Measured as "international reserves," the kitty came to USD 31,825 million as of the same date. However, while back in 1994 the country had USD 33 billion in short-term, dollar-denominated debt, such obligations are now down to as little as USD 3 billion. Rather than having difficulties repaying what it owes abroad, Mexico recently incurred the wrath of Citibank by pre-paying USD 2.5 billion in loans and thus depriving the institution of hundreds of millions in interest. Mexico now has credibility in the eyes of the world and there is no risk of it slipping into international-liquidity difficulties.

The government not only announced last month that it has no intention of drawing on outstanding cash from its USD 4.1-billion stand-by facility with the IMF, but indicated that it was considering to make repayments to the tune of USD 3.6 billion ahead of schedule. It is also working on a scheme to retire USD 6.15 billion in Brady bond obligations through debt swaps (the total external public debt stood at USD 83,388 million at the end of March 2000). Moreover, the government has expanded as well as extended the USD 23.7-billion "emergency" financing program unveiled in June of last year. The package has been increased to USD 26.4 billion (including USD 19.74 billion in loan facilities from a variety of sources, plus USD 6.7 billion in rainy day credits from NAFTA partners) and can now be drawn on until the end of 2001, providing the incoming government a comfortable transition period on this front.

Peso Buoyancy

The favorable external-liquidity prospects have been reflected in the local financial markets ever since the election result has become known. The peso – which proved its resilience before, when it recuperated from levels below MXN 10:USD 1 hit during the Russian crisis in 1998 and from nadirs under 11:1 during the Brazil crisis in 1999 – is likely to exhibit considerable strength in the months ahead, although the Central Bank will take care not to let it climb too high for comfort, using interest rates and monetary policy rather than direct market intervention to curb its uptrend.

OUR FORECAST

Currency	8/02/00	End-Sep 2000	End-Dec 2000	End-Mar 2001	End-Jun 2001	End-Sep 2001
Mexican peso	9.3460	9.5000	9.8000	10.000	10.500	10.750

ECONOMIC INDICATORS A
(Compiled by S.J. Rundt & Associates, Inc.)

MEXICO	1993	1994	1995	1996	1997	1998	1999
REAL GDP (PCT CHG. OVER PREV. PERIOD	0.40	3.50	-6.20	5.10	7.10	4.80	3.70
EXCHANGE RATE (END OF PERIOD)	3.11	5.33	7.64	7.87	8.14	9.88	9.44
PCT CHG. FROM PREV. PERIOD	0.64	-41.65	-30.24	-2.92	-3.32	-17.61	4.66
GDS. EXPORTS: FOB (BLN US$)	51.89	60.88	79.54	96.00	110.43	117.50	136.70
GDS. IMPORTS: FOB (BLN US$)	65.37	79.35	72.45	89.47	109.81	125.24	142.06
TRADE BALANCE (BLN US$)	-13.48	-18.47	7.09	6.53	0.62	-7.74	-5.36
CUR. ACC. BOP (MLN US$)	-23400	-29662	-1576	-1923	-7449	-15786	-14013
OVERALL BOP (MLN US$)	7232	-17199	-16312	3863	13997	3193	17
TOTAL RESERVES NOT INCL. GOLD (BLN US$)	25.11	6.28	16.85	19.43	28.80	30.14	31.78
GOLD RESERVES (MLN. FINE TROY OUNZES)	0.48	0.43	0.51	0.26	0.19	0.24	0.15
IMPORT COVER RATIO *	4.61	0.95	2.79	2.61	3.15	2.89	2.68

EXCHANGE RATES ARE ADJUSTED FOR CURRENCY REFORM
* TOTAL NON-GOLD RESERVES DIVIDED BY AVERAGE MONTHLY IMPORTS (EXPRESSED IN MONTHS)

ECONOMIC INDICATORS B
(Compiled by S.J. Rundt & Associates, Inc.)

MEXICO	1993	1994	1995	1996	1997	1998	1999
CONSUMER PRICES (PCT CHG. YEAR ON YEAR)	9.80	7.00	51.97	27.70	15.72	18.61	12.32
WHOLESALE PRICES (PCT. CHG. YEAR ON YEAR)	8.40	6.79	39.15	36.30	18.51	19.41	12.47
IND. PRODUCTION (PCT. CHG. YEAR ON YEAR)	-1.50	4.68	-7.33	10.40	9.30	6.70	5.40

ECONOMIC INDICATORS C
FOREIGN DEBT PROFILE
(Source: World Bank, US$ mln)

MEXICO	1994	1995	1996	1997
DEBT OUTST.-ALL DEBTORS	140,006	166,104	157,125	149,690
DEBT OUTST.-LONG TERM	96,824	112,976	113,778	112,095
DEBT OUTST.-SHORT-TERM	39,323	37,300	30,068	28,507
DISBURSEMENTS-ALL CREDITORS	16,130	44,152	31,335	30,234
PRINCIPAL REPAYMENTS-ALL	12,706	15,679	29,064	28,795
INTEREST PAYMENTS-ALL DEBTORS	6,556	8,053	8,339	8,395

Economic Trends At a Glance

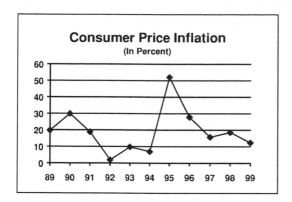

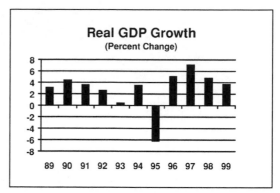

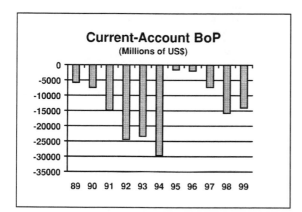

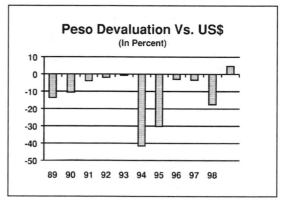

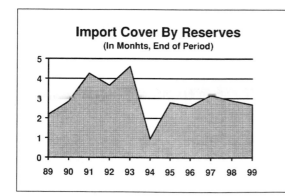

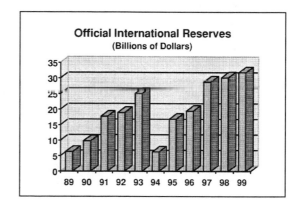

NUMERICAL RISK RATING
Graded from 1 (best) to 10 (worst)

COUNTRY: Mexico

General	Weight	Grade	Current Score	Previous Score
a. Threats to stability from the outside (1) none, to (10) major systemic disruption	0.04	1	0.04	0.04
b. Stability of the government (1) no change, to (10) collapse anticipated	0.08	4	0.32	0.56
c. Character of legal opposition (1) Constructive, to (10) obstructive	0.06	4	0.24	0.12
d. Influence of illegal opposition (1) non-existent, to (10) revolution imminent	0.08	2	0.16	0.16
e. Social stability (1) calm, to (10) state of turmoil	0.12	3	0.36	0.48
f. Labor-management relations (1) peaceful conditions, to (10) frequent strikes	0.12	6	0.72	0.60
g. Official treatment of foreign investment (1) encouraging, to (10) extensive limitations	0.08	2	0.16	0.16
h. Risk of expropriation without full compensation (1) virtually nil, to (10) very high	0.08	1	0.08	0.08
i. Attitude of local bureaucracy (1) fair and efficient, to (10) corrupt and difficult	0.08	6	0.48	0.48
j. Government intervention in the economy (1) minimal, to (10) pervasive	0.12	4	0.48	0.48
k. Government ownership of economic entities (1) very limited, to (10) extensive	0.06	4	0.24	0.24
Country-Specific: l. Economic well-being of the middle class (1) strong improvement, to (10) bad deterioration	0.08	3	0.24	0.32
TOTALS	1.00		3.52	3.72

NUMERICAL RISK RATING
Graded from 1 (best) to 10 (worst)

Domestic Economic Factors

General	Weight	Grade	Current Score	Previous Score
a. Overall condition of the economy, next 12 months (1) very good, to (10) severe problems	0.06	2	0.12	0.12
b. Real GDP growth, next 12 months (1) more than 10%, to (10) contraction over 10%	0.06	3	0.18	0.12
c. Expected real GDP growth by past standards (1) marked acceleration, to (10) sharp slow-down	0.08	6	0.48	0.32
d. Growth of industrial production, next 12 months (1) more than 10%, to (10) fall exceeding 10	0.06	2	0.12	0.18
e. Expansion of capital investment, next 12 months (1) over 10%, to (10) decline of over 10%	0.06	1	0.06	0.06
f. Expansion of consumer demand, next 12 months (1) over 10%, to (10) decline of over 10%	0.06	2	0.12	0.12
g. Current inflation (CPI or COL) (1) less than 5%, to (10) more than 100%	0.05	3	0.15	0.15
h. Trend in inflation, next 12 months (1) major slow-down, to (10) sharp acceleration	0.09	3	0.27	0.36
i. Availability/cost of local finance, next 12 months (1) abundant & inexpensive, to (10) extremely tight	0.09	4	0.36	0.45
j. Access to financing abroad, next 12 months (1) readily available, to (10) totally barred	0.08	3	0.24	0.24
k. Availability/cost of labor, next 12 months (1) ample pool, to (10) extreme scarcity	0.05	2	0.10	0.10
l. Monetary policy, next 12 months (1) very accommodative, to (10) extremely tight	0.06	7	0.42	0.36
m. Fiscal policy (1) highly stimulative, to (10) extremely tight	0.06	6	0.36	0.30
n. Level of taxation (1) relatively low, to (10) very steep	0.04	4	0.16	0.16
o. Trend in taxation (1) big cuts impending, to (10) stiff boosts likely	0.04	4	0.16	0.20
Country-specific p. Real growth of the tourist sector, next 12 months (1) more than 10%, to (10) decline of over 10%	0.06	2	0.12	0.12
TOTALS	1.00		3.42	3.36

NUMERICAL RISK RATING
Graded from 1 (best) to 10 (worst)

External-Accounts Factors:

General	Weight	Grade	Current Score	Previous Score
a. Overall condition of the external accounts (1) very good, to (10) severe liquidity strains	0.06	3	0.18	0.18
b. Trend in terms of trade, next 12 months (1) highly positive, to (10) highly adverse	0.06	6	0.36	0.30
c. Volume growth of exports, next 12 months (1) more than 10%, to (10) decline of over 5%	0.08	2	0.16	0.16
d. Volume growth of imports, next 12 months (1) more than 10%, to (10) decline exceeding 10	0.06	2	0.12	0.12
e. Trend of trade balance, next 12 months (1) sharp improvement, to (10) major worsening	0.06	6	0.36	0.36
f. Trend of current-account BoP, next 12 months (1) sharp improvement, to (10) major worsening	0.06	6	0.36	0.42
g. Official restrictions on capital movements (1) free movement, to (10) transfers prohibited	0.05	2	0.10	0.10
h. Trend in restrictions on capital movements (1) major easing, to (10) harsh tightening	0.09	5	0.45	0.45
i. Short-term capital flows, next 12 months (1) large net inflows, to (10) large net outflows	0.09	1	0.09	0.09
j. Volatility of capital flows (1) relatively low, to (10) very strong	0.08	6	0.48	0.40
k. Overall balance of payments, next 12 months (1) major improvement, to (10) serious worsening	0.05	3	0.15	0.20
l. Official restrictions on trade (1) open economy, to (10) closed economy	0.06	2	0.12	0.12
m. Trend in restrictions on trade, next 12 months (1) major easing, to (10) harsh tightening	0.06	5	0.30	0.30
n. Percent change in currency value, next 12 months (1) rise over 20% vs. $, to (10) fall of over 50%	0.04	6	0.24	0.28
o. Import coverage by gross reserves, next 12 months (1) over 12 months, to (10) less than one month	0.04	5	0.20	0.20
Country-specific p. Avg. oil prices next 12 months/past 12 months (1) rise of over 20%, to (10) decline of over 20%	0.06	6	0.36	0.36
TOTALS	1.00		4.03	4.04

Rundt's World Business Intelligence

No. 2,254   October 12, 2000

Trends You Should Know About

STORM CLOUDS OVER THE MIDDLE EAST

In light of the almost warlike eruption of violence between Palestinians and Israel in the past couple of weeks, which so far has seen more than 90 killed and thousands injured, it seems hard to believe that up until September 28, when Israeli Right-wing politician Ariel Sharon made his ill-fated visit to a site that is holy to Moslems as well as Jews (Jerusalem's Haram al-Sharif or Temple Mount), the two sides were still talking peace. Now, only 13 days later, this process is in tatters and world leaders, aware that "time is short and the stakes are high and the price of failure is more than any of us wants to pay" (to use the words of UN General Secretary Kofi Annan), are struggling to prevent an even worse blow-up.

One can argue that Sharon should not have made his provocative visit to Haram al-Sharif, especially not at so tricky and sensitive a point in time, or that the government of Prime Minister Ehud Barak should have found a way of preventing him from going where he was sure to stir up bitter emotions. One can also reason that the main responsibility for the clashes lies with Yasser Arafat, who instead of counseling restraint called for a general strike, closed schools to put children on the streets, and ordered clips of the intifada (an earlier uprising of Palestinians against Israel) to be broadcast on state television. Apologists for Arafat claim that he does not have sufficient control to have prevented the violence. In fact, though, his Tanzim militias and the Palestinian police could undoubtedly have stopped the rock-throwing youths, had they not been so busy turning their guns on Israeli soldiers.

There is not much to be gained at this point from trying to apportion blame. The immediate task at hand is clearly to stop the fighting, and -- luckily -- the clashes have diminished considerably as these lines are being written. In the short run, a decisive factor will be whether, and under what conditions, Israel can negotiate the release of its three soldiers taken hostage by Syrian-backed Hezbollah guerrillas in Lebanon. Hezbollah is said to be demanding, in return, the release of more than 15 of its members held captive in Israel, and while the Israelis would probably accept an exchange of this sort, it is by no means certain that Hezbollah would ultimately let go of the valuable bargaining chip it believes to be holding. Syria's influence on the terrorist organization is not nearly as clear as some commentators make it out to be. It has not been since Bashar al-Assad took over the Presidency from his late father.

Beyond the immediate concerns, the outlook is dire. Not only is bitterness between the Israelis and the Palestinians now once again running deep, but the televised pictures of the clashes that have been beamed around the globe have kindled outrage across the Arab world, making it extremely difficult even for moderate leaders such as Egypt's President Hosni Mubarak to argue for moderation. There have been anti-Israeli protests in Jordan, Syria, Lebanon and Yemen. Rather than supporting a new U.S.-led summit with the goal of restarting the peace process, Arab states are now planning a top-level meeting of their own in Cairo on October 21-22, at which it will be evident that the balance has shifted heavily from the moderates to the militants.

We said earlier in these Briefs that Arafat's Palestinian Authority at the Camp David talks, when it rejected extensive Israeli offers of concessions, made it plain for all to see that it had little real interest in peace. But with emotions in the region being what they are, the quest for peace is not a process that can simply be suspended in time, in expectation of a better negotiating climate. There is either progress or backsliding. The longer it takes for the talks to be resumed, the closer the region will skid toward hostilities on a much larger scale.

Argentina

As if the mood of consumers and investors in the Plata Republic were not already depressed enough, political uncertainty is now adding to the clouds over the outlook. Even if President de la Rua's governing alliance survives the resignation of Vice President Alvarez, which is not entirely certain yet, it has undoubtedly been weakened by the events of last week and the crisis could imperil the government's ability to pass key legislation.

In our issue of September 21 we stressed that -- while we find little to quibble with in the 10-month-old government's economic policies -- the coalition administration of President Fernando de la Rua has been singularly unsuccessful in getting public opinion on its side, leaving business and consumer confidence to ebb to a new low. With consumers keeping their purse strings tight and businesses not investing, the Argentine economy has been listless, showing little inclination to stage a strong rebound from last year's recession and appearing to be headed for a real GDP gain of less than 2% this year, rather than the 4%-5% officials had initially anticipated.

Needed all along has been a turn of events that would have strengthened the people's trust in the government's ability to lead the country out of stagnation. What Argentines got instead last week was a political crisis that has further undermined confidence and has tarnished the President's once impeccable image. Mr. de la Rua took office with a firm promise that he would jump-start the depressed economy and weed out corruption in the political system. The people and the local media granted him a fairly lengthy honeymoon following his election last October, but of late, reflecting the nation's growing impatience, the newspapers have been replete with headlines decrying what editorial writers called "paralysis" and "disorder" in the administration.

The Last Thing Argentina Needed

Things came to a head when a Federal judge began to investigate whether members of de la Rua's Cabinet had paid bribes to up to 11 senators to pass a new labor code last April. Vice President Carlos Alvarez, popularly known as "Chacho," who was widely regarded as "the most honest guy in the government" and who reportedly had helped to unearth evidence of the alleged bribes, called for "heads to roll" over the scandal and became ever more insistent in his open criticism of the administration's failed attempts to perk up business activity. When President de la Rua yielded to the clamoring, however, and announced a government revamp last week in which half the faces in his Cabinet changed, he strengthened the hand of Economy Minister Jose Luis Machinea and confirmed or promoted officials suspected of being involved up to their ears in the bribery affair.

The former Cabinet chief Rodolfo Terragano and Infrastructure Minister Nicolas Gallo both offered their resignations. De la Rua merged the Infrastructure Ministry into the Economy Ministry, giving Machinea more clout, even though he stripped the national tax bureau AFIP from the latter portfolio and put it under the purview of the Cabinet chief's office. The new Cabinet Chief, Chrystian Colombo, is a close ally of the President and was previously the head of the state-owned Banco Nacion. De la Rua's brother, Jorge, was promoted to Justice Minister from the post of presidential Chief of Staff. He replaces Ricardo Gil Lavedra, a highly respected judge.

A Questionable "Clean-up"

Rather than firing the two members of his official family who are said to be most directly implicated in the corruption scandal, the President confirmed Intelligence Chief Fernando de Santibanes in his job and moved Labor Minister Alberto Flamarique closer to his own office by making him his new Chief of Staff.

This blatant effort by de la Rua to surround himself with trusted and loyal aides in the confrontation with his Vice President so irked Alvarez that he quit. Soon afterwards, having held his post for just 24 hours, Alberto Flamarique also threw in the towel, telling reporters that he no longer felt able to continue his job under such pressure.

Added Complications

Admittedly, the Vice President's role in government is not so crucial as to make or break an administration. There have been instances before when a VP left and was not replaced, without much impact on the handling of government affairs, and President de la Rua may well decide to follow these precedents. Moreover, Alvarez, who defected from the Peronist camp in 1991 and formed the Left-leaning Frepaso alliance, was never entirely trusted by the conservative business sector and by the financial markets. But as the leader of Frepaso, he heads the junior coalition partner of de la Rua's Radicals in an arrangement that even before the eruption of last week's crisis forced the government to bargain for deals with smaller parties in order to muster a parliamentary majority.

Frepaso has 36 congressmen and women in the 257-member Chamber of Deputies. Were the Alliance to break up, as many local pundits are convinced it will, this would put the President and his new team in a precarious position. Alvarez and a number of Frepaso deputies indicated late last week that they would remain in the ruling coalition and that the party intends to retain all the executive positions it now holds, but this marriage of convenience, at the very least, has been badly shaken. Its longer-term survival, and with it the semblance of governability the President seeks to preserve, is no longer as unquestioned as it once was.

Investment Will Suffer Further

Only time will tell what effect this state of affairs will have on the administration's ability to push key economic legislation through parliament, starting with the budget for 2001. So, one should not take at face value Economy Minister Machinea's assurances that economic policies and their implementation will in no way be affected by Alvarez' resignation. In the financial markets, bonds fell and the Argentine bourse tumbled on the news, and it must be assumed that political uncertainty, added to the already prevailing sense of gloom, can only further damage investment.

Argentina has done remarkably well in meeting the IMF's prescriptions for fiscal restraint. The deficit of USD 3,815 million reported for this year's first nine months was clearly below the USD 3,850-million ceiling targeted by the Fund as part of its USD 7.2-billion loan program. Moreover, Minister Machinea lately has been hinting that the government will be in a position to lower taxes next year, reversing some of the hikes that have been widely blamed for stifling the recovery that seemed to get underway in late-1999. But the economy is so sluggish that consumer prices in September fell by 0.2%, to where they were 0.7% lower than 12 months earlier. (10/12/00)

Bolivia

It appears that the government is succeeding in putting an end to the widespread strikes and protests that have troubled the nation for the past three weeks, but the unrest has already left its mark on the economy, paring growth and boosting inflation. We also doubt that any social peace now engineered will hold for any length of time.

This small Andean country, with a population not much greater than that of New York City, has had its share of popular unrest over the years. Despite its remarkable wealth in natural resources it remains desperately poor and the restiveness of labor and peasant movements generally focuses on complaints over how the economy is being run.

The latest wave of such unrest is just now coming to an end, after a three-week period during which coca-growing peasant farmers and teachers were on a nation-side strike and set up extensive road blocks that prevented the movement of goods and people between the major cities. Toward the end, under pressure from the local business community which found the disturbances crippling, the government saw itself forced to plan for a major step-up of airlifts to overcome food shortages that had cropped up and was contemplating the declaration of a state of emergency.

By then, the situation had become so bad that housewives began threatening to loot grocery stores and businessmen in Santa Cruz warned that they would launch a tax boycott unless the government put a halt to the demonstrations, using whatever force necessary to reopen the roads. President Hugo Banzer, no doubt, contemplated the use of force, but he is still trying hard to live down his old reputation as a brutal dictator (which he was back in the 1970s).

Besides, with only two years left in his elected five-year term he is increasingly looking like a lame duck. His coalition government, in which half the Ministers are members of his Right-wing Democratic Nationalist Action Party while the others belong to the Social-Democrat Revolutionary Leftist Movement and the populist Civic Solidarity Union, is split on policy. And he has, presumably, not forgotten what happened earlier this year, in April, when the government under similar circumstances did impose a two-week long state of siege and the police went on strike.

Concessions Rather Than Force

This time around, the government agreed to a broad range of demands by the farmers to avert a collapse of its authority and prevent paralysis of the shaky economy. It promised to prop up corn prices, reverse a land titling process, and return water rights to the Indian peasants. It granted the striking teachers a USD 240-million bonus over the course of the next year, suspended coca eradication in the Yungas region, and offered indemnification to the families of those who were injured or killed in confrontations with the security forces. But by then, according to Economy Minister Jose Luis Lupo, Bolivia had suffered losses of at least USD 120 million in damaged roads, spoiled food, and missed exports.

Lasting Consequences

The unrest has pushed up food costs so sharply that consumer prices in September jumped by 1.84%, rendering inflation for this year's first nine months 4.48%. October results will hardly be much better, and the official goal of keeping monetary erosion below 4.5% this year now appears to be out of reach. The IMF's local representative, Eliahu Kreis, insists that the two weeks of disturbances will pare economic growth by a full percentage point to 2.0%-2.5% in 2000 from the organization's earlier forecast of 3.0%-3.5%.

We find this prediction exaggerated. As we pointed out in our Briefs of August 17, Bolivia is on the brink of a major expansion of natural gas exports and world market conditions for other mining products have improved considerably. Even the IMF expects inflows of foreign direct investment to grow to USD 1 billion this year, from USD 800 million in 1999. But it is true that most of this influx is concentrated in capital-intensive, export-oriented industries which create few local jobs. And the government's coca-eradication program will remain a contentious issue as well.

Confrontation Over Coca

Urged on by the United States, Bolivia has destroyed most of the illegal coca plantations (those used for the production of cocaine rather than for medical purposes and the farmers' own use), in a campaign that by some estimates has deprived the economy of USD 400 million annually (equivalent to roughly 5% of GDP). Of the 38,000 hectares of leaf in the jungle area of Chapare, only 2,300 hectares are reported to remain, and these are to be destroyed shortly. There are still around 14,500 hectares in the Yungas region near La Paz, of which perhaps 2,500 are illegal. Although the government has now given this area a reprieve, it remains determined to complete the job there as well.

No Time For an Increase In Aid

Much as the program has pleased Washington, it has ired the peasant farmers who for generations used to make a decent living from coca leaf and find it difficult to grow legal cash crops with an even remotely similar earning power. The U.S. has shown its appreciation by adding USD 110 million to an already generous aid package this year, but Bolivians, looking at the massive USD 1.3-billion package Colombia has just been granted, feel that they deserve much more. They would like to receive not only financial aid, but also a Caribbean-Initiative-like reduction or lifting of U.S. tariffs on imports of textiles manufactured in Bolivia. Such a concession, it is felt in La Paz, could spawn a major industry and generate a very large number of jobs. The Clinton Administration, however, though sympathetic to such clamoring, is near the end of its term and there is next to no chance that the U.S. Congress would seriously consider a White House request for more Bolivian aid during the remainder of this year. (10/12/00)

Canada

The economy remains in the best shape it's been in for decades, with strong investment and brisk productivity gains heralding continued growth with minimal inflation. While business conditions broadly follow the U.S. pattern, Canada continues to run a sizeable foreign trade surplus. Prime Minister Jean Chretien seems to be preparing for an early election. He is doing everything he can to steal his opponents' thunder and the prospects of his winning a third term look good, the resurgence of the Canadian Alliance party notwithstanding.

R ecently published official data for the second quarter show that real GDP gained at an annual clip of 4.7% during the period, down only slightly from 5.1% in January-March. All sectors are contributing to the strong performance. Business investment forged ahead by 19.5% per annum, while exports expanded 8.5% and domestic demand rose by 3.6%. Investment is being driven by heavy outlays on high-tech equipment & machinery and overall growth is benefitting from strong sales of computers & peripherals, a trend that points to increasing productivity gains down the road that should enable the economy to continue expanding without generating inflationary bottlenecks and pressures.

Strength and Stability

The labor market in Canada is not nearly as strained as that in the United States. In fact, the official unemployment rate climbed unexpectedly to 7.1% in August from 6.8% in July and 6.6% in June as the 86,000 people who joined the labor force in that month far outweighed the 30,000 new jobs that were created. We believe, though, that the ranks of the jobless have since contracted again to under 7% as students recently returned to school. Inflation is, and will stay, low. The headline rate dipped to an annual 2.5% in August from 3.0% in July. Core inflation, which excludes the volatile food and energy components and is being targeted by the Bank of Canada with a 1%-3% range, was just 1.5% in August.

The Canadian Central Bank has been following the U.S. Federal Reserve in gradually ratcheting interest rates higher, but like the latter, it is now no longer confronted with an urgent need to maintain the upward push. It is fairly confident (as are we) that its upward revised prediction of real GDP growth of 4.25%-4.75% this year will be met without excessive price pressures, especially as the boom is occurring against a solid fiscal backdrop. In the financial year ended last March 31, the Federal Government wound up with a surplus of CAD 12.3 billion, four times what was projected in the original budget and the largest black entry in Canada's history. Still-preliminary results for the first four months of the current fiscal year (April-July) show a surplus of CAD 11.37 billion, nearly triple the government's earlier projection.

Healthy Fiscal Position

While seasonal factors together with tax cuts that took effect in July will cause the accumulation of excess revenues to slow in the months ahead, Ottawa will still be left with a handsome kitty with which to woo the voters ahead of the next elections. Last year's entire surplus is being used to retire Federal debt, which has been paid down to the tune of almost CAD 19 billion, to 58.9% of GDP from 71.2% in fiscal 1996/97. Most of this year's positive entry, however, will be used for further tax cuts and additional increases in spending. Eight out of ten Provinces are also expected to operate in the black this year.

Since many outside observers (particularly in the exchange markets) still have a tendency to regard Canada's economy as basically resource-based, it is well worth noting that the services sector today accounts for more than two-thirds of the country's output, while industry makes up around 25% and primary production a mere 6%. In other words, there has been a very significant shift away from basic resources to services and value-added production, which makes it easier for exporters to resist down-trends in world market prices and to re-orient their overseas sales in the event of a marked slackening of U.S. demand, which currently absorbs some 85% of Canadian exports.

Strong Exports

Canada's foreign trade surplus contracted in July to CAD 4.19 billion from the record of CAD 5.12 billion set in June, but the positive result for the year's first seven months still came to a most impressive CAD 28.9 billion, for an increase of CAD 10.4 billion over the like 1999 span. In the coming months, slowing business activity in the United States and consequently decelerating Canadian exports (especially sales of cars and automotive parts & equipment) will join higher interest rates in putting a brake on the economy, but we expect the dampening effect to be fairly mild as Canada will continue to benefit from the CAD's low exchange rate, higher consumer spending on the back of tax cuts, stepped-up outlays by governments on all levels, and continued growth in investment.

The Bank of Canada will help to pave the way for a soft landing of the economy, inter alia by making its interest-rate policy more transparent and predictable. Starting in November, it will halt its past practice of surprising the markets with the timing of its moves and will set eight dates, spaced over the course of the year, for its key policy announcements (preserving the right, to be sure, to take interim steps "in extreme cases"). By giving its course better predictability and greater transparency (it promises to be explicit as it can on what motivates its decisions), the BoC hopes to promote stability in the markets, since "monetary policy functions better if people understand the whys and wherefores." With this change, the bank is closing ranks with a slew of other leading CBs, including the U.S. Federal Reserve, the Bank of England, the European Central Bank, the Bank of Japan, the Swedish Riksbank, and the Reserve Banks of Australia and New Zealand.

Pre-Election Generosity

Given current economic boom conditions and the prospect for a slow-down next year, together with the handy availability of a big budget surplus for putting the voters in a good mood, most political analysts believe that Prime Minister Jean Chretien will opt to hold early elections this year. The PM appears determined to seek a third consecutive term, even though there has been some talk in Liberal circles that a fresh face at the helm might make it easier for the ruling party to fend off the predictable challenge from the conservative Canadian Alliance under its young, charismatic and energetic leader Stockwell Day. The Liberals have little to fear from the other parties in the opposition camp, including the Progressive Conservatives, the Reform Party, the socialist New Democrats, and the separatist Parti Quebecois.

Last month, M. Chretien clinched a healthcare accord with provincial governments under which the latter will see Federal transfers to them increased by CAD 23.4 billion over five years. The quid pro quo is that the Provinces will have to furnish Ottawa independently verified reports on healthcare delivery, which allows the Federal Government to claim that it is ensuring national standards while the Provinces can say that they have fought off outright control by Ottawa. Healthcare is arguably the Number One concern of the electorate, and the hefty increase in Federal spending on it pre-empts an important election issue which the Alliance had wanted to work in its favor.

Already in June, the Prime Minister unveiled CAD 700 million in new subsidies and grants for Atlantic Canada, the country's poorest region where the Liberals suffered badly in the 1997 elections. Soon afterwards the government loosened rules on jobless benefits, reversing changes that had been highly unpopular in the Maritimes and parts of Quebec. There are persistent rumors that Finance Minister Paul Martin will soon unveil a mini-budget in which Ottawa will spend most of the anticipated fiscal surplus on election goodies, among them most likely a cut in fuel taxes, personal income tax cuts, increases in allowable contributions to tax-sheltered retirement savings plans, perhaps a reduction in capital gains imposts, and special tax relief for the technology sector.

Time Is of the Essence

Mr. Martin has been playing his cards close to his chest and has so far refused to set a date for the interim budget -- or even to confirm that there will be one. The same holds true for Prime Minister Chretien, who does not have to seek a fresh mandate until the middle of 2002 and is well aware that Canadian voters on previous occasions (in 1997, for instance) used the ballot box to express their displeasure over being called to fresh polls substantially before the end of the traditional four years. Doing so now would not be without risk for Chretien. His Liberals have 160 out of 301 seats in the House of Commons against the Alliance's 58, and it would not take much in terms of losses at the polls to push them into a minority position.

At that, recent opinion surveys have had the Liberals running consistently about 19 points ahead. This is down from 40 points (thanks to the popularity of the Alliance and Stockwell Day), but it is a reasonable margin that, to boot, is more likely to decrease than to increase next year. While M. Chretien seems to have been having fun keeping everybody guessing, it appears that the Prime Minister's office has sent instructions to Liberal campaign workers to begin gearing up. The odds are, thus, that there will be early elections, only about 3-1/2 years into the government's current term. The earliest they could be held would be November 27. (10/12/00)

Egypt

Despite the escalation of oil prices & revenues, the economy has been in a slump for the past half year. The government of Prime Minister Atef Obeid, in power since October 1999, expects GDP growth to pick up. To propel the expansion, it plans to pursue the economic restructuring. The authorities have injected hard currency into the market to curb the Egyptian pound's depreciation.

C iting the economic slump, local business analysts project a GDP advance of 4.3% in the year to next June 30. A gain in this neighborhood would mark a deceleration from the 5.5% estimated by Prime Minister Atef Obeid for 1999/00 and the 6.0% seen in 1998/99. The public-sector budget for 2000/01 anticipates a GDP advance of 7.0%. Puzzlingly, Obeid, who was named Chief of Government a year ago, is claiming credit for an economic "turn-around" that is not evident. The 5.5% at which he puts GDP growth in 1999/00 is less than the 6.0% for which the government had aimed. Still, he recently said that the "recession" was over and that the economy was back on track.

Government to Step Up Restructuring

The Prime Minister says that foreign investors are coming back amid the surge in oil prices and revenues. He promises to encourage the inflow of foreign capital by selling stakes in the petroleum, telecommunications, and energy sectors. A program is underway to restructure the financial sector and make it more competitive. As part of the process, the bond market is to be activated and diversified. According to Obeid, the government plans to "conclude the privatization of government and public shares in joint-venture banks by the end of this year." He warns, however, that it will take up to 17 months more to appraise the four largest state banks in advance of denationalization.

Minister of Finance Medhat Hassanien says that the government aims to increase the inflow of foreign direct investment to USD 3-5 billion annually from USD 1 billion p.a. currently. To enhance Egypt's appeal, he proposes to expand tax holidays for investors as part of a broader fiscal restructuring. Among other things, he is calling for abolition of the capital gains tax. The government is studying proposals for Customs reform. Hassanien says that state-owned economic authorities are to be converted into independent holding companies, and that the increase in revenues from the transformed entities should offset the tax losses.

FX Infusion to Relieve Pressure On Pound

The Egyptian pound remains weak, despite the rise in oil earnings. The economy is in the grips of a foreign-exchange squeeze, as a result of which stock prices hit four-year lows two months ago. In May, the authorities adopted a "crawling peg" system of exchange-rate depreciation. Before then, the pound had been effectively pegged to the U.S. dollar for nine years. Partly reflecting the exchange-rate reform, the pound weakened to EGP 3.65 per U.S. dollar on October 5 from pounds 3.44:USD 1 at the start of 2000. At bureaux de change, the dollar fetched up to EGP 3.80 a week ago.

To help meet FX needs, the Central Bank of Egypt (CBE) injected USD 400 million into the banking system on October 5. The institution evidently acted at the behest of the government's economic team, which the day before discussed the FX crunch at a meeting chaired by President Hosni Mubarak. Thereafter, Prime Minister Obeid vowed to stick to the policy of non-intervention in currency trading, expressing confidence that the markets would stabilize with the easing of demand for hard currency.

The infusion of hard currency should reduce exchange-rate volatility, but it does not have a fundamental impact on the FX shortage, which is complicated by tight domestic liquidity. The local-currency money supply climbed to EGP 255.276 billion in June from EGP 234.569 billion in the like month of 1999. The 8.8% rise was partly offset by consumer-price inflation of 2.8% in the year ended on June 30, 2000, making for a real increase in the domestic money supply of 6.0%. In April, the government launched a drive to clear by early 2001 EGP 25 billion (USD 7 billion) in IOUs to private-sector suppliers. It anticipates for 2000/01 a budget deficit of 3.4%, but the forecast strikes us as optimistic. Last year's shortfall was 4.2% of GDP, four times more than had been originally projected.

FX Reserves Dropped

Some bankers fear defaults on the foreign debt, but such concerns are baseless at this point. CBE reports that Egypt's foreign reserves stood at USD 14.642 billion in July, down from USD 17.582 billion a year before. Last month, Prime Minister Obeid put external debts at USD 27.2 billion and estimated the current-account deficit at 1.2% of GDP.

In August, the Prime Minister outlined a plan to spur economic growth. The proposal includes import curbs to control a "dangerous" rise in purchases from abroad. Many imports, Obeid charges, compete with domestic goods, thus hampering Egypt's GDP expansion. He puts imports in calendar 1999 at EGP 54.0 billion (USD 15.2 billion), versus EGP 44.0 billion in 1997. He says that foreign trade was in the red by an average of USD 11.54 billion p.a. in the three years through 1999. (Deficits of USD 13,035.7 million and USD 12,298.5 million were seen in 1998 and 1999, respectively, versus a shortfall of USD 9,292.5 million in 1997.) Last year, the government made a first attempt to restrict imports, requiring 100% cash cover for letters of credit.

Regional Turmoil Affects Egypt

The break-down in negotiations between Israel and the Palestinians and the likelihood that turmoil in the occupied lands will persist are roiling efforts to strengthen Egypt's role as a regional economic hub. Last month, Prime Minister Obeid promised that Cairo would soon initial an economic partnership agreement with the European Union (EU), which is Egypt's main trading partner. He said that the government was waiting for the EU's response to a request for aid to support industrial modernization, which the accord calls for. Last week, the Egyptian government hosted a conference that brought together prospective trade partners from Europe, Africa and the Middle East.

The flare-up in fighting between Jews and Arabs in Israel and occupied parts of the West Bank has put President Mubarak on the spot. While Egypt has a peace treaty with Israel (going back to 1979), it must remain conscious of its pivotal role in the Arab world. As a military leader in the region, Egypt might be sucked into the conflict if it spills beyond Israel's borders. On his first foreign trip as President, Syria's new Head of State visited Egypt last week. Days later, Mubarak met with the Prime Minister of Israel and the President of the Palestinian Authority. If the Jewish-Arab blood-letting persists, Cairo may be compelled to give up its carefully cultivated image as an even-handed peace maker. Last week-end, the police broke up big anti-Israel demonstrations in Cairo. The clash between popular opinion and public policy threatens to embolden Egypt's armed Islamic movement. (10/12/00)

Iraq

International economic sanctions, in place for ten years, are eroding fast. The escalation of oil-export prices and earnings is enabling Iraq to rebuild its economy. Some of the revenues come from illegal shipments to neighboring countries. Friendly governments are helping Iraq break out of its isolation.

The United Nations imposed economic sanctions in August 1990, after Iraqi armed forces invaded neighboring Kuwait. The Security Council relaxed curbs in December 1996, approving the Oil-for-Food program. Under this scheme, Iraq was permitted to ship a stipulated amount of petroleum, with the revenues going into a UN escrow account. Iraq's oil exports came to around USD 34.6 billion in the 45 months through September. Besides the food, pharmaceuticals and other "humanitarian" goods originally earmarked as import priorities, Iraq has also been permitted to buy oil-field equipment, tankers and irrigation systems. The United States and Britain have disallowed some imports, asserting that they could have military applications. Import contracts for more than USD 2.0 billion of nominally civilian goods (13.5% of outstanding orders) are, thus, blocked.

More Money For Imports

The sanctions were eased last December to allow Iraq to export as much oil as it wants. Four months ago, the Security Council drew up a list of capital goods that Iraq is permitted to procure abroad. Baghdad can import these goods on the say-so of UN officials, without the Security Council's item-by-item approval. Under pre-existing trade review & approval procedures, finalization of oil-export contracts was typically delayed by as much as three weeks.

China, Russia and France — among Iraq's most constant friends -- are pushing for a further loosening of sanctions on Iraq. Some USD 8.0 billion of the money that Iraq has earned from UN-supervised oil exports over the past four years has gone for reparations to Kuwait and other parties seeking damages arising from the invasion of the neighboring Emirate. Under a Security Council deal of September 27, USD 15.9 billion is to be set aside to reimburse the Kuwait Petroleum Corporation for oil production lost during Iraq's seven-month occupation. Under the accord, however, the proportion of Iraq's oil-export revenues reserved for reparations is to be reduced to 25% from 30% in December. Every year, Iraq will save some USD 1.0 billion (at current oil-export prices) that can be used for imports.

Key decisions on proposals to ease trade restrictions have been held up by Baghdad's defiance of the international community, including refusal to let UN arms inspectors monitor Iraq's arms-development & – procurement program. The government has barred the inspectors since December 1998.

Iraq's Rehabilitation

The UN recently put Iraq's petroleum production at 2.6-2.8 million barrels per day (bpd). This was equivalent to roughly 4.0% of world output in late September. The escalation of world oil prices over the past year has heightened Iraq's role as a supplier and enhanced its clout in producers' forums. These effects have been strengthened in recent weeks by the rise of political tensions in the Middle East.

These developments are promoting Iraq's emergence from isolation. In mid-August, the government reopened Saddam International Airport. Last month, Russia and France allowed charter flights to Baghdad. A passenger airliner arrived from Jordan on September 27, the first from an Arab country in more than a decade. These flights were made with the authorization of the Security Council, and could have been blocked by vetoes from Britain or the U.S. Both the latter countries want, however, to avoid a falling-out with other Security Council members. Iraqi Minister of Transport Ahmad Murtada Ahmad Khalil says that Russia plans by mid-October to initiate scheduled commercial flights to Iraq. In August, passenger train service resumed between Iraq and Syria after a hiatus of 19 years. Last week, Turkey, a close regional ally of the U.S. and a member of NATO, upgraded its diplomatic relations with Iraq to ambassadorial level.

Illegal Exports Supplement Income

Under UN supervision, Iraq was exporting 2.4 million bpd of oil worth USD 16-20 billion per annum in late September. On top of revenues from internationally administered oil sales, Iraq smuggles out an estimated 10 million tons of petroleum, on which it earns some USD 2.0 billion p.a. Most of the illegal oil shipments end up in Iran or the United Arab Emirates. Iranian military officials usually take USD 50-60 per ton to clear the contraband, but they occasionally seize cargoes to exert pressure on smugglers for more money. In addition, while Iraq claims to be in dire need of foodstuffs and medical equipment, it ships grain and hospital machinery to neighboring Jordan. It uses part of the proceeds from illegal exports to import whisky, cigarettes and weapons.

In 1994, Iraq recognized Kuwait as an independent country. Border tensions have flared over the past month, however, with Kuwait accusing Iraq of stealing the Emirate's oil through a pipeline laid during the occupation. Likewise, Iraqi Minister of Oil Amir Muhammad Rasheed has charged that the Emirate is lifting oil from a zone shared by the two countries. The outbreak was a key factor in a surge in world oil prices at the start of this month. Such tension could continue to exert upward pressure on prices, partly offsetting the deflationary effects of agreements by major petroleum producers to raise output. (10/12/00)

Korea (South)

The Central Bank has raised interest rates. While the increase aims to curb inflation, it will also aggravate the debt-service burdens of the ailing industrial conglomerates. GM and Fiat have stepped in with a new bid to buy Daewoo Motor Co. Doubts remain about the corporate restructuring, however, as a U.S. company this week withdrew its bid for a big Korean steel-maker.

I n an attempt to curb inflation, the Bank of Korea (BoK) raised its overnight call rate by one-quarter of a percentage point, to 5.25%, on October 5. It was the first increase since February. Inflation is being driven by soaring oil prices, as winter arrives in the Northern Hemisphere. While the volume of oil imports rose only 3.1% (year-on-year) in January-August (to 591.8 million barrels), the bill for foreign petroleum shot up to USD 15.82 billion from USD 8.03 billion in the like period of 1999. The surge was a factor in the narrowing of the current-account BoP surplus to USD 6.0 billion from USD 16.6 billion. Foreign trade was in the black by USD 6.58 billion in the first eight months of 2000.

Consumer-price escalation quickened to 3.9% (y/y) last month from 2.7% in August and 0.8% in September 1999, and another pick-up may be in store. M-2 growth was 30.6% (y/y) last month, off from 35.3% in August but up from 26.6% in September 1999. In a contribution to the fight against inflation, the government is trying to correct fiscal drift. Minister of Planning & Budget Jeon Yun-churl expects a deficit in 2000 of 1.7% of GDP, half of the 3.4% projected at the start of the year.

Rate Hike Hits Ailing Chaebols

The government had urged the Central Bank to hold the line on interest rates, asserting that an increase would tend to discourage investment and aggravate the financial obligations of heavily indebted corporations. Ford Motor Company last month withdrew a USD 7.0-billion bid for Daewoo Motor Company, and DaimlerChrysler and Hyundai Motor Company said that they were no longer interested. These moves came as a blow to Korean Development Bank and Daewoo's other creditors, who have tried for more than a year to find a buyer and reduce their exposure.

Other multinationals, including General Motors and Fiat S.p.A. (which are working together), are still interested in Daewoo. GM had a 15-year partnership with Daewoo that ended in 1992. But reflecting a decline in expectations, creditors are studying a proposal to divide up the company and sell it piece by piece, if negotiations with remaining suitors fall through. The creditors have injected KRW 2.1 trillion (some 1.9 billion) into Daewoo Motor since August 1990, when the company and 11 other affiliates of the Daewoo Group were put under debt work-out plans.

Cost of Bail-Out Escalates

After Ford pulled out of talks to buy Daewoo, the government expressed concern over the impact on the local company's creditors. The Cabinet this week approved a proposal to spend another KRW 40 trillion (USD 35.84 billion) to prop up ailing banks and reform the financial sector. (The government must now obtain the National Assembly's authorization.) As of the end of August, the government had spent KRW 109.6 trillion (USD 96.4 billion) over three years for the financial-sector bail-out. Mainly due to the rising cost of the rescue operation, the Cabinet is calling for a 6.3% increase (to KRW 101.0 trillion, or USD 90.0 billion) in fiscal spending in 2001.

The cost of the bail-out threatens to go even higher. Nabors Industries, Inc. (of the U.S.) this week rescinded a USD 480-million bid for Hanbo Iron & Steel Co. Minister of Finance Jin Nyum says that the government is in no hurry to sell off Hanbo and will keep it afloat until another buyer is found. Hanbo's creditors threaten to sue Nabors.

Popular Resistance a Factor

With the cost of the bail-out sky-rocketing, the government is accusing some officials of sabotaging negotiations with foreign suitors of ailing companies. President Kim Dae-jung has ordered an investigation into the collapse of the deals to sell Daewoo and Hanbo. His aides say, furthermore, that those responsible will be punished. Business executives warn that the search for scapegoats is unhelpful and could derail ongoing efforts to find buyers for other companies. In fact, the government has rejected proposed concessions that might enhance the appeal of some entities to investors. Most people oppose any "fire sale" of public assets.

The National Assembly this week passed a law authorizing the creation of financial holding companies. Some officials argue that the gathering of banks, insurance firms and brokerages into groups will spur the rehabilitation of the financial sector. Such reorganizations would fall short of the mergers that trade unions fear would lead to mass lay-offs. Last week, six banks operating under government-approved debt work-outs announced plans to lay off 2,800 workers. In July, such a proposal triggered a strike that led the government to vow never to compel banks to merge. The government plans to inject KRW 6.0 trillion (USD 5.4 billion) into four troubled banks by the end of next month. Thereafter, it is to unite the institutions under a holding company. The authorities hope that the restructuring will prompt stronger financial institutions to consolidate voluntarily.

Privatization Drive to Be Relaunched

Despite the potential for a popular backlash, the government proposes to repeal the 30% ceiling on foreign ownership of Pohang Iron and Steel Company, a reform intended to relaunch the privatization drive. On the drawing boards are plans to sell to foreign investors a 25% stake in Hanjung (a machinery maker) and a 20% interest in Korea Tobacco & Ginseng. Planning & Budget Minister Jeon says that resistance to market forces has undermined many companies and that the government should promote adjustment by denationalizing and deregulating the economy. He also considers privatization a key to fiscal management. He aims to balance the public-sector budget by 2003.

International monetary reserves climbed to USD 92.5 billion on September 30 from USD 65.5 billion a year before and USD 3.0 billion in December 1997. Korea's external liabilities dropped to USD 142.1 billion (including short-term obligations of USD 47.8 billion) on July 31 from USD 159.2 billion (with short-dated IOUs of USD 63.6 billion) at the end of 1997. (10/12/00)

Oman

Like many of its neighbors, Oman is reaping a windfall from the escalation of world petroleum prices. The Sultanate is, however, also seeing a surge in non-oil exports. The bonanza is being used to relaunch industrial projects shelved when oil prices were low. Oman, which expects to join the WTO before the end of this year, plans to ease curbs on foreign ownership of local companies in 2001.

T hanks in part to the escalation of oil prices and revenues, the foreign-trade surplus widened to 1.05 billion rials (USD 2.73 billion) in January-June from OMR 180 million in the comparable term of last year. (Since 1986, the rial has traded at OMR 1.00 per USD 2.60.) According to the Economy Ministry, imports rose 5.0% (year-on-year), to OMR 945 million from OMR 900 million in the first half of 1999. But aggregate exports jumped almost 84.3%, to OMR 1,990 million from OMR 1,080 million. Reflecting a surge in Oman's oil-export prices to USD 25.70 per barrel in the more recent period from USD 14.50 in January-June 1999, earnings from foreign petroleum sales climbed 68.0%, to OMR 757.4 million from OMR 450.8 million. More surprisingly, non-oil exports shot up 95.9%, to OMR 1,232.6 million from OMR 629.2 million.

Economic Recovery Complete

The Central Bank of Oman interprets the increase in the surplus as evidence that Oman is "coming out of a recession." In fact, the economic slump ended in 1999. We estimate that GDP expanded by 10.35% in real terms last year. The gain followed a contraction of 10.67% in 1998. Last year's increase did not, thus, quite return the economy to the 1997 level. Oman's international monetary reserves (excluding gold) dropped to USD 509.3 million on June 30 from USD 1,495.3 million a year before and USD 1,094.2 million two years earlier. Admitting that they have clamped down on imports, officials express confidence that foreign trade will be in the black again in July-December.

Oman is not a member of the Organization of Petroleum Exporting Countries and is not subject to the cartel's production restrictions, but it sometimes voluntarily follows OPEC's guidelines. Production of crude oil has been running at 850,000-900,000 bpd.

Fiscal Restraint

The government is taking a fiscally conservative approach to the windfall. The export surge is reflected in an improvement in public finances, with some officials saying that the budget deficit in 2000 will be some OMR 100 million less than the OMR 349 million projected at the start of the year.

The budget presupposes an average petroleum-export price of USD 14.50 pb, and earmarks everything over that for a new oil reserve. While the fund is intended to cushion the effects of fluctuations in prices and revenues, the Commerce & Industry Ministry is urging the government to use it to step up spending. The administration has done so -- but very cautiously. The Ministry of the Economy reports that public spending rose to OMR 1.30 billion in January-July from OMR 1.19 billion in the like period of 1999, an increase of 9.2%. The budget allows for an increase in outlays to OMR 2.440 billion in 2000 as a whole from the OMR 2.094 billion actually spent last year.

Diversification Drive Relaunched

As reflected in the foreign-trade figures, Oman has made some headway in its drive to diversify the economy away from oil & gas, which in 1999 accounted for 46.9% of GDP. The Finance Ministry promises to use the export windfall to relaunch high-visibility projects that ground to a halt in late 1998 and early last year. Among development priorities is an aluminum smelter in Sohar (a northern town officially designated a regional industrial center). Joining Oman in the USD 2.5-billion project are the governments of Abu Dhabi and Dubai (two of the seven United Arab Emirates). Omani officials say that accords on the venture will probably be concluded by the end of 2000. Another priority is a free-trade zone proposed for Salalah (in the south). The government last month awarded the development contract to a U.S. company (Hillwood Development). Several petrochemicals projects will probably be taken off the shelf and reactivated.

Officials of the Commerce Ministry say that the government proposes to invest USD 7.0 billion in industry over the coming ten years in pursuit of economic diversification. The drive aims in part to reduce Oman's dependence on foreign labor. Expatriates account for about one-quarter of the Sultanate's 2.4 million people. Under the government's "Omanization" policy, employers are required to systematically upgrade nationals.

Opening to Foreign Capital

The government has also opened the economy to foreign capital and private management to improve efficiency. Effective from January 1, the ceiling on foreign ownership of local companies is to be raised to 70% from the current 49%. (For special projects the government sometimes allows a higher cap.) Starting in 2003, 100% foreign ownership is to be permitted in the banking, insurance and brokerage industries. Minister of State For Development Mohammed bin Moussa al-Youssef says that the government will likely offer to the private sector minority stakes in telecommunications and other state-controlled sectors.

Three months ago, a working group of the World Trade Organization accepted Oman's draft protocol of accession. The Emirate is expected to be formally admitted to the WTO in November. (10/12/00)

Poland

President Aleksander Kwasniewski has handily won re-election. His victory and the ascendancy of his SLD pose new problems for the current minority government, threatening to hamper decision-making on economic matters. Political support for fiscal restraint is waning, thus increasing the probability that monetary policy will be tightened.

Twelve people ran for the Presidency in the October 8 elections. Heading the list was President Aleksander Kwasniewski, seeking re-election to the post that he first won in 1995. Prominent among his challengers were Marian Krzaklewski, the leader of Solidarity Electoral Action (AWS), and independent Andrzej Olechowski. The latter, a business-oriented former Finance Minister, was backed by the Freedom Union (UW), which did not put up a candidate. Also running was Lech Walesa, one of the founders of the Solidarity trade-union movement and Poland's President until he was beaten by Kwasniewski.

All along, voter-preference surveys had shown Kwasniewski and his Democratic Left Alliance (SLD) ahead of rivals. In the view of many people, he has risen above partisan politics and ended the constant bickering that was a staple of national life under the more quarrelsome Walesa. The latter, Poland's first post-Communist Head of State, presided during an especially stormy spell. Understandably, most Poles are happy to have that period behind them.

Kwasniewski Won Decisively

While the victory of Kwasniewski was expected, the depth of his political base was surprising. Ahead of the elections, some of his backers feared that he might fail to win the 50% of the vote necessary to avoid a run-off. In fact, Kwasniewski garnered 53.7% of the ballots, according to the State Electoral Committee. Olechowski was the runner-up, with 17.0%. Krzaklewski came in third with 15.6%. Defeated again was Walesa, who won less than 1.0% of the votes, marking a stunning repudiation of a once-towering figure.

On the surface, Kwasniewski's victory leaves the make-up of government unchanged. But there has been a fundamental shift in the political dynamic that threatens to undermine the administration of P.M. Jerzy Buzek. The outcome of last Sunday's poll augurs well for SLD, which is preparing for general elections that must be held by October 2001. They may be called as early as next Spring, if Buzek's minority government fails to win Legislative approval of its budget for 2000 by January 31. The government has until November 15 to unveil the document.

New Trouble For Minority Government

The Buzek administration has been hobbled since June, when Leszek Balcerowicz pulled his UW out of its coalition with AWS. With Parliamentary elections approaching and SLD in the ascendant, the government is more lame and vulnerable than ever. Kwasniewski's victory raises the stakes and heightens the probability of insuperable disagreements on major policy matters. Poland's electoral laws favor major parties. Politicians of smaller parties are not likely to cooperate with Buzek and his AWS as long as the momentum lies with SLD.

This shift in the political dynamic also provides the government with convenient excuses for shortcomings. As we reported two weeks ago, Parliament has rejected a bill to gradually raise value-added-tax rates to European Union levels, thereby lowering revenue expectations for 2001 by more than 1.7 billion zlotys (USD 374 million). The Finance Ministry now proposes to hold the line on personal tax rates in 2001, saying that a plan (outlined earlier this year) to reduce them from the current 19%, 30% and 40% has become unrealistic.

Threat of Fiscal Indiscipline

Days ahead of the elections, Minister of Finance Jaroslaw Bauc warned that higher-than-forecast outlays by state agencies were also playing havoc with his budget forecasts. He projected for 2000 a deficit of not less than 2.30% of GDP. The forecast compares favorably with the 2.75% anticipated at the start of the year. It marks a dimming of the fiscal outlook, however, since July, when Bauc said that the budget would be in the red by only 2.00% of GDP. A factor in the set-back is mismanagement at the Social Security Office (ZUS), health funds and other public agencies. Earlier this year, ZUS underwent an overhaul as part of Bauc's plan to reduce the fiscal gap to 1.7% of GDP in 2001.

In the wake of Kwasniewski's victory, political support for fiscal restraint is waning. Before the balloting, Poles had voiced objections to austerity. The advent of Parliamentary elections dims the outlook for the belt-tightening proposed by Bauc for 2001 and for the reduction of inflation. The Monetary Policy Council (RPP) warns that it will again raise interest rates if the fiscus begins to drift. An increase would tend to discourage investment and hamper economic expansion. As part of efforts to reduce domestic liquidity, the National Bank of Poland is studying a proposal to introduce in 2001 a new deposit interest rate. If it decides to do so, the institution will carry out repurchase operations at this rate.

Economic Slow-Down Feared

If interest rates remain at current heights, 8.0%-12.0% in real terms, GDP growth will likely recede from the 5.0% officially anticipated for 2000 to 2.0%-4.0% p.a. in the medium-term future. A slow-down can be avoided by a relaunch of the economic restructuring drive. The minority government lacks the muscle, however, to push through reforms. (10/12/00)

Yugoslavia

The "people's revolution" against strongman Milosevic is still running its course, so it is understandable that chaos prevails in the political arena as well as on the economic front. It will take some time for the dust to settle -- for newly elected President Kostunica to gain full control of the levers of power and for macro-economic conditions to stabilize. Then, of course, the key question will be whether Kostunica will prove to be the man the West thinks he is. By and large, though, the omens are good.

S
lobodan Milosevic, who for 13 years had ruled Yugoslavia with an iron fist, took almost everyone by surprise last Friday, when -- after a lengthy period of refusing to bow to the will of the electorate -- he addressed the nation on the only major television station still under his control. Congratulating the opposition leader Vojislav Kostunica on his election victory he claimed that he had "just gotten official information" on the poll results and on a ruling by the Constitutional Court confirming his opponent's victory. Wishing the country "success over the next term," he said that his Socialist Party would be strong in opposition and that he would play a part.

After all the talk that he would not shy away from starting a civil war to hang on to power, his reign, thus, ended with a whimper. Soon after his address, the head of the army let it be known that the uniformed services, "strictly respecting constitutional rulings, did not take part in the political struggle and are ready to accept the people's will and all the legitimate decisions of the electoral institutions." Nothing was heard from Milosevic's Interior Ministry special police force, but the fact that these paramilitaries gave no indication of any desire to stop or reverse the flow of events was, in itself, good news.

New Government

Kostunica was sworn in as the truncated (now consisting of only Serbia and Montenegro) country's new President and began to move quickly to consolidate his position. He and other opposition leaders set up a "crisis committee," a quasi-government in which they are inviting representatives of Montenegro to take part. With their support, Kostunica will have a majority in the Federal parliament and will also control the Serbian legislature, which has far more power. Once he has firmly established his authority, presumably with the help of a formal transition government, he plans to call new Federal elections and charge the emerging parliament with the drafting of a new, democratic constitution. Long before that, a Serbian parliamentary poll is to be held on December 19.

Sanctions Are Being Lifted -- Gradually

The European Union was quick to respond to the turn of events by lifting its oil embargo and flight ban on Yugoslavia. Its Foreign Ministers agreed to free up about USD 300 million in aid during the next seven years and to invite Belgrade into a network of Balkan assistance programs, including a free trade pact that should allow duty-free access to the Common Market for most of Yugoslavia's exports. Brussels said, however, that the restrictions on moving financial assets out of Yugoslavia and a ban on visas for Mr. Milosevic, his family, and a circle of close associates would remain in place for now, to make sure that the strongman and his cronies cannot flee the country with looted assets. Washington has indicated that it, too, will ease sanctions in coming days, but wants to make sure that Pres. Kostunica first accepts all elements of the Dayton peace accords.

Representatives of Russia (which supplies Yugoslavia with most of its oil and gas), the United States, and the so-called "contact group" (including, in addition to the U.S., France, Germany, Italy and the United Kingdom) have been meeting in London to coordinate policy toward Belgrade. Meanwhile, Yugoslav workers committees (frequently squabbling among themselves) have taken on the task of cleaning out protegees of the old regime from lucrative posts at thousands of state companies, factories, hospitals, banks, mines, hotels and universities in a campaign that at least in the short term is raising havoc with the management of these entities.

Doctors unions have taken charge of the Health Ministry. The directors of the country's largest bank, Beogradska Banka, were forced to resign. The 18-party Democratic Opposition of Serbia bloc (DOS) has taken over the Customs service and named the owner of one of the largest trading companies, Dusan Zabunovic, its temporary chief. At the Central Bank, Kostunica loyalists engineered several "computer crashes" before taking over the institution's management, to prevent the transfer abroad of potentially large sums by members of the Milosevic clique.

Economic Conditions Will Get Worse

It is obvious that this wholesale sacking of experienced (if politically tainted) business managers across the country is creating chaos in the remnants of an economy that has been devastated by years of war, sanctions and international isolation. In the short run, the resulting scenes of mounting confusion will undoubtedly get worse and the new government has yet to discover how bad the situation really is. For instance, while Serbia alone has accumulated around USD 14 billion in debt and interest to an assortment of foreign creditors, official international monetary reserves amount to only USD 385 million, less than the holdings of neighboring Albania, which arguably ranks as Europe's poorest country.

Spokesmen for Kostunica have already hinted that in the weeks and months to come Yugoslavia will not be able to meet all its financial obligations abroad. To get back on its feet, it will need very generous assistance from abroad, much more than has been promised so far. Independent estimates indicate that to repair the damage done by NATO's bombing campaign will swallow up roughly USD 4 billion. Belgrade has an agreement in principle on a rescheduling of debt owed to government creditors under the Paris Club umbrella, but it also needs a pact with commercial creditors of the London Club, from whom the new administration hopes (too optimistically, we think) to gain 80% forgiveness of its obligations.

An Interesting Plan

Kostunica has an economic blue-print, which -- according to its architect Mladjan Dinkic, who is widely expected to become the next Yugoslav Central Bank Governor -- seeks to combine elements of Polish shock therapy with Slovenia's model of gradual privatization and Scandinavia's generous social security systems. Key elements of the plan call for a monetary reform that would introduce a new currency by 2001, wage hikes that would push average monthly pay up to 250 German marks by the end of next year from only DEM 90 now, a simplification of the fiscal system via a reduction of the number of taxes to six from around 250, and institutional reform aimed to tighten monetary control, bring in immediate (if partial) price and trade liberalization, and promote privatization and private sector development.

None of this sounds unrealistic or ill-conceived. But one must keep in mind that it will be a horrendous task to give even a veneer of normality to an economy that at the present time cannot by any stretch of the imagination be called market-oriented, has factories operating at dismally low rates of capacity (if they operate at all), must contend with a badly battered infrastructure, can offer a job to only one in two workers, and does not even have a worthwhile currency of its own. For all practical purposes, the German mark is the circulating tender, although the dinar in the curb market has strengthened to about 24 per DEM 1 from under 40:1 prior to the collapse of Milosevic's regime.

Pitfalls Ahead

There are still big political challenges ahead as well. Kostunica and his supporters are not yet in full control of the secret police and there are reports, as these lines are being written, of units of this force banding together for acts of terrorism. To depoliticize the army and police will not be easy. Kostunica himself is certainly not a great friend of the United States. He has all along resented -- and continues to resent -- the air war NATO waged, and his views concerning Kosovo are hard to distinguish from those of Milosevic. The DOS coalition supporting him is a hodgepodge of groups with greatly differing interests and ideologies. It managed to unite because of its common distaste for Milosevic's regime. Now that the strongman has, at least temporarily, removed himself from the scene, the alliance may prove difficult to hold together. It also remains to be seen how the new administration decides to approach the question of Montenegro, where secessionist tendencies remain quite strong.

In the end, almost everything will depend on whether or not Kostunica proves to be the man the West thinks he is. He will undoubtedly to what he can to preserve what is left of Serbian pride. He is an avowed nationalist who condemns the international war crimes tribunal and has no intention of handing Milosevic over to the court. He will try hard to retain Russia's support even while he works to mend relations with the West. But in almost every other respect, he is the exact opposite of his predecessor. Large and anything but charismatic, he is quiet-spoken and betrays in his choice of words his background as a constitutional lawyer and political scientist. Though fiercely patriotic and unwavering in his support for the Bosnian and Kosovo Serbs, he is also fervent about the rule of law, the value of free elections, the importance of reliable, transparent institutions, and the need for negotiation. From what we know of Kostunica, he may well turn out to be the right man in the right place at the right time. But human beings have a remarkable ability to surprise, particularly in times of crisis. (10/12/00)

Zimbabwe

Citing the country's debt-payment arrears, the World Bank has frozen aid. It is not likely to resume assistance until the IMF does so. Officials call the BoP situation critical. They propose to step up spending and domestic borrowing. The government is cracking down on the opposition, following a call for President Mugabe's overthrow.

The World Bank last week cut off funding for Zimbabwe. It said that no further money would be forthcoming until the government made past-due payments on USD 889 million in outstanding loans. The institution allows a country up to six months after the scheduled remittance date to make payment. It puts Zimbabwe's overdue remittances at USD 47 million. As a result of the World Bank's action, the African Development Bank is expected to halt assistance. Many other official creditors were already withholding aid.

The World Bank says it is continuing to "talk to the government" in search of an agreement on a policy package that would allow it to normalize relations with Zimbabwe. Under its assistance policy, the World Bank can refinance part of a country's arrears. But officials also link prospects for a resumption of lending to Harare's working out a new economic program with the International Monetary Fund. While the latter institution has already stopped lending to Zimbabwe, it sent a mission to Harare last month for talks with the government. Still, prospects for a near-term resumption of IMF aid are dim.

BoP Situation Is Critical

Minister of Finance Simba Makoni admitted last week that Zimbabwe is in a "very critical balance-of-payments situation.. We are living from hand to mouth as far as foreign receipts are concerned." The cycle of tobacco auctions, which runs from April to October and is the source of the bulk of Zimbabwe's FX earnings, is almost over for this year. Tobacco revenues have, furthermore, been lower than usual, due to the seizure and occupation of hundreds of commercial farms. In addition, some exporters are refusing to repatriate FX earnings, hoping thereby to force the authorities to further devalue the local dollar. The unit has been downgraded by 28% against the greenback since August. A rise in world prices for cotton, another of Zimbabwe's exports, has not substantially increased the FX inflow.

The country's international monetary reserves fell to USD 165.8 million at the end of August from USD 221.2 million a year before. Finance Minister Makoni acknowledges that hopes for assistance from the IMF are slim, saying that talks with the institution depend on its assessment of the draft 2001 budget, which is to be presented to Parliament at the end of this month.

IMF's Conditions

Makoni says that, while the IMF and Harare are discussing "the way forward, I don't think we should generate unrealistic expectations about how soon dollars and cents can flow." He said that another round of talks with the IMF may be held in January, provided that the 2001 budget is found satisfactory. While taking note of "the rapid deterioration of the country's economic and fiscal situation," the IMF says that Harare must also address issues of "governance" (i.e., rooting out bureaucratic corruption) to get back into the good graces of creditors. To qualify for new money, the Fund says, Zimbabwe must in addition make "clear progress" on reduction of the fiscal deficit and implementation of structural reforms.

As of August, Zimbabwe had received only 10% of the USD 200 million in foreign aid that it had anticipated for 2000, according to Makoni. The government had counted on this money to close gaps in this year's budget. Last month, it called for an increase of 35.527 billion Zimbabwe dollars (USD 699.3 million) in the spending allocation for 2000 to cover wage hikes for state workers and reduce public-sector debt-payment arrears. Business analysts estimate that such an increase would drive up the public debt-to-GDP ratio to 20.0% this year from an average 10.0% in the decade through 1999. For 2000, the government had anticipated a debt-to-GDP ratio of 14.9%.

Fiscus Deteriorating

Among other effects, the suspension of World Bank aid makes it more difficult and more costly for Zimbabwe to borrow. In the first 8-1/2 months of 2000, the government raised over ZWD 40 billion on the domestic market at interest rates exceeding 50% p.a. Due mainly to the quickening of inflation and the escalation of the debt-servicing bill, private economists expect the government's budget to be in the red by around 22.0% of GDP in 2000, versus the 3.8% projected a year ago. Other factors in the deterioration of the fiscus include a surge in the public-sector payroll and a steep rise in military spending. If the domestic debt climbs to the privately projected ZWD 150 billion by the end of 2000, financing costs will skyrocket to ZWD 75 billion annually. Business economists expect real GDP to fall by 5.0-6.0% in 2000. For next year, the World Bank projects a contraction of 6.0%-10.0%.

Exchange-rate depreciation and the widening of the fiscal gap are key factors in inflation. The government puts the consumer price rise in August at 53.6% (year-on-year), versus 53.4% in July and 68.8% in August 1999 and a record-high 70.4% last October, but business analysts say that inflation is actually running at around 65.0% p.a. To curb monetary erosion, the Reserve Bank of Zimbabwe (RBZ) slashed its discount rate to 55.0% in mid-September from 70.0% six weeks before. With interest on bank holdings now nominal, many investors jumped into the stock market last month, pushing up the prices of local equities. This anomaly is, however, not likely to endure. The market is in the midst of a hard-currency crunch and many companies are on the brink of bankruptcy. Despite RZB's counter-offensive, fuel-price hikes of up to 101% (effected on September 1) are aggravating inflationary pressures.

MDC Chief Issues Strong Challenge to Mugabe

The leader of the opposition Movement for Democratic Change (MDC) was detained and questioned this week over a recent call for the violent overthrow of the government. On September 30, Morgan Tsvangirai called on the international community to "stop Africa's Milosevic" – i.e., President Robert Mugabe. He accused Mugabe of committing genocide and destroying the economy. He said that Zimbabwe, along with the President, now faces international isolation.

Tsvangirai warned Mugabe: "If you don't want to go peacefully, we will remove you violently." (The President's current term expires in March 2002.) Following the speech, the police detained three deputies of MDC, which won 57 of the 120 Parliamentary seats up for grabs in the June 2000 elections. MDC's supporters countered with demonstrations that were broken up by the police. Minister of Information Jonathan Moyo called Tsvangirai a criminal and other officials urged that he be tried for treason.

Government Retreats

Evidently fearing a show-down and a possible backlash, the government backtracked. The police released Tsvangirai after the interrogation and freed the MDC deputies. Officials toned down their anti-MDC rhetoric. But the change of heart had Machiavellian undercurrents. While easing pressure on MDC, the government pardoned thousands of people accused of "politically motivated" crimes in the first six months of 2000 –- i.e., in the run-up to the June elections. The vast majority of them are members or supporters of the ruling Zimbabwe African National Union-Patriotic Front. The amnesty does not apply to those suspected of involvement in murder, rape, theft or weapons possession. Thirty people were killed in pre-election violence.

Tsvangirai briefly toned down his rhetoric while the heat was on, saying that he does not advocate the use of force or unconstitutional means. As soon as the pressure eased, he taunted the government. "You cannot go about concocting charges.. against people who are innocent. The government is panicking, groping in the dark." In some quarters, his call to arms has raised expectations of imminent, sweeping change. A show-down with the government is still probable. (10/12/00)

ৼৼৼৼৼৼ

Chapter 8

Standard & Poor's Ratings Group

Sovereign Credit Ratings: A Primer

David T Beers, London (44) 171-826-3646; Marie Cavanaugh, New York (1) 212-208-1579

Standard & Poor's sovereign credit ratings—which now cover local and foreign currency debt issued by governments in 77 countries and territories (*see table 1*)—are an assessment of each government's capacity and willingness to repay debt according to its terms. Sovereign ratings are not "country ratings," an important and often misunderstood distinction. Sovereign ratings address the credit risks of national governments, but not the specific default risks of other issuers. Ratings assigned to other public and private sector entities in each country can, and frequently do, vary. Ratings of some issuers may be the same as the sovereign's, while others are lower. In rare cases, the ratings of some issuers may be even higher. In all instances, however, the sovereign's ratings set the benchmark for the ratings assigned to other issuers under its jurisdiction.

Standard & Poor's Ratings Group offers ratings in seven major areas: 1) long-term debt; 2) commercial paper; 3) preferred stock; 4) certificates of deposit; 5) money market funds; 6) mutual bond funds; and 7) insurance companies claims-paying ability. Ratings are based on consideration of the likelihood of default; the nature and provisions of the obligation; and the protection afforded by and relative position of the obligation in the event of bankruptcy, reorganization, or other arrangement under the laws of bankruptcy and other laws affecting creditors' rights.

S&P's rating methodology in country assessments results in a forecast of debt-servicing capacity. Its determination of credit risk incorporates Political Risk (the willingness of a sovereign to repay debt on time) and Economic Risk (the government's ability to repay its obligations).

Political Risk considers the stability of political institutions and the degree of popular participation in the political process. It includes an assessment of the following: 1) the form of government and adaptability of political institutions; 2) the extent of popular participation; 3) the orderliness of leadership succession; 4) the degree of consensus on economic policy objectives; 5) the integration of global trade and the financial system; and 6) internal and external security risks. The key Economic Risk factors are: 1) the income and economic structure of the country; 2) fiscal policy and budgetary flexibility; 3) monetary policy and inflation pressures; and 4) public and private sector debt burdens and debt service track record.

S&P rates countries in each debt category with a triple-letter rating system (AAA to D) reflecting least to most risk for the investor.

Table 1					
Standard & Poor's Sovereign Credit Ratings					
Issuer	Local Currency	Foreign Currency	Issuer	Local Currency	Foreign Currency
Austria	AAA	AAA	Colombia	A	BBB-
France	AAA	AAA	Slovak Republic	A	BBB-
Germany	AAA	AAA	Tunisia	A	BBB-
Japan	AAA	AAA	Egypt	A-	BBB-
Liechtenstein	AAA	AAA	Greece	A-	BBB-
Luxembourg	AAA	AAA	Hungary	A-	BBB-
Netherlands	AAA	AAA	Malaysia	A-	BBB-
Norway	AAA	AAA	Poland	A-	BBB-
Singapore	AAA	AAA	Thailand	A-	BBB-
Switzerland	AAA	AAA	Croatia	BBB+	BBB-
United Kingdom	AAA	AAA	Lithuania	BBB+	BBB-
United States	AAA	AAA	Uruguay	BBB+	BBB-
			Oman	N.R.	BBB-
Canada	AAA	AA+			
Denmark	AAA	AA+	India	BBB+	BB+
New Zealand	AAA	AA+	Korea	BBB+	BB+
Sweden	AAA	AA+	Philippines	BBB+	BB+
Belgium	AA+	AA+	South Africa	BBB+	BB+
Ireland	AA+	AA+	Trinidad & Tobago	BBB+	BB+
Taiwan	AA+	AA+	Panama	BB+	BB+
Australia	AAA	AA	El Salvador	BBB+	BB
Finland	AA	AA	Mexico	BBB+	BB
Italy	AA	AA	Morocco	BBB	BB
Spain	AA	AA	Argentina	BBB-	BB
Bermuda	N.R.	AA	Peru	BBB-	BB
Cyprus	AA+	AA-	Costa Rica	BB+	BB
Portugal	AA-	AA-			
			Jordan	BBB-	BB-
Iceland	AA+	A+	Paraguay	BBB-	BB-
Malta	AA+	A+	Bolivia	BB+	BB-
Slovenia	AA	A	Brazil	BB+	BB-
Hong Kong	A+	A	Lebanon	BB	BB-
Kuwait	A+	A			
Czech Republic	AA	A	Romania	BB	B+
Chile	AA	A-	Dominican Republic	BB	B+
Israel	AA-	A-	Kazakhstan	BB-	B+
			Venezuela	N.R.	B+
Estonia	A-	BBB+	Turkey	N.R.	B
China	N.R.	BBB+	Cook Islands	B-	B-
Latvia	A-	BBB			
Qatar	N.R.	BBB	Indonesia	B-	CCC+
			Pakistan	N.R.	CCC-
			Russia	N.R.	CCC-
Ratings as of 10/15/98. N.R.—Not rated.					

Defaults by sovereign issuers of bank and bond debt—the risk the ratings address—have declined in recent years, at least until 1998. Since 1975 (and even earlier), in fact, no sovereign issuer has defaulted on local or foreign currency debt rated by Standard & Poor's. Will such defaults occur in the future? Judging from the volume of bond issuance by emerging market sovereigns in the 1990s, many with ratings in the speculative-grade ('BB+' ratings or lower) category (*see table 1*), Standard & Poor's believes that they will. The default rates for sovereign issuers, over time, should broadly parallel the default rates for similarly rated corporate issuers.

If defaults occur more frequently in the sovereign sector, as we expect, this will not be an unprecedented development. Defaults on foreign currency bonds took place repeatedly, and on a substantial scale, throughout the 19th century and as recently as the 1940s. Sovereign default rates fell to low levels only in the first three decades after the Second World War (*see chart 1*), when cross-border sovereign bond issuance also was minimal. Defaults on bank loans, the main vehicle for financing governments in the 1970s and 1980s, peaked in 1990 and have fallen steadily since then.

Chart 1
Sovereign Foreign
Currency Bond
Defaults: 1820-1997

1820	4.5
1830	13.9
1840	11.7
1850	11.5
1860	6.5
1870	9.7
1880	9.5
1890	7.5
1900	6.2
1910	6.2
1920	4.8
1930	17.2
1940	17.7
1950	4.9
1960	2
1970	1
1980	1.2
1990	2.3

Source: Debt Cycles in the World Economy, Westview Press, 1992 and Standard & Poor's.

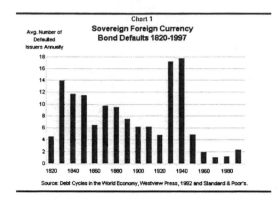

Chart 1

Sovereign Foreign Currency Bond Defaults 1820-1997

Avg. Number of Defaulted Issuers Annually

Source: Debt Cycles in the World Economy, Westview Press, 1992 and Standard & Poor's.

Past defaults reflected a variety of factors, including wars, revolutions, lax fiscal and monetary polices, and external economic shocks. As the 1990s draw to a close, fiscal discipline, debt management, and the contingent liabilities arising from weak banking systems, in particular, represent significant policy challenges for many sovereigns. The associated credit risks, which for a time may seem manageable, can mushroom quickly—as events in a number of emerging market countries since 1997 have shown. Given these factors, it would be surprising if a new sovereign default cycle did not emerge over the next decade. Standard & Poor's believes, therefore, that understanding sovereign ratings, what they mean, and the criteria behind them, is more relevant than ever.

Behind the Ratings

Standard & Poor's appraisal of each sovereign's overall creditworthiness is both quantitative and qualitative. The quantitative aspects of the analysis incorporate a number of measures of economic and financial performance as outlined below. The analysis is qualitative because Standard & Poor's ratings indicate future debt service capacity.

The ratings service uses both a "top down" and a "bottom up" analyses to determine sovereign ratings. "Top down" analyses consider global systemic factors, which past experience suggests influence both the timing and magnitude of sovereign defaults. Examples include quarterly analysis of default trends throughout the sector *(see Sovereign Defaults in 1998: A Turning Point?, November 1998)* and regular examination of global financial sector risks *(see Global Financial System Stress: Leading Indicators Signal Pressure in 16 Countries, September 1998)*.

The "bottom up" analyses focus on the credit fundamentals affecting each government. It divides the analytical framework into eight categories so that all important factors that contribute to sovereign default are considered in turn *(see box)*. Each category relates to both economic and political risk, the key determinants of credit risk. Economic risk addresses the government's ability to repay its obligations on time and is a function of both quantitative and qualitative factors. Political risk addresses the sovereign's willingness to repay debt.

SOVEREIGN RATINGS METHODOLOGY PROFILE

Political Risk
- Form of government and adaptability of political institutions
- Extent of popular participation
- Orderliness of leadership succession
- Degree of consensus on economic policy objectives

- Integration in global trade and financial system
- Internal and external security risks

Income and Economic Structure
- Living standards, income, and wealth distribution
- Market vs. nonmarket economy
- Resource endowments and degree of diversification

Economic Growth Prospects
- Size and composition of savings and investment
- Rate and pattern of economic growth

Fiscal Flexibility
- General government operating and total budget balances
- Tax competitiveness and tax-raising flexibility
- Spending pressures

Public Debt Burden
- General government financial assets
- Public debt and interest burden
- Currency composition and structure of public debt
- Pension liabilities
- Banking, corporate, other contingent liabilities

Price Stability
- Trends in price inflation
- Rates of money and credit growth
- Exchange rate policy
- Degree of central bank autonomy

Balance of Payments Flexibility
- Impact of fiscal and monetary policies on external accounts
- Structure of the current account
- Composition of capital flows

External Debt and Liquidity
- Size and currency composition of public external debt
- Importance of banks and other public and private entities as contingent liabilities of the sovereign
- Maturity structure and debt service burden
- Level and composition of reserves and other public external assets
- Debt service track record

Willingness to pay is a qualitative issue that distinguishes sovereigns from most other types of issuers. Partly because creditors have only limited legal redress, a government can (and sometimes does) default selectively on its obligations, even when it possesses the financial capacity for timely debt service. In practice, of course, political and economic risks are related. A government that is unwilling to repay debt usually is pursuing economic policies that weaken its ability to do so. Willingness to pay, therefore, encompasses the range of economic and political factors influencing government policy.

As part of the committee process that Standard & Poor's uses to assign credit ratings, each government is ranked on a scale of one (representing the highest score) to six (the lowest) for each analytical category in relation to the universe of rated and unrated sovereigns. There is, however, no exact formula combining the scores to determine ratings. The analytical variables are interrelated and the emphasis can change when, for example, differentiating the degree of credit risk between a sovereign's local and foreign currency debt.

Because the default frequency of sovereign local currency debt differs significantly from that of foreign currency debt, both types of debt are analyzed. While the same political, social, and economic factors affect the government's ability and willingness to honor local and foreign currency debt, they do so in varying degrees. A sovereign government's ability and willingness to service local currency debt is supported by its taxation power and its ability to control the domestic financial system, which gives it potentially unlimited access to local currency resources.

To service foreign currency debt, however, the sovereign must secure foreign exchange, usually by purchasing it in the currency markets. This can be a binding constraint, as reflected in the higher frequency of foreign than local currency debt default (*see Sovereign Defaults Continue to Decline in 1998, September 1998*). The primary focus of Standard & Poor's local currency credit analysis is on the fiscal, monetary, and inflation outcomes of government policies that support or erode incentives for timely debt service. When assessing the default risks on foreign currency debt, Standard & Poor's places more weight on the interaction between fiscal and monetary policies, the balance of payments and its impact on the growth of external debt, and the degree of each country's integration in the global financial system.

Local Currency Ratings Factors

Key economic and political risks that Standard & Poor's considers when rating sovereign debt include:
- Stability of political institutions and the degree of popular participation in the political process,
- Income and economic structure,
- Fiscal policy and budgetary flexibility,
- Monetary policy and inflation pressures, and
- Public and private sector debt burdens and debt service track record.

These factors, more than any others, directly affect the ability and willingness of governments to ensure timely local currency debt service. Further, because fiscal and monetary policies ultimately influence the country's external balance sheet, they also affect the ability and willingness of governments to service foreign currency debt.

The stability and perceived legitimacy of a country's political institutions are important considerations. They set the parameters for economic policymaking, including how quickly policy errors are identified and corrected. France's 'AAA' credit standing, for instance, in part reflects the country's democratic political framework. Policymaking is transparent and, as a result, the government's response to policy errors is predictable over time. Kazakhstan's evolving political institutions, by contrast, constrain its 'B+' foreign currency and 'BB-' local currency ratings; the future direction of economic policy is less predictable for this reason.

A country's economic structure also factors into the analytical process. Because of its decentralized decision-making process, a market economy, with legally enforceable property rights, is less prone to policy error and more respectful of the interests of creditors, than one where the state dominates. If market reforms succeed in the transition economies of Central and Eastern Europe, the credit standing of at least some of the region's sovereigns ultimately could converge with those of Western Europe, where market economies are well entrenched (*see Rating the Transition Economies, February 1997*).

A government in a country with a growing standard of living and income distribution regarded as broadly equitable can more readily support high public debt levels and withstand unexpected economic and political shocks, than can one with a poor or stagnant economy. But a sovereign with a recent history of default, generally, must manage with lower levels of leverage to rebuild its credibility than one that has maintained an unblemished debt record. The United Kingdom, rated 'AAA,' has a track record of honoring its obligations over centuries punctuated by war and financial distress. In contrast, Argentina's ('BB' foreign currency and 'BBB-' local currency) ratings still reflect the legacy of many years of economic mismanagement, including default. Its credit standing, while improving, is by no means as strong as Britain's, although the Argentine government now has less debt in relation to national income. These factors, in turn, influence the conduct of fiscal and monetary policies, and their impact on future changes in the public debt burden.

Fiscal Policy

When evaluating fiscal policy, Standard & Poor's focuses on three related issues:
- The purpose of public sector borrowing;
- Its impact on the growth of public debt; and
- Its implications for inflation.

Deficit financing can be an appropriate policy tool for any government. Public sector infrastructure projects, for example, can be prudently financed through borrowing when they generate revenues sufficient to cover future debt service. Singapore, rated 'AAA', has transformed itself into a prosperous manufacturing- and service-based economy over the past 40 years partly by astute investment in its public infrastructure.

More typically, governments borrow to finance combinations of consumption and investment that increases public debt. Still, analysis of public finance is complicated by the fact that the taxation and monetary powers unique to sovereigns can permit them to manage widely varying debt levels over time. Depending on their political support, policymakers can raise taxes to meet their obligations. But a growing tax burden can adversely affect the economy's growth prospects. Moreover, public opinion often favors the lowest possible tax burden—so much so that proposals to raise taxes occasionally drive governments from office. Efforts to cut spending can be stymied by powerful interests that benefit from government programs. Absent a political consensus favoring conservative fiscal principles, sovereigns can succumb to the temptation to print money owing to their monopoly over the currency and control of the banking system.

Inflation and Public Debt

Standard & Poor's regards the rate of inflation as the single most important leading indicator of sovereign local currency credit trends. Significant monetization of budget deficits fuels price inflation, which can undermine popular support for governments. As a result, policymakers usually respond with measures to contain it. If they do not, and price increases accelerate, serious economic damage and an erosion of public trust in political institutions can result. These conditions are fertile ground for a sovereign default. Inflation benchmarks, and their relationship to different local currency rating categories, are shown in table 2 *(on the next page)*.

Table 2	
Local Currency Rating Category	Annual Inflation (%)
B	50-200
BB	25-100
BBB	10-50
A	7-25
AA	4-15
AAA	0-10

In evaluating price pressures in each country, Standard & Poor's considers their behavior in past economic cycles. The analysis is based, in part, on the level and maturity structure of the public debt burden—total borrowing of central, regional, and local governments in relation to GDP—together with the likely extent of future borrowing. Off balance sheet, public sector pensions, and contingent liability items—such as banks and other enterprises—are scrutinized for their possible contribution to inflation. Related indicators include rates of money and credit expansion. Taking all these factors into account, the rating service makes a conservative assessment of average inflation, as measured by the consumer price index, over the next cycle.

In addition, Standard & Poor's looks at institutional factors affecting inflation. For instance, an autonomous central bank with a public mandate to ensure price stability can be a strong check on fiscal imbalances; less so a central bank tied closely to the government. Among industrial countries, Germany (AAA) and the U.S. (AAA) provide excellent examples of central banks where strong traditions of independence have evolved over the years. Similar examples among emerging market issuers include the central banks of Chile ('A-' foreign currency and 'AA' local currency) and Israel ('A-' foreign currency and 'AA-' local currency). On the other hand, Mexico's credit standing ('BB' foreign currency and 'BBB+' local currency) does not benefit from the Banco de Mexico's formal autonomy, given the federal government's continued influence over the institution.

The depth and breadth of a country's capital markets also can act as an important discipline. The sovereign has fewer incentives to default on local currency obligations when they are held by a broad cross-section of investors, rather than concentrated in the hands of local banks. For this reason, the establishment of mandatory, privately funded pension funds in a number of countries—such as Chile and Argentina—helps bolster their credit standing by creating an influential new class of bondholders. The experience of many OECD countries suggests that, even when public debt is high, creditworthiness can be sustained over long periods when policymakers are responsive to constituencies with vested interests in safeguarding the value of money.

Foreign Currency Rating Factors

The same economic and political factors that affect a sovereign's local currency credit standing also impact its ability and willingness to honor foreign currency debt—often to a greater degree because of the binding constraints the balance of payments can impose. As a result, Standard & Poor's analysis of foreign currency debt focuses on how government economic policies influence trends in public and private external debt over time.

In addition, from a political risk perspective, the extent of each country's integration in the global trade and financial systems must be considered. A high degree of integration generally gives the government strong incentives to meet its external obligations because of the correspondingly high political and economic costs of default.

Sudan (N.R.), in default on its foreign currency bank loans since 1979, has struggled almost continuously in recent years with civil insurrection and the breakdown of effective administration—its political and economic links with the outside world are at a low ebb. By contrast, Luxembourg (AAA) is a small country that is highly integrated with Europe and the rest of the world. As a result, it has very strong incentives to play by the international financial rules of the game. All sovereigns fall somewhere between these two extremes in their integration in the global economy.

At the same time, relations with neighboring countries must be examined with an eye for potential security risks. National security is a concern when military threats place significant burdens on fiscal policy, reduce the flow of potential investment, and put the balance of payments under stress. As Iraq's invasion of Kuwait ('A' foreign currency and 'A+' local currency) in 1990 demonstrated, the very existence of the sovereign can sometimes come into question. Lebanon ('BB-' foreign currency and 'BB' local currency) and Qatar ('BBB' foreign currency) are two other examples of sovereigns whose credit standing is constrained by their vulnerable geopolitical positions.

Balance of Payments Flexibility

Standard & Poor's balance of payments analysis focuses on the impact of economic policy on the external sector, as well as its structural characteristics. In the short run, policymakers' ability to manage financial pressures from abroad partly depends on the structure of merchandise trade, services, transfers, and the like. Yet, balance of payments pressures do not appear spontaneously or reach large magnitudes for structural reasons alone. In most cases, they can be traced back to flawed economic policies. The ratings service's approach reflects the premise that the macro- and microeconomic policies discussed earlier affect balance of payments behavior.

For this reason, the size of a country's current account deficit, even when very large, may not by itself be an important rating consideration. The tendency for some countries to run current account surpluses and others to run current account deficits is well documented. It is the product of many factors, not all of them negative, and not all related to government policies. Singapore ran very large current account deficits for much of its modern history, ones readily financed because they were not the by-product of fiscal mismanagement. However, Thailand's ('BBB-' foreign currency and 'A-' local currency) foreign exchange crisis in 1997 is a sharp reminder that large current account deficits can also be a symptom of serious underlying weaknesses—in this case a financial sector whose asset quality had weakened dramatically after years of rapid domestic credit growth. And as Mexico's debt servicing crisis in 1995 illustrated, current account deficits are a concern when government policies result in a public external debt structure that is vulnerable to sudden changes in investor sentiment.

External Financial Position

Consequently, Standard & Poor's examines each sovereign's external balance sheet alongside its analysis of balance of payments flows. The main focus is on trends in the public external debt position, the magnitude of contingent liabilities of the government, and the adequacy of foreign exchange reserves to service its and (especially in a crisis) the private sector's foreign currency debt. To complete the picture, Standard & Poor's calculates an international investment position. This is the broadest measure of a country's external financial position. It adds the value of private sector debt and equity liabilities to public sector external indebtedness denominated in local and foreign currencies.

Four important variables are:

- Net public external debt,
- Net external debt of financial institutions,
- Net external debt of the nonbank private sector, and
- Total debt service.

Public external debt includes the direct and guaranteed debt of the central government, obligations of regional and local governments, and the nonguaranteed debt of other public sector entities. Net public external debt equals total public sector debt minus public financial assets, including central bank reserves. The debt of other levels of government are analyzed, and generally consolidated with those of the national government, if legal and political circumstances expose the sovereign to internal and external financial risks from this source.

To measure the magnitude of public debt, Standard & Poor's compares it with annual flows of exports of goods and services (along with net public and private transfers where they are positive). For the 77 sovereigns with public ratings in October 1998, the median net public external debt-to-export ratio is 60%. Sovereigns with this degree of leverage currently include Denmark ('AA+' foreign currency and 'AAA' local currency), Israel ('A-' foreign currency and 'AA-' local currency), and Egypt ('BBB-' foreign currency and 'A-' local currency).

Other sectors' external debt also are measured in this way. Financial institutions' net debt equals their total external liabilities minus total external assets. Net debt of the nonfinancial private sector equals their total debt minus loans abroad. Debt of the private sector is examined because, in some circumstances, it can become a liability of the state.

Problems in the financial sector, in particular, can impair the sovereign's credit standing when they lead to official rescues of failing banks. Korea ('BB+' foreign currency) and Thailand are sovereigns whose foreign and local currency ratings were sharply downgraded in 1997-1998, in part because of the escalating cost of supporting their banking sectors. Currently, Malaysia's banks weigh on the sovereign's ('BBB-' foreign currency and 'A-' local currency) credit standing. Asset quality is rapidly deteriorating, and the system already relies on substantial official financial support. By contrast, New Zealand's banking sector poses relatively little risk to the sovereign's credit standing. Asset quality is generally sound and, importantly, the system's largest institutions are owned by creditworthy foreign banks.

Sovereign external debt also is evaluated in terms of its maturity profile, currency composition, and sensitivity to changing interest rates. Along with new borrowings, these factors influence the size of future interest and amortization payments. Debt service—including interest and principal on both short- and long-term debt—therefore is compared with projected exports. Debt contracted on concessional terms, to some extent, can offset a high public debt burden. Poland, for instance, has relatively high public external debt, around 82% of exports in 1998. But favorable terms on restructured foreign currency debt mean that debt service is low at 10% of exports.

International Liquidity

Central bank reserves are another external indicator, one whose importance varies across the ratings spectrum. Reserves usually act as a financial buffer for the government during periods of balance of payments stress. They include foreign currency and gold holdings, with the latter valued at market prices. Reserve adequacy is measured in relation to imports, and to projected current account deficits and total debt service. Whether a given level of reserves is adequate or not is judged in relation to the government's financial and exchange rate policies and, consequently, their vulnerability to changes in trade and capital flows.

Access to funding from the IMF and other multilateral and bilateral official sources is a related factor to consider. However, the mixed experience of recent Fund-led programs in Asia and Russia underscores the limited availability of official resources in relation to the funds deployed by banks and cross-border investors. Reserve levels, consequently, deserve particular scrutiny during periods of global financial volatility, as in the latter part of 1998, when bond markets effectively closed their doors to emerging market issuers.

The U.S. maintains very low reserves. It can do so because the U.S. dollar generally has floated against other currencies since 1971. The dollar's unique status as the key currency financing global trade and investment also reduces the need for gold and foreign exchange. Most other high investment-grade sovereigns with floating currencies and little foreign currency debt also require relatively modest reserves.

At lower rating levels, though, international liquidity is more critical when, as is often the case, government debt is denominated in foreign currencies and significant amounts of local currency debt are held by cross-border investors. Public finance setbacks and other economic or political shocks, consequently, can impair financial market access. Most Latin American sovereigns fall into this category and generally maintain above-average reserves as a result. Argentina and Hong Kong (foreign currency 'A' and local currency 'A+') also require above-average levels of international liquidity because their currency boards issue notes backed by foreign exchange. Lebanon, which maintains reserves equal to nearly a year's worth of imports, is something of a special case. It does so because the economy's highly dollarized nature is intertwined with the country's vulnerable geopolitical position, which creates the need for an especially large financial cushion to maintain investor confidence.

Local and Foreign Currency Rating Distinctions

Any divergence between a sovereign's local and foreign currency ratings reflects the distinctive credit risks of each type of debt. For example, long-standing political stability, fiscal and monetary policies resulting in relatively low inflation, and a high degree of international economic integration are characteristics of sovereign issuers of 'AAA' rated local currency debt. The manageable public external debt burdens of these issuers, in turn, result in foreign currency debt ratings at the upper end of the investment-grade spectrum.

Differences between local and foreign currency debt ratings can widen to some degree with sovereigns that are further down the ratings scale. These sovereigns, typically, fall into one of two categories: Sovereigns in the first category have long records of timely service on both local currency and foreign currency debt. Inflationary pressures are moderate and public finances are relatively sound, but foreign currency indebtedness may be relatively high or is likely to become so over time. Sovereigns in the second category also have unblemished local currency debt servicing track records, but relatively recent histories of foreign currency default. The local and foreign currency debt ratings assigned to them balance often substantial improvements in inflation and public finances with the risks inherent to still-heavy foreign currency debt burdens.

At the lower end of the rating scale, however, such rating differences sometimes narrow. A number of sovereigns in this category have emerged from local or foreign currency debt default quite recently, and still carry the risk of policy reversals that can result in renewed default. Other sovereigns in this category may not have defaulted, but face high inflation and other forms of social and political stress that carry a material risk of local currency default after payment of foreign currency debt can no longer be assured.

Canada ('AA+' foreign currency and 'AAA' local currency) is a good example of a government shouldering a public debt burden on the order of 90% of GDP—well above the OECD country average—but where the political commitment to low or moderate rates of inflation seems well entrenched. Conversely, when public finances are weak and inflation is left unchecked, the stage can be set for an accelerating spiral that leads to default. Government-inspired indexation of debt and other contracts to price inflation often abets the process, as in the defaults of Brazil ('BB-' foreign currency and 'BB' local currency) earlier this decade. But not all countries that have experimented with indexation suffer hyperinflation and default. Chile and Israel have long records of timely local currency debt service. Relatively conservative fiscal policies have underpinned their general credit standing in recent years by helping to unwind inflation and to contain the external debt burden.

Ratings of EU states joining the EMU present a special case. Governments entering EMU, due to start in January 1999, will cede monetary and exchange rate responsibilities to the new European Central Bank. As a result, Standard & Poor's now rates each government's local currency, including euro-denominated, debt and foreign currency debt the same. Economic and fiscal factors, already important, will be the dominant criteria for differentiating credit quality of sovereigns inside EMU going forward (*see Local and Foreign Currency Ratings Converge for EMU Issuers, June 1998*). Local and foreign currency ratings for Liechtenstein (AAA), Panama (BB+), and the Cook Islands (B-) are the same because these countries, too, are part of monetary unions.

As these examples illustrate, a number of factors must be examined when considering whether distinctions between local and foreign currency ratings are appropriate. The default frequency of sovereign local currency debt, generally, is much lower than that of foreign currency debt, but local currency defaults do occur. Russia's August 1998 default on its rouble-denominated debt is a particularly instructive case. Ironically, its experience shows why most sovereigns resist the temptation to take such a drastic step. Governments rarely default on local currency debt because control over the domestic banking system gives them access to some finance, even when foreign currency debt is in default. Russia defaulted on its rouble debt, in part, because a substantial portion was held by nonresidents seeking to reduce their holdings. (In such cases, Standard & Poor's usually rates local currency debt the same as, or only slightly higher than, foreign currency debt.) As a result of its default, however, Russia suddenly cut itself off from *all* financial markets, both domestic and external. The government, therefore, crippled the real economy, generated intense inflationary pressures, and sharply raised the default risk on its foreign currency debt.

Sovereign Rating Changes

Until recently, rated sovereigns formed an exclusive club of the world's most creditworthy governments. In 1980, Standard & Poor's rated just a dozen sovereign issuers—all at the 'AAA' level. Rating downgrades were relatively rare over the remainder of that decade and, when they occurred, usually were of modest dimensions. Today, the sovereign sector is far more heterogeneous. The 77 sovereigns Standard & Poor's monitors carry ratings between 'AAA' and 'CCC-'. Given this range of credit quality, rating changes occur more frequently.

Current economic and financial indicators alone do not determine ratings. Sovereign ratings measure future debt service capacity, and the future, of course, is uncertain. As a result, Standard & Poor's rating committees consider reasonable "worst-case" scenarios over a three- to five-year time horizon to gain a better understanding of future downside risks. The government's medium-term financial program, when available, is scrutinized alongside independent forecasts. The ratings service then looks at the interaction between public finances, external debt, and other variables, such as real export growth, asset quality trends affecting the local banking system, and changes in overseas interest rates.

Rating changes occur whenever new information significantly alters Standard & Poor's view of likely future developments. (Analysts generally meet with government officials at least once annually, but the timing of on-site meetings itself is not a factor determining when the agency raises or lowers ratings or changes rating outlooks.) For example, Ireland's foreign currency rating was upgraded to 'AA+' (and converged with its local currency rating) from 'AA' in May 1998, in light of its improved fiscal performance and declining public debt burden. By contrast, Kazakhstan's foreign and local currency ratings were downgraded to B+/BB- from BB-/BB+ in September 1998. These actions stemmed from the government's ineffective response to mounting fiscal and current account deficits at a time when, along with other emerging market issuers, its ability to attract capital inflows had greatly diminished.

As these examples illustrate, the impact of public finances on external debt usually is a key factor driving changes in foreign currency credit ratings. Similarly, significant changes in the inflation outlook figure in local currency rating changes. However, the implications of rating changes can vary across the credit spectrum. Fiscal pressures were behind the loss of New Zealand's 'AAA' foreign currency rating in 1983 and subsequent downgrades to 'AA-' though 1991. Still, the erosion in its credit quality was neither sudden nor very great. This reflects an important characteristic of most high investment-grade sovereigns, namely their ability to correct financial imbalances and even to bounce back in credit terms over time. Following a sustained tightening of budgetary policy, New Zealand's foreign currency rating was upgraded to 'AA' in December 1994 and to 'AA+' in January 1996. (Renewed fiscal weakness resulted in a rating outlook change to negative from stable in September 1998.)

Again, Russia tells a rather different story. Currently, Standard & Poor's considers its foreign currency debt to have the highest default risk in the sovereign sector. The government's credit standing has fallen steeply since it was first assigned a 'BB-' foreign currency rating in October 1996. The rating was lowered in four steps to 'CCC-' this year and the outlook remains negative. If anything, since the onset of Russia's crisis in the summer of 1998, policymakers have embraced heterodox policies, which suggests that the country's economic troubles will persist for a long time to come. Often in such cases, a number of financial crises, and defaults, may occur before there is renewed support for genuine economic stabilization and reform.

Sovereign Ratings and Corporate Credit Risk

Sovereign credit risk is always a key consideration in the assessment of the credit standing of banks and corporates. Sovereign risk comes into play because the unique, wide-ranging powers and resources of each national government affect the financial and operating environments of entities under its jurisdiction. Past experience has shown that defaults by otherwise-creditworthy borrowers can stem directly from the imposition of exchange controls, often, though not always, linked to a sovereign default.

In the case of foreign currency debt, the sovereign has first claim on available foreign exchange and controls the ability of any resident to obtain funds to repay creditors. To service debt denominated in local currency, the sovereign can exercise its powers to tax, to control the domestic financial system, and even to issue local currency in potentially unlimited amounts. Given these considerations, the credit ratings of international borrowers most often are at, or below, the ratings of the relevant sovereign. When obligations of issuers are rated higher than the sovereign's, this reflects both their stand-alone credit characteristics and other factors mitigating sovereign credit risk. (See *"Understanding Sovereign Risk,"* January 1997 and *"Less Credit Risk for Borrowers in Dollarized Economies,"* May 1997.)

Ratings Definitions

ISSUE CREDIT RATING DEFINITIONS

A Standard & Poor's issue credit rating is a current opinion of the creditworthiness of an obligor with respect to a specific financial obligation, a specific class of financial obligations, or a specific financial program (including ratings on medium term note programs and commercial paper programs). It takes into consideration the creditworthiness of guarantors, insurers, or other forms of credit enhancement on the obligation and takes into account the currency in which the obligation is denominated. The issue credit rating is not a recommendation to purchase, sell, or hold a financial obligation, inasmuch as it does not comment as to market price or suitability for a particular investor.

Issue credit ratings are based on current information furnished by the obligors or obtained by Standard & Poor's from other sources it considers reliable. Standard & Poor's does not perform an audit in connection with any credit rating and may, on occasion, rely on unaudited financial information. Credit ratings may be changed, suspended, or withdrawn as a result of changes in, or unavailability of, such information, or based on other circumstances.

Issue credit ratings can be either long-term or short-term. Short-term ratings are generally assigned to those obligations considered short-term in the relevant market. In the U.S., for example, that means obligations with an original maturity of no more than 365 days—including commercial paper. Short-term ratings are also used to indicate the creditworthiness of an obligor with respect to put features on long-term obligations. The result is a dual rating, in which the short-term rating addresses the put feature, in addition to the usual long-term rating. Medium-term notes are assigned long-term ratings.

Long-Term Issue Credit Ratings

Issue credit ratings are based, in varying degrees, on the following considerations:
- Likelihood of payment—capacity and willingness of the obligor to meet its financial commitment on an obligation in accordance with the terms of the obligation;
- Nature of and provisions of the obligation;
- Protection afforded by, and relative position of, the obligation in the event of bankruptcy, reorganization, or other arrangement under the laws of bankruptcy and other laws affecting creditors' rights.

The issue rating definitions are expressed in terms of default risk. As such, they pertain to senior obligations of an entity. Junior obligations are typically rated lower than senior obligations, to reflect the lower priority in bankruptcy, as noted above. (Such differentiation applies when an entity has both senior and subordinated obligations, secured and unsecured obligations, or operating company and holding company obligations.) Accordingly, in the case of junior debt, the rating may not conform exactly with the category definition.

AAA

An obligation rated 'AAA' has the highest rating assigned by Standard & Poor's. The obligor's capacity to meet its financial commitment on the obligation is extremely strong.

AA

An obligation rated 'AA' differs from the highest rated obligations only in small degree. The obligor's capacity to meet its financial commitment on the obligation is very strong.

A

An obligation rated 'A' is somewhat more susceptible to the adverse effects of changes in circumstances and economic conditions than obligations in higher rated categories. However, the obligor's capacity to meet its financial commitment on the obligation is still strong.

BBB

An obligation rated 'BBB' exhibits adequate protection parameters. However, adverse economic conditions or changing circumstances are more likely to lead to a weakened capacity of the obligor to meet its financial commitment on the obligation.

Obligations rated 'BB', 'B', 'CCC', 'CC', and 'C' are regarded as having significant speculative characteristics. 'BB' indicates the least degree of speculation and 'C' the highest. While such obligations will likely have some quality and protective characteristics, these may be outweighed by large uncertainties or major exposures to adverse conditions.

BB

An obligation rated 'BB' is less vulnerable to nonpayment than other speculative issues. However, it faces major ongoing uncertainties or exposure to adverse business, financial, or economic conditions which could lead to the obligor's inadequate capacity to meet its financial commitment on the obligation.

B

An obligation rated 'B' is more vulnerable to nonpayment than obligations rated 'BB', but the obligor currently has the capacity to meet its financial commitment on the obligation. Adverse business, financial, or economic conditions will likely impair the obligor's capacity or willingness to meet its financial commitment on the obligation.

CCC

An obligation rated 'CCC' is currently vulnerable to nonpayment, and is dependent upon favorable business, financial, and economic conditions for the obligor to meet its financial commitment on the obligation. In the event of adverse business, financial, or economic conditions, the obligor is not likely to have the capacity to meet its financial commitment on the obligation.

CC

An obligation rated 'CC' is currently highly vulnerable to nonpayment.

C

A subordinated debt or preferred stock obligation rated 'C' is CURRENTLY HIGHLY VULNERABLE to nonpayment. The 'C' rating may be used to cover a situation where a bankruptcy petition has been filed or similar action taken, but payments on this obligation are being continued. A 'C' also will be assigned to a preferred stock issue in arrears on dividends or sinking fund payments, but that is currently paying.

D

An obligation rated 'D' is in payment default. The 'D' rating category is used when payments on an obligation are not made on the date due even if the applicable grace period has not expired, unless Standard & Poor's believes that such payments will be made during such grace period. The 'D' rating also will be used upon the filing of a bankruptcy petition or the taking of a similar action if payments on an obligation are jeopardized.

Plus (+) or minus (-)

The ratings from 'AA' to 'CCC' may be modified by the addition of a plus or minus sign to show relative standing within the major rating categories.

r

This symbol is attached to the ratings of instruments with significant noncredit risks. It highlights risks to principal or volatility of expected returns which are not addressed in the credit rating.

N.R.

This indicates that no rating has been requested, that there is insufficient information on which to base a rating, or that Standard & Poor's does not rate a particular obligation as a matter of policy.

Short-Term Issue Credit Ratings

A-1

A short-term obligation rated 'A-1' is rated in the highest category by Standard & Poor's. The obligor's capacity to meet its financial commitment on the obligation is strong. Within this category, certain obligations are designated with a plus sign (+). This indicates that the obligor's capacity to meet its financial commitment on these obligations is extremely strong.

A-2

A short-term obligation rated 'A-2' is somewhat more susceptible to the adverse effects of changes in circumstances and economic conditions than obligations in higher rating categories. However, the obligor's capacity to meet its financial commitment on the obligation is satisfactory.

A-3

A short-term obligation rated 'A-3' exhibits adequate protection parameters. However, adverse economic conditions or changing circumstances are more likely to lead to a weakened capacity of the obligor to meet its financial commitment on the obligation.

B

A short-term obligation rated 'B' is regarded as having significant speculative characteristics. The obligor currently has the capacity to meet its financial commitment on the obligation; however, it faces major ongoing uncertainties which could lead to the obligor's inadequate capacity to meet its financial commitment on the obligation.

C

A short-term obligation rated 'C' is currently vulnerable to nonpayment and is dependent upon favorable business, financial, and economic conditions for the obligor to meet its financial commitment on the obligation.

D

A short-term obligation rated 'D' is in payment default. The 'D' rating category is used when payments on an obligation are not made on the date due even if the applicable grace period has not expired, unless Standard & Poor's believes that such payments will be made during such grace period. The 'D' rating also will be used upon the filing of a bankruptcy petition or the taking of a similar action if payments on an obligation are jeopardized.

Local Currency and Foreign Currency Risks

Country risk considerations are a standard part of Standard & Poor's analysis for credit ratings on any issuer or issue. Currency of repayment is a key factor in this analysis. An obligor's capacity to repay foreign currency obligations may be lower than its capacity to repay obligations in its local currency due to the sovereign government's own relatively lower capacity to repay external versus domestic debt. These sovereign risk considerations are incorporated in the debt ratings assigned to specific issues. Foreign currency issuer ratings are also distinguished from local currency issuer ratings to identify those instances where sovereign risks make them different for the same issuer.

ISSUER CREDIT RATING DEFINITIONS

A Standard & Poor's Issuer Credit Rating is a current opinion of an obligor's overall financial capacity (its creditworthiness) to pay its financial obligations. This opinion focuses on the obligor's capacity and willingness to meet its financial commitments as they come due. It does not apply to any specific financial obligation, as it does not take into account the nature of and provisions of the obligation, its standing in bankruptcy or liquidation, statutory preferences, or the legality and enforceability of the obligation. In addition, it does not take into account the creditworthiness of the guarantors, insurers, or other forms of credit enhancement on the obligation. The Issuer Credit Rating is not a recommendation to purchase, sell, or hold a financial obligation issued by an obligor, as it does not comment on market price or suitability for a particular investor.

Counterparty Credit Ratings, ratings assigned under the Corporate Credit Rating Service (formerly called the Credit Assessment Service) and Sovereign Credit Ratings are all forms of Issuer Credit Ratings.

Issuer Credit Ratings are based on current information furnished by obligors or obtained by Standard & Poor's from other sources it considers reliable. Standard & Poor's does not perform an audit in connection with any Issuer Credit Rating and may, on occasion, rely on unaudited financial information. Issuer Credit Ratings may be changed, suspended, or withdrawn as a result of changes in, or unavailability of, such information, or based on other circumstances. Issuer Credit Ratings can be either long-term or short-term. Short-Term Issuer Credit Ratings reflect the obligor's creditworthiness over a short-term time horizon.

Long-Term Issuer Credit Ratings

AAA

An obligor rated 'AAA' has EXTREMELY STRONG capacity to meet its financial commitments. 'AAA' is the highest Issuer Credit Rating assigned by Standard & Poor's.

AA

An obligor rated 'AA' has VERY STRONG capacity to meet its financial commitments. It differs from the highest rated obligors only in small degree.

A

An obligor rated 'A' has STRONG capacity to meet its financial commitments but is somewhat more susceptible to the adverse effects of changes in circumstances and economic conditions than obligors in higher-rated categories.

BBB

An obligor rated 'BBB' has ADEQUATE capacity to meet its financial commitments. However, adverse economic conditions or changing circumstances are more likely to lead to a weakened capacity of the obligor to meet its financial commitments.

Obligors rated 'BB', 'B', 'CCC', and 'CC' are regarded as having significant speculative characteristics. 'BB' indicates the least degree of speculation and 'CC' the highest. While such obligors will likely have some quality and protective characteristics, these may be outweighed by large uncertainties or major exposures to adverse conditions.

BB

An obligor rated 'BB' is LESS VULNERABLE in the near term than other lower-rated obligors. However, it faces major ongoing uncertainties and exposure to adverse business, financial, or economic conditions which could lead to the obligor's inadequate capacity to meet its financial commitments.

B

An obligor rated 'B' is MORE VULNERABLE than the obligors rated 'BB', but the obligor currently has the capacity to meet its financial commitments. Adverse business, financial, or economic conditions will likely impair the obligor's capacity or willingness to meet its financial commitments.

CCC

An obligor rated 'CCC' is CURRENTLY VULNERABLE, and is dependent upon favorable business, financial, and economic conditions to meet its financial commitments.

CC

An obligor rated 'CC' is CURRENTLY HIGHLY-VULNERABLE.

Plus (+) or minus (-)

Ratings from 'AA' to 'CCC' may be modified by the addition of a plus or minus sign to show relative standing within the major rating categories.

R

An obligor rated 'R' is under regulatory supervision owing to its financial condition. During the pendency of the regulatory supervision the regulators may have the power to favor one class of obligations over others or pay some obligations and not others. Please see Standard & Poor's issue credit ratings for a more detailed description of the effects of regulatory supervision on specific issues or classes of obligations.

SD and D

An obligor rated 'SD' (Selective Default) or 'D' has failed to pay one or more of its financial obligations (rated or unrated) when it came due. A 'D' rating is assigned when Standard & Poor's believes that the default will be a general default and that the obligor will fail to pay all or substantially all of its obligations as they come due. An 'SD' rating is assigned when Standard & Poor's believes that the obligor has selectively defaulted on a specific issue or class of obligations but it will continue to meet its payment obligations on other issues or classes of obligations in a timely manner. Please see Standard & Poor's issue credit ratings for a more detailed description of the effects of a default on specific issues or classes of obligations.

N.R.

An issuer designated N.R. is not rated.

Public Information Ratings

Ratings with a 'pi' subscript are based on an analysis of an issuer's published financial information, as well as additional information in the public domain. They do not, however, reflect in-depth meetings with an issuer's management and are therefore based on less comprehensive information than ratings without a 'pi' subscript. Ratings with a 'pi' subscript are reviewed annually based on a new year's financial statements, but may be reviewed on an interim basis if a major event occurs that may affect the issuer's credit quality.

Outlooks are not provided for ratings with a 'pi' subscript, nor are they subject to potential CreditWatch listings. Ratings with a 'pi' subscript generally are not modified with '+' or '-' designations. However, such designations may be assigned when the issuer's credit rating is constrained by sovereign risk or the credit quality of a parent company or affiliated group.

Termination Structure

T subscript: Termination structures are designed to honor their contracts to full maturity or, should certain events occur, to terminate and cash settle all their contracts before their final maturity date.

Short-Term Issuer Credit Ratings

A-1

An obligor rated 'A-1' has STRONG capacity to meet its financial commitments. It is rated in the highest category by Standard & Poor's. Within this category, certain obligors are designated with a plus sign (+). This indicates that the obligor's capacity to meet its financial commitments is EXTREMELY STRONG.

A-2

An obligor rated 'A-2' has SATISFACTORY capacity to meet its financial commitments. However, it is somewhat more susceptible to the adverse effects of changes in circumstances and economic conditions than obligors in the highest rating category.

A-3

An obligor rated 'A-3' has ADEQUATE capacity to meet its financial obligations. However, adverse economic conditions or changing circumstances are more likely to lead to a weakened capacity of the obligor to meet its financial commitments.

B

An obligor rated 'B' is regarded as VULNERABLE and has significant speculative characteristics. The obligor currently has the capacity to meet its financial commitments; however, it faces major ongoing uncertainties which could lead to the obligor's inadequate capacity to meet its financial commitments.

C

An obligor rated 'C' is CURRENTLY VULNERABLE to nonpayment and is dependent upon favorable business, financial, and economic conditions for it to meet its financial commitments.

R

An obligor rated 'R' is under regulatory supervision owing to its financial condition. During the pendency of the regulatory supervision the regulators may have the power to favor one class of obligations over others or pay some obligations and not others. Please see Standard & Poor's issue credit ratings for a more detailed description of the effects of regulatory supervision on specific issues or classes of obligations.

SD and D

An obligor rated 'SD' (Selective Default) or 'D' has failed to pay one or more of its financial obligations (rated or unrated) when it came due. A 'D' rating is assigned when Standard & Poor's believes that the default will be a general default and that the obligor will fail to pay all or substantially all of its obligations as they come due. An 'SD' rating is assigned when Standard & Poor's believes that the obligor has selectively defaulted on a specific issue or class of obligations but it will continue to meet its payment obligations on other issues or classes of obligations in a timely manner. Please see Standard & Poor's issue credit ratings for a more detailed description of the effects of a default on specific issues or classes of obligations.

N.R.

An issuer designated N.R. is not rated.

Local Currency and Foreign Currency Risks

Country risk considerations are a standard part of Standard & Poor's analysis for credit ratings on any issuer or issue. Currency of repayment is a key factor in this analysis. An obligor's capacity to repay foreign currency obligations may be lower than its capacity to repay obligations in its local currency due to the sovereign government's own relatively lower capacity to repay external versus domestic debt. These sovereign risk considerations are incorporated in the debt ratings assigned to specific issues. Foreign currency issuer ratings are also distinguished from local currency issuer ratings to identify those instances where sovereign risks make them different for the same issuer.

RATING OUTLOOK DEFINITIONS

A Standard & Poor's Rating Outlook assesses the potential direction of a long-term credit rating over the intermediate to longer term. In determining a Rating Outlook, consideration is given to any changes in the economic and/or fundamental business conditions. An Outlook is not necessarily a precursor of a rating change or future CreditWatch action.

- Positive means that a rating may be raised.
- Negative means that a rating may be lowered.
- Stable means that a rating is not likely to change.
- Developing means a rating may be raised or lowered.
- N.M. means not meaningful.

CreditWatch

CreditWatch highlights the potential direction of a short- or long-term rating. It focuses on identifiable events and short-term trends that cause ratings to be placed under special surveillance by Standard & Poor's analytical staff. These may include mergers, recapitalizations, voter referendums, regulatory action, or anticipated operating developments. Ratings appear on CreditWatch when such an event or a deviation from an expected trend occurs and additional information is necessary to evaluate the current rating. A listing, however, does not mean a rating change is inevitable, and whenever possible, a range of alternative ratings will be shown. CreditWatch is not intended to include all ratings under review, and rating changes may occur without the ratings having first appeared on CreditWatch. The "positive" designation means that a rating may be raised; "negative" means a rating may be lowered; and "developing" means that a rating may be raised, lowered, or affirmed.

DUAL RATINGS DEFINITIONS

Standard & Poor's assigns "dual" ratings to all debt issues that have a put option or demand feature as part of their structure. The first rating addresses the likelihood of repayment of principal and interest as due, and the second rating addresses only the demand feature. The long-term debt rating symbols are used for bonds to denote the long-term maturity and the commercial paper rating symbols for the put option (for example, 'AAA/A-1+'). With short-term demand debt, Standard & Poor's note rating symbols are used with the commercial paper rating symbols (for example, 'SP-1+/A-1+').

MONEY MARKET FUND RATING DEFINITIONS

Money market fund ratings assess the safety of invested principal.

AAAm

Safety is excellent. Superior capacity to maintain principal value and limit exposure to loss.

AAm

Safety is very good. Strong capacity to maintain principal value and limit exposure to loss.

Am

Safety is good. Sound capacity to maintain principal value and limit exposure to loss.

BBBm

Safety is fair. Adequate capacity to maintain principal value and limit exposure to loss.

BBm

Safety is uncertain. Vulnerable to loss of principal value.

Bm

Safety is limited. Very vulnerable to loss of principal value.

CCCm

Extremely vulnerable to loss of principal value.

Dm

Fund has failed to maintain principal value; realized or unrealized losses exceed 0.5% of net asset value.

G

The letter 'G' follows the rating symbol when a fund's portfolio consists primarily of direct U.S. government securities.

Plus (+) or minus (-)

The ratings may be modified by the addition of a plus or minus sign to show relative standing within the rating categories.

A money market fund rating is not directly comparable with a Standard & Poor's issue-specific rating due to differences in investment characteristics, rating criteria, and creditworthiness of portfolio investments. For example, a money market fund portfolio provides greater liquidity, price stability, and diversification than a long-term bond, but not necessarily the credit quality that would be indicated by the corresponding issue rating. Ratings are not commentaries on yield levels.

A money market fund rating is not a recommendation to buy, sell, or hold any security held or issued by the fund, inasmuch as it does not comment as to yield or suitability for a particular investor. Further, the rating may be changed, suspended, or withdrawn as a result of changes in or unavailability of information relating to the fund. The ratings are based on current information furnished to Standard & Poor's by the issuer or obtained by Standard & Poor's from other sources it considers reliable. Standard & Poor's does not perform an audit in connection with any rating and may, on occasion, rely on unaudited financial information. The ratings may be changed, suspended, or withdrawn as a result of changes in, or unavailability of, such information, or based on other circumstances.

BOND FUND CREDIT QUALITY RATING DEFINITIONS

Managed fund credit quality ratings, identified by the 'f' subscript, are assigned to bond funds and other actively managed funds that exhibit variable net asset values. These ratings are current assessments of the overall credit quality of a fund's portfolio. The ratings reflect the level of protection against losses from credit defaults and are based on an analysis of the credit quality of the portfolio investments and the likelihood of counterparty defaults.

AAAf

The fund's portfolio holdings provide extremely strong protection against losses from credit defaults.

AAf

The fund's portfolio holdings provide very strong protection against losses from credit defaults.

Af

The fund's portfolio holdings provide strong protection against losses from credit defaults.

BBBf

The fund's portfolio holdings provide adequate protection against losses from credit defaults.

BBf

The fund's portfolio holdings provide uncertain protection against losses from credit defaults.

Bf

The fund's portfolio holdings exhibit vulnerability to losses from credit defaults.

CCCf

The fund's portfolio holdings make it extremely vulnerable to losses from credit defaults.

Plus (+) or minus (-)

The ratings from 'AAf to CCCf' may be modified by the addition of a plus (+) or minus (-) sign to show relative standing within the major rating categories.

The credit ratings are not a recommendation to purchase, sell, or hold any security held or issued by the fund, inasmuch as they do not comment as to market price, yield or suitability for a particular investor. The ratings are based on current information furnished to Standard & Poor's by the fund or obtained by Standard & Poor's from other sources it considers reliable. Standard & Poor's does not perform an audit in connection with any rating and may, on occasion, rely on unaudited financial information. The ratings may be changed, suspended, or withdrawn as a result of changes in, or unavailability of, such information, or based on other circumstances.

BOND FUND VOLATILITY RATINGS DEFINITIONS

A bond fund volatility rating is a current opinion of a fixed-income investment fund's sensitivity to changing market conditions relative to the risk of a portfolio composed of government securities* and denominated in the base currency of the fund. Volatility ratings evaluate the fund's sensitivity to interest rate movements, credit risk, investment diversification or concentration, liquidity, leverage, and other factors.

S1

Bond funds that possess low sensitivity to changing market conditions are rated S1. These funds possess an aggregate level of risk that is less than or equal to that of a portfolio comprised of government securities maturing within one to three years and denominated in the base currency of the fund. Within this category, certain funds are designated with a plus sign (+). This indicates the fund's extremely low sensitivity to changing market conditions. These funds possess an aggregate level of risk that is less than or equal to that of a portfolio comprised of the highest quality fixed-income instruments with an average maturity of six months or less.

S2

Bond funds that possess low to moderate sensitivity to changing market conditions are rated S2. These funds possess an aggregate level of risk that is less than or equal to that of a portfolio comprised of government securities maturing within three to seven years and denominated in the base currency of the fund.

S3

Bond funds that possess moderate sensitivity to changing market conditions are rated S3. These funds possess an aggregate level of risk that is less than or equal to that of a portfolio comprised of government securities maturing within seven to 10 years and denominated in the base currency of the fund.

S4

Bond funds that possess moderate to high sensitivity to changing market conditions are rated S4. These funds possess an aggregate level of risk that is less than or equal to that of a portfolio comprised of government securities maturing beyond 10 years and denominated in the base currency of the fund.

S5

Bond funds that possess high sensitivity to changing market conditions are rated S5. These funds may be exposed to a variety of significant risks including high concentration risks, high leverage, and investments in complex structured and/or illiquid securities.

S6

Bond funds that possess the highest sensitivity to changing market conditions are rated S6. These funds include those with highly speculative investment strategies with multiple forms of significant risks, with little or no diversification benefits.

The ratings are based on current information furnished by the fund to Standard & Poor's or obtained by Standard & Poor's from other sources it considers reliable. Standard & Poor's does not perform an audit in connection with any rating, and may rely on unaudited financial information. The ratings may be changed, suspended, or withdrawn as a result of changes in, or unavailability of, such information, or based on other circumstances. The rating is not a recommendation to purchase, sell, or hold any security held or issued by the fund, inasmuch as it does not comment on market price, yield, or suitability for a particular investor.

INSURER FINANCIAL STRENGTH RATING DEFINITIONS

A Standard & Poor's Insurer Financial Strength Rating is a current opinion of the financial security characteristics of an insurance organization with respect to its ability to pay under its insurance policies and contracts in accordance with their terms. Insurer Financial Strength Ratings are also assigned to health maintenance organizations and similar health plans with respect to their ability to pay under their policies and contracts in accordance with their terms.

This opinion is not specific to any particular policy or contract, nor does it address the suitability of a particular policy or contract for a specific purpose or purchaser. Furthermore, the opinion does not take into account deductibles, surrender or cancellation penalties, timeliness of payment, nor the likelihood of the use of a defense such as fraud to deny claims. For organizations with cross-border or multinational operations, including those conducted by subsidiaries or branch offices, the ratings do not take into account potential that may exist for foreign exchange restrictions to prevent financial obligations from being met.

Insurer Financial Strength Ratings are based on information furnished by rated organizations or obtained by Standard & Poor's from other sources it considers reliable. Standard & Poor's does not perform an audit in connection with any rating and may on occasion rely on unaudited financial information. Ratings may be changed, suspended, or withdrawn as a result of changes in, or unavailability of such information or based on other circumstances.

Insurer Financial Strength Ratings do not refer to an organization's ability to meet nonpolicy (i.e. debt) obligations. Assignment of ratings to debt issued by insurers or to debt issues that are fully or partially supported by insurance policies, contracts, or guarantees is a separate process from the determination of Insurer

Financial Strength Ratings, and follows procedures consistent with issue credit rating definitions and practices. Insurer Financial Strength Ratings are not a recommendation to purchase or discontinue any policy or contract issued by an insurer or to buy, hold, or sell any security issued by an insurer. A rating is not a guaranty of an insurer's financial strength or security.

Insurer Financial Strength Ratings

An insurer rated 'BBB' or higher is regarded as having financial security characteristics that outweigh any vulnerabilities, and is highly likely to have the ability to meet financial commitments.

AAA

An insurer rated 'AAA' has EXTREMELY STRONG financial security characteristics. 'AAA' is the highest Insurer Financial Strength Rating assigned by Standard & Poor's.

AA

An insurer rated 'AA' has VERY STRONG financial security characteristics, differing only slightly from those rated higher.

A

An insurer rated 'A' has STRONG financial security characteristics, but is somewhat more likely to be affected by adverse business conditions than are insurers with higher ratings.

BBB

An insurer rated 'BBB' has GOOD financial security characteristics, but is more likely to be affected by adverse business conditions than are higher rated insurers.

An insurer rated 'BB' or lower is regarded as having vulnerable characteristics that may outweigh its strengths. 'BB' indicates the least degree of vulnerability within the range; 'CC' the highest.

BB

An insurer rated 'BB' has MARGINAL financial security characteristics. Positive attributes exist, but adverse business conditions could lead to insufficient ability to meet financial commitments.

B

An insurer rated 'B' has WEAK financial security characteristics. Adverse business conditions will likely impair its ability to meet financial commitments.

CCC

An insurer rated 'CCC' has VERY WEAK financial security characteristics, and is dependent on favorable business conditions to meet financial commitments.

CC

An insurer rated 'CC' has EXTREMELY WEAK financial security characteristics and is likely not to meet some of its financial commitments.

R

An insurer rated 'R' is under regulatory supervision owing to its financial condition. During the pendency of the regulatory supervision, the regulators may have the power to favor one class of obligations over others or pay some obligations and not others. The rating does not apply to insurers subject only to nonfinancial actions such as market conduct violations.

N.R.

An insurer designated 'N.R.' is NOT RATED, which implies no opinion about the insurer's financial security.

Plus (+) or minus (-) signs following ratings from 'AA' to 'CCC' show relative standing within the major rating categories.

CreditWatch highlights the potential direction of a rating, focusing on identifiable events and short-term trends that cause ratings to be placed under special surveillance by Standard & Poor's. The events may include mergers, recapitalizations, voter referenda, regulatory actions, or anticipated operating developments. Ratings appear on CreditWatch when such an event or a deviation from an expected trend occurs and additional information is needed to evaluate the rating. A listing, however, does not mean a rating change is inevitable, and whenever possible, a range of alternative ratings will be shown. CreditWatch is not intended to include all ratings under review, and rating changes may occur without the ratings having first appeared on CreditWatch. The "positive" designation means that a rating may be raised; "negative" means that a rating may be lowered; "developing" means that a rating may be raised, lowered or affirmed.

'pi' Ratings, denoted with a 'pi' subscript, are Insurer Financial Strength Ratings based on an analysis of an insurer's published financial information and additional information in the public domain. They do not reflect in-depth meetings with an insurer's management and are therefore based on less comprehensive information than ratings without a 'pi' subscript. 'pi' ratings are reviewed annually based on a new year's financial statements, but may be reviewed on an interim basis if a major event that may affect the insurer's financial security occurs. Ratings with a 'pi' subscript are not subject to potential CreditWatch listings.

Ratings with a 'pi' subscript generally are not modified with '+' or '-' designations. However, such designations may be assigned when the insurer's financial strength rating is constrained by sovereign risk or the credit quality of a parent company or affiliated group.

National Scale Ratings, denoted with a prefix such as 'mx' (Mexico) or 'ra' (Argentina), assess an insurer's financial security relative to other insurers in its home market. For more information, refer to the separate definitions for national scale ratings.

Quantitative Ratings, denoted with a 'q' subscript, were discontinued in 1997. The ratings were based solely on quantitative analysis of publicly available financial data.

Short-Term Insurer Financial Strength Ratings

Short-Term Insurer Financial Strength Ratings reflect the insurer's creditworthiness over a short-term time horizon.

A-1

An insurer rated 'A-1' has a STRONG ability to meet its financial commitments on short-term policy obligations. It is rated in the highest category by Standard & Poor's. Within this category, certain insurers are designated with a plus sign (+). This indicates that the insurer's ability to meet its financial commitments on short-term policy obligations is—EXTREMELY STRONG.

A-2

An insurer rated 'A-2' has a GOOD ability to meet its financial commitments on short-term policy obligations. However, it is somewhat more susceptible to the adverse effects of changes in circumstances and economic conditions than insurers in the highest rating category.

A-3

An insurer rated 'A-3' has an ADEQUATE ability to meet its financial commitments on short-term policy obligations. However, adverse economic conditions or changing circumstances are more likely to lead to a weakened ability of the insurer to meet its financial obligations.

B

An insurer rated 'B' is regarded as VULNERABLE and has significant speculative characteristics. The insurer currently has the ability to meet its financial commitments on short-term policy obligations; however, it faces major ongoing uncertainties which could lead to the insurer's inadequate ability to meet its financial obligations.

C

An insurer rated 'C' is regarded as CURRENTLY VULNERABLE to nonpayment and is dependent upon favorable business, financial, and economic conditions for it to meet its financial commitments on short-term policy obligations.

R

See definition of "R" under Long-Term Ratings.

Plus (+) or minus (-)

Ratings from 'AA' to 'CCC' may be modified by the addition of a plus or minus sign to show relative standing within the major rating categories.

Standard & Poor's ratings and other assessments of creditworthiness and financial strength are not a recommendation to purchase or discontinue any policy or contract issues by an insurer or to buy, hold, or sell any security issued by an insurer. In addition, neither a rating nor an assessment is a guaranty of an insurer's financial strength.

INSURER FINANCIAL ENHANCEMENT RATING DEFINITIONS

A Standard & Poor's Insurer Financial Enhancement Rating is a current opinion of the creditworthiness of an obligor with respect to insurance policies or other financial obligations that are predominantly used as credit enhancement and/or financial guarantees. When assigning an Insurer Financial Enhancement Rating, Standard & Poor's analysis focuses on capital, liquidity, and company commitment necessary to support a credit enhancement or financial guaranty business. The Insurer Financial Enhancement Rating is not a recommendation to purchase, sell, or hold a financial obligation, inasmuch as it does not comment as to market price or suitability for a particular investor.

Insurer Financial Enhancement Ratings are based on information furnished by the obligors or obtained by Standard & Poor's from other sources it considers reliable. Standard & Poor's does not perform an audit in connection with any credit rating and may, on occasion, rely on unaudited financial information. Insurer Financial Enhancement Ratings may be changed, suspended, or withdrawn as a result of changes in, or unavailability of, such information or based on other circumstances. Insurer Financial Enhancement Ratings are based, in varying degrees, on all of the following considerations:

1. Likelihood of payment-capacity and willingness of the obligor to meet its financial commitment on an obligation in accordance with the terms of the obligation;
2. Nature of and provisions of the obligations; and
3. Protection afforded by, and relative position of, the obligation in the event of bankruptcy, reorganization, or other arrangement under the laws of bankruptcy and other laws affecting creditors' rights.

Criteria for Multilateral Lending Institutions

Helena Hessel, New York (1) 212-438-7349

Standard & Poor's credit analysis of multilateral lending institutions reflects their special character-istics as financial institutions created, owned, and controlled by a group of sovereign governments. Stan-dard & Poor's rating methodology for a sovereign-supported financial institution balances sovereign governments' willingness and ability to provide support and the institution's stand-alone financial strength.

Membership Support

Strong membership support is essential to the creditworthiness of any sovereign-supported institution. The strength of this support depends on three broad factors:
- Political and economic purpose;
- Ownership structure; and
- Size, form, and timeliness of capital contributions.

Purpose.

For a multilateral lending institution to be viable, it must serve abiding economic and political pur-poses, which its member states fully support. An important consideration is the extent to which an equi-table distribution of financial benefits and costs is maintained among shareholders, given that a multilat-eral lending institution's purpose changes over time as it adapts to the evolving needs of its membership.

Ownership Structure.

The credit support a multilateral lending institution enjoys depends on its member nations' credit-worthiness and on the manner and extent to which this creditworthiness has been extended. Because a multilateral lending institution's debt obligations are not guaranteed by member governments, member-ship support must be judged indirectly. Callable capital is an important indicator of the owners' willing-ness to support the institution, although it does not represent a guarantee. It is available only to meet the multilateral lending institution's debt obligations, not to fund loans. Moreover, it only assures ultimate debt repayment, as the timeliness of call procedures cannot be ensured. Standard & Poor's places more weight on callable capital from 'AAA' rated member states than on the callable capital committed by other investment-grade countries.

Standard & Poor's assesses the decision-making process of a multilateral lending institution by examining the distribution of voting power among member countries. To ensure the willingness of donor member countries to provide additional capital, the distribution of voting power should broadly parallel the benefits of membership. As such, it should foster maintenance of prudent financial policies that safeguard investments and minimize the likelihood of recourse to callable capital.

Capital Contributions.

Standard & Poor's evaluates the size, composition, and timeliness of capital contributions, which provide the most tangible test of membership support. The appropriate size depends on the scale, diversity, risk characteristics, and growth of a multilateral lending institution's assets. The composition of capital contributions has important implications for the ownership structure, the portion of subscribed capital that is paid in, and the quality of callable capital. In this regard, the willingness of 'AAA' shareholders to maintain or even increase their shares is key. Timeliness of capital increases is inferred by member governments' willingness to act well before any potential lending or borrowing constraints imposed by statutory limitations on gearing or leverage are encountered.

Standard & Poor's gives greatest weight to the paid-in portion of subscribed capital, focusing on the amount available in convertible currencies. Paid-in capital represents a good faith deposit, which enhances the credibility of callable capital and helps ensure timely debt repayment. Since paid-in capital requires a budgetary outlay for member governments, it represents a more difficult political decision than callable capital. As a contingent claim, callable capital has no immediate budgetary cost. Therefore, paid-in capital is a more direct and sensitive measure of members' willingness to support a multilateral lending institution. A secondary consideration is that higher paid-in capital improves profitability.

Table A Nonperforming Loan Experience For Multilateral Lending Institutions	-- Year ended Dec. 31 -- Nonaccrual loans outstanding*/ disbursed loans outstanding (%)				Nonaccrual loans outstanding -- loan loss provisions*/ 'AAA' callable capital + paid-in capital + reserves (%)			
	1998	1997	1996	1995	1998	1997	1996	1995
African Development Bank	14.1	9.4	10.1	13.9	10.7	6.0	7.8	13.7
Asian Development Bank	0.2	0.2	0.1	0.2	(0.0)	(0.0)	(0.0)	(0.0)
Corporacion Andina de Fomento	0.9	0.7	1.0	0.5	(32.6)	(27.8)	(23.5)	(20.5)
Council of Europe Social Development Fund	0.7	0.7	0.7	0.5	(0.3)	(0.7)	(1.0)	(2.5)
European Bank for Reconstruction and Development	5.0	2.6	0.3	0.5	(1.9)	(0.3)	(1.0)	(0.4)
EUROFIMA	0.0	NA	0.0	0.0	0.0	NA	0.0	0.0
European Investment Bank	0.0	0.0	0.0	0.0	(0.3)	(0.3)	0.5	0.6
Inter-American Development Bank	0.0	0.0	0.0	0.0	(2.0)	(1.9)	(2.0)	(2.3)
International Bank for Reconstruction and Development**	1.8	1.9	2.2	2.3	(1.4)	(1.1)	(0.9)	(0.8)
International Finance Corporation **$	11.1	9.2	4.9	5.6	(2.3)	(4.4)	(6.2)	(3.7)
Nordic Investment Bank	0.0	0.0	0.3	0.4	0.1	(1.4)	1.8	1.3

*All loans to countries with any losses in nonaccrual status. For African Development Bank, Asian Development Bank, Corporacion Andina de Fomento public loans, Inter-American Development Bank, and International Bank for Reconstruction and Development loans are placed in nonaccrual after 180 days; for Corporacion Andina de Fomento private loans and Nordic Investment Bank's ordinary loans after 90 days; for International Finance Corporation automatically after 90 days, or, at option of management, after 60 to 90 days, for European Bank for Reconstruction and Development (EBRD) private loans after 60 days and public loans after 30 days. Other MLIs have no explicit policies. ** Fiscal year ends June 30 of the following year. $ Exclude equity investments

Statutory And Policy Controls

Standard & Poor's evaluates multilateral lending institutions' statutory and policy controls to assess their prudence and the extent to which they ensure financial soundness. These limits are designed to control credit and market risk exposures and to ensure sufficient liquidity. Emphasis is placed on statutory limitations, expressed in each multilateral lending institution's Articles of Agreement, since amendments to the agreements require broad membership approval. Importance also is attached to policy guidelines established by a multilateral lending institution's board of directors, although these are more easily changed than statutes.

Statutory and Policy Controls	Table B		
	Gearing Ratio	**Debt Leverage**	**Liquidity**
African Development Bank	Loans outstanding plus undisbursed commitments and guarantees cannot exceed 100% of subscribed capital, reserves and surplus.	Senior debt limited to 80% of callable capital of non-borrowing members. Total debt limited to 100% of usable capital (defined as paid-in capital, reserves, and callable capital of AA and AAA rated shareholders.	Must be greater than the average of the coming two years' annual debt service requirements plus anticipated loan disbursements net of scheduled principal repayments, if positive.
Asian Development Bank	Loans outstanding plus undisbursed commitments, equity investments, and guarantees cannot exceed 100% of subscribed capital and reserves.	No explicit policy. Policy target of limiting debt and guarantees to 95% of callable capital of members with convertible currencies.	Must be 100% of market-based facility loans and no less than 40% of undisbursed loan commitments.
Corporacion Andina de Fomento	Loans outstanding plus equity investments and guarantees limited to 400% of paid-in capital, reserves, and retained earnings.	Debt limited to 350% of paid-in capital, reserves, and retained earnings.	Must be no less than 30% of the sum of current portion of long-term debt, increase in short-term debt and project loan disbursements, or 30% of the total undisbursed project loans, whichever is larger.
Council of Europe Social Development Fund	Loans outstanding cannot exceed 600% of subscribed capital, reserves, and retained earnings.	Long-term debt (over 2 years) is limited to 400% of subscribed capital reserves. Subordinated Debt, retained earnings and short-term debt are limited to 300% of subscribed capital, reserves, Subordinated Debt and retained earnings.	The sum of bank deposits and the Treasury Portfolio with a maturity of less than 18 months should be no less than the sum of the stock of project and cash requirements over the next three years.

Statutory and Policy Controls *(continued)*	Gearing Ratio	Debt Leverage	Liquidity
EUROFIMA	Target minimum 6% ratio of subscribed capital plus reserves to total assets.	No explicit policy.	No explicit policy. Management guideline to maintain liquidity equal to two months of projected debt service. No undisbursed loan commitments.
European Bank for Reconstruction and Development	Loans outstanding plus guarantees plus equity investment cannot exceed 100% of subscribed capital, reserves, and surplus.	No explicit policy. Gearing ratio implicitly limits net debt to 100% of subscribed capital and reserves.	Must be no less than 45% of projected net cash requirements over next three years.
European Investment Bank	Loans outstanding plus guarantees cannot exceed 250% of subscribed capital.	No explicit policy. Gearing ratio implicitly limits net debt to 250% of subscribed capital.	Target is to maintain overall liquidity in a range of 25% to 40% of the net annual cash flow.
Inter-American Development Bank	Loans outstanding plus guarantees cannot exceed paid-in capital plus the general reserve and the callable capital of non-borrowing members. Also, target reserves-to-loans ratio at 20%-25%.	Debt and guarantees, net of qualified liquid assets and special reserve, limited to 100% of callable capital of non-borrowing members.	Targets annual range of 70%-90% of sum of 50% of projected year-end undisbursed balance of signed loans plus 33% of projected net cash requirements for that and the succeeding year.
International Bank for Reconstruction and Development	Loans outstanding plus the present value of guarantees cannot exceed 100% of subscribed capital, reserves, and surplus. Also, target reserves to loan ratio at 13 to 15%.	No explicit policy. Gearing ratio implicitly limits net debt to 100% of subscribed capital and reserves.	Target liquidity at 100% of six month's debt service plus anticipated disbursements on committed loans net of repayments.
International Finance Corporation	Paid-in capital, retained earnings, and general loan loss reserves must be at least 30% of risk weighted assets (on- and off-balance sheet)	Statutes restrict debt and guarantees to 400% of subscribed capital and retained earnings.	Liquid assets plus undrawn borrowing commitments from IBRD must cover at least 65% of next three years' estimated net cash requirements. (Operating target: 70%)
Nordic Investment Bank	Ordinary lending ceiling is set at 250% of authorized capital.	No explicit policy. Gearing ratio implicitly limits net debt to 250% of authorized capital.	Target liquidity equal to 100% of projected cash requirement for the coming year.

Statutory and policy controls fall into three categories:
* Gearing and leverage;
* Asset/liability management; and
* Lending.

Gearing and Leverage.

Standard & Poor's judges the conservatism of gearing and leverage limits given the inherent risks of multilateral lending institution' activities and the strength of their capital. The analysis of gearing restrictions, which limit outstanding loans relative to capital and reserves, emphasizes the quality of multilateral lending institutions' assets and capital. Asset quality depends on the underlying structure of the loan portfolio and its repayment record. Quality of capital mainly reflects the paid-in share of subscribed capital and the callable capital of the more creditworthy member countries. The quality of callable capital is important as a gauge of the ability of member states to meet a capital call in the unlikely event a multilateral lending institution cannot service its debt. Standard & Poor's expects very conservative gearing ratios for development finance institutions due to the inherent risks of lending to developing nations, while European multilateral lenders are viewed as needing less-conservative gearing ratios because of their better-quality loan portfolios.

The analytical approach in evaluating leverage—outstanding debt compared to capital and reserves—broadly resembles that for gearing in its emphasis of the relative level and quality of capital. Standard & Poor's evaluates the different leverage definitions adopted by the multilateral lending institution. For example, the regional development banks effectively limit debt to the callable capital of the most creditworthy members. In addition, Standard & Poor's distinguishes between leverage limits that are explicitly stated in a multilateral lending institution's Articles of Agreement and those that are implied through statutory restrictions on gearing. The latter are judged to be less restrictive in that they effectively limit debt net of liquid resources, not gross debt. In such instances, the quality of liquid assets takes on added importance in Standard & Poor's analysis.

Asset/Liability Management.

Standard & Poor's evaluates the extent to which a multilateral lending institution's asset/liability management policies safeguard against market and liquidity risks. Such risks are inherent in multilateral lending institution' business of providing long-term (and, until recently, almost exclusively fixed-rate) loans funded strictly with capital market borrowings. Attention is drawn to where assets and liabilities are not closely matched, thereby introducing potential currency, maturity, and interest rate risks. For example, while multilateral lending institutions generally pass on currency risks to the borrowers, some multilateral lenders allow for small currency mismatches in their investment operations. The extent of interest rate risk is also evaluated, along with an assessment of how these risks are being reduced through such techniques as pricing loans on a pooled cost of funds, resetting rates frequently, and gradually adopting variable lending rates.

Liquidity management plays a particularly crucial role in safeguarding financial flexibility, notably when adverse market conditions constrain a multilateral lending institution's access to long-term funds. Liquidity also helps to ensure timely repayment to multilateral lending institution bondholders in the event that a capital call is delayed by political resistance within the institution or a shareholder government. Lacking a natural deposit base, multilateral lenders must maintain sufficient liquid assets to meet a portion of future cash requirements. Standard & Poor's judges the adequacy of liquid resources in view of the structure of the institution's lending and funding operations and its reliance on callable capital. Particularly close attention is paid to liquidity relative to the level of undisbursed loan commitments and to a multilateral lending institution's debt amortization profile. For example, prudence suggests that multilateral lenders that shift their loan portfolios in favor of faster-disbursing loans require increased liquid holdings.

Conservative liquidity management also dictates close correspondence of liquid resources with a multilateral lending institution's debt service requirements for the next year.

Table C		
Delinquent Loan Policies		
	Sanctions	**Accounting**
African Development Bank	No new commitment and disbursements when arrears exceed one month. All disbursements to the country suspended after one month	Nonperforming loans placed on nonaccrual after six months as of July 1.
Asian Development Bank	Members notified when arrears exceed 30 days. No new commitments when arrears exceed 60 days. No disbursements on current loans when arrears exceed 90 days.	Delinquent loans placed on nonaccrual after six months. Loan loss provisions made for private sector loans after six months in arrears; for public sector loans after 12 months.
Corporacion Andina de Fomento	All further loan disbursements and new commitments are suspended the day a debtor falls into arrears. A penalty fee is charged the day a debtor falls into arrears.	Delinquent loans to private sector entities placed on nonaccrual after 90 days and to public sector entities after 180 days. There are no specific provisions but general loan and equity securities loss provisions, which amounted to 3% of the portfolio in 1997 ($109.4 million). As a basis for comparison, loans equivalent to only 12% of the loan and equity securities loss provisions built in 1998 were written off during the year.
Council of Europe Social Development Fund	Charge penalty rate on overdue amounts. The Fund may suspend, cancel or demand repayment of all loans of the same borrower in case of failure to fulfill any contractual obligation.	Regarding unpaid principal and interest due for more than 90 days, a 100% interest provision has been set up. Specific provisions are established when there is a risk of either partial or total non-recovery of principal or interest.
EUROFIMA	Charge penalty rate on overdue interest. Delinquent railway must surrender applicable rolling stock and forfeit all installments already paid.	No explicit policy.
European Bank for Reconstruction and Development	All loan disbursements to the country are suspended when arrears on public loans exceed 30 days and private loans exceed 60 days. No new commitments when arrears on public loans exceed 60 days.	General loan loss provisions policy for private sector loans was refined in 1995. It shifted from an automatic provisioning policy at a rate of 5% for loans and 8% for equity investments, to a risk-based provisioning policy linked to the 'riskiness' of these loans. General provisions at the rate of 3% of outstanding sovereign exposure introduced in July 1997.

Table C *(continued)*		
Delinquent Loan Policies		
	Sanctions	**Accounting**
European Investment Bank	No explicit policy on EC loans. For non-EC loans, disbursements halted on all own-source and EC source EIB loans to the country when arrears exceed 90 days.	No explicit policy. Specific provisions are made at the end of the financial year on a risk-based provisioning policy. Transfers to a fund for general banking risk are made at management's discretion.
Inter-American Development Bank	No new sovereign loans are approved or signed if the sovereign's arrears exceed 30 days. If arrears exceed 120 days, disbursements on sovereign loans are suspended and no new sovereign loans are considered. Sovereign arrears do not trigger sanctions for private sector borrowers within the country. Arrears on loans to private sector borrowers without a sovereign guarantee do not trigger sanctions for any other private or public sector borrowers. For private sector borrowers in arrears, additional disbursements are suspended and the IADB charges a penalty rate on overdue amounts.	All sovereign and sovereign guaranteed loans to a country are placed on nonaccrual after 180 days. Private sector loans may be placed on nonaccrual after 60 days at the option of management, and are automatically placed on nonaccrual after 180 days. General loan loss provisions are maintained at 3% of outstanding loans.
International Bank for Reconstruction and Development	All loan disbursements to the country are suspended when arrears exceed 60 days. No new projects can be submitted to the Board when arrears exceed 30 days (45 days when borrower is not a sovereign). Partial interest rate waivers are given only to borrowers without arrears over 30 days during the previous six months.	Loans placed on nonaccrual when arrears exceed 180 days. General loan loss provisions maintained at 3% of outstanding loans.
International Finance Corporation	Charge penalty rate on overdue amounts. Generally, disbursements suspended for loans in arrears, though management has discretion to continue disbursing net of arrears.	Loans automatically placed on nonaccrual after 90 days, or, at option of management, after 60 to 90 days. Case-by-case specific loss provisions. General loss reserve set according to multiparameter guidelines, currently at about 6% of disbursed investments, excluding specific reserves.
Nordic Investment Bank	Charge penalty rate on overdue amounts. No new products can be submitted to the Board when arrears exceed 30 days.	Ordinary loans placed on nonaccrual if arrears exceed 90 days. Project Investment Loans placed on nonaccrual when arrears exceed 180 days. General loan loss provision made at management's discretion.

Lending.

Standard & Poor's analysis of lending policies centers on the measures multilateral lenders have adopted to manage credit risk. Their prudential controls on loan concentrations, requirements of government and other quality guarantees, and preferred creditor status have contributed to the multilateral lending institutions' generally excellent loan repayment record.

Loan policy is evaluated from the standpoint of how effectively it limits the risk of concentrating loans with individual borrowers or in particular countries and economic sectors. In this regard, loan approval and monitoring procedures are important considerations. The credit risk of a multilateral lending institution's loan portfolio is also inferred by judging how commercially viable are the various loan categories. For example, self-supporting project lending is generally seen as less risky than social policy loans or policy-based lending. Standard & Poor's evaluates whether credit risk is mitigated by collateral backing a loan, either in the form of mortgages or guarantees provided by member governments, public authorities, or banks. Guarantees are judged as to the creditworthiness of the ultimate obligor.

In the eyes of their borrowers, multilateral lenders enjoy preferred creditor status that, while funda-mentally a political expression, reflects the borrowers' incentives to place priority on loan repayment to the multilateral lending institutions. Therefore, Standard & Poor's focuses on multilateral lenders' poli-cies that reinforce these incentives. The incentives include committed loans yet to be disbursed, the availability of generally lower-cost funds at longer-term maturities, technical assistance, and the threat of sanctions. These incentives are reinforced by the almost universal policy among multilateral lenders of not participating in loan reschedulings.

9568c	Table D
Lending Rate Policies	
African Development Bank	A multi-currency pool-based variable rate scheme adjusted semi-annually to main-tain a 50 basis point spread was introduced on July 1, 1990. Beginning October 1,1997 the bank will offer single currency loans at a variable, fixed, or floating rate. Existing variable rate loans may be converted to single-currency variable rate loans at the direction of the borrower on or before March 31, 1998. An annual commit-ment fee of 1% is charged on undisbursed loans.
Asian Development Bank	Variable lending rate adjusted semi-annually based on the cost of borrowing since June 30, 1986 plus a spread of 40 basis points. Commitment fee of 75 basis points is levied on increasing percentage of undisbursed loan amount.
Corporacion Andina de Fomento	Variable lending rates set at LIBOR plus a spread, depending on the tenor and risk of the transaction and market conditions, plus a surveillance fee of 100 basis points. On project loans, a loan origination fee of 100 basis points of the loan amount and a commitment fee of 75 basis points per year on undisbursed loan balances are charged.
Council of Europe Social Development Fund	Lending rate based on actual cost of funds (including issuance fees) plus a spread of 25 basis points. Social loans carry a 1% interest rate. No commitment fees.
EUROFIMA	Lending rates are set at the actual cost of funds (including fees) plus an annual commission of 2.5 to 50 basis points on the initial principal amount, depending on the credit quality of the client.

9568c	Table D (continued)
Lending Rate Policies	
European Bank for Reconstruction and Development	For private sector loans, variable and fixed rates to be based on prevailing market rates while considering the cost of funds and loan risks. For public sector loans a new pricing scheme, maintaining a uniform 1% margin over LIBOR was introduced in April 1994. A minimum front-end fee of 1% and a commitment fee on undisbursed loans of 1% and 0.5% on fixed and variable rate loans.
European Investment Bank	Fixed lending rate based on actual funding cost of the currency lent plus a spread of an average 12 basis points for EU countries and about 25 basis points for non-EU countries. Variable rate loans are repriced quarterly at a spread over the effective average cost of funds.
Inter-American Development Bank	Most loans are priced semi-annually at a rate based on effective funding costs over the previous six months, plus a spread covering administrative and other costs to meet income targets. Charges, which may be waived, include an annual fee of 0.75% on the convertible currency portion of undisbursed loans, and a 1% one-time charge on the principal amount.
International Bank for Reconstruction and Development	Variable lending rate for single currency and currency pool loans adjusted semiannually to maintain a spread over the Bank's cost of funding allocated to these products. The Bank continues to waive 50 basis points on undisbursed balances and in fiscal 1999 waived 5 basis points on interest on disbursed and outstanding balances.
International Finance Corporation	Lending rates are based on prevailing market rates while considering cost of funds and loan risks. A front-end fee of 1% at signing. Annual commitment fees on undisbursed loans of 1% and 0.5% for fixed and variable rate loans respectively.
Nordic Investment Bank	Market based lending rates are set at disbursement. Commitment fees are usually charged on undisbursed loans.

Financial Performance

Steady financial performance is an important multilateral lending institution rating consideration because it serves to safeguard the institution's capital base and shield it from unforeseen operating and financial shocks. In contrast to profit-maximizing financial institutions, a multilateral lender's profits are not expected to be a primary means of bolstering capital in line with asset growth. Most multilateral lending institution capital needs are met by new capital subscriptions from shareholders, with much provided as callable capital.

Asset Quality.

Asset quality is rooted in the composition of the loan portfolio and is ultimately evidenced in the record of loan payments to the multilateral lending institution. In assessing the degree of concentration risk, Standard & Poor's focuses foremost on the creditworthiness of the recipient countries, with particular attention paid to countries that are or have recently rescheduled their debt to other creditors. This analysis concentrates on such ratios as loans to rescheduling countries relative to both disbursed loans and the sum of 'AAA' callable capital, paid-in capital, and reserves. More broadly, Standard & Poor's identifies disproportionate shares of the loan portfolio extended to particular borrowers, economic sectors, or countries. In this regard, Standard & Poor's calculates measures of risk assets by netting from gross exposures those loans guaranteed by highly rated governments and other obligors. The repayment record is scrutinized, with reported problem loan statistics adjusted to reflect differing accounting practices among multilateral lenders and the exceptional occurrence of rescheduling. As a matter of policy, most multilateral lending institutions would not write off a loan to a member government unless it withdrew from the organization. When loan arrears occur, Standard & Poor's evaluates all loans to countries with arrears relative to total disbursed loans and 'AAA' callable capital, paid-in capital, and reserves. Arrears are subject to a duration analysis to assist in judging whether the delinquencies reflect administrative difficulties or more fundamental factors affecting the capacity and willingness to repay.

Capital Adequacy.

A crucial rating consideration is the ability of a multilateral lending institution's capital base to protect both the institution and its creditors from loan losses. Capital adequacy relates to both the quality and relative levels of capital. In assessing the quality, Standard & Poor's places primary emphasis on "core" capital, comprised of paid-in capital and reserves. The proportion and trend over time of paid-in capital serves as a tangible sign of membership support. However, only capital paid with convertible currencies is included in Standard & Poor's ratio analysis. Moreover, only unencumbered reserves are included in the capital base but are netted from loans in calculating gearing ratios. For example, general country risk reserves would be included, but specific loan-loss provisions would not. Broader measures of the capital base would incorporate callable capital. Standard & Poor's emphasizes a restrictive sub-set of callable capital that is attributable to 'AAA' rated countries. It places secondary importance on the broader category of investment-grade countries, which includes all countries assessed by Standard & Poor's to have a 'BBB' or better capacity to service their debt.

The capital base is judged relative to both risk assets and debt. A key measure of gearing is the ratio of disbursed loans to 'AAA' callable capital, paid-in capital, and reserves. The same ratio adjusted to exclude the 'AAA' callable capital serves to indicate the ability to absorb financial shocks without the need to resort to capital calls. Among various leverage definitions examined, Standard & Poor's concentrates on the ratio of debt net of liquid assets relative to 'AAA' callable capital, paid-in capital, and reserves. Analysis of net leverage ratios highlights the sizable liquidity positions some multilateral lenders hold for various policy reasons (*see Liquidity section*), which, if not considered, would overstate multilateral lending institution leverage. A variety of gross leverage ratios are also assessed.

Liquidity.

To judge the adequacy of a multilateral lender's liquid assets requires an appreciation of the wide differences among multilateral lending institutions regarding their levels of undisbursed loans, funding practices, and the conservatism of their investment policies. In the context of the above considerations, liquidity analysis focuses on the relation of liquid assets to the sum of undisbursed loans and the next year's debt service. Liquid assets are also compared to total debt to evaluate the ability of a multilateral lending institution's readily available resources to meet its obligations.

Profitability.

Standard & Poor's assesses multilateral lending institutions' profitability mindful of their primary objectives to cover costs, maintain margins sufficient to build adequate reserves, and provide borrowing member nations with attractive loan terms. In particular, Standard & Poor's recognizes that profit maximization is not an objective for the conservatively leveraged multilateral lenders, which are themselves ultimately an expression of cooperation among the member countries.

In analyzing profitability, Standard & Poor's disaggregates net earning trends to highlight the relative contributions of loan spreads, commitment fees, earnings from liquid investments, and operating costs. Key analytical considerations include the size and timing of cost-free, paid-in capital contributions, the record of loan repayments, the effects of interest rate and other market risks, and operating efficiency. A key measure of profitability is the ratio of net operating income to average total assets. The numerator comprises interest earnings, commission fees, investment and other earnings, less interest expenses, borrowing fees, and other expenses. A narrower profitability definition is based on net income, which excludes from net operating income any contributions to special multilateral lending institution programs or reserves. Care is taken to ascertain the impact of loan loss provisions, interest arrears, and extraordinary gains/losses on such profitability measures. All measures are adjusted for differences in the accounting treatment of interest accruals and other practices to ensure consistent comparison over time and across institutions.

Rating Regional and Local Governments

Jane Eddy, New York (1) 212-438-7996

Standard & Poor's rates regional and local governments in 25 countries. In all cases, the analytical methodology is the same, focusing on a range of economic, system, and administrative factors, budgetary performance and flexibility, and the entity's financial position. These credit features are evaluated in a composite manner, not in isolation from each other. The analytical steps taken allow for an international rating scale despite the vast differences between local and regional governments worldwide with respect to their structures, competencies, and legal latitudes. The general approach for specific issuers takes into account the distinct characteristics of the country of which these governments are a part, especially those characteristics related to intergovernmental arrangements and the macroeconomic environment.

While regional and local governments differ in the scope of their activities, Standard & Poor's evaluation recognizes that they bear identical responsibilities: delivering public services supported directly or indirectly from taxes and fees levied on residents or transferred from other governmental authorities. Their common task is to balance the level and cost of these services with available revenues.

Sovereign Factors

Before Standard & Poor's rates any issue or issuer, the creditworthiness of the sovereign government must be determined. For both foreign and local currency debt, the relative sovereign ratings generally represent the upper limit for any local/regional government domiciled in that country. The reason for this policy is that the central government has a wide range of powers and resources that render its credit standing superior to that of any subsovereign government. For example, the central government has first claim on foreign exchange reserves to service external debt obligations. It also has the power to tax and print national currency. Further, to the specific point of municipalities, the sovereign usually can impinge on these entities' autonomy by setting the terms of intergovernmental transfers of both revenues and expenditure responsibilities, mandating spending, and controlling debt authorization. Finally, subsovereign credits are influenced by the larger macroeconomic environment, such as the prevailing inflation rate and other features of monetary and fiscal policies that are incorporated into sovereign ratings.

Economy

The economic base, growth, and diversity of a region or locality are among the most critical determinants of a rating. Fiscal health is intimately linked to economic prosperity in almost all cases. Most revenue sources-from sales, property, and income taxes to various licenses and user fees-are affected by economic growth patterns.

Demographics

The absolute size, density, growth rate, and age distribution of the population is assessed in light of their ability to influence future revenue growth and the demand for public services. A declining or rapidly growing population will likely constrain government finances by shrinking revenues or dramatically accelerating service demands, respectively. However, high population growth due to significant in-migration of working-age population and, in particular, of skilled workers could be a positive.

An important aspect of demographics is the size of the dependent population, that is, the portion under 15 or over 65. These groups place the greatest burden on locally delivered services, such as education and health care, and contribute the least to revenues.

Overall, a stable, moderately growing population with a low dependent population is the optimal demographic profile. Population size by itself is not a consideration, but in some cases might be a measure of economic diversity.

Economic Structure

This part of the analysis focuses on the depth, diversity, and prosperity of the local or regional economic base to gauge the likely stability of government revenue growth. Factors considered include labor force characteristics, employment mix, and income levels. Medium-term variations in the growth of employment, personal income and output, and the unemployment level are the best historical indicators of an economic base's stability.

One objective of this analysis is to assess whether employment is concentrated in a few sectors (e.g., mining, banking, textile manufacturing, etc.) or individual companies, and, if so, to evaluate the health and prospects of these sectors and companies. Reliance on a few primary job segments and output suggests a greater vulnerability to business and/or commodity cycles and that sector's competitive position. The leading employers and taxpayers are weighed in relation to the type of industry involved, recent and anticipated investments, and status of the physical plant. Unemployment and underemployment levels are independently examined within the context of migration and changes in labor force participation.

Another consideration is economic prosperity. In general, the higher the level of per-capita income and wealth, the more flexibility a government retains to raise taxes or restrict services. Standard & Poor's measures this flexibility by looking at both per-capita income and GDP levels. As much as possible, the unaccounted-for contribution of the underground economy to local incomes is ascertained. Finally, income distribution is pertinent, as a highly skewed distribution can create social and spending pressures that are obscured by examining only average figures.

Growth Prospects

Standard & Poor's evaluates the outlook for an economy based on recent trends in employment, output, and investment, adjusted for any recent structural or policy changes. Independent economic forecasts are useful, but their accuracy is not taken for granted. Standard & Poor's emphasizes long-term structural trends and their implications for future growth, not developments related simply to business cycles. The optimal pattern is for real per-capita income or GDP growth of 2%-3% per year, or 5%-6% per year for less-developed countries.

Growth trends are placed in the context of the area's demographic profile and economic structure. The competitive position of local industries is a critical consideration, as is location (e.g., the existence of an up-to-date port facility and proximity to major markets, etc.), resource endowments (minerals, energy, and a skilled labor force, etc.), and infrastructure adequacy. Other measures of a vibrant economy include recent and anticipated levels of private and public investment, construction activity, and retail sales growth.

System Structure and Management

Intergovernmental Structure

Local and regional government ratings take into account the intergovernmental system's stability and supportiveness, factors that often weigh heavily in a rating decision.

Intergovernmental transfers can be a revenue source and/or a service responsibility and, as such, can either enhance or constrain budgetary flexibility. The capacity of a higher level of government to mandate spending (or service standards) by a lower level of government without a corresponding transfer of revenues or taxing authority is a definite negative factor. Transfers are examined in terms of their size, predictability, and the ease with which they can be adjusted to meet changing circumstances. In the emerging markets, these arrangements are usually new and subject to change, creating a less predictable operating environment.

Standard & Poor's looks at the composition of revenue transfers between general revenue-sharing allocations, specific-purpose grants, and equalization payments. Fiscal equalization is perhaps the most important transfer program from a ratings perspective. Equalization schemes are designed to ensure that political subdivisions can provide reasonably comparable levels of public services with similar tax efforts. Certainly, these programs raise the credit profile of the recipients-economically disadvantaged regions. If the equalization system quickly adapts to changing fortunes, this type of system is a positive, even for those that are net contributors, in that they provide a safety net of varying importance during difficult times. The evaluation incorporates any explicit mechanisms for assisting governments facing financial stress and the historical evidence of such support. Barring predictable financial assistance being available well in advance of an acute financial crisis, no sovereign guarantee is acknowledged in the rating. However, a track record that demonstrates general intergovernmental supportiveness may be cited as an extraordinary item incorporated into the entity's stand-alone rating.

Revenue and Expenditure Balance

Another rating consideration is whether the structure of government yields service responsibilities that are well matched with revenue-raising authority. This determination requires an assessment of the degree to which the municipality's revenue capability and service provisions are controlled or mandated by higher levels of government or by law at the local level. On the expenditure side, the focus is on the portion of the budget driven by service mandates and standards, or other nondiscretionary spending. The match would be considered poor if a local government faces service mandates that entail spending growth that exceeds the pace of revenue growth; this dilemma would be exacerbated if revenues are tightly circumscribed and inelastic.

A final area of interest is borrowing authority. Some subsovereign governments must receive central government approval for debt sales, especially for external borrowing. Likewise, some local laws require voter approval for debt issuance. The former requirement can be a positive, as it ensures coordination with the central government and compliance with all authorization principles. However, either restriction can be problematic if it limits financial flexibility and the necessary capital access to maintain public infrastructure.

Management Systems and Policy

The focus here is on the consistency and rigor of budgetary and financial policies as demonstrated over several administrations and political alignments.

Management structure, systems, and controls are useful indicators of future financial stability and the lack of reliance on a few key administrators. Institutionalized rules governing debt issuance and mandating a balanced budget are strengths. However, absent such legal requirements, policy guidelines are considered, as is management's compliance with them. A government's attitude toward maintaining operating balances is examined in light of past performance. Budget forecasting and monitoring systems are assessed, including expenditure controls, revenue collection procedures, and cash management systems. Control over spending is measured by a medium-term comparison of expenditure growth to economic expansion. Similarly, the ability to limit budget variances is an important factor.

Another consideration is the timeliness and comprehensiveness of financial reporting practices, planning documents, mid-year fiscal reports, and cash flows. Standard & Poor's does not perform an audit, but relies on issuers to supply adequate and timely financial reports, preferably prepared by an independent certified public accountant in accordance with generally accepted government accounting standards in the country.

The ability of a government to act quickly is also incorporated into the rating. A large, fragmented legislature or a government in which there is an unbridgeable rift between the executive and legislative branches is usually viewed negatively.

Fiscal Flexibility and Performance

Analyzing fiscal performance involves reviewing the base and relative growth trends of revenues and expenditures, the flexibility to adjust revenues and expenses, and the level of budgetary imbalances experienced over a five-year period.

Revenue Sources And Flexibility

Evaluating the revenue structure focuses on the major sources, their changing importance over time, and their suitability with respect to the economic base. The first step distinguishes between own-source revenues and transfer receipts. Own-source revenues are closely scrutinized, as they represent the resources most directly under the municipality's control. Historical movements of these revenues are analyzed in the context of trends in economic activity. Diversification of sources is important, as is their vulnerability to tax policy changes. Likewise, the stability of intergovernmental transfers is examined in light of governmental transfer and tax policies, economic growth, and the fiscal capacity of the higher authority responsible for these transfers.

A key area of examination is the potential for generating additional revenue. This evaluation emphasizes total and comparative tax burdens and the proportion of revenues under the municipality's control. Estimating the tax burden involves a comparison of tax and fee levels relative to other similar jurisdictions in the country; this contrast is enhanced by comparing own-source revenues per capita or as a percentage of income or output. To facilitate international comparisons, the per-capita tax and fee burden imposed by the central government or other overlapping jurisdictions is added to that of the rated local government.

The relevance of any legal limits on revenue raising is assessed by determining the proportion of own-source revenues. Other things being equal, a higher own-source revenue share suggests greater revenue flexibility. Finally, the willingness of management to tap its available revenue-raising capacity is evaluated based on its track record during past periods of budgetary pressure.

Expenditure Trends And Flexibility

The assessment of expenditures emphasizes the proportion of discretionary expenses, the political will to curb spending, and the tendency of expenditure pressures to heighten during economic downturns.

Discretionary spending is defined as nonessential capital and current outlays. Generally, there is greater latitude to defer or discontinue capital expenditures, at least over the short term, so a greater percentage of internally generated capital spending usually implies a higher degree of discretion. To gauge this flexibility, Standard & Poor's estimates the minimum level of capital spending needed to maintain existing infrastructure and to complete new projects of an essential and urgent nature. Also, assuming supportable debt levels, the capital costs may be legitimate items for bond financing.

On the operating side, debt service and personnel costs are considered nondiscretionary, and their growth relative to the size of the budget is monitored closely. Consequently, labor relations are critical, and the wage settlement process, timing, and results, as well as the significance of labor disputes, are reviewed. Finally, where service standards are set by a higher level of government, the municipality has inherently less control over its budget.

The political will to limit or cut expenses is discerned through examining historical performance. The trend in personnel and salary levels is a useful measure of the capacity to control spending, especially when compared to regional or national trends. As in the case of revenues, the vulnerability of operating expenditures to economic cycles is assessed by comparing the variance in the growth rate of spending over an economic cycle relative to the variability in the growth of personal income or economic output.

Budgetary performance and financing requirements. When evaluating budgetary performance, an important factor is the magnitude of variances between initial budget projections and final outcomes. Significant recurring differences raise questions about the adequacy of forecasting techniques, budget controls, and management's ability and willingness to make intra-year adjustments.

The operating balance measures the government's capacity to manage its recurrent activities and helps to identify any structural mismatch between on-going income and expenses. Persistent operating deficits indicate that the revenue base is inadequate to sustain the municipality's range of services, or conversely, point to management's lack of commitment to accepting the burden of raising sufficient funds. Continual use of borrowing to finance operations does not bode well for a government's capacity to honor its current expenses, together with an accumulating debt service expense. As part of this analysis, the definition of operating revenues and expenses is scrutinized to determine the degree of conservatism. For example, conservative accounting of expenditures includes spending on capital maintenance and subsidies to the private sector, even where such transfers are for investment purposes.

Prudent management of a municipality's capital needs is best measured by studying the amount of capital investment made over the medium-term from sources such as operating surpluses and capital grants. The ratio of net borrowing requirements to total revenues indicates the pace of debt accumulation relative to resources available for repayment.

Financial Position

Liquidity

The evaluation of an issuer's liquidity position emphasizes the appropriateness of internal liquidity, investment policies, and committed bank or other credit lines to the seasonality of revenues and expenses. This analysis factors in any outstanding short-term or variable-rate debt or bonds with bullet maturities.

The average and minimum reserves and cash balances relative to total expenditures and debt service are important to the analysis. A heavy reliance on short-term debt or debt with an irregular maturity profile can pose a significant risk in the absence of credible refunding options. Cash management and its coordination with long-term borrowings often reflect the strength of budgetary planning and controls. Finally, the confidence placed on the level of reserves must reflect the prudence of investment guidelines and practices pertaining to credit and market risk exposures.

Debt Burden

The burden posed by debt is measured by comparing annual charges and year-end stocks with available resources. Several measurements of debt are used, including the government's direct and guaranteed debt and the total tax-supported debt burden, including the obligations of the municipality's nonself-supporting enterprises and trusts. As in the case of evaluating a community's taxes, an entity's debt burden cannot be looked at in isolation, but needs to be viewed more broadly by including the public debt of overlapping jurisdictions and the central government. This approach allows comparisons between communities that provide a dramatically different range of services.

Emphasis is placed on the ratios of net direct debt to budget and net tax-supported public sector debt relative to GDP and on a per-capita basis. Net direct debt ratios exceeding 100% of revenue and net tax-supported debt ratios that exceed 25% of GDP usually indicate a heavy burden. Finally, the proportion of revenues required to service debt is closely evaluated as are the trends thereof.

Analysis of debt management concentrates on the structure and composition of tax-supported debt, including its maturity and currency profiles and interest-rate sensitivity.

Off-Balance-Sheet Liabilities

A particularly complex part of the analysis focuses on off-balance-sheet liabilities defined as total public sector debt, including all public sector enterprises (e.g., banks, utilities, housing companies, etc.), unfunded pension liabilities, and other contingent obligations relative to budgetary revenues. Key issues include the likelihood that guarantees will be called upon, the need to support public enterprises' operations and debt service, and the probable demand on budgetary resources posed by public pensions.

The health of public enterprises is evaluated based on their stand-alone profitability, adjusted for any subsidies and the historical need for capital injections. These entities' credit quality determines the likelihood and the potential magnitude of any governmental intervention. The burden posed by pensions takes into account any actuarial studies, the evolution of pension contributions and payments relative to the budget, and the adequacy of plans to amortize outstanding liabilities.

Exceeding Sovereign Ratings

Jane Eddy, New York (1) 212-438-7996

Over the past few years, a series of sovereign defaults, as well as the so-called Asian meltdown, have served to highlight the challenges even strong, creditworthy companies face during times of sovereign stress. The urgency of determining the complex effects the macroeconomic environment has on issuers of infrastructure debt has been highlighted by two interactive trends.

First, an increasing number of utilities and transportation-related entities located in noninvestment-grade countries have requested ratings as they have been privatized or made more independent financially. Second, more issuers have structured debt to mitigate transfer and convertibility problems (the inability to access and send offshore hard currency due to actions by the sovereign government).

In most cases, these risks limit foreign currency ratings of domiciled entities to those of the sovereign government. To offset these risks, companies use political risk insurance, sell debt backed by future export receivables, or craft transactions to take advantage of the preferred credit status of entities like the International Finance Corp. or the InterAmerican Development Bank.

While several transaction or corporate credit ratings have been enhanced by the elimination of transfer and convertibility risk, Standard & Poor's remains mindful of the fact that "country risk" encompasses a far greater scope of considerations that influence creditworthiness. To determine how a company's ability to service local and foreign currency obligations might be affected by other types of country risk, only some of which are indicated by the sovereign's local and foreign currency ratings, it is useful to study the performance of infrastructure entities in countries that recently defaulted on local and/or foreign currency debt, including Ecuador, Indonesia, and Russia. This commentary touches on these case studies and explains the country risk issues of concern, aside from the transferability and convertibility of currency.

Case Studies

A review of past events indicates that there is variation in the ability of private sector borrowers to continue servicing their debt in the face of a sovereign crisis and default. Many factors influence this capacity. In Indonesia, on Jan. 27, 1998, the government announced a temporary freeze on debt servicing, but claimed that this act was not a moratorium, because companies with U.S. dollars could voluntarily continue paying creditors. Due to the rapidly depreciating rupiah, however, defaults were widespread because of most companies' poor liquidity coupled with their lack of currency hedging, high local interest rates, and the impact of depressed operation condition. Banks reported a level of nonperforming loans of about 75%. It is estimated that some 220 of Indonesia's leading companies defaulted in 1998. These companies were also disadvantaged by their debt structures, which included high levels of short-term debt and a lack of refinancing sources. Additionally, project finance transactions were harmed by the government's failure to approve needed tariff increases for the off-take utility, PLN, which led to PLN's default on its contractual obligations. For most or all of the defaults in Indonesia, transferability and convertibility insurance would not have salvaged the defaulted transactions. Indeed, this cover would have been irrelevant.

In Ecuador, few corporations issued debt in the capital markets, and bank loan information is difficult to obtain. The sovereign government defaulted on its foreign currency obligations in 1999. Following the crisis, while no transferability or convertibility controls were implemented, the poor condition of the banking system indicates that corporate loans went into default owing to the macroeconomic fallout, inflation, the severe devaluation of the sucre, and the interactive problems of and with the banks. Access to working capital was greatly constrained, and bank deposits were frozen for six to 12 months.

In Russia, the government placed a moratorium on debt service payments by banks (which was probably moot, as most banks were deeply insolvent, given their investment in GKOs) but never put any restriction on the ability of corporates to service debt. Some defaulted, while others continued to pay. Certainly the effects listed above relative to macroeconomic, credit, and currency conditions applied here. Further, while access to bank deposits was generally not limited (some banks were closed, but for only a few days), there is evidence of a slowdown in access to funds and foreign exchange, given the disarray of the banking system. Further, infrastructure companies with fixed tariffs were hit hard, especially those dependent on imported equipment and other supplier links. Nonetheless, the picture is mixed, as some issuers, even those most tightly linked to the central government, Russian cities, and regions, continue to service debt.

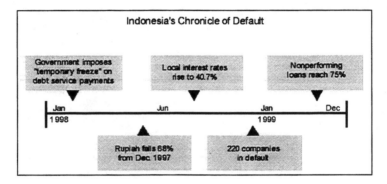

Standard & Poor's Perspective

In 1997, Standard & Poor's published a study that identified 31 countries where private sector foreign currency default was significant at the time of sovereign defaults occurring between 1975 and 1995. In these cases, defaults by the private sector were triggered by the sovereign in 21 countries, or 68% of the total.

However, the historical evidence of direct sovereign interference is mixed, and some analysts believe that this risk is actually diminishing. The integration and transformation of the structure of the capital markets from ones more heavily dominated by bank lending to bonds, has made it more difficult for governments to intervene in the cross-border flows of private issuers, both as a practical matter, in terms of the difficulty of enforcing prolonged exchange controls, and as a matter of incentive. Thus, it was easier for countries in the 1980s, for example, to convince banks to exercise forbearance on their exposure to private creditors than it is to negotiate with a wide group of bondholders. Nonetheless, it is still more common for private issuers in defaulting countries to default within a relatively short time frame, but increasingly, this is due to indirect sovereign risk, not direct intervention.

On an ongoing basis Standard & Poor's analyzes the empirical evidence in two ways: first, to better define the circumstances in which governments are least prone to use current and/or capital account restrictions as an economic policy tool or to interfere with private sector debt service and, second, to fine-tune globally the indirect risks that affect corporates in emerging markets.

Country Risk Factors of Importance to Infrastructure

Among the array of country risk factors that create the most severe problems on the heels of a sovereign default, the following have the greatest effect on infrastructure-related entities.

Macroeconomic volatility.

Recessions of varying depths cut or reverse the growth in demand for all types of services. In addition, consumers' purchasing power can drop significantly. In emerging countries, it is not unusual for utilities' bad debt accounts and the level of theft to rise during an economic downturn. This further pressure on liquidity is compounded by the fact that issuers in most emerging regions typically have no access to committed credit lines.

Currency depreciation.

Debtors with loans, fuel contracts, or equipment needs linked to, or denominated in, foreign currency, such as U.S. dollars, will be greatly stressed by a devaluation. To date, no political risk insurance (PRI) policies cover this risk. Hedging facilities are infrequently available, especially for tenors of longer than three years, and are expensive for entities in emerging countries.

Government regulation.

Governments under political and economic stress have a long history of "changing the rules of the game" through amending contract or concession arrangements. Most commonly, governments use a roll-back of automatic tariff adjustments for inflation or tax increases as a means of achieving other macroeconomic goals.

Access to capital.

Even the strongest private sector issuers have had difficulties accessing local or international capital markets or banks loans during periods of stress. Investor interest can change swiftly, and local banking systems are often illiquid during a crisis. Even if credit is available, international investors quickly bid up demanded spreads due to perceived higher risk.

Liquidity restrictions.

When confronting a solvency crisis, a government can temporarily close down the banking system. Once banks are reopened, it is not unusual for governments to freeze bank accounts or convert assets into long-term securities, greatly restricting or eliminating borrowers' access to funds.

Inflation.

Excessive inflation is often associated with sovereign economic crises, as governments hike interest rates sharply to strengthen their countries' currencies. How much inflation impinges on financial performance is a function of a company's pricing flexibility and know-how for keeping revenues increasing in line with or ahead of costs. Additionally, the regulatory allowance for the timely pass-through of inflation is critical.

Local interest rates.

The effect of rising local interest rates can bear some relationship to inflation rates, but the link is often imperfect. Therefore, even if a regulator allows for inflation adjustments, these may not compensate for higher local interest rates. For example, local borrowing rates in Brazil hit 40% for some months in 1999, while inflation fell below 10%. The compounding problem for credits in emerging markets, even those that do not have the misfortune of having to refinance during a period of high prevailing rates, is the fact that most local borrowing rates are in a variable mode.

Conclusion

A review of the recent examples of the performance of the corporate and project sectors during a sovereign default (as summarized above), reinforces Standard & Poor's approach, which acknowledges the importance of many types of country risks aside from transfer risk, on a company's ability to meet local and foreign currency obligations. The likelihood of only some of these risks occurring is indicated by the relevant sovereign's local and foreign currency ratings. Standard & Poor's will maintain its practice of evaluating each company and country individually to determine if an entity can withstand the severe effects that occur upon a sovereign default.

Section III
Economic and Financial Risk

Institutional Investor

Bank of America
World Information Services

Chapter 9

Institutional Investor

By Harvey D. Shapiro

Institutional Investor addresses the single issue of "creditworthiness" in its 100-point index. Every six months, bankers from around the world are asked to rate more than 135 countries on a scale of zero (very high chance of default) to 100 (least chance of default).

The responses, from up to 100 banks, are then weighted according to the worldwide exposure of the bank and the level of sophistication of the bank's analytical model. The weighted average becomes the Institutional Investor's Credit Rating. The ratings are published in both worldwide and regional lists that indicate changes from the previous six months and one year.

"The 1980s were a series of concentric, vicious circles in which third-world debt problems pushed the confidence of bankers lower and lower," muses one U.K. banker. "But now we've entered an era of virtuous circles in which positive developments seem to bring more positive developments."

Indeed, as proof of this new buoyancy, the composite creditworthiness of the world's nations, as measured by *Institutional Investor*'s exclusive semi-annual country credit survey, has increased 0.6 points in the current survey, to 36.7. This substantial rise is broadly based, with 52 countries moving up by one or more points, the amount *Institutional Investor* regards as statistically significant, while only eight declined by a point or more — and four of the laggards were located in Eastern Europe.

WINNERS AND LOSERS

"There is kind of a generic improvement in high-risk countries under way," says a sovereign risk analyst at one New York bank. "The political and economic imperatives of the global economy mean that country risk is generally down, whether you're talking about Vietnam or India or all of Latin America." She adds: "This is not an era in which countries are likely to default on their obligations if at all possible. They recognize that it's important to be a part of the global economic system."

The reason credit raters are handing out so many upgrades,notes another banker, is "not just a halo effect from a few good countries. The general shift to a globalized financial system has reduced country risk across the board because more countries are desperately trying to attract foreign capital." Not all bankers are quite so sanguine. "The survey's respondents may feel things are better because they're able to do new kinds of business," says one London banker. "What is rising is not confidence in the ability to repay the old kind of debt instruments but rather in the security of new kinds of financial instruments, which are often shorter-term and asset-backed or linked." Whatever the instruments, there is a basic feeling that countries are more willing and able to meet all of their financial obligations. "Standing behind obligations is a matter of attitude as much as economics, and that new attitude heartens lenders and investors," concludes this U.K. banker.

THE SIX-MONTH RECORD (SEPTEMBER 1993 TO MARCH 1994)			
Who's up the most?		Who's down the most?	
Country	Change in Institutional Investor credit rating	Country	Change in Institutional Investor credit rating
Slovenia	4.8	Ukraine	-3.1
Czech Republic	3.1	Georgia	-2.8
Argentina	3.0	Belarus	-2.0
Israel	2.9	Angola	-1.9
Lebanon	2.7	Yugoslavia	-1.7
Tunisia	2.6	Cameroon	-1.6
Peru	2.5	Iran	-1.6
Philippines	2.5	Belgium	-1.0
Morocco	2.4	Guinea	-0.9
Vietnam	2.4	Italy	-0.9
Cyprus	2.3	Russia	-0.9
Egypt	2.3	Algeria	-0.8
Kuwait	2.3	Croatia	-0.8
Mauritius	2.3	Gabon	-0.8
Seychelles	2.3	Zaire	-0.8

THE ONE-YEAR RECORD (MARCH 1993 TO MARCH 1994)			
Who's up the most?		Who's down the most?	
Country	Change in Institutional Investor credit rating	Country	Change in Institutional Investor credit rating
Slovenia	10.8	Iran	-4.3
Lebanon	5.7	Yugoslavia	-3.4
Argentina	5.1	Ukraine	-3.1
Czech Republic	5.1	Angola	-3.0
Mauritius	4.9	Italy	-2.5
Chile	4.7	Cameroon	-2.1
Botswana	4.6	Russia	-2.1
Vietnam	4.4	Algeria	-1.9
Swaziland	4.1	Belarus	-1.9
Tunisia	4.1	Kenya	-1.9
Israel	3.8	Zaire	-1.9
Colombia	3.6	Nigeria	-1.7
Morocco	3.6	Belgium	-1.5
Peru	3.6	Croatia	-1.4
Poland	3.6	Spain	-1.1

THE LONG WAY BACK

Despite all this, the ratings are still struggling to recover from the brutal 1980s. In March 1981 the global average rating was 50.7, versus the current 36.7; the Asia-Pacific region was at 60.4, compared with the current 47.8; and Eastern Europe, now at 22.5, was at 53.1.

The average rating change in the current survey was 1.091, compared with 0.821 points in the last survey, which was also considered a volatile one. Two changes made in the preparation of this year's rankings temper the comparisons. First, Togo and Malta have been added. Second and more important, in response to passage of the North American Free Trade Agreement, Mexico has been moved out of the Latin America ratings and into North America with the U.S. and Canada. The immediate effect is a sharp decline in the North America regional ranking, which averages the ratings of the three countries. "But if the Nafta critics are right, perhaps Mexico will soon be carrying the other two," laughs one New York banker.

The **Middle East** tied with Latin America (when Mexico is excluded) as the most active region in the survey. Nine of the 14 countries there rose a point or more and only one fell at all, yielding a net rise of 1.3 points. "There are almost two groups in the region," a U.K. banker explains. The northern group is closely associated with Israel. Buoyed by signs of a peace pact between Israel and the Palestinians, they racked up sizable increases: 2.9 points for Israel, 2.7 for Lebanon, 2.3 for Egypt and 1.0 for Jordan.

The prospect of peace between Israel and the Palestinians has "a halo effect on the rest of the Middle East," this banker claims, which explains all of the increases in Middle Eastern ratings. But a Dutch banker disagrees, arguing that Saudi Arabia has cast a separate halo over its neighbors. "Some people were taking the view that its finances were rocky and its political situation was becoming less stable, but those views have died down," he says. Besides Saudi Arabia's own modest rise (0.7 points), there were big increases in Kuwait (2.3), Oman (1.8), Qatar (1.8) and the United Arab Emirates (1.6).

Meanwhile, Cyprus continues to soar — its 2.3-point increase puts it up 5.4 points over two and a half years. Cyprus has been riding on its image as the Miami of the Middle East — a peaceful offshore center offering access to all points in a turbulent region. It's a role that Beirut once played and, some say, that Tel Aviv might someday assume.

The one exception to the regional upturn was Iran, which fell 1.6 points on concern over its internal political situation. And despite the general rise, one New York banker warns against excessive optimism in the region. "If Israel and its neighbors can make peace, their prospects are very exciting," he says. "But you have to ask yourself, 'What are the long-term prospects of Saudi Arabia and the other quasi-medieval monarchies in the region?'"

HOW THE RATINGS ARE COMPILED

The country-by-country credit ratings developed by Institutional Investor are based on information provided by leading international banks. Bankers are asked to grade each of the countries on a scale of zero to 100, with 100 representing those with the least chance of default.

The sample for the study, which is updated every six months, ranges from 75 to 100 banks, each of which provides its own ratings. The names of all participants in the survey are kept strictly confidential. Banks are not permitted to rate their home countries. The individual responses are weighted using an Institutional Investor formula that gives more importance to responses from banks with greater worldwide exposure and more sophisticated country-analysis systems.

Latin America continues its transformation from economic basket case to one of the hottest emerging markets. The regional rating (including Mexico) rose 1.4 points over the past six months and is up 5.8 points since bottoming out at 20 in March 1990. When Mexico, which had been the region's second-strongest credit, is rated as part of North America, Latin America still chalks up a 1.3-point rise, widening its lead over Eastern Europe and Africa. Even better, the gain rests on increases in 21 of the 23 countries in the region. The only two countries that didn't show at least some increase were troubled Haiti, which fell a half a point, and Venezuela, which was unchanged.

Among the region's major countries, Argentina and Chile led the surge, rising 3.0 and 2.1 points, respectively, and Colombia rose 2.0 points. Meanwhile, Peru was up 2.5 points and Barbados rose 2.1 points, while 12 countries rose one to two points. Even Brazil, with its political scandals and hyper-inflation, advanced a full point. "Its growth was better — 3.2 percent last year — and its relations with external debt negotiators seem more pragmatic," says a New York banker. "But its inflation was something like 2,500 percent last year, so I wouldn't get too enthusiastic. Despite some recent progress, if you do a hierarchy of who's been able to implement economic reform, Brazil is widely acknowledged as being last on the totem pole."

What's going on in places like Barbados, Guatemala and Uruguay to warrant increases of about two full points each? "Nada," says this banker. "There are individual differences and specific achievements that account for ratings changes in Chile, which has been improving for a long time. But most of the others are benefiting from debt reduction programs, general economic improvements and the conclusion of the General Agreement on Tariffs and Trade, which has eased fears that Latin America could be isolated from the major trading blocs of North America, Europe and Asia."

Like Latin America, the **Asia-Pacific** region basked in a warm glow of investor enthusiasm. Its 0.9-point rise reflects ratings increases in 19 of the region's 22 countries, and the other three countries had only minor declines.

The Philippines and Vietnam led the region's gainers, rising 2.5 and 2.4 points, respectively, because "the flood of press coverage has been virtually universally positive, and it is seen as the next rapidly developing Asian economy," one U.K. banker says. "Although it's a long way from being a newly industrialized country, it is, in fact, likely to show strong growth over the medium term."

Meanwhile, Malaysia rose 1.8 points, mostly because it's the fastest-growing economy in the region after China, a Hong Kong banker notes, "yet it has managed growth without overheating the economy and without anyone taking the prime minister's speeches too seriously." He adds that New Zealand's 1.4-point rise is "probably a reward for several years of better economic management after going through a dreadful period in the 1980s."

Other ratings moves were more surprising. Why did India climb 1.6 points? "India improved its current account deficit," one U.K. banker says, "and the government has moved toward a free market. But from a banking point of view, its aggressive stance toward Western banks makes it surprising that its rating has moved up that much." Next door, Pakistan is up 1.1 points, "probably because the view is that the political situation is a little bit better," this banker explains. "Prime Minister Benazir Bhutto has come to a reasonable accommodation with her political rivals." That accommodation was favorable enough to permit Morgan Stanley & Co. to raise $185 million in equity capital for the Pakistan Investment Fund at the end of 1993.

But one Dutch banker insists that things aren't all that good in India or Pakistan, nor do objective conditions warrant the strong increases in the Philippines (2.5), Sri Lanka (2.2) and Bangladesh (1.3). And, he asks, "who's in a position to know of any reasons to change the rating of Nepal [up 1.1]?" Rather, he says, "there is a sense that the Asian Century is upon us, and therefore anything Asian will do well."

All the more surprising then that China, the biggest Asian country and the fastest-growing economy in the world, moved up only 0.7 points, and its once and future window to the world, Hong Kong, actually slipped 0.1 points. Both changes could be statistical blips, but the absence of further gains for China may reflect a sense that the economy "has established its strength, and now analysts are waiting to see how well the growth will be managed," says one U.K. banker.

"You know bankers are feeling better when **Africa** goes up," notes a Dutch banker. Africa's rating (excluding Togo) reached 20.7, up 0.4 points on a same-country basis since the last survey. The addition of Togo pushed the regional rating down to 20.6, but the upturn reflects significant gains in ten countries and declines in only two. The two regional leaders, Mauritius (up 2.3) and Botswana (1.0), were simply extending their string of gains reflecting good economic performance that has been noticed abroad. In the cases of Tunisia (up 2.6) and Morocco (2.4), one French banker explains that "the good news was there is no bad news. Muslim fundamentalism seems to have retreated somewhat, and they have not caught cold from Algeria."

Further south, Zimbabwe rose 1.0 points "because the drought through all of southern Africa has now broken," a U.K. banker says. That, along with political stability, also explains increases in the Seychelles (2.3), Swaziland (1.8 points) and Mali (1.4). Uganda's strong rise (1.7) is dismissed as an aberration in a country that has long bumped along at the bottom of the ratings.

However, the 1.9-point decline of Angola clearly reflects that "the political situation and fighting have gotten worse, and people can see that on television," says one New York banker. Cameroon's 1.6-point drop also reflects concern about political stability, though some of those interviewed express surprise at the severity of the decline.

South Africa remains the big question. The country moved upward slightly — 0.7 points — but bankers are still taking a wait-and-see attitude until after the nationwide elections.

By contrast, bankers have made up their minds about **Eastern Europe**. After years of plummeting scores, this time its regional rating remains unchanged at 21.8. But that conceals a growing split in the region. Six countries rose smartly, while four fell significantly.

The biggest gainer in Eastern Europe, and in the survey, was Slovenia, up 4.8. "There is business afoot there," says a U.K. banker, "and there is also a feeling that it's immune from some of the more disastrous problems in the surrounding area." A German banker adds: "Non-Europeans have discovered that Slovenia is not Yugoslavia. It was always the wealthiest part, and it has divorced itself from the rest and is doing very nicely, thank you. There is no fighting there, and it has a strong tourism sector. Europeans have strong nerves."

Meanwhile, the Czech Republic rose 3.1 points, the second-biggest increase in the survey. "It's everybody's favorite," one German banker says, adding that it pulled Slovakia up a point in its wake; that country's rise is thanks to the recognition that "Slovakia is doing better than people thought without the Czechs," says a New York banker. Two of the other Eastern European leaders, Poland and Hungary, rose 1.9 and 1.3 points, respectively. "There are not necessarily signs of great strength economically, but of stability, and that is very reassuring," says a German banker.

The big puzzle among the gains was Romania's 1.0-point rise. "I suppose it's because it's got no debt," says one U.K. banker, adding, "Former president Nicolae Ceau• escu brought down the economy to pay it off, but its financial ratios are strong even if its politics are unreformed and its economy is in poor shape."

As the region's six best credits got better, its seven worst credits all got even worse in the eyes of survey respondents. One of the sizable declines was the remnants of Yugoslavia, down another 1.7 points and now rated 6.6, putting it ahead of only North Korea, Sudan and Liberia. Meanwhile, three major pieces of the former Soviet Union also declined sharply. Ukraine (down 3.1), Georgia (2.8) and Belarus (2.0) all fell "because in each of those entities, there have been intense economic and political problems," one New York bank country risk analyst says, adding, "The nationalist aspirations of some of Russia's key actors are perceived by many as creating risks for these nations."

Though the rating increases tallied by the stronger credits in Eastern Europe reflect "the confidence that continuity creates," a German banker says, the nations of the old Soviet Union are regarded as ever more dicey. "What has all of us worried about the region is not things like a rescheduling, but catastrophic events," this banker adds.

The **Western European** countries, in contrast to their eastern neighbors, are a haven of stability. The region (excluding Malta) chalked up a rating of 75.3, up 0.2 points from the last survey. Western Europe remains the Greenwich meridian of the survey; its current rating is precisely the same as the regional rating in September 1990 and only marginally different from the 73.6 registered in March 1986 or the 74.8 recorded in September 1981. Indeed, through the entire 14-and-a-half year history of the survey, Western Europe has remained within a 5.7-point band, between 71.8 and 77.5.

In the current survey most of Western Europe barely moved; the only significant changes were Denmark, which rose 1.1 points, and Belgium and Italy, which fell 1.0 and 0.9 points, respectively. "Denmark has been improving over some considerable period," says a U.K. bank economist. "It went through a bad patch in the early 1980s, but it has recovered from that. Its debt levels are under control, its external position is much improved and it suffered less than anybody else from the recession in 1993 — there was only a marginal decline in its economy. For a relatively small country, it has strong numbers and people are recognizing this." Denmark ranked third among sovereign issuers in the international bond market last year, raising some $9.8 billion.

"For Belgium, like Italy, there are concerns with the domestic debt," says a New York banker. "With the increased integration of different economies, people start to understand that domestic debt is important in looking at country risk, and that's what's going on here." A U.K. banker argues that Belgium fell "because of the magnitude of the budget deficit and the suspension of belief that the authorities are going to do something significant about it." Belgium was the ninth-largest borrower in the international bond market in 1993, raising some $2.5 billion, according to IFR Securities Data.

Italy fell because of its tangled political travails and the financial community's concern over "the somewhat perverse Italian attitudes toward what many people consider state debt," says the U.K. banker. "At one point it appeared that it would abrogate certain of these debts." Despite such concerns, however, Italy managed to raise $12.7 billion in the international bond markets last year, making it the second-largest user of those markets.

There was good news in **North America**, but because of the Nafta-inspired inclusion of Mexico under North America, its rating slid. The old North America — the U.S. and Canada — rose 0.2 points, to 85.8, the highest level in three and a half years. This result stemmed from signs of an economic recovery in the U.S., which boosted that country's rating 0.5 points, and pushed it from fourth to third place in the global rankings, reversing positions with Germany.

But the addition of Mexico lowers the regional rating to 72.8, below Western Europe. The prospect of Nafta, along with support for the policies of Mexican President Carlos Salinas de Gortari, led respondents to boost Mexico 1.3 points (despite signs of an economic downturn). Its rating of 46.9 is 8.2 points higher than it was two and a half years ago. However, Mexico's rating is 35 points below Canada's and almost 43 below the U.S.'s. No other region has such a range between its highest- and lowest-rated countries.

Most bankers believe that Mexico's ability to benefit from its large and wealthy neighbors should fuel its economy. But as a New York banker says, Mexico, like many other countries, has seen its ratings rise "because it has made it clear it intends to participate in the global economy." That desire to enter global markets has much to do with the broad range of ratings increases this year. "As long as the emerging markets keep waving the 'invest here' signs instead of the 'Yankee go home' signs, the confidence level of foreign lenders and investors should keep going up," says a U.K. banker.

Associate Editor Kit Purcell prepared the statistical material accompanying this feature.

ANATOMY OF CREDITWORTHINESS

OECD countries		
1979	1994	Rating factor
1	1	Economic outlook
5	2	Debt service
2	3	Financial reserves and current account
9	4	Fiscal policy
3	5	Political outlook
6	6	Access to capital markets
4	7	Trade balance
7	8	Inflow of portfolio investments
8	9	Foreign direct investment

Quantifying a country's appeal to foreign providers of capital is a difficult feat, but investors and lenders do it all the time. What is it that shapes a country's ratings, and how has it evolved over the years?

To answer that question, *Institutional Investor* asked participants in its semiannual country credit survey to rank the factors they currently use in establishing a country's rating and to indicate how they thought these factors ranked in 1979, when the survey began. These results, which appear below, were tallied for three categories of countries: OECD economies, emerging countries and the rest of the world.

The poll shows that analysts rely on economic, financial and political variables. But they combine the general outlook with a review of specific statistics, including financial reserves and current-account figures, inflow of investment, and debt service measures. "We're trying to combine balance-sheet concepts, as embodied in things like the current account, with big-picture things: How's the economy? How stable is the regime?" explains one bank's country risk analyst in London.

Emerging countries		
1979	1994	Rating factor
1	1	Debt service
3	2	Political outlook
2	3	Economic outlook
4	4	Financial reserves and current account
5	5	Trade balance
6	6	Foreign direct investment
9	7	Fiscal policy
8	8	Inflow of portfolio investments
7	9	Access to capital markets

Surprisingly, the biggest changes in the factors used to formulate the ratings were those applied to the OECD countries. Since 1979 debt service has jumped from the fifth- to the second-most-important factor, and fiscal policy has climbed from ninth to fourth. "The basic size of a country's obligations and its ability to keep its fiscal house in order have proved more important," one New York banker says, while political outlook has declined from third to fifth. "That just reflects the fact that there is less reason to be concerned about politics in the industrialized nations," one London banker points out, adding, "The kind of debt repudiation harangues and socialist murmurings that used to scare bankers are largely absent from political discourse these days."

Although the factors that shape the ratings have remained constant over time, the survey showed that the importance bankers give each of them differs according to where the bankers are located.

Rest of world		
1979	1994	Rating factor
1	1	Debt service
2	2	Political outlook
4	3	Financial reserves and current account
3	4	Economic outlook
5	5	Trade balance
6	6	Fiscal policy
9	7	Foreign direct investment
7	8	Inflow of portfolio investments
8	9	Access to capital markets

In rating the emerging countries, European bankers ranked foreign direct investment as fifth in importance, while Asian bankers put it in seventh place and Western Hemisphere bankers rank it ninth. By contrast, bankers in the Americas rank fiscal policy fifth, European bankers seventh and Asian bankers ninth.

On the whole, however, there is substantial consistency, both geographically and chronologically, in the attributes that determine the country credit ratings. "I suppose the term 'creditworthiness' has become somewhat less meaningful because the mechanisms for providing capital have evolved beyond the syndicated sovereign loan," a New York banker says. "But the concept remains valid and important." And, he adds, assessing it isn't all that hard: "It's like the U.S. Supreme Court said about pornography: I know it when I see it."

INSTITUTIONAL INVESTOR'S 1994 COUNTRY CREDIT RATINGS

Sept 1993	Mar 1994	Country	Institutional Investor credit rating	Six-month change	One-year change
1	1	Switzerland	92.2	0.2	0.2
2	2	Japan	91.0	-0.7	0.0
4	3	United States	89.7	0.5	1.1
3	4	Germany	89.4	-0.4	-0.9
5	5	Netherlands	88.4	-0.4	-0.8
6	6	France	88.2	0.0	0.6
7	7	United Kingdom	86.0	0.6	1.4
8	8	Austria	85.6	0.3	0.3
9	9	Luxembourg	84.6	0.0	0.1
10	10	Canada	81.9	-0.1	-0.1
11	11	Singapore	81.4	0.5	1.2
13	12	Taiwan	79.0	0.9	0.5
12	13 *	Belgium	78.8	-1.0	-1.5
13	14 *	Norway	78.8	0.7	1.7
15	15	Denmark	77.8	1.1	2.5
16	16	Spain	74.7	-0.5	-1.1
17	17	Sweden	74.5	0.1	-0.7
18	18	Italy	72.6	-0.9	-2.5
19	19	Ireland	70.7	0.7	1.3
20	20	Finland	69.9	0.5	0.3
21	21	South Korea	69.5	0.6	0.9
22	22	Australia	68.9	0.8	1.0
23	23	Portugal	67.3	0.6	1.2
25	24	Malaysia	66.6	1.8	2.7
26	25	New Zealand	66.1	1.4	2.3
24	26	Hong Kong	66.0	-0.1	0.4
27	27	Thailand	61.1	0.3	1.1
28	28	UAE	59.9	1.6	2.0
–	29	Malta	58.7	–	–
29	30	Saudi Arabia	58.6	0.7	0.6
30	31	China	58.0	0.7	1.7
31	32	Iceland	55.8	0.9	0.7
32	33	Qatar	54.7	1.8	2.5
34	34	Chile	53.6	2.1	4.7
36	35	Oman	52.5	1.8	1.7
33	36	Bahrain	52.0	0.4	1.0
35	37	Indonesia	51.7	0.2	0.6
37	38	Kuwait	51.5	2.3	2.6
38	39	Cyprus	51.1	2.3	2.3
40	40	Czech Republic	49.7	3.1	5.1
39	41	Greece	49.1	0.5	1.2
41	42	Mexico	46.9	1.3	1.7
43	43	Hungary	46.1	1.3	1.8
44	44	Botswana	45.7	1.0	4.6
42	45	Turkey	45.6	0.5	0.3
46	46	Israel	43.4	2.9	3.8
45	47	Mauritius	43.3	2.3	4.9
48	48	Tunisia	42.9	2.6	4.1
47	49	Colombia	42.4	2.0	3.6
49	50	India	40.0	1.6	1.4
50	51	South Africa	38.9	0.7	-0.9
51	52	Venezuela	37.6	0.0	-1.0
52	53	Barbados	37.3	2.1	1.5
53	54	Uruguay	36.0	1.8	2.3
54	55	Morocco	35.8	2.4	3.6
55	56	Argentina	35.6	3.0	5.1
61	57	Slovenia	33.4	4.8	10.8
56	58	Papua New Guinea	32.8	0.4	0.4
57	59	Slovakia	31.6	1.0	0.6
58	60	Trinidad & Tobago	30.8	1.4	1.2
64	61 *	Philippines	30.5	2.5	3.4
62	62 *	Poland	30.5	1.9	3.6
67	63	Egypt	29.8	2.3	2.7
60	64	Libya	29.4	0.6	0.8
68	65 *	Paraguay	28.8	1.6	1.0
66	66 *	Pakistan	28.8	1.1	-0.1
65	67 *	Brazil	28.8	1.0	1.1
70	68	Zimbabwe	27.9	1.0	0.2
59	69	Iran	27.8	-1.6	-4.3
73	70	Sri Lanka	27.7	2.2	2.2
71	71	Costa Rica	27.6	0.8	2.8
63	72	Gabon	27.4	-0.8	-0.6
72	73	Ghana	27.1	1.1	2.9
74	74 *	Swaziland	26.3	1.8	4.1
69	75 *	Algeria	26.3	-0.8	-1.9
75	76	Romania	25.4	1.0	1.2
80	77	Seychelles	23.7	2.3	3.0
79	78	Jamaica	23.6	1.7	1.7
78	79	Nepal	23.2	1.1	1.5
77	80	Syria	23.1	0.4	0.7
76	81	Kenya	22.8	-0.2	-1.9
81	82	Ecuador	22.5	1.2	1.7
85	83 *	Panama	22.1	1.2	1.7
83	84 *	Jordan	22.1	1.0	1.1
88	85	Vietnam	21.9	2.4	4.4
90	86	Dominican Republic	21.0	1.8	2.5
86	87	Senegal	20.9	0.8	0.9
84	88	Estonia	20.7	-0.2	-0.7
97	89	Guatemala	20.1	2.0	1.3
95	90	Bangladesh	20.0	1.3	0.7
89	91 *	Bulgaria	19.8	0.3	0.9
102	92 *	Lebanon	19.8	2.7	5.7
81	93	Cameroon	19.7	-1.6	-2.1
87	94	Latvia	19.6	-0.4	0.1
94	95	Bolivia	19.5	0.8	1.4
91	96	Nigeria	18.6	-0.5	-1.7
93	97	Lithuania	18.4	-0.6	-0.5
92	98	Russia	18.1	-0.9	-2.1
98	99	Kazakhstan	17.7	0.1	1.9
109	100	Peru	17.5	2.5	3.6
101	101	Malawi	17.4	0.1	1.2
107	102	El Salvador	17.3	2.0	2.1
99	103	Burkina Faso	17.2	-0.3	–
103	104	Benin	16.8	-0.1	–
107	105	Mali	16.7	1.4	–
104	106	Cote d'Ivoire	16.4	0.2	-0.3
106	107	Honduras	16.2	0.6	0.5
105	108 *	Congo	15.5	-0.3	0.3
100	109 *	Belarus	15.5	-2.0	-1.9
–	110	Togo	15.4	–	–
96	111	Ukraine	15.1	-3.1	-3.1
110	112	Uzbekistan	14.3	-0.1	-0.2
111	113	Tanzania	13.9	-0.1	1.0
114	114	Myanmar	13.3	0.3	0.9
116	115 *	Zambia	13.1	0.7	1.4
111	116 *	Guinea	13.1	-0.9	–
113	117	Croatia	12.8	-0.8	-1.4
115	118	Angola	10.7	-1.9	-3.0
120	119	Ethiopia	10.6	0.8	2.1
118	120 **	Mozambique	10.3	0.6	1.9
121		Albania	10.3	-0.2	-0.8
123	122	Uganda	10.1	1.7	2.8
119	123	Afghanistan	9.9	-0.4	–
122	124	Nicaragua	9.1	0.4	0.8
117	125	Georgia	8.9	-2.8	–
128	126	Grenada	8.5	1.0	1.2
127	127	Cuba	7.9	0.2	-0.3
125	128	Haiti	7.5	-0.5	0.2
130	129 *	Sierra Leone	7.2	0.6	0.5
129	130 *	Iraq	7.2	0.0	-0.2
126	131	Zaire	6.9	-0.8	-1.9
124	132	Yugoslavia	6.6	-1.7	-3.4
131	133	North Korea	6.5	0.2	-0.8
133	134	Sudan	6.1	0.4	-0.9
132	135	Liberia	6.0	0.0	0.0
		Global average rating	37.6	0.6	-0.1

*Order determined by actual results after rounding
**Actual tie

Chapter 10

Bank of America
World Information Services

COUNTRY OUTLOOKS

Country Outlooks brings you Bank of America's business briefings on 30 countries. These 30 countries are of great importance to planners and decisions makers in business and government.

In its Country Risk Monitor, Bank of America evaluates country risk based on 10 economic ratios. For 80 countries, an ordinal ranking is created for each of the ratios. A rank of one indicates the least difficulty or problem; a rank of 80 is associated with the most difficulty.

The ranks are then averaged across the 10 variables and a comprehensive ranking of the averages is created to provide a picture of relative risk. The Country Risk Monitor provides rankings for the current year, historical data for the previous four years, and projections for the next five years.

The rankings will be particularly useful for investors in the financial and banking industries but can also serve as an indicator of stability for firms in other business sectors. Bank of America also provides a Country Outlook for each of the 80 countries covered, plus the rankings and ratios for each of the 10 included variables.

Each Country Outlook portrays in depth the business, financial and economic environment expected over the coming two years. The outlook includes a table of key economic indicators at the end. These indicators show two years of historical data, the current-year estimate, and forecasts for the two years covered by the outlook.

The writing style in the outlooks is concise. Facts are clearly stated with projections made on the basis of preceding analysis. Standardized format allows for quick access to those sections of each outlook that may be of greatest interest.

Though standardized, the format also is flexible to permit special treatment of unusual and important events. When a country faces an issue such as growing external indebtedness, falling commodity prices for its principal exports, changing economic policy, or labor unrest, the issue is dealt with in depth.

Country Outlooks may be used independently from our other products but is also a complement to Country Data Forecasts and Country Risk Monitor. Used separately, it supports marketing, investment and planning and policy decisions.

An example of our *Country Outlook* on Poland follows. This outlook was taken directly from our product. It shows you exactly what type of information is available for 30 countries. You will see how clearly and concisely the information is presented.

Country Outlook
Poland

July 1993

Overview — As the first Central European country to embark on the transformation to a market economy, Poland is an important model. In January 1990, the government adopted a "shock adjustment" program and major structural reforms. Since that time the country has grappled with complex restructuring of large state-owned companies, and a shift in trade away from Eastern Europe toward western countries. This year Poland is showing the first strong signs of economic recovery. Output is rising, inflation has eased, and private sector employment is expanding rapidly.

Local entrepreneurs and foreign investors have benefited from a recovery in domestic demand and improved sales, but operating costs will remain high as inflation and indirect taxes rise through the balance of 1993. Despite the pressure of a national election campaign, the government has taken difficult steps to limit the budget deficit and is financing more debt through the domestic capital markets. This will allow the central bank to follow a more flexible monetary policy in support of economic recovery.

Strong import demand in Poland and weakness among its main trading partners will push Poland's trade balance into deficit in 1993. The current account will, however, benefit from lower debt service payments as a result of Poland's debt reduction agreement with the Paris Club governments. This may be complemented in 1994 with a Brady-style agreement with commercial bank creditors.

Growth and Employment — After two and a half years of deep recession, the Polish economy is experiencing solid recovery. National output rose slightly in the second half of 1992, but was held down by a severe drought which hurt the agricultural sector. In 1993, GDP will register 2.5 percent growth. Industrial production is rising at a fast 5 percent pace, but performance remains erratic as many troubled state enterprises await restructuring. The key areas of improvement are in the chemical, electromachinery, and clothing industries. Agriculture will rebound this year as the effects of the drought ease. The major source of new growth is the private sector which now accounts for nearly two-thirds of employment and half of national output. With economic recovery and some easing of interest rates, business investment will rise an estimated 5 percent next year. These trends will contribute to an economic growth rate of 3.5 percent in 1994.

Unemployment has risen sharply over the past year, despite the general improvement in the economy. The total number of jobless reached 2.6 million, or 14.2 percent of the work force, in June. These figures will increase later this year as uncompetitive coal mines and steel mills close. To counter this trend, the national government has offered special credits to small businesses and to companies in areas with the highest concentration of unemployed. Still, the scale of joblessness has compelled the government to cut back its generous unemployment compensation program, focusing instead on retraining and youth job creation programs.

Business Conditions — The sharp rebound in output and domestic demand will provide a solid boost to domestic companies. However, business costs will remain relatively high as companies face rising input costs and the introduction of new taxes. Producer prices, which affect business more directly, have risen about 28 percent over the past year, although they slowed recently to 22 percent annual pace. Tax obligations are another significant business cost. In December 1992, the government was forced to introduce a series of special taxes, including a 6 percent temporary import surcharge, a 3 percentage point rise in the turnover tax (a type of sales tax at each stage of production), and limits on depreciation allowances. Lower business payrolls are offsetting these costs somewhat. Average wages decreased in most sectors during the first part of 1993, while real wages have fallen nearly 10 percent in the past six months. A result, enterprise profitability (pre-tax profit compared to sales) rose 4.4 percent in the first quarter of 1993. This trend is likely to expand to more sectors, as losses tend to be concentrated in a few sectors such as coal mining, transportation equipment, and railways.

Poland has embarked on an ambitious program to privatize small and large scale businesses. In 1993, the government plans to make private an additional 400 small to medium-sized state companies through leases or sales to employees, management, and Polish investors. Large-scale privatization is proceeding more slowly as the government will gradually transfer control of 600 large scale state enterprises to 20 National Investment Funds, which will oversee the restructuring and sale of these firms. In addition, the government expects to transfer ownership of approximately 250 firms through direct sales or share issuance to the public. Through these various measures the Ministry of Finance will receive up to $350 million in revenues during 1993. The major problem is the near bankruptcy of many state firms. This poses serious difficulties for the banking system, and will require a program of debt write-offs and conversion of local loans into equity to resolve the most difficult cases.

Fiscal Policy — The Polish government suffered a serious setback during 1992, as the budget deficit approached 7 percent of GDP. This prompted the IMF to suspend its Stand-by program and threatened to derail the second stage of the debt reduction package offered by Western governments. In early 1993, the Polish Cabinet gained initial legislative approval for a budget which called for spending of Zloty 514 trillion (US$29 billion) and revenues of Zloty 434 trillion (US$24.5 billion). This budget stressed the need to stabilize tax revenues, primarily through a temporary import surcharge and the introduction of value-added tax. The VAT, introduced in July 1993, will carry a basic rate of 20 percent for most goods, with a 7 percent rate for certain goods essential to the cost of living.

The initial budget aimed to limit the fiscal deficit to 5 percent of GDP. However, weaker revenues in the late spring widened this deficit sharply, requiring politically difficult cuts in social benefits and public payrolls. Conflict over pension cuts sparked a vote of "no-confidence" in June, forcing national elections to be held in September. Despite this uncertainty, the current Cabinet is expected to present a 1994 budget in the early autumn, with new spending reductions and an overall deficit equal to 4.5 percent of GDP. This budget will contain important reforms, including a restructuring of the social insurance programs and a transfer of revenues to local governments.

Monetary Policy — Throughout most of 1992, the National Bank of Poland (NBP) exerted tight control over credit and increased interest rates in order to moderate inflationary pressures. Inflation averaged 45 percent in 1992 due to large public deficits, escalating real wages, and higher agricultural prices. Consumer price increases have slowed this year, averaging about 35 percent and will drop below 30 percent in 1994. With the easing of inflation, the NBP was able to cut the refinancing rate to 29 percent in February. The NBP has also shifted its emphasis away from credit rationing, which was required in 1992 to ensure financing for the government deficit. The National Bank now relies on open market operations to control the short-term money supply, while the government is able to finance more than 15 percent of its deficit through the issue of treasury instruments. A greater problem for the NBP is the weakness of the nine major state banks. Non-performing loans of insolvent state companies represent nearly one-third of the total assets at these state banks. The IMF and World Bank are providing funds to recapitalize these banks and to restructure the state enterprise sector. Once these banks are recapitalized, most will be privatized, as Wielkopolski Bank Kredytowy was sold to a group of Polish and foreign investors earlier this year.

Another key aspect of Polish monetary policy is support for the convertibility of the zloty exchange rate. In early 1992, the National Bank of Poland devalued the zloty by approximately 13 percent to improve the country's trade competitiveness. Since that time the NBP has devalued the zloty at a rate of 1.8 percent per month against the U.S. dollar. In late 1992 and early 1993, the zloty appreciated in real terms. The National Bank plans to maintain the same pace of devaluation through 1993, but with the trade balance shifting sharply into deficit by mid-year the NBP may come under pressure to accelerate the pace of devaluation.

Trade and Current Account — Poland's convertible currency trade registered a strong $500 million surplus in 1992. Export growth will slow markedly in 1993, reflecting the slowdown in West European economies which account for nearly 60 percent of Poland's export markets. Total exports will actually decline slightly to about $13.9 billion. At the same time, Polish imports are increasing rapidly in tandem with the domestic economic boom. In the first four months of 1993 imports rose 22 percent. Some of this may be attributable to importers accelerating purchases before the VAT went into effect on July 1st. The government imposed a temporary 6 percent import surcharge to moderate import growth, but total imports are still likely to increase more than 10 percent, to $14.9 billion. This would result in a trade deficit of $1 billion. Other structural problems are emerging in Poland's trade with OECD countries. The European Community has introduced permanent anti-dumping duties on Polish steel exports and has issued complaints against Polish sales of live animals and certain other products into the community. Poland contends that the trade relations are asymmetrical. It is lowering import barriers as a condition of its EC Association Membership, while the European Community is raising barriers to key Polish exports such as specialty steel, electrical machinery, and textiles. These disputes may be resolved through a series of EC trade negotiations or in the context of the General Agreement on Tariffs and Trade (GATT). Once the European economies begin to recover in 1994, exports will begin to expand again, and the trade deficit will remain steady at $1 billion.

The burgeoning trade deficit poses some concerns for the current account and overall balance of payments. Poland's services account will show a small surplus, but the traditionally large inflow of private transfers from Poles living abroad will be offset by Polish citizens transferring assets out of Poland. Poland will also save nearly $2 billion in 1993 from the third year of the Paris Club debt reduction agreement. This will hold the current account deficit to about $1.3 billion, but the deficit will widen in 1994 with the resumption of higher interest payments to all creditors.

Capital Account, Debt, and Reserves — Poland will readily finance its small current account deficit and add to its foreign exchange reserves during 1993. The major sources of funds will be a new IMF Stand-by program, with drawings of $680 million, credits of $700 million from the World Bank and EBRD, and net foreign investment of $500 million. Despite major new foreign investment projects by Fiat, International Paper, and Coca-Cola, Poland's foreign investment flows remain significantly below those of other Central European countries. Foreign investment may accelerate once national elections stabilize the political situation, and agreement is reached between the Polish government and the commercial banks on a Brady-style debt reduction package. By 1994, Poland's total external debt is expected to fall to $43 billion, while external debt service will absorb only 19-20 percent of goods and services exports. Official foreign exchange reserves remain relatively stable at $3.5 billion, equivalent to 3.5 months of goods and services imports.

Key Economic Indicators Country: Poland					
	History		Current	Forecast	
	1991	1992	1993	1994	1995
GDP Per Capita ($)	2,107	2,157	2,290	2,420	2,540
Real GDP Growth (%)	-7.2	-1.0	2.5	3.5	5.0
Nominal GDP ($M)	80,559	83,071	88,900	94,500	99,700
Exports Merchandise FOB ($M)	12,760	13,997	13,900	15,100	16,600
Imports Merchandise FOB ($M)	12,709	13,485	14,900	16,100	17,600
Trade Balance ($M)	51	512	-1,000	-1,000	-1,000
Current Account Balance ($M)	-1,359	-400	-1,300	-1,700	-2,000
Reserves with Gold ($M) Year-end	4,100	4,000	3,900	4,200	4,600
Total External Debt ($M) Year-end	46,034	47,079	48,100	43,300	44,100
Money Growth (Ml) (%) Year-end	25.7	35.0	30.0	30.0	20.0
Consumer Price Inflation (%) Year-end	76.0	44.0	30.0	30.0	20.0
Exchange Rate (L.C./$) Year-end	10,957	15,767	19,300	25,100	30,100

COUNTRY DATA FORECASTS

Country Data Forecasts is a comprehensive strategic planning tool that neatly lays out the major economic, financial, and demographic environment in each of 80 countries. For each country covered by *Country Data Forecasts,* there are two pages of data showing 23 key economic indicators in a format covering six years of history, an estimate for the current year, and **five years of forecasts.** Bank experts have chosen the 23 indicators on the basis of many years of first-hand experience in country analysis and business needs. Rather than loading you down with reams of data on every aspect of each economy, *Country Data Forecasts* shows just those series from which a comprehensive picture of an economy can be easily drawn.

Country Data Forecasts projects data such as income per capita, growth and size of the economy, inflation rates, trade performance, international indebtedness, and the exchange rate. Summary data tables and graphs give you global and regional perspectives.

Country Data Forecasts offers you a quick but comprehensive picture of an economy. The data format facilitates comparison among individual economies or between economies and regional trends.

The next pages show data on Indonesia and Mexico from *Country Data Forecasts.* These pages were taken directly from our product. They show you exactly what information is offered for 80 countries. You will see how clearly and concisely the information is presented.

Country Data Forecasts
Country: Indonesia

Economic Indicator	1987	1988	1989	1990	1991	1992
Population (Millions)	170.2	173.4	176.5	179.3	182.5	185.8
Percent Change	1.9%	1.9%	1.8%	1.6%	1.8%	1.8%
GDP Per Capita ($)	446	486	535	596	638	685
Percent Change	-6.9%	9.0%	10.1%	11.4%	7.0%	7.4%
Real GDP Per Capita ($)	573	595	628	664	696	723
Percent Change	1.6%	3.8%	5.6%	5.7%	4.7%	3.9%
GDP ($M)	75,923	84,300	94,455	106,859	116,476	127,273
Percent Change	-5.1%	11.0%	12.0%	13.1%	9.0%	9.3%
Real GDP ($M)	97,497	103,152	110,889	119,094	126,955	134,318
Percent Change	3.6%	5.8%	7.5%	7.4%	6.6%	5.8%
GDP (Local Currency Millions)	124,817,000	142,105,000	167,185,000	196,919,000	227,163,000	258,363,838
Percent Change	21.6%	13.9%	17.6%	17.8%	15.4%	13.7%
Consumer Price Change, year-end	9.2%	5.6%	6.3%	9.5%	9.5%	4.9%
Exports Merchandise FOB ($M)	17,206	19,509	22,974	26,807	29,430	32,502
Percent Change	19.5%	13.4%	17.8%	16.7%	9.8%	10.4%
Imports Merchandise FOB ($M)	12,532	13,831	16,310	21,455	24,626	26,481
Percent Change	5.0%	10.4%	17.9%	31.5%	14.8%	7.5%
Trade Balance ($M)	4,674	5,678	6,664	5,352	4,804	6,021
Current Account Balance ($M)	-2,098	-1,397	-1,108	-4,093	-5,049	-3,676
Int'l Reserves Without Gold ($M) year-end	5,592	5,048	5,454	7,459	9,258	11,600
Int'l Reserves With Gold At Market Prices ($M) year-end	7,102	6,300	6,700	8,700	10,400	12,600
Total External Debt ($M), year-end	55,000	57,300	61,132	72,300	79,548	82,663
Exchange Rate (L.C./$), year-end	1,650	1,731	1,797	1,901	1,992	2,062

Date: August, 1993
Data are expressed in nominal terms unless otherwise indicated.
Real GDP is at constant 1980 prices and 1980 exchange rates.

Country Data Forecasts
Country: Indonesia

Economic Indicator	1993	1994	1995	1996	1997	1998
Population (Millions)	189.1	192.5	196.0	199.5	203.1	206.8
Percent Change	1.8%	1.8%	1.8%	1.8%	1.8%	1.8%
GDP Per Capita ($)	749	817	891	971	1,051	1,132
Percent Change	9.3%	9.1%	9.1%	9.0%	8.2%	7.7%
Real GDP Per Capita ($)	754	788	823	859	896	933
Percent Change	4.3%	4.5%	4.4%	4.3%	4.3%	4.1%
GDP ($M)	141,566	157,217	174,714	193,714	213,361	234,052
Percent Change	11.2%	11.1%	11.1%	10.9%	10.1%	9.7%
Real GDP ($M)	142,646	151,775	161,337	171,340	181,963	192,881
Percent Change	6.2%	6.4%	6.3%	6.2%	6.2%	6.0%
GDP (Local Currency Millions)	297,430,517	342,732,754	393,106,586	449,416,353	512,598,899	582,204,704
Percent Change	15.1%	15.2%	14.7%	14.3%	14.1%	13.6%
Consumer Price Change, year-end	8.6%	8.0%	7.8%	7.5%	7.3%	7.0%
Exports Merchandise FOB ($M)	36,800	42,000	47,200	53,200	60,000	68,000
Percent Change	13.2%	14.1%	12.4%	12.7%	12.8%	13.3%
Imports Merchandise FOB ($M)	29,400	33,000	36,800	41,000	45,500	51,000
Percent Change	11.0%	12.2%	11.5%	11.4%	11.0%	12.1%
Trade Balance ($M)	7,400	9,000	10,400	12,200	14,500	17,000
Current Account Balance ($M)	-3,200	-3,000	-2,900	-2,300	-2,000	-1,500
Int'l Reserves Without Gold ($M) year-end	13,000	14,300	15,700	17,200	18,800	20,500
Int'l Reserves With Gold At Market Prices ($M) year-end	14,100	15,400	16,900	18,400	20,100	21,800
Total External Debt ($M), year-end	84,800	86,600	88,500	89,900	91,300	92,500
Exchange Rate (L.C./$), year-end	2,140	2,220	2,280	2,360	2,445	2,530

Date: August, 1993
Data are expressed in nominal terms unless otherwise indicated.
Real GDP is at constant 1980 prices and 1980 exchange rates.

Country Data Forecasts
Country: Mexico

Economic Indicator	1987	1988	1989	1990	1991	1992
Population (Millions)	81.2	82.8	84.5	86.1	87.8	89.5
Percent Change	2.0%	2.0%	2.0%	2.0%	2.0%	1.9%
GDP Per Capita ($)	1,528	2,177	2,714	3,043	3,415	3,741
Percent Change	-6.1%	42.5%	24.7%	12.1%	12.2%	9.5%
Real GDP Per Capita ($)	2,430	2,415	2,440	2,499	2,539	2,555
Percent Change	-0.4%	-0.6%	1.1%	2.4%	1.6%	0.7%
GDP ($M)	124,014	180,291	229,271	262,166	299,977	334,958
Percent Change	-4.2%	45.4%	27.2%	14.3%	14.4%	11.7%
Real GDP ($M)	197,220	199,981	206,180	215,252	223,001	228,799
Percent Change	1.6%	1.4%	3.1%	4.4%	3.6%	2.6%
GDP (Local Currency Billions)	193,462	403,130	564,006	734,851	904,431	1,038,371
Percent Change	144.5%	108.4%	39.9%	30.3%	23.1%	14.8%
Consumer Price Change, year-end	159.2%	51.7%	19.7%	29.9%	18.8%	11.9%
Exports Merchandise FOB ($M)	20,655	20,566	22,765	26,838	27,121	27,531
Percent Change	28.8%	-0.4%	10.7%	17.9%	1.1%	1.5%
Imports Merchandise FOB ($M)	12,222	18,898	23,410	31,271	38,184	48,538
Percent Change	6.9%	54.6%	23.9%	33.6%	22.1%	27.1%
Trade Balance ($M)	8,433	1,668	-645	-4,433	-11,063	-21,007
Current Account Balance ($M)	3,968	-2,443	-3,958	-7,117	-13,282	-22,700
Int'l Reserves Without Gold ($M) year-end	0	5,279	6,329	10,270	17,726	18,942
Int'l Reserves With Gold At Market Prices ($M) year-end	1,234	6,327	6,740	10,600	18,100	19,300
Total External Debt ($M), year-end	107,265	100,914	97,420	109,700	114,666	127,000
Exchange Rate (L.C./$), year-end	2,210	2,281	2,630	2,943	3,073	3,123

Date: August, 1993
Data are expressed in nominal terms unless otherwise indicated.
Real GDP is at constant 1980 prices and 1980 exchange rates.

Country Data Forecasts
Country: Mexico

Economic Indicator	1993	1994	1995	1996	1997	1998
Population (Millions)	91.3	93.2	95.0	96.9	98.9	100.8
Percent Change	2.0%	2.0%	2.0%	2.0%	2.0%	2.0%
GDP Per Capita ($)	4,077	4,314	4,537	4,904	5,300	5,728
Percent Change	9.0%	5.8%	5.2%	8.1%	8.1%	8.1%
Real GDP Per Capita ($)	2,570	2,608	2,646	2,724	2,804	2,887
Percent Change	0.6%	1.5%	1.5%	2.9%	2.9%	2.9%
GDP ($M)	372,365	401,886	431,141	475,256	523,932	577,578
Percent Change	11.2%	7.9%	7.3%	10.2%	10.2%	10.2%
Real GDP ($M)	234,748	242,964	251,468	264,041	277,244	291,106
Percent Change	2.6%	3.5%	3.5%	5.0%	5.0%	5.0%
GDP (Local Currency Billions)	1,177,000	1,322,000	1,478,000	1,676,000	1,900,000	2,155,000
Percent Change	13.4%	12.3%	11.8%	13.4%	13.4%	13.4%
Consumer Price Change, year-end	9.0%	8.0%	8.0%	8.0%	8.0%	8.0%
Exports Merchandise FOB ($M)	31,400	36,100	41,500	47,700	54,900	63,100
Percent Change	14.1%	15.0%	15.0%	14.9%	15.1%	14.9%
Imports Merchandise FOB ($M)	55,300	63,500	72,000	80,600	90,300	101,100
Percent Change	13.9%	14.8%	13.4%	11.9%	12.0%	12.0%
Trade Balance ($M)	-23,900	-27,400	-30,500	-32,900	-35,400	-38,000
Current Account Balance ($M)	-25,200	-25,900	-28,100	-29,400	-30,700	-31,500
Int'l Reserves Without Gold ($M) year-end	23,000	25,000	27,500	30,000	33,500	35,000
Int'l Reserves With Gold At Market Prices ($M) year-end	23,300	25,400	27,900	30,400	33,900	35,400
Total External Debt ($M), year-end	130,000	132,500	142,500	152,500	160,500	167,500
Exchange Rate (L.C./$), year-end	3.20	3.38	3.48	3.58	3.68	3.78

Date: August, 1993
Data are expressed in nominal terms unless otherwise indicated.
Real GDP is at constant 1980 prices and 1980 exchange rates.

COUNTRY RISK MONITOR

INTRODUCTION

Country Risk Monitor ranks 80 countries in terms of ratios of key economic performance indicators. The ratios measure aspects of economic activity that enable comparison of economic management, economic performance, and country risk among the countries. According to annual ratio values, countries are objectively given a risk ranking for each of the past four years, the current year, and five future years. For each year, *Country Risk Monitor* also compares countries' ratio values to the averages of 14 important country groups.

Country Risk Monitor quickly shows a nation's present and future economic health and its relative country risk.

Application of *Country Risk Monitor* to country risk analysis for decision purposes is an extension of the common-size ratio analysis that is often used for evaluating the financial viability and creditworthiness of business units.

Country Risk Monitor uses data on economic performance as a basis of comparison across the 80 countries. Country rankings and ratio values show exactly where a specific economy stands relative to other economies or benchmark group of economies. *Country Risk Monitor* supports business and marketing decisions that must choose between alternative country risks.

COUNTRY RISK MONITOR RATIOS — SIGNIFICANCE OF VALUE AND RANK

In *Country Risk Monitor*, economies are evaluated and assigned annual rankings according to the values of 10 ratios. These ratios and their significance in country risk rankings are as follows:

- **Debt Service to Export Ratio** — countries are ranked from low ratio values to high values. Higher values indicate greater amount of interest and principal payments on external debt as compared to the foreign exchange cash-flow generated by exports. A country whose foreign exchange earning exports are low relative to debt payments may have to lower domestic business activity and imports to economize on foreign exchange. A lower debt service to export ratio is associated with less country risk.

- **External Debt to Export Ratio** — countries are ranked from low ratio values to high values. Higher external debt relative to exports that earn foreign exchange indicates a higher debt payment burden that undermines growth prospects and the ability to import. A country with a high debt burden relative to exports may choose to impose foreign exchange controls to limit outflow of funds and grant export subsidies. A lower external debt to export ratio is associated with less country risk.

- **External Debt to GDP Ratio** — countries are ranked from low ratio values to high values. Higher values indicated more outstanding external indebtedness relative to the size of the economy. Any level of debt can be sustained easier by a larger, more diversified economy. A lower external debt to GDP ratio is associated with less country risk.

- **External Debt to the International Reserve Assets (with gold) Ratio** — countries are ranked from low ratio values to high values. International reserve assets are composed of foreign exchange, gold, and special asset allocations from the International Monetary Fund. Such reserve assets are a means of servicing debt. Higher external debt relative to reserve holdings indicates a lower liquidity cushion and a greater likelihood that the government will impose reserve-building austerity policies that economize on imports and encourage exports. <u>A lower external debt to reserve asset ratio is associated with less country risk</u>.

- **International Reserve Assets (with gold) to Import Ratio** — countries are ranked from high ratio values to low values. Reserves can be used to pay for import needs necessary to sustain economic performance. Higher reserve holdings relative to imports allow a country to pay for import needs without new external borrowing or policy adjustments such as exchange rate devaluation. <u>A higher international reserve asset to import ratio is associated with less country risk.</u>

- **Coverage — Months of Imports Covered by Existing International Reserve Assets (with gold)** — countries are ranked from high to low values (number of months). Higher values indicate greater economic security. Higher values allow for a longer continuation of necessary import flows should all new additions (e.g. from new borrowing or export earnings) to the stock of international reserves suddenly cease. <u>More months of coverage is associated with less country risk</u>.

- **Exports to GDP Ratio** — countries are ranked from high ratio values to low values. Higher ratio values indicate an open economy that is able to export successfully relative to its economic size. An economy with higher values can more successfully sustain given external debt levels as exports earn foreign exchange. <u>A higher export to GDP ratio is associated with less country risk</u>.

- **Current Account Balance to GDP Ratio** — countries are ranked from high ratio values to low values. This ratio value ranges from high positive (current account surplus) to high negative (current account deficit). Much external indebtedness today arises from current account deficit financing needs. A larger current account surplus (or smaller deficit) relative to the size of the economy decreases the need for external indebtedness, and makes it less likely that the economy will incur new external indebtedness that is not serviceable. <u>A higher current account balance to GDP ratio is associated with less country risk</u>.

- **Government Budget Balance to GDP Ratio** — countries are ranked from high ratio values to low values. This ratio ranges from high positive values (government budget surplus) to high negative values (government budget deficit). A larger government budget surplus (or smaller deficit) relative to the size of the economy makes it less likely that the government consumption is fueling domestic demand, import needs, and inflation, all of which can cause external cash flow and debt problems. Countries faced with large government budget deficits relative to their economic size more likely will have to compress government spending or raise taxes. Either step will slow down business activity in the economy. <u>A higher government budget balance to GDP ratio is associated with less country risk</u>.

- **Country Per Capita GDP to G-7 Per Capita GDP Ratio** — countries are ranked from high ratio values to low values. This ratio value compares an economy's per–capita income position to that of the average per capita income of the United States, Canada, Japan, West Germany, Great Britain, France, and Italy. Generally, economies whose per capita income is high relative to key industrial economies will have more flexibility in adapting to adverse changes in the global economic environment. <u>A higher ratio value is associated with less country risk</u>.

USING COUNTRY RISK MONITOR

I. NOTE ON RANKING — A consistent method is used for ranking economies in *Country Risk Monitor*. To arrive at a ranking based on the values of each ratio, the 80 countries are ranked in ascending order of country risk from "1" to "80". Top rank is "1", indicating least country risk in terms of the ratio considered.

II. When using *Country Risk Monitor,* you will first find summary ranking tables. These show comprehensive annual rankings of the 80 countries. To arrive at these comprehensive annual rankings, *Country Risk Monitor* calculates for each year the average of each country's "1" to "80" rankings for the ten individual ratios. These averages are then ordered by size and assigned a comprehensive ranking from "1" to "80".

The results are first shown alphabetically by country and then by absolute ranking. These tables show data for the past four years, the current year, and five future years, tracking changes in these summary rankings.

III. You will see that *Country Risk Monitor* is divided into 10 main sections. **There is one section for each country risk ratio.** In each section you will find the following tables:

Benchmark Table

This table shows the average ratio values for each of 14 benchmark country groupings. The benchmark country groupings are:

- World
- Problem Countries
  (countries whose international
   debt is under restructuring)
- Non-Problem Countries
- Low Income
  (under $2,500 per capita income)
- Middle Income
  ($2,500-$15,00 per capita income)
- High Income
  (over $15,000 per capita income)

- Industrial
- All developing countries
- OPEC
- Non-OPEC developing countries
- Asia
- Latin America
- Middle East
- Africa

Comparison Tables

(1) <u>Ratio values.</u> These tables show the annual values of the ratio for each of the 80 countries for the past four years, the current year, and five years in the future.

(2) <u>Alphabetical listing.</u> A second set of tables displays an alphabetical listing of the 80 countries showing the annual "1" to "80" rank position of each country on the basis of its ratio value. Data are for the past four years, the current year, and five future years.

(3) <u>Listing by ranking.</u> These tables list countries from "1" to "80" according to rank and show the associated ratio value. Data are for five future years.

Debt Service Divided by Exports (Percent) ***
Benchmark Ratios

Benchmark Country Groups	1989	1990	1991	1992	1993	1994	1995	1996	1997	1998	Avg
World	28.1	26.6	28.0	27.2	24.3	23.8	23.4	22.9	22.1	21.7	24.8
Industrial Countries	23.4	22.5	23.1	22.0	21.7	21.5	21.3	20.6	19.6	18.5	21.4
Asia	19.4	18.7	17.4	15.9	14.9	14.1	13.4	12.8	11.9	11.1	15.0
Latin America	39.0	35.8	33.6	30.1	26.7	26.8	26.6	26.9	27.2	26.1	29.9
Middle East	15.1	16.5	44.3	44.4	25.8	22.5	21.0	20.5	19.2	18.1	24.8
Africa	33.3	30.5	28.6	29.5	28.3	28.1	27.9	27.2	26.2	25.1	28.5
Non-OPEC Developing	31.5	29.7	25.9	25.3	24.2	24.2	24.1	23.8	23.5	23.7	25.6
OPEC	24.3	23.1	45.3	44.2	29.5	26.5	25.0	23.9	21.9	20.2	28.4
Developing	29.9	28.3	30.0	29.3	25.3	24.7	24.3	23.9	23.2	23.0	26.2
High Income (Over $15000)	18.0	17.7	18.5	17.3	17.2	17.1	17.1	16.7	15.9	15.1	17.0
Medium Income ($2500 – $15000)	24.4	22.2	20.6	20.1	19.7	19.5	19.5	18.9	18.5	18.1	20.1
Low Income (Under $2500)	36.3	34.6	38.3	37.5	31.4	30.4	29.7	29.2	28.1	27.8	32.3
Non-Problem Countries	21.7	20.5	20.1	19.5	18.8	18.6	18.4	17.8	17.1	16.4	18.9
Problem Countries	37.6	35.8	39.9	38.7	32.5	31.7	31.0	30.6	29.7	29.6	33.7

*** Lower ratio values indicate less country risk.

Date: August, 1993

Debt Service Divided by Exports (Percent) ***World Results											
Country	1989	1990	1991	1992	1993	1994	1995	1996	1997	1998	Avg
Algeria	72.9	61.7	68.0	66.4	62.0	55.8	51.9	46.6	43.2	40.5	56.9
Argentina	77.5	64.0	58.3	57.4	51.3	48.6	46.8	46.3	49.3	46.1	54.6
Australia	30.1	30.9	32.0	33.1	30.6	29.2	28.7	28.1	27.3	26.1	29.6
Austria	8.9	7.1	7.1	6.9	6.9	6.9	6.8	6.7	6.4	6.0	7.0
Bahrain	4.4	4.2	4.3	4.3	4.8	5.1	5.5	5.6	5.4	5.3	4.9
Belgium	10.0	8.3	7.2	6.4	6.3	6.6	7.1	7.3	7.1	6.8	7.3
Bolivia	70.7	51.2	45.6	40.0	33.7	33.7	34.2	35.2	38.2	36.1	41.9
Brazil	41.9	43.5	40.0	29.7	26.5	25.3	25.0	24.5	25.5	23.2	30.5
Bulgaria	74.4	59.8	24.0	23.0	21.6	15.7	16.1	16.4	16.8	14.4	28.2
Canada	25.9	25.5	24.8	22.9	21.6	20.9	20.9	21.0	20.0	19.0	22.2
Chile	26.1	23.9	21.5	18.9	15.9	15.9	17.3	16.8	15.0	13.5	18.5
China	11.4	12.3	14.8	13.7	12.2	10.5	9.0	7.8	6.8	5.9	10.4
Colombia	51.4	42.7	39.9	42.1	28.1	22.7	22.9	21.6	19.7	17.7	30.9
Costa Rica	29.7	22.0	17.4	13.9	13.1	14.1	15.5	17.0	17.9	17.9	17.8
Czech Republic	20.5	16.4	14.6	12.8	14.3	15.1	16.3	11.7	11.8	16.8	15.0
Denmark	33.0	29.3	30.3	25.6	24.0	22.7	21.6	19.4	16.6	14.4	23.7
Dominican Republic	21.8	35.2	27.6	23.8	22.7	23.3	24.7	25.9	27.8	26.6	25.9
Ecuador	52.9	50.2	46.8	41.5	34.6	36.0	35.1	35.3	32.0	30.1	39.5
Egypt	47.6	34.3	27.4	18.9	16.9	15.4	14.7	13.4	12.0	10.7	21.1
Ethiopia	37.5	36.9	29.4	35.1	27.7	26.4	26.4	26.8	26.9	26.5	30.0
Finland	29.2	31.3	38.7	37.0	37.2	35.4	33.2	30.9	28.5	25.8	32.7
France	9.8	11.3	10.7	8.9	8.8	8.9	9.0	9.3	9.2	8.9	9.5
Gabon	21.2	17.8	20.2	21.9	21.7	21.9	22.1	22.1	21.9	20.9	21.2
Germany	17.0	16.4	18.6	19.8	20.8	21.7	22.3	22.8	23.1	23.2	20.6
Ghana	51.0	36.2	26.8	29.9	29.2	31.1	33.1	32.9	31.9	30.2	33.2
Greece	46.1	42.0	44.9	52.8	56.1	55.6	53.2	48.9	44.5	40.9	48.5
Hong Kong	2.2	2.0	2.0	1.8	1.8	1.7	1.7	1.7	1.7	1.6	1.8
Hungary	47.4	47.1	33.8	30.1	26.7	26.8	27.5	29.1	31.7	32.8	33.3
Iceland	26.7	25.8	25.9	26.0	26.4	26.5	26.5	25.7	24.4	23.2	25.7
India	32.1	29.5	31.7	30.2	28.9	28.3	28.0	26.4	23.7	21.3	28.0
Indonesia	35.8	33.2	31.1	28.7	27.4	25.1	23.1	21.1	19.5	17.8	26.3
Iran	4.7	8.8	11.9	14.5	18.4	18.3	20.9	22.0	22.7	22.3	16.5
Iraq	20.4	35.4	281.7	274.2	103.3	72.0	56.1	52.9	42.4	35.7	97.4
Ireland	23.2	22.3	23.4	19.7	19.1	18.4	17.1	15.8	14.2	12.9	18.6
Israel	28.4	23.4	24.6	20.2	19.9	20.8	20.4	19.9	19.3	18.6	21.6
Italy	20.3	21.5	23.2	19.9	20.2	21.3	23.4	24.6	25.3	25.7	22.6
Ivory Coast	49.8	52.1	55.9	49.0	44.0	45.7	46.4	46.4	44.5	42.7	47.7
Jamaica	38.8	33.9	28.1	21.8	20.2	28.7	20.9	22.2	24.9	24.9	26.5
Japan	17.2	16.4	14.9	13.2	12.0	11.1	10.1	9.2	8.5	8.0	12.1
Kenya	30.8	31.9	29.6	29.0	29.5	31.0	29.5	29.6	27.8	27.1	29.6

*** Lower ratio values indicate less country risk.

Debt Service Divided by Exports (Percent) *** World Results										
Country	1989	1990	1991	1992	1993	1994	1995	1996	1997	1998	Avg
Korea, South	11.8	10.7	7.1	7.9	7.6	7.0	6.4	5.9	5.3	4.7	7.4
Kuwait	6.2	8.6	20.1	15.6	16.6	18.5	19.7	18.7	17.2	15.4	15.7
Libya	5.9	4.1	3.7	4.4	5.4	5.3	6.1	5.0	4.9	5.0	5.0
Madagascar	43.7	38.7	32.7	40.0	38.9	36.7	34.8	33.3	32.1	31.4	36.2
Malaysia	12.5	9.1	7.5	6.4	7.5	6.6	5.3	4.3	3.5	3.0	6.6
Mexico	38.0	35.2	32.4	28.6	27.3	25.9	25.2	24.9	23.6	23.4	28.5
Morocco	50.3	46.3	43.3	42.5	40.2	40.1	40.0	38.5	37.1	35.8	41.4
Netherlands	17.8	15.5	15.5	16.8	17.1	17.1	17.2	17.2	17.3	17.4	16.9
New Zealand	34.5	34.7	32.4	29.2	26.3	25.3	25.0	24.3	23.1	21.4	27.6
Nigeria	26.1	22.9	25.3	27.7	29.2	30.3	30.8	29.9	27.4	24.6	27.4
Norway	27.6	23.8	20.7	18.1	18.5	18.7	18.3	17.5	16.2	15.0	19.4
Pakistan	28.7	27.4	28.2	28.2	23.4	21.0	19.0	17.6	16.7	15.8	22.6
Panama	8.5	10.4	9.6	8.6	7.3	7.3	7.3	6.8	6.3	6.3	7.8
Papua New Guinea	32.9	36.6	29.7	25.9	23.2	22.5	21.9	21.7	20.8	20.6	25.6
Paraguay	17.4	13.7	10.4	10.9	9.6	10.1	10.6	11.0	10.7	11.1	11.6
Peru	41.5	50.7	66.5	62.2	58.4	60.2	64.6	69.5	74.5	73.1	62.1
Philippines	27.8	27.0	23.2	18.4	18.5	18.2	17.5	17.1	16.2	16.1	20.0
Poland	65.3	40.8	26.2	23.5	23.6	27.2	26.6	26.6	24.5	20.1	30.4
Portugal	20.3	16.8	19.3	18.0	16.8	18.2	19.6	19.4	18.5	17.8	18.5
Russia	18.6	48.1	32.5	33.3	36.6	44.7	46.1	47.7	49.8	49.4	40.7
Saudi Arabia	7.0	5.6	5.7	6.1	7.0	8.1	8.9	9.6	10.5	10.8	7.9
Singapore	4.5	4.0	3.1	2.3	2.2	2.4	2.2	1.9	1.9	1.7	2.6
South Africa	12.5	15.3	12.1	10.4	11.9	12.2	12.9	14.0	15.5	16.9	13.4
Spain	15.9	16.6	20.1	20.8	20.8	21.5	21.6	21.1	20.5	19.8	19.9
Sudan	11.7	9.8	6.0	14.7	19.4	21.1	24.2	23.0	21.8	20.2	17.2
Sweden	20.5	25.0	24.4	22.9	22.8	21.9	20.8	20.0	18.3	16.6	21.3
Switzerland	23.5	22.0	22.4	20.2	21.2	22.0	22.3	21.9	20.9	19.9	21.6
Syria	27.9	28.8	15.9	29.1	32.3	32.4	32.9	33.7	34.4	35.1	30.2
Taiwan	3.0	2.5	1.9	1.5	1.3	1.4	1.8	2.1	2.0	1.9	1.9
Tanzania	22.1	27.0	22.7	26.2	25.1	24.9	24.7	23.8	22.8	22.8	24.2
Thailand	16.4	13.4	11.7	10.5	9.3	8.2	7.5	6.9	6.4	5.8	9.6
Tunisia	26.3	29.4	28.5	24.6	22.2	22.4	22.3	22.2	22.0	21.7	24.1
Turkey	41.6	33.8	34.5	29.8	27.0	25.7	23.7	21.9	20.2	18.6	27.7
Ukraine	37.1	46.8	52.0	73.8	96.6	95.0	94.4	88.3	78.5	118.4	78.1
United Arab Emirates	8.3	6.5	6.8	7.2	6.8	6.2	5.6	4.9	4.5	4.1	6.1
United Kingdom	13.0	14.7	16.4	16.8	17.4	17.9	18.6	19.0	18.4	17.8	17.0
United States	26.5	25.5	22.9	21.9	21.5	21.7	22.0	22.0	21.5	20.8	22.6
Uruguay	39.0	38.2	36.8	31.0	30.0	29.1	28.8	27.9	26.6	26.0	31.3
Venezuela	30.0	22.4	22.6	21.8	21.6	20.9	19.8	18.5	16.7	15.4	21.0
Zimbabwe	22.6	23.1	26.7	31.2	28.6	28.8	26.9	27.1	27.5	25.4	26.8

*** Lower ratio values indicate less country risk.

Debt Service Divided by Exports
World Rankings 1994

Rank	Country	Ratio	Rank	Country	Ratio
1	Taiwan	1.4%	41	Sweden	21.9%
2	Hong Kong	1.7%	42	Gabon	21.9%
3	Singapore	2.4%	43	Switzerland	22.0%
4	Bahrain	5.1%	44	Tunisia	22.4%
5	Libya	5.3%	45	Papua New Guinea	22.5%
6	United Arab Emirates	6.2%	46	Colombia	22.7%
7	Malaysia	6.6%	47	Denmark	22.7%
8	Belgium	6.6%	48	Dominican Republic	23.3%
9	Austria	6.9%	49	Tanzania	24.9%
10	Korea, South	7.0%	50	Indonesia	25.1%
11	Panama	7.3%	51	Brazil	25.3%
12	Saudi Arabia	8.1%	52	New Zealand	25.3%
13	Thailand	8.2%	53	Turkey	25.7%
14	France	8.9%	54	Mexico	25.9%
15	Paraguay	10.1%	55	Ethiopia	26.4%
16	China	10.5%	56	Iceland	26.5%
17	Japan	11.1%	57	Hungary	26.8%
18	South Africa	12.2%	58	Poland	27.2%
19	Costa Rica	14.1%	59	India	28.3%
20	Czech Republic	15.1%	60	Jamaica	28.7%
21	Egypt	15.4%	61	Zimbabwe	28.8%
22	Bulgaria	15.7%	62	Uruguay	29.1%
23	Chile	15.9%	63	Australia	29.2%
24	Netherlands	17.1%	64	Nigeria	30.3%
25	United Kingdom	17.9%	65	Kenya	31.0%
26	Portugal	18.2%	66	Ghana	31.1%
27	Philippines	18.2%	67	Syria	32.4%
28	Iran	18.3%	68	Bolivia	33.7%
29	Ireland	18.4%	69	Finland	35.4%
30	Kuwait	18.5%	70	Ecuador	36.0%
31	Norway	18.7%	71	Madagascar	36.7%
32	Israel	20.8%	72	Morocco	40.1%
33	Venezuela	20.9%	73	Russia	44.7%
34	Canada	20.9%	74	Ivory Coast	45.7%
35	Pakistan	21.0%	75	Argentina	48.6%
36	Sudan	21.1%	76	Greece	55.6%
37	Italy	21.3%	77	Algeria	55.8%
38	Spain	21.5%	78	Peru	60.2%
39	Germany	21.7%	79	Iraq	72.0%
40	United States	21.7%	80	Ukraine	95.0%

Debt Service Divided by Exports
World Rankings 1998

Rank	Country	Ratio	Rank	Country	Ratio
1	Hong Kong	1.6%	41	Switzerland	19.9%
2	Singapore	1.7%	42	Poland	20.1%
3	Taiwan	1.9%	43	Sudan	20.2%
4	Malaysia	3.0%	44	Papua New Guinea	20.6%
5	United Arab Emirates	4.1%	45	United States	20.8%
6	Korea, South	4.7%	46	Gabon	20.9%
7	Libya	5.0%	47	India	21.3%
8	Bahrain	5.3%	48	New Zealand	21.4%
9	Thailand	5.8%	49	Tunisia	21.7%
10	China	5.9%	50	Iran	22.3%
11	Austria	6.0%	51	Tanzania	22.8%
12	Panama	6.3%	52	Germany	23.2%
13	Belgium	6.8%	53	Brazil	23.2%
14	Japan	8.0%	54	Iceland	23.2%
15	France	8.9%	55	Mexico	23.4%
16	Egypt	10.7%	56	Nigeria	24.6%
17	Saudi Arabia	10.8%	57	Jamaica	24.9%
18	Paraguay	11.1%	58	Zimbabwe	25.4%
19	Ireland	12.9%	59	Italy	25.7%
20	Chile	13.5%	60	Finland	25.8%
21	Denmark	14.4%	61	Uruguay	26.0%
22	Bulgaria	14.4%	62	Australia	26.1%
23	Norway	15.0%	63	Ethiopia	26.5%
24	Venezuela	15.4%	64	Dominican Republic	26.6%
25	Kuwait	15.4%	65	Kenya	27.1%
26	Pakistan	15.8%	66	Ecuador	30.1%
27	Philippines	16.1%	67	Ghana	30.2%
28	Sweden	16.6%	68	Madagascar	31.4%
29	Czech Republic	16.8%	69	Hungary	32.8%
30	South Africa	16.9%	70	Syria	35.1%
31	Netherlands	17.4%	71	Iraq	35.7%
32	Colombia	17.7%	72	Morocco	35.8%
33	Portugal	17.8%	73	Bolivia	36.1%
34	Indonesia	17.8%	74	Algeria	40.5%
35	United Kingdom	17.8%	75	Greece	40.9%
36	Costa Rica	17.9%	76	Ivory Coast	42.7%
37	Israel	18.6%	77	Argentina	46.1%
38	Turkey	18.6%	78	Russia	49.4%
39	Canada	19.0%	79	Peru	73.1%
40	Spain	19.8%	80	Ukraine	118.4%

Section IV
Political Risk

Political Risk Services
The PRS Group, Inc.

IHS Energy Group

Control Risks Group (CRG)

Chapter 11

Political Risk Services
The PRS Group, Inc.

Using Political Risk Forecasts

Individuals holding nearly any position of responsibility in an internationally oriented firm can use political risk forecasts. Typical users include the president, vice president, manager, director, planner, finance officer, international officer, security officer, economist, researcher, market analyst, and librarian. This variety is evidence of the importance of political risk information. The many uses also present companies with a challenge to determine how to maximize political risk information throughout the organization, especially in the major areas of need. A discussion of how to apply our risk ratings follows, and a summary of applications appears in Table 1 on the next page.

Political Risk Services (PRS) provides a decision-focused political risk model with three industry forecasts at the micro level. The PRS system forecasts risk for investors in two stages, first identifying the three most likely future regime scenarios for each country over two time periods and then by assigning a probability to each scenario over each time period, 18 months and five years. For each regime scenario, PRS's expert consultants then establish likely changes in the level of political turmoil and 11 types of government intervention that affect the business climate.

After calculating consolidated scores for all regimes (100% of possibilities), the PRS system converts these numbers into letter grades (on a scale from A+ to D) for three investment areas: *financial transfers* (banking and lending), *foreign direct investment* (e.g. retail, manufacturing, mining), and *exports* to the host country market. PRS' unique system provides only industry specific forecasts, not a generic macro level assessment, as is usually the case.

Users can customize the PRS forecasting model to individual projects or the particular exposures of a firm with an optional weighting system, adding or subtracting variables and adjusting the model to fit specific firm or project attributes.

PRS *Country Reports* forecast the risk of doing business in 100 countries. PRS completely revises these 100 reports on a quarterly basis. Each includes comments and analysis on recent events, profiles of key political players, and wide-ranging forecast scenarios, as well as basic historical and political background and data on the government, political entities, the environment, and the economy, including key sectors.

Commodity and Currency Forecasting

Many business managers must make decisions or advise decision-makers on the future prices of currencies, precious metals, and such commodities as wheat, sugar, tin, and bauxite. Some managers make such forecasts because their business responsibilities require it, while others buy and sell against future prices as a direct profit-making activity. Such people also subscribe to forecasting services that are based on the analysis of various economic trends. At the same time, they realize the importance of understanding how political events can determine not only underlying trends, but also how buyers and sellers behave and react.

Country Lending Decisions

Banks, insurance companies, and public institutions, such as export credit agencies, frequently assess the amount of exposure they have in each country in proportion to their total exposure. This assessment may be necessary because of internal portfolio management policies or because of governmental regulations. Country limits are often established and modified according to levels of political and economic risk as well as market factors. Most lenders and insurers recognize the need to assess political factors along with economic data. Many business people use qualitative descriptions of risk, as well as quantitative indicators, as part of the weighting scheme they use to set country limits.

Credit Management

A credit manager is concerned not only with collecting bills, but also with establishing terms of credit that may affect the firm's competitiveness. Deciding whether to require a letter of credit for a particular transaction within a given country, for example, requires that the credit manager anticipate political developments. There is a need, therefore, to assess evolving conditions in foreign countries, along with performing the traditional analysis of an individual customer. Credit managers use political risk forecasting to anticipate such risk factors as the potential for the imposition of exchange controls, political upheaval that may lead to capital flight, or a breakdown of administrative processes in a country.

Table 1. Most Frequent Uses of Country and Political Risk Information

Type of Use	Percent Using
General background	51%
Evaluating risks to specific projects or investments	36%
Briefing upper–level management	32%
Supplement to other outside sources	30%
Briefing before overseas trips	28%
Strategic planning	27%
Supplement to information from foreign subsidiaries	25%
Briefing colleagues	21%
Making decisions about security	19%
Determining new business opportunities	18%
Identification of key people and institutions	16%
Tempering upper management's "inside information"	16%
Sales or marketing decisions	15%
Supplement to headquarters research and analysis	15%
Preparing for negotiations	10%
Giving perspective to news stories	9%
Planning and evaluating insurance coverage	9%
Assistance in public information activities	5%
Briefing employees going overseas	4%

Source: Political Risk Services Client Survey.

Finance

Treasurer's offices are among the more frequent users of political risk forecasts. Given the constant fluctuation in international currency values and the difficulties encountered in moving capital and profits across national boundaries, the decisions made by a finance officer heavily influence the profitability of most multinational corporations. The procedures leading to financial decisions are among the most sophisticated employed within most business firms. Until recently, however, economic analysis and financial forecasting models dominated such decision-making, and the process downplayed the role of political factors. Major political events, such as the Iranian revolution, revolutions in East Europe, and the collapse of Communist control in the Soviet Union, and less spectacular developments, such as regime changes that led to declining currency values, have conclusively illustrated the need for political analysis.

Despite the clear need for such analysis, the generalized and disparate forms of political information from both traditional and newer sources hinder their use in financial decision-making. This kind of information is simply not consistent with the precise and sophisticated procedures used for financial decisions. That is why financial officials find concise summaries, comparisons, and rankings useful for assessing the political environments within which various financial decisions must take place.

Government Affairs

Offices dealing with government affairs may have a research function or a public relations function, or both. Whatever the balance of their priorities, government affairs officers look to political risk forecasts to provide an objective, independent perspective. If these offices already have access to analysts specializing in a country, independent forecasts are used as a check on their perceptions and understanding of evolving political conditions. From this perspective and their own analysis, they can develop public relations activities and advise their management on future government actions. Government affairs offices also find political risk forecasts useful as a resource in preparing briefings for top management before their overseas visits.

Headquarters–Field Communications

The regular and well-integrated use of political information is one of the best ways to improve the relationship between field offices and a firm's headquarters. Relations between headquarters and the field often thwart the potential role of local offices as useful sources of information about the country. Typically, headquarters requires field officers to evaluate the country in which they operate. However, it tends to disbelieve their reports, suspecting the field staff of being too optimistic and provincial. For their part, those in the field believe that headquarters never reads the required reports and operates solely on a crisis-oriented basis, rather than constantly staying informed about the political environment of its field operations.

The regular sharing and dissemination of information about the climate for business can help alleviate difficulties and problems of communication between headquarters personnel and those in the field. Basing their dialogue on a regular, routine procedure for political risk assessment can help build a consensus on the strengths and weaknesses of the localized political environments. Whether field and headquarters agree with a particular assessment is not as important as a clear understanding of their individual positions based on regular evaluations. Adopting a format like one described in this book allows for detailed and precise analysis of similarities and differences in viewpoint.

Marketing

Political events and governmental policies can have a direct impact on stability and growth in current markets and on the potential for new markets. Clients can use political risk forecasts to anticipate patterns in government procurement, regulations affecting imports, and general trends that are influenced by government decisions, such as economic growth, unemployment, and inflation. Marketing analysts assess the degree to which political events may increase market opportunities. They must also stay alert for potential threats and the possibility that turmoil might disrupt transportation, communications, and commercial activities. In some developing economies, particularly where government priorities shift frequently and where sales are highly sensitive to those priorities, a new government or a new policy emphasis can open or close significant markets. For businesses dealing with government buyers, political risk forecasts can provide profiles of individuals and descriptions of domestic political systems that can be essential in formulating sales strategies.

Project Decisions

Corporations frequently organize their work around particular projects or marketing activities. The project director or team focuses largely on the commercial viability of each project. The political stability of a country and the trends in its government policies are critically important in assessing the benefits and costs of proposed projects. Political risk forecasts can be used as a basis for making these political assessments, particularly at the initial stage, during the process of selecting countries as potential project sites.

Risk Management

Sometimes assigned to a single office and sometimes decentralized, the function of anticipating major risks can be vital. Risk management officers use political risk forecasts to help determine whether to buy political risk insurance, whether to borrow money locally, and how to structure contracts in a way that minimizes risk. They can use detailed, qualitative descriptions of local political conditions, as well as systematic ratings that allow for country-by-country comparisons and alert them to changing conditions.

Security Decisions

Corporate security often has an image of being essentially an operation encompassing technical hardware and the personnel for enforcement. However, many officials who are responsible for corporate security have the responsibility of providing political risk assessments that are incorporated into the firm's decision-making. These officials feel that assessing future political trends is important for planning investments in security equipment and programs. Their estimates keep top management informed about potential risks to the security of new and ongoing operations, as well as personnel security issues.

Strategic Planning

Strategic planning involves identifying future trends and analyzing how the corporation can take advantage of those trends. Such analysis traditionally concentrated heavily on economic trends, but since political decisions and events substantially influence these trends, planners now incorporate political risk analysis. Current planning activities involve an attempt to assess the impact of political and economic trends, but strategic planners can find it difficult to incorporate political analysis into their traditional economic and business research. Political analysis, by its nature, is qualitative, dealing with more abrupt and sweeping factors. Many planners have found systematic risk ratings particularly useful because they allow for the cross-country comparisons that are an integral part of their analytical approach. Most firms use risk information for many reasons and in several different offices.

Country and political forecasts, summarized in the survey of international business officials in Table 1, have many and varied applications. Organizations can apply analysis methods in different ways to successfully achieve the same goal—anticipating and planning for the political, economic, and financial risks involved in international business.

The *Political Risk Services* Rating System

A series of risk ratings summarize the in-depth analyses and forecasts provided in each *Country Report*, consisting of approximately 70 pages. Underlying these risk ratings is the Prince Model (See Appendix PRS -A at the end of this chapter).

Each *Country Report* provides the current level and likely changes of the following 17 risk components (12 covering our 18-month forecast and five covering our five-year forecast), which are also used in compiling the risk scores.

18-Month Risk Factors

Twelve factors are analyzed from an 18-month forecast perspective, including political turmoil, which is included in both the 18-month and the five-year forecasts.

> *Turmoil.* Actions that can result in threats or harm to people or property by political groups or foreign governments, operating within the country or from an external base:
> * Riots and demonstrations
> * Politically motivated strikes
> * Disputes with other countries that may affect business
> * Terrorism and guerrilla activities
> * Civil or international war
>   - Street crime that might affect international business personnel
>   - Organized crime having an impact on political stability or foreign business
> Not included in turmoil are legal, work-related labor strikes that do not lead to violence.
>
> *Equity Restrictions.* Limitations on the foreign ownership of businesses, emphasizing sectors where limitations are especially liberal or especially restrictive.
>
> *Operations Restrictions.* Restrictions on procurement, hiring foreign personnel, or locating business activities, as well as the efficiency and honesty of officials with whom business executives must deal and the effectiveness and integrity of the judicial system.
>
> *Taxation Discrimination.* The formal and informal tax policies that either lead to bias against, or special advantages favoring international business.
>
> *Repatriation Restrictions.* Formal and informal rules regarding the reparation of profits, dividends, and investment capital.
>
> *Exchange Controls.* Formal policies, informal practices, and financial conditions that either ease or inhibit converting local currency to foreign currency, normally a firm's home currency.
>
> *Tariff Barriers.* The average and range of financial costs imposed on imports.
>
> *Other Import Barriers.* Formal and informal quotas, licensing provisions, or other restrictions on imports.
>
> *Payment Delays.* The punctuality, or otherwise, with which government and private importers pay their foreign creditors, based on government policies, domestic economic conditions, and international financial conditions.

Fiscal and Monetary Expansion. An assessment of the effect of the government's spending, taxing, interest rate and other monetary policies. The assessment is based on a judgment as to whether the expansion is inadequate for a healthy business climate, acceptably expansionist, or so excessively expansionist as to threaten inflation or other economic disorder.

Labor Policies. Government policies, trade union activity, and productivity of the labor force that create either high or low costs for businesses.

Foreign Debt. The magnitude of all foreign debt relative to the size of the economy and the ability of the country's public and private institutions to repay debt service obligations promptly.

Five-Year Risk Factors

Four additional factors are analyzed from a five-year forecast perspective. (Turmoil is included in both the 18-month and the five-year forecasts.)

Investment Restrictions. The current base and likely changes in the general climate for restricting foreign investments.

Trade Restrictions. The current base and the likely changes in the general climate for restricting the entry of foreign trade.

Domestic Economic Problems. The ranking of the country according to its most recent five-year performance record in per capita GDP, GDP growth, inflation, unemployment, capital investment, and budget balance.

International Economic Problems. The ranking of the country according to its most recent five-year performance record in current account (as a percentage of GDP), the ratio of debt service to exports, and the annual percentage change in the value of the currency.

We use these 17 factors in our summary risk ratings, first estimating the current risk level of each factor and then forecasting the change in its risk level under each of the three most likely regime scenarios. The numerical equivalents of these current and forecast levels are then used to calculate the risk scores. As an example, consider Figure 1 on the following page, which shows the current level and forecast levels of the 17 risk factors for Morocco, as of November 2000. (For the five-year forecasts, the "Base Level" is the equivalent of the 18-month "Current Level." The Base Level for turmoil and restriction is estimated from the political climate, and the Base for domestic and international economic problems is computed from the country's rankings.)

Figure 1: **Risk Factors for Morocco, November 2000**

18-Month Forecast of Regimes & Probabilities

Risk Factors	Current Level	Most Likely Regime Monarchy 70%	Second Most Likely Regime Military 25%	Third Most Likely Regime Fundamentalists 5%
Turmoil	Moderate	Same	MORE	MORE
Investment Restrictions				
Equity	Moderate	SLIGHTLY LESS	SLIGHTLY MORE	MORE
Operations	Moderate	Same	MORE	MORE
Taxation	Moderate	SLIGHTLY LESS	SLIGHTLY MORE	MORE
Repatriation	Low	Same	SLIGHTLY MORE	MORE
Exchange	Moderate	SLIGHTLY LESS	SLIGHTLY MORE	MORE
Trade Restrictions				
Tariffs	Moderate	SLIGHTLY LESS	SLIGHTLY MORE	MORE
Other Barriers	Moderate	SLIGHTLY LESS	MORE	Same
Payment Delays	Moderate	Same	MORE	MORE
Economic Policy				
Expansion	Moderate	Same	MORE	MORE
Labor Costs	Low	Same	Same	Same
Foreign Debt	High	SLIGHTLY LESS	MORE	MORE

Five-Year Forecast of Regimes & Probabilities

	Base Level	Most Likely Regime Monarchy 70%	Second Most Likely Regime Military 25%	Third Most Likely Regime Fundamentalists 5%
Turmoil	Moderate	Same	MORE	MORE
Restrictions				
Investment	Moderate	SLIGHTLY LESS	SLIGHTLY MORE	MORE
Trade	Moderate	SLIGHTLY LESS	SLIGHTLY MORE	MORE
Economic Problems				
Domestic	High	Same	SLIGHTLY MORE	MORE
International	Moderate	SLIGHTLY LESS	Same	MORE

After country specialists provide the current and forecast levels, the next step is to convert them into their numerical equivalents, based on the following tables:

For Current Levels and Base Level of Restrictions = Value

Very Low	=	-1
Low	=	0
Moderate	=	1
High	=	2
Very High	=	3

<u>For Domestic and International Economic Rankings = Value</u>

Best 25%	=	0
Second 25%	=	1
Third 25%	=	2
Worst 25%	=	3

For Forecast Levels	=	Value
LESS	=	-1.0
SLIGHTLY LESS	=	-0.5
Same	=	0.0
SLIGHTLY MORE	=	+0.5
MORE	=	+1.0
MUCH MORE	=	+2.0

Figure 2, below, illustrates the conversion of Morocco's risk levels shown in Figure 1. For example, the current "Moderate" level of turmoil is represented by a "1," the forecast for the "Same" level under the monarchy is represented by a "0," and the forecast for "More" turmoil under either the military or fundamentalists is represented by a "1"under each of those regimes.

Figure 2: Numerical Equivalents of Morocco's Risk Factors, November 2000

Risk Factors	CL	18-Month Forecast		
		Regime 1	Regime 2	Regime 3
		Monarchy 70%	Military 25%	Fundamentalists 5%
Turmoil	1	0	1	1
Investment Restrictions				
Equity	1	-0.5	0.5	1
Operations	1	0	1	1
Taxation	1	-0.5	0.5	1
Repatriation	0	0	0.5	1
Exchange	1	-0.5	0.5	1
Trade Restrictions				
Tariffs	1	-0.5	0.5	1
Other Barriers	1	-0.5	1	0
Payment Delays	1	0	1	1
Economic Policy				
Expansion	1	0	1	1
Labor Costs	0	0	0	0
Foreign Debt	2	-0.5	1	1
		Five-Year Forecast		
	Base	Regime 1	Regime 2	Regime 3
		Monarchy 70%	Military 25%	Fundamentalists 5%
Turmoil	1	0	1	1
Restrictions				
Investment	1	-0.5	0.5	1
Trade	1	-0.5	0.5	1
Economic Problems				
Domestic	2	0	0.5	1
International	1	-0.5	0	1

Each of the 17 factors is assigned a risk value based on its current level and the sum of three products: each forecast level times the probability of the corresponding regime. For example, the risk value for turmoil is 1.3, calculated by the 1 (the current level) plus 0*.70 (the forecast level for the Monarchy, which has a probability of .70), plus 1*.25 (the corresponding figures for the Military regime), plus 1*.05 (the corresponding figures for the Fundamentalist regime). In formula terms, this process is:

1+ (0*0.70)+(1*0.25)+(1*0.05)
=1+0+.25+.05
= 1.3

As illustrated in Figure 3, the same calculations are performed for each of the 17 risk factors based on the analysis for Morocco.

Figure 3: Risk Values for Morocco, November 2000

Risk Factors	CL	18-Month Forecast Regime 1 Monarchy 70%	Regime 2 Military 25%	Regime 3 Fundamentalists 5%	Risk Values
Turmoil	1	0	1	1	1.3
Investment Restrictions					
Equity	1	-0.5	0.5	1	0.825
Operations	1	0	1	1	1.3
Taxation	1	-0.5	0.5	1	0.825
Repatriation	0	0	0.5	1	0.175
Exchange	1	-0.5	0.5	1	0.825
Trade Restrictions					
Tariffs	1	-0.5	0.5	1	0.825
Other Barriers	1	-0.5	1	0	0.9
Payment Delays	1	0	1	1	1.3
Economic Policy					
Expansion	1	0	1	1	1.3
Labor Costs	0	0	0	0	0
Foreign Debt	2	-0.5	1	1	1.95

	Base Level	Five-Year Forecast Regime 1 Monarchy 70%	Regime 2 Military 25%	Regime 3 Fundamentalists 5%	Risk Values
Turmoil	1	0	1	1	1.3
Restrictions					
Investment	1	-0.5	0.5	1	0.825
Trade	1	-0.5	0.5	1	0.825
Economic Problems					
Domestic	2	0	0.5	1	2.175
International	1	-0.5	0	1	0.7

Creating a General Risk Summary from Specific Risk Forecasts

The resulting numerical scores can be used in a variety of ways. For example, PRS uses the numerical risk scores to calculate unified risk scores, producing the PRS Risk Index, providing a basic, convenient way for users to compare countries directly.

The PRS Risk Index

This overall measure of risk for a country is calculated by using all 17 risk components. Each factor's contribution to the index is based on its risk value, computed as described above.

Each of the 17 factors has a theoretical range of -1.0 (in case of a "Very Low" current level and a forecast of no change under any of the three regime) to +4.0 (in case of a very high current level and a forecast of more restrictive policies).

The 17 risk values are summed, and the resulting total is scaled so that a raw score of 0 or less (representing very low risk) is reported as 100 and a score of 68 (representing very high risk) is reported as 0.

The index ranges from 0, for countries with the most unfavorable climate for international business, to 100, for countries with the most favorable climate. In the case of Morocco, the raw score is 17.4, which is converted to an PRS Risk Index of 74 (representing moderate risk), by the formula

$$((RS-68)/(-68))*100$$

where RS is the raw score obtained by summing all 17 risk values.

Sectoral Risk Scores

The 17 risk values can also be used selectively to calculate 18-month and five-year risk scores for different categories of risk values. In each *Country Report* we report summary ratings for four categories of risk: turmoil, financial transfer, direct investment, and export market. Turmoil risk is reported in a scale of Very Low, Low, Moderate, High, and Very High. The other three risk categories are reported in alphabetical scales, from least risky (A+) to most risky (D-).

As described previously, the rating for turmoil risk is based on the "risk value," which is calculated from the current level and forecasts of change for three potential regime scenarios, according to the following table:

−1	Very Low
0	Low
1	Moderate
2	High
3	Very High

Terminology Used in PRS Risk Ratings

Turmoil Risk Ratings

Very Low Risk. Countries in which disorderly politics are almost unknown, and where crime represents virtually no risk to business operations.

Low Risk. Most discontent is expressed peacefully, and the extremely rare occurrences of violence from political causes almost never affect international business directly or indirectly.

Moderate Risk. International business can sometimes be affected by occasional riots, acts of terrorism, and significant levels of labor unrest or other kinds of discontent.

High Risk. Levels of violence or potential violence may seriously affect international business.

Very High Risk. The turmoil level creates conditions that approach a state of war.

Economic Sector Risk Ratings

The risk scores for financial transfer, investment, and export markets are summarized in alphabetical scores, based on the risk values of the factors used, according to the following table:

< = 0.25	=	A+	1.51-1.75	=	C+
0.26-0.50	=	A	1.76-2.00	=	C
0.51-0.75	=	A-	2.01-2.25	=	C-
0.76-1.00	=	B+	2.26-2.50	=	D+
1.01-1.25	=	B	2.51-2.75	=	D
1.26-1.50	=	B-	>2.75	=	D-

Financial Transfer Risk. The term "transfer" in our risk summaries refers to the risk from financial transfer, inconvertibility from the local currency to the desired foreign currency, and the transfer of foreign currency out of the country. The transfer could be for the payment of exports, repatriation of profits or capital, or for any other business purpose. The 18-month letter grades are determined by combining the current level and forecasts of change under the three most likely regime scenarios for these four equally weighted factors:

1. Repatriation restrictions on international business.
2. Payment delays facing exports to that country.
3. Policy related to fiscal and monetary expansion.
4. Governmental foreign borrowing.

Five-year letter grades are determined by three equally weighted factors:

1. The average score obtained from the 18-month calculations.
2. The level of turmoil forecast for the 18-month period and the level forecast under the three most likely five-year regime scenarios.
3. The average rank of the country on the indicators of international financial problems and the forecasts of change under the three most likely regime scenarios.

The "A" Countries. No exchange controls, repatriation restrictions, or other barriers to financial transfer, and little likelihood that controls will increase in the forecast period.

The "B" Countries. Modest or sporadic delays in financial transfers, and a reasonable chance that delays will be high in the forecast period.

The "C" Countries. Modest to lengthy delays and even blockage of financial transfers, a reasonable chance that barriers will increase, and little chance that they will decrease, within the forecast period.

The "D" Countries. Oppressive exchange controls and long delays for the transfer of currency, and little chance that conditions will improve within the forecast period.

Direct Investment Risk. The term "direct investment" or "investment" refers to the risks facing foreign investment in wholly owned subsidiaries, joint ventures, and other forms of direct ownership of assets or equities in a foreign country. The 18-month letter grades are determined by these seven equally weighted factors, each combining the current level and the forecasts of change under the three most likely regimes.

1. Turmoil
2. Equity Restrictions
3. Restrictions on Local Operations (labor, management, and procurement)
4. Taxation Discrimination
5. Repatriation Restrictions
6. Exchange Controls
7. Labor Costs

Five-year letter grades are determined by four equally weighted factors:

1. The average score obtained from the 18-month calculations.
2. The level of turmoil forecast for the 18-month period and the level forecast under the three most likely five-year regime scenarios.
3. The relative strength of forces supporting and opposing restrictions on international investment and the forecasts of change under the three most likely five-year regime scenarios.
4. The average rank of the country on indicators of domestic economic problems and the forecasts of change under the three most likely five-year regime scenarios.

The "A" Countries. Few restrictions on equity ownership in most industries; few controls on local operations, the repatriation of funds, or foreign exchange; taxation policy that does not discriminate between foreign and domestic business. Little likelihood that restrictions will increase, and little threat from political turmoil.

The "B" Countries. Some threat on equity ownership, frequently in the form of a requirement for partial ownership by nationals; restrictions on local operations, particularly regarding local procurement; few restrictions on repatriation, but some exchange controls possible; some threat to business from political turmoil; and a possibility that restrictions and turmoil may increase.

The "C" Countries. Considerable restriction on equity ownership, including a requirement that nationals hold a majority percentage; considerable restriction on local operations, repatriation, and foreign exchange; some taxation discrimination possible; and a serious threat of political turmoil. A serious chance that restrictions and turmoil will remain high or increase during the forecast period.

The "D" Countries. Considerable restriction on equity ownership, including a prohibition against equity ownership by foreigners; substantial regulation of local operations, repatriation, and foreign exchange; taxation discrimination; political turmoil that may present a serious threat. A serious chance that restrictions and turmoil will remain high or increase during the forecast period.

Export Market Risk. The term "export market" or "export" refers to the risks facing exporters to the country, especially risks related to market conditions, barriers to imports, and delays or difficulties in receiving payment for goods. The 18-month letter grades are determined by these six equally weighted factors, each combining the current level and the forecasts of change under the three most likely regimes. These are the six factors:

1. Turmoil
2. Exchange Controls
3. Tariffs
4. Other Trade Barriers
5. Payment Delays
6. Foreign Debt

Five-year letter grades are determined by five equally weighted factors:

1. The average score obtained from the 18-month calculations.
2. The level of turmoil forecast for the 18-month period and the level forecast under the three most likely five-year regime scenarios.
3. The relative strength of forces supporting and opposing restrictions on trade and the forecasts of change under the three most likely five-year regime scenarios.
4. The average rank of the country on indicators of domestic economic problems and the forecasts of change under the three most likely five-year regime scenarios.
5. The average rank of the country on indicators of international economic problems and the forecasts of change under the three most likely five-year regime scenarios.

The "A" Countries. Stable politically and economically, low trade barriers and adequate foreign reserves to allow for prompt payment, and little chance that conditions will deteriorate.

The "B" Countries. Some protectionist sentiment and a poor foreign exchange position may lead to moderate tariff and non-tariff barriers to trade, modest delays in payment resulting from poor economic conditions, and some chance the business climate will deteriorate.

The "C" Countries. Substantial protectionist sentiment and weak foreign exchange position, producing high tariff and other barriers to trade; the risk of prolonged payment delays or non-payment, requiring conservative credit policies; little chance that conditions will improve and a serious chance that they will deteriorate.

The "D" Countries. High tariff and non-tariff barriers resulting from a combination of protectionist sentiment and a lack of foreign currency; prolonged payment delays or non-payment likely, little chance conditions will improve, and a serious chance they will deteriorate further.

Adjusting PRS Ratings for Your Own Use

Political Risk Services produces its risk ratings for 100 *Country Reports*, using the measures of interest to most businesses. The system employed by PRS facilitates cross-country comparisons. The PRS system can also be used to calculate risk scores for individual business projects or other specific situations of concern to an individual firm. PRS treats each of the 17 underlying risk factors as equal in calculating country risk ratings, in order to make the system applicable to general use, but individual businesses can easily adapt the same system by giving variable weightings to the 17 risk factors (including, of course, giving zero weighting to factors not relevant to a particular project).

Figure 4 (below) illustrates the use of a worksheet to give variable weighting to a sample start-up project in a hypothetical country.

Figure 4: Start-up Operations							
Unweighted Risk Index =	63						
Weighted Risk Index =	58		Alpha =	C+			
REGIMES -->		Leftist Coalition	Centrist	Military			Score * Weight
		50%	40%	10%	Score	Weight	
18- MONTH	CL						
Turmoil	2	0.5	0	1	2.35	2.00	4.70
Investment							
Equity	1	0.5	-0.5	1	1.15	1.00	1.15
Operations	2	0.5	-0.5	1	2.15	1.00	2.15
Taxation	1	1	-1	0	1.10	0.00	0.00
Repatriation	1	0	-0.5	1	0.90	0.00	0.00
Exchange	1	0	-0.5	1	0.90	0.00	0.00
Trade							
Tariffs	1	0.5	-0.5	0.5	1.10	1.00	1.10
Other Barriers	1	0.5	-0.5	1	1.15	1.00	1.15
Payment Delays	0	0.5	0	1	0.35	1.00	0.35
Economic Policy							
Expansion	2	1	-0.5	1	2.40	0.00	0.00
Labor Costs	1	1	0	-1	1.40	1.00	1.40
Foreign Debt	1	0	0	0	1.00	0.00	0.00
5-YEARS							
REGIMES ---->		Leftist Coalition	Centrist	Military			
RISK FACTORS		50%	35%	15%			
Turmoil	2	0	1	2	2.65	2.00	5.30
Restrictions							0.00
Investment	1	0	-0.5	0	0.83	1.00	0.83
Trade	1	0	-0.5	0.5	0.90	0.00	0.00
Economic Problems							
Domestic	2	0.5	-0.5	1	2.23	1.00	2.23
International	1	0	-0.5	0.5	0.90	0.00	0.00
Environmental conrols	1	1	0	0	1.50	2.00	3.00
							0.00
							0.00
						14.00	23.35
Scores / Weights =	1.668					Weights	Weighted
Max Risk =	56						Score
Customized Risk =	58.30		Alpha =	C+			

As Figure 4 shows, the project managers give zero weights to taxation, repatriation restrictions, exchange controls, economic expansion, and international economic problems. Their reasoning is that in the first years of the project they will not be earning substantial income; consequently, considerations of taxation and international finance are of minor importance. The analysts have also added an additional factor, environmental controls, a factor that is important to their project. Their calculations produce a moderately high risk rating, only a 58 on a 0-100 scale in which the higher the score, the lower the risk. (The weighting makes the country look more risky than its unweighted index score of 63.) In alphabetical terms the score translates to nothing better than a C+, a mediocre outlook, at best.

However, compare the Start-up Operation in Figure 4 with Figure 5 (on the next page), which shows the risk ratings for the same project under the assumption that the project is under way, producing income some of which is to be repatriated. Because the policy outlook indicates relatively low restrictions on such projects, the substantial weight given to factors affecting international financial transactions improves the risk score, producing a score of 70, equivalent to a B, and a substantially reduced risk outlook.

Figure 5: Mature Project							
Unweighted Risk Index =	63						
Weighted Risk Index =	70		Alpha =	B			
REGIMES -->		Leftist Coalition	Centrist	Military			
		50%	40%	10%	Score	Weight	Score * Weight
18- MONTH	Current						
Turmoil	2	0.5	0	1	2.35	3.00	7.05
Investment							
Equity	1	0.5	-0.5	1	1.15	3.00	3.45
Operations	2	0.5	-0.5	1	2.15	3.00	6.45
Taxation	1	1	-1	0	1.10	5.00	5.50
Repatriation	1	0	-0.5	1	0.90	10.00	9.00
Exchange	1	0	-0.5	1	0.90	10.00	9.00
Trade							
Tariffs	1	0.5	-0.5	0.5	1.10	1.00	1.10
Other Barriers	1	0.5	-0.5	1	1.15	1.00	1.15
Payment Delays	0	0.5	0	1	0.35	1.00	0.35
Economic Policy							
Expansion	2	1	-0.5	1	2.40	0.00	0.00
Labor Costs	1	1	0	-1	1.40	1.00	1.40
Foreign Debt	1	0	0	0	1.00	7.00	7.00
5-YEARS							
REGIMES ----->		Leftist Coalition	Centrist	Military			
RISK FACTORS		50%	35%	15%			
Turmoil	2	0	1	2	2.65	2.00	5.30
Restrictions							0.00
Investment	1	0	-0.5	0	0.83	5.00	4.13
Trade	1	0	-0.5	0.5	0.90	0.00	0.00
Economic Problems							
Domestic	2	0.5	-0.5	1	2.23	1.00	2.23
International	1	0	-0.5	· 0.5	0.90	5.00	4.50
Environmental conrols	1	1	0	0	1.50	5.00	7.50
					0.00		0.00
					0.00		0.00
						63.00	75.10
Scores / Weights =	1.1921					Weights	Weighted
Max Risk =	252						Score
Customized Risk =	70.20		Alpha =	B			

The calculations on the worksheet are straightforward extensions of the procedures described in earlier in this chapter. The customized scores are calculated, then weighted by the values assigned by individual analysts. These weighted scores are then divided by the unweighted scores (as in any calculation of a weighted average) and converted according to the standards previously described. Figure 6 (below) is a blank worksheet you can use to prepare your own calculations.

Figure 6. Customized Worksheet

RISK CALCULATIONS FOR _____

PROJECT_____COUNTRY _____TIME-FRAME_____

DATE _____PREPARED BY _____

Risk or Restriction	Current Level	Regime 1 F x P	Regime 2 F x P	Regime 3 F x P	Score x Weight	Weighted =SCORE
Turmoil	_____	+ (_x_)	+ (_x_)	+ (_x_)	= __x__	=___
Equity Restrictions	_____	+ (_x_)	+ (_x_)	+ (_x_)	= __x__	=___
Local Operations Restrictions	_____	+ (_x_)	+ (_x_)	+ (_x_)	= __x__	=___
Taxation Discrimination	_____	+ (_x_)	+ (_x_)	+ (_x_)	= __x__	=___
Repatriation Restrictions	_____	+ (_x_)	+ (_x_)	+ (_x_)	= __x__	=___
Exchange Controls	_____	+ (_x_)	+ (_x_)	+ (_x_)	= __x__	=___
Tariff Barriers	_____	+ (_x_)	+ (_x_)	+ (_x_)	= __x__	=___
Other Barriers	_____	+ (_x_)	+ (_x_)	+ (_x_)	= __x__	=___
Payment Delays	_____	+ (_x_)	+ (_x_)	+ (_x_)	= __x__	=___
Fiscal/Monetary Expansion	_____	+ (_x_)	+ (_x_)	+ (_x_)	= __x__	=___
Labor Costs	_____	+ (_x_)	+ (_x_)	+ (_x_)	= __x__	=___
Foreign Debt	_____	+ (_x_)	+ (_x_)	+ (_x_)	= __x__	=___

FACTORS SPECIFIED BY USER:

_____	_____	+ (_x_)	+ (_x_)	+ (_x_)	= __x__	=___
_____	_____	+ (_x_)	+ (_x_)	+ (_x_)	= __x__	=___
_____	_____	+ (_x_)	+ (_x_)	+ (_x_)	= __x__	=___

SUMS: WEIGHTS   WEIGHTED SCORES

SUM OF WEIGHTED SCORES/SUM OF WEIGHTS =____/___ = _____
                 WEIGHTED
                 MEAN

F = FORECAST
P = PROBABILITY

Long-Term Economic Forecasting

Our reports also include five-year economic forecasts based on the expected policies and other considerations for each of the three forecast regimes.

Gathering Data

Our country and economic specialists provide the information from which we produce the forecasts. Our forecasts are structured to make a clear statement of:

1. Current estimates.
2. A one-year estimate or forecast for each of the three indicators under each of the three alternative regime scenarios in Section H of the report.
3. A five-year forecast average for each of the three indicators under each regime scenario.

Our forecasts are based on the following considerations:

1. World and regional economic trends
2. How those trends affect the country
3. Local conditions affecting the economy of the country
4. Turmoil and social conditions under the three most likely regimes
5. Business and economic policies expected under each of the three most likely regimes

Sources of Our Forecasts and Data

Independent Analysts

Country specialists carefully selected for their professional expertise prepare each *Country Report*. These experts draw on their experience in such primary roles as academic researcher, consultant to government and business, government specialist, or adviser to multinational banks, trade associations, and manufacturers. We select each specialist based on a track record of objective and accurate research on the country to which the specialist is assigned. Many analysts have access to classified host government data, which they share on a confidential basis.

These specialists provide draft materials that are assessed and consolidated into forecasts by our editorial staff working with our directors, William D. Coplin and Michael K. O'Leary. The quality of the forecasts depends on both the quality of the specialists who participate in the study and the effectiveness of the questionnaire procedures we use to obtain a systematic analysis.

Country specialists crosscheck our information. Each may add information or make corrections. This process is especially important for many less-developed countries, for which information regarding unemployment, wages, and debt service is rarely available from the usual sources. Most of our country specialists have access to government documents and specialized publications that contain this data. These experts also contribute information on recent social trends—such as population growth—and update the political information.

Timely Data: The Starting Point of Every Country Report

Each of our *Country Reports* includes a comprehensive Fact Sheet that provides 30 categories of information on the country, its government, its leaders, and social conditions. It also contains 27 economic variables and indexes covering the most recent 10 years for each country.

Not only is this compilation of economic data comprehensive and extensive, it is also more up-to-date than any other source of which we are aware, printed or online. In addition to gathering data from official sources we routinely make updated estimates of the current year's figures for each variable.

Of course, estimates during a particular year need to be adjusted as a more complete picture evolves. We completely revise and update both the data and forecasts for each country on a quarterly basis. Our policy of keeping our data as timely as possible does mean that many of the figures we report, especially the most recent, require updating over time. We believe that the inevitability of revision and updating is no reason to delay the reporting of the best estimates as they become available.

Other Sources

Our country specialists provide the basic source of all political, economic, and social background. For the economic data contained in each country's databank and fact sheets, our primary source is *International Financial Statistics (IFS)*. This monthly publication of the International Monetary Fund (IMF) is the most reliable, comprehensive, and timely source available for making comparisons between countries. News sources, regional and technical journals, and electronic news services help us track day-to-day events that may necessitate changes in our Fact Sheets. Our research and editorial staff also relies on publications of individual governments, the World Bank, regional international banks, agencies of the

US and other governments, and embassies. We also maintain direct personal contact with officials and researchers in these organizations in order to obtain information and estimates quickly and reliably.

Compiling Our Structured Analyses

A detailed, comprehensive protocol elicits comparable information on the country from each specialist. Some draft text; others update, revise, and review the initial analysis. The structure of the protocol yields the underlying information necessary for the analysis, and also allows for thorough and systematic comparisons between country specialists.

Our *Country Reports,* updated quarterly, are backed by this sophisticated team of political and economic analysts, making up the world's largest private sector network exclusively devoted to political risk forecasting. Purchasing our products and services is the same as hiring a network of analysts, specialists, and researchers. Each month, our team produces hundreds of pages on the Internet, in print, and on CD-ROM, providing users with the most up-to-date political and economic analyses available.

Our political risk assessments begin with independent estimates made by specialists whose professional involvement in the country's business environment includes years of field research, regular visits, personal contacts, and residency. This input is then consolidated and synthesized.

Our Only Goal: Unbiased Forecasts and Timely, Accurate Data

Our forecasts avoid the inevitable biases found in other sources of risk analysis. Financial institutions tend to be excessively optimistic in their forecasts, especially regarding those countries in which they themselves hold a substantial stake. Governments generally make projections about a country—either optimistic or pessimistic—depending on the state of diplomatic relations with the country. They rarely provide forecasts inconsistent with their own objectives. By contrast, insurance companies, concerned as they are with loss and risk, are inclined toward chronic pessimism.

Newspapers tend to cover stories that relate to the latest events, following a country closely when it is newsworthy, and otherwise ignoring it. They also will emphasize those countries in which their reporters are located or where they happen to be visiting. Internal corporate sources are perhaps the most suspect of all. They are overwhelmingly motivated to shape their views around the interests of top corporate officials. The staffs of foreign divisions of corporations are notorious for their tendency to become apologists for their own country, usually reporting back to headquarters based on information provided by the officials of the host government and others most protective of the status quo.

In short, all these other sources provide reports and analyses shaped by their interests and particular points of view. By contrast, our own self-interest is simple: to provide the most accurate, timely, and objective information, analysis, and forecasting possible. We neither advocate nor discourage investments in any country. We simply try to provide the most comprehensive and useful *Country Report* possible for each country that we monitor.

The following pages provide a sample of one such *Country Report.*

1-Mar-2001

South Korea
Country Forecast
Highlights

MOST LIKELY REGIMES AND THEIR PROBABILITIES	
18-Month:	MD Coalition 45%
Five-Year:	MD Coalition 45%

FORECASTS OF RISK TO INTERNATIONAL BUSINESS				
	Turmoil	Financial Transfer	Direct Investment	Export Market
18-Month:	Moderate	B+	B+	B+
Five-Year:	Low	B+	A- (B+)	B+

( ) Indicates change in rating.   * Indicates forecast of a new regime.

KEY ECONOMIC FORECASTS			
Years	Real GDP Growth %	Inflation %	Current Account ($bn)
1996-2000(AVG)	5.5	3.8	8.67
2001(F)	4.4	2.2	5.10
2002-2006(F)	4.2	2.6	6.20

Delayed Reforms Threaten Economy

Key Points To Watch...

✓ Unfulfilled structural reforms and the fear of political backlash are slowing economic growth in the 2001–2006 forecast period to about one-half the estimated 10% achieved in 2000...

✓ Inflation fell to less than 2% in 2000, but will rise to average 2.6% annually over the forecast period...

✓ Kim Dae Jung's victory in December 1997 ensures that he will remain president until after the next presidential election, scheduled for December 2002...

✓ Progress in restoring the economy and in fostering reconciliation with North Korea will lay the basis for a successful bid for the presidency in 2002 by an MD candidate backed by Kim Dae Jung (who himself is not eligible for re-election)...

✓ Kim Dae Jung's efforts to reorganize the chaebols will be diluted by the struggle to contain unemployment...

Slow Progress in Economic Restructuring

✓ The dismantling of the Daewoo and the Hyundai groups was a major test for government efforts at corporate restructuring. After substantial delays, state creditor banks are dismembering the two as part of bankruptcy or debt-restructuring programs; the conglomerates' executives are beginning to respond, with reluctance...

✓ The government will continue to privatize and shrink the public sector. Although it will also try to simplify investment procedures, bureaucratic obstacles will still thwart foreign investment...

✓ The replenished foreign exchange reserves will avert the need for exchange controls, allowing the second phase of foreign exchange liberalization to proceed as scheduled in 2001, removing most remaining restrictions. The government will maintain its attractive tax incentives to increase foreign investment in priority sectors...

✓ The slowing economy and the impact of unemployment from industrial restructuring will provoke labor disturbances...

✓ Foreign businesses are likely to become targets of labor hostility, especially as the easing of investment restrictions increases the number of foreign investors, but labor hostility to foreign companies probably will be less intense than it was during the late 1980s and early 1990s.

Economic Forecasts for the Three Alternative Regimes

	Regime 1			Regime 2			Regime 3		
	Growth (%)	Inflation (%)	CACC ($bn)	Growth (%)	Inflation (%)	CACC ($bn)	Growth (%)	Inflation (%)	CACC ($bn)
2001	4.4	2.2	5.10	4.2	2.4	4.90	4.1	2.6	4.70
2002-2006	4.2	2.6	6.20	3.9	2.7	5.80	3.3	3.1	3.20

Political Fact Sheet

CAPITAL:
Seoul

CONSTITUTION:
February 25, 1988

ADMINISTRATIVE SUBDIVISIONS:
9 provinces, 5 special cities

POPULATION:
2000, 46.13 million

AREA:
98,477 sq. km.

OFFICIAL LANGUAGE:
Korean

STATUS OF PRESS:
free

SECTORS OF GOVERNMENT PARTICIPATION:
banking, steel, communications, utilities

CURRENCY EXCHANGE SYSTEM:
managed float

EXCHANGE RATE:
2/16/2001 $1=1243.00 won

ELECTIONS:
Presidential elections are held every five years. Last, December 18, 1997; next, scheduled December 2002. National Assembly elections are held every four years. Two-thirds of the members are chosen by direct vote, the remainder by proportional representation. Last election, April 13, 2000; next, scheduled April 2004.

HEAD OF STATE:
President Kim Dae Jung (1998)

HEAD OF GOVERNMENT:
Prime Minister Lee Han-dong (2000)

OFFICIALS
Jin Nyum, *Deputy Prime Minister; Finance*
Han Kap-soo, *Agriculture & Forestry*
Shin Kook-hwan, *Commerce, Industry & Energy*
Kim Yoon ki, *Construction*
Lee Don-hee, *Education*
Lee Joung-binn, *Foreign Affairs & Trade*
Choi In-kee, *Government Administration & Home Affairs*
Choi Sun-chong, *Health & Welfare*
Ahn Byong-yup, *Information & Communications*
Kim Chung-kil, *Justice*
Kim Ho-jin, *Labor Affairs*
Choe Sung Tae, *National Defense*
Pak Chae-Kyu, *National Unification*
Jeon Yun-churl, *Planning & Budget*
So Chong-ok, *Science & Technology*

LEGISLATURE:
Unicameral: 273-member National Assembly. Distribution of seats: Grand National Party (GNP), 133; Millennium Democratic Party (MD), 115; United Liberal Democratic Party (ULDP), 17; others, 8.

Political Risk Services

1-Mar-2001

South Korea
Databank

Domestic Economic Indicators	1991-1995 Average	1996-2000 Average	1991	1992	1993	1994	1995
GDP (Nominal, $bn)	367.92	436.94	294.18	307.94	345.72	402.52	489.26
Per Capita GDP ($)	8305	9472	6795	7040	7825	9015	10850
Real GDP Growth Rate (%)	7.8	5.5	9.4	6.1	5.8	8.6	8.9
Inflation Rate (%)	6.2	3.8	9.3	6.2	4.8	6.2	4.5
Capital Investment ($bn)	135.03	139.81	113.11	112.61	125.03	144.92	179.49
Capital Investment/GDP (%)	36.8	31.6	38.4	36.6	36.2	36.0	36.7
Budget Revenues ($bn)	67.82	89.56	50.21	56.11	63.23	76.06	93.47
Budget Revenues/GDP (%)	18.3	20.6	17.1	18.2	18.3	18.9	19.1
Budget Expenditures ($bn)	68.13	100.10	54.97	57.64	61.10	74.83	92.12
Budget Expenditures/GDP (%)	18.5	23.2	18.7	18.7	17.7	18.6	18.8
Budget Balance ($bn)	-0.32	-10.54	-4.76	-1.53	2.13	1.23	1.35
Budget Balance/GDP (%)	-0.2	-2.6	-1.6	-0.5	0.6	0.3	0.3
Money Supply (M1, $bn)	37.64	37.72	29.66	31.49	36.18	40.46	50.40
Change in Real Wages (%)	7.6	3.7	7.6	9.5	6.1	9.3	5.4
Unemployment Rate (%)	2.4	4.3	2.3	2.4	2.8	2.4	2.0
International Economic Indicators							
Direct Foreign Investment ($bn)	1.02	6.01	1.18	0.73	0.59	0.81	1.78
Forex Reserves ($bn)	21.32	53.72	13.31	16.64	19.70	25.03	31.93
Gross Reserves (ex gold, $bn)	21.87	54.28	13.70	17.12	20.23	25.64	32.68
Gold Reserves ($bn)	0.03	0.06	0.03	0.03	0.03	0.03	0.03
Gross reserves (inc gold, $bn)	21.91	54.33	13.73	17.15	20.26	25.67	32.71
Total Foreign Debt ($bn)	54.76	145.99	40.80	41.90	47.50	58.60	85.00
Total Foreign Debt/GDP (%)	14.6	34.5	13.9	13.6	13.7	14.6	17.4
Debt Service ($bn)	8.15	21.36	5.18	5.65	8.07	11.00	10.85
Debt Service/XGS (%)	7.3	11.9	6.0	6.1	8.0	9.3	7.0
Current Account ($bn)	-4.73	8.67	-8.32	-3.94	0.99	-3.87	-8.51
Current Account/GDP (%)	-1.3	2.9	-2.8	-1.3	0.3	-1.0	-1.7
Current Account/XGS (%)	-4.3	4.7	-9.6	-4.3	1.0	-3.3	-5.5
Merchandise Exports ($bn)	89.68	141.19	70.54	76.20	82.09	94.96	124.63
Merchandise Imports ($bn)	92.39	128.38	77.34	77.95	79.77	97.82	129.08
Trade Balance ($bn)	-2.71	12.81	-6.80	-1.75	2.32	-2.86	-4.45
Exports of Services ($bn)	14.66	25.78	10.01	10.72	12.95	16.81	22.83
Income, credit ($bn)	2.84	3.38	2.91	2.45	2.51	2.84	3.49
Transfers, credit ($bn)	3.45	5.87	2.84	3.24	3.38	3.67	4.10
Exports G&S ($bn)	110.63	176.22	86.30	92.61	100.93	118.27	155.05
Liabilities ($bn)	0.17	10.10	0.19	-0.05	0.10	0.43	0.16
Net Reserves ($bn)	21.74	44.24	13.54	17.20	20.16	25.24	32.55
Liquidity (months import cover)	2.78	4.26	2.10	2.65	3.03	3.10	3.03
Currency Exchange Rate	778.278	1093.836	733.35	780.65	802.67	803.45	771.27
Currency Change (%)	-1.8	-9.8	-3.6	-6.4	-2.8	-0.1	4.0
Social Indicators							
Population (million)	44.19	46.19	43.30	43.75	44.19	44.64	45.09
Population Growth (%)	1.0	0.5	1.0	1.0	1.0	1.0	1.0
Infant Deaths/1000	15	10	19	17	15	13	11
Persons under Age 15 (%)	24	22	26	25	24	24	23
Urban Population (%)	73	77	71	72	73	74	74
Urban Growth (%)	3.0	2.6	2.9	2.9	2.9	3.0	3.1
Literacy % pop.	96	97	95	96	96	96	96
Agricultural Work Force (%)	20	16	21	21	21	21	17
Industry-Commerce Work Force (%)	27	26	27	27	27	27	27
Services Work Force (%)	53	58	52	52	52	52	56
Unionized Work Force (%)	12	12	12	12	12	12	12
Energy - consumption/head	3031	3141	2569	2863	3000	3294	3431
Energy - Imports as % Exports	18	17	17	17	18	19	18

Political Risk Services
1-Mar-2001

South Korea
Databank

Domestic Economic Indicators	1991-1995 Average	1996-2000 Average	1996	1997	1998	1999	2000
GDP (Nominal, $bn)	367.92	436.94	520.21	476.49	317.08	406.94	464.0
Per Capita GDP ($)	8305	9472	11425	10360	6830	8685	10060
Real GDP Growth Rate (%)	7.8	5.5	7.1	5.5	-5.8	10.7	9.8
Inflation Rate (%)	6.2	3.8	5.0	4.4	7.5	0.8	1.5
Capital Investment ($bn)	135.03	139.81	191.41	167.26	94.41	113.75	132.24
Capital Investment/GDP (%)	36.8	31.6	36.8	35.1	29.8	28.0	28.5
Budget Revenues ($bn)	67.82	89.56	104.76	96.69	68.13	88.67	89.55
Budget Revenues/GDP (%)	18.3	20.6	20.1	20.3	21.5	21.8	19.3
Budget Expenditures ($bn)	68.13	100.10	104.22	102.73	80.23	107.51	105.79
Budget Expenditures/GDP (%)	18.5	23.2	20.0	21.6	25.3	26.4	22.8
Budget Balance ($bn)	-0.32	-10.54	0.54	-6.04	-12.10	-18.84	-16.24
Budget Balance/GDP (%)	-0.2	-2.6	0.1	-1.3	-3.8	-4.6	-3.5
Money Supply (M1, $bn)	37.64	37.72	49.15	36.83	25.39	37.33	39.89
Change in Real Wages (%)	7.6	3.7	7.3	0.8	-10.6	13.9	7.0
Unemployment Rate (%)	2.4	4.3	2.0	2.6	6.8	6.3	3.7
International Economic Indicators							
Direct Foreign Investment ($bn)	1.02	6.01	2.33	2.84	5.41	9.33	10.12
Forex Reserves ($bn)	21.32	53.72	33.24	19.71	51.96	73.70	90.00
Gross Reserves (ex gold, $bn)	21.87	54.28	34.04	20.37	51.97	73.99	91.01
Gold Reserves ($bn)	0.03	0.06	0.04	0.04	0.07	0.07	0.08
Gross reserves (inc gold, $bn)	21.91	54.33	34.07	20.40	52.04	74.06	91.09
Total Foreign Debt ($bn)	54.76	145.99	120.00	153.00	149.80	135.00	172.14
Total Foreign Debt/GDP (%)	14.6	34.5	23.1	32.1	47.2	33.2	37.1
Debt Service ($bn)	8.15	21.36	13.39	18.11	20.22	21.58	33.53
Debt Service/XGS (%)	7.3	11.9	8.3	10.4	12.1	11.9	17.0
Current Account ($bn)	-4.73	8.67	-23.01	-8.17	40.37	24.48	9.70
Current Account/GDP (%)	-1.3	2.9	-4.4	-1.7	12.7	6.0	2.1
Current Account/XGS (%)	-4.3	4.7	-14.3	-4.7	24.2	13.5	4.9
Merchandise Exports ($bn)	89.68	141.19	129.97	138.62	132.12	145.16	160.10
Merchandise Imports ($bn)	92.39	128.38	144.93	141.80	90.50	116.79	147.90
Trade Balance ($bn)	-2.71	12.81	-14.96	-3.18	41.62	28.37	12.20
Exports of Services ($bn)	14.66	25.78	23.41	26.30	25.57	26.53	27.08
Income, credit ($bn)	2.84	3.38	3.67	3.88	2.68	3.24	3.43
Transfers, credit ($bn)	3.45	5.87	4.28	5.29	6.74	6.42	6.61
Exports G&S ($bn)	110.63	176.22	161.33	174.09	167.11	181.35	197.22
Liabilities ($bn)	0.17	10.10	0.40	19.96	15.95	7.38	6.79
Net Reserves ($bn)	21.74	44.24	33.67	0.44	36.09	66.68	84.30
Liquidity (months import cover)	2.78	4.26	2.79	0.04	4.79	6.85	6.84
Currency Exchange Rate	778.278	1093.836	804.45	951.29	1401.44	1188.82	1123.18
Currency Change (%)	-1.8	-9.8	-4.3	-18.3	-47.3	15.2	5.5
Social Indicators							
Population (million)	44.19	46.19	45.54	45.99	46.43	46.86	46.13
Population Growth (%)	1.0	0.5	1.0	1.0	1.0	0.9	1.6
Infant Deaths/1000	15	10	10	10	11	11	7
Persons under Age 15 (%)	24	22	23	23	22	22	22
Urban Population (%)	73	77	74	74	79	79	81
Urban Growth (%)	3.0	2.6	3.3	3.3	2.1	2.1	2.1
Literacy % pop.	96	97	97	97	97	97	98
Agricultural Work Force (%)	20	16	17	17	17	17	11
Industry-Commerce Work Force (%)	27	26	27	27	27	27	22
Services Work Force (%)	53	58	56	56	56	56	67
Unionized Work Force (%)	12	12	12	12	12	12	12
Energy - consumption/head	3031	3141	3141	3141	3141	3141	3141
Energy - Imports as % Exports	18	17	17	17	17	17	17

Current Data

1-Mar-2001

South Korea Country Forecast

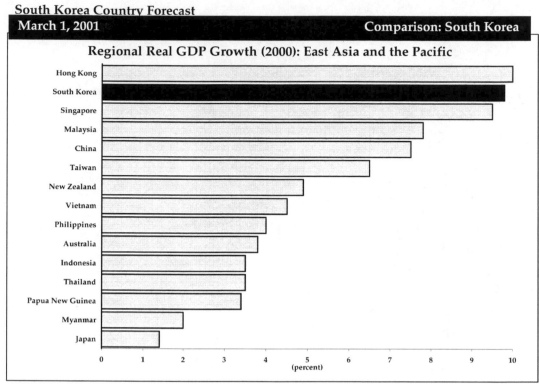

Regional Real GDP Growth (2000): East Asia and the Pacific

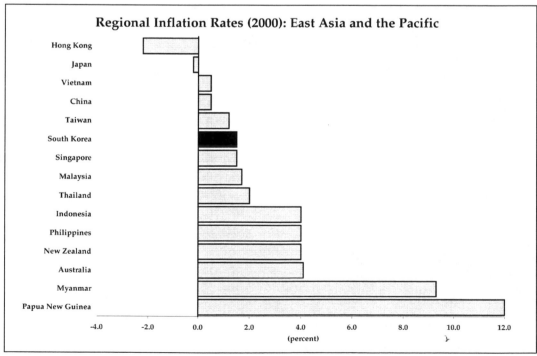

Regional Inflation Rates (2000): East Asia and the Pacific

1-Mar-2001   Current Data

South Korea Country Forecast

Regional Current Account/GDP (2000): East Asia and the Pacific

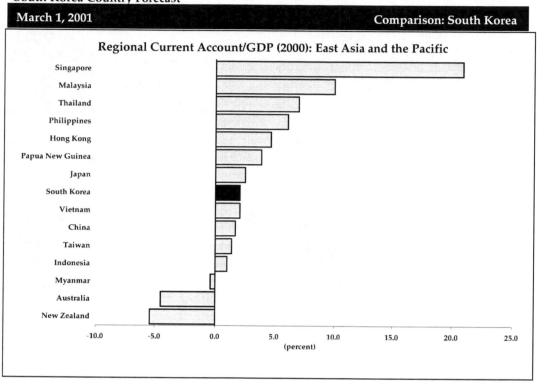

Economic Performance Profile
Country's Ranking Relative to All Countries
Covered by Political Risk Services
1996-2000

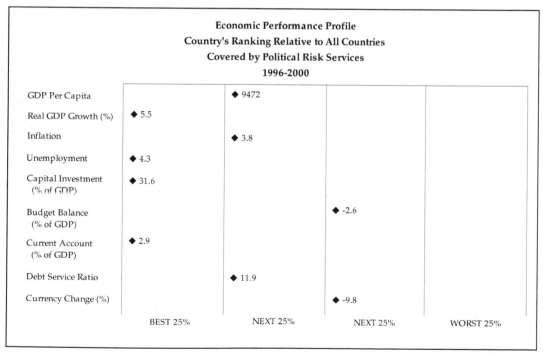

	BEST 25%	NEXT 25%	NEXT 25%	WORST 25%
GDP Per Capita		◆ 9472		
Real GDP Growth (%)	◆ 5.5			
Inflation		◆ 3.8		
Unemployment	◆ 4.3			
Capital Investment (% of GDP)	◆ 31.6			
Budget Balance (% of GDP)			◆ -2.6	
Current Account (% of GDP)	◆ 2.9			
Debt Service Ratio		◆ 11.9		
Currency Change (%)			◆ -9.8	

Current Data   1-Mar-2001

Political Risk Services

South Korea Country Forecast

1-Mar-2001

Social Indicators

as of 2000

Energy (kg. oil equivalent)

Per Capita Consumption:	3141
Imports as % of Exports:	17

Population

Annual Growth	-1.6%
Infant Deaths per 1,000	7
Persons Under Age 15	22%
Urban Population	81%
Urban Growth	2.1%
Literacy	98%

Work Force Distribution

Agriculture (%)	11%
Industry-Commerce (%)	22%
Services (%)	67%
Unions (%)	12%

Ethnic Groups

Korean

Languages

Korean

Religions

Christian (34%), Buddhist (19%), Confucianist (2%), other (45%)

Current Data

1-Mar-2001

South Korea
Country Forecast
Comment & Analysis

2001 Budget Draws Criticism at Home and Abroad

In February 2001, the IMF warned that the budget process requires additional reform, citing the failure of the government to institute international best practices. The IMF called on the government to consolidate all spending into the state budget and eliminate supplementary budgets. It charged that the extent of extra-budgetary spending produced haze that interfered with the transparency of the budget process. IMF representatives also called upon the government to reduce its direct involvement in the corporate and financial sectors, in part by giving the central bank full operational independence.

The 2001 budget bill won passage in the National Assembly in late December 2000 by 186–38, with 14 abstentions. However, to secure the bill's approval, the government had to accept a cut of slightly less than 1% of the $90.2 billion budget it presented to the Assembly. Total spending for the year amounts to $89.2 billion.

Legislators took $2.4 billion from state reserve funds and several other items and boosted subsidies to farmers and fishermen by $1.6 billion. State reserve funds lost the most, $842.6 million, followed by $502 million in reductions on interest payments for state bonds.

Farmers and fishermen will get an additional $587.7 million for debt relief, and engineers building up the nation's infrastructure have $750 million more at their disposal.

The National Assembly left the nearly $450 million the administration wanted for inter-Korean cooperation projects untouched. Legislators also agreed to the government's proposed spending on the National Intelligence Service. However, they also mandated the government inform the National Assembly Committee on Foreign Affairs and Trade and the Special Committee on Inter-Korean Exchanges and Assistance about how the money is used.

Political Risk Services   **South Korea Country Forecast**

1-Mar-2001   Reproduction without written permission of The PRS Group is strictly prohibited.

The Assembly also allocated $44.5 million, about half of the total earmarked for road construction, to build expressways in southeastern Kyongsang Province, the power base of the main opposition Grand National Party (GNP).

Some Chungchong Province assemblymen issued statements denouncing the budget's apparent bias in favor of GNP constituents. However, if such bias exists, it certainly failed to quiet the GNP's criticism of the government. GNP representatives Kim Yong-kap and Kim Won-wung denounced as unwarranted the expenditures on inter-Korean projects and the Saemangum Breakwater along the west coast. Opposition leader Lee Hoi-chang also criticized the government for front-loading 63% of budget expenditures for 2001 in the first half of the year in an effort to boost the slowing economy.

Financial Reforms Lagging

The IMF's call for financial reforms echoed President Kim Dae-jung's warning in January 2000 that the financial sector must learn to stand on its own and not rely on the government to lead the reform process.

Kim's warning came just days after Lee criticized the government's economic policies, emphasizing the enormous volume of bad loans still carried by financial institutions, despite more than $85 billion in public funds injected into the sector since the 1997 financial crises erupted.

In particular, Lee criticized the government's handling of the Hyundai group, which announced in early 2001 that the state-run Korea Development Bank (KDB) would take over $3.8 billion of debt from Hyundai Electronics and Hyundai Engineering and Construction. Lee accused the government of forcing the KDB to take on the debt of weak companies.

Corruption

The urgency of financial reforms has been highlighted by a series of corruption scandals that have troubled the government since late 2000.

In January 2001, the National Assembly began public hearings on allegations that former Culture and Tourism Minister Park Jie-won pressured a financial institution to extend illegal loans to a venture firm. Park resigned from the government in September 2000 over the issue.

At the end of October 2000, a third businessman was arrested under allegations of offering bribes to the government financial supervisory service (FSS).

Political Risk Services

1-Mar-2001

South Korea Country Forecast

Reproduction without written permission of The PRS Group is strictly prohibited.

Jang Song-Whan, is accused of using about $1 billion in bonds to bribe FSS officials to overlook irregularities at financial service firms. An Internet entrepreneur, Chung Hyun-Joon, and his financier were arrested a week earlier on similar charges.

On November 7, a former senior director of the FSS, Chang Rae-chan, was found dead at a hotel in the capital. He had been wanted for questioning in regard to the bribery scandal. The official Yonhap news agency said Chang had committed suicide.

Chaebols

South Korea is beset by strikes at a time when the economy is struggling to recover in the face of high world oil prices. Until mid-2000, most strikes involved the loss of job security and automatic pay rises, rather than actual layoffs. However, as the chaebols actually begin to restructure, the level of strike action can only rise sharply.

In that vein, time seems to be up for the massive industrial conglomerates that have dominated the economy for decades. Their rapid expansion of the chaebols through massive loans has proved unsustainable and, in retrospect, foolhardy. The companies' creditors have deemed 52 of them as "non-viable." They include the country's largest building firm, Hyundai Engineering and Construction Corporation, the carmaker Daewoo Motor, and Samsung Automobile.

At the end of October, Hyundai Engineering and Construction defaulted on its loans. Dong Ah Construction said it was planning to apply for receivership after creditors refused to grant new loans.

On November 8, Daewoo was declared bankrupt after it defaulted on payments of more than $39 million. Creditor banks say they will not approve fresh funds for the company unless the unions agree to plans for restructuring. Company officials are holding emergency talks with trade union members in an attempt to win approval for the company's self-rescue plan announced in October.

Growing Social Strains

All of this means that the liquidation, sale, or merger of these firms is unavoidable. The headache for the government is that the resultant layoffs will impose massive social and economic strains of their own. Hyundai and its subsidiaries alone employ about 100,000 people. The Dongwon Economic Research Institute estimates that the closure of all 52 firms could put up to 200,000 people out of work. South Korea's official unemployment rate stood at 3.7% at the end of 2000, representing about 800,000 unemployed.

In November 2000, 900 workers at Samsung Automobile held a rally and set fire to several vehicles in the southeastern city of Taegu. They are demanding that Samsung bosses must guarantee their jobs.

They will certainly not be the last to do so. In December, thousands of workers in the financial sector struck in response to feared job losses that would results from plans to merge two banks. The week-long strike ended with a threat from union officials, who warned that a new walkout was possible if the union was not included in future talks on merger plans. The strike by bank workers followed on the heels of a walkout by telephone workers, which succeeded in forcing the government to delay plans to privatize Korea Telecom by 2002.

Appeasement of China Draws Rebuke

Developments in the international arena have provided the government with little respite from its domestic troubles. At the end of October 2000, Seoul decided not to allow a visit by the Tibetan spiritual leader, the Dalai Lama. Foreign ministry spokesman, Lee Nam-Soo, gave no reason for the ban, but officials indicated it was intended to avoid a diplomatic row with China, which considers the Tibetan leader a separatist.

The decision was strongly criticized by the South Korean Buddhist group, which had invited the Dalai Lama to visit the country on November 16. The group has launched a campaign to press for Foreign Minister Lee Joung-Binn's resignation over the issue.

An editorial in the *Korea Times* newspaper commented: "Not only the members of the private citizens' groups who invited the religious leader, but also the general public will doubt the nation's diplomatic ability against the arrogant pressures by the Chinese authorities."

The Chinese Premier Zhu Rongji visited South Korea after the October 2000 Asia-European summit and the Chinese Embassy had put pressure on Seoul to postpone the Dalai Lama visit until 2001.

A February 2001 visit by Russia's President Putin was apparently more productive. The two presidents showed a meeting of minds on a wide range of diplomatic issues. President Kim even, by his silence during a joint press conference, allowed the inference that he endorsed Putin's criticism of the proposed US missile shield system.

Closer Ties to North Create Potent Issue for Opposition

The rapprochement with North Korea proceeds slowly but surely. A new shipment of aid made its way to North Korea in January 2001. The shipment, donated by religious

Political Risk Services

1-Mar-2001

South Korea Country Forecast

Reproduction without written permission of The PRS Group is strictly prohibited.

and civic groups, included food, livestock, and medical and school supplies valued at $917,000.

In February, months of negotiations finally bore fruit as military officials from the North and South agreed to a code of conduct designed to prevent clashes between soldiers from the two countries who are engaged in the reconstruction of a railway line across the heavily militarized border zone.

The issue had erected roadblocks to resolving other matters, including the creation of a standing procedure for further reunions between family members in the North and South. Another reunion was held in late February.

The process of repairing ties between the two countries has been hampered by several incidents since mid-2000 on both the international and domestic political fronts. At the end of October, the North was angered when two US warplanes violated its airspace during a military exercise by US and South Korean forces. Although the US later apologized for the intrusion, North Korea said the exercises were threatening the atmosphere of goodwill.

On November 3, North Korea threatened to suspend further reunions of families after the head of the South Korean Red Cross, Chang Choong-Shik, was quoted by a magazine as saying that there was no freedom in the North.

The state-controlled North Korean Red Cross said that Chang's comments were incompatible with his status and that as long as he remained head of the South Korean Red Cross it could not deal with him and had no choice but to reconsider future family reunions.

On November 8, economic talks were resumed in Pyongyang. The talks are to concentrate on reaching agreement on investment guarantees, trade settlement systems and the avoidance of double taxation.

In mid-November 2000, the National Assembly was suspended after politicians clashed over the government's 'sunshine policy' with North Korea. Opposition lawmaker Kim Yong-kap accused South Korea's governing Millennium Democratic Party (MD) of acting like a subsidiary of North Korea's Communist Workers' Party.

He said he opposed government plans to amend the National Security Law, which he said was part of Pyongyang's strategy to place South Korean society under North Korean leader Kim Jong-il's control. His comments and his refusal to retract them created uproar in the Assembly.

Likewise, government aid packages to North Korea are coming under growing criticism in the media as economic hardship in the South increases. The GNP has in the past taken a hard line on the North. Although it has reluctantly supported President Kim's efforts to improve relations between the two countries, it may well be tempted to reverse its position in order to tap into the popular mood.

South Korea
Country Forecast
Forecast Scenarios

SUMMARY OF 18-MONTH FORECAST

REGIMES & PROBABILITIES	MD Coalition 45%	GNP Coalition 35%	Divided Government 20%

SUMMARY OF FIVE-YEAR FORECAST

REGIMES & PROBABILITIES	MD Coalition 45%	GNP Coalition 40%	Divided Government 15%

MOST LIKELY REGIME SCENARIO

18–Month Forecast Period:
MD Coalition (45% Probability)
Five–Year Forecast Period:
MD Coalition (45% Probability)

MD Coalition	Growth (%)	Inflation (%)	CACC ($bn)
2001	4.4	2.2	5.10
2002-2006	4.2	2.6	6.20

Kim Dae Jung's victory in December 1997 ensures that he will remain president until after the next election, scheduled for December 2002. Progress in restoring the economy and in fostering reconciliation with North Korea will lay the basis for a successful bid for the presidency in 2002 by an MD candidate backed by Kim (who himself is not eligible for re-election).

One disappointment for Kim was the withdrawal of his party's partner, the ULDP, from the ruling coalition just before the April 2000 parliamentary elections. The ULDP split from the coalition over election law revisions passed in February, siding with the opposition GNP against a bill proposed by the MD calling for a change in the voting system to a one person-two ballot system. The ULDP was already disappointed that the MD did not make good on its promise to include in its platform a proposal to adopt a parliamentary Cabinet system to replace the current presidential system. The defection was a great setback to Kim's MD, which had hoped to share nominations with the ULDP in order to improve its chances of defeating the GNP. However, newly selected Prime Minister Pak Tae-chun, a ULDP member, agreed to continue to cooperate with President Kim in running state affairs, in effect remaining in his post and signaling some cooperation between the two parties. In May 2000, Pak resigned and was replaced by the head of the ULDP, Lee Han Dong. There is some hope that the two parties might renew their alliance in the future.

The April 2000 elections were a victory for the opposition GNP, which maintained a parliamentary plurality. The MD took second position, winning 115 seats to the GNP's 133 seats, thus making it more difficult for the ruling party to push through key legislation. The ULDP fared very poorly, winning only 17 seats. Two minor parties that won a total of only three seats between them were the New Korean Party of Hope (NKPH) and the Democratic People's Party (DPP).

Part of the reason for the ULDP's poor showing in the elections was the fact that, along with other party candidates, its leader, former Prime Minister Kim Jong Pil, was blacklisted by a civic group as unfit to run for office. Civic groups played a significant role in the election campaign by publishing lists of candidates that they felt unworthy of office because of past corruption, human rights violations, or poor military records. Many GNP and MD candidates were also blacklisted, as the electors displayed their frustration with political corruption.

Slow Progress in Economic Restructuring

Kim Dae Jung's goal of reorganizing the chaebols will be tempered by the struggle to contain unemployment, and by substantial entrenched opposition to restructuring within the chaebol system.

The dismantling of the Daewoo and the Hyundai groups has been a major test for the government in its corporate restructuring process. State creditor banks are dismembering the two as part of a debt-restructuring program. However, the process is far from complete, especially for Hyundai. In January 2001, the GNP charged that the government was back-tracking on reforms by forcing the KDB to take on the loans of struggling chaebols. The allegations arose after Hyundai reported that the KDB would assume $3.8 billion of debt from Hyundai Electronics and Hyundai Engineering and Construction.

The revelations have fed fears of another financial crisis, which emerged in May 2000 following the disclosure that Hyundai was experiencing cash flow problems. The scare has highlighted concerns that Korean banks are still vulnerable to another financial crisis because of their heavy exposure to the highly indebted conglomerates. An increased pace of structural reform will have to be achieved, especially corporate restructuring, if the economy is to be kept healthy.

Clearly, the government must take substantial steps to further reduce intervention in the economy. In late January 2001, Finance Minister Jin Nyum was named deputy prime minister in a move to indicate official commitment to bringing new momentum to reform efforts. However, critics remain unimpressed, particularly in light of Jin's spotty record on reform during his tenure as finance minister.

The government will continue to privatize and shrink the public sector. Although it will also try to simplify investment procedures, bureaucratic obstacles will still thwart foreign investment.

The replenished foreign exchange reserves will avert the need for exchange controls, allowing the second phase of foreign exchange liberalization to proceed as scheduled in 2001, removing most remaining restrictions. The government will maintain its attractive tax incentives to increase foreign investment in priority sectors.

The government still hopes to meet the obligations of its OECD membership by lowering individual tariffs, reducing the basic tariff rate, and attempting to reach agreement on trade issues with the US, Japan, and other OECD members.

The government will ease trade restrictions according to established timetables. Pressure from international quarters (particularly the US and the EU), and concerns about access to markets will prompt the government to follow through with planned trade liberalization. Healthy surpluses in the external balances will limit resistance to trade liberalization. The chief opposition will come from agricultural interests.

Domestic and International Threats of Turmoil

Under any likely government, the chief determinants of instability will be the course of relations with North Korea, the degree of success in achieving sustained economic recovery, and the state of relations with organized labor. The potential for North Korea to resume the development of nuclear weapons and further clashes between the military forces of the two countries will depend on the progress of North-South negotiations following the summit talks. The North-South summit and the deterioration of North Korean conventional military capabilities in the 1990s make the chances of a new Korean war remote.

The buoyant recover in 1999–2000 has helped to soften the impact of unemployment from industrial restructuring, but slowing growth, combined with further reforms will provoke additional labor disturbances. Foreign businesses are likely to become targets of labor hostility, especially as the easing of investment restrictions increases the number of foreign investors, but labor hostility to foreign companies probably will be less intense than it was during the late 1980s and early 1990s.

Demonstrations by organized labor will undermine social order. Professionals in the health care and education fields are inclined to go on strike to protect wages or prerogatives. In addition, fears of massive job losses as a result of the restructuring of the chaebols will provoke a series of protests and strikes.

The annual spring riots by university students do not in themselves threaten the business climate. Recent elections, including the 2000 legislative elections, were peaceful. Likewise, the establishment of greater civilian control over the military has not prompted any retaliation by the armed forces, although pockets of resentment remain.

Slight Slowing of the Economic Revival

After contracting in 1998, the economy returned to healthy annual growth of more than 10% in 1999 before slowing to an estimated 9.8% in 2000. Growth should slow to a more troubling average of 4.2% through 2006, not enough to reduce the high unemployment. Inflation fell to less than 1% in 1999, and rose to 1.5% in 2000; inflationary pressures are weakening in light of the slowing economy, and the

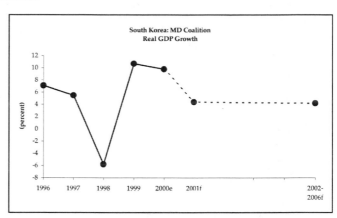

government should easily meet its 3% inflation ceiling; the rate is expected to average 2.6% annually through 2006. The inflation will not fall further because of price pressures resulting from higher wage and oil costs. The fall in growth rates may delay the goal of a balanced budget, as the deficit will persist at least through 2004.

Political Risk Services

1-Mar-2001

South Korea Country Forecast

Over the longer term, sustained recovery will depend on the recovery of the US economy and other markets, and restructuring of the financial and corporate sectors. The government has taken significant steps to open the economy to foreign investors, and its commitment to further reforms will help to maintain investors' confidence. However, labor unrest may

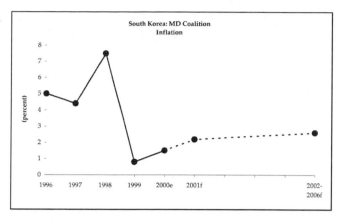

deter investors, especially early in the forecast period. Tightened fiscal policy later in the forecast period will offset inflationary pressures arising from the revival of demand.

Recovery Program Reduces Current Account Surplus

The decline in the current account surplus since 1998 when it surpassed $40 billion (some 13% of GDP) is largely due to the rising imports associated with the economic recovery.

Both imports and exports are expected to slow, at least in the early part of the forecast period, resulting in a declining current account surplus averaging $6.2 billion annually through 2006.

The surplus will fall as imports begin to recover and the stronger won reduces the competitiveness of exports. Increased interest payments and greater remittances by foreign investors will combine with a narrowing trade surplus to diminish the positive current account balance, possibly even producing a return to deficit later in the period. Nevertheless, the surpluses for most of the period will ensure healthy levels of foreign exchange reserves. The debt service ratio will rise substantially after 2000 as rescheduled debt payments fall due. Korea was able to repurchase funds drawn under the SRO ahead of schedule, and its sovereign credit rating was raised to investment grade.

SECOND MOST LIKELY REGIME SCENARIO

18-Month Forecast Period:
GNP Coalition (35% Probability)
Five-Year Forecast Period:
GNP Coalition (40% Probability)

GNP Coalition	Growth (%)	Inflation (%)	CACC ($bn)
2001	4.2	2.4	4.90
2002-2006	3.9	2.7	5.80

While Kim Dae Jung has achieved economic success and some significant reforms, many economic risks lie ahead. Kim has alienated broad sectors of organized labor; his government has been tainted by scandals; and the opposition has sought to stir up regional animosities in an effort to undermine the president's efforts to broaden the support base of his party. The fracture of the ruling coalition, with the departure of the ULDP from its alliance with Kim's MD, has also weakened Kim's power in the National Assembly. As a result, the outcome of the 2000 elections was disappointing for the ruling MD as the opposition GNP retained its plurality. Consequently, the GNP could begin to assert itself in the legislature even while Kim remains president. Such a revival could set the stage for the election of a GNP president in the December 2002 election.

A center-right government headed by a GNP leader such as Lee Hoi-chang, who narrowly lost the 1997 presidential election to Kim Dae Jung, would maintain the reconciliation talks with North Korea. However, it would probably urge businesses to be more cautious in investing there. Consequently, it could take longer for talks to result in any real progress.

Filling in Some of the Policy Gaps

A government dominated by the GNP would take a more conservative approach to promoting economic recovery and attracting foreign investment. It would place more emphasis on appeasing the chaebols, slowing the rate of corporate restructuring.

The GNP would also be more cautious in pursuing trade liberalization. Deterioration in the balance of payments could stimulate some restrictive policies, but the central role of exports in the economic recovery program would limit the government's willingness to increase trade barriers.

Aid to Social Calm

More moderate policies might help decrease labor unrest, as the government would be unwilling to lay off workers after the labor unrest of the late 1990s and 2000. However, this regime would remain under pressure to sustain some reforms in investment and restructuring in order to maintain support from the IMF.

Recovery Would Remain on Track

Real GDP growth would average 3.9% per year through 2006, and inflation would average 2.7% annually. The current account would remain in surplus, but would fall to average $5.8 billion annually over the forecast period, partly as a result of lower growth in imports. Reforms already under way and the achievement of debt rescheduling in 1998 should help to prevent an unmanageable increase in debt.

THIRD MOST LIKELY REGIME SCENARIO

18-Month Forecast Period:
Divided Government (20% Probability)
Five-Year Forecast Period:
Divided Government (15% Probability)

Divided Government	Growth (%)	Inflation (%)	CACC ($bn)
2001	4.1	2.6	4.70
2002-2006	3.3	3.1	3.20

Democratic institutions are still weak, the party structure is fluid, and party affiliation is determined more by regional loyalties and personal ties than by policy goals. Because of the tendency of individuals to switch parties and for parties to split in response to the thwarted ambitions of political leaders, it is possible that no single party or cohesive grouping of parties would be able to establish political dominance. The MD-ULDP partnership was the first coalition government in Korea's history, but it could very well establish a pattern for years to come, whether or not a parliamentary system is introduced. The tensions that caused its breakup highlight the instability that would threaten any such government. Even before the elections of 2002, the greater activity of the GNP may lead to a stalemate between the legislature and President Kim. Furthermore, the next president might well face the prospect of having to rule without a working majority in the National Assembly.

Slowing Reforms

Even if the president were inclined to pursue economic reforms, the lack of a majority in the National Assembly would thwart their passage and implementation. Efforts to build a majority would produce compromises that limited the scope of liberalization.

Although such a regime would have greater difficulty in securing economic legislation, it would continue to liberalize trade restrictions according to the established timetables.

Turmoil

Political uncertainty and instability would contribute to greater turmoil. This government's inability to develop a cohesive policy toward North Korea would heighten tensions between the two countries. Its failure to establish firm economic policies would threaten the sustainability of the economic recovery, leading to further labor unrest.

Worsened Economic Prospects

Annual GDP growth would slow to an average of just 3.3% over the 2001–2006 forecast period. Inability to carry out desperately needed reforms and continued wariness among investors caused by political instability would lead to weaker economic performance. Business groups would seek out political allies to protect their interests, delaying economic recovery and pushing up annual inflation, which would average 3.1% through 2005.

The current account surplus would average just $3.2 billion per year over the forecast period. The weak economic performance would restrain both exports and imports, maintaining a smaller but persistent surplus in the trade balance. This regime's greater difficulty in carrying out necessary reforms would revive wariness among investors, slowing inflows of foreign capital.

Forecast Summary

SUMMARY OF 18-MONTH FORECAST

REGIMES & PROBABILITIES		MD Coalition 45%	GNP Coalition 35%	Divided Government 20%
RISK FACTORS	**CURRENT**			
Turmoil	Moderate	Same	Same	Same
Investment				
Equity	Moderate	SLIGHTLY LESS	Same	Same
Operations	High	Same	Same	Same
Taxation	Low	Same	Same	Same
Repatriation	Moderate	Same	Same	Same
Exchange	Moderate	SLIGHTLY LESS	SLIGHTLY LESS	Same
Trade				
Tariffs	Moderate	SLIGHTLY LESS	SLIGHTLY LESS	SLIGHTLY LESS
Other Barriers	High	SLIGHTLY LESS	SLIGHTLY LESS	SLIGHTLY LESS
Payment Delays	Moderate	SLIGHTLY LESS	SLIGHTLY LESS	Same
Economic Policy				
Expansion	Moderate	SLIGHTLY MORE	SLIGHTLY MORE	SLIGHTLY MORE
Labor Costs	Moderate	SLIGHTLY MORE	SLIGHTLY MORE	MORE
Foreign Debt	Moderate	SLIGHTLY LESS	Same	Same

SUMMARY OF FIVE-YEAR FORECAST

REGIMES & PROBABILITIES		MD Coalition 45%	GNP Coalition 40%	Divided Government 15%
RISK FACTORS	**BASE**			
Turmoil	Low	Same	Same	SLIGHTLY MORE
Restrictions				
Investment	Moderate	SLIGHTLY LESS	SLIGHTLY LESS	Same
Trade	Moderate	SLIGHTLY LESS	SLIGHTLY LESS	SLIGHTLY LESS
Economic Problems				
Domestic	Moderate	Same	SLIGHTLY MORE	MORE
International	Moderate	Same	SLIGHTLY MORE	MORE

* When present, indicates forecast of a new regime

Political Risk Services

1-Mar-2001

South Korea
Country Forecast
Political Framework

Players To Watch

Kim Dae Jung: President Kim will encourage economic recovery by creating foreign investment opportunities, promoting trade liberalization, and furthering privatization efforts. His economic policy will focus on retaining low interest and inflation rates...

Grand National Party: Since the opposition GNP holds a plurality in parliament, President Kim will have to work with it to pass any economic programs. The GNP is a center-right party, and thus will tend to favor the chaebols' interests. Kim will have to take this into consideration when proposing restructuring of the large Korean corporations...

Chaebols: These huge conglomerates are largely owned by a small group of families. Because of the country's economic difficulties, the chaebols have become the target of a major debt restructuring by the government...

Labor: Labor has displayed its political power several times in recent years. Particularly from 1996 into 2000, the unions have often successfully fought to protect workers' rights. This extends to the government's proposed economic reforms, such as layoffs suggested in 1998. Labor unrest reached such proportions as a result that the government was forced to modify its proposals. Trade unions will continue to play an important role in politics...

Millennium Democratic Party: As the ruling party, the MD maintains a liberal view of economic recovery and reform. Its members favor extensive foreign investment and trade liberalization, and also favor reconciliation talks with North Korea. However, as second in power in parliament, the MD must contend with the center-right GNP to pass any legislation that would affect business interests, such as the debt restructuring of chaebols...

...more on these and other Players on the following pages

POLITICAL PLAYERS

Chaebols

The power of the business community is largely concentrated in the hands of a small group of families who own the country's huge conglomerates. Their dominant role has encouraged preferential treatment from the government, enabling them to form business relationships and gain access to credit at the expense of smaller firms. Although weakened by the country's economic difficulties, the huge conglomerates have exploited their extensive web of business and financial relationships to block reform, virtually daring the government to let them fail.

Plans to streamline the business activities of the chaebols and reduce the worrisome debt-to-equity ratios are a central component of the reforms outlined in the agreement with the IMF. Nevertheless, the government has hesitated to apply pressure on the chaebols to proceed with restructuring. The five largest concerns, Daewoo, Hyundai, LG, Samsung, and SK, account for the majority of exports, and the government fears setting back an export-led recovery. Concerns about the political and economic fallout of business failures encouraged the government and financial agencies to continue to provide financial support to prop up ailing firms. Moreover, the government showed ambivalence about pushing for restructuring at the expense of thousands of jobs, as long as unemployment remained at record highs.

Strong signs of an economic recovery in 1999 emboldened Kim Dae Jung to take a more forceful approach with the chaebols, leading to some progress in restructuring the corporate sector since the beginning of 2000. However, the failure of the chaebols to undertake sweeping reform on their own has placed the government in the position of intervening more directly in economic activity.

Grand National Party (GNP)

The GNP was formed in November 1997 through the merger of the New Korea Party (NKP) and the Democratic Party (DP), which combined their forces in an effort to counter the alliance of Kim Dae Jung and Kim Jong Pil. In the April 2000 parliamentary elections, the GNP won 133 seats, maintaining its plurality in the legislature.

The NKP won 139 seats in the 1996 elections for the National Assembly, and succeeded in recruiting a sufficient number of independents and defectors from other parties to form a working majority. Subsequently, the political fortunes of the NKP, and its successor, the GNP, were hurt by corruption scandals tainting Kim Young Sam's administration and the breakdown in the leadership of the party as Kim's term neared its end. He was unable to prevent the designation of a bitter personal rival, Lee Hoi Chang, as party chairman in March 1997.

The NKP's 1997 merger with the DP, which won 15 seats in the 1996 elections, gave the resultant GNP a total of 154 seats in the National Assembly. From its inception, the fractious party was susceptible to defections by self-serving members attracted by other parties. The potential for damaging internal discord became apparent when Rhee In Je broke with the ruling party and formed the New People's Party after failing to gain the party's nomination. Rhee attracted more than 19% of the votes in the 1997 presidential election, enabling Kim Dae Jung to narrowly defeat the GNP's Lee.

Continued strife within the party and the GNP's weak showing in the June 1998 local elections prompted additional defections that eliminated the party's majority. By the middle of 1999, the GNP held just 136 seats in the National Assembly, despite winning two by-elections in July. President Kim Dae-jung has continued to exploit factionalism within the party in an effort to lure one of the GNP's two large blocs into his camp, hoping to free himself of dependence on the ULDP.

Kim Dae Jung (President)

Kim's victory in the December 1997 presidential election after three previous unsuccessful bids represented an astounding comeback for the leading member of the democratic opposition. Only one year earlier, he had run a losing campaign for a congressional seat. The key to his victory was the partnership he formed with the ULDP, which allowed Kim to expand his base of support beyond Cholla Province and exploit the divisions within the GNP. However, a subsequent break with the ULDP and the second-place finish of his MD party in the April 2000 parliamentary elections has made his control of a legislative majority tenuous, despite the continued cooperation of the ULDP's representatives in Parliament.

Kim was born in 1924 in Mokpo and is a former member of the Party for Peace and Democracy (PPD), the New Democratic Party (NDP), and the DP. He became a political dissident, serving prison terms in 1976–1978 and 1980–1982. He unsuccessfully ran for president in 1971, 1987, and 1992.

Kim's social democratic inclinations raised fears that he would not follow through on IMF-mandated reforms, particularly since during the campaign he had claimed that he would renegotiate the agreement with the IMF. Even before officially taking office, however, he began indicating his acceptance of the agreement. He also secured the cooperation of labor union leaders to pass a law that increased employers' ability to lay off workers. Reform efforts were slowed by the government's lack of a majority in the National Assembly until September 1998, as the GNP successfully blocked or diluted key legislative items. During the period when he enjoyed a legislative majority, Kim took a more forceful approach to reform, including the restructuring of the corporate sector. In May 1999, and again in August 2000, the president reorganized his Cabinet to place allies and technocrats in control of economic policy, a clear sign that he has no intention of allowing the country's improved economic conditions to weaken the reform drive.

Labor

Trade union membership has remained stable at about 12% of the labor force after declining in the early 1990s. Until 1998, the government refused to register unions that were not affiliated with one of the country's two legally recognized labor groupings, the Federation of Korean Trade Unions and the Independent Korean Federation of Clerical and Financial Workers. Although the government has banned political activities by unions, it has aided the FKTU by suppressing unions seeking to challenge the FKTU's dominant position in the union movement. The best known example is Chonnohyop (National Association of Trade Unions), a fledgling alternative labor federation founded in 1990. However, as part of a compromise agreement reached with labor following widespread demonstrations in late 1996 and early 1997, the government extended official recognition to the Korean Confederation of Trade Unions , a body that claims 560,000 members and has adopted a more militant stance than the FKTU.

Labor displayed its political power in late 1996 and early 1997 by forcing Kim Young Sam's administration to modify proposed labor reforms designed to reduce workers' rights and make it easier for employers to fire workers. In the wake of labor protests, the government passed a revised law in March 1997 that delayed the planned changes for two years. Labor's success marked a partial return to the power it had exercised between 1987 and 1989, when demonstrations played an important part in forcing the ouster of President Chun Doo Hwan and bringing about direct presidential and legislative elections. In early 1998, an agreement between the government and the labor unions established a Tripartite Commission of government, employers, and labor representatives to deal with labor issues related to the structural reforms needed to address the country's economic problems, including layoffs.

Despite the cooperative stance adopted by labor in early 1998, mass strikes organized by the KCTU in 1998–1999 have provided evidence of the organization's capacity for disrupting the reform process, and have made it clear that labor will not tolerate bearing the entire burden of economic sacrifice demanded by reforms. The unions have rejected plans for layoffs, and have called instead for job-sharing and a shorter workweek. Hyundai's announcement of 1,500 layoffs in mid-1998 touched off weeks of protests that included the occupation of factories by workers. Faced with the unwelcome prospect of sending in riot police to drive out the workers, the government acceded to Hyundai's decision to offer the unions a compromise that would produce a substantially smaller number of layoffs and obligated the company to provide six months of job training. The compromise, which marked a setback for corporate restructuring, followed a decision by Daewoo Motor to halt layoffs until 2000 in the interests of maintaining social stability. Both companies nevertheless remain in trouble. Daewoo declared bankruptcy in early November 2000 after failing several times to persuade its unionized workers to accept layoffs. Although the government has pledged to save Hyundai from a similar fate, the government's efforts to prop up the ailing conglomerate has left it vulnerable to sharp attacks from both the opposition and international lending institutions.

In early 1999, the labor organizations and employers both withdrew from the Tripartite Commission. Signs of economic recovery have diminished the sense of urgency that encouraged labor's cooperative posture in early 1998, and the unions and employers have each accused the other of refusing to share the cost of restructuring. A fresh round of strikes in April 1999 stimulated concerns that unrest could discourage foreign investors. Yet another round exactly one year later was instigated by the KCTU and college students over wages and hours. Sporadic strikes by employees of individual firms slated for restructuring continued to present difficulties for the government into early 2001.

Lee Han-dong (Prime Minister)

Lee was appointed prime minister by President Kim in May 2000, shortly after Park Tae-chun resigned in the wake of a scandal over tax evasion. Lee is the head of the ULDP, the MD's former coalition partner, and his appointment might eventually lead to an informal renewal of that alliance.

Lee, born in 1934, graduated with a law degree from Seoul National University's Law College. He served six terms in the legislature before being appointed prime minister, a mainly ceremonial position. Lee favors the adoption of a parliamentary system of government in place of the current presidential system. His ULDP broke off its coalition with the MD in February 2000 on the grounds that Kim had broken a pledge to pursue such reform.

Military

The military has receded in importance, although it still retains the ability to influence many political decisions. President Kim Young Sam's installation of new senior commanders was designed to enhance civilian control, as were some of the personnel changes made by President Roh Tae Woo. The prestige and political influence of the armed forces has declined since the early 1990s, undermined by several episodes in which North Korea infiltrated South Korea's territory. The armed forces also suffered from the dismissal of Defense Minister Lee Yang-ho and his subsequent jailing for corruption and for leaking government secrets. The forces have also endured the celebrated trials of former generals Chun and Roh, who were convicted of murder and treason in 1997. Public sentiment has moved decidedly against military involvement in politics. The military's share of the budget has been reduced to less than 20%.

Military morale is low, particularly among the officers. Although discontent within the military leadership could tempt some officers to consider a coup, there is widespread recognition that such a move would inflict substantial harm and disrupt the process of economic recovery.

Millennium Democratic Party (MD)

The MD was chosen to succeed President Kim Dae Jung's National Congress for New Politics (NCNP) as the ruling party. The NCNP decided to merge with the MD in order for the new party to gain legitimacy and the legal rights and obligations of the former. At its formation in 2000, the new party named as its goals a global-level economy, an information-oriented nation, advanced education, healthy social construction, and wider social participation by women. Its charter is founded on principles of democracy, productive welfare, and a market economy. Its parliamentary representation is 42%, putting it in second place to the 48% held by the opposition GNP.

Students

The activist tradition among South Korea's 1.2 million college students makes them a potentially significant political force. Student bodies contain no more than 5% radical leftists, but they are well-organized and dominate campus politics, especially in the universities around Seoul. The radical movement is split into two factions, Chanmintu and Minmintu. Chanmintu, which favors North Korea and accepts direction from Pyongyang, controls Chondaehyop, the national student federation that outwardly leads student protest activities. Since the radicals virtually control another 10% of the student population, the number of students involved in demonstrations sometimes exceeds 100,000.

Public sympathy for radical student activism has declined as a result of such events as the killing of eight combat police officers by student demonstrators in Pusan in 1989 and the dispatch of a student delegation to the Pyongyang Youth Festival. The collapse of global communism has also weakened the appeal of leftist radicals. Fewer students are supporting radical action, and moderates are gaining at the expense of radicals in campus elections. The students took no significant role in the 1992 parliamentary and presidential elections.

The number of political protests by radical students against both the government and the US has declined. In 1994 and 1995, student groups shifted their emphasis away from political matters toward environmental concerns, women's rights, and campus issues. However, there was a revival of student unrest in league with labor in April 2000, when thousands of college students and militant KCTU members rioted on the basis of wage and workweek demands. Moreover, radical students have exploited the growing controversy in 2000 over the US military presence in South Korea and revision of the agreement under which the troops operate.

United Liberal Democratic Party (ULDP)

The ULDP was formed in early 1995, when Kim Jong Pil created the party as a political vehicle following his departure from the Democratic Liberal Party (DLP). Kim broke with the DLP over what he perceived to be Kim Young Sam's intention to thwart his presidential ambitions. The party failed to meet its leader's expectations in the April 1996 legislative elections, although it won 50 seats, making it the second largest party in the opposition after the NCNP.

Until February 2000, the ULDP was the junior partner in the ruling coalition, a position it secured through an agreement with the NCNP during the 1997 presidential campaign. However, the ULDP withdrew from the government two months before the April 2000 parliamentary elections, claiming that the new ruling MD had failed to deliver promised electoral and governmental reforms. The move proved disastrous for the ULDP; it won only 17 seats in the 2000 elections, and no longer holds the balance of power in the National Assembly. It has nevertheless expressed its willingness to continue to cooperate with the MD in making policy.

Appendix A
Political Risk Services

The Prince Model

A unique feature of Political Risk Services' approach to political risk forecasting is the use of systematic and uniform analysis by independent country experts. The Prince Model forms the basis for this analysis. The model was designed by the directors of Political Risk Services, William D. Coplin and Michael K. O'Leary. Since its development in 1969, Coplin and O'Leary have enhanced and expanded its uses. A publication describing the use of the Prince Model is *Power Persuasion* (Reading, Mass.: Addison-Wesley, Inc., 1985). *Power Persuasion* illustrates how to use the system to achieve personal and business goals in corporate setting, using the term "power persuasion" instead of Prince Model to identify the system.

The Prince Model, a general political forecasting model, can be applied to forecasting a policy initiative, support for a current or potential regime, participation in political violence, passage of a new law, issuing a regulation, or, indeed, any collective action. The model has evolved over many years of refinement and application. It is useful in a wide variety of political situations and is one of the few approaches to political forecasting that is both systematic and relevant to decision-makers. The Prince Model provides a means for rigorous analysis, producing calculations that result in forecasts of the probability of specific political outcomes. At the same time, it uses the invaluable and unique expertise of specialists — both to supply information for the model and to adjust calculations produced by the model according to their own qualitative and subjective knowledge about a given country. The Prince Model generates probability scores for the most likely regime, turmoil, and restrictions on international investment and trade. This procedure shows how to illustrate the results of analyzing the political forces underlying these probabilities.

Constructing the Model

Data for the Model. In using the Prince Model, the first step is to attain the input of expert analysts. Experts provide information on the key political players that will affect each of the future decisions and outcomes covered in our reports.

Players and Their Positions. These players may be individuals, groups, or ministries within the government, or opponents of the government, as well as individuals or groups within the society as a whole, such as business, unions, or ethnic organizations. Players may also include foreign individuals or institutions, such as the International Monetary Fund or foreign governments. Each player's role is assessed according to the following estimates:

> *Position.* This indicates the firmness with which each player either supports or opposes the outcome being forecast. For group players, certainty is a function of the extent to which there is consensus of support or opposition among the membership. Certainty is measured on a scale ranging from +1 (*little certainty*) to +5 (*extremely high certainty*). The same 1-5 scale (using negative numbers) is used to estimate the firmness of opposition. The firmness of a neutral player's orientation is not taken into account in computing the Prince Score for that player.

> *Power.* This indicates the degree to which each player can exert influence, directly or indirectly, to support or oppose a particular factor, relative to all other players. A player's power can have a variety of bases, and the exercising of power takes many forms. Power may be based on such factors as group size, wealth, physical resources, institutional authority, prestige, and political skill. Power is measured on a scale ranging from 1 (*little power*) to 5 (*extremely high power*).

Priority. This indicates the importance attached to supporting or opposing a particular factor, relative to all other concerns facing that player. Priority is measured on a scale ranging from 1 (*little importance*) to 5 (*extremely high importance*).

The model is the basis of estimating: (1) the stability of the most likely regime; (2) the likelihood of turmoil; (3) future restrictions on international investment; and (4) the future level of restrictions on trade. The current levels and forecast levels of instability and policy restrictions are used to calculate risk ratings, as described in the following sections.

Applying the Model

The Prince political forecasting system can be used to determine the probability of any collective action or event, such as the following examples that might apply to business:
- Procurement decisions
- Government support
- Disruptive protests
- Procurement priorities
- A new health and safety regulation
- Changing operational restrictions
- Budget decisions
- Import and export regulations
- International sanctions
- Joint venture rules
- Tax rates
- Concessions
- Work stoppages
- Environmental regulations
- Repatriation restrictions

Steps in the Prince System

1. Define the event or action.
2. Identify the players involved.
   - "Veto" players, players that have the power to block the action.
   - "Influence" players, others that may influence Veto Players.
3. Estimate the position of each player, using the range of –5 (*strong opposition*) to +5 (*strong support*), and 0 for a *neutral* position.
4. Estimate the power of each player on a +1 to +5 scale. (Negative power values are not allowed.)
5. Estimate each player's priority on a +1 to +5 scale. (Negative priority values are not allowed.)
6. Calculate the event's probability as follows:

Calculating the Probability of an Event

1. Multiply each player's position, power, and priority to calculate the Prince score.
(If the player has a zero – neutral – position, multiply power and priority, and mark the Prince score for special treatment, as indicated below.)
2. Sum the Prince scores of players supporting the action.
3. Sum Prince scores of all neutral players.
4. Find the numerator: add Step 2 + 1/2 of Step 3.
5. Find the denominator: add supportive scores, neutral Prince scores, and absolute value of opposing Prince scores.
6. Compute the probability in the range of 0.0 - 1.0: divide Step 4 by Step 5. (Report as a percentage.)

Interpreting the probability
 Less than 40%: action is unlikely to occur.
 40% - 60%: uncertain whether action will occur
 Greater than 60%: action is likely to occur.

See Figure A-1 for an illustrative example of a Prince forecast. See Figure A-2 for a blank Prince Chart. For additional information on the Prince terms and procedures, see the references in the body of the chapter.

Figure A-1: Forecast of Proposal to Tighten Environmental Regulations

Tighten environmental regulations   71% Probability

Player	Position	Power	Priority	Score	Support	Neutral	Oppose
Government Party	3	4	3	36	36	--	--
Manufacturers	-3	3	4	-36	--	--	-36
Green Party	5	2	4	40	40	--	--
Opposition Party	-3	2	2	-12	--	--	-12
Green Peace	5	1	5	25	25	--	--
Recycling firms	5	1	5	25	25	--	--
Trade union leaders	0	3	3	9	--	9	--
				--	--	--	--
				--	--	--	--
				--	--	--	--
				--	--	--	--

1. Multiply each player's position, power, and priority to calculate the Prince score.
(If the player has a zero – neutral – position, multiply power and priority, and mark the Prince score for special treatment, as indicated below.)

2. Sum supportive scores. 126
. .

3. Sum neutral scores. 9

4. Find the numerator: add Step 2 + 1/2 of Step 3. . . . . 130.5

5. Find the denominator: add supportive and neutral
   scores, and absolute value of opposing scores 183

6. Compute the probability in the range of 0.0 - 1.0:
   divide Step 4 by Step 5. (Report as a percentage.). 71%

Interpreting the probability
Less than 40%: action is unlikely to occur.
40% - 60%: uncertain whether action will occur
Greater than 60%: action is likely to occur.

Figure A-2: Blank Prince Chart

					___% Probability		
Player	Position	Power	Priority	Score	Support	Neutral	Oppose
___	___	___	___	___	___	___	___
___	___	___	___	___	___	___	___
___	___	___	___	___	___	___	___
___	___	___	___	___	___	___	___
___	___	___	___	___	___	___	___
___	___	___	___	___	___	___	___
___	___	___	___	___	___	___	___
___	___	___	___	___	___	___	___
___	___	___	___	___	___	___	___
___	___	___	___	___	___	___	___
___	___	___	___	___	___	___	___

1. Multiply each player's position, power, and priority to calculate the Prince score. (If the player has a zero – neutral – position, multiply power and priority, and mark the Prince score for special treatment, as indicated below.)

2. Sum supportive scores. . . . . ___

3. Sum neutral scores. . . . . ___

4. Find the numerator: add Step 2 + 1/2 of Step 3. . . . . ___

5. Find the denominator: add supportive and neutral
   scores, and absolute value of opposing scores . . . . ___

6. Compute the probability in the range of 0.0 - 1.0:
   divide Step 4 by Step 5. (Report as a percentage.). . . . ___
. . . . .

Interpreting the probability
Less than 40%: action is unlikely to occur.
40% - 60%: uncertain whether action will occur
Greater than 60%: action is likely to occur.

Appendix B
Political Risk Services

TERMINOLOGY AND DATA SOURCES

This section defines the terms used for the variables in our Country Reports and all related publications, including Country Forecasts. The referenced source indicates the most frequently used authority. When a description includes more than one source, the primary source of information is indicated by an asterisk. "PRS research files" refers to data files we maintain, primarily from news sources and the reports of our country specialists. The relevant date for each category is our date of publication, except where noted.

Geographic & Political Data

Capital: The designated seat of government of the country (*World Almanac*).

Population: A mid-year estimate of the total number of people living in the country (**IFS, World Factbook, World Almanac*).

Area: The total area of the country in square kilometers (*World Almanac*).

Official Language: The officially designated language(s) of the government (**World Almanac, National Trade Data Bank, World Factbook*).

Constitution: The date of promulgation of the country's current constitution (**World Almanac, World Factbook, National Trade Data Bank*).

Head of State: The formal leader of the country, and the year of the leader's accession (**Chiefs of State and Cabinet Members of Foreign Governments, World Almanac*).

Head of Government: The administrative leader of the government, and the year of accession (**Chiefs of State and Cabinet Members of Foreign Governments, World Almanac*).

Officials: A listing of major government officials and their posts. Priority is given to the following: Deputy Prime Minister, Agriculture, Commerce, Defense, Development, Energy, Finance, Foreign Affairs, Industry, Interior, Labor, Mining, Planning, Security, and Trade (**Chiefs of State and Cabinet Members of Foreign Governments*, PRS research files).

Administrative Subdivisions: The number and type of administrative districts in the country (**World Almanac, World Factbook*).

Legislature: The types of national legislative bodies and the distribution of seats among the major political parties (**embassies, PRS research files, World Factbook*).

Elections: The national election schedule and terms of office; the date of the most recent election; and the date of the next election or the date by which the next election must be held, as appropriate (**embassies, PRS research files*).

Status of the Press: The freedom accorded to the news media to report and editorialize (*PRS research files).

Sectors of Government Participation: The areas of the economy in which the government exercises control or ownership (*National Trade Data Bank*, PRS research files).

Currency Exchange System: A description of the exchange characteristics of the currency (*IFS*, PRS research files).

Exchange Rate: The value of the currency in relation to the US dollar on the most recent date available. The dollar is reported in relation to the deutschmark (*IFS*, PRS research files).

Domestic Economic Indicators

Gross Domestic Product (GDP): One year's nominal value of the total final output of goods and services the country's economy produced within a country's territorial jurisdiction, regardless of the foreign or domestic ownership of the source of the production (*IFS, Trends in Developing Economies, OECD Economic Surveys*, PRS research files).

Per Capita: The ratio of GDP to population (*IFS, Trends in Developing Economies, OECD Economic Surveys*, PRS research files).

Real Growth Rate: The annual percent change in GDP, adjusted by the inflation rate (*IFS, Trends in Developing Economies, OECD Economic Surveys*, PRS research files).

Inflation: The annual percent change in a consumer price index (*IFS, Trends in Developing Economies, OECD Economic Surveys*, PRS research files).

Capital Investment: The annual value of gross fixed capital formation (*IFS*).

Investment/GDP: The value of capital investment as a percentage of gross domestic product (*IFS*).

Budget Revenues: One year's nonrepayable and nonrepaying government receipts, plus grants received from other governments (domestic or foreign) and international institutions (*IFS, Trends in Developing Economies*, PRS research files).

Budget Revenues/GDP: Revenues, as defined above, as a percentage of gross domestic product (*IFS, Trends in Developing Economies*, PRS research files).

Budget Expenditures: One year's nonrepayable and nonrepaying payments by governments, plus government acquisition of claims on others (loans and equities), minus repayments of lending and sales of equities previously purchased (*IFS, Trends in Developing Economies*, PRS research files).

Budget Expenditures/GDP: Expenditures, as defined above, as a percentage of gross domestic product (*IFS, Trends in Developing Economies*, PRS research files).

Budget Balance: The difference between (a) revenue and applicable grants received and (b) expenditure and lending, minus repayments (includes foreign lending) (*IFS, Trends in Developing Economies*, PRS research files).

Budget Balance/GDP: Budget balance, as defined above, as a percentage of gross domestic product (**IFS, Trends in Developing Economies*, PRS research files).

Money Supply (M1): The year-end stock of money in the economy. Components of M1 include currency in circulation, commercial bank deposits, NOW accounts, credit union share drafts, mutual savings bank demand deposits, and nonbank travelers checks (**IFS*, PRS research files).

Change in Real Wages: The annual percent change in real (inflation-adjusted) wages (**IFS, Foreign Labor Trends*, PRS research files).

Unemployment Rate: The year's average percentage of the labor force without work during the period cited (**National Trade Data Bank, OECD Economic Outlook*, PRS research files).

International Economic Indicators

Foreign Direct Investment: One year's investment by foreign citizens in domestic business; usually involves majority stock ownership of the enterprise (**IFS*, PRS research files).

Forex Reserves: The year-end value of foreign currency (excluding gold) held by a central bank for purposes of exchange intervention settlement of intergovernmental claims (**IFS*, PRS research files).

Gross Reserves (ex gold, $bn): The year-end value of assets denominated in foreign currency and SDRs, excluding gold, held by a central bank (*IFS*).

Gold Reserves ($bn): The year-end value of gold reserves held by a central bank (*IFS*).

Gross Reserves (inc gold, $bn): The year-end value of assets denominated in foreign currency and SDRs, plus gold, held by a central bank (*IFS*).

Total Foreign Debt: The year-end value of gross indebtedness by private and public sector domestic borrowers to foreign entities (**Trends in Developing Economies*, PRS research files).

Total Foreign Debt/GDP: Total Foreign Debt, as defined above, as a percentage of gross domestic product (**Trends in Developing Economies*, PRS research files).

Debt Service ($bn): The year's sum of interest and principal repayments on external public and publicly guaranteed debt (**IFS, Trends in Developing Economies*, PRS research files).

Debt Service/XGS (Debt Service Ratio): The year's sum of interest and principal repayments on external public and publicly guaranteed debt as a percentage of exports of goods and services (**PRS research files, Trends in Developing Economies*).

Current Account: The year's total balance of payments on goods and services and all transfer payments: the difference between (a) exports of goods and services, plus inflows of unrequited official and private transfers, and (b) imports of goods and services, plus unrequited transfers to the rest of the world (**IFS, Trends in Developing Economies, OECD Economic Surveys*, PRS research files).

Current Account/GDP: Current account, as defined above, as a percentage of gross domestic product (**IFS, Trends in Developing Economies, OECD Economic Surveys*, PRS research files).

Current Account/XGS (%) Current account, as defined above, as a percentage of exports of goods and services. (*IFS, Trends in Developing Economies, OECD Economic Surveys*, PRS research files).

Merchandise Exports: The year's value of merchandise exports, measured free-on-board (*IFS, Trends in Developing Economies*, PRS research files).

Merchandise Imports: The year's value of merchandise imports, measured free-on-board (*IFS, Trends in Developing Economies*, PRS research files).

Foreign Trade Balance: The year's value of merchandise exports, measured free-on-board, minus the year's value of merchandise imports, measured free-on-board (*IFS, Trends in Developing Economies*, PRS research files).

Exports of Services ($bn): The year's value of exports of services (*IFS, Trends in Developing Economies*, PRS research files).

Income, credit ($bn): The year's value of income received (*IFS*).

Transfers, credit ($bn): The year's value of transfer payments received, excluding those for exceptional financing (*IFS*).

Exports G&S ($bn): The year's value of exports of goods and services. (*IFS, Trends in Developing Economies*, PRS research files).

Liabilities ($bn): The foreign liabilities of the monetary authorities. (*IFS*).

Net Reserves ($bn): The year-end value of gross reserves, including gold, minus liabilities (*IFS*).

Liquidity (months import cover) Estimated annual net liquidity expressed as months of cover and calculated as the official reserves of the individual countries, including their official gold reserves calculated at current free market prices, but excluding the use of IMF credits and the foreign liabilities of the monetary authorities. (*IFS*, PRS research files).

Currency Exchange Rate: The national currency value in relation to the US dollar; for the dollar, the value in relation to the deutschmark (*IFS*, PRS research files).

Currency Change: The annual percent change in the national currency value in relation to the US dollar (*IFS*, PRS research files).

Principal Exports: The country's primary exports and main export partners (*World Factbook, National Trade Data Bank, World Almanac*)

Principal Imports: The country's primary imports and main import partners (*World Factbook, National Trade Data Bank, World Almanac*).

Social Indicators

Population Growth: The average annual percent change in the population, resulting from a surplus (or deficit) of births to deaths and the balance of migrants entering and leaving a country. The rate may be positive or negative (**IFS, World Population Data Sheet, World Factbook*).

Infant Deaths/1000: One year's total deaths of children under one year of age per 1,000 live births in a calendar year (*World Development Report, World Population Data Sheet*).

Persons under Age 15: The percentage of the population age zero to 14 years, inclusive (**World Almanac, World Population Data Sheet*, PRS research files).

Urban Population: The mid-year percentage of the population living in urban areas (**World Development Report, World Population Data Sheet, World Almanac, World Factbook*).

Urban Growth: The average annual percent change in the urban population of the country (**World Development Report, World Factbook*).

Literacy: The year-end percentage of persons age 15 and over who can read and write (**World Development Report, World Almanac*, PRS research files).

Ethnic Groups: Groups with which significant percentages of the population identify themselves (**World Almanac, World Factbook, National Trade Data Bank*).

Languages: Languages spoken by significant percentages of the population (**World Almanac, National Trade Data Bank, World Factbook*).

Religions: The religious preferences of significant percentages of the population (**World Almanac, National Trade Data Bank, World Factbook*).

Agriculture Work Force: The year-end percentage of the work force employed in agricultural production (**World Almanac, World Factbook*).

Industry-Commerce Work Force: The year-end percentage of the work force employed in industrial production and commerce (**World Almanac, World Factbook*).

Services Work Force: The year-end percentage of the work force employed in service-oriented production (**World Almanac, World Factbook*).

Unionized Work Force: The year-end percentage of the work force that is organized, independent of the government (**World Factbook, National Trade Data Bank*).

Energy - consumption/head: The amount of energy consumed per person in kg. oil equivalent (*World Development Report*).

Energy - Imports as % Exports: The ratio of the value of fuel imports to the value of total merchandise exports (*World Development Report*).

Chapter 12

The IHS Energy Group's
Political Risk Ratings and Ranking Index

Terry Hallmark, Ph.D. & Kevin Whited
IHS Energy Group

INTRODUCTION

Political risk analysis has played a prominent role in the strategic planning of major international oil and service and supply companies for roughly three decades. In the early years, the chief or central concern of oil companies was the threat of a sudden, uncompensated nationalization or expropriation of company interests abroad – but by the mid-1980s, the relationship between foreign operators and host country governments had changed. The political leadership and other key players in lesser-developed and newly-industrialized countries eventually came to the realization that uncompensated takeovers cut off much needed technology, sources of energy, and most importantly, in the case of exporters, hard currency earnings from crude oil and natural gas sales. As a result, what emerged in most host-countries was a far more congenial relationship with foreign oil operators, along with a liberalization of petroleum legislation and fiscal regimes to make the exploration and exploitation of hydrocarbons more economically attractive.

While this shift in posture was certainly a plus for the international oil and gas industry, at a certain level it made distinguishing between countries on the basis of political risk more difficult, and in many instances it shifted the focus of risk assessment more toward the policy arena. At the same time, the experiences of operators in places like Angola and elsewhere suggested that traditional political risks like widespread violence or political instability – even in the form of civil war – did not necessarily constitute a prohibitive risk to foreign oil company investment. And, even in those countries where the threat to oil company interests was both immediate and extensive – Colombia and Nigeria come readily to mind – operators showed themselves willing to forego the risks present and continue to explore for and produce oil and natural gas. So long as the prospectivity was relatively high, access to markets remained open and acceptable fiscal terms guaranteed a sufficient after-tax rate of return on investment.

Armed with the understanding that foreign oil companies are able and willing to work in almost any country in the world, and believing that political risk assessment is really useful only to the degree that it is industry specific, Petroconsultants – now

The IHS Energy Group's Political Risk Ratings and Ranking Index provides a more focused risk assessment than most ratings systems. Clearly a micro level assessment, the rating was built specifically for the petroleum industry. This rating system goes one stage further than that of PRS by looking within the FDI category at industry-specific indicators in the host country's environment.

The IHS Index is actually a country risk assessment, although predominantly political risk. The Index is a composite of political risk (60%), socio-economic risk (20%), and Commercial Petroleum risk (20%), but some of the socio-economic and commercial indicators are employed as political risk attributes in other models.

The variables included in IHS that are counted as political risk elsewhere are 1) War and External Threats; 2) Civil and Labor Unrest; 3) Internal Violence; 4) Regime Instability; 5) Environmental Activism; 6) Ethno-Linguistic Factionalism; 7) Constraints on Foreign Oil Company Investment; 8) Restrictions on Repatriation/Convertibility; and 9) Threat of Adverse Changes in Contracts/Fiscal Terms. Only two variables are strictly economic.

The IHS Index has another important feature that can be transported to other models. It contains a mechanism for segmenting a countrywide risk assessment into a regional breakdown when an industry has only local vulnerabilities. IHS, like PRS, also advises users on how to modify the model to fit a specific firm within the industry.

the IHS Energy Group – set out in 1986 to identify political risks to international oil companies and establish a systematic way in which countries might be ranked and compared according to the risks associated with upstream exploration and production ventures. Out of this effort came the *Country Petroleum Risk Environment Index* – which has gone through several permutations over the years. The index is now a part of the IHS Energy Group's *Petroleum Economics and Policy Solutions* service and is known as the *Political Risk Ratings and Ranking Index*.

THE POLITICAL RISK RATINGS & RANKING INDEX

The IHS Energy Group's *Political Risk Ratings and Ranking Index* is a weighted composite of three distinct indices designed to reflect the potential impact of non-technical factors that affect a particular country's petroleum investment climate: (1) Political Risks; (2) Socio-economic Risks; and (3) Commercial Risks. The weight assigned to a particular index reflects its capacity to affect the country's petroleum environment (for good or ill). Those weights are assigned as follows: Political Risks (0.60), Socio-economic Risks (0.20), Commercial Risks (0.20).

The three indices are comprised of the weighted averages of scores ranging from 0-5 (with 0 signifying no risk and 5 maximum risk) assigned to 11 petroleum risk variables that are grouped under the appropriate index. The score for each index is derived using the following formula:

$$I = \sum_{i}^{n} C_i * w_i$$

where

I = index
w = weights
C_i = score on individual variable
$\sum w$ = 1

The variables used to construct the three indices directly influence the investment or operational climates of upstream exploration plays. In the case of variables based on subjective or qualitative assessments, observations gleaned from surveys conducted with operators familiar with the host country were utilized, as were analyses by political scientists, economists and industry experts and current users; the quantitative economic data were taken from readily available sources such as the International Monetary Fund and World Bank. The various weights are based on the importance of a particular variable or its capacity to affect a country's petroleum environment, for good or ill.

The Political Risks Index (weight = 0.60)

The Political Risk index consists of four familiar variables or indicators that typically form the basis of macro-level political risk assessment:

1. <u>War and External Threats</u>: including conflicts over issues of sovereignty and border disputes (weight = 0.10);

2. <u>Civil and Labor Unrest</u>: including strikes, protests and demonstrations against the government (weight = 0.25);

3. <u>Internal Violence</u>: as evidenced by bombings, assassinations, kidnappings, low-intensity guerrilla warfare and crime (weight = 0.35);

4. Regime Instability: based on the assessed risk of a change in leadership through either a regularly scheduled election or unanticipated development such as a coup or death (weight = 0.30).

The Socio-Economic Risks Index (weight = 0.20)

The Socio-Economic Risk Index consists of four social and economic factors that can adversely affect a host country's investment climate:

1. Economic Instability: based on the performance, liquidity and structural soundness of a country's economy (weight = 0.25);

2. Energy Vulnerability: based on energy supply and demand, dependence on imported oil, and the oil import bill as a percentage of total exports (weight = 0.20);

3. Environmental Activism: based on level of activity and opposition to oil exploration by the environmental lobby (weight = 0.30);

4. Ethno-linguistic Factionalism, based on level of unrest and threat to industry posed by tensions between rival ethnic, religious or linguistic groups (weight = 0.25).

The Commercial Petroleum Risks index (weight = 0.20)

The Commercial Petroleum Risk index identifies certain risks that are neither strictly political nor economic in origin, but nevertheless pose operational constraints:

1. Constraints on Foreign Oil Company Investment: resulting from sanctions, border or sovereignty disputes, interest group opposition, or other government policies (weight = 0.35);

2. Restrictions on Repatriation/Convertiblity: restrictions in the free repatriation of capital and revenues and/or restrictions on currency convertibility (weight = 0.25);

3. Threat of Adverse Changes in Contracts/Fiscal Terms: the threat of unanticipated negative changes in contracts and/or agreed fiscal terms (weight = 0.40).

Recap: A rating between 0 and 5 is assigned according to the perceived significance or actual performance for each of the 11 variables. The score is then multiplied by the weight assigned to that variable. The particular index rating for a country is the sum of all of its weighted scores, with a perfect risk-free score being zero (0) and five (5) signifying maximum risk. Finally, the ratings from the three indices are then weighted again and aggregated to establish the overall rating.

CASE STUDY: BOLIVIA

In early 2000, Bolivia had an overall *Political Risk RRI* rating of 2.03, with political risks rated 2.11, socio-economic risks rated 2.48 and commercial risks rated 1.29. The ratings for the individual variables were as follows:

Political Risks

	Rating		Weight		Score
War/External Threats	1.20	x	0.10	=	0.12
Civil and Labor Unrest	3.10	x	0.25	=	0.78
Internal Violence	2.00	x	0.35	=	0.70
Regime Instability	1.70	x	0.30	=	0.51
Political Risk Rating					2.11

Socio-Economic Risks

	Rating		Weight		Score
Economic Instability	2.70	x	0.25	=	0.68
Energy Vulnerability	0.80	x	0.20	=	0.16
Environmental Activism	2.70	x	0.30	=	0.81
Ethno-Linguistic Factionalism	3.30	x	0.25	=	0.83
Socio-Economic Risks Rating					2.48

Commercial Petroleum Risks

	Rating		Weight		Score
Constraints on Investment	1.20	x	0.35	=	0.42
Repatriation Restrictions	1.40	x	0.25	=	0.35
Threat of Adverse Contract Changes	1.30	x	0.40	=	0.52
Socio-Economic Risks Rating					1.29

Weighting and summing the sub-indices ratings in the following fashion produces the final or overall *Political Risk Ratings and Ranking Index* rating:

	Rating		Weight		Score
Political Risks	2.11	x	0.60	=	1.27
Socio-Economic Risks	2.48	x	0.20	=	0.50
Commercial Petroleum Risks	1.29	x	0.20	=	0.26

Political Risk RRI **Rating**   **2.03**

As a result of Bolivia's *Political Risk Ratings and Ranking Index* rating of 2.03, the nation ranked 64 out of 111 countries covered by the *Petroleum Economics and Policy Solutions* service in 2000. Thus, the client or user has some sense of how Bolivia "stacks-up"against the other 110 countries, and the mere intellectual exercise of reviewing the weights and ratings assigned to the variables requires one to think about the configuration of risks present in Bolivia. Moreover, breaking the index down into sub-parts allows one to see where a country might be particularly strong or attractive, while isolating potential areas of concern. In the case of Bolivia, one can see – based on the ratings assigned – that ethno-linguistic factionalism and civil and labor unrest pose the greatest risks, followed by ecnomic instability and environmental activism

Of course, no methodolgy is perfect, and any indexing scheme presents certain problems. For one thing, any attempt to establish an index requires the generation of a summary measurement, which necessarily entails a condensation of data or information. No matter how sound the weighting scheme, the aggregation of the ratings causes the individual variables or ratings to be muted and the relationship between the variables to be blurred. More importantly, while the index can serve the purpose of establishing a basis for cross-country or cross-regional comparisons, it sheds no real light on the exact nature present in a particular country. That is, regardless of how precisely one defines the variable or risk category, the particular characteristics of the risk will vary from country to country, even if the rating for a particular risk or variable is the same in different countries. And of course there is always the potential for disagreement over the subjectively assigned ratings or the particular weights employed. However, the IHS Energy Group's *Petroleum Economics and Policy Solutions* service is produced digitally and allows the client to change the default weights assigned in the *Political Risk Ratings and Ranking Index*, should some other weight for a variable seem more appropriate.

SUB-NATIONAL RATINGS

One other difficulty is the fact that the variables and ratings are, in many instances, assigned at the macro or country level. In some instances, as is the case with regime instability or energy vulnerability, a rating assigned for the whole country is appropriate. In other instances, though – say, for example, with civil and labor unrest, internal violence or ethno-linguistic factionalism – the risk or threat may be confined to a certain geographic area or exploration operations may be offshore and unaffected by events onshore. Consequently, in 2000, the *Political Risk Ratings and Ranking Index* began incorporating sub-national ratings where appropriate. The scheme is exactly the same as that used in the rest of the *Index* – a 0 to 5 rating scale, with the rating signifying the level of threat or intensity of the variable in a given area and the weight signifying industry presence or interest. So, for example, Angola – which has endured 25 years of civil war – was recently divided into sections and the ratings and weights for Internal Violence assigned in the following way, based on the rationale listed:

Section 1: Cabinda   Rating: 4.0; Weight: 0.40

The enclave of Cabinda is home of most of Angola's current production and is threatened by indigenous separatists.

Section 2: Offshore Angola Rating: 0.5; Weight: 0.35

Offshore Angola has seen significant levels of foreign oil company investment recently but has not yet matched Cabinda's production levels and UNITA rebels pose only a very slim threat.

Section 3: Northwest Angola   Rating: 4.4; Weight: 0.25

The oil center of Soyo, located in northwest Angola, has limited onshore oil production and is occasionally attacked by UNITA rebels (most recently in September 2000).

Section 4: West-Central Angola   Rating: 4.7; Weight: 0.0

This section of Angola has seen the most intense fighting between government forces and UNITA rebels, but has no oil or license holders.

Section 5: East-Central Angola   Rating: 4.0; Weight 0.0

This area has seen less fighting than West-Central Angola, and it has no oil or license holders.

Section 6: Southwest Angola   Rating: 3.5; Weight: 0.0

This area has seen some fighting but has no oil.

Section 6: Southeast Angola   Rating: 3.5; Weight: 0.0

Like Southwest Angola, this area has seen some fighting but has no oil.

Once the ratings for the various sections are multiplied by the assigned weight, the scores are summed and the single rating derived is used for Internal Violence rating. Previously, in 1999, when the Internal Violence rating was applied at the macro level, Angola was assigned a rating of 3.9. Under this current system the rating for Internal Violence is 2.30 – which seems to be a better reflection of the level of threat actually facing oil operators in Angola. This sub-national rating system is applied in the same way to distinguish between northern Algeria (where violence is rife) and the southern half of the country (where there are licenses and oil and natural gas production), different parts of the Indonesian archipelago and the Niger Delta and onshore Nigeria.

CONCLUSION

Winston Churchill once remarked that "the future is eminent, but obscure." Because this or any indexing scheme blurs the variables and cannot say much about the exact nature of the risks present in a country, the *Political Risk Ratings and Ranking Index* can only be used as a tool for comparing countries at the most superficial level. It can only serve as a first step. The political risk assessment process must eventually move toward some effort to understand the exact nature of the risks present in a given country, and to ascertain the manner and extent to which the risks adversely affect a foreign oil company investment. Yet, by breaking the risks down into groups, and assigning certain ratings and weights – even to certain areas in a country – the *Index* forces users to contemplate the configuration of circumstances surrounding a particular investment, in addition to providing some standard for cross-country and cross-regional comparisons. In doing so, the aim is to make the future a little less obscure, if no less eminent.

Chapter 13

Control Risks Group (CRG)

Sandy Markwick

INTRODUCTION

The global economy has presented corporations with unprecedented opportunities in newly emerging economies. New opportunities bring new risks. Political instability and violence persist in many regions. Legal and regulatory infrastructures are often inadequate or opaque and hybrid economic systems dominated by political patronage and corrupt business elites are common. Complexity is compounded by greater accountability demanded of corporate investors from pressure groups and Non-Governmental Organizations (NGOs).

This article discusses the services offered by Control Risks Group (CRG) in the field of business, political and security risk assessment and consulting. It begins with an introduction to the company and describes our basic analytical tools. It then outlines the contents and approach of our customized political risk projects and our online subscription service *Country Risk **Forecast**.*

Control Risks Group (CRG) provides separate macro and micro ratings and political risk advice. It is essentially an attribute-defined model, although decisions and policies are considered – at the micro level.

Macro level risk assessments are obtained in three major areas: Political Risk, Security Risk, and Travel Risk. Each is rated on a 5-point Likert-type scale ranging from "Insignificant Risk" to "Extreme Risk." Political Risk assesses political stability, economic stability, and campaign issues. Security Risk takes into account violent/terrorist groups, crime, and border conflict/border war. Travel Risk covers matters such as crime, the possibility of strikes, terrorism, and war conditions. The CRG ratings cover 118 countries.

CRG accompanies its ratings with customized written assessments and tailors its ratings and reports to micro level risk, i.e., analyzing the particular exposures of individual investing firms in specific circumstances. This coverage of both macro and micro aspects of political risk, along with its contributions on Security and Travel risk, are important contributions from CRG.

ABOUT CONTROL RISKS GROUP (CRG)

Control Risks Group (CRG) is an independent consulting company specializing in political and security risk management. CRG assesses types and levels of risk associated with investment projects worldwide and then recommends strategies to mitigate these risks. The group provides a variety of crisis management, investigative and security consulting services to corporations, governments, financial institutions and private clients worldwide. CRG has offices in London, New York, Washington DC, Mexico City, Bogota, Rio de Janeiro, The Hague, Bonn, Moscow, Tokyo, Manila, Melbourne and Sydney.

The Research Team

Successful political risk analysts are country specialists typically through a combination of living, working and studying in their regions of interest. Linguistic ability is a clear advantage in gaining access to regional sources and an understanding of local culture and people.

The core team of risk analysts at CRG consists of 20 analysts and editors. Typical academic backgrounds are history, economics, regional studies and political science. All the analysts have studied or worked in their specialists regions and re-visit them regularly to deepen their understanding and to develop and maintain contacts. The analysts have a wide network of informal contacts. Sometimes these contacts may be commissioned to contribute their expert knowledge to our reports where necessary.

In addition to the full-time analysts, CRG employs local 'stringers' to provide up-to-date input from the ground and to conduct research at short notice. Stringers may be local or foreign journalists, businesspeople, academics, lawyers or retired diplomats. Stringers are selected for their skills as political observers and understanding of business issues.

The analytical team also benefits from the expertise and experience of our overseas office and consultants from other parts of CRG who are constantly travelling on international assignments.

Final products always undergo a thorough editing process to ensure reports meet high standards of analysis and clarity.

Sources

Our analysts draw on multiple sources to assist their own expert analysis. Analysts draw on their wide range of informal contacts including government ministers, bureaucrats, opposition politicians, activists, local and foreign business people, local and foreign journalists, academics, foreign diplomats, expert economists and other observers such as opinion pollsters. In addition, at CRG we have access to huge quantity of public information available. Since the advent of the Internet, the quantity of information available to the public has increased dramatically. The task of a good analyst is to select high quality information from the bulk of misleading, subjective or irrelevant material.

A similar judgment is required when using personal contacts and confidential sources. Analysts must ask themselves a number of questions:

- Is the source in a position to know?
- Does the source have his/her own agenda?
- Is there any supporting evidence from other sources?

CUSTOMIZED POLITICAL RISK CONSULTING

In political risk, as in most other areas of business, managers and planners have to live with a degree of uncertainty. But uncertainty is not the same as ignorance. Companies who enter high-risk areas without assessing the possible consequences are acting irresponsibly both to their employees and to their shareholders.

Equally, companies who refuse even to consider problem areas may be missing vital opportunities. Investors in a 'dangerous' country where the situation is improving will be a step ahead of their more cautious competitors.

The job of a political risk analyst, like a stock market analyst, is to identify both risks and opportunities – and then to help find ways of turning high risks into high returns.

What issues are addressed in political risk consulting?

Customized analysis is just that – *customized* to the particular needs of clients, usually corporate investors. The scope and consulting varies widely. Clients' concerns may be limited to a single, (though crucial) question. They may be seeking recommendations on the best way to react to events in the host country where an investment is taking place. Alternatively, corporate investors may require comprehensive analysis of risks associated with particular projects *before* committing to large investments. Such reports are proactive and seek recommended long term strategies to mitigate risk.

In-depth political risk consulting involves several components.

- **Macro risk.** Initially, an evaluation of the macro-political and economic environment of the host country is necessary. What is the nature of the government? Is it stable? Do the institutions of government function well? If not, personalities will be more important. Who are the key personalities? Who really makes the decisions and what is their power base? Are investment regulations stable? What pressure is the government and its policies under from the economy, the political opposition or other power groups?

- **Micro risk.** Country risk analysis of this type is a necessary requirement, but is insufficient on its own. Macro political risk analysis should be complemented by an assessment of risks associated with the particular project itself. Who are the winners and losers that will result from the proposed project? What strategies can be implemented to strengthen support for the project? What political conditions exist in the relevant geographic location? What is the relationship between central government and regional government? What is the attitude of local communities to the proposed project? Are there any armed opposition groups in the area? If so, what is their attitude towards the presence of a foreign company? What are the security risks to people and operations?

- Furthermore, micro analysis of a proposed project should determine the best structure for an investment. If a company is involved in a partnership with a local firm, how can you retain sufficient control? What does the company know about its partners reputation, background and political connections. What cultural nuances should a company be aware of when embarking on business transactions overseas?

Forecasting

Political risk analysis is an art, not a laboratory science, which lends itself to precise predictions. Corporate planners look for a basis of comparison, particularly if they have to make a choice between proposed sites. However, numerical expressions of the likelihood of future political events are bound to be problematic because of the number of variants involved. Analysts offer considered judgements, nor measurements. Numerical ratings are of very little value unless they are backed by written, qualitative assessment, to explain how the analyst came to a conclusion.

In our in-depth assessment we prefer to draw up distinct scenarios to help companies build-in contingencies. Scenarios are tailored to the requirements of the client and include 'business as usual' outcomes as well as 'surprise' developments. This process requires historical understanding, but also creative imagination. When drawing up scenarios it is often best to bring together a multi-disciplinary team with a range of approaches. It is illuminating to include, for example, both experts with impressive experience, but who may be stuck in a particular perspective and younger analysts who may perhaps be less blinkered and less respectful of conventional wisdom. Companies can then test their management plans against each of the variant scenarios.

The use of outside consultants to provide regular country assessments and project-based political risk analysis can provide vital objectivity to country and project risk assessments because they have no personal stake in any of the various management options. There can be a tendency within corporations for project managers to become zealous supporters of a potential investment that can blind management to real risks.

Who commissions reports?

Consulting is conducted for small- and medium-sized companies as well as large multinational corporations. One of the effects of globalization has been to encourage smaller companies that were formerly domestic to seek opportunities overseas. In addition, banks providing finance for investment project will seek CRG assessments of political risks before proceeding. Government departments such as investment or aid agencies and transnational organizations occasionally commission reports too.

The are numerous management functions within corporations that commission political risk consulting. Typically, comprehensive assessments of proposed new venture projects will support executives with an international business development function, including strategic planners and project managers. Such reports will also support corporate in-house analysts - a function which may exist in the largest corporations.

Consulting with a more limited scope, perhaps addressing questions of personnel security or asset protection may be conducted for security departments, travel departments or human resources executives. Risk managers too are frequent end-users of CRG reports.

ON-LINE INFORMATION – COUNTRY RISK *FORECAST*

CRG publishes electronically Country Risk *Forecast*, a subscription service with in-depth daily analysis and information of political, security, business and travel issues in 118 countries worldwide. Analysis of key political, security or investment issues in other countries is provided when they occur. In addition, we provide Political, security and travel risk ratings for all countries from Anguilla and Afghanistan to Zambia and Zimbabwe.

Senior management and business development managers use CRF to assess potential new markets and review investment conditions. For security personnel, CRF provides practical examination of risks to staff and assets. CRF also provides authoritative advice to staff who are travelling and helps travelling executives judge the security of a destination or route

Country Risk *Forecast* contains several features designed to help busy executives keep in touch with developments affecting their business and staff from day to day.

What's New	This lists in headline form the issue/developments our analysts are assessing that day.
Executive Update	This is a synopsis of each story in just one paragraph.

Business Travel Update A summary of issues affecting international business travellers currently and in the months ahead.

Each in-depth country file is divided into divided into three main sections:

1. Business Essentials

Risk Ratings   This includes separate risk ratings for political, security and travel risk on our five-point scale of risk: *Insignificant-Low-Medium-High-Extreme*.   (See sample report for definitions)

What Really Counts   A brief overview of the main political and security issue affecting business.

Update   This is our latest forecast/analysis of political, security and travel developments updated daily.

2. Business planner

The Keys   What is the structure and composition of government? Who's who in the opposition? What are the issues and players that drive politics?

Political Risk and Business   Analysis of political stability, economic stability, operations obstacles and external political risks.

Security Environment   Analysis of crime, kidnapping/extortion, violent/terrorist groups, organized criminal gangs and any border conflicts.

Significant Events   A chronology of selected major political and security incidents.

3. Business Traveller

Getting There   Travelling to the country. Major airlines serving the country with a comment on the national airline. Any land routes. Preferred carriers and routes.

Arrival   General information and advice on arrival at the country's international airport(s) - including security and airport procedures; and travel to city centers.

Getting Around   Travel within the country including air, road (taxi and rental cars) and rail. information and advice.

Staying Safe   Recommendations on how not to become a victim of local crime threats.

Businesswomen	Any issues affecting the safety and security of women travellers.
Main Business Destinations	City information and advice, including details of arrival at the international airport and getting to the center, travelling around; any 'no go' areas; advice on hotels.
Practicalities	A range of issues (which vary according to the country) including: language, money, business practice, public holidays, climate, embassy addresses.
Health	Inoculations required, advice, recommended hospitals and doctors (provided by *US Assist*).
Map	A country map with links to and from Main Business Destinations and to adjoining countries.

Other features of Country Risk *Forecast* include:

- **Regional and international issues**
- **Alerts**
- **Worldwide risk ratings**

MULTI-CLIENT STUDIES

CRG prepares a series of special reports for general release. These provide scope for more detailed analysis than is possible in regular on-line services.

- **No Hiding Place.** A special report examining the increasing scrutiny of international business from Non-   Governmental Organizations (NGOs) and pressure groups.

- **Outlook 98.** CRG's annual preview of risks to international business.

- **Other CRG titles include:**

  Oil and Gas Quarterly
  Algeria Monthly Briefing
  Living and working in...(series providing practical information for expatriate employees and their families living overseas).

Turkey Country File – from Country Risk *Forecast*

TURKEY BUSINESS ESSENTIALS

RISK RATING

POLITICAL RISK RATING	MEDIUM
SECURITY RISK RATING	LOW MEDIUM in Istanbul, Ankara, Izmir, Adana HIGH in south-east
TRAVEL RISK RATING	LOW MEDIUM in Istanbul, Ankara, Izmir, Adana HIGH in south-east

WHAT REALLY COUNTS

Foreign companies will find the private sector easier to deal with than the public sector. The private sector has developed strategies for minimising the effects of political instability, patronage and corruption on business operations. These factors, combined with an unstable economy, mean that foreign companies undertaking public-sector contracts face lengthy delays for decisions and payment. Political and economic instability will remain for the foreseeable future. An unwieldy bureaucracy presents investors with serious problems, though successive governments have simplified the investment environment. Foreign companies that offend strong nationalist sensitivities will face difficulties operating in Turkey.

Kurdish separatist terrorism targeting state and tourist-related interests has replaced ultra-leftist and Islamic extremist activity as the prime security threat in western Turkey. Around 20,000 people have been killed in the separatist Kurdish Workers' Party (PKK)'s 12-year insurgency, mostly in the south-east. Travel to the area is unsafe. However, business travellers to Istanbul and Ankara are unlikely to encounter significant difficulties as long as they take sensible precautions.

UPDATE

- ♦ **Government to investigate links between security forces, organised crime**
- ♦ **Court confirms casino ban**
- ♦ **Islamist Refah party banned**
- ♦ **Local environmentalist group blocks mining company**

23 Jan 98
Government to investigate links between security forces, organised crime

Prime Minister Mesut Yilmaz on 22 January said that he would step up official investigations into the links between the security forces and organised crime.

Yilmaz is attempting to control widespread anger at revelations that two members of the security forces were involved in gang killings in December 1997. He is also attempting to counter fears that the government will not carry out an effective probe into 'mafia' corruption. Proof of links between the mafia and the security forces first emerged in late 1996 when a senior police officer and a leading member of a criminal family died in a car crash while travelling in the same vehicle. An initial investigation into links was dismissed as a cover up, forcing the government to sponsor a second inquiry.

Yilmaz indicated that the new inquiry was unlikely to complete its report for some months. However, damaging leaked excerpts from the draft report claim that rival intelligence agencies have been using right-wing organised crime gangs to kill rivals in return for being been allowed to smuggle drugs and run extortion rackets without official interference.

22 Jan 98
Court confirms casino ban

The constitutional court on 21 January rejected a final appeal against legislation banning casinos.

The legislation, which was initially passed in mid-1997, will come into effect from 11 February. It includes foreign-owned casinos, though foreign operators have yet to receive details of compensation, if any, that the government will offer them.

The challenge to the casino legislation was launched in the belief that the legislation, which was introduced by Necmettin Erbakan's Islamist Refah government, would be overturned following the fall of his administration. However, Prime Minister Mesut Yilmaz has continued to support the law. In part this reflects broad Islamic unease at casinos, even within Turkey's secular parties, and the desire to win support from openly Islamist groups such as Refah. More significantly the government is attempting to crack down on the organised crime groups that control of some casinos, which have been used to launder cash from drug sales and other smuggling operations. However, the move unlikely to have a significant impact. It will prove difficult to crack-down on the many illegal casinos, which will be boosted by the ban, that operate alongside the 80 or so licensed gambling centres.

16 Jan 98
Islamist Refah party banned

The constitutional court on 16 January outlawed the Islamist Refah party and banned its leader Erbakan from political leadership for five years for 'acting against the principles of the secular state'.

The decision to ban Refah was expected, and is a warning from the secular political forces in the military and administration to the Islamist movement not to challenge the secular state. However, it falls short of a dangerous ban on Islamist politics that would have risked driving the movement underground.

Although Refah has been outlawed, its supporters have formed a new party known as 'Virtue', which is likely to be allowed to contest the next elections. Erbakan has been banned from high-ranking political office, but has not been banned from political activity altogether. Moreover, support for Islamist parties seems unlikely to dissipate, and the ban may even boost support for them.

Refah successfully positioned itself not simply as a religious party but as a genuine opposition force to the status quo. Its concern for social welfare and its well-organised relief programmes in poor neighbourhoods also won it considerable support. High inflation and growing, localised unemployment seem certain to ensure this support.

However, the loss of its high-profile leader will weaken the party. There is no apparent successor. Refah's organisational capacity will also be damaged, as the state treasury is likely to seize its assets. The military, which has exerted its influence through the courts to have the party banned, much as it did through parliament to have the Refah-led government brought down, will hope that this makes clear the parameters within which Islamic political parties are allowed to operate. Other parties will compete to win Refah's supporters away from the new Islamist political grouping, and many of the 'secular' parties include Islamist elements within them. However, it will take several months to assess their success.

Refah leaders condemned the decision to ban the party as 'political' and claimed that it cast a deep shadow over Turkish democracy. However, they did not call on their supporters to demonstrations, and said that they hoped there would not be violence. Despite their calls, there is a risk of clashes between pro-Refah activists and the police.

Local environmentalist group blocks mining company

A local environmentalist group on 14 January appeared to have successfully prevented the Gutlem Mining Company from developing a lignite mine close to the Kaz Mountain National Park, north-eastern Anatolia.

The small Turkish-owned mining project is of relatively little significance, but the decision to halt the development highlights the growing importance attached to environmental concerns at popular and governmental levels. The mining company believed that it had been granted a licence to mine in the area in April 1997 by the ministry of energy and the mine works general directorate. The culture and environmental ministry did not formally agree the project but is understood to have given tacit approval.

However, local activists launched a campaign against the mine, which would have required the removal of several hundred hectares of trees and plant life in a recognised area of natural beauty. Under pressure from the activists, the ministry of energy appears to have reconsidered the mining licence, claiming that it permitted only a survey of the area, and not extraction. The culture and environment ministry subsequently announced that it would take the entire region under its protection, effectively barring all mining activity.

The local environmentalist movement in Turkey is at an early stage of development and currently lacks the weight to challenge major projects. This is particularly true in cases involving foreign companies, which the government is keen to protect from NGO pressure. However, local groups have had some success in troubling foreign operators. The Eurogold company has had its mining licence endangered by a local campaign group that has used legal and violent tactics against the company.

Links have begun to emerge between local and international environmental groups such as Greenpeace, which has established offices in Turkey. In general, the powerful international campaigning groups have focused on high-profile issues such as a planned nuclear power station in the north-west and the pollution of the Bosporus. However, they have also involved themselves in occasional localised issues - a trend that seems set to continue as they gain wider support and influence.

TURKEY BUSINESS PLANNER

1 - THE KEYS

Key Facts

Structure and composition of government

The Grand National Assembly (parliament) is elected by a modified first-past-the-post system, for a maximum term of five years. Parliament elects a president directly for a five-year term. There is no upper house of parliament. The president invites the leader of the party (or coalition) able to command a simple majority to act as prime minister, and selects a cabinet from ruling party deputies. The president, prime minister, several ministers and senior military and paramilitary officers serve on the National Security Council (known by its Turkish initials as MGK), which has the ultimate say on domestic security and foreign policy. The next general election is scheduled for 2000.

President	Süleyman Demirel
Prime Minister	Mesut Yilmaz
Government	Minority coalition between centre-right Motherland Party (Anap), leftist Democratic Left Party (DSP). Centre-left Republican People's Party (CHP) supports government but not formal member of coalition.
Opposition	Islamist Refah (Welfare) party, centre-right True Path Party (DYP), extreme right Nationalist Action Party (MHP).
International links	Customs union with EU came into effect Jan 1996.

Key Players

- *The military*

The military continues to be one of the most powerful forces in politics and views itself as protector of the Turkish state from internal and external threats. It sees Islamist and radical Islamism as one of the prime threats facing Turkey. Since January 1997 it has attempted to suppress such ideas, including forcing the resignation of Islamist Refah prime minister Necmettin Erbakan in June. The military influences government policy through the powerful National Security Council (MGK). Chief of Staff Gen. Ismail Karadayi and his senior generals would intervene if they believed that Turkey's national and secular identity was under threat. However, this pressure will continue to be applied through legal channels and a military coup is highly unlikely.

- *Mesut Yilmaz and the Motherland party (Anap)*

Prime Minister Yilmaz leads a minority government that was formed under military pressure to prevent Refah from regaining power. The government is likely to prove temporary and will pave the way for early elections in 1998. Yilmaz could emerge as prime minister after this as part of the military's continuing campaign to exclude Refah from power. The struggle to keep his government in power and the lead up to elections means that the government is unlikely to enact economic reforms to address the country's weaknesses (see ECONOMIC SITUATION).

- *Necmettin Erbakan, Refah and conservative religion*

Former prime minister Necmettin Erbakan, the leader of the Islamist Refah party resigned in June 1997 as part of a dispute with the military-led secular establishment. A pragmatist, Erbakan realises that a radical Islamic agenda is anathema to most Turks and presents himself as a moderate. Refah – divided between pragmatists and radicals, traditionalists and modernists – bases its support among religious conservatives who dominate in several Anatolian towns and the first- and second-generation immigrants who now comprise the majority of the population in Istanbul, Ankara and Izmir.

- ### *Tansu Çiller and the True Path party (DYP)*

US-educated Tansu Çiller served as premier from 1993-96 and is now allied to Refah. Her Western outlook tends to reassure secular Turks and the international community. She has survived frequent attempts to unseat her from within her own DYP and the fierce personal animosity with Motherland Party (Anap) leader Yilmaz prevents what many see as a logical merger of the two parties. Her 'betrayal' of the secularist cause, when she agreed to form a coalition government with Refah, lost her much support among her previous power base among urban women. It also angered the military, which is attempting to prosecute her.

- ### *Industry and commerce*

Industry and commerce have played an important role in politics since the 1980s. The giant industrial concerns of Sabanc, Koç and Eczadeba, and the business federation TUSIAD dominate business life, and politicians ignore their opinions at their peril. The trade union federations continue to wield considerable political influence.

2 - POLITICAL RISK AND BUSINESS

Political Stability

The political environment

Civil society and democratic institutions have flourished since the military withdrew from political life in 1983 (following the 1980 military coup). However, government corruption, political patronage, petty party squabbling and the low calibre of senior public officials alienate the dynamic entrepreneurial classes in Istanbul, Izmir and Adana, and obstruct economic development. These problems also contribute to the rise of the Islamist Refah party, which emerged as the largest single party in the December 1995 general elections.

The two largest secularist parties, Mesut Yilmaz' Motherland (Anap) and Tansu Çiller's True Path Party (DYP), agreed in March 1996 to form a coalition. However, personal animosity between Yilmaz and Çiller, combined with shrewd political manoeuvring by Refah, forced the coalition's collapse in June. Çiller then formed a coalition with the Refah but since January 1997, the secular establishment led by the military has attempted to undermine this government. It forced Refah from office in June 1997 and Yilmaz took over as head of a minority coalition.

The military

The military is content to exercise its influence through the powerful National Security Council (MGK). The escalation since 1992 of the Kurdish insurgency in the east and south-east prompted President Süleyman Demirel to give the army a free hand against the insurgents. While prime minister in 1994, Çiller courted the military's approval by dissolving the pro-Kurdish Democracy Party (DEP) and putting all 16 deputies on trial. The move prompted criticism of Turkey's human rights record in Europe and the US.

Islamists vs. secularists

Attempts by military-led secular elements in the political establishment to counter an upsurge in radical Islamist ideas are the main source of political instability. A series of religiously-inspired proposals by Refah, while in power, alarmed the military and led for calls for a clampdown on radical Islamist activity. The military presented a 20-point plan to counter such activity in March 1997. This plan included demands to reform the education system and close religious schools.

Refah Prime Minister Necmettin Erbakan initially refused to implement the plan, but was forced to do so. Interior Minister Meral Aksener in April 1997 ordered provincial governors to crack down on Islamist schools, hostels and other organisations and to dismiss civil servants sympathetic to radical Islamist causes.

The military, with the help of the judiciary, the police and the secular political parties, has maintained the pressure on Erbakan and Refah, which they view as encouraging the rise of Islamism. The state prosecutor asked the constitutional court to outlaw Refah in May as it undermined the secular nature of the state.

The dispute between the secularist and Islamist elements in Turkish politics will continue to paralyse the government for the foreseeable future and perpetuate the weaknesses in the Turkish political system. Turkey has suffered a series of weak coalition governments in recent years that has prevented economic reform and caused widespread disillusionment with the traditional political parties. Economic problems and this disillusionment have fuelled support for Refah, which is expected to increase its share of the vote in the next general election (whenever it is held).

Economic Stability

All major political parties and other key elements in the political system such as the military are committed to an open economy and the principles of free trade. In 1983 the then prime minister, the late Türgat Özal, started the process of economic liberalisation, inspired by the reforms that the then British prime minister Margaret Thatcher was implementing in the UK. Successive Turkish governments have continued the process of economic liberalisation, inspired by the reforms that the then British prime minister Margaret Thatcher was implementing in the UK. Successive Turkish governments have continued the process and created an attractive environment for foreign investors. The results have been a boom in the private sector, especially in manufacturing and the service sector (such as banking).

The economy faltered with a currency crisis in early 1994, but an austerity programme drawn up by then prime minister Çiller, combined with the economy's inherent resilience, turned the situation around by mid-1995. Istanbul is one of the most dynamic business centres in the Mediterranean, and hundreds of foreign companies are making profitable investments in the country. A customs union with the EU makes the country an attractive base for European manufacturing companies looking to exploit markets in Western Europe, the Middle East and the former Soviet union countries.

A series of weak coalition governments since elections in 1995 have delayed the privatisation programme and damaged confidence both in the local business community and among foreign investors. However, the economy remains strong enough to withstand these pressures. Day-to-day bureaucratic management of economic affairs remains good. The tax collection system is efficient, giving whatever government is in power a secure revenue base.

Operational Obstacles

Infrastructure

Turkey's infrastructure is adequate but in many areas, especially rural areas, less developed than in Western Europe, Japan or North America. Most intercity roads are paved but there are few multi-lane highways. This creates hazardous driving conditions as road transport is the main form of moving both goods and people. Major routes, especially the main west-east roads, become very crowded. Goods vehicles and coaches rarely observe speed limits or lane discipline. Rail travel is slow and unreliable. However, numerous Istanbul-based shipping lines serve the long coast line.

Turkey's power-generating capacity has not kept pace with its economic growth and there is an increased risk of power shortages. The government in late 1997 announced restrictions on street lighting to ease pressure on electricity generators. Water and telecommunications services are reliable, even in rural areas. Shortages or interruptions to services are rare and usually the result of unusual weather conditions, earthquakes (common in eastern Turkey) or accidents.

Corruption

Corruption and the Middle Eastern tradition of bahi - a 'share' - play a major role in politics, in the government, in the administration, in business and in the media. Most Turks claim that all politicians and public servants are corrupt. Tansu Çiller faces a parliamentary investigation into allegations of corruption during her three-year tenure as premier. Even investigating commissions into corruption allegations are packed with political appointees.

Business people constantly complain of officials asking for kickbacks, commissions and 'gifts' in return for favours. Tenders for national government as well as municipalities' contracts are unlikely to be awarded to companies that do not respect these unofficial rules. Some companies – often owned by relatives of politicians – win all the contracts for which they tender.

Turkey's privatisation programme is seen as a 'cash cow' for corrupt government officials and business people. The government is committed to privatising most loss-making state economic enterprises but already the media is claiming that the agency responsible for the programme, the OIB, expects bidders to offer money.

Foreign business executives will encounter direct or indirect requests for bribes or benefits at most levels of the civil service. This ranges from customs officers at airports and border crossings, to police officers, the traffic police, officials in state-run banks and bureaucrats.

Contracts and tendering process

The tendering process for public-sector contracts is cumbersome (see bureaucracy) and not transparent. Foreign companies are likely to face requests for bribes. Even if a contract is tendered, changing political priorities caused by budgetary problems may lead to the suspension of contracts. In early 1997 the Istanbul municipality cancelled a contract to install electrical systems in the city's railway system after it had been awarded.

Bureaucracy

Red tape and the slowness of decision-making frustrate investors. Political control of civil service appointments means that politicians give jobs at all administrative levels to supporters. Many senior officials hold their positions as a reward for political patronage, and tenures tend to be tied to governmental changes at municipal, provincial or national level.

Legal shortcomings

The legal environment for investors is considered one of the most favourable in the world. A liberal investment regime has improved further with the establishment in 1996 of a customs union with the EU. Profits can be repatriated freely and tax-free zones in Trabzon, Istanbul, Mersin and Antalya have attracted many foreign firms. Laws are generally well worded and the judiciary is well trained. Although not entirely free of political influence, it is independent in commercial matters.

The taxation system has been simplified and there are plans for further overhauls. Foreign investors benefit from attractive tax holidays.

Human rights issues

There is considerable international pressure on Turkey to improve its poor human rights reputation. The human rights group Amnesty International (AI) issues reports regularly and produces press advertisements highlighting its concerns. AI also attempts to persuade foreign companies with interests in Turkey to pressure the government over human rights, but the organisation has a policy of not calling for boycotts. Foreign, especially high-profile, companies known to operate in Turkey may receive requests from AI to hold discussions and/or to put pressure on the Turkish government. Companies that decide not to co-operate with AI are unlikely to face negative publicity but companies that co-operate discreetly gain some beneficial international publicity.

Exiled Kurdish opposition groups stage publicity campaigns to discourage tourists from visiting the country. These campaigns usually take the form of poster and leaflet campaigns in Western European cities.

Vested interests

Prominent families dominate many Turkish private companies, including large corporations such as the Sabanc and Koç groups. In some cases, such families or companies enjoy monopolies or near monopolies on the supply of goods and services. Foreign companies attempting to break into such markets will face considerable obstacles. There is almost no legislation preventing monopolistic practices (anti-trust laws).

Indigenous peoples

Kurdish groups both in Turkey and internationally campaign for recognition of their rights in Turkey. This campaign takes many forms, from the separatist Kurdish Workers' Party (PKK)'s insurgency, to poster and leaflet campaigns. Foreign business operating in the Kurdish-dominated south-east, where the insurgency is centred, risk attacks on their facilities and personnel.

Campaign Issues

The Turkish environmental lobby is an increasingly important force in politics, and finds a sympathetic voice in the media. International groups such as Greenpeace enjoy growing support among the urban liberal intelligentsia, and have launched campaigns against coastal pollution in the Aegean and the construction of nuclear power stations at Gökova and Akkuyu (in the south-west). Greenpeace in 1996 launched a campaign against Royal Dutch/Shell oil company for alleged environmental pollution at a former installation in the south-east during the 1970s.

Several other environmentalist groups sprang up in the early 1990s. One focuses on pollution of the Bosphorus waterway, a campaign supported enthusiastically by the government. However, the authorities are more likely to adopt a heavy-handed approach, with arrests of demonstrators common.

Uniquely for a Muslim country, dog ownership is high in the towns and cities and animal rights awareness is growing. In 1996 there were even demonstrations against Island animal rights awareness is growing. In 1996 there were even demonstrations against Islamist municipalities summarily killing stray dogs and cats.

3 - SECURITY ENVIRONMENT

Violent/Terrorist Groups

Kurdish separatists
Kurdish Workers' Party (PKK)

Founded in 1974; strength c.15,000; leader Abdullah Ocalan ('Apo'); active in south-east, Istanbul, Izmir, Antalya.

Objective: autonomy for south-east Turkey.

Ultra-leftists
Revolutionary People's Liberation Party-Front (DHKP-C)

Founded in 1994 from remnants of Dev Sol; strength c.2,000; leader Dursun Karata; active in Istanbul, Ankara, Izmir.

Objective: establishment of Marxist-Leninist state

TIKKO

Founded in early 1970s; strength c.500; active in Tunceli, Istanbul.

Objective: establishment of socialist state

Other groups all active mainly in Istanbul:

Turkish People's Liberation Party - Front (THKP-C); Marxist-Leninist Armed Propaganda Unit (MLAPU); Revolutionary Communist Party (DKP); Union of Communist Fighters (KFB); People's Revolutionary Pioneers (HDO); Turkish Communist Labour Party (TKEP); Resistance Movement.

Islamic extremists
Great Eastern Islamic Raiders-Front
(IBDA-C)   Founded in 1993; strength c.1,000; active in Istanbul,
                                           Ankara.

                                           Objective: establishment of Islamic republic

Hezbollah   Founded in 1979; strength c.500; active in south-east.

                                           Objective: establishment of Islamic republic

Islamic Action   Founded in 1987; strength c.300; has Iranian links; ac-
                                           tive in Istanbul, Ankara.

                                           Objective: establishment of Islamic republic

Islamic Jihad of Turkey (IJT)   Founded in 1990s; strength less than 100; active in An-
                                           kara

Ultra-rightists
Grey Wolves   Founded in 1960s; strength c2,000; active nationwide.

Kurdish separatist terrorism

The separatist Kurdish Workers' Party (PKK) embarked on an insurgency against the government in 1984. By 1996 more than 21,500 people had lost their lives. Kurdish demands range from improved civil rights and ethnic recognition to a separate Kurdish nation state. The PKK originally adopted a Marxist platform, but by 1995 was trying to present itself as an Islamic nationalist organisation. The government insists that the PKK is a terrorist organisation and tries to drive a wedge between pro- and anti-PKK Kurds with its system of pro-government village guards. Most secular Turks reject any substantial concessions to Kurdish ethnicity as
inimical to the constitution.

The PKK's leadership is based in Lebanon, Syria and Europe, and this gives the organisation's field commanders a large degree of freedom. The guerrillas operate mainly in remote mountainous areas - the lowlands north of the Syrian border are rarely affected - from which they launch roadblock ambushes against the security forces and, increasingly, civilians. They also frequently raid security installations, police stations and, occasionally, towns.

The insurgency has affected foreign business operations in Kurdish areas, and few companies operate in remote parts of the region. The US oil company Mobil suspended operations at its Selmo field in 1993 following several PKK attacks and extortion attempts. Guerrillas also attacked rigs belonging to Royal Dutch/Shell combine twice in 1993.

In a bid to gain international attention, in 1993 the PKK abducted 19 Westerners in remote areas of the east or south-east, releasing them unharmed after a few weeks. Although the organisation staged only two kidnaps in 1994-95, foreigners and Turkish security force personnel remain prime targets for kidnaps in east and south-east Turkey. Most Western embassies have warned their nationals not to visit the east or south-east unless essential.

The large number of ethnic Kurds in western cities - Istanbul, Izmir, Ankara, Antalya and Adana - provides a fertile breeding ground for PKK recruits and cover for terrorism. Kurdish terrorism affects Istanbul in particular. PKK sympathisers and agents have planted bombs at popular tourist sites, in up-market shopping centres and bus stations, outside Turkish businesses, on cross-Bosphorus ferries and at railway stations.

The PKK has in the past targeted foreign business, and is the prime suspect for a spate of bomb attacks on commercial targets such as Toyota-Sa, the US-owned Bank of Boston, the US-Turkish Koc-Amerikan Bank and Coca-Cola company, and the five-star Marmara Hotel in Istanbul in September 1992.

The PKK also aims to damage Turkey's economy by frightening off tourists. The group's sympathisers staged a series of bombings in places frequented by tourists in Istanbul in 1994 and again in 1995, killing three foreign tourists and injuring more than 40. After repeated warnings, the group planted three bombs in 1994 in the popular Mediterranean resorts of Fethiye and Marmaris. A foreign tourist was killed and nine others were injured. The terrorists struck in 1995 for the first time in Istanbul's central Beyoglu district, which is popular with tourists and the location of many consulates and business premises. A Jordanian and a Turk were killed and several Western tourists were injured when bombs packed with nails exploded in crowded Istiklal Caddesi. In an exceptional incident, ultra-leftists in 1995 held 16 foreign tourists hostage inside the historic Galata Tower in Istanbul during a protest against deaths in police custody. The hostages were released unharmed after two hours. Despite high security, Kurdish separatists planted a bomb in the five-star Marmara Hotel in central Istanbul; in 1994, killing three. Although there were no attacks against the tourist trade in 1996, the PKK is capable of resuming its anti-tourism campaign at any time.

Ultra-leftists

Security force crackdowns and infighting have reduced the ability of ultra-leftist terrorists to strike at Turkish and foreign interests in Istanbul and other western cities. Bombings occur much less frequently than in 1991-92. The arrests in 1993 of up to 100 Dev Sol (Revolutionary Left) members have restricted the group to a handful of attacks, such as the killings of policemen and bombings of state symbols. However, Dev Sol re-emerged following the arrest in 1994 of its leader Dursun Karata in France for the assassination of a former justice minister in Ankara. (Dev Sol adopted the name the People's Revolutionary Liberation Party-Front (DHKP-C) at about this time.)

Although weakened, ultra-leftist groups are capable of inflicting serious damage at any time. DHKP-C gunmen murdered one of Turkey's leading industrialists and two other company employees at the Sabanci headquarters in Istanbul in 1996. Ultra-leftists have also targeted Western and (less frequently) Japanese interests in western Turkish cities, staging small-scale bomb attacks on the US-Turkish company General Motors, the Japanese-Turkish company Toyotara and US and British diplomatic premises in Istanbul and Izmir during 1992. Dev Sol assassinated three Western businessmen (two US nationals and a Briton) in Istanbul and Adana in 1992.

Islamic extremists

Islamic radicalism and extremism flourish on the fringes. The latest active group, the Great Islamic Eastern Raiders-Front (IBDA-C), is suspected of links to hardline nationalists within military intelligence. The group mounts occasional waves of bombings of secularist and state targets in Istanbul and Ankara and, less often, of historic mosques.

Fundamentalist unrest is rare, but can be volatile. Fundamentalists attacked the organisers of a leftist cultural festival in Sivas in 1993. Thirty-six people, including a German tourist, were killed when the mob burnt down a hotel.

Islamic extremists also stage protests against international events. Protesters threw fire bombs in 1995 at the Russian consulate-general in central Istanbul's Beyoglu district in support of the Chechens. Islamic extremists also struck over New Year 1994-95, targeting bars and nightclubs in protest at hotels organising parties to celebrate New Year, a date which Islamists consider to be a foreign import.

Iranian-backed Islamic extremists pose a minor but growing threat in the east and south-east. The main groups, Hezbollah and Islamic Jihad of Turkey (IJT), stage occasional well-planned attacks, usually assassinating pro-PKK journalists, politicians and civilians. The Iranian-backed Islamic Action (IA) in 1993 murdered prominent journalist Ugur Mumcu and narrowly failed to kill Jewish-Turkish business-man Jak Kahmi.

Ultra-rightists

The Grey Wolves is believed responsible for isolated attacks, including the attempted assassination of then prime minister Turgut Ozal in June 1988. The organisation has been increasingly popular since 1993, when membership was estimated at 20,000.

Alevi unrest

The large, mainly secularist Alevi minority is a potential source of unrest. It is increasingly resentful at what it perceives as institutionalised discrimination.. Sectarian unrest involving the Alevi minority flared up in 1995 after a 15-year lull. More than 30 people were killed in four days of intermittent rioting and clashes between Alevis (protesting against perceived state tolerance of Islamic fundamentalism) and the security forces in Istanbul. Widespread public frustration at the social effects of the 1994 economic crisis and government austerity measures fuelled a rapid heightening in tensions after the violence.

Violence flared up again in 1995 when members of a right-wing extremist group fired shots in the air while driving around Istanbul's Alevi-dominated Kagithane district. Two policemen and a protester were injured after locals took to the streets in protest.

Crime

A rise in petty crime has accompanied Turkey's increasing popularity as a European tourist destination. Mugging, car crime and burglaries of residences in Istanbul and other western towns are rising. However, strict policing keeps crime down in most areas. Crime levels in Istanbul are considerably lower than in Western cities of equivalent size.

Foreign companies could inadvertently become involved with organised criminal gangs that have close links with politicians, the security forces and some businesses. Foreign companies should carry out a thorough investigation of potential joint venture partners. Organised criminal gangs also maintain relations with the main trade unions. There is concern that gangs will increasingly attempt to infiltrate legitimate business for money-laundering purposes. In the past, organised criminals have used Turkey's legitimate casino industry for money-laundering. In July 1997 the government announced a ban on all casinos, with effect from January 1998. Organised criminal gangs will be forced to seek other channels for money-laundering.

Kidnapping and Extortion

The PKK occasionally kidnaps Turks and foreigners travelling on main roads in the south-east. Kidnaps are invariably carried out to generate international publicity, and victims are usually released unharmed after a few days or weeks. The frequency of kidnaps peaked in mid-1993.

Border Conflict/Border War

Greece

Turkey's relations with Greece undergo periodic strain, occasionally pushing the two countries to the brink of military conflict. Tensions persist over the control of the Aegean sea and of Cyprus. a resolution of the island's partition - Turkish troops have in effect occupied the north since 1974 - appears as remote as ever, and there is occasional violence along the dividing 'green line'. The EU's decision to ratify a customs union with Turkey in 1995 has not improved Turco-Greek relations, though full-scale war remains unlikely.

Syria

Syria allows the PKK to maintain its headquarters in Damascus as a means of exerting pressure on Turkey, which controls water flowing into Syria through the Euphrates and Tigris rivers. There has been a long-running war of words between the two countries apparently spilt over into a series of bombings in Syria in 1996, allegedly carried out by Syrian Turks backed by Turkish intelligence. However, there is little prospect of bilateral tensions fuelling a war.

The Caucasus

Turkey's ethnic and cultural links to Azerbaijan force it to support the Baku government against Armenian rebels in Azerbaijan's Armenian-dominated enclave Nagorno Karabakh. However, conflict there and other unrest in Armenia, and Georgia are unlikely to spill over the Turkish border.

4 - SIGNIFICANT EVENTS

22 Jan 98
Prime Minister Mesut Yilmaz said that he would step up official investigations into links between security forces, organised crime.

21 Jan 98 W Turkey
Police seize 400lb (183kg) heroin.

21 Jan 98 Ankara
Constitutional court rejected appeal against law banning casinos.

21 Jan 98 Istanbul
US Secretary of Commerce William Daley said that US supported Baku-Ceyhan pipeline.

20 Jan 98 Ankara
Refah MPs reportedly offered greater co-operation with government in return for easing ban.

20 Jan 98 Ankara

Police in Anatolia seized 3,000lb (1,500kg) of narcotics in 1997 according to official figures; government blamed separatist Kurdish Workers' Party (PKK) for drug smuggling.

20 Jan 98 Ankara

Constitutional court reportedly reviewing appeal on decision to ban casinos. Appeal rejected 21 Jan; ban to take effect from 11 Feb.

16 Jan 98

Constitutional court outlawed Islamist Refah party, banned its leader former prime minister Necmettin Erbakan from political leadership for five years.

14 Jan 98

Reports emerged that local environmental group had successfully prevented mining company from operating.

13 Jan 98 Istanbul

Policeman, special forces officer reportedly among 7 arrested for attack on intercity bus in December 1997.

13 Jan 98 Istanbul

Investigation into corrupt tendering process for renovation of Turkish Grand National Assembly building initiated.

13 Jan 98 (Germany) Bonn

Turkish embassy condemned German government's decision to no longer brand PKK as terrorist organisation.

12 Jan 98 Istanbul

Constitutional court froze Refah's funds.

7 Jan 98

Figures showed Turkish exports rose 14% in 1997, debt repayment by 10%.

4 Jan 98 Adana

Security forces foiled leftist People's Revolutionary Liberation Party Front (DHKP-C) attempt to bomb US airbase.

30 Dec 97 Istanbul

Train bomb exploded at Bakirkoy station: 6 injured.

17 Dec 97

Prime Minister Mesut Yilmaz threatened to withdraw Turkey's EU membership bid by Jun 1998 if EU did not review Turkey's rejected application (see 14 Dec).

17 Dec 97 Ankara

Police clashed with 1,000 demonstrating at Court of Appeals for release of 5 students imprisoned for membership of illegal organisation, arrested protesters arriving at city railway station, prevented others from entering by road; around 430 arrested.

15-16 Dec 97

Minister responsible for customs Rifat Serdarolu threatened to boycott tenders from EU companies for customs projects; State Minister Iin Çelebi threatened non-tariff trade barriers against EU goods; leading Confederation of Turkish Labour Unions (Turk-Is) urged boycott of EU goods.

15 Dec 97 Ankara

Prime Minister Yilmaz, Russian Prime Minister Viktor Chernomyrdin signed $13.5bn gas deal supplying Turk$13.5bn gas deal supplying Turkey, other accords on energy sector co-operation, investment incentives, taxation.

15 Dec 97 Mardin prov

12 killed when minibus struck land-mine.

14 Dec 97 (Luxembourg)

EU summit rejected Turkey's bid to begin membership talks or preparatory membership talks; Prime Minister Yilmaz rejected EU's offer of 'Conference of Europe' membership.

11 Dec 97 (N Iraq)

Turkish planes, helicopters attacked suspected rebel bases.

11 Dec 97 Ankara

Turkey announced that it would hold controversial joint military exercises with Israel, US on 5-9 Jan 1998.

10 Dec 97 Ankara

Government comfortably survived no-confidence motion.

10 Dec 97 Istanbul

Crowd gathered to protest against Turkish human rights record on anniversary of Universal Declaration of Human Rights.

9 Dec 97 Istanbul

Prosecutors investigating Istanbul's Islamist mayor for 'provoking hatred' in speeches said prosecution likely.

TURKEY BUSINESS TRAVELLER

5 - GETTING THERE

Air travel to Turkey is straightforward. In addition to state carrier Turkish Airlines (THY), most European and several North American, Middle Eastern and Asian carriers operate direct services to Istanbul. THY and several Turkish private airlines offer connecting services to Ankara, which is the hub of the domestic network, Izmir and more than ten other regional cities.

Land travel is possible, though not recommended. Few business visitors arrive by sea.

6 - ARRIVAL

Major international airports

The main international airport is Istanbul's Atatürk (formerly Yesilkoy). There also are international airports at Ankara, Izmir (west Turkey) and Adana (south Turkey). Dalaman international airport (south-west Turkey) is used mainly by foreign charter airlines.

Airport security

Security at all Turkey's airports is adequate. Passengers are normally required to produce identification to enter airport perimeters and terminals. Passports and flight tickets are generally sufficient. Leave plenty of time to pass through security checks especially at peak times. Passengers and baggage are screened on entry to airport terminals; hand baggage is searched again on entry to departure lounges. Passengers are politely frisked. They must show passports and boarding cards (which are stamped) and complete exit forms. Passengers may be required to identify their baggage on the tarmac before it is loaded.

Airport procedures

British and US visitors need to purchase visas at a marked desk immediately before passport control. Payment is in exact foreign paper currency only: check with consulates for current prices before departure.

On arrival, there are random baggage searches at customs. Officials can be obstinately suspicious about expensive consumer durables (but not cameras). However, Turks and residents are more likely to attract their attention than short-term business visitors.

Travel to and from the airport

Taxis are the best means of transport from the airports to city centres, but the national carrier Turkish Airlines (THY) runs a good, frequent bus service.

7 - MAIN BUSINESS DESTINATIONS

Istanbul

Atatürk airport

Atatürk airport is 15 miles (24km) from the centre of Istanbul. There are three terminals at Atatürk: international, domestic and mixed. The international terminal dates from the 1970s and is often over-crowded. Facilities are basic, though gradually improving. Facilities at the domestic terminal are rudimentary, though adequate. The new, mixed terminal will handle both international and domestic flights. Facilities are of a similar standard to Western airports.

Taxis are the most reliable and convenient form of transport into Istanbul. The journey to the Taksim/Maçka area takes around 50 minutes and costs around $15; to Levent, 55 minutes and around $20. Add on another 25 minutes and $10 for destinations on the Asian side of the Bosphorus. Journey times can lengthen considerably at peak periods and in the evening. Buses are overcrowded and, because of

Istanbul's acute traffic problems, very time-consuming. Several five-star hotels operate courtesy buses: check when booking.

Crime

Crime is not a major problem, but foreign business visitors should beware of pickpockets in Beyazit, the Grand Bazaar and many other tourist attractions. Muggings are possible in Beyolu and around Taksim Square.

Avoid bars in the Beyolu district (at the southern end of Istiklal Caddesi, the main shopping street). Touts lure foreigners into bars with promises of free drinks before presenting them with a bill of around $100.

Getting around

Try to use licensed yellow taxis, though these can be scarce at peak periods (08.00-09.00; 17.15-18.00). Ensure that the driver switches on the meter when setting off, and check the current starting price with local contacts. Drivers rarely speak English: it is advisable to learn basic directions in Turkish, or carry written details of your destination, specifying house number, street and district. Leave plenty of time for travelling to appointments as there is almost continuous traffic congestion in most areas of the city, particularly on the first Bosphorus Bridge. Drivers often refuse a tip unless they have done some special service. Shared taxis (dolmus) are in widespread use, but visitors unfamiliar with the system should stick to individual taxis.

Do not use public buses: they are crowded and unpleasant. a tramway (Metro) runs from Eminonu (near the Galata Bridge) to Aksaray, though it is crowded. There are also train services on each shore, but these do not serve business districts and have been subject to sabotage attacks.

Bosphorus ferries (linking Istanbul's European and Asian shores) are a good way of seeing the city's two halves. The PKK has mounted small-scale bombings and arson attacks against ferries, but further attacks of this kind are unlikely.

Areas to avoid

Women should avoid the red light district of Aksaray. As well as having an unpleasant atmosphere, the area has a higher than average level of sexual attacks. Women should also keep away from the Islamic fundamentalist stronghold of Fatih. Foreign women are often jostled and may suffer verbal and physical sexual harassment.

Protests

Demonstrations – occasionally violent – sometimes occur in the central Taksim Square and outside Sultanahmet Mosque and Aya Sofya Museum (in the south-central Sultanahmet district). All large crowds should be avoided.

Hotels

There are many luxury hotels suitable for foreign business visitors: those in the central Taksim-Harbiye area are most convenient. All major credit cards, except American Express, are widely accepted. Expatriates favour the suburbs along the European shore of the Bosphorus (such as Bebek and

Etiler), the central Macka district, or quieter suburbs on the Asian shore such as Caddebostan and Fener-bahce.

<table>
<tr><td colspan="2">*Recommended hotels*</td></tr>
<tr><td>Conrad</td><td>A US-managed 1990s-built hotel in Beikta, near the newer business districts of Levent and Etiler, though distant from Taksim and the Old City. a popular venue for conferences and seminars.</td></tr>
<tr><td>Çiraan Kempinski</td><td>A sumptuous former Ottoman palace on the Bosphorus, converted into Istanbul's premier hotel in the 1990s. The only disadvantage is its relative remoteness from business and tourist centres.</td></tr>
<tr><td>Istanbul Hilton</td><td>A favourite centrally-located business hotel near Taksim. Built in the 1950s but recently refurbished.</td></tr>
<tr><td colspan="2">*Others*</td></tr>
<tr><td>Divan</td><td>A recently refurbished 1950s-built hotel near Taksim, with famous restaurants.</td></tr>
<tr><td>Hyatt Regency</td><td>US-managed five-star hotel near Taksim.</td></tr>
<tr><td>Parksa Hilton</td><td>A popular four-star 1980s-built hotel near the Taksim-Maçka business districts.</td></tr>
</table>

Business entertaining

Istanbul has numerous restaurants suitable for entertaining business contacts. The PKK has mounted attacks on tourist-frequented restaurants late at night. Therefore, it is best to leave restaurants and nightclubs before midnight - though the PKK only rarely targets upmarket restaurants or hotels - the most notable being a bomb attack in the coffee-shop of the Marmara Hotel (in central Istanbul) on New Year's Eve 1994-95, in which one customer was killed.

Ankara

Esenboa Airport

Esenboa Airport is 19 miles (31km) north of Ankara. If arriving on a domestic flight that connected with an international flight at Istanbul, visitors should ask to be dropped at the international arrivals gate to pass through immigration, retrieve baggage that will have been transferred from their international flight, and pass through customs. Taxis are available immediately in front of the baggage reclaim: the journey to the Gaziosmanpaa, Çankaya and Kavakldere diplomatic and business districts takes around 40 minutes. THY operates a bus to the Ulus area, but this is not recommended for business travellers.

Crime

Streets are generally safe even at night. Shanty town areas (the gecekondus) are not inherently dangerous but are best avoided, particularly at night.

Getting around

Taxis are the most convenient method of transport within the city and are available at most times of the day and night.

Hotels

There is a limited range of international-standard hotels in Ankara. All are located in the government/business districts of Gaziosmanpaa, Kavakldere and Çankaya.

Recommended hotels

Hilton — Well-established 1980s-built five-star hotel in Kavakldere. The meeting place of the Ankara elite.

Sheraton — A 1980s-built round tower hotel situated next to the US-style Karum shopping mall in Kavakldere. Well equipped with business centres and popular with business travellers.

Other

Best Otel — A smaller, four-star hotel situated opposite the US embassy, popular with journalists and business travellers.

Business entertaining

Ankara is shaking off its image as the boring provincial sister of Istanbul. There is an increasing number of international-standard restaurants in the hilly districts of Çankaya, Gaziosmanpaa and Kavakldere, where most expatriates and diplomats live. The restaurants at Ankara Citadel are popular with expatriates and the Ankara elite.

8 - GETTING AROUND

By Air

Turkish Airlines THY

The mainly state-run THY-Turkish Airlines dominates Turkey's domestic and international airline sectors.

Smaller airlines

Smaller carriers - Istanbul Airlines, Onur Air, Sultan Airlines and MAS Air - operate some domestic routes and charter services from European airports.

Safety

THY has a better than average safety record. The airline has one of the youngest fleets in the world, mainly Airbus A-320s and B-737s. Service standards and reliability have improved markedly during the 1990s. The carrier is particularly popular for services via Istanbul to airports in central Asia. Other Turkish carriers tend to operate older aircraft, some of them Soviet-made.

However, as Turkey's 'flag-carrier', THY offices abroad and check-in desks at foreign airports are potential targets for several terrorist groups including Turkish ultra-leftists, Kurdish separatist rebels and Greek leftist extremists. Attacks, which are rare, are typically small-scale and result in only minor damage. They are usually in protest at events in Turkey, such as major clashes between Kurdish separatists and the security forces, or round-ups of ultra-leftists. In Europe, THY offices in Germany, France and Belgium are frequently targeted. Offices in Greece, the Netherlands and the UK are also singled out.

Tight security at THY premises and airports in western Turkish cities reduces the risk of terrorist attacks. Security on board THY aircraft is high, but in-flight attacks or hijack attempts are possible in Turkey and abroad. Security measures on other airlines are similar.

Strike history

The last serious strike action on THY was a five-week stoppage between April-May 1991.

By Road

Turkey has one of the highest traffic accident rates in the world: an average of 30 people are killed every day, a rate much higher than in the UK or France. Most accidents are caused by appalling driving on overcrowded and badly-maintained roads.

By taxi

Travel by taxi is marginally safer than driving yourself in a hired car, though taxis are often involved in accidents in urban areas.

By car

Car hire is expensive: international car hire firms charge around $90 per day at peak times. Basic insurance is usually included, but a collision damage waiver is not. Drivers must carry their licence and car hire documents at all times, and must by law wear front seat belts, though local drivers often ignore this. Visitors should go straight to the nearest police station if involved in an accident.

By public transport

Travel on inter-city buses should be avoided: they are uncomfortable and safety records are poor. Kurdish separatist bomb explosions on three buses outside Ankara in 1994 killed three passengers and injured 20. Kurdish terrorists hijacked an Ankara-Istanbul bus near Kocaeli in 1994, killing two passengers and injuring 26.

By Train

'Express' trains operate between Ankara, Izmir and Istanbul. These are comfortable (first class compartments are air-conditioned) but slow, often taking twice as long as bus services. Travel only on express services, as local commuter trains in and around Istanbul have been the targets of arson attacks. Reservations are recommended.

9 - STAYING SAFE

Crime

Despite the international publicity attracted by the Kurdish separatist campaign against tourism, petty pilfering and bag snatching are the main security hazards for foreign business visitors in Turkey. Crime levels in Istanbul and Izmir are similar to those in many European cities; crime rates are lower in

Ankara. Foreign business visitors should keep an eye on their belongings at all times, and should not flaunt expensive items, like cameras.

Mafia-style organised gangs carry out frequent armed bank robberies in Istanbul: foreign exchange transactions are best carried out in hotels. Street violence is unusual, but it is unwise to get into disputes with locals: these can turn nasty. For example, a dispute between rival tour bus operators apparently prompted the stoning of a bus as it left Antalya airport for the resort of Alanya in September 1993. A British tourist was seriously injured in the incident.

Fraudsters also target foreigners for various scams. The most common involves one or two smartly dressed men, who claim to be plainclothes policemen investigating illegal currency transaction, approaching a foreigner. They demand to see the foreigner's foreign currency and then run off with it or surreptitiously exchange it for scrap paper. Under no circumstances should visitors approached in this way hand over wallets or foreign currency. Instead, they should offer to go to the nearest police station to sort out the matter. This usually deters the fraudsters. Business visitors as well as tourists are targeted for this scam.

The other common scam involves serving drinks that contain a sleeping drug. When the victim regains consciousness, their money and other valuables are missing. This scam usually occurs in downmarket bars that business visitors should avoid.

Urban terrorism

Istanbul and the other major western industrial towns (Bursa, Izmir, Ankara and Adana) are often affected by waves of terrorist bombings. However, the risk of being caught up in incidents is slight as long as you take sensible precautions.

Bombings are the work of Kurdish separatists, ultra-leftists and Islamic activists. Their most regular targets in urban areas are Turkish official and business premises (particularly Turkish banks), offices of political parties and police stations or security force installations. In addition, bombings are sometimes directed at high-profile Western business and diplomatic premises. There are usually waves of attacks during and in the run-up to elections and national holidays, particularly those with political significance (see Significant security dates).

In January 1996 extremists shot and killed two leading industrialists in their headquarters in Istanbul. However, short-stay visitors are unlikely targets. Ultra-leftist assassins typically mount sophisticated surveillance on their intended victims, who tend to be selected because of their position within high-profile companies.

Islamic extremists stage sporadic protests and occasional bombings against perceived Western indifference to Muslim suffering (for example in Chechnya and the former Yugoslavia). Most bomb attacks in towns and cities take place at night, minimising the risk of injuries. Nevertheless, visitors to Istanbul and Ankara should:

- avoid establishments serving alcohol outside the major hotels, particularly those in downmarket neighbourhoods;

- avoid lingering outside Russian, UN and Western diplomatic premises in Istanbul and Ankara because of the risk of fire bomb attacks; and

• change money in hotels rather than in banks because of the risk of being caught up in an attack.

Terrorism against the tourist trade

The main Kurdish separatist guerrilla group, the PKK, aims to damage Turkey's economy by deterring tourists. The group mounted a spring and summer bombing campaign against the tourist trade in 1993 and 1994, and to a more limited extent in 1995. PKK attacks against Turkish and foreign state and business premises in urban areas have generally been intended to cause alarm rather than indiscriminate injuries. However, the PKK has occasionally been ruthless in its campaign against the tourist trade: attacks have taken place in crowded places during the day and some foreigners have been killed.

The PKK threatened to resume its anti-tourist campaign in 1996, but did not stage any attacks. This was largely because of the vigilance of the security forces, who uncovered several plots. There is a significant chance that the PKK will resume its campaign in 1998. If so, it is likely to strike at larger Mediterranean and Aegean resorts such as Antalya, Kuadas, Bodrum, Marmaris and Fethiye. The PKK typically plants bombs in public places and in restaurants frequented by tourists, though in one attack in 1993 a grenade was thrown at a hotel. The group's quest for publicity makes it unlikely to stage attacks in smaller, lesser-known resorts.

The Kurdish insurgency in the south-east

The PKK has kidnapped foreign tourists in the south-east. The victims were seized while climbing on Mounts Ararat (Van province) and Nemrut (Bitlis province), and while travelling on tour buses. The PKK has stated that foreigners are kidnapped because they visit the region without its permission, and has repeatedly warned tourists to avoid the area. However, the real reason for the kidnaps is to publicise the Kurdish cause in the West: hostages are invariably released unharmed. The most recent kidnap was of two Polish-Americans in September 1996, though there are suspicions that the two 'victims' collaborated with their 'abductors' for propaganda reasons.

All travel to south-eastern Turkey is hazardous and is best avoided unless absolutely necessary. Inform your embassy or consulate of travel plans. The safest way to reach the area is by air from Ankara to Diyarbakir.

Road travel in the region should be avoided if possible. If travel is unavoidable, keep to main towns and consult the security forces before visiting remote areas. All foreigners in east or south-east Turkey should obtain an escort from the security forces, even for the shortest journeys. Do not travel on any road after 18.00; guerrillas often plant mines, erect roadblocks, and stage ambushes or holdups. Military or goods vehicles are most affected, but attacks on private cars, including those driven by foreigners, are increasing. Guerrillas tend to detain drivers for short periods before robbing them. The main Idil-Sirnak, Diyarbakir-Malatya and Diyarbakir-Silvan highways are under virtual guerrilla control. The Ankara-Diyarbakir-Tehran (Iran) express train - the 'Kuratan' - no longer operates east of Diyarbakir.

Sectarian unrest

Sectarian unrest involving Turkey's large Alevi minority flared up in Istanbul in 1995 after a 15-year lull. Certain districts of western Istanbul - particularly Gaziosmanpaa - are the likely locations for further trouble, though it is unlikely that foreign business visitors would visit such districts. It is also wise to keep away from Kagithane and Cevdet Paa (on the European side), and Altunizade (on the Asian side). Outside Istanbul, high-density suburbs of Ankara, Izmir and Bursa are most likely to witness any repeat of the March 1995 unrest.

The police

The police can arrest and hold individuals for up to 24 hours without charge for 'suspicious' or 'indecent' behaviour or inability to provide sufficient proof of identity. In practice, they are unlikely to challenge well-dressed visiting business people. Police officers may not speak much English, but are courteous to foreigners. Blue-uniformed Market Police (Belediye Zabitasi) ensure that merchants do not cheat customers.

10 - BUSINESSWOMEN

Turkish men are accustomed to dealing with visiting foreign businesswomen, though the older generation may appear patronising. Many Turkish women work in the financial sector, particularly in Istanbul, and middle-class women usually work until marriage. Women also are reasonably well represented in local and national government, though this mainly confined to the 'liberal' western cities. However, women at senior executive level are rare – politician Tansu Çiller is a novelty – and traditional roles are predominant in rural areas.

Businesswomen travelling alone are likely to encounter attitudes similar to those in southern Europe. Outside the main hotels, a woman eating alone will feel uncomfortable at best and harassed at worst, though travelling alone in taxis or by air should not present particular problems.

It is never wise for a woman to walk around after dark, though violent sexual attacks against women are rare outside traditionally dangerous areas of Istanbul. In an exceptional series of events, three Dutch women tourists were raped and had their throats slit near the Mediterranean resort town of Alanya in May 1995. The women were kidnapped while travelling in a minibus, which had picked them up outside their hotel. Two days earlier, a Russian dancer was raped and murdered on the Alanya-Manavgat road. Police arrested the minibus driver and three accomplices for the attacks.

11 - PRACTICALITIES

Language

Most Turkish business people and administrators have spent periods studying or working abroad and have a good working knowledge of English or German. Similarly, visitors are unlikely to encounter language problems with hotel clerks or company receptionists, though a few words of Turkish will always be appreciated. It is a good idea to familiarise yourself with Turkish pronunciation, particularly with regard to placenames.

Money

Turkey's spiralling inflation rate means that US dollars and German Deutschmarks are an unofficial second currency to the Turkish lira. Visitors should take time to familiarise themselves with currency denominate Deutschmarks are an unofficial second currency to the Turkish lira. Visitors should take time to familiarise themselves with currency denominations, as the multiples of million liras are confusing at first. Private exchange shops and hotels are the best places to change money. It is best to change small amounts as rates can go up and down at short notice. In Istanbul, many souvenir shops and hotels quote their prices directly in US dollars or other foreign currency. Only use well-known traveller's cheques as you are likely to encounter problems with lesser-known brands. Most credit cards are accepted in main business centres.

Communications

The internal and international telephone service is reliable and comparable to the West. However, call charges are steep and hotels often add a surcharge. Telephone directories are widely available but difficult to use without some knowledge of Turkish.

The postal system is generally comparable to that in most Western countries. Fax machines are common in main business centres and in all business-class hotels. It is best to post letters through hotels rather than trusting street boxes (they can easily be mistaken for garbage cans).

Other information

The Islamic environment

Although run on a secular basis, Turkey is a predominantly Muslim country. The big cities are cosmopolitan and attitudes are generally similar to those in the West. Most urban middle-class Turks drink alcohol and dress as they would in any Western city, though it is a good idea to err on the side of caution. Do not wear shorts or revealing T-shirts in public and in smaller places. Islamist-run municipalities in Istanbul, Ankara and elsewhere often impose stricter drinking laws. During the Muslim fasting month of Ramadan attitudes are relatively relaxed, particularly in main cities. However, visitors are advised to be discreet and should not smoke, eat or drink out of doors, especially in strongly Islamic provincial towns like Konya. Never imitate or otherwise draw attention to the ezan (call to prayer).

Local taboos

There are laws against insulting or mocking the 'father' of the Turkish Republic Kemal Ataturk, the Republic, the Turkish flag and even Turkish currency. Offenders, including foreigners, can be arrested. Turks will be deeply offended by a jocular comment about the 'father' of their Republic, even in private. Visitors should apologise at the first sign of offence.

Turkey does not acknowledge that an Armenian state existed within its current borders and bans all atlases and maps that show otherwise. Turks are highly sensitive to allegations about the 1915 Armenian massacre: all discussions relating to Armenia should be avoided. Kurdish culture is suppressed and Kurds are seen only as 'mountain Turks'. Discussion of the Kurdish issue may invite accusations of peddling Kurdish propaganda and could lead to your arrest. Turks also are sensitive about their country's human rights record - avoid criticising Turkey's treatment of political prisoners or Turkish jails.

Business hours

	Mon-Fri	Sat
Banks	08.30-12.00; 13.00-17.00	
Offices	08.30-12.00; 13.00-17.30	
Shops	Ankara 09.00-12.00; 13.30-19.00	Ankara 09.00-12.00; 13.30-19.00
	Istanbul 09.00-13.00; 14.00-19.00	Istanbul 13.00-20.00

Public holidays 1998

1 Jan	New Year's Day
30 Jan (approx)*	Seker Bayram (Eid al Fitr)
8 Apr (approx)*	Kurban Bayram (Eid al-Adha)
23 Apr	National Sovereignty and Children's Day
19 May	Youth and Sports Day
30 Aug	Victory Day
28 Oct (half day), 29 Oct	Foundation of the Turkish Republic

* denotes holidays that begin on the afternoon of the previous day. Seker Bayram celebrates the end of the fasting month of Ramadan. Like Kurban Bayram, its date is approximate and depends on sightings of the moon.

Note: the weekend in Turkey runs from Saturday morning to Sunday night. All official departments and most businesses are closed on Saturday.

Notable dates

30 Dec 1997-29 Jan 1998
19 Dec 1998 - 17 Jan 1999 (approx)

Ramadan. During Ramadan, business hours are shortened. However, restrictions on eating, drinking and smoking in public during daylight hours are much less widespread than in other Islamic countries, and less strictly enforced in business centres than in rural areas.

Significant security dates

21-24 Mar

Nevruz (Nowrouz - Kurdish New Year); upsurge in anti-government guerrilla activities in Kurdish areas.

1 May

May Day; large rallies in all main towns, cities, risk of street clashes, ultra-leftist terrorist attacks.

16 Jun

Anniversary of general strike (1970); terrorist attacks on Turkish state targets possible.

15 Aug

Anniversary of start of Kurdish insurgency (1984); probable upsurge in anti-government guerrilla activities.

11 Sep

Anniversary of military coup (1980); attacks by extreme right-wingers possible.

Climate

The Marmara and the Aegean and Mediterranean coasts have a typical Mediterranean climate with hot summers and mild winters. Winters can be severe in the central Anatolian plateau and in the Eastern highlands.

Maximum temperatures in Istanbul: January 46F (8C); July 82F (28C)

Embassy addresses in Ankara
Country telephone code: +90; city telephone code: 312

Australia	Nenehatun Caddesi 83, Gaziosmanpasa, Ankara 06680
	Tel: 436 1180
Belgium	Mahatma Gandi Caddesi 55, Gaziosmanpasa, Ankara
	Tel: 446 8247
Canada	Nenehatun Cad. 75, Gaziosmanpasa
	Tel: 436 1275
Denmark	Kirlangiç Sokak 42, 06700 Gaziosmanpasa, Ankara
	Tel: 468 7760
Finland	Farabi Galip Dede Sokak 1/20, PO Box 22, Kavaklidere, 06692 Ankara
	Tel: 426 5921
France Paris	Caddesi 70, Kavaklidere, Ankara
	Tel: 468 1155
Germany	Atatürk Bulvari 114, Kavaklidere, TR 06540 Ankara
	Tel: 426 5465
Ireland	*see Istanbul listings below*
Italy	Atatürk Bulvari 118, Ankara
	Tel: 426 5460
Japan	Resit Galip Caddesi 81, Gaziosmanpasa, Ankara.
	Postal address: PO Box 31, Kavaklidere, Ankara
	Tel: 446 0500
Korea (South)	Cinnah Caddesi Alacam Sok 5, 06690 Cankaya, Ankara.
	Tel: 468 4822
Netherlands	Ugur Mamcu Caddesi 16, Gaziosmanpasa, 06700 Ankara
	Tel: 446 0470
New Zealand	Level 4, Iran Caddesi 13, Kavaklidere 06700 (PO Box PK 162 Kavaklidere 06692) Ankara
	Tel: 467 9054
Norway	Kelebek Sokak 18, Gaziosmanpasa, (PK 82-06692 Kavaklidere) Ankara
Spain	Abdullah Cevdet Sokak 8, 06680 Çankaya, Ankara
	Postal address: PK 48, 06552 Çankaya, Ankara
	Tel: 438 0392
Sweden	Katip Celebi Sokak 7, 06692 Kavaklidere, Ankara
	Tel: 428 6735
Switzerland	Atatürk Bulvari 247, Kavaklidere, Ankara
	Tel: 467 5555
UK	Sehit Ersan Caddesi 46/A, Çankaya, Ankara
	Tel: 468 6230
US	Atatürk Bulvari 110, Ankara
	Tel: 468 6110

Consulate addresses in Istanbul
City telephone code: +212

Australia	Tepecik Yolu 58, Etiler, Istanbul Tel: 257 7050
Belgium	Siraselviler Caddesi 73, 80060 Taksim, Istanbul Tel: 243 3300
Denmark	c/o Vitsan, Bilezik Sokak 2, Findikli, 80040 Istanbul *Postal address*: PO Box 689, Sisli, 80255 Istanbul Tel: 245 0385
France	Istikal Caddesi, Taksim, Istanbul Tel: 243 1852
Germany	Inönü Caddesi 16-18, Istanbul Tel: 251 5404
Ireland	*Honorary Consul* Cumhuriyet Caddesi, Pegasus Evi 26/A 80200, Harbiye, Istanbul Tel: 246 6025
Italy	Tom Tom Kaptan Sokak 15, 80073 Istanbul Tel: 243 1024
Japan	Inönü Caddesi 24, Gumussuyu, Taksim, Istanbul Tel: 251 7605
Netherlands	Istikal Caddesi 393, Beyoglu, PO Box 39, 80072 Istanbul Tel: 251 5030
New Zealand	Level 24, Maya Akar Center 100/102, Buyukdere Caddesi, Estentepe 80280, Istanbul Tel: 275 2989
Norway	Kemakes Caddesi 227, Frank Han 3rd floor, Karaköy, Istanbul
UK	Mesrutiyet Caddesi 34, Tepebasi, Beyoglu, PK 33 Istanbul 80072 Tel: 293 7540
US	104-108 Mesrutiyet Caddesi, Tepebasi, Ankara Tel: 251 3602

12 - HEALTH

U S Assist City Profile - Turkey (Istanbul, Izmir)

Important: Every effort has been made to assure the accuracy of the information contained in this document at the time of preparation. This document is reviewed and updated every 6 months; however, information is subject to change over time. For additional information regarding U S Assist services, contact a U S Assist Corporate Account Executive at (301) 214-8200.

Istanbul

Date Prepared: 1 November 97 (expires: 1 November 98)

Important: This document is reviewed and updated every 6 months; however, information is subject to change over time. For additional information regarding U S Assist services, contact a U S Assist Corporate Account Executive at (301) 214-8200.

Overview

The quality of medical care in Turkey varies significantly depending on the city and medical facility. Istanbul offers the highest level of care in Turkey.

There can be a significant decline in the quality of medical care provided at facilities outside of Istanbul. In Izmir, medical care is below standards found in the U.S. English-speaking physicians are not readily available. Appropriate selection of a physician, clinic, or hospital may help avert medical problems and reduce risks during an emergency.

Hospital/Emergency Care

It is recommended that you do not receive medical care at the public hospitals, unless absolutely necessary as in the case of a medical emergency. Private hospitals offer the best care in the region and should be the primary resource for American expatriates seeking care even though there may be closer public hospitals. If you are in need of emergency medical care after hours, the hospitals have 24-hour Emergency Rooms.

The information provided is a referral and not a recommendation. Although the provider meets the standards required in our selection process, *U S Assist* cannot be held responsible for an individual's performance.

Hospital

International Cinar Hospital
Istanbul Street 82
Istanbul
Tel. (90 212) 663-3000, 900-1530
Fax 663-2862

Ege University Hospital
Poskot 35100
Izmir
Tel. (90 232) 388-1880

Outpatient Care

Outpatient care should be sought with physicians who are associated with private hospitals including the hospitals listed on this document. They generally spend most of their time at the hospital. Doctors in all specialties maintain private consulting rooms within the hospital itself and outpatient visits can be scheduled within a day or two for minor or routine medical consults. Most physicians have advanced training in Germany, the U.K. or the U.S. and most are fluent in English.

U S Assist clients have access to international hospital and physician referral services. For more detailed information regarding *U S Assist* services, contact a *U S Assist* Account Executive at (301) 214-8200.

Dental Care

A complete dental exam prior to travel and on each visit to the U.S. is recommended. Based on infection considerations, specifically lack of water purity and standardized instrument sterilization, dental care in Turkey is questionable and *U S Assist* cannot endorse the quality or safety of dental care in Izmir. The decision to seek dental care must be based upon the risks balanced by the benefits of invasive dental care. You should see a medical doctor for treatment of pain and return to Western Europe for definitive care.

Pharmaceuticals

Istanbul has a large number of pharmacies. There are pharmacies open nights, weekends and holidays in Izmir and in every district of Istanbul. All local pharmacies keep a sign in their windows showing the nearest open pharmacy during non-business hours. The variety of drugs stocked in the Turkish pharmacies is comparable to that of Europe and most foreign brand drugs are manufactured in Turkey under license from the American or European manufacturers. Generally, Turkey is very lenient about over-the-counter medications. Most drugs can be purchased without a prescription.

It is always advisable to bring an adequate supply of all prescriptions. U S Assist clients have access to emergency prescription replacement services. For more detailed information regarding U S Assist services, contact a *U S Assist* Account Executive at (301) 214 8200.

Required Immunizations

There are no immunizations that are required for entry into Turkey. U S Assist clients have access to immunization recommendations customized for each individual traveller and trip. For further information, contact a *U S Assist* Corporate Account Executive at (301) 214-8200.

Food and Water Precautions

Food and water borne diseases are the number one cause of illness to travellers in this region. Exercising caution with food and water can help reduce the risk of getting traveller's diarrhea and other infectious illnesses. Avoid drinking tap water and using ice cubes. Drink bottled water or commercially canned or bottled beverages that have not been previously opened. Beverages made with boiled or purified water are safer. Use boiled or canned milk; milk bought at the market is likely to be unpasteurized. Buy unpeeled fruits and vegetables; peel and cook them yourself before eating. Cook meats well before serving; eat only meats that have been cooked thoroughly and recently, not rewarmed. As a general rule, avoid salads, dairy products made with unpasteurized milk, and food cooked at roadside stands.

Insect Precautions

Many diseases are transmitted by the bite of infected insects. The first line of defense is to wear protective clothing; the second is to use repellent on the exposed areas of skin. The most effective repellent contain DEET, an ingredient found in most insect repellents. Repellents should be used according to label directions and sparingly on children.

Risk Definitions

POLITICAL RISK

Insignificant

The government is stable and there is a high degree of political continuity. There are no significant extra-constitutional threats to the authority of the government AND there is no arbitrary treatment of business by government or in the courts.

Low

Political and commercial institutions are strong. Any changes of government are likely to take place through constitutional process. Political and economic stability is secure enough to withstand occasional internal disputes or outbreaks of unrest AND courts and other government authorities respect business rights.

Medium

Political and economic stability is secure in the short term but cannot be guaranteed in the longer-term because political and state institutions lack authority or are evolving OR the economy is weak. Legal guarantees are weak. In some Medium risk countries there is a latent threat of military or other illegal intervention.

High

Political, economic and legal institutions are highly vulnerable or have ceased to function effectively. The government could be ousted by non-constitutional means OR the government is only maintained in office by the presence of international peace-keeping force.

Extreme

Law and order has broken down and government has ceased to function outside very narrow circles: the economy is in ruins. There are no protections for foreign business except possible political patronage.

SECURITY RISK

Insignificant

Virtually no politically-motivated violence, and a low level of violent crime. However, extremely isolated attacks by foreign terrorists may occur.

Low

Occasional violence perpetrated by terrorists or criminals. This affects companies or individual members of their staff only infrequently.

Medium

Internal unrest or violence frequently perpetrated by terrorists or criminals, though there are no areas completely outside the state's control. Violence occasionally affects companies or individual members of their staff, but there is no sustained threat directed specifically against foreign companies.

High

There is a sustained campaign of terrorist or criminal violence specifically directed against companies' personnel and property OR there is a high risk of collateral damage from attacks on nearby targets. There is a probability - not a possibility - of encountering security problems.

Extreme

The government is unable to maintain law and order. In extreme cases conditions verge on war or civil war. Business operations become untenable or are set to become so. Foreign companies must strongly consider withdrawal.

TRAVEL RISK

Insignificant

The crime risk is very low. No terrorist groups are active and, although isolated incidents are possible, the security threat to travellers is minimal.

Low

There are occasional demonstrations or terrorist incidents, but these provide no more than incidental threats to business travellers. There is a limited amount of criminal activity but this provides little risk to travellers provided they exercise common-sense discretion.

Medium

There is a high crime rate in certain areas or significant political unrest which could disrupt business travel at short notice. Terrorist attacks occasionally disrupt travel.

High

A terrorist campaign or high levels of violent crime directly affect business travellers. Business travel is possible, but only after careful planning.

Extreme

Conditions of war or civil war exist or are about to: law and order are in imminent danger of breaking down. It is strongly advisable that travel should be avoided.

Appendices

Appendix A
"Internet Resources for Country & Political Risk Analysis"
by Doris Walsh, Toni Siragusa, and Llewellyn D. Howell

Appendix B
"The Overseas Private Investment Corporation:
A Management Application—MidAmerican Energy in Indonesia"
By Llewellyn D. Howell

Appendix A

Internet Resources for Country & Political Risk Information
Doris Walsh, Toni Siragusa, and Llewellyn D. Howell

Though not an all-inclusive list, the following websites represent a useful start for anyone gathering information related to country and political risk through the Internet. The websites listed below are divided into four sections:

a) Websites for the firms represented in the chapters of this book
b) Sites that relate to other firms dealing with political or country risk assessment
c) Sites that provide economic statistics, country market data, and risk data
d) Academic websites related to political risk, including specific courses or syllabi

All sites were active in early 2001, but may have changed addresses since then or been removed from the Internet over time.

How to use the addresses:

Each of the addresses given follows the initial http:// in a URL. If there is no "www" indicated, do not add one; simply type the address following the http://.

Firms Represented in *The Handbook,* 3rd Edition

www.icrgonline.com

International Country Risk Guide (ICRG) is a journal of financial, political and economic risk in 140 countries. The publication also includes extensive statistical tables to help customers forecast risk. The PRS Group, Inc., publishes ICRG on a monthly basis, on the Internet, in print, and on CD-ROM. The journal and risk ratings tables are fee-based, but the journal includes the tables.

www.beri.com

Business Environment Risk Intelligence (BERI) is a private source for risk ratings, analyses, and forecasts for over 140 countries. Economic, financial, monetary, operating, and political conditions are integral components of the zero (worst case) - 100 (best case) system for assessing countries. BERI provides reports on 50 countries three times a year that are written by professionals who are area experts. Fee-based.

www.eiu.com

The Economist Intelligence Unit (EIU) offers fee-based analyses with forecasts on the political, economic and business environment for over 180 countries. Based in London, their reports are written with the help of "information gatherers" worldwide and edited by area experts.

www.euromoney.com

Euromoney magazine's website offers online fee-based subscriptions, the site also has free links to back issues from 1995 onward and editorials on current events by staff members. Also has free information available on several countries and financial instruments.

www.moodys.com

Moody's Investors Service (Moody's) is a fee-based company, which employs financial analysts to research and analyze mainly fixed-income securities. Their publications include credit ratings on securities and obligations for both private firms and sovereign nations.

www.rundtsintelligence.com
S. J. Rundt & Associates, Inc., is a 48-year old consulting and publishing firm dedicated to helping multinational companies, exporters, importers, banks and investors assess risks and opportunities in their international strategies and transactions. Their reports cover over 185 countries. Some of the weekly *World Business Intelligence* publication is available to read on the website. Fee-based.

www.standardandpoors.com
Standard and Poor's is a rating, research, and risk analysis firm assessing the international financial marketplace. Not only do they provide credit ratings and risk analyses for companies and mutual funds, they also offer risk management consulting and databases. Fee-based.

www.iimagazine.com
Institutional Investor's Online Magazine covers issues ranging from global money management to bonds to emerging markets. There are links to reports and articles that are a good resource for international finance research.

www.bankofamerica.com
Bank of America's World Information Services offers country outlooks on over 30 countries. Their website does not have sample entries, but is a good resource for learning more about the company and the many services it offers.

www.prsgroup.com
The PRS Group, Inc., offers a complete overview of its publications and services, including details about its two forecasting services, Political Risk Services and ICRG, and sample publications. The site has sample reports for all of its publications available after a quick registration. Some of PRS's services are cross-referenced in this index.

www.prsonline.com
Launched in 2001, this new website is a joint venture of The PRS Group, Inc., and CountryWatch.com. The site combines PRS's Political Risk Services Country Reports (country analysis and forecasts, economic data and forecasts) with CountryWatch.com's comprehensive political, economic, cultural, business, and environmental information and data, as well as its unique CountryWire™ service. Fee based.

www.ihsenergy.com
IHS Energy Group is a company that provides the energy and petroleum industries with information, analysis, databases and consulting. They have dozens of different products, specifically, the Country Petroleum Risk Environment, which is a county and industry specific political risk appraisal. The website has samples of their services but no additional links.

www.crg.com
Control Risks Group (CRG) assists its clients in understanding and dealing with political, security and operational risks. These range from government stability and the threat of terrorist attack to the influence of rival interests on local decision-makers, organized crime, corruption, and the challenges posed by pressure groups.

Other Firms/Organizations/Groups Related to Political Risk

www.macivorgrant.com/Risk/polrisk.asp
MacIvor Grant is a consulting firm that produces political risk analyses, business intelligence, corporate investigations, and crisis management support for customers worldwide. Includes political and security risks as well as trade and pressure group risks. Focused on emerging markets. Fee-based.

www.s2a.com
Summit Analytical Associates provides analytical expertise and tools to analyze public policy and manage political risk exposure and capitalize on opportunities in emerging markets. They offer fee-based reports on political risk in emerging markets.

www.aon.com
Aon is a Fortune 500 Company - insurance brokerage, risk management products and consulting, personal lines, warranties, and human resources services and consulting. A political risk office is located in Aon Risk Services, Aon Trade Credit. Fee-based services.

www.ilprc.com
International Legal & Political Risk Consultancy identifies and prepares its clients for risks associated with global business management in Australasia, East Asia, and North America. Focus is on import/export and high technology. Offers fee-based reports.

www.asiarisk.com
Political and Economic Risk Consultancy, Ltd. (PERC) is a consulting firm specializing in strategic business information and analysis for companies doing business in the East and Southeast Asia. PERC produces a range of risk reports, paying attention to variables such as corruption, intellectual property rights risk, labor quality, and other systemic strengths and weaknesses.

www.political-risk.net
The site is a contact point for services related to political risk assessment training and education. Through the site maintained by Howell International, Inc., firms may arrange for lectures, seminars, workshops, courses, and consulting on questions of political risk assessment or analysis. Fee-based services.

members.aol.com/infomundo/index.htm
Website for Infomundo Publishing, through which two instructional tools may be obtained: The Country Risk Tool Kit and the International Quantitative Analysis Tool Kit.

www.delcredere.be
Ducroire/Delcredere is a Belgian company that offers political risk and financial insurance and services. The company offers a risk assessment for 238 countries as well as a review of the international press, which is updated daily. Country risk is determined by assessing a combination of the type of commercial transaction (export credits or investments), the nature of the risk (political events/foreign currency shortage or general state of suspension of payments in the country), and the credit period (less or more than 1 year). The site also includes an insurance premium calculator for non-payment risk on export credits.

Data Sources

Government-related organizations providing data

www.oecd.org
This is the official web site of the Organization for Economic Co-operation and Development. Basic indicators are included for all OECD countries as well as a synopsis of economic surveys for countries as they are released.

www.un.org
This is the starting place for UN statistics for the analysis of socio-economic development at the world, regional and country levels. Provides information on hundreds of issues ranging from human rights and social development to animal breeding. This fabulous free resource has listings by department and by subject for easy access. Available in several languages.

www.worldbank.org
Through this site you can access World Bank statistics on most countries of the world as well as ordering World Bank publications that include thousands of data items for most countries of the world.

www.stat-usa.gov
A service of the U.S. Department of Commerce, this site provides access to many U.S. government reports and links to other U.S. government sites. Some information is fee-based. Divided into two sections: global trade and country economic data.

www.census.gov
The U.S. Census Bureau site provides links to statistical sites for most countries that have such a site. These country statistical sites often have the most up-to-date releases of economic information as well as press statements from government officials, etc. Many developing countries have much better and more up-to-date materials on their web sites than can be found in printed materials.

www.cia.gov/cia/publications/facttell
This site takes you to the Central Intelligence Agency's *World Factbook,* a brief statistical overview of countries around the world. It includes a useful narrative of the current political economy, but will need to be supplemented by one of the other sites suggested that is more up-to-date on current events.

www.opic.gov
Website for the Overseas Private Investment Corporation (OPIC), an agency of the U.S. government. Contains information on political risk insurance and a list of web resources for each country in which they provide insurance for U.S. companies.

www.efic.gov.au
The Export Finance & Insurance Corporation (EFIC), the Australian equivalent of OPIC. EFIC offers political risk insurance for a few variables: currency inconvertibility, expropriation/confiscation, and war/civil damage. Also contains links to Australian government websites.

Non-governmental sources.

Most of these sources are fee-based. Some sites simply provide more detailed information about a consultancy or company's offerings; others include data or the possibility of actually downloading a report.

www.countrywatch.com
CountryWatch.com covers 191 countries, providing comprehensive political, economic, cultural, business, and environmental information and data, including its unique country-specific *CountryWire* ™ service that offers daily-updated news from 10 newswire services. Fee based.

www.euromonitor.com
Euromonitor publishes an annual *World Economic Factbook* that includes 207 countries covering demographic and economic factors as well as descriptions of the political situation and the most recent election. This web site also includes information on myriad industry-specific reports that Euromonitor publishes, all fee-based.

www.worldopinion.com
This site from Survey Sampling, Inc. in Westport, Ct., includes hundreds of links for market research and opinion polling organizations as well as releases of the latest data from opinion polls around the world, many of which are political or security related.

www.transparency.org
This is Transparency International's home page. TI is an NGO monitoring levels of perceived corruption worldwide. Although not about political risk specifically, this site examines an important variable from most political risk models: corruption. Contains a world ranking of corruption by country and an index of other sites for organizations dedicated to fighting corruption worldwide.

www.cpss.org
A non-profit organization, The Center for Political and Strategic Studies is dedicated to educating the United States public about complex international and domestic events. They offer publications and symposiums. The publications are available for free on the website.

tradecredit.aig.com
American International Group's (AIG) website on insurance for companies investing abroad includes specific political risk sections with periodic and specific reports from AIG's country risk analysts. Offers country risk analyses for a fee; provides example analyses.

www.steningsimpson.com.au
This is a good place to look for events that have happened in the past 24 hours. The site is maintained by Stening Simpson Group, political risk insurance brokers based in Australia. Offers country risk ratings and world alerts. Fee based.

kins.kroll-ogara.com/
Timely and focused risk assessments on a range of security concerns including crime, political instability and terrorism. Informative travel advisories help clients plan safe, hassle-free trips to nearly 300 cities worldwide.

www.countrydata.com
Current and historical data for 140 countries. Includes historical economic data and risk ratings for most countries. Trend data on 25 separate economic indicators available by month, year, item, and country. The site also offers 26 ICRG monthly risk indicators (including historical data back to 1984) and 24 current risk indicators from Political Risk Services in nearly any combination. A service of The PRS Group, Inc., the publishers of this handbook. Fee-based.

www.stratfor.com
Stratfor's website provides regular news reports on critical current issues. Although the longer reports are subscription-based, short updates can be obtained free of charge. Useful in keeping up with critical world events.

www.keesings.com
Keesing's Worldwide is a publisher providing information specialists with regular international news reports and resources to communicate with leaders around the world. Since 1931 *Keesing's Record of World Events* has brought the world written news reports covering every significant event. *Keesing's Record of World Events* Online Archive consists of 40 years and 30,000 pages of contemporary world history with original international news reports.

Academic and Informational Websites Related to Country or Political Risk

www.riskworld.com

Provides links to all other websites that deal with any sort of risk including political risk. Contains several different sections including a bookstore, organizations and news services. Links to hundreds of websites and articles for free.

www.duke.edu/~charvey/Country_risk/couindex.htm

Campbell Harvey, a professor at Fuqua School of Business, Duke University, includes Country Risk Analysis on his Internet site. Contains notes from his classes, which cover economic as well as political risk. Data is country specific.

www.grai.com

The site for Global Risk Assessments, Inc. (GRA), a private international business information and intelligence service. This site provides more than 100 hotlink references to help you navigate the field of international information. The website provides a contact to obtain the GRA publication series, four volumes of articles on the nature and quality of political and country risk assessments. A quality source for political risk linkages.

www.lphpitman.co.uk

LPH Putnam Limited is a British insurance company that offers political risk insurance on a wide variety of variables. This is an interesting site to visit in order to see how political risk is defined in the private sector.

www.mcm.ca

A political risk insurance brokerage, Millennium is based in Canada. They offer insurance on thirteen different variables for companies worldwide. A good site to see current events reported from a Canadian perspective.

www.morrisx2.com

Morris & Morris Middle East Consultants offers business, security, environmental and political risk analyses for the Middle East and Islamic countries. A good resource for recent events in the Middle East.

www.worldcapitalforum.com

This site is maintained by the "Dr. Heynen Political Risk Management Advisory in International Affairs". This site has literally hundreds of links arranged by topic. An excellent source for world news, they have links to every major international paper and foreign policy magazine.

www.edc-see.ca

Export Development Corporation's website. A Canadian, private counterpart to OPIC and EPIC, this company offers risk protection for Canadian businesses in the world market. In addition to insurance, they provide business intelligence and financial services as well. Many articles on the Canadian market are available to read for free.

www.ucis.pitt.edu/reesweb/

This site, maintained by the Center for Russian and European Studies at the University of Pittsburgh, provides all types of information about the region including political information and links to other important information sources for the region.

www.subcontinent.com/sapra.html

If you want to view things from a different perspective, this site comes from an India think tank, which focuses on peace and conflict studies, political risk, terrorism, and security issues pertinent to South Asia.

www.harperrisk.com
Harper Risk Inc. is a consulting and administration firm offering services in risk management and insurance. Their home page contains a list arranged alphabetically and by subject on insurance, fact-finding and political risk websites. Fee based.

www.internationalaffairs.com
InternationalAffairs.com is an internet company owned by Oxford Analytica which provides an extensive list of sites arranged by topic. Arranged in several categories, this site mainly contains links to publications, political and non-governmental organizations, and nonprofit think tanks and statistical organizations.

www.acad.polyu.edu.hk/~mspeter/politica.htm
This is the course syllabus for a Political Risk class offered by Hong Kong Polytechnic University. The site also has lecture notes and links to many related websites, both in English and Chinese.

www.mgt.smsu.edu/jashw/im-polrisk/coutline.html
Syllabus and lecture notes on an introductory course offered by Southwest Missouri State University. The site also contains a list of related topics and resources. Must have a java-enabled browser to utilize.

§ § §

Acknowledgements: The authors compiled this list with the assistance of: Philippe Minerbo, Claude Chiricescu, Steve Johnston, Rodolfo Bay, Fabio Teixeira, Lori Murphree, Cristian Oprescu, Alberto Lopez Nunez, Louis Bergman, Kevin Matthews, Kirk Hickey, Charles Liu, Loay Ghazaleh, Ashwin Gopalaswamy, Maulik Parekh, Mesut Aslantas, Javier Bolanos Cacho, Reka Csersnyes, Jeffrey Dewolf, Marcell Faller, Emily Giacomini, Gustavo Grisa, Warren Harris, Kristin Johnson, Patrick Ostrander, Neil Phillips, Michael Rubel, Josephine, Savarino, Jordan Trajkov, Seung Lim Yoo, and Ed Whiting.

Appendix B

The Overseas Private Investment Corporation (OPIC)
An Application of Risk Management—The MidAmerican Energy Holdings Case
Llewellyn D. Howell

OPIC Political Risk Insurance and Guarantees as a Management Tool

The Overseas Private Investment Corporation (OPIC)[1] is a self-sustaining U.S. government agency that supports American private investment in developing nations and emerging market economies around the world by selling financial services that are not commercially available. These services include long-term political risk insurance and limited recourse project financing. OPIC earns revenues from the sale of these services and, in fiscal year 2000, produced a profit of $185 million.

In addition to helping establish long-term economic stability in developing nations, OPIC-backed projects help increase the size of the American economy. Projects approved in fiscal year 2000 generated roughly $20 billion in U.S. exports and helped to create and support more than 57,000 new American jobs. Operating as a quasi-private corporation, OPIC had $4,035,000,000 in reserves at the end of fiscal year 2000.

OPIC had its structural beginnings as a unit of the Agency for International Development (AID) but became an independent institution within the U.S. government in 1971. Its operational roots were in the 1948 Marshall Plan for European recovery, beginning with insurance against currency inconvertibility. In the 1950s insurance was expanded to cover protection against expropriation when the Marshall Plan was restructured to supplement direct aid programs for developing countries.

In 1961, administration of the insurance program was transferred to the newly established AID. In 1969 the U.S. government decided that a separate, business-oriented agency could provide more effective support for American investors entering the international marketplace and OPIC was established in 1971. OPIC today reports paid insurance claims beginning with the 1966 fiscal year.

While the agency continues to face challenges from some elements of Congress, its mandate has regularly been renewed.[2] OPIC continues to operate as a small, independent agency in the executive branch of the federal government. It can offer up to $400 million in total project support for any one project--up to $200 million in project finance and up to $200 million in political risk insurance. OPIC has coverage available for equity investments, parent company and third party loans and loan guarantees, technical assistance agreements, cross-border leases, capital market transactions, contractors' and exporters' exposures, and some forms of investment.

---

[1] A complete picture of OPIC services is provided in OPIC publications "Executive Summary," Washington, D.C.: n.d.; "Investment Insurance," Washington, D.C.: n.d.; "Investment Finance," Washington, D.C.: n.d.; and "Investor Services," Washington, D.C.: n.d. All may be obtained by writing to Investor Services, Overseas Private Investment Corporation, 1100 New York Avenue, NW, Washington, D.C. 20527. Internet access to the same information may be obtained at http://www.opic.gov. Some of the text below is adapted from that Internet site.

[2] See Daniel B. Moskowitz, "OPIC Gets A Boost," *International Business*, May 1996, pp. 36-37.

OPIC can also help secure loans or appropriate financing with terms up to 15 years for companies with significant equity or management participation by U.S. businesses. OPIC loans can be as little as $250,000 or as much as $200 million per project on either a project finance or corporate finance basis.

OPIC clients are exclusively American companies; OPIC does not provide direct government-to-government aid or grants. In early 1998, OPIC had about 400 active clients, including small, medium and large U.S. businesses. Demand for OPIC services has increased, in large measure, due to the demand for large-scale private sector infrastructure projects in the developing world.

U.S. companies are well positioned to compete for new infrastructure projects that have significant potential to increase U.S. exports and create U.S. jobs. OPIC helps these companies compete with their foreign counterparts for these export-intensive infrastructure projects. Importantly, OPIC helps small U.S. businesses make investments in new markets, offering the kind of individualized support that small businesses need to bring their goods and services abroad. In fiscal 2000, forty percent of OPIC's activities involved small businesses.

OPIC's political risk insurance serves firms in political risk management in two ways. First, simply acting as insurance it provides *protection* in case actual losses do occur. Investors thereby have confidence that good business practices will result in a profitable venture and that the company will survive even though the social and political environment may deteriorate after the venture is undertaken. Second, OPIC insurance (and that from the Multilateral Investment Guarantee Agency (MIGA) of the World Bank) provides a more direct form of management through its *deterrence* function. Deterrence is provided as a management tool—that is, to manage political risk by preventing or containing negative outcomes—by linking the weight of the U.S. government to host government choices or actions on expropriation, contract repudiation, or currency convertibility.

Host governments are fully aware that if they illegally interfere with an OPIC insured investment and fail to compensate the American investor, the U.S. government will inherit the debt, become the owner of the equity involved, and then link that debt to other financial interactions that are supported by the U.S. The U.S. government can prevent new loans to the host government, refuse new political risk insurance (thereby preventing new investment), discourage investors from other countries, and seize host government assets in the United States. Host governments will usually be loath to seize or otherwise interfere with an American investment if they understand the potential consequences. OPIC insurance as a management tool then becomes a matter of just having it and making its presence known to the host government.

OPIC supports business projects in virtually every industrial and economic sector including agriculture, energy, construction, natural resources, telecommunications, transportation and distribution, banking, and services among others. It provides political risk insurance to U.S. investors, contractors, exporters, and financial institutions involved in international transactions. Specifically, OPIC insurance is available to:

• citizens of the United States;
• corporations, partnerships, or other associations created under the laws of the United States, its states or territories, and beneficially owned by U.S. citizens (OPIC deems a corporation organized under the laws of the United States or its states and territories to be beneficially owned by U.S. citizens if more than 50 percent of each class of its issued and outstanding stock is owned by U.S. citizens either directly or beneficially).;

- foreign corporations at least 95 percent owned by investors eligible under the above criteria; and
- other foreign entities that are 100 percent U.S. owned.

OPIC Political Risk Insurance

Insurance is available for investments in new ventures or expansions of existing enterprises, and can cover equity investments, parent company and third party loans and loan guaranties, technical assistance agreements, cross-border leases, assigned inventory or equipment, and other forms of investment. Coverage is also available for contractors' and exporters' exposures, including unresolved contractual disputes, wrongful calling of bid, performance, advance payment and other guaranties posted in favor of foreign buyers, and other risks.

OPIC insurance can cover the following three political risks:

- *currency inconvertibility* - deterioration of the investor's ability to convert profits, debt service and other remittances from local currency into U.S. dollars;
- *expropriation* - loss of an investment due to expropriation, nationalization or confiscation by a foreign government; and
- *political violence* - loss of assets or income due to war, revolution, insurrection or politically motivated civil strife, terrorism and sabotage. Political violence claims are separated into the categories "war damage" and "civil strife damage."

OPIC also has specialized insurance programs for: financial institutions, leasing arrangements, oil and gas projects, natural resource projects and contractors and exporters. OPIC can insure up to $200 million per project. OPIC does not insure against currency devaluation, nor does it guarantee that investors will earn a profit.

Currency inconvertibility coverage compensates investors if new currency restrictions prevent the conversion and transfer of remittances from insured investments. Currency restrictions may take the form of new, more restrictive foreign exchange regulations or a failure by exchange control authorities to act on an application for hard currency. OPIC inconvertibility coverage insures earnings, returns of capital, principal and interest payments, technical assistance fees, and other similar remittances related to insured investments in eligible projects. The coverage does not protect against the devaluation of a country's currency. Rather, OPIC insures investors against the consequences of conversion restrictions that occur after an insurance contract is issued.

Expropriation coverage protects against the nationalization, confiscation, or expropriation of an enterprise, including "creeping" expropriation - government actions that for a period of at least six months deprive the investor of fundamental rights in a project. The coverage excludes losses due to lawful regulatory or revenue actions by host governments and actions provoked or instigated by the investor or foreign enterprise.

For equity investments, compensation is based on the book value of the investment as of the date of expropriation. For loans, payment is based on outstanding principal and accrued interest. With some limited exceptions, OPIC covers total expropriation only; to receive compensation, an investor must assign to OPIC all rights to an insured investment.

Insurance for specialized risks peculiar to a specific project are available upon request and will be rated on a case-by-case basis. Coverage for expropriation of funds only - unlawful host government retention of foreign exchange intended to be remitted as investment earnings - may be purchased for a reduced premium in conjunction with currency inconvertibility coverage.

Insurance may be available to cover losses resulting from the unlawful breach of specific host government obligations identified by the U.S. investor at the outset as vital to the successful operation of the project. Coverage is available on a case-by-case basis and will be individually rated.

Political violence coverage compensates for property and income losses caused by violence undertaken for political purposes (as in the example provided in the Keene Industries case below). Declared or undeclared war, hostile actions by national or international forces, civil war, revolution, insurrection, and civil strife (including politically-motivated terrorism and sabotage) are all examples of political violence covered by OPIC. An investor may choose to insure for all these risks or to exclude civil strife. Actions undertaken primarily to achieve labor or student objectives are not covered.

Table 1*: OPIC Claims Paid Since 1994				
Investor	Country	Type of Claim	Industry	Settlement Amount
Code for Types of Losses -- A – Inconvertibility; B – Expropriation; C – War Damage; F – Civil War				
FY94				
Agronom	Zaire	F	Farming	$185,885
Tea Importers	Rwanda	F	Tea	$53,966
Haitian Tropical	Haiti	F	Farming	$305,900
TOTAL				$497,520
FY95				
Charles Hoyt	Haiti	F	Tanning	$319,091
Tea Importers	Rwanda	F	Tea	$178,429
TOTAL				$497,520
FY96				
Andre Greenhouses Inc.	Dominican Republic	F	Agriculture	$21,000
Nord Resources Corp. 6/	Sierra Leone	F	Mining	$2,000,000
TOTAL				$2,021,000
FY97				
Tea Importers	Rwanda	F	Tea	$8,317
C&W Trading Company Inc.	Rwanda	F	Tea	$1,561
Alliant Techsystems, Inc	Belarus	B	Services	$5,900,000
TOTAL				$5,909,879
FY98				
African Holding Company	Zaire	F	Manufacturing	$3,950,000
Nord Resources Corp	Sierra Leone	F	Mining	$14,204,500
TOTAL				$18,154,500
FY99				
Joseph Companies Inc.	Jamaica	B	Manufacturing	$1,494,00
Alliant Techsystems, Inc.	Ukraine	B	Services	$17,700,000
TOTAL				$19,194,000
FY2000				
MidAmerica Energy	**Indonesia**	**B**	**Power**	**$217,500,000**
FC Schaffer & Associates	Ethiopia	F	Manufacturing	$9,563
Citibank, N. A.	Sudan	B	Banking	$1,055,607
TOTAL				$218,565,170
* Source: OPIC, "Insurance Claims Paid to Date: OPIC and Its Predecessor Agency," OPIC, September 30, 2000				

OPIC pays compensation for two types of losses: *business income losses* and *damage to tangible property*. An investor may purchase one or both coverages.

Business income coverage (BIC) protects the investor's share of income losses resulting from damage to the insured property caused by political violence. With an "off-site" rider, OPIC may also compensate for income losses resulting from damage to specific sites outside the insured facility, such as a critical railway spur, power station, or supplier.

Compensation is based on what the project would have realized in net income but for the damage, plus the project's continuing, normal operating expenses that must be paid during the time the damage is being repaired. OPIC will also pay for expenses that reduce the business income loss, such as renting a temporary facility. Compensation is paid until productive capacity can reasonably be restored, not to exceed one year.

Assets coverage compensates for loss of or damage to tangible property caused by political violence. Compensation is based on the investor's share of the adjusted cost of the property or replacement cost. Adjusted cost is defined as the least of the original cost of the item, the fair market value at the time of loss, or the cost to repair the item. OPIC may pay replacement cost up to twice the investor's share of the lost or damaged property's original cost, provided the property is actually replaced within three years.

Table 1 lists the claims paid by OPIC since 1994.[3] It shows a clear dominance of political violence—especially civil strife—as the source of most claims during this period. Until the end of the Cold War, most losses were a result of expropriation and inconvertibility. As the structural umbrellas of democratic capitalism and Communism fell away at the end of the 1980s, many countries deteriorated into ethnic chaos and structural uncertainty. Many of these costs of fragmentation continue but increased problems from maturing but often erratic governments are evident beginning in 1997.

The case provided below is an example of this increasingly common political risk problem faced by OPIC-insured claimants at the beginning of the 21th Century: government interference in operations and, ultimately, a takeover of assets of the investor (expropriation).[4] The MidAmerican case illustrates both the *protection* and *deterrence* features of political risk insurance. In this case, protection is afforded to Mid-American but the MidAmerican case is then used by the U.S. government to pressure the Indonesian government and deter it from acting in a similar manner in the future. In establishing the deterrent function, the U.S. government successfully diverted potential investment away from Indonesia and threatened to seize Indonesian assets to obtain payment for the OPIC-MidAmerican equity. The aftermath of the case and the process of establishing deterrence will be described below in the section "Establishing Deterrence."

Set in the Southeast Asia state of Indonesia, the case offers a useful picture of the problems faced by investors operating in potentially profitable emerging markets.

The Indonesian Context

Indonesia was receiving significant investor attention at the end of the Twentieth Century because of three main factors: 1) a population of roughly 200,000,000 million (at 210 million by 2001); 2) an abundance of human and natural resources; and 3) a great demand for economic development in which private enterprise and foreign investment could play an important role. As singular as these factors were,

---

[3] For the complete listing of claims paid since 1966, see OPIC, "Insurance Claims Experience to Date: OPIC and Its Predecessor Agency," OPIC: Washington, DC, September 30, 2000.

[4] See OPIC, "Insurance Claims Experience to Date...."

Indonesia's history and socio-political development were contextual elements that, in many ways, counter-balanced the advantages of this emerging market.

Indonesia's history is a rich one, replete with episodes of empire, war, fragmentation, cultural expansionism, Asian and European colonialism, revolution, and, ultimately, unification and independence only in 1949. Prior to this date, "Indonesia" as a single political entity never existed. One of the Indonesian government's primary problems is the population's lack of experience in self-rule for a system in this form. When the Dutch and other colonial powers arrived in Indonesia in the 16th Century, the archipelago consisted of more than 13,600 islands, about 300 distinct ethnic groups, and 225 dialects. Rule was generated through numerous sultanates, monarchies, and chief-ruled tribal territories. It was the Dutch who brought together these many diverse units and created the country we now know as Indonesia.

Adding to the political fragmentation of the region was the multidimensional sources of religious thought and the origins of philosophies of governance. In a quasi-colonial manner, Indians had ruled or influenced many of the major political entities of the Indonesian archipelago prior to the arrival of the Europeans. The Indians had brought with them Hinduism, Buddhism, and Islam, which became layered in a mix that underlies the nature of modern Sunni Islam in Indonesia. In all of these religious manifestations, political power was vested in single male leaders whose right to rule was granted by the deities or heaven. Rule was singular, patriarchal, and hierarchical. To this the Dutch added nothing and subtracted nothing.

Prior to the arrival of the European colonialists, significant and powerful empires existed in the region that form the historical basis of nationalism today. Sri Vijaya, based at Palembang in southern Sumatra, reached through Java to the East and to the area of Bangkok (before it existed) in Thailand to the north. It was a Buddhist empire born in 670AD and lasting until 1365AD, nearly 700 years. It was during this period that Buddhist culture and thought spread throughout the archipelagic region influencing social order, commerce, and art. Madjapahit was a Hindu empire with a capital in eastern Java that originated in about 1100AD and continued until 1500AD. Malacca was the first major Islamic state in the region—located in what is Malaysia today—originating in 1400AD and remaining powerful until defeated by a major Portuguese naval force in 1511AD. Each of these historically and culturally powerful states was ruled under provisions that were religious. All political power was derived from above, not below. The concepts of democratic institutions and governance were vague and foreign until well into the independence period.

The Indonesian entity's first relief from Dutch rule came in 1942 when the Japanese interrupted, and really concluded, European control of this configuration of states. A sense of Indonesian nationalism was born and was fostered between 1942 and 1945, leading to the independence movement that, in turn, led to revolution against the returning Dutch. After the successful conclusion of that revolt in 1949, Indonesia was ruled in the same manner that its components had been ruled for several millennia. It should have come as no surprise that the revolutionary leader Sukarno built his own patriarchal empire as Indonesia's first president (1949-1968). Despite the leanings of his successor (General Suharto, 1968-1998) toward the West, it should not be difficult to understand why the political system remained uniquely hierarchical and personalized. A nearby sultanate—Brunei—remains a personal possession and fiefdom of its leader to the present.

Throughout these millennia of continuity, Indonesia has remained authoritarian in institutional construction because its belief systems, culture, and experience make it so. Law and legal concepts had their origins in heaven and neither the Dutch nor the Japanese did anything to alter these underpinnings.[5] Really only the Asian financial crisis of 1997 and Indonesia's economic collapse brought to bear the force to alter the course of Indonesian history.[6] It brought down the last of the great Indonesian patriarchs, brought to power B. J. Habibie as a temporary president, and laid the groundwork for the first democratic election in 1999. President Abdurrahman Wahid has struggled to escape history, tradition, and inertia to establish political and legal institutions and practices that conform to the demands of a global, democratic, and market-oriented social system. The OPIC-MidAmerican Energy Holdings story bridges this transition and felt both the negative and positive reverberations of a major culture in transition. It is an exciting and informative narrative, reflecting both the dangers of investment in emerging economies and a roadmap to management and progress for both host governments and investors.

Important, too, in an examination of this case are the pre-loss circumstances of the investment and its early operation. Many of the methods described in this *Handbook* incorporate "authoritarianism," "democratic accountability," or "military in politics" among the variables to be examined in building an index of risk.[7] The MidAmerican Energy-Indonesia case is rich with detail on the political, social, and cultural environments that led to the events generating the losses and is thus a useful tool in understanding both the need for risk forecasts and the ingredients necessary in creating an effective model and risk index.

The MidAmerican Energy Holdings Case

In this instance, MidAmerican Energy Holdings suffered insured losses at the hands of the Indonesia government of General Suharto, which, in response to the 1997 Asian financial crisis, began a process continued by subsequent governments of Indonesia (GOI). By unilaterally altering the contractual relationship between MidAmerican and the government, the GOI action eventually turned into what the courts and OPIC established to be a case of expropriation. The case describes the circumstances under which these losses occurred and the justification for claims under terms of MidAmerican's OPIC coverage.

What follows below, beginning with "Memorandum of Determinations" through the statement "End of Memorandum," is the case as defined by the official documents of OPIC. The format is that provided by OPIC, providing readers with a description of the arguments and exact terminology necessary in establishing proof of loss and demonstrating the cohesion between the specific loss and the equally explicit terms of the insurance contract.[8]

MEMORANDUM OF DETERMINATIONS
Expropriation Claim of MidAmerican Energy Holdings Company
(formerly CalEnergy Company, Inc.),
Contracts of Insurance Nos. E374, E453, E527, and E759

On May 28, 1999, MidAmerican Energy Holdings Company (formerly CalEnergy Company, Inc.) (the "Insured") filed an application for compensation (referred to herein as the "Original Claim" (a copy

---

[5] See "Doing Business and Investing in Indonesia," PriceWaterhouseCoopers (www.pwcglobal.com), 1998.
[6] The IMF forces at work are described in the *Economist Intelligence Unit* (*EIU*) reports from "Business Asia" dated 20 April 1998, 15 June 1998, 13 July 1998, and 28 June 1999.
[7] See, for example, the *International Country Risk Guide*'s (*ICRG*), December 1997 evaluation of the role of these variables, "Indonesia," pp. 142-144.
[8] The author is indebted to Robert C. O'Sullivan, Associate General Counsel for Insurance Claims at OPIC for his advice and assistance in identifying this case and provision of other OPIC data cited here.

of which is attached as Exhibit A)) for expropriation under four Contracts of Insurance (Nos. E374, E453, E527, and E759 (the "Contracts") (copies of which are attached as Exhibits B through E, inclusive)) relating to, two geothermal power projects (referred to as the "Dieng Project" and the "Patuha Project" or collectively as the "Projects" and each as a "Project") in Indonesia. The insured has since filed three amendments to the Original Claim dated June 8, 1999, June 22, 1999, and September 27, 1999, respectively (copies of which are attached as Exhibits F through H). The Original Claim, as amended, requests compensation in the amount of $211,710,971.91.

On October 1, 1999, the Insured filed a separate application for compensation (referred to herein as the "Second Claim" (a copy of which is attached as Exhibit I)) for expropriation under the Contracts. The Insured has not withdrawn the Original Claim, as amended, and the two claims assert distinct but not mutually exclusive grounds for compensation. The Second Claim was amended on October 22, 1999 and on November 12, 1999 (copies of these amendments are attached as Exhibits J and K). The Second Claim, as amended, requests compensation in the amount of the $217,500,000. This amount is the sum of the active amounts of coverage under all of the Contracts.

The Contracts provide two alternative bases for an expropriation claim, the first dependent on acts of the government of Indonesia (the "GOI") that are not breaches of contracts between the Insured or the Foreign Enterprises (as defined below) and the GOI, PLN (as defined below), or Pertamina (as defined below). The Original Claim requests compensation under this basis for coverage. (The provisions of the Contracts relevant to the Original Claim are Sections 4.01(a) and 4.01(i). For ease of reference only, these provisions will be referred to as "4.01(a)" and a claim under them as an "A Claim.")

The second basis for an expropriation claim is that the Foreign Enterprises have received arbitral awards against PLN or Pertamina under the project agreements (as defined below), as well as against the GOI based on the GOI Support Letters (as defined below). The Second Claim requests compensation under this second basis for coverage. (The provisions of the Contracts relevant to the Second Claim are Sections 4.01(b) and 4.01(ii). For ease of reference only, these provisions will be referred to as "4.01(b)" and a claim under them as a "B Claim.")

Acting through its majority-owned subsidiaries Himpurna California Energy Ltd. ("HCE") in connection with the Dieng Project and Patuha Power Ltd. ("PPL") in connection with the Patuha Project, the Insured had entered into contractual arrangements (discussed below) with P.T. Perusahaan Umum Listrik Negara ("PLN"), the wholly state-owned Indonesian electricity company, Perusahaan Pertambangan Minyak Dan Gas Bumi Negara ("Pertamina"), the wholly state-owned natural resources company, and the GOI for the development of two separate geothermal fields, the construction of generation facilities thereon, and the long-term sale of the electricity to be generated. (Himpurna California Energy Ltd. and Patuha Power Ltd. are referred to herein as the "'Foreign Enterprises" and each a "Foreign Enterprise").

The Original Claim (as amended) asserts that the GOI took a number of actions, including directing PLN to breach its contracts in respect of the Projects, that meet the requirements for compensation under 4.01(a). The Second Claim asserts that the Foreign Enterprises have received arbitral awards as required by 4.01(b) and otherwise met the requirements of the Contracts. On October 19, 1999, OPIC received copies of those awards dated October 16, 1999, which awards have remained unpaid through the date of this determination.

SUMMARY OF EVENTS

The Foreign Enterprises each entered into several agreements with PLN, Pertamina, and the GOI relating to the Projects. Pursuant to separate Joint Operating Contracts (each a "JOC") between each Foreign Enterprise and Pertamina, the Foreign Enterprises were to develop and operate their respective geothermal fields for a period of forty-two (42) years. Although Pertamina continued to have an interest in the fields as required under Indonesian law, each Foreign Enterprise, acting as contractor for Pertamina, had the exclusive right to develop the field and to build generation facilities thereon.

Each Foreign Enterprise, PLN, and Pertamina then entered into an Energy Sales Contract ("ESC") providing that PLN would purchase electricity generated from the field or, in the event it did not purchase the electricity, it would nevertheless be obligated to pay a fixed amount for the unused capacity. PLN's purchase obligation ran directly to Pertamina, as the owner of the field, but the payment obligations were assigned to the Foreign Enterprises irrevocably. The term of the ESCs coincided with the term of the related JOCs. The two insured Projects were each to be developed in four staged units. It is unclear whether this structure was agreed upon because of the engineering requirements of the Projects or due to economic or other reasons, but each Foreign Enterprise had the discretion to vary the timing and other aspects of each unit's development.

Each of the Projects also received a letter signed on behalf of the Government of Indonesia by the then-Minister of Finance that provided that the GOI "would cause" Pertamina and PLN "to honor their obligations" under the relevant JOC and ESC (collectively, the "GOI Support Letters" and each a "GOI Support Letter"). The GOI Support Letters, the JOCs, and the ESCs are referred to herein as the "Project Agreements."

The development of geothermal and other forms of power generation capacity requires long-term investment. The Insured undertook to make this investment using a combination of equity and debt raised through limited recourse project financing of the Foreign Enterprises. In order to attract the necessary levels of investment, power developers and their lenders require commensurate commitments from the proposed purchasers of the power to be generated, including take-or-pay purchase arrangements. Furthermore, to keep interest costs down, the construction of generation capacity is designed to minimize the period of construction before commercial production commences and income accrues to the project from sales of power. The structure of these contractual' arrangements, including the payment obligations and the construction schedule, as well as the dispute resolution mechanism built into the Project Agreements, were all standard in the industry, and essential elements of the Insured's decision to invest in the Projects.

Upon the applications of the Insured and Kiewit Energy Company, Inc. ("Kiewit"), which at that time owned a fifty percent (50%) equity interest in each of the Foreign Enterprises, OPIC issued two contracts of insurance (E374 and E527) in connection with the Dieng project in April of 1996 and, upon subsequent application of the same two companies, issued two contracts of insurance (E453 and E759) in connection with the Patuha Project in August and September of 1997. The contracts of Kiewit were assigned, with OPIC's consent, to the Insured in connection with the Insured's subsequent acquisition of Kiewit's interests in the Foreign Enterprises.

On September 20, 1997, Presidential Decree 39/1997 ("PD39") was issued by the GOI. This presidential decree had the force of law and affected the rights of all parties, including the state-owned enterprises, Pertamina and PLN, in connection with independent power projects (IPPs) being developed at that time in Indonesia. This decree divided Indonesia's various independent power projects into three categories: those that were to be "continued," those that were to be "reviewed," and those that were to be "postponed." PD39 classified the Dieng project as continued in part (units 1, 2, and 3) and postponed in part (unit 4) and the Patuha project as reviewed in part (unit 1) and postponed in part (units 2, 3, and 4).

PD39 set out the criteria on the basis of which the IPPs had been classified into the three categories.[9] Under those criteria, each of the Projects should have been placed in the "continued" category since both Foreign Enterprises had begun construction or development. In fact, Dieng unit 1, the furthest developed, was near completion.

In addition to this inconsistency in classification of the Projects under PD39, a second inconsistency was reflected in the division of the projects into their separate units for purposes of application of PD39. ✓ No basis for treating the units as separate projects exists under the Project Agreements or PD39's stated criteria. The Project Agreements allowed the Foreign Enterprises to develop the Projects in stages or units, and provided that PLN was to be kept informed of the development schedule. However, financing and development were managed on a Project-wide basis, and these were the aspects of project status on which by its terms PD39 classification depended.

The Insured attempted without success to have the misclassification corrected. The Insured believed that the projects would be reclassified as "continued" and did not stop its development activities at that time. Although neither PLN nor the Insured ceased to perform under the Project Agreements as a result of the decree, from the time PD39 was promulgated, the ability of the Foreign Enterprises to retain commitments for project financing became increasingly doubtful, and the further development of the Projects became increasingly uncertain. The lenders refused to permit disbursement of loan funds for the purpose of constructing additional units unless clarification of the status of the Projects, including the units that were "continued," could be obtained from the GOI or PLN. Such clarification was not forthcoming, and no units other than Dieng unit 1 were ever completed.

The stated intent of PD39 was to establish a transparent process for quickly determining which of the reviewed and postponed IPPs should be continued, based on factors to be developed during the course of the review process. A high level committee was to be created. However, on November 1, 1997, a new presidential decree (Presidential Decree 41/1997) was issued modifying PD39. This decree reclassified certain of the IPPs without any reference to, the committee. Patuha unit 1 was reclassified as "continued." While this further decree did not purport to change the plan to put in place a committee to oversee the review process, the effect of the decree was to make the role of any PD39 committee uncertain. Indeed, at that time no review committee had been established. On December 16, 1997 the Foreign Enterprises each asked PLN to confirm its intention to carry out its obligations under the ESCs, but no response has ever been received.

On January 10, 1998, Presidential Decree 41/1997 was itself rescinded by the terms of Presidential Decree 5/1998. The status of the Projects reverted to that announced in PD39, but a further four months had passed and no committee had been established. Also, if the Projects' original classification under PD39 had been in error, that error remained uncorrected. PD39 used the terms "postponed" and "reviewed" concerning part of the Dieng project and all of the Patuha project. The GOI has even now (more than two years later) failed to commence any meaningful steps to address the possibility of any continuation of the projects so classified.

---

[9] PD39 provided that projects were postponed if they were "not yet in progress" and continued if "the construction process are [sic] underway." Reviewed projects were to be evaluated by a committee and then assigned to one of the other classifications. Presidential Decree 39/1997 1 8 (Sept. 20, 1997).

During the spring of 1998, the Insured attempted to obtain assurances, as required by its lenders, from the GOI and PLN that they would comply with the Project Agreements, both in connection with the continued parts of the Dieng project and in connection with the parts of the Projects classified as postponed or reviewed. The Foreign Enterprises wrote a series of letters to PLN, to the Minister of Finance, to the Minister of Mines, and to the Minister of State-Owned Enterprises seeking assurances that the ESCs would be respected. They received no response to their repeated requests from either the GOI or from PLN. The then President-Director of PLN subsequently admitted in testimony that he failed to respond because he required direction from the GOI, which was withheld.[10]

On March 3, 1998, however, a memo from the legal bureau of the Ministry of Mines and Energy of the GOI stated that it did not intend to require the cancellation of all "power agreements." Indeed the Original Claim acknowledges that during this period the Insured was "repeatedly assured by U.S. and GOI officials that the Joint Review Process would focus on the PD39 criteria and a review of whether the Project was the product of 'KKN' (corruption, collusion [sic], or nepotism). If the Project Agreements met the PD39 criteria and had been negotiated in a transparent process, [the Insured] was assured they would be continued.[11]

In June of 1998, PLN (through its President-Director) made several public statements implying that the Project Agreements of both of the Projects would be repudiated. These statements were followed by clear breaches of the Project Agreements of the Dieng Project. On June 4, 1998, PLN failed to make the first payment due under the ESC relating to that Project, even though the first unit had been "continued" under PD39. PLN's breach of its payment obligations was followed by an instruction from PLN to the Foreign Enterprise on July 8, 1998, "to dispatch Dieng Unit 1 to 0 MW," which had the effect of shutting the plant down.[12] Under the ESC, however, PLN's payment obligations continued whether it took power from the Dieng plant or not. PLN has made no payments since then on these obligations.

During the period since the promulgation of PD39, no compensation has been paid to the Insured or the Foreign Enterprises under the Project Agreements or otherwise. Additionally, the GOI and its wholly owned enterprise, PLN, have made it clear (both publicly and in direct conversations with OPIC) that, in their view, the Dieng and Patuha projects are not needed. PLN has begun a program (referred to as "rationalization") of selectively renegotiating similar arrangements for other IPPs affected by PD39 and has indicated that none of the reviewed or postponed projects will receive payments in accordance with their original project documents. PLN has indicated that the "continued" projects (those in the same category as units 1 through 3 of the Dieng Project) will be considered on a case-by-case basis and paid if the relevant project is needed (apparently, at significantly reduced levels).

PLN has informed OPIC directly that its basis for "rationalization" discussions has been that the GOI and PLN are not bound by their prior agreements.[13] Given the delay and the approach of the GOI and

---

[10] Himpurna California Energy Ltd. (Bermuda) v. PT. (Persero) Perusahaan Listruik Negara (Indonesia), Final Award ¶ 164; Patuha Power Ltd. (Bermuda) v. PT. (Persero) Perusahaan Listruik Negara (Indonesia), Final Award ¶ 164.

[11] Original Claim p. 5 (May 28, 1999).

[12] Himpurna California Energy Ltd. (Bermuda) v. PT. (Persero) Perusahaan Listruik Negara (Indonesia), Final Award 1 33; Patuha Power Ltd. (Bermuda) v. PT. (Persero) Perusahaan Listruik Negara (Indonesia), Final Award ¶ 33.

[13] These statements have been made frequently in conversations between representatives of PLN and OPIC. Among these meetings are those held on July 15, 1999 with PLN director of planning Dr. Hardiv H. Situmeang and representatives of OPIC, EID/MITI, and the Export-Import Bank of Japan, and meetings on October 11, 1999 with the President-Director of PLN, Adhi Satriya, and representatives of the same organizations and of the World Bank and the ADB.

PLN to the IPPs, the categories under PD39 are not meaningful in practice and the classification of Dieng units 1 through 3 as "continued" is of no significance. The GOI has treated all IPPs as postponed or cancelled.

The Insured has attempted to discuss compensation with the GOI but has been unsuccessful. The Foreign Enterprises have pursued their right under the Project Agreements to arbitrate disputes with PLN and the GOI and, in August of 1998, jointly commenced arbitration under the terms of the Project Agreements.

At the insistence of the GOI and PLN, the arbitration proceedings were split into two separate proceedings, the first against PLN and, after a determination of that action, the second against the GOI. Both Foreign Enterprises received awards against PLN in May 1999 (the "PLN Awards"), and against the GOI in October 1999 (the "GOI Awards"). However, no payment has been made with respect to any of the awards.

During the arbitration against PLN, PLN argued, inter alia, that the Foreign Enterprises had breached the Project Agreements and that therefore performance and payment by PLN was excused. The final PLN Awards issued in favor of each of the Foreign Enterprises determined that no such breach existed.[14]

Having obtained unsatisfied awards against PLN, the Foreign Enterprises proceeded with their arbitration against the GOI. However, in. June of 1999 Pertamina sought to enjoin both the second arbitration and the enforcement of the PLN Awards, and PLN separately sought to enjoin the enforcement of the PLN Awards. On July 23, 1999 Pertamina obtained from an Indonesian court an order enjoining the Insured from attempting to collect on the PLN Awards and from pursuing other remedies under the Project Agreements. (OPIC has received no information concerning the disposition of the separate action regarding enforcement of the PLN Awards, and apparently there have been no hearings on that action.) In addition, the GOI has threatened to use its police powers-to fine and imprison any person attempting to take any action under the remedies sections of the Project Agreements or otherwise participate in violation of the terms of the injunction.[15]

Notwithstanding the injunction, the duly constituted arbitral panel for the second arbitration unanimously determined that it could proceed outside of Indonesia and scheduled hearings during the week of September 21, 1999 in The Hague, The Netherlands.[16] The GOI declined to participate in these hearings, presenting no case on the merits, and failing to appear for the hearings. In addition, the GOI made an unsuccessful attempt to obtain an injunction against the proceedings from a court in The Netherlands. The Dutch court ruled on September 21 against enjoining the proceedings.

At the same time, according to affidavits of one of the arbitrators and other witnesses, copies of which are attached at Exhibit L, the GOI instructed the arbitrator whom it had appointed pursuant to the

---

[14] Himpurna California Energy Ltd. (Bermuda) v. PT. (Persero) Perusahaan Listruik Negara (Indonesia), Final Award ¶¶ 296-297, 350-369; Patuha Power Ltd. (Bermuda) v. PT. (Persero) Perusahaan Listruik Negara (Indonesia), Final Award 11 297-298.

[15] Himpurna California Energy Ltd. (Bermuda) v. Republic of Indonesia, Interim Award (1 74 (Sept. 26, 1999); Patuha Power Ltd. (Bermuda) v. Republic of Indonesia, Interim Award ¶ 74 (Sept. 26, 1999).

[16] "Procedural Order of 11 August 1999," quoted in Himpurna California Energy Ltd. (Bermuda) v. Republic of Indonesia, Interim Award ¶ 105, at 49-50; see also Patuha Power Ltd. (Bermuda) v. Republic of Indonesia, Interim Award ¶ 105, at 49-50.

Project Agreements not to participate in the scheduled hearings. According to the affidavits of these witnesses, the arbitrator reported that when he arrived in The Netherlands, he was met by a number of persons who informed him that they were to escort him back to Jakarta and would not permit him to participate in the scheduled hearings. The arbitrator has since confirmed that he was met by officials of the GOI who delivered a letter purportedly from persons acting on behalf of the Indonesian courts informing him that the injunction was outstanding and that his participation in the procedure would be contrary to that injunction. He was escorted to Jakarta before the start of the hearings and was therefore not able to participate in them or to take part in further deliberations of the arbitral tribunal.[17]

The arbitral tribunal nevertheless issued interim awards with respect to its jurisdiction in favor of each of the Foreign Enterprises on September 26, 1999, determining that the GOI was in default under the terms of appointment due to its failure, without sufficient cause, to submit documentary evidence for the hearing, and that the tribunal had the jurisdiction to decide the case on the evidence before it. On October 16, 1999, the tribunal issued final awards without the participation of the Indonesian arbitrator. Those awards found that the GOI was responsible under the terms of the GOI Support Letters for causing PLN to honor and perform its obligations to the Foreign Enterprises, including the obligation to make payment on the PLN Awards, and that the GOI was therefore liable for damages to the Foreign Enterprises in the aggregate amount of $577,000,000.

DETERMINATIONS UNDER THE CONTRACTS

As noted above, the Contracts contain alternative methods of covering events of expropriation. Section 4.01(a), which contains the provisions governing A Claims, provides that compensation is payable if acts (other than acts that constitute breaches of contracts) attributable to the GOI(i) deprive the Insured of its fundamental rights in its investments, (ii) violate international law, and (iii) continue for a period of six months. Section 4.01(b), which contains the provisions governing B Claims, provides that compensation is payable if valid, final arbitral awards have been obtained against PLN or Pertamina pursuant to the Project Agreements as a result of acts not covered by section 4.01(a),[18] such awards have also been obtained against the GOI pursuant to the GOI Support Letters, such awards have not been paid for a period of 90 days, the nonpayment constitutes a violation of international law and deprives the investor of its fundamental rights in the insured investment, and the Foreign Enterprises were not in breach of the Project Agreements.

THE A CLAIM

I. Acts attributable to the GOI.

The first step in evaluating the elements of an A Claim is to determine if the alleged expropriatory "act or series of acts, excluding (I) any breach or alleged breach of any provision of any Project Agreement,"[19] is "attributable to a foreign governing authority."[20]

---

[17] Himpurna California Energy Ltd. (Bermuda) v. Republic of Indonesia, Interim Award ¶¶ 140-146; Patuha Power Ltd. (Bermuda) v. Republic of Indonesia, Interim Award ¶¶ 140-146.

[18] Such acts are those that are breaches of the Project Agreements or otherwise excluded by 4.03(b). (See infra p. 21 for a discussion of § 4.03(b).)

[19] Contract of Insurance E374 § 4.01(i); Contract of Insurance E527 § 4.01(i). The language of the corresponding provision, §4.01(a), in Contracts of Insurance E453 and E759, reads: "except for (x) any breach or alleged breach of any provision of any Project Agreement. . . ."

[20] Contract E374 § 4.01(i)(a); Contract E527 § 4.01(i)(a); Contract E453 § 4.01(a)(i); Contract E759 § 4.01(a)(i).

There have been a number of acts attributable to the GOI that have directly affected the rights of the ✓
Insured in its investments in the Foreign Enterprises:

> (i)   Then-President Soeharto issued PD39, which interrupted the development of the
> Investor's projects.

> (ii)   The GOI refused to respond to requests for explicit assurances that the Projects
> would be permitted to continue. The result of this failure was a withdrawal of financing and the
> Foreign Enterprises' inability to continue development and to complete construction of the
> Projects.

> (iii)   The GOI failed to establish an effective review process under PD39 or to offer
> compensation for the deprivation of the value of the Insured's investments.

> (iv)   The courts of Indonesia interfered in the exercise of the dispute resolution provi-
> sions of the Project Agreements and the enforcement of a properly issued arbitral award.[21]

> (v)   The GOI further interfered in the arbitral process by using its personnel in an at-
> tempt to disrupt and cause a postponement (or even cancellation) of the tribunal's sessions.

While other direct or indirect actions of the GOI may also have deprived the Insured of fundamental
rights in its investments, it is not necessary to consider such actions here to the extent that they relate to
breaches of the Project Agreements (which are excluded from consideration in connection with an A
Claim) rather than to government actions separate from breaches of those Project Agreements.[22]

II. The acts of the GOI are violations of international law.

The Draft Convention on the International Responsibility of States for Injuries to Aliens (1961)[23] defines a taking as "unreasonable interference with .the use, enjoyment, or disposal of property as to justify
an inference that the owner will not be able to use, enjoy, or dispose of the property within a reasonable
time after the inception of such interference." This definition would include an act or series of acts that
deprived an investor of the benefit of its investment without compensation from the state or a third party.
The Iran-U.S. Claims Tribunal found takings in Iran's deprivation of fundamental property or contract
rights of several American companies notwithstanding the lack of a formal decree of nationalization.[24]
Additionally, arbitral tribunals have recognized that rights under contracts are property subject to expropriation.[25]

---

[21] Under applicable principles of international law, the acts of the judiciary are attributable to the state. If the courts
take actions that result in interference with a property right, the state may be held responsible for compensation, just
as it would had the action been taken by the legislative or executive arm of the state. Islamic Republic of Iran v.
U.S., Award No. 586-A27FT (Iran-U.S. Cl. Trib. Jun. 5, 1998).

[22] The contractual exclusion from OPIC coverage under the A Claim does not imply that the GOI is not responsible
for such actions, however.

[23] 15 Although this document is a draft and has not been accepted by any state, it reflects the opinions of experts on
customary international law in this area. "Although in the form of conventions requiring ratification or accession,
they have been widely accepted as generally declaratory of existing law and therefore actually given legal effect even
prior to their formal entry into force." Oscar Schachter, International Law in Theory and Practice 71 (1991).

[24] See, e.g., Starrett Housing v. Islamic Republic of Iran, 23 I.L.M. 1090 (Iran-U.S. Cl. Trib. 1993).

[25] Libyan Am. Oil Co. v. Libyan Arab Republic, 20 I.L.M. 1, 60 (I.C.J. 1977); see also O'Connell, 2. International
Law 763-68 (2d. ed. 1970).

The deprivation of property is a violation of international law if prompt, adequate, and effective compensation is not paid.[26] The GOI has failed to pay or offer to pay any compensation and has interfered with the Insured's attempts to use contractual and judicial means to obtain compensation. The acts of the Indonesian courts (which are attributable to the GOI) and acts of the GOI in connection with the tribunal hearings in The Hague were intended to deny the Foreign Enterprises their rights under the Project Agreements, and under the terms of appointment agreed to by the GOI, to arbitration as a form of dispute resolution.[27] As a signatory to the Convention on the Recognition and Enforcement of Foreign Arbitral Awards of June 10, 1958, the GOI additionally had an international law obligation to assure that entities investing in Indonesia were afforded appropriate protection for the rights to arbitration contained in the Project Agreements.[28] The GOI has failed to comply with this obligation and has instead taken steps to prevent the exercise of those rights.

While there could be debate over whether the acts described could also be viewed as breaches of the Project Agreements, it is not necessary to resolve that question definitively here, and this determination does not do so, because of the existence of an alternative basis on which compensation is payable under the Contracts, as described below. What is clear is that the acts of the GOI directly and adversely affected the rights of the Insured in its investments, that no compensation has been provided therefor, and that the GOI has taken extraordinary measures to frustrate the Insured's attempts to obtain compensation through the arbitration process to which the GOI had agreed, all in violation of international law.

III. The acts attributable to the GOI have deprived the Insured of its fundamental rights in the investments.

The terms of PD39 interfered with the carefully constructed contractual arrangements established under the Project Agreements. Even if the Projects were eventually permitted to continue, the two years of delay to date caused by PD39 and the failure to implement the review process, without any indication by the GOI of an intent or willingness to perform or to attempt to perform its obligations under the Project Agreements, have deprived the Insured of important rights in the Projects. The effective abrogation of the Project Agreements has deprived the Insured of any possibility of recouping its investment other than through compensation from the GOI. Although the Dieng Project was continued in part, the refusal of the GOI to give reasonable assurances of its and PLN's compliance with their respective agreements caused the withdrawal of financing for the remainder of the Project, depriving the insured of an important element of its fundamental rights in its investment.

By permitting Pertamina to seek and to obtain an injunction against the enforcement of the PLN Awards, which had been rendered by a tribunal constituted in accordance with the terms of the Project Agreements and terms of appointment agreed to by th-a GOI, and by issuing that injunction, the GOI has interfered with the right of the Foreign Enterprises to enforce the awards against PLN. The PLN Awards probably have no value outside of Indonesia, since it is unlikely that PLN has assets outside of Indonesia. The dispute resolution mechanisms established in the Project Agreements and the rights to independent arbitration are vital to development of any large-scale project with substantial government involvement. These provisions are customary in international power project financing and necessary both to attract

---

[26] See O'Connell, 2 International Law 776-77 (2d. ed. 1970).

[27] This conclusion would be true even if the acts of the GOI are characterized as having merely been to inform one of the members of the tribunal of the injunction.

[28] The Convention on the Recognition and Enforcement of Foreign Arbitral Awards, Jun. 10, 1958, art. II, 9 U.S.C. § 201 (1999) [hereinafter "New York Convention"].

financing and to assure prompt and fair resolution of controversies with a foreign counter-party. The rights established by such provisions are an essential element of the Project Agreements. By interfering with these rights, therefore, the GOI has deprived the Insured of an important element of its fundamental rights in the insured investment, and has additionally deprived the Insured and the Foreign Enterprises of the value of the PLN Awards.

Under the laws of Indonesia, the only permitted purchaser of power for transmission or distribution is PLN, and the development of independent power generation capacity is prohibited except in connection with contractual arrangements providing for the purchase of that power by PLN. Since no separate market for electricity exists, or is permitted to exist, the Insured has no prospect of operating its project outside of the scope of its agreements with the GOI and its wholly owned companies, PLN and Pertamina. Thus, by depriving the Insured and the Foreign Enterprises of the benefits of the Project Agreements, the GOI has deprived the Insured of its fundamental rights in its investments.

The Insured and the Foreign Enterprises have been deprived of fundamental rights in the insured investments both because the Insured has been deprived of its ability to develop the Projects and because the right to arbitration and to enforce the PLN Awards has been interfered with and effectively denied.

IV. The expropriatory effect has continued for a period of six months.

The Insured's rights in its investments were first affected by PD39 in September of 1997. However, at that time, there remained the possibility that the review process would proceed and that the Projects could (perhaps after a delay) be completed in accordance with the provisions of the Project Agreements. When completion no longer seemed possible after the events of June and July of 1998, the Foreign Enterprises pursued arbitration, first against PLN and subsequently against the GOI pursuant to the GOI Support Letters. During the period since PD39 was issued, the Investor has been deprived of its rights in its investment manifested in the ability to sell electricity, to continue development, and, ultimately, to obtain compensation following arbitration. However, while it may not be necessary for all of these effects to have occurred in order to meet the requirements of the Contracts, the precise time at which the those requirements were met does not need to be decided here because of the existence of an alternative basis on which compensation is payable under the Contracts. The effects of the acts of the GOI have not been mitigated and continue. The date on which the Insured was deprived of its fundamental rights in the Projects as required by 4.01(a) is not decided here.

THE B CLAIM

As noted above, the second alternative basis for a claim for expropriation provided under the Contracts requires that the Foreign Enterprises obtain "a valid final arbitral award against. . . PLN. . . pursuant to the [ESC] as a result of events not constituting total expropriation under subparagraph (a) above, and a valid final arbitral award [against the GOI] under the [GOI Support Letter]" the GOI fails for a period of 90 days to pay such award in violation of international law, depriving the Insured of fundamental rights; and the Foreign Enterprise is not in material breach of the Project Agreements.

I.   The Foreign Enterprises have obtained Arbitral Awards against PLN and the GOI.

The Foreign Enterprises each obtained final arbitral awards against PLN on May 4, 1999 which were based on breaches of the Project Agreements The tribunal was constituted pursuant try terms of appointment executed by PLN and each of the Foreign Enterprises. Hearings in the two proceedings were held jointly in Jakarta. Both PLN and the Foreign Enterprises were represented and heard.

On October 16, 1999, a second tribunal, also constituted in accordance with the terms of appointment executed by the GOI and the Foreign Enterprises, issued final awards against the GOI. These awards were issued following a determination, in interim awards dated September 26, 1999, that the GOI was in default under the terms of appointment of the arbitral panel because it had failed, without showing sufficient cause for such failure, to present either its case in chief or to appear at the scheduled hearing. In making the final awards, the tribunal evaluated the evidence presented on the issues and concluded that the GOI was responsible under the GOI Support Letters for the nonperformance by PLN as determined in the proceedings against PLN. The tribunal awarded damages to the Foreign Enterprises in an amount in excess of the amounts in the PLN Awards.

Due to the absence (for the reasons detailed at page 9 above) of the GOI-appointed arbitrator, the tribunal deliberated with only two of three members present. In deciding to proceed on this basis the tribunal took into account the cause of the third arbitrator's absence, the role played by the courts and possibly other instrumentalities of the GOI in causing such absence, and the stage of the proceedings. The decision to proceed with a truncated tribunal is consistent with international arbitral practice in situations involving the absence or other withdrawal of an arbitrator without valid excuse.[29] The awards state that the tribunal would have reached the same result even if the GOI had not been directly involved in causing the absence of the GOI-appointed arbitrator.[30]

In reaching this conclusion, the tribunal stated that in determining whether a withdrawing member of the tribunal should be replaced or whether the tribunal should proceed as a truncated tribunal, the remaining members may exercise their discretion, taking into consideration the stage of the proceedings at which the withdrawal occurs.[31] The tribunal evaluated this matter and determined that the circumstances of this arbitration were such that the proceedings should continue with only two arbitrators. Fully deliberated interim awards[32] had been issued, which determined that the GOI was in default of the terms of appointment and that the tribunal was to proceed on the evidence before it at that time. In these circumstances, the appointment of a replacement arbitrator would have resulted in a delay that would have benefited the GOI; the remaining members of the tribunal determined that the GOI should not so benefit and exercised their discretion to continue accordingly.[33]

Given in these circumstances and all other factors relevant to the issuance of the final awards, such awards are valid as required by the Contracts.

---

[29] See Stephen Schwebel, "International Arbitration: Three Salient Problems" 71-72, 87-89 (1987).

[30] Therefore, in deciding that the awards are valid it is not necessary to determine whether the GOI acted in any way improperly in connection with the arbitrator's nonattendance at the hearings in The Netherlands. However the statements of the GOI and, its counsel acknowledge that the GOI contacted the arbitrator and sought his absence, that the injunction issued by the courts of Indonesia was a basis for his absence, and that the courts (perhaps together with other agencies of the GOI) communicated with the arbitrator to persuade him not to attend. The purpose of these efforts was apparently to delay or prevent the continuation of the tribunal's deliberations.

[31] Himpurna California Energy Ltd. (Bermuda) v. Republic of Indonesia, Final Award ¶¶ 69-70 (Oct. 16, 1999); Patuha Power Ltd. (Bermuda) v. Republic of Indonesia, Final Award ¶¶ 69-70 (Oct. 16, 1999).

[32] The awards state that all three arbitrators were involved in the discussions and had agreed on the findings as set forth in the awards (conditionally, since the discussions preceded the GOI's nonattendance at the hearing in The Hague). The Indonesian arbitrator did not sign the interim award. Himpurna California Energy Ltd. (Bermuda) v. Republic of Indonesia, Interim Award ¶¶ 145-147; Patuha Power Ltd. (Bermuda) v. Republic of Indonesia, Interim Award ¶¶ 145-147.

[33] Himpurna California Energy Ltd. (Bermuda) v. Republic of Indonesia, Final Award ¶ 78: Patuha Power Ltd., (Bermuda) v. Republic of Indonesia, Final Award ¶ 78.

Although the arbitral awards against the GOI were issued on October 16, 1999 and have not remained unpaid for ninety days, OPIC is justified in making its determination at this time and waiving the remainder of the time period. The Insured and the Foreign Enterprises are under an injunction issued by an Indonesian court prohibiting them from making any attempt to enforce the award. Any such attempt would make the Insured, the Foreign Enterprises, and any persons acting on their behalf subject to criminal sanctions and fines of $1,000,000. Additionally, the PLN Awards have been outstanding, unpaid, for six months. While failure to pay the PLN Awards is not sufficient to establish OPIC's liability under the Contracts, the GOI's efforts to avoid their enforcement and its refusal to acknowledge its obligations under the GOI Awards indicate that the GOI will not honor the GOI Awards within the full 90-day period. The Insured should not be expected to incur the sanctions threatened against it by attempting to enforce the awards, and a delay in making a payment to the Insured would serve no purpose.

II. Non-payment of the arbitral award is a violation of international law.

The Restatement (Third) of Foreign Relations Law states that ". . . a state may be responsible. . . if, having committed itself to a special forum for dispute settlement, such as arbitration, it fails to honor such commitment: or if it fails to carry out a judgment or award rendered by such domestic or special forum."[34] Article II of the New York Convention recognizes the importance of these provisions and each signatory (including Indonesia) undertakes to support and enforce agreements to arbitrate (whether such proceeding is otherwise subject to the Convention, or not).[35]

The economic crisis that continues to affect Indonesia does not afford a defense to Indonesia's obligation to pay the amount of the awards. The GOI has stated that it is not able to pay the amount of the GOI Awards and will not do so. Similar arguments have been raised and rejected in other contexts.[36] According to the notes explaining the Harvard Draft Convention,

> The poverty of a country or its asserted inability to pay may not be set up as a defense to international responsibility. As in connection with the taking of property, a State can easily allege that it did not have enough funds for its own governmental purposes and therefore would not be in a position to discharge its obligations to aliens. The acknowledgement of any such defense would involve an international court in. . . inquiries into the internal affairs of States.[37]

Therefore, the failure of the GOI to make payment constitutes a violation of international law.

III. The nonpayment has deprived the Insured of its fundamental rights in the insured investment.

As discussed in connection with the A Claim, the Insured's ability to develop the Projects and to sell electricity generated has been effectively denied pursuant to PD39 and its implementation. The sole remaining source of recovery of its investment is through the arbitration process set out in the Project

---

[34] Restatement (Third) of Foreign Relations Law § 712 cmt. h (1999).

[35] New York Convention, supra note 19, art. II, ¶ 1.

[36] See e.g., Societe Commercial de Belgique (Socobel) Case, P.C.I.J., Ser. C, No. 87, pp. 101; see also Harvard Draft Convention on the International Responsibility of States for Injuries to Aliens, art. 17(2), reprinted in Louis B. Sohn & R.R. Baxter, Responsibility of States for Injuries to the Economic Interests of Aliens, 55 Am. J. Int'l L. 545, 576 (1961).

[37] Sohn & Baxter at 572-73.

Agreements. By failing to pay the awards the GOI has deprived the Insured of all of its remaining rights in the Projects.

IV. The Foreign Enterprises are not in material breach of the Project Agreements.

The Foreign Enterprises have been unable to develop the Projects in accordance with the Project Agreements. However, it was established in the arbitration proceedings between the Foreign Enterprises and PLN that the Foreign Enterprises had complied with their undertakings to the extent not otherwise excused by the actions of PLN and that the Foreign Enterprises were not in default under the Project Agreements.

NO EXCLUSION APPLIES TO THE PAYMENT OF COMPENSATION

Section 4.03(a) of the Contracts provides for an exclusion from coverage if "the preponderant cause [of the expropriation] is unreasonable actions attributable to the Investor, including corrupt practices." This exclusion is not applicable here. The GOI has acted on several different levels in connection with the Projects, including actions of the then president of Indonesia in issuing presidential decrees broadly applicable across the power sector. Those actions can not be considered as having been taken in reaction to acts of the Insured.

The GOI and PLN have asserted that the Insured was involved in "KKN" (corruption, cronyism, and nepotism) and have alleged that the Projects were awarded to the Insured due to corruption. When specific allegations of corruption have been requested, however, no response has been forthcoming. It should be noted that the identical allegations, without specifics, have. been made in connection with all IPPs in Indonesia. OPIC has received no evidence of any corrupt practices in this case. The tribunal in the proceedings of the Foreign Enterprises against the GOI confronted this issue. In the course of pointing out that no evidence of corruption had been presented to it the tribunal found

> ". . . unsupported allegations are not enough to demonstrate corruption. Not only is it not illegal to have local partners; it is in many situations intelligent and indeed commendable business practice. . . . Much more is needed; the criticised conduct must be proved. . . [and] shown [to have run] afoul of defined legal structures. . . . But to punish parties who are apparently doing no more than to seek to enforce contractual claims, and to pretend to justify such punishment by unsupported allegations, is no part of this struggle [against corruption]."[38]

Section 4.03(b)of the Contracts, as amended by section 10.03, provides an exclusion if the expropriatory action covered by section 4.01(a) is "taken by the foreign governing authority in its capacity or through its powers as a purchaser from, or supplier, creditor, shareholder, director[,] or manager of, the foreign enterprise."[39] The actions on which determination of the A Claim would be based were not taken by the GOI in these capacities. Although PLN was a purchaser from and Pertamina a supplier to the Foreign Enterprises, any determination of the A Claim would have to rely on the acts of the GOI itself, not on the acts of Pertamina or PLN. The GOI was not a purchaser from, supplier to, or creditor, shareholder, director, or manager of any of the Foreign Enterprises. Although the Original Claim asserted actions of the GOI in directing PLN's failure to perform under the ESCs and to pay the PLN Awards, such acts did not form the basis for this determination.

---

[38] Himpurna California Energy Ltd. (Bermuda) v. Republic of Indonesia, Final Award 9(9(99-100; Patuha Power Ltd. (Bermuda) v. Republic of Indonesia, Final Award 9[1 99-100.
[39] Contracts at § 4.03(b).

The B Claim is not subject to the exclusion contained in section 4.03(b).

AMOUNT OF COMPENSATION

Pursuant to section 5.01 of the Contracts, as amended, compensation for expropriation is based on the book value of the insured investment, subject to certain adjustments and limitations. The book value of the insured investment is determined by reference to the unaudited, but management certified, financial statements for the Foreign Enterprises dated as of October 16, 1999. The Insured will certify to OPIC that the amounts reflected in these financial statements as due to affiliates reflect amounts actually advanced by the Insured to the Foreign Enterprises and that the Foreign Enterprises received such funds. Section 10.14 of each of the Contracts provides that amounts invested as Secondary Investments (as defined in the Contracts) shall be evidenced in a form acceptable to OPIC. The Secondary Investments were made as book entries only and are reflected as such on the records of the Insured and the Foreign Enterprises. This form is determined to be acceptable since it is the norm in connection with interaffiliate loans of this kind. After consultation with accounting experts, OPIC has determined that the book value of the insured investment throughout the relevant period exceeded the applicable limitation set out below.

The amount of compensation is not subject to any of the adjustments contained in section 5.03, as amended.

Pursuant to section 5.04, as amended, the amount of compensation is limited to the active amount as of the date the expropriatory effect commenced, and cannot exceed the Investor's share of the award against the GOI. The active amount at all relevant times was $217,500,000, which is less than the Investor's share of the such award, and less than the book value of the insured investment, and thus constitutes the amount of compensation payable under the Contracts.

Further details regarding the calculation of book value are contained in Schedule A hereto.

Procedures relevant to the Claims

Section 8.01(b) provides that an application for compensation must be filed within six months after the Insured has reason to believe the requirements of Article IV have been met. The Insured filed the Original Claim eleven months after the date on which it asserts in the Original Claim that the expropriatory effect commenced. However, it is not necessary to determine whether the requirements of Article IV had been met more than six months before the Original Claim was filed, because it is clear that the period has not elapsed with respect to the Second Claim. The Insured has kept OPIC fully apprised of developments in connection with the Projects.

As a condition to payment, the Insured will assign to OPIC, in a form and in substance satisfactory to OPIC, all of the shares related to the insured investment as required by Section 8.02 and by Section 10.12 of Contracts E374 and E527 and by Section 10.13 of Contracts E453 and E75-9.

DUTIES OF THE INSURED

The Foreign Enterprises are majority owned and are controlled by the Insured, which acquired the interests that originally belonged to Kiewit. The Insured has certified that the eligibility requirements of .all the Contracts have been satisfied.[40]

The Insured was assigned the interests of Kiewit with the consent of OPIC.

The Insured has continued to bear the risk of loss of at least 10% of the book value of its interest in the Foreign Enterprises. The Insured has maintained private insurance as well as the coverage under the Contracts. The aggregate amount of all coverages has not exceeded 90% of the book value of the insured investment.

Pursuant to section 9.01.9 of the Contracts, the Insured is required to preserve the Projects, to pursue available judicial and administrative remedies, and to negotiate in good faith with the GOI. The Insured refused in December 1998 and in January 1999 to attend meetings among PLN, OPIC, and itself to discuss the Projects, which, if pursued, might have resulted in a resolution of the dispute and mitigated its losses. Since the Insured was at that time involved in arbitration with PLN and since other IPPs who were engaged in ongoing discussions have not been successful in resolving their contract disputes with PLN, this refusal should not be treated as a violation of this provision of the Contracts. It will be a condition of payment that the Insured provide OPIC with a certificate in connection with the provisions of this section with regard to preservation of the property of the Foreign Enterprises.

Additionally, the Insured will, as a condition to payment, transfer its interests in the Foreign Enterprises in accordance with the provisions of the section of 8.02 and make appropriate arrangements for the transfer of the insured investments to OPIC.

It will be a condition of payment that the Insured and the Foreign Enterprises each provide to OPIC a certificate confirming that they have complied with the environmental and worker rights requirements of Sections 9.01.12 and 9.01.13 as amended by Section 10.08 and of Section 10.10 of Contracts E374 and E527 and of Section 10.11 of Contracts E453 and E759.

CONCLUSION

For the foregoing reasons OPIC concludes that compensation in the amount of $217,500,000 should be paid to the Insured.

OVERSEAS INVESTMENT CORPORATION
END OF MEMORANDUM
****

OPIC's Power: The Aftermath

On November 18, 1999, two years after the initial GOI pronouncement of a change in status in Mid-American's projects, MidAmerican announced that OPIC and Lloyd's had paid in full its claims under its

---

[40] See Second Claim Exhibit 21 (Oct. 1, 1999).

political risk insurance policies.[41] The two insurers paid a total of $290 million, with OPIC's share being $217.5 million. Upon payment of the claim, project equity became the property of OPIC (and Lloyd's). As a matter of normal practice, paid OPIC claims become the responsibility of the host country's government, making the claim paid to MidAmerican effectively Indonesian government debt to the U.S. government.[42] At that point begins the second phase of this OPIC-MidAmerican case. It was now OPIC's turn to pursue the changing Indonesian governments for compensation for what was now a loss to the United States government. Development was slow. President Suharto's successor, B. J. Habibie, took a confrontational stance toward private power producers, as with MidAmerican, in his effort to resolve the disputes.

By November, the GOI, now led by the newly elected (October 1999) and democratic government of Abdurrahman Wahid, initially continued to pursue solutions to its critical financial problems by attempting to alter or cancel contracts with foreign power producers operating in Indonesia. Since the GOI had refused to pay the MidAmerican arbitration award, it had taken no lesson from its expropriation of the two projects. The state-owned electric company, Perusahaan Listrik Negara (PLN), was given approval in late November 1999 to file a suit to cancel a multi-billion dollar power purchase agreement with Paiton Energy Company. The GOI still seemed to feel that it had gotten away with the MidAmerican expropriations and now was moving on to even bigger pickings.

It was widely suggested and acknowledged that the GOI should "'not saw off the branch you're sitting on'....If PLN makes good on its threat to nullify a 30-year power purchase contract with Paiton," wrote *The Business Times* of Singapore, "the country's ability to attract sorely needed foreign investors could be compromised, especially the variety who are willing to sink US$2.5 billion into large infrastructure projects."[43] But the GOI continued anyway, ignoring the precedents of Western contract law and potential repercussions.

As the new government slowly settled in, both the recognition of global economic integration and the decidedly different ruling style of President Wahid began to have an impact. Kwik Kian Gie, Indonesia's top economics minister, announced that "Mr. Wahid prefers the negotiating table to the courts in handling these disputes."[44] As a religious leader, as well as someone inclined toward democratic processes, President Wahid might well have been expected to take this course. It should also be recognized, though, that many Asians are masters of negotiation and that court processes of adjudication are essentially foreign.

Extending the effort to relieve pressure on potential foreign investors, the GOI removed the Suharto-Habibie regime President Director of PLN and installed Kuntoro Mangkusubroto, giving him a mandate to negotiate their way out of the troubling foreign investment quagmire. Negotiations with OPIC continued through another full year. In March of 2000, Finance Minister Bambang Sudibyo stated that "The government [GOI] will not pay OPIC's claim of around $290 million because the government doesn't have the money."[45] The bargaining process was on course.

---

[41] PR Newswire, November 18, 1999.

[42] "Indonesian Government Won't Pay OPIC for Calenergy Claim," *Dow Jones International News*, March 7, 2000.

[43] See T. M. Callahan, "US$2.5b Indon Power Play," *Business Times* (Singapore), November 27, 1999, Weekend p. 9.

[44] Jay Solomon, "Indonesia Ends Legal Battles in Power Sector," *The Asian Wall Street Journal*, December 21, 1999, p. 1.

[45] "Indonesian Government Won't Pay OPIC for Calenergy Claim," *Dow Jones International News*, March 7, 2000.

The U.S. Ambassador to Indonesia, Robert Gelbard, indicated formally on March 8 that he was "dismayed" at Indonesia's assertion that it wouldn't pay for the claims. Outside the direct exchanges, Dow Jones Newswires obtained documents that indicated that OPIC had "threatened to seize Indonesian assets abroad if the government fails to settle the claim."[46] In July Gelbard explicitly said that the U.S. was losing patience with delays in negotiations between the two countries and explicitly threatened to retaliate by seizing Indonesian assets.[47]

The GOI continued to stall. It claimed that OPIC had never submitted an invoice to the GOI. It continued to argue that "corruption, collusion, and nepotism" on the part of Suharto's government and MidAmerican had tainted the contracts. It made the claim that MidAmerican had defaulted on its payments to local Indonesian contractors for the amount of $40 million.[48] But by the end of July, right after the U.S. threats became explicit, Finance Minister Kwik Kian Gie announced that progress was being made in the negotiations with OPIC.[49] He also announced that a letter of intent would be signed shortly with the IMF that would allow the next disbursement of funds to help the country's ailing economy.

In October, PLN finally said that it would pay the claim.[50] However, this still wasn't the final step. PLN President-Director Kuntoro Mangkusubroto also indicated that PLN was now negotiating payment terms with OPIC. It turned out that this agreement was to be met with terms similar to those obtained from the Paris Club of creditors to Indonesia, wherein the debt was actually rescheduled, with a grace period, instead of paid. OPIC rejected the terms on October 23.[51]

In January, 2001, the two sides announced that they had "finally" reached an agreement. OPIC now would accept the offer to allow Indonesia to pay the debt under Paris Club terms, with a four-year grace period and then the debt payment over 20 years. There was to be an interest rate of one percentage point above the rate set by the creditors' respective central banks.[52] But that deal, too, fell through.

As negotiations continued, PLN then offered to pay $217 million of the $290 million claim, then upped that offer to $240 million. Playing for its long-range deterrence capability, OPIC rejected the offer as too low and the GOI acknowledged that it was "under tremendous political pressure to settle the case to maintain foreign investor confidence."[53]

On March 5, 2001, PLN sacked its President-Director, Kuntoro Mangkusubroto, without explanation.[54] Speculation was heavily on the likelihood that the firing had something to do with the stalled OPIC negotiations. PLN also announced that it faced bankruptcy unless the government wrote off its $7.7 billion long-term debt.

As of March, 2001, the OPIC-GOI negotiations remained unresolved and the U.S.-Indonesian relationship remained clouded. More critically, deterrence was having its effect. Foreign investment into Indonesia remained minimized, but most importantly the GOI had been sensitized to contract

---

[46] "Interview: US Dismayed at Indonesia Min's OPIC Statement," *Dow Jones International News*, March 8, 2000.

[47] "US Threatens Indonesia Over Unpaid Power Claim – Min," Dow Jones International News, July 25, 2000.

[48] Editorial, "Asset Seizure Threat," *Jakarta Post*, July 28, 2000.

[49] "Government Says PLN Makes Progress in Talks with OPIC," *Jakarta Post*, July 29, 2000.

[50] "Indonesia to Pay Claim in Dispute Over Power Deal—State Utility PLN," *Asian Wall Street Journal*, October 12, 2000, p. 3.

[51] "Indonesia Says OPIC Rejects PLN Payment Terms—Report," *Dow Jones International News*, October 25, 2000.

[52] "OPIC, Indonesia's PLN Reach Agreement Over Failed Power Deals," *Asia Pulse*, January 2, 2001.

[53] "OPIC Rejects PLN's $240-Million Payout for MidAmerican's 400-MW Projects," Electric Utility Week, January 22, 2001, p. 21.

[54] "Indonesia's PLN Say Govt Sacks Chief," *Reuters English News Service*, March 6, 2001.

interference and seizure such as in the case of MidAmerican. In late February the GOI announced that it was planning to set up a co-insurance scheme with the World Bank to protect power projects in the country against risk that may stem from social and political uncertainties.[55] The U.S. government has been consistent and persistent in pursuing the act of expropriation against an OPIC-insured firm. MidAmerican was protected and the government of Indonesia is being precluded from dealing in an authoritarian and illegal manner with much needed foreign investors, at great cost to its own development and progress. Its intended behavior towards Paiton was deterred.

A subtler note about the MidAmerican case is that MidAmerican knew enough to obtain political risk insurance before starting its venture in Indonesia. Awareness of the political environment is essential in today's investment climate. A second observation is with regard to the persistence of OPIC and the U.S. government in pursuing the GOI to conform to now global legal standards covering government dealings with foreign investors. In a globalized economy, there is much less room for the authoritarian and arbitrary practices of the last century. For governments to survive and development to proceed, international legal standards must be observed and prevail.

---

[55] "Indonesia Looks into Co-Insurance Scheme for Future IPPs [Independent Power Producers]," *Jakarta Post*, February 28, 2001.